the Unofficial Guide® to

Florida with Kids

3rd Edition

the Unofficial Guide® to Florida with Kids

3rd Edition

Pam Brandon

Wiley Publishing, Inc.

For Steve, Katie, and Will, who show me the way.—P. B.

Published by:
Wiley Publishing, Inc.
909 Third Ave.
New York, NY 10022

Produced by Menasha Ridge Press
Cover design by Michael J. Freeland
Interior design by Michele Laseau

For information on our other products and services or to obtain technical support please contact our Customer Care Department within the U.S. at (800) 762-2974, outside the U.S. at (317) 572-3993 or fax (317) 572-4002

Wiley also publishes its books in a variety of electronic formats. Some content that appears in print may not be available in electronic formats.

ISBN 0-7645-6684-9

ISSN 1526-1727

Manufactured in the United States of America

5 4 3 2 1

Contents

Part Seven Southeast Florida 365

List of Maps

List of Maps *(continued)*

Acknowledgments

In a state that's the number-one tourist destination in the world, it was an enormous task to compile this comprehensive guide. My biggest thanks go to Doris Ramirez, my research assistant who tirelessly stuck with me 'til the end, and to writer Nicole Palovich, who jumped in to work on chapters I had barely started. Along the way, friends including Dorothy Jordan, Beth Dunlop, Irene Brandon, and Jennifer Jenkins shared personal insights gained from traveling with their own children. The Florida Division of Tourism supplied maps and stacks of press materials. And kudos to special folks we encountered along the way, like innkeeper Nancy Noloboff in St. Augustine and Peggy Weber in Palm Beach, who went above and beyond duty to help us understand their little corners of the Sunshine State. Finally, thanks to my own children, Will and Katie, and my husband, Steve, who patiently helped evaluate hotels, restaurants, and attractions. I couldn't have done it without them.

Thanks to the staff at Menasha Ridge Press: Molly Merkle, Gabbie Oates, Annie Long, Steve Jones, my managing editor Nathan Lott, and Bob Sehlinger.

—Pam Brandon

Introduction

The Dynamics of Family Travel

Don't even think about planning a family trip until you answer this question: What does each member of the family want to get out of the vacation?

It seems like a simple question, but it'll take more time and thought to answer than you might realize. It means assessing your current relationship with your kids and your spouse. It means taking stock of your children's passions and fears, as well as your own. It means attaching a budget to everyone's wishes. And it invariably means compromise.

Start by asking yourself some questions. Is this vacation a time for togetherness, for time alone for you while the children are entertained, or for a little of both? Are you a single dad who doesn't get to see the kids much? Are you an at-home mom who never gets a break? Are you looking for exhilarating adventures or a laid-back getaway? Do you want intellectual stimulation for you and the kids? How well do your kids handle spontaneity?

Because your family's dynamics change with every birthday, the answers may surprise you. One child may be more eager for adventure than you realize; another might look forward to peace and quiet without your realizing it.

The Pleasures of Planning

It's best to decide what you want to do and come up with some options to start the ball rolling. Then call a family meeting and include your kids in the planning process. Let everyone ask questions. Show some brochures or books about the places you have in mind so the children feel like they have enough information to be taken seriously. Pull out maps and a globe. Jump on the Internet. Teenagers in particular are quite vocal about expressing their choices, and they appreciate it when they can influence the planning process. The getaway is much more enjoyable when everyone wants to be there.

This shared planning time can be a great routine to continue as the trip itself gets under way. Remember, your kids may not be able to easily visualize your destination or the plane ride or cab ride you'll take on the way. And if you're traveling from place to place during your vacation, each new day dawns on the unknown. So keep the brochures and guidebooks handy, and break the itinerary down into manageable chunks. Offer an advance agenda every now and then, referring again to your original planning sessions ("Remember we thought the Bubbling Brook motel sounded like a good one?") and letting the kids develop anticipation rather than anxiety.

It's essential to be realistic when you plan a family vacation. Parents of young children may have to concede that the days of romantic sunsets are over for a while if there's a toddler tugging at their shorts. With infants and toddlers, the best vacations are the simple ones. They don't really need to see the sights; the idea is to be somewhere comfortable and intriguing for the adults, with a pleasant environment in which to relax and enjoy your children. Simple beach resorts are ideal for parents of the youngest group of kids. School-age kids revel in attractions created for their enjoyment—theme parks, amusements parks, arcades, rides. The metropolitan regions can also be a blast with elementary-age kids. Teens may seem reluctant, but if a pilgrimage to a special point of interest for them (a certain skateboard shop, a movie-star hangout) is included, the whole trip becomes "worthwhile." And they thrive in safe, explore-it-on-your-own situations, like Disney's Magic Kingdom or a low-key resort town like Seaside in the Florida Panhandle.

Free Florida Publications for Visitors

Travelers can contact any of the following for free information:

Florida Attractions Association, P.O. Box 10295, Tallahassee, Florida 32302; (850) 222-2885. Official guide map to Florida attractions with information on museums, parks and natural attractions, theme parks, cruises, and tours.

For a **Florida State Parks Guide,** Florida Vacation Guide, free maps, Florida Events Calendar, and Florida Trails: A Guide to Florida's Natural Habitats, call toll-free (888) 7-FLAUSA or visit www.flausa.com.

For **canoeing information** in Florida State Parks write or call the Department of Environmental Protection, Division of Parks and Recreation, Mail Station 536, 3900 Commonwealth Boulevard, Tallahassee, Florida 32399-3000; (850) 488-9872.

For **historical sites,** write or call the Department of State, Bureau of Historic Preservation, R. A. Gray Building, 500 S. Bronough Street, Tallahassee, Florida 32399-0250; (850) 245-6333.

Less Is More than Enough

As you plan, we urge you to leave plenty of downtime in the schedule. Some of my family's most memorable moments are simple breakfasts on the beach or early-evening walks to nowhere, when the conversation flows naturally. Kids treasure moments, not places or days. Give your children plenty of room to run and play; a morning collecting seashells or an afternoon at the hotel pool can be more satisfying than standing in line at a crowded theme park attraction.

A good rule of thumb may sound stringent: no more than two "activities" in a day. If you spend the morning at a museum and plan to go to dinner at a chaotic theme restaurant, go back to the hotel in the afternoon to rest and swim. If you're driving from Miami to Orlando, plan to go to Walt Disney World the next day. Then you can stop on the way to Orlando for a picnic at the beach or at the funny little town that time forgot. Remember that travel itself is an "activity."

Also, plan some activities that allow you to take a break from each other. The quarters get a little close after a week together in a hotel room, particularly if children are of significantly different ages. Schedule an afternoon during which mom and dad split duties, giving each other a break; take advantage of child and teen programs offered in many resorts to make sure there's at least one evening alone with your spouse. Everyone benefits from a little elbow room.

Reconnections

Family vacations are a necessary indulgence in today's hurried-up world, a time for togetherness without the day-to-day distractions. Whether it's a car trip on a budget or a transcontinental flight, it's a time to reconnect with your family, especially teenagers. And the best times are the serendipitous moments—a heart-to-heart conversation on an evening hike or silly "knock-knock" jokes while standing in line for the roller coaster. Roles are relaxed when schedules are flexible, and kids can have the opportunity to see their parents as interesting companions, not just bossy grown-ups. We can all learn from one another when there's time to listen and when we take the time to see the world through a loved one's eyes.

A seasoned traveler friend once scoffed at the notion of traveling with young children "since they don't remember anything." Our well-traveled teenage daughter is a better listener and communicator and is more patient, tolerant, and flexible than many girls her age. Both our kids have struck up instant friendships with children around the globe; on a recent jaunt, Katie learned about British fashion magazines from a UK teen, and young Will giggled and communicated in single-word Spanish sentences with a young girl in a Cuban restaurant in Miami. With an open heart and all the innocence of childhood, new impressions may sink in even more deeply than with adults.

Our children have a greater understanding of the rest of the world as a result of traveling to new places and exposure to new ideas. And siblings have formed a special bond from traveling together, a bond less likely to be formed at home, where they have separate classrooms, separate friends, separate rooms. As parents, it's up to us to be sure there's some fun in a trip for each member of the family. And as a family, we all need to remember to indulge our fellow traveling companions from time to time. Remember, your responses to challenges on the road—delayed flights, long lines, unsatisfactory accommodations—will influence the way your children will deal with frustrations. Be patient, be calm, and teach your children these important lifelong skills.

Vacations are times for adventure, relaxation, shared experiences, time alone . . . whatever your family decides. Our goal in this book is to evaluate each destination with that in mind—recognizing that your family has needs, based on ages, backgrounds, and interests, that are quite different from any other family's—and provide you with some structure to analyze your family's needs and create a vacation that works.

We have traveled the world with our two children, from France and Spain to the American Northwest and the hills of West Virginia. Yet some of our most wondrous trips have been in our own backyard: the sugary beaches in the Florida Panhandle, an old-fashioned inner-tube ride down the chilly Ichetucknee River, or snorkeling in the warm waters of the Florida Keys. The Sunshine State is incredibly diverse, and there is an endless variety of getaways, from the high energy of man-made attractions at Walt Disney World to the stillness and natural beauty of the Everglades. We can't imagine ever tiring of exploring our home state, whether we're stalking the newest amped-up amusement park or finding the next serene beach.

This book is not meant to be a compendium of every family-priced hotel or every advertised attraction, though we have striven to cover a variety of interests for a variety of ages. Instead of compiling a family-travel yellow pages, we've edited out the less worthy places to better draw attention to the destinations that will make your trip a hit.

Dozens of families have contributed their opinions to this book; it is evaluative and opinionated, and it offers advice on the best ways for families to have fun together and to further relationships.

Survival Guide for Little Kids

Think Small Little ones love little pleasures: splashing in the hotel pool, playing hide-and-seek in the lobby, stacking up rocks on the beach. Don't overload them.

Seek Creative Transportation For young children, getting there is often more fun than being there. When Will was three, his greatest joy and memory from his first trip to Walt Disney World was the monorail ride between the Magic Kingdom and the Ticket and Transportation Center. Seek out the ferries, trolleys, shuttles, trains, surreys, and double-decker buses, and you'll be rewarded with a cheap thrill that's as fun for little ones as a theme park ride.

Limit the Shopping Our rule at attractions is a firm one: No shopping, not even looking, until we are leaving the place. Young children can get consumed by and panicky about choosing a souvenir, and they'll enjoy the museum or theme park more if they can focus on the activities, not the trinkets.

Give Them a Voice Even a three-year-old will benefit from feeling like he has some control over his vacation. When possible, let him make simple choices for the family—like "Should we walk to the beach or ride the trolley?"

Allow for Lots of Downtime Bring books or quiet hobbies to amuse yourself during nap times or playtimes. Remember, children's ability to tackle the big world is much more limited than yours.

Accept Some Slowness It's stressful enough to get a kindergartner out the door to school each morning, so don't keep up the stress on vacation. They need a break from being rushed, too. If they're happy playing in their pajamas for an extra half-hour, the museum can wait. Conversely, accept that the times you like to be more leisurely—like dinnertime—lead to impatience in children.

Survival Guide for School-Age Kids

Give Them Their Own Space Whether it's a backpack, a carry-on train case, or one of those shoe bag–like hanging pockets that fit over the car seat in front of them, each kid needs a portable room of his or her own in which to stow gum, cards, books, disposable cameras, and souvenirs.

Make a New Routine At least until middle-school years, most kids do best with a certain amount of predictability, so it's a kindness to create little travel routines and rituals within your changed life. Knowing that his parents will always stop sightseeing by 3 p.m. to swim (or will never check out without one last hour in the pool) is a comforting thought to many a fourth-grader. Knowing that you will have $5 spending money each day can do away with shopping anxiety. Having set turns as map reader can add some fun to a 100-mile drive.

Avoid Eating Breakfast Out Many savvy traveling parents never eat breakfast in a restaurant. School-age kids are at their brightest and best in the morning, and waiting for table service at a ho-hum restaurant can start the day on the wrong foot. We pack fruit and cereal and carry milk and juices in coolers or to kitchenettes, or pop for room service—it's the least expensive and most wonderfully indulgent time to do so.

Beware Befuddled Expectations School-age kids are old enough to have some reference points and young enough to have great gaping holes in their mental pictures of the world. Our kids have imagined that they'd find the "Under Toad" at the seashore, and they've worried that an ostrich would peck out the car window at Lion Country Safari. Ask what's going on in their minds. Listen. Don't overpromise.

Watch the Diet It's fun to let vacation time be a time of special treats, but overindulgence in junk food, sweets, and caffeinated drinks may contribute to behavior changes in kids who aren't sleeping in their own beds and are full of adrenaline as it is.

Remember that Kids Hate Scenery Drive them through it if you must, but don't make them actually look at too much of it.

Give Them a Ship's Log A roll of tape and a blank book are all that's needed to turn ticket stubs, menus, brochures, and postcards from a clutter of trash into a wonderful scrapbook that's always ready to be shared and enjoyed.

Hotels and Motels Are Not Just for Sleeping Allow time for getting ice, playing in the pool, reviewing all items and prices in the minibar, packing and unpacking, using the hair dryer, putting laundry into the laundry bags, trying out the vending machines, and so on.

Hit the Playgrounds Check your maps and ask ahead about public playgrounds with climbing and sliding equipment, and on days when you'll be sightseeing, driving, or absorbing culture, allow for an hour's lunch or rest stop at the playground. Even on city vacations, try to set aside at least one day for pure physical fun at a beach or water theme park or ski slope.

Just Say Yes to Ranger Tours They are often designed with schoolkids in mind, and we'd have never seen sea turtles lumbering ashore or a nesting bald eagle if we didn't check the schedule at state or national park information centers and make a point to join ranger walks.

Survival Guide for Teenagers

Don't Try to Fool Them Don't try to tell them they'll have more fun with you than with their friends. They won't. But if you offer them the possibility of doing things they might want to tell their friends about later, they'll be interested.

Respect Their Culture Let your teenager play an active role in planning the vacation. Ask her opinion of your arrangements. Often our daughter will offer a great suggestion or an alternative that we may not have considered. And look for pop culture landmarks—movie locations, palaces of fashion or music or sport. Add a ball game to the itinerary.

Night Moves A vacation is a great time to go with your teenager to a music club, to a midnight movie, or on a moonlight hike. Go to the theater or the ballet; check out a jazz club. If you have other kids needing earlier bedtimes, let parents switch-hit on going out at night with the older kids.

Give Them Options You don't need to go everywhere with everyone. If your younger child wants to see the dinosaurs at the museum, this is the time for a split plan: mom and son see the dinosaurs, dad and daughter shop or take in a movie or a play. If you have a teenager who appreciates his sleep time, let him snooze late at least one morning. Slip out with younger siblings and take a walk or read a book. Also, set wake-up time before everyone says good-night so there are no grouchy morning risers (at least not because they've been awakened too early without warning).

Give Them Freedom Before age 12, kids are bound to parents, preferring to stay in your orbit; when adolescence hits, they're programmed to push away from you. Choose a vacation spot that is safe and controlled enough to allow them to wander or spend time with other teenagers. If you can't do that, look for an afternoon or evening at a controlled hangout place like a mall. Give them the night to themselves at Universal Studios Florida. Send them off for a surf lesson in Ft. Pierce or sign them up for a one-day scuba class in the Florida Keys.

Compromise on the Headphone Thing Headphones can allow teens to create their own space even when they're with others, and that can be a safety valve, but try to agree before the trip on some nonheadphone parameters so you don't begin to feel as if they're being used to keep other family members and the trip itself at a distance. If you're traveling by car, take turns choosing the radio station, CD, or audio tape for part of the trip.

Don't Make Your Teenager the Built-in Baby-sitter It's a family vacation, a time to reconnect, not for avoiding the kids. A special night out for parents also should be special for the kids; let them order videos and room service, for example, or participate in age-appropriate hotel programs.

Make Your Peace with Shopping Look for street markets and vintage stores; spend some time in surf shops and record stores. If you go with your teenager, you may find the conversation in such an environment flows easily. Or hit the outlets. Many a summer vacation has included a day of back-to-school shopping.

Just Say Yes to at Least One Big-Ticket Excursion Teenagers will get a lot out of a half-day adventure. What look at first like expensive tours (often available through hotel sports desks or concierges) have been memorable and important experiences for our kids, which we, as parents, are simply not able to offer by ourselves. A canoe or snorkel trip, a horseback trail ride, a fishing excursion... each was worth every cent.

A Word on Homework

Both our elementary school and high school kids have faced a load of homework or a special project that had to be worked on during "vacation" time. If a surprise major assignment comes up and plans can't be changed, there will be an unavoidable strain on the trip. Parents should consider strategies such as bringing along a laptop computer, scheduling vacation fun in half-day chunks so the homeworked kid gets some work and some play, planning a marathon session at a library at the vacation spot, or a combination of these. Or, shamelessly beg the teacher for a reprieve.

A Few Words for Single Parents

Because single parents generally are working parents, planning a special getaway with your children can be the best way to spend some quality time together. But remember, the vacation is not just for your child—it's for you, too. You might invite along a grandparent or a favorite aunt or uncle; the other adult provides nice company for you, and your child will benefit from the time with family members.

Don't try to spend every moment with your children on vacation. Instead, plan some activities for your children with other children. Look for hotels with supervised activities, or research the community you'll be visiting for school-vacation offerings at libraries, recreation centers, or temple or church day camps. Then take advantage of your free time to do what you want to do: read a book, have a massage, take a long walk or a catnap.

Tips for Grandparents

A vacation that involves different generations can be the most enriching experience for everyone, but it is important to consider the needs of each family member, from the youngest to the oldest.

- If you're planning to travel alone with your grandchildren, spend a little time getting to know them before the vacation. Be sure they're comfortable with the idea of traveling with you if their parents are not coming along.
- It's best to take one grandchild at a time, two at the most. Cousins can be better than siblings, because they don't fight as much.
- Let your grandchildren help plan the vacation, and keep the first one short. Be flexible and don't overplan.
- Discuss mealtimes and bedtime. Fortunately, many grandparents are on an early dinner schedule, which works nicely with younger children. Also, if you want to plan a special evening out, be sure to make the reservation ahead of time.
- Gear plans to your grandchildren's age levels, because if they're not happy, you're not happy.

- Choose a vacation that offers some supervised activities for children in case you need a rest.
- If you're traveling by car, this is the one time we highly recommend headphones. Teenagers' musical tastes are vastly different from most grandparents', and it's simply more enjoyable when everyone can listen to his or her own style of music.
- Take along a night-light.
- Carry a notarized statement from parents for permission for medical care in case of an emergency. Also be sure you have insurance information.
- Tell your grandchildren about any medical problems you may have so they can be prepared if there's an emergency.
- Many attractions and hotels offer discounts for seniors, so be sure you check ahead of time for bargains.
- Plan your evening meal early to avoid long waits. And make reservations if you're dining in a popular spot, even if it's early. Stash some crayons and paper in your bag to keep kids occupied.
- A cruise may be the perfect compromise—plenty of daily activities for everyone, but shared mealtimes.
- If planning a family-friendly trip seems overwhelming, try Grandtravel (call (800) 247-7651), a tour operator–travel agent aimed at kids and their grandparents.

For Travelers with Disabilities

Facilities for the physically challenged are plentiful in Florida. All public buildings have some form of access for those who use wheelchairs. In addition, many public buses are equipped with wheelchair lifts. Most of the state's attractions offer facilities and services for those with physical challenges, and many hotels have specially equipped rooms.

The Florida Department of Commerce, Division of Tourism publishes a free Florida planning companion for travelers with disabilities, offering information about services and accessibility at places throughout the state. Call (888) 7-FLAUSA for a copy, or log onto www.flausa.com.

How the *Unofficial Guide* Works

Organization

Our informal polls show that most families tend to choose a vacation spot based on geography—a place that's new and different, or familiar and comfortable. So we've divided Florida into seven regions, with family-friendly information in each area:

- Northwest Florida, stretching from Pensacola on the state's western border, east to the Suwannee River
- Northeast Florida, including historic districts such as St. Augustine and Fernandina Beach, and myriad state parks, springs, and lakes that dot the region

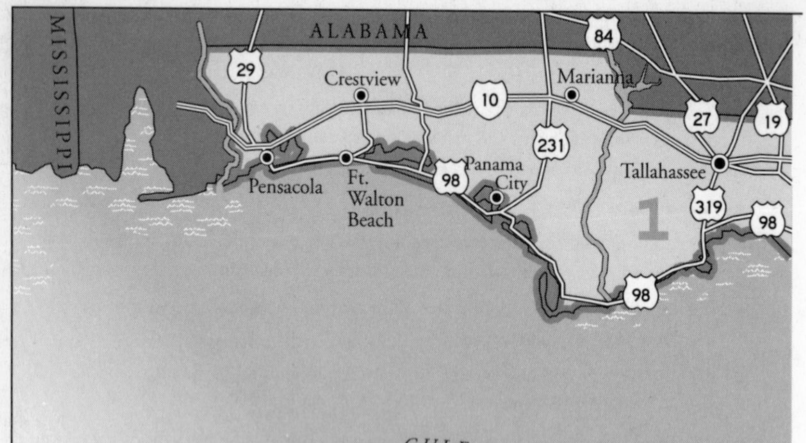

Florida Touring Zones

1 Northwest Florida
2 Northeast Florida
3 Central East Florida
4 Central Florida
5 Central West Florida
6 Southwest Florida
7 Southeast Florida

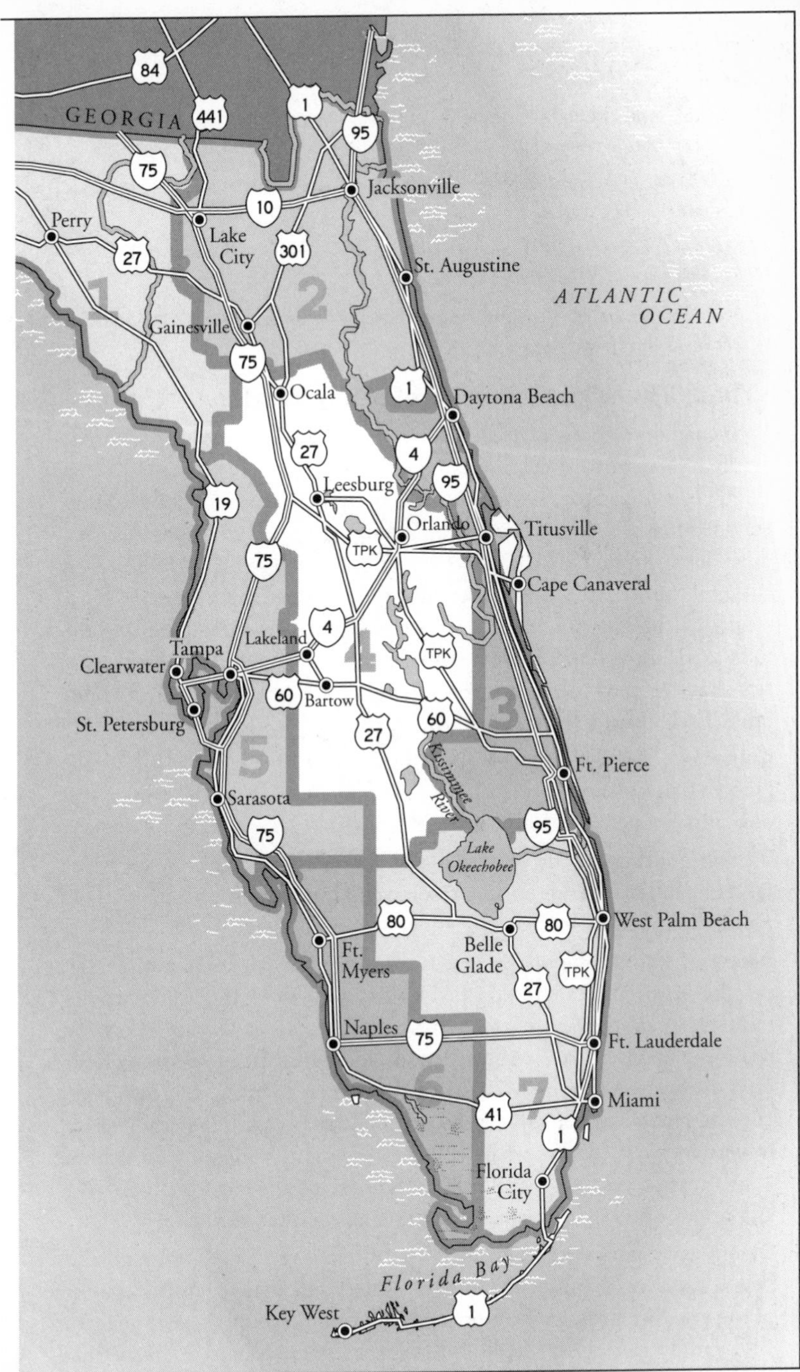
GEORGIA
ATLANTIC
OCEAN
Jacksonville
St. Augustine
Perry
Lake
City
Gainesville
Ocala
Daytona Beach
Leesburg
Orlando
Titusville
Cape Canaveral
Lakeland
Tampa
Clearwater
St. Petersburg
Bartow
Kissimmee
River
Ft. Pierce
Sarasota
Lake
Okeechobee
West Palm Beach
Belle
Glade
Ft.
Myers
Naples
Ft. Lauderdale
Miami
Florida
City
Florida Bay
Key West
84
441
1
95
75
10
27
301
19
4
TPK
60
80
41
1
2
3
4
5
6
7

- Central East Florida, from the hard-packed sands of Daytona Beach south to Vero Beach
- Central Florida, from the majestic Ocala National Forest to Orlando's five-star man-made attractions
- Central West Florida, tracing the shoreline of the Gulf of Mexico and the islands scattered along the coast
- Southwest Florida, guarded on the east by the Everglades, on the west by an incredible string of Gulf Coast islands
- Southeast Florida, from stylish Palm Beach to the 149-mile-long chain of coral known as the Florida Keys

What's There to Do besides Disney World?

Each chapter recommends the best beaches, the best outdoor adventures, family resorts, attractions, and family-friendly restaurants.

The *Unofficial Guide* system for attractions includes an "appeal to different age groups" category, indicating a range of appeal from one star (★), don't bother, up to five stars (★★★★★), not to be missed. A ♥ indicates an author's favorite beach or outdoor adventure in a particular region.

If you're looking for some healthy family bonding, stretch beyond the man-made attractions. Have a sense of adventure and plan some activities that are new and exciting—not necessarily strenuous, but memorable. Each chapter has specific spots for:

Camping We'll give you plenty of options all over Florida; if it's your family's first experience, you might opt for a cabin; we list them in several of Florida's state parks and identify them with a ▲Δ.

Birding Sitting quietly to watch and identify birds isn't for everyone (and of course it sounds boring to some children), but it teaches good listening skills and patience.

Biking Cycling, one of the best ways to experience an area firsthand, can be enjoyed year-round in Florida. However, the state's cooler months, October to May, are the best cycling season. For beginners, we recommend miles of paved bicycle trails, including the fun and easy Rails to Trails Conservancy paths. You don't even have to bring your own bike; you can rent them at many resorts and bike shops, and many shops have trailers for rent to tow small children (five and under) safely behind you—much safer than bicycle seats. Helmets are the law for children 16 and under, and it is strongly advised that all cyclists wear helmets.

Diving and Snorkeling Florida is the number-one dive destination in North America, thanks to warm, clear waters and favorable weather most of the year. We list plenty of spots where even the youngest swimmers in your family can don a mask and snorkel for a look at the fascinating world under the sea.

Fishing With more than 8,000 miles of tidal shoreline, plus some 4,500 square miles of inland water, Florida offers plenty of options for fishing: from the shore, bridges, piers, jetties, or boats. Florida is the only place in the United States where anglers can realistically catch snook, bonefish, and permit—three of the most revered game fish in all the world. More sailfish and tarpon are caught in Florida than anywhere else in the United States. And Florida's lakes are well known among bass anglers. Rivers are the place to hook black bass, redfish, catfish, and more. If you don't have a rod and reel, you can rent them at many of the public marine fishing piers for a few dollars. Also check to see if you need a fishing license, usually available at local bait and tackle shops.

Hiking There may not be mountains, but pine forests, hammocks, and savannahs, all winding through Florida's state parks, can be enjoyed by families of all interest and fitness levels.

Canoeing and Kayaking If you want to see an alligator, maybe even a black bear, one of the best ways is a peaceful canoe ride on the Florida Canoe Trail System, with 33 scenic wonders through 950 miles of waterways. Kayaking is another way to get close to nature.

What's "Unofficial" about This Book?

The material in this guide has originated with the authors and researchers and has not been reviewed, edited, or in any way approved by attractions, restaurants, or hotels we describe. Our goal is to help families plan a vacation that's right for them by providing important details and honest opinions.

Readers care about the author's opinion. Authors, after all, are supposed to know what they are talking about. This, coupled with the fact that the traveler wants quick answers (as opposed to endless alternatives), dictates that authors should be explicit, prescriptive, and above all, direct. The *Unofficial Guide* tries to do just that—it spells out alternatives and recommends specific courses of action. It simplifies complicated destinations and attractions and allows the traveler to feel in control in the most unfamiliar environments. The objective of the *Unofficial Guide* is not to have the most information or all the information but to have the most accessible, useful information, unbiased by affiliation with any organization or industry.

This guide is directed at value-conscious, consumer-oriented families who seek a cost-effective, though not spartan, travel style.

Letters and Comments from Readers

We expect to learn from our mistakes, as well as from the input of our readers, and to improve with each book and edition. Many of those who use the *Unofficial Guides* write to us making comments or describing their own discoveries and lessons learned. We appreciate all such input, positive and critical, and encourage our readers to continue writing to us. Readers' comments and observations are frequently incorporated in revised editions of the *Unofficial Guide* and contribute immeasurably to its improvement.

How to Write the Author

Pam Brandon
The Unofficial Guide to Florida with Kids
P.O. Box 43673
Birmingham, AL 35243

When you write, be sure to put your return address on your letter as well as on the envelope—sometimes envelopes and letters get separated. And remember, our work takes us out of the office for long periods of time, so forgive us if our response is delayed.

Getting Ready to Go

Weather and When to Go

Florida weather can be quite varied—Florida stretches through two time zones (Eastern and Central)—and though South Florida rarely dips below the 70s, it snows on occasion in the Panhandle.

When to travel in the Sunshine State depends on what you plan to do. If you're here for the Central Florida attractions, the least crowded times (and the best weather) are January through March and September through Thanksgiving. For camping, nothing beats the winter months, with cooler weather and hibernating mosquitoes. Summertime is best for inexpensive beach vacations and trips to the Panhandle and Northern Florida.

Average summertime temperatures range from the low to mid-80s, though they can soar into the 90s, especially in the south, and humidity makes it seem much hotter. Keep in mind the afternoon thunderstorms and sweltering temperatures if you plan to camp; unless you're on the ocean, it's extremely humid and mosquitoes can be unbearable. Still, if you can stand the heat and humidity, bargains are plentiful at the beach.

Summer travelers should stash rain ponchos, sunscreen, and bottled water, no matter what the activity.

November through April offers the lowest humidity, blue skies, and plenty of sunshine. But it's also peak tourist season in the southern half of the state, starting just before Christmas and ending just after Easter. Lines get long at major tourist destinations; small attractions get inundated; and finding a hotel room that's both convenient and affordable is more difficult.

The "shoulder seasons"—during April and May and from September to November—are great times to visit any part of the state. Temperatures are milder, and hotel rates are lower. In general, popular tourist sights are busier on weekends than weekdays, and Saturdays are busier than Sundays.

Of course, family travel schedules often center around school holidays, which tend to be the busiest times to travel. But consider taking your children out of school for special family trips—a well-planned week of family travel is just as enriching as five days in a classroom. Make it clear that traveling is a privilege, and agree that all missed work must be made up upon return. Talk with teachers ahead of time.

Pack Light

We limit ourselves to two carry-on bags each, one of which is a backpack, no matter what the duration of the trip or how we are traveling. If you have small children, an extra T-shirt and pair of shorts stashed in your backpack comes in handy in emergencies. A Florida trip generally is casual, though you may want to pack one nice outfit for dressing up for a special evening out.

T-shirts, shorts, and bathing suits are perfect year-round in most of Florida, and you can take along a small bottle of detergent for handwashing if necessary. Vacation is much more enjoyable if you don't have a bunch of bags to haul around busy airports or hotel lobbies.

Let your children pack their own backpack, then ask them to wear it around the house to check out how comfortable it will be on a long trip. Our children have become savvy packers, aware that each piece counts. Of course, you should check their bags before departing, just to be sure the essentials are all there.

Finally, you may want to take along a "surprise bag" for cranky young travelers. Sticker books, a card game, or a new book are perfect, lightweight diversions to bring out when everyone's patience is starting to wear thin.

What to Take with You: A Checklist

No matter what your means of transportation, be sure you take along (and have handy at all times):

- Sunglasses and hats to protect you from the sun
- Sunscreen, at least 15 SPF
- Emergency information—whom to contact at home in case of an accident or emergency, medical insurance cards, and your pediatrician's telephone number (they can often diagnose and call in a prescription by phone)
- A travel-size bottle of antibacterial gel (the kind that doesn't require water)

- Basic first-aid kit—children's aspirin and aspirin substitute, allergy medication, Dramamine for motion sickness, insect repellent, bandages, gauze pads, thermometer, cough syrup, decongestant, medication for diarrhea, antibiotic cream, tweezers, and fingernail scissors
- Prescription medications
- Unscented baby wipes that can be used for any clean up
- A small sewing kit with scissors
- A small night-light to ease fear of darkness
- A couple of extra paperback books, especially for teenagers (our daughter fell in love with Agatha Christie novels when she was forced to read her first one on a trip after she finished the book she brought)
- A folding cooler, perfect for carrying fruit, drinks, even sandwiches to theme parks, on walks, or in the car
- Lightweight windbreakers for cool evenings at the beach
- Inexpensive rain ponchos for surprise rainstorms
- Comfortable walking shoes for nature trails, botanical gardens, and beachside strolls (as well as theme parks)
- Each child should bring along some cash of her or his own, even just a few dollars (tell them it is theirs to spend on souvenirs or whatever they choose; when it's their money, they're much more judicious shoppers)
- A sense of humor; traveling with children can be trying at times

Remembering Your Trip

When you choose a destination, write or call for information. The travel brochures can later become part of a scrapbook commemorating your trip.

Purchase a notebook for each child and spend some time each evening recording the events of the day. If your children have trouble getting motivated or don't know what to write about, start a discussion; otherwise, let them write, or draw, whatever they want to remember from the day's events.

Collect mementos along the way and create a treasure box in a small tin or cigar box. Months or years later, it's fun to look at postcards, seashells, or ticket stubs to jump-start a memory. We used seashells from a trip to Sanibel Island on Florida's West Coast to create a wind chime for our back porch.

Add inexpensive postcards to your photographs to create an album, then write a few words on each page to accompany the images.

Give each child a disposable camera to record his or her version of the trip. Our five-year-old snapped an entire series of photos that never showed anyone above the waist—his view of the world (and the photos are priceless).

Nowadays, many families travel with a camcorder, though we recommend using one sparingly—parents end up viewing the trip through the lens rather than enjoying the sights. If you must, take it along, but only record a few moments of major sights (too much is boring anyway). And let the kids tape and narrate.

Another inexpensive way to record memories is a palm-size tape recorder. Let all family members describe their experiences. Hearing a small child's voice years later is so endearing, and those recorded descriptions will trigger an album's worth of memories, far more focused than what many novices capture with a camcorder.

Getting There

By Car

Driving is certainly the most economical way to travel, but if you're covering a lot of miles, it's time consuming and can try the patience of every passenger. For starters, don't pull any punches with your kids about just how long you'll be in the car.

If it's a long trip, leave before daylight. Take along small pillows and blankets (we use our children's baby blankets) and let the kids snooze. When they're fully awake a few hours down the road, stop for breakfast and teeth brushing.

Be sure there are books, crayons and paper, and a couple of laptop games (though not the electronic kind with annoying beeps). Parents can stash a few surprises to dole out along the way—sticker books, action figures, magazines. We take along a deflated beach ball to blow up, a Frisbee, or a "koosh" ball for impromptu playtimes at rest stops.

Be sure you have maps, and chart your trip before you leave home. Share the maps with the children so they'll understand the distance to be covered. To get a free, easy-to-read Official Transportation Map call Visit Florida toll free at (888) 735-2872. Along with an overall map, it lists attractions region by region, public recreation areas, state forests, and national parks.

Major Florida highways are I-4, connecting the Tampa Bay area on the west coast to the Daytona Beach area on the east coast via Orlando; I-10, connecting Jacksonville on the east coast with the Alabama state line west of Pensacola; I-75, entering Florida from Georgia through Lake City to the Tampa Bay area on the west coast, south through Ft. Myers and Naples where it crosses the state to Ft. Lauderdale (the Naples–Ft. Lauderdale segment is commonly called Alligator Alley); I-95, from the Georgia line near Jacksonville down the east coast to Miami; and the Florida Turnpike, from its northern entrance at Wildwood to the Miami-Homestead area.

Seat belts for drivers and front-seat passengers are the law in Florida. Child car safety seats are mandatory for children under age four or who weigh less than 40 pounds.

Snacks are great, but leave the drinks (preferably water, since it doesn't stain or get sticky when spilled) until the last moment, or else frequent rest room stops will prolong the journey. Rest areas are all along Florida's major highways, and most are open around the clock. Pack a picnic for mealtimes, and everyone can take a walk or stretch.

Small pillows and your own CDs or tapes make the journey peaceful. Take turns letting everyone choose a favorite. If kids fight over music, make them take turns choosing. To solve the seat fights, we rotate turns, either weekly or daily, for who gets to choose a seat first.

Don't forget to always lock your car, and never leave wallets or luggage in sight. Keep valuables locked in the trunk.

By Train

Amtrak serves several Florida destinations on both the east and west coasts: Jacksonville (Northeast Florida); Winter Park, Orlando, and Kissimmee (Central Florida); Tampa, St. Petersburg (Central West Florida); Ft. Myers (Southwest Florida); West Palm Beach, Ft. Lauderdale, and Miami (Southeast Florida).

We have taken the train from Orlando to Miami, and for youngsters, it's interesting for about the first hour of the six-hour trip. But with books, games, and activities to occupy the time, it's a leisurely and relatively inexpensive way to travel, with time to unwind and spend quality time with your family. You can stand up and stretch or go for a walk, and there's more leg room than in an airplane or car (and no traffic jams). Many trains offer sleeping and dining cars, but remember—it's 26 hours from New York to Miami and the fare is not much less than cut-rate airfares. If you opt for a longer trip, book first class and a sleeping car.

Amtrak offers a children's discount—ages 2–15 ride half-price when accompanied by a full-fare-paying adult. Each adult can bring two children for the discount; children under age two ride free.

Train stations are generally not close to major attractions, so car rentals need to be arranged in advance for transportation at your destination. If you want to take the train and bring your own car, Amtrak's Auto Train runs daily from Lorton, Virginia (12 miles south of Washington, D.C.) to Sanford, just north of Orlando. Your vehicle travels in an enclosed car carrier at the end of the train.

For reservations and information call (800) USA-RAIL or check the Internet at www.amtrak.com.

By Plane

Every region of Florida is served by major airlines, so choosing a flight is a matter of time and economics. Booking as far in advance as possible can save hundreds of dollars for a family of four. We don't recommend flying standby, particularly with smaller children. Taking the chance of spending hours in an airport doesn't make sense, no matter how flexible you think you are or how much money you can save.

Takeoff and landing bother some children's ears, particularly if they have a cold; take along gum for older children or a bottle or sipper cup for babies and toddlers. Most of your fellow passengers would agree that the best babies on airplanes are sleeping babies, so if possible, book your flights around nap times, which ensures a peaceful flight for you and a happy child as you land.

Pack a few nutritious snacks, like pretzels, dried fruit, or crackers, and a small bottle of water. Food and beverage service takes a while on a packed flight (and food isn't always served). If you or your child wants or needs a special meal, be sure to call the airlines at least 48 hours in advance to request it.

Bring your own child safety seat; though airlines allow children under two to fly free on a parents' lap, it's much safer if they're in their own seat. Although the extra seat will be full price, the authors feel it is worth having the peace of mind. Remember, your car seat must have a visible label that states it is approved for air travel.

If You Rent a Car

Florida has some of the nation's most competitive rates for car rentals, and almost every major company is located at the larger airports. Recreational vehicles and convertibles also can be rented, though they are considerably more expensive.

Every major car rental agency and dozens of smaller companies have operations in Florida, so rates are quite competitive and booking in advance can save up to 20 percent. To rent a car, you will need a valid driver's license, proof of insurance, and a major credit card. Some companies have minimum age requirements.

Ask about extras. Many companies offer child car safety seats, cellular phones, and area maps.

If there are more than four in your family, you might want to consider renting a minivan. They cost a little more, but the comfort is worth it.

Making Yourself at Home in a Hotel

What to Look for in a Hotel

Some families want every moment planned, others just want advice on interesting hotels that other families recommend. Many of our recommendations are suites or apartments, since the best vacations give everyone a space of their own. Four in a hotel room may be economical, but adjoining rooms or an apartment or condominium may save your sanity and be worth the extra dollars.

Here are some important questions you might want to ask before booking a reservation:

- Do kids stay free?
- Is there a discount for adjoining rooms? How much?
- Can you rent cribs and roll-away beds?
- Does the room have a refrigerator? A microwave?
- Is the room on the ground floor? (particularly important if there are small children)
- Is there a swimming pool? Is it fenced? Is there a lifeguard?
- Is there a laundry on the premises?
- Is there a family-friendly restaurant? A breakfast buffet? Other family-friendly restaurants nearby?
- Is there a supervised children's program? What are the qualifications of the staff? How much does it cost? How do you make a reservation?
- Is there in-room baby-sitting? What are the qualifications of the caregivers? How much does it cost per hour? How do you make a reservation?
- Are the rooms "childproof"? Can patio or balcony doors be securely locked and bolted?
- Is there an on-site doctor or a clinic nearby that the hotel recommends?

Childproof Your Room

When you arrive at the hotel, some childproofing may be in order. Be sure the front door and any patio or balcony doors and windows can be securely locked and bolted. Some hotels offer electrical outlet coverings if you have toddlers and protective covers for sharp furniture corners. They will also remove glass objects or other knickknacks that might be easy for a toddler to break. And if the minibar is stocked with junk food and alcoholic beverages, it should be locked.

Resort-Based Children's Programs

Many large hotels offer supervised programs for children, some complimentary, some with fees. We've included several throughout Florida that offer exemplary activities in their respective regions.

If you decide to take advantage of the kids programs, call ahead for specific children's events that are scheduled during your vacation. Ask about cost and the ages that can participate; the best programs divide children into age groups. Make reservations for activities your child might want to participate in. You can always cancel after arrival.

After check-in, visit with the kids program staff. Ask about counselor-child ratio and whether the counselors are trained in first aid and CPR. Briefly introduce your children to the staff and setting, which typically will leave them wanting more, thereby easing the separation anxiety when they return to stay.

Some hotels offer in-room baby-sitting, but if your hotel does not, a national, nonprofit referral program called Child Care Aware will help you locate good, quality sitters. You can call (800) 424-2246, Monday through Friday, 9 a.m. to 4:30 p.m. EST. Or, visit the website www.childcareaware.org.

Be sure to ask if the sitter is licensed, bonded, and insured. To ease your children's anxiety, tell them how long you plan to be away, and be sure they feel good about the person who will be caring for them. Finally, trust your own instincts.

Chain Hotel Toll-Free Numbers

This guidebook gives details on some of the hotels in Florida with outstanding children's programs. However, for your convenience we've listed toll-free numbers for the following hotel and motel chains' reservation lines:

Best Western	(800) 528-1234 U.S. & Canada (800) 528-2222 TDD (Telecommunication Device for the Deaf)
Comfort Inn	(800) 228-5150 U.S.
Courtyard by Marriott	(800) 321-2211 U.S.
Days Inn	(800) 325-2525 U.S.
Doubletree	(800) 222-8733 U.S.
Doubletree Guest Suites	(800) 222-8733 U.S.
Econo Lodge	(800) 424-4777 U.S.
Embassy Suites	(800) 362-2779 U.S. & Canada
Fairfield Inn by Marriott	(800) 228-2800 U.S.
Hampton Inn	(800) 426-7866 U.S. & Canada
Hilton	(800) 445-8667 U.S. (800) 368-1133 TDD
Holiday Inn	(800) 465-4329 U.S. & Canada
Howard Johnson	(800) 654-2000 U.S. & Canada (800) 544-9881 TDD

Hyatt	(800) 233-1234 U.S. & Canada
Marriott	(800) 228-9290 U.S. & Canada
	(800) 228-7014 TDD
Quality Inn	(800) 228-5151 U.S. & Canada
Radisson	(800) 333-3333 U.S. & Canada
Ramada Inn	(800) 228-3838 U.S.
	(800) 228-3232 TDD
Renaissance Hotel	(800) 468-3571 U.S. & Canada
Residence Inn by Marriott	(800) 331-3131 U.S.
Ritz-Carlton	(800) 241-3333 U.S.
Sheraton	(800) 325-3535 U.S. & Canada
Wyndham	(800) 822-4200 U.S.

Special Challenges to a Sunshine State Vacation

Most families with children visit Florida during the summer months, when school is out—and the Sunshine State bakes in heat and humidity. So before starting off on a day of touring or a visit to the beach, parents should keep some things in mind.

Overheating, Sunburn, and Dehydration Due to Florida's subtropical climate, parents with young children on a day's outing need to pay close attention to their kids. The most common problems of smaller children are overheating, sunburn, and dehydration. A small bottle of sunscreen carried in a pocket or fanny pack will help you take precautions against overexposure to the powerful subtropical sun. Be sure to put some on children in strollers, even if the stroller has a canopy. Some of the worst cases of sunburn we have seen were on the exposed foreheads and feet of toddlers and infants in strollers. To avoid overheating, rest at regular intervals in the shade or in an air-conditioned museum, hotel lobby, restaurant, or public building.

Don't count on keeping small children properly hydrated with soft drinks and water fountain stops. Long lines at popular attractions often make buying refreshments problematic, and water fountains are not always handy. What's more, excited children may not inform you or even realize that they're thirsty or overheated. We recommend renting a stroller for children six years old and under, and carrying plastic water bottles.

Blisters Blisters and sore feet are common for visitors of all ages, so wear comfortable, well-broken-in shoes or sandals. If you or your children are susceptible to blisters, carry some precut Moleskin bandages;

they offer the best possible protection, stick great, and won't sweat off. When you feel a hot spot, stop, air out your foot, and place a Moleskin over the area before a blister forms. Moleskin is available by name at all drugstores. Sometimes small children won't tell their parents about a developing blister until it's too late. We recommend inspecting the feet of preschoolers two or more times a day.

Sunglasses If you want your smaller children to wear sunglasses, it's a good idea to affix a strap or string to the frames so the glasses won't get lost and can hang from the child's neck while indoors.

The Beach To avoid a severe sunburn that can ruin a child's—and your—vacation, listen to this advice offered by Larry Pizzi, operations supervisor of the Miami Beach lifeguards: "Put your kids in light or pastel-colored T-shirts, gob the sunscreen on exposed skin, and give 'em little hats. Be particularly careful on windy days, because kids don't feel the sun burning."

More advice: "Don't let little kids swim alone—it's still the ocean out there," Pizzi says. "And don't leave your children alone on the beach—it's easy for them to get disoriented. Mark your street number so you don't get lost." For more advice on the hazards of the beach and ocean swimming, see our Swimming Hazards section on page 404.

Safety

- Discuss safety with your family before you leave home.
- Discuss what to do if someone gets lost. If you are going to a crowded theme park or anywhere there's a possibility you and your child could get separated, write your child's name on adhesive tape and tape it inside his shirt. Be sure young children know their full name, address, and phone number (with area code).
- Carry photos of your kids for quick ID.
- Travelers checks are the easiest way to protect your money.
- In emergencies, call 911 for assistance in reaching paramedics, law enforcement officials, or the fire department.
- Teach your children to find the proper authorities if they are lost. Tell them to approach a security guard or store clerk— "a grown-up who is working where you're lost."
- Before heading out for a stroll, if you are unsure about the safety of an area, ask the front desk manager or concierge in your hotel.
- Always lock your car when it is parked.
- Always try to keep your gas tank full.
- At night, try to park your car under a streetlight or in a hotel parking garage. Never leave wallets, checkbooks, purses, or luggage in plain view within the car. It's best to lock your luggage out of sight in the trunk.

- Keep your wallet, purse, and camera safe from pickpockets. A "fanny pack," worn around the waist, is the most convenient way to stash small items safely.
- Leave your valuables at home, but if you must bring them along, check with your hotel to see if there is a safe.
- Be sure you lock sliding doors that lead to your hotel balcony or porch while you are in your room and always when you leave. Never open the hotel room door if you are unsure who is at the door.
- Keep medicine out of reach of small children; it's easy to forget and leave it out in hotel rooms.
- Check with the front desk, hotel security, or guest services at attractions for lost property. Report lost or stolen travelers checks and credit cards to the issuing companies and to the police.
- Crime can happen anywhere, so use common sense and take necessary precautions.

Part One

Northwest Florida

Slip off your shoes and step onto the pure, white sand of an unspoiled Panhandle beach and you're in for an unexpected delight: sand so sugary and fine it squeaks beneath your feet. Add the gentle lapping waves and you'll be reminded of the Caribbean—minus Customs and a long, expensive flight over the ocean.

The pace is slow in this part of Florida—perhaps because the Panhandle is in the central time zone, an hour behind the rest of the state.

Stretching from the historic city of Pensacola on the state's western border to the shores of the Suwannee River on the east, Northwest Florida has miles and miles of pristine beaches, much of it undeveloped and protected as the Gulf Islands National Seashore. And not only are there dreamy beaches, but also countless lakes and streams, clean rivers, and pine forests. Add a laid-back ambience, cordiality, and down-home goodness, and you've got an ideal vacation spot for good, old-fashioned family fun.

There are no big cities here, rather an armful of charming little towns, from the high-energy Panama City Beach to rustic Cedar Key (with something in between for everyone). For history, Tallahassee, the state capital, exudes Southern charm with oak-lined streets and antebellum mansions; nearby Apalachicola is full of historically significant structures that provide a rare glimpse into Florida's past.

Navarre Beach, just east of Pensacola, officially begins the Emerald Coast, named for the color of the Gulf of Mexico. Heading east, there are dozens of tiny beach communities all along the way, including Ft. Walton Beach, Destin, Grayton Beach, and the nouveau-Victorian town of Seaside. But Panama City is still the mecca for Southerners in the summertime, with dozens of inexpensive beachside motels, tacky souvenir shops, fast-food joints, and colorful amusement parks. Just minutes to the east it gets quiet again, with pristine places like nearby St. Andrews State Recreation Area, one of the most beautiful beaches in the United States.

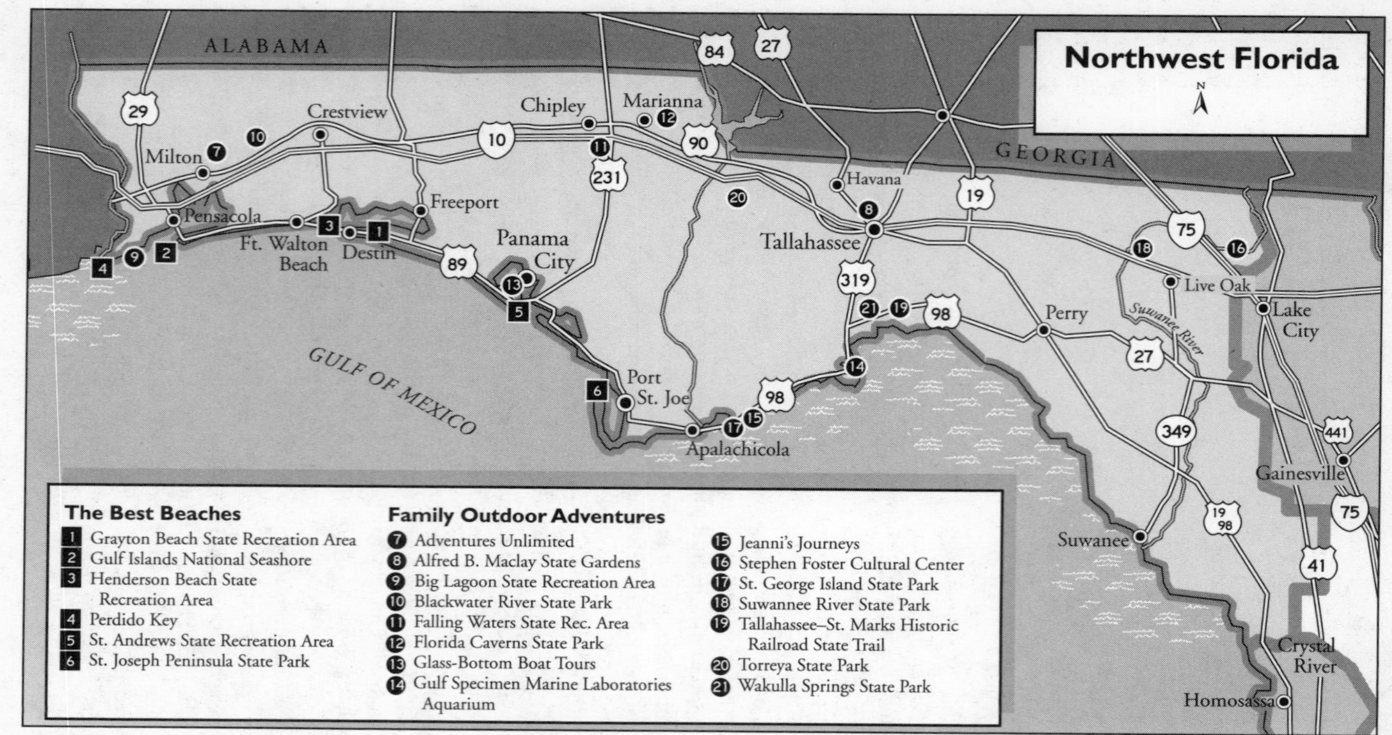
Northwest Florida
N
ALABAMA
GEORGIA
GULF OF MEXICO
Milton
Crestview
Chipley
Marianna
Havana
Tallahassee
Pensacola
Ft. Walton Beach
Destin
Freeport
Panama City
Port St. Joe
Apalachicola
Perry
Live Oak
Lake City
Gainesville
Suwanee
Suwanee River
Crystal River
Homosassa
29
10
84
27
90
231
19
75
319
98
89
349
441
41
19 98
The Best Beaches
1 Grayton Beach State Recreation Area
2 Gulf Islands National Seashore
3 Henderson Beach State Recreation Area
4 Perdido Key
5 St. Andrews State Recreation Area
6 St. Joseph Peninsula State Park
Family Outdoor Adventures
7 Adventures Unlimited
8 Alfred B. Maclay State Gardens
9 Big Lagoon State Recreation Area
10 Blackwater River State Park
11 Falling Waters State Rec. Area
12 Florida Caverns State Park
13 Glass-Bottom Boat Tours
14 Gulf Specimen Marine Laboratories Aquarium
15 Jeanni's Journeys
16 Stephen Foster Cultural Center
17 St. George Island State Park
18 Suwannee River State Park
19 Tallahassee–St. Marks Historic Railroad State Trail
20 Torreya State Park
21 Wakulla Springs State Park

Head inland to the Blackwater, Escambia, and Yellow Rivers near Pensacola, and the Suwannee River near the eastern border for canoeing, kayaking, and boating. Stop for a walk through the eerie limestone caverns in Marianna or for a dip in Wakulla Springs. This part of the state is full of outdoor adventures.

Getting There

By Plane Oskaloosa County Air Terminal, (850) 651-7160, 1 mile east of Destin; Bay County International Airport, (850) 763-6751, 4 miles northwest of Panama City; Pensacola Regional Airport, (850) 436-5005, 3 miles northeast of Pensacola; Tallahassee Regional Airport, (850) 891-7800, 5 miles southwest of Tallahassee, and Williston Regional Airport, (352) 528-4900, 1 mile southwest of Williston.

By Train The Amtrak transcontinental Sunset Limited stops in Pensacola near the bayfront, at 980 E. Heinberg Street, and at 918H Railroad Avenue in Tallahassee; (800) USA-RAIL or www.amtrak.com.

By Car From the east or west take I-10, US 90, or US 98.

How to Get Information before You Go

Apalachicola Bay Chamber of Commerce, 99 Market Street, Suite 100, Apalachicola 32320; (850) 653-9419; www.baynavigator.com.

Emerald Coast Convention Center and Visitor Bureau, P.O. Box 609, Ft. Walton Beach 32549; (800) 322-3319 (U.S. & Canada); www.destin-fwb.com.

Hamilton County Tourist Development Council, 207 N.E. First Street, Room 106, Jasper 32052; (386) 792-1300.

Navarre Beach Tourist Information Center, P.O. Box 5337, Navarre 32566; (850) 939-3267 or (800) 480-SAND (U.S. only); www.navarrefl.com.

Panama City Beach Convention and Visitors Bureau, P.O. Box 9473, Panama City Beach 32417-9473; (800) 722-3224 (U.S. & Canada); www.800pcbeach.com.

Pensacola Convention and Visitor Center, 1401 E. Gregory Street, Pensacola 32501; (850) 434-1234, (800) 874-1234 (U.S. only); www.visitpensacola.com.

South Walton Tourist Development Council, P.O. Box 1248, Santa Rosa Beach 32459; (800) 822-6877 (worldwide); www.beachesofsouthwalton.com.

Tallahassee Area Convention and Visitors Bureau, 106 E. Jefferson Street, Tallahassee 32301; (800) 628-2866 (U.S. & Canada); www.seetallahassee.com.

The Best Beaches

Grayton Beach State Recreation Area, Grayton Beach Grayton, one of the oldest townships on the Gulf Coast, has 356 acres for camping (with just 37 campsites), easy-to-navigate nature trails with self-guided leaflets, and some of the best beaches around (rest rooms and showers; no lifeguards). Campfire interpretive programs are available to summer campers. Cost to camp is $9–13, or $3.25 per vehicle for the day. Santa Rosa; (850) 231-4210.

Gulf Islands National Seashore This is an astounding, stretch of undeveloped beaches, islands, and keys between Destin, Florida, and Gulfport, Mississippi, protected as a National Seashore since 1971. There are historic forts and other structures and myriad wildlife—more than 280 species of birds have been spotted here. Camping, swimming, boating, fishing, and ranger-guided fort tours and nature hikes are favorite family activities.

Though much of the protected seashore is not accessible by car, there are two easy entrances; one at Perdido Key (see above) and the other at Fort Pickens on Santa Rosa Island (both have additional information on the entire stretch of the Gulf Islands National Seashore). On the way to Fort Pickens, you'll pass three public beaches; the first two offer parking only, and the third, called Langdon Beach, has rest rooms, outdoor showers, and a picnic area. There are lifeguards during the peak summer season.

Fort Pickens was a fortress that saw combat during the Civil War, but it's best remembered as the home of Geronimo, an Apache medicine man who was imprisoned there from 1886 to 1888. The fort and museum are open daily 9:30 a.m.–5 p.m. April–October and 8:30 a.m.–4 p.m. November–March. Seven-day admission permits are $8 per vehicle. Also popular is bicycling on the 6-mile, round-trip, oyster-shell trail that begins and ends at the Fort Pickens Visitor Center. The fort is located at 1400 Fort Pickens Road, Santa Rosa Island; (850) 934-2635. Take US 98 and SR 399 to Pensacola Beach then follow signs west to Fort Pickens. For Fort Pickens campground reservations, call (850) 934-2621 or (800) 365-2267. A campsite runs $20 per night.

Henderson Beach State Recreation Area This beach is sugar white and home to gulls, brown pelicans, and the protected sea turtle. There are 208 acres, with several boardwalks for easy access to the beach. There are two pavilions with rest rooms and showers. Hours are 8 a.m.–sunset daily. Entrance fee is $2 per vehicle, per day. Entrance is just east of Destin on US 98; (850) 837-7550.

Perdido Key Fifteen miles west of Pensacola, Perdido Key is a barrier island with spectacular, powdery beaches. The eastern third of the island, known as Johnson Beach Area, is part of the Gulf Islands National Seashore, with great beachside hiking on 7 clear miles of pristine sand and rolling dunes. There are rest rooms and showers but no lifeguards. Hours are 7 a.m.–sunset daily. Seven-day admission permits are $8 per vehicle; (850) 492-7278.

St. Andrews State Recreation Area, Panama City This is one of the most popular parks in the state, where you can camp right on the waterfront. There are miles of beautiful beaches (though it can get crowded in the summer, there are no lifeguards), two fishing piers, and a boat ramp that makes it fun for families who want to get out on the water. A nature trail leads through habitats fragrant with wild rosemary that are home to wading birds, alligators, and many small animals—even a herd of deer. There are picnic areas, a playground, rest rooms, and open-air showers. Admission is $4 per car; open 8 a.m.–sunset. The campground has 176 tent sites, with picnic shelters, a playground, rest rooms, and showers. Cost to camp is $8–15.

A ferry runs from St. Andrews a few hundred yards across the inlet to Shell Island, a 7.5-mile-long, 10-mile-wide barrier island where you can look for shells, swim, or just enjoy the solitude, peace, and quiet. The shuttle runs every 30 minutes during the summer from 9 a.m. to 5 p.m.; off-season, 10 a.m.–3 p.m. Fare is $9.50 for adults, $5.50 for children ages 12 and under. 4607 State Park Land, Panama City Beach; (850) 233-5140.

St. Joseph Peninsula State Park, Port St. Joe This beach gets high ratings, and its towering dunes make it a hiker's paradise. There are rest rooms and showers but no lifeguards. The park encompasses 2,516 acres on a 14-mile-long island off the Gulf Coast, surrounded by the Gulf of Mexico and St. Joseph Bay. Camping, cabins, hiking trails, and miles of natural beach make this perfect for families looking for an active, but quiet, getaway. Bird-watching is excellent (more than 209 species have been noted), and shelling is good. An 18-mile round-trip trail starts at the state park and runs to the end of the preserve, and the island is never more than a mile wide so you're always within sight or earshot of the Gulf. Hikers need to register, because only 20 are allowed each day in the preserve. Entry is $3.25 per vehicle; camping is $8–15. Eight cabins rent for $70 in the summer, $55 in the off-season (minimum stay five nights in summer and two nights off-season). Campfire programs and guided walks are scheduled seasonally. Located near Port St. Joe off CR 30-E, off US 98; (850) 227-1327.

Family Outdoor Adventures

Adventures Unlimited Santa Rosa County has been designated as the Canoe Capital of Florida by the state legislature, and Adventures Unlimited, an 88-acre park at the confluence of the Coldwater River and Wolfe Creek, is a great starting place to get your family out on Santa Rosa's streams, said to have the purest water of any in the state.

Santa Rosa County is thickly forested with several of the best canoeing and tubing streams in the state: Coldwater Creek, Juniper Creek, Sweetwater Creek, and the Blackwater River. Together they provide more than 100 miles of paddling past juniper, cypress, and oak. The rivers flow over and around beautiful white sand and sand bars, so it's easy to wade or swim to a sandy bottom, with an average depth of 2–3 feet, and the little beaches are perfect for an impromptu picnic.

Perfect for families with small children is a 2-hour, 4-mile trip on the Coldwater, where the current keeps your canoe or tube moving; you only have to paddle on occasion to stay in the main current. Adventures Unlimited takes you upstream to start back towards the main landing.

A family of two adults and two children under 8 years old can rent a canoe for about $30. Reservations are advised, especially on weekends. Go in the spring or fall, and you may have the river all to yourself—and that's when the creeks and rivers are at their best.

If you want to stay overnight, Adventures Unlimited can outfit you with everything necessary except clothes and food: a canoe, tents, sleeping bags. At Tomahawk Landing, for a two-night minimum stay, they also have air-conditioned cabins with full kitchens, and the Old Schoolhouse Inn with eight bedrooms—but no phones, TVs, or clocks. Cabins start at $39; guest rooms in the inn start at $79. SR 6, 15 miles north of Milton; from US 90 in Milton, turn north on Highway SR 87; go 12 miles and follow the signs on the right. Turn right and go 4 miles to Adventures Unlimited Tomahawk Landing; (850) 623-6197; www.adventuresunlimited.com.

Alfred B. Maclay State Gardens In the hills near Tallahassee, Maclay State Gardens are just too pretty to pass up when the azaleas and snowy dogwoods are in bloom from January through April (optimum time is mid-March). The ornamental gardens are open 8 a.m.–5 p.m., and they're a great place for a long, peaceful walk. You can also swim, canoe, and boat here. Admission year-round is $3.25 per vehicle. To visit the formal gardens from January through April, cost is an additional $3 for adults and $1.50 for children ages 6–11. The gardens are a half-mile north of I-10 in Tallahassee on US 310; (850) 487-4556.

Big Lagoon State Recreation Area With sandy beaches and salt marshes, Big Lagoon is home to myriad birds and animals—cardinals are common in the uplands, while great blue herons frequent the marshes and the lagoon. Elaborate boardwalks and an observation tower at the east beach give a panoramic view of Big Lagoon and Gulf Island National Seashore across the Intracoastal Waterway. Activities include swimming, picnicking, and nature study. Camping on 75 sites is $8. Located on CR 292A, about 10 miles southwest of Pensacola; (850) 492-1595.

Blackwater River State Park The Blackwater is considered one of the purest sand-bottom rivers in the world, and it is still in a natural state for most of it length. Canoes can be rented at the park, and the run is especially good for novice paddlers because of an easy current with no whitewater. Camping on 31 sites is around $8, $10 with electricity.

There are easy nature trails and decent fishing here, too. Pets are permitted. Located 15 miles northeast of Milton, off US 90; SR 1, Box 57-C, Holt; (850) 983-5363.

Falling Waters State Recreation Area, Chipley. The name comes from a 67-foot waterfall (the only one in Florida) that tumbles into a 20-foot-wide cylindrical sinkhole. The water's unknown final destination remains mysterious. Nature trails guide you through primeval Florida. There's a nice picnic area near the falls. Camping on 24 sites is $8. Located 3 miles south of Chipley off SR 77A; (850) 638-6130.

Florida Caverns State Park, Marianna A bizarre series of connecting caves containing limestone stalactites, stalagmites, columns, rimstone, flowstone, and draperies are found at Florida Caverns State Park. All the enchanting formations are composed of calcite, which is dissolved from the limestone when the surface water containing carbonic acid percolates through the rock and into the cave. Guided tours (45 minutes, with up to 25 per tour) are provided every day. You'll see the Waterfall Room, the Cathedral Room, and the Wedding Room—all impressive. The air is dry, there's no humidity, and it's always 65°.

Picnicking, swimming on a man-made white-sand beach, fishing, and canoeing are available. There are two horse trails with rentals. Camping on 32 sites is $8–12. Admission to the park is $3.25 per vehicle, with admission to the caves $4 for adults, $2 for children ages 2–12. Florida Caverns is located 3 miles north of Marianna on SR 167; (850) 482-1228.

Glass-Bottom Boat Tours This family-run charter out of Treasure Island Marina in Panama City Beach is an easy way to get out on the water for a peek under the sea, especially fun when curious dolphins swim alongside the boat. You might see puffer fish, seahorses, and other exotic marine life, and the guides even bring along a shrimp net to scoop out treasures for a closer look. The boat heads to Shell Island, where you get to spend about 45 minutes on shore collecting shells. It's about 3 hours round trip, and they advise you to call ahead for reservations, as the boat fills up fast, especially in the summertime. Prices are $15, $14 for seniors, and $8 for children. Treasure Island Marina on Thomas Drive; (850) 234-8944.

Gulf Specimen Marine Laboratories Aquarium If you make the trip to Wakulla Springs, just a few miles south is the tiny town of Panacea, where you'll find this amazing laboratory of sea life. Author-explorer Jack Rudloe owns the place, and you'll be lucky if he's around and not out scouting for more Florida marine life to add to his living collection. He'll take his time walking you through the gurgling lab, wall to wall with open tanks teeming with unusual seal life (he also conducts research and stocks biomedical labs around the world). The meanest fish in the ocean? Not the sharks he feeds while you watch, but the innocent-looking flounder, says Rudloe, as he demonstrates their ferocious bite. Kids can touch sea cucumbers, blowfish, sea anemones, and more. 300 Clark Drive at Palm Street south of US Highway 98, Panacea; (850) 984-5297; www.gulfspeciman.org. Open Monday–Friday 9 a.m.–5 p.m., Saturday 10 a.m.–4 p.m., and Sunday noon–4 p.m. Admission is $4, $2 under ages 12.

Jeanni's Journeys Owner Jeanni McMillan returned to St. George Island after spending two years in Singapore and has been camping and exploring the Panhandle for nearly 25 years. Parents, rest assured: Jeanni is a jack-of-all-trades, with a captain's license, a divemaster certificate, a lifeguard certificate, a Florida teaching certificate, and a certificate in first aid and CPR. She'll arrange family trips to the barrier island for snorkeling, shelling, and dolphin watching kayak and canoe trips to neat places like undeveloped St. Vincent or Little St. George Island. Her kids-only trips include sand-sculpting on the beach, rainy day art projects, night critter identification, and a 3-hour fishing adventure in Apalachicola Bay (children must be at least 9 years old for the fishing trip). Kids-only trips range from $25 to $50; others are based on the excursion. 139 E. Gorrie, Street, St. George Island, open from March 5 through December 31; (850) 927-3259; www.sgislandjourneys.com.

WHY IS THE SAND SO WHITE AND THE OCEAN SO BLUE-GREEN IN THE PANHANDLE?

The unusual whiteness of the sand is the result of quartz crystals washing down from the Appalachian Mountains centuries ago. Over time, the crystals have been bleached, ground, smoothed, and polished. Millions and millions have been deposited along this coastline.

The Gulf water appears to be green because of light reflecting off the photosynthetic, micro-algae that are suspended in the clear water. The blue hues in the Gulf that usually are at greater depths are the result of all the colors of light, except blue, being absorbed by the water.

Stephen Foster State Folk Culture Center This center is worth a stop if you are in the vicinity just to learn a little about Mr. Foster, the composer who penned "The Old Folks at Home." The 247-acre center honors the memory of Foster and serves as a gathering place for those who perpetuate the crafts, music, and legends of early and contemporary Floridians. The center is most enjoyable when there are special events, so check as you plan your trip.

It's fun to get out on the river made famous by the song, the beautiful Suwannee. For families it's a great biking spot, too, with an easy, four-mile ride that's part of the Florida National Scenic Trail. You may spot deer, turkey, gray foxes, or gopher tortoises. Camping on 32 sites is $8, $10 with electricity. Admission to the park is $3.25 per car, and there are additional fees for some events. Located in White Springs, on US 41 N. (3 miles from I-75 and 9 miles from I-10); (386) 397-4331.

The little burg of White Springs is excellent bicycling territory, noted as headquarters of the Suwannee Bicycle Association. There are more than 700 miles of clearly marked trails, from short ones up to 100 miles. For information call (386) 397-2347 on weekends only.

St. George Island State Park This little jewel is a best-kept secret, where you can see Florida in its almost-natural state. With 9 miles of sandy shores and grass flats, it's a bird-watcher's paradise, with trail boardwalks and observation platforms for an easy hike. Though the beach is outstanding, be sure to take a little time to explore the bay side of the island, alive with birds and other wildlife. Some of the best shelling on this part of the Gulf Coast is here, and you can even harvest your own oysters. There are picnic areas, rest rooms, showers, and a campground with 60 sites. $4 per vehicle; $8–12 to camp. Located on St. George Island, 10 miles southeast of Eastpoint, off US 98; (850) 927-2111.

There are plenty of seafood restaurants on the island; we highly recommend Finni's Grill & Bar, 40 W. Gorrie Street, (850) 927-3340, for burgers, pasta, or the delicious Deviled Crab Cuban. Finni's is closed on Mondays.

Suwannee River State Park, Live Oak It's doubtful that Stephen Foster ever saw the river he made famous with "The Old Folks at Home," but it's a lovely spot for camping, fishing, picnicking, and canoeing; it also has five short nature trails (look for the amazing Balance Rock). The River Trail is a little over 9 miles, part of the Florida National Scenic Trail, beginning on the CR 141 bridge on the Withlacoochee River, half a mile from the state park, and continuing to the park's northern boundary. Admission is $3.25 per car; open daily, 8 a.m.–sunset. The park is 13 miles west of Live Oak, off US 90; (904) 362-2746. Camping is $8–10 and $2 for pets. To rent a canoe, see Suwannee Canoe Outpost on SR 129; (386) 364-4991. Cost per adult for a full day is $16, for a half day is $14, and for an hour is $9. Children ages 3–12 pay half-price on all trips. Reservations are recommended. Closed Wednesday.

Tallahassee–St. Marks Historic Railroad State Trail From 1837 until 1984 the Tallahassee–St. Marks Railroad was the oldest railroad in Florida; it transported cotton and other products to the port of St. Marks on the Gulf Coast. Now an easy, 16-mile trail starts at Tallahassee and ends at St. Marks, a wide, paved path with a parking lot on SR 363, just south of Tallahassee at the entrance to the trail; (850) 922-6007. You can rent bikes or

A CALENDAR OF FESTIVALS AND EVENTS

March

Natural Bridge Battlefield Reenactment Tallahassee. Civil War life is revisited at the annual reenactment of the 1865 Natural Bridge battle featuring soldiers garbed in authentic uniforms bearing antique weapons. (850) 922-6007.

April

Eglin Air Show Ft. Walton Beach. Every other year (counting from 2001). The event includes Thunderbirds and model aircraft in flight; displays of military aircraft, including some from WWII; and food vendors. (850) 882-3933 or (800) 322-3319.

Ft.Walton Beach Seafood Festival Seafood, seafood, and more seafood at this annual food fest. Also a vintage car show, 1960s rock and roll, and arts and crafts. (800) 322-3319.

Spring Farm Days and Pioneer Breakfast Tallahassee Museum of History and Natural Science. Experience springtime activities on an 1880s farm in the South—sheep shearing, wool spinning, and "yarn" telling by costumed pioneers. (850) 576-1636.

Springtime Tallahassee Downtown Tallahassee. The annual celebration of Florida's capital city in full bloom featuring a parade, arts and crafts, entertainment, and more. (850) 224-5012.

Stephen Foster Storytelling Fest Stephen Foster State Folk Culture Center, White Springs. A two-day event featuring popular storytellers from around Florida. Sponsored by the Stephen Foster Citizen Support Organization, the Florida Storytellers Guild, and the Florida Park Service. (386) 397-4331.

in-line skates at St. Marks Trail Bikes and Blades at the north entrance; (850) 656-0001. Bikes rent for $9 for 2 hours, $16 for 4 hours, and they'll give you a good deal if you're renting bikes for the whole family. Open Monday–Friday noon–sunset and Saturday–Sunday 9 a.m.–6 p.m.

Torreya State Park, Bristol High bluffs along the Apalachicola River are a rare sight in Florida—steep rises 150 feet above the river are forested by hardwood trees and plants more commonly found in the Appalachian Mountains of north Georgia. So if you're homesick for autumn colors, this place ought to cure your urge to travel farther north. A moderate, 7-mile loop trail takes you past hundreds of plants more common to the Appalachian mountains—mountain laurel, wild ginger,

May

Destin May Festival First weekend in May. Seafood, rides, arts and crafts, plus local and national musical entertainment. (800) 651-7131.

Florida Folk Festival Every Memorial Day weekend at Stephen Foster State Culture Center, White Springs, musicians and artisans pay tribute to the old arts. (386) 397-4331.

Suwannee Bicycle Festival The Suwannee Bicycle Festival, held the first weekend in May, is a three-day extravaganza of bicycle rides and outdoor activities. For more information contact the Suwannee County Chamber of Commerce, (386) 397-2347.

June

Billy Bowlegs Festival Destin–Ft. Walton Beach. Pirates aboard flag-flying fleets 500-strong invade the harbor to "capture" the Emerald Coast in honor of local legend Billy Bowlegs. Includes treasure hunts, fishing competitions, a parade, and contests for kids. (850) 651-7131.

Fiesta of Five Flags Pensacola. This event commemorates the founding of Pensacola in 1559 and the five different government flags that have flown over the city. Includes parades, a Spanish fiesta, a children's treasure hunt, sand-sculpture contest, and more. (850) 433-6512.

July

Blue Angels Air Show Pensacola. The world-famous fliers do aerial acrobatics just 100 yards off the Pensacola Beach Fishing Pier. (850) 452-SHOW.

and wild hydrangea, for instance. Wildlife such as deer, beaver, bobcat, and gray fox live here, and more than 100 species of birds have been spotted. You'll also see plenty of torreya, a rare species of tree that grows only along the Apalachicola River bluffs. Camping on 35 sites is $8. Located off SR 12 on CR 1641, 13 miles north of Bristol; (850) 643-2674.

Wakulla Springs State Park This memorable state park is home of the world's largest and deepest freshwater springs—every minute 600,000 gallons of crystal-clear water bubble from a cave 185 feet below the surface. There's an abundance of wildlife—about 2,000 waterfowl make the park their migratory winter home, along with alligators, deer, bears, snakes, and bobcats.

A CALENDAR OF FESTIVALS AND EVENTS *(continued)*

September

Native American Heritage Festival Tallahassee Museum of History and Natural Science. Canoe sculpting, roof thatching, native arts and crafts, and traditional Indian games show lifestyles and traditions of several area Indian tribes. (850) 576-2531.

Pensacola Seafood Festival Pensacola. In the historic Seville Square area. Local seafood dishes, children's area, an antiques show, and continuous entertainment. (850) 433-6512.

October

Monarch Butterfly Festival St. Marks National Wildlife Refuge. A celebration of the butterflies' migration. (850) 925-6121.

Destin Seafood Festival Destin. Everything from shark kabobs to barbecued shrimp to fried alligator and crawfish cheese bread at this annual eat-in. Also music and crafts. (800) 322-3319.

Halloween Howl Tallahassee Museum of History and Natural Science. Haunted trail, tricks and treats, storytelling, music, movies, and magic shows are part of this annual event. (850) 576-2531.

November

Blue Angels Homecoming Air Show World-famous pilots do thrilling aerial acrobatics just 100 yards off the Pensacola Fishing Pier. (850) 452-SHOW.

Glass-bottom boat tours operate over the spring when the water is clear, and there are also 30-minute riverboat cruises on the spring run. The guides love to tell the stories about the old Tarzan movies that were filmed here and how the bones of Ice Age creatures have been recovered from the depths of the 35-million-year-old limestone caverns. Boats run daily from 9:45 a.m.–5 p.m. during daylight savings time; 11 a.m.–3 p.m. the rest of the year. Cost is $4.50 adults, half price for children ages 3–12 and free for those younger. The park is also great for picnicking, nature walks, swimming, and snorkeling in a designated area near the head of the spring.

Bicycling, though a bit challenging, is a real treat on a 10-mile (round-trip) trail—cyclists warn about ravenous horseflies in the summertime.

Annual Florida Seafood One of the biggest events in Northwest Florida, the little town is packed for this all-you-can-eat extravaganza. (850) 653-9419.

Old Tyme Farm Days Live Oak, Spirit of the Suwannee Music Park. Celebrate rural American life and heritage with farming activities, demonstrations, vendors, music, and more. (386) 364-1683.

Annual Rural Folklife Days Stephen Foster State Folk Culture Center, White Springs. Demonstrations featuring cane grinding, syrup making, lye soap making, quilting, and other farm traditions associated with folk life in the South. Cosponsored by the Florida Department of State. (386) 397-4331.

December

Christmas Festival of Lights Stephen Foster State Folk Culture Center, White Springs. A one-day celebration of the holiday season. Features decorations, music, and much more. Highlight is the lighting of the park for the season. Donations of canned goods and small toys to be distributed to needy families are accepted as admission to the program. (904) 397-4331.

Annual Winter Festival Tallahassee. A celebration of lights, music, and the arts. Festivities include a lighting ceremony, 3K jingle bell run, night-time parade, eight stages of entertainment, and Santa's enchanted forest. (850) 891-3860.

Check in with the ranger before setting out, as the last 3 miles are a bit remote; ask the state park attendant for a map as you pay your user fee. Located 14 miles south of Tallahassee on SR 267 at SR 61; (850) 922-3632.

If you're in luck, you can book a room at the Wakulla Springs Lodge. This beautiful old lodge features rare Spanish tiles, marble floors, and paintings of old Florida on the ceiling beams. Rooms are simple and spacious. The dining room has a wood-burning fireplace, tall windows that overlook the springs, and food that is pure Southern. You'll think time has stood still. Phones are provided in each room. No TV. Rates run $80–90 on the weekends; $70–90 weekdays. 1 Springs Drive, 14 miles south of Tallahassee via SR 61; (850) 224-5950; www.wakullacounty.com.

Pensacola

Warm, Southern heritage and warmer Gulf beaches are the best drawing cards any tourist destination could dream up, and Pensacola has a rich Southern history and some of the prettiest beaches in the United States. The city is in the heart of the Gulf Islands National Seashore, which flanks the city with a pair of barrier islands—Perdido Key to the west and Santa Rosa Island to the east.

Santa Rosa Island is home to Pensacola Beach, with miles of unspoiled white sand and a minimum of traffic. Much of Santa Rosa is protected from development but accessible to visitors. You'll find everything from tall condominiums to historic Fort Pickens, a Civil War fortress that is popular with campers (see Gulf Islands National Seashore on page 28).

Pensacola's restored downtown reflects much of the 400-year-old city's history—a town that has changed hands more than a dozen times and flown five flags—Spain, France, England, the United States, and the Confederacy.

Youngsters enjoy the U.S. Museum of Naval Aviation at Pensacola Naval Air Station, known as the cradle of naval aviation for its role in the development of aviators and aircraft, as well as their use by the military. The museum is one of the three largest air and space museums in the world. And you can see the Blue Angels soar skyward off Pensacola Beach during special events in July and November.

Family Resorts

Best Western Pensacola Beach

16 Via de Luna Drive, Pensacola Beach • (850) 934-3300 or (800) 528-1234
fax (850) 934-4366.

Oversized rooms right on the Gulf beach all have microwaves, refrigerators, coffeemakers, and wet bars. Rooms don't have balconies, a plus for families with small children, but there are some very pretty ocean views.

Free breakfast is served every morning. There are two outdoor pools and a playground for children right on the beach. Children up to age 18 stay free with parents. Rates start at $169 in the summer and $109 in the winter, parking and a Continental breakfast included.

The Dunes

333 Fort Pickens Road, Pensacola Beach • (850) 932-3536 or (800) 83-DUNES fax (904) 932-7088.

The Dunes offers spacious rooms with balconies with lovely views of the Gulf of Mexico or the bay and an undeveloped dune preserve next door. There are a heated pool, a bike path, and volleyball nets on the beach. A nanny service is offered through the hotel. Rates start at $150 in the summer, $115 in the winter; kids ages 18 and under stay free with parents.

Take a Free Ride

At Pensacola Beach, a free island trolley runs May–September, Friday–Sunday, 10 a.m.–3 p.m. There are 2 routes: parallel to the beach on Via de Luna and Fort Pickens Road, and along Pensacola Beach Boulevard from the Bob Sikes Bridge to Casino Beach, (850) 595-3228.

Attractions

Fort Barrancas

1801 Gulf Breeze Parkway, Gulf Breeze • (850) 455-5167

Hours - April–October, 9:30 a.m.–5 p.m.; November–March, Wednesday–Sunday, 8:30 a.m.–4 p.m.

Admission - Free

Appeal by Age Group -

Pre-school ★★	Teens ★★★	Over 30 ★★★
Grade school ★★★	Young Adults ★★★	Seniors ★★★

Touring Time - Average 1 hour; minimum 45 minutes

Rainy-Day Touring - Not recommended

Author's Rating - ★★; interesting history lesson

Restaurants - No

Alcoholic beverages - No

Handicapped access - No

Wheelchair rental - No

Baby stroller rental - No

Lockers - No

Pet kennels - No

Rain check - No

Private tours - No

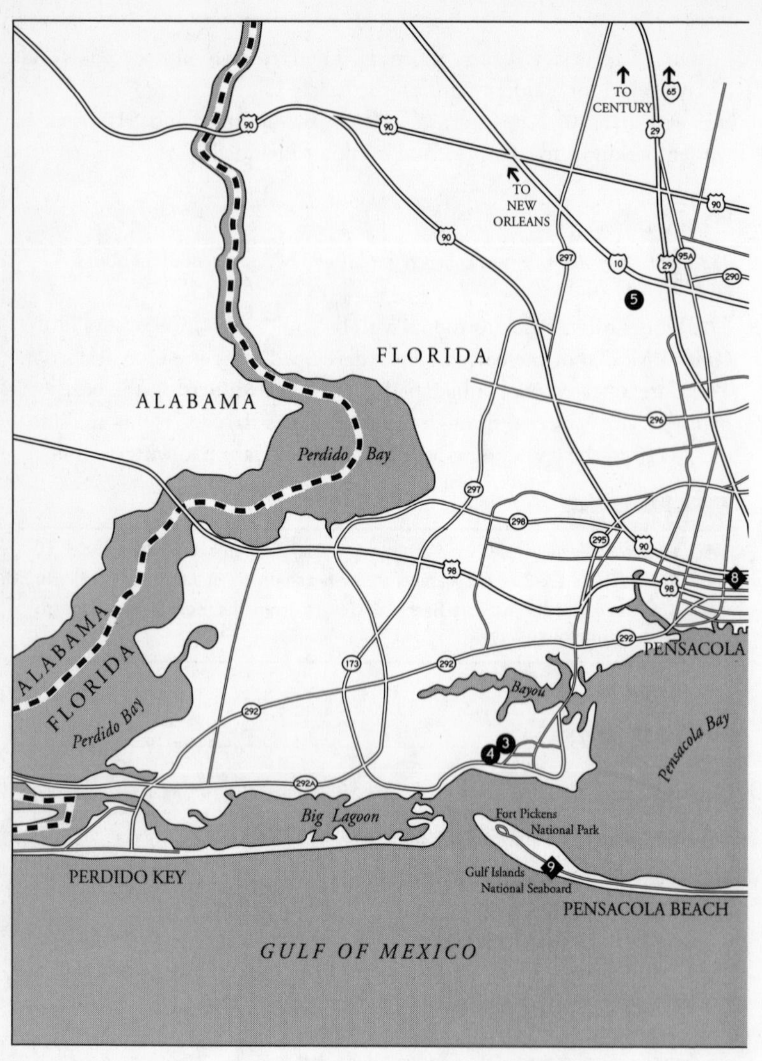
TO
CENTURY
65
90
90
29
TO
NEW
ORLEANS
90
90
297
10
29
95A
290
5
FLORIDA
ALABAMA
296
Perdido Bay
297
298
295
90
98
8
98
292
PENSACOLA
ALABAMA
FLORIDA
173
292
Bayou
292
Perdido Bay
Pensacola Bay
3
4
292A
Big Lagoon
Fort Pickens
National Park
Gulf Islands
National Seaboard
9
PERDIDO KEY
PENSACOLA BEACH
GULF OF MEXICO

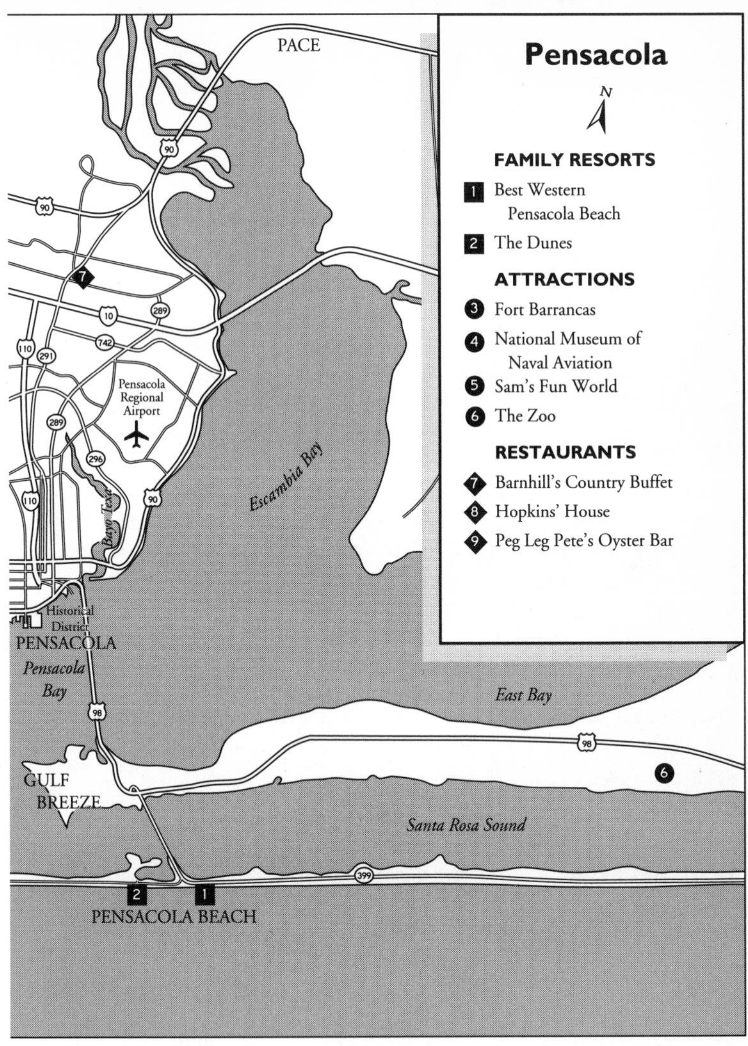

Pensacola
N
FAMILY RESORTS
1 Best Western Pensacola Beach
2 The Dunes
ATTRACTIONS
3 Fort Barrancas
4 National Museum of Naval Aviation
5 Sam's Fun World
6 The Zoo
RESTAURANTS
7 Barnhill's Country Buffet
8 Hopkins' House
9 Peg Leg Pete's Oyster Bar
PACE
Pensacola Regional Airport
Escambia Bay
Historical District
PENSACOLA
Pensacola Bay
East Bay
GULF BREEZE
Santa Rosa Sound
PENSACOLA BEACH

Description and Comments Fort Barrancas was started by the Spanish in 1797 and finished by American troops between 1839 and 1844. The fort was restored by the National Park Service and is part of Gulf Island National Seashore. Kids enjoy exploring the old fort; guided tours are available.

HISTORIC PENSACOLA VILLAGE

More than 400 years of history are displayed in historic Pensacola Village, with ten restored buildings and museums in a four-block area, and a dining and entertainment complex. Now preserved by the state, the village hosts costumed characters who demonstrate crafts and daily chores. Charming boutiques and restaurants are now part of the historic area, bounded by Government, Zaragossa, Adams, and Alcanz streets. Start at the T.T. Wentworth Jr. Florida State Museum at 330 S. Jefferson Street to purchase tickets.

Important landmarks include the Museum of Industry, the Museum of Commerce, the French Creole–style Charles Lavalle House, the Victoria Dorr House, the Quina House, and the Julee Cottage Black History Museum. The Julee Cottage Musuem is located at 205 E. Zaragossa Street. Admission is $6 adults, $5 seniors ages 65 and older and military, $2.50 children ages 4–16, free ages 4 and under, $13 families. Open Memorial Day–Labor Day, daily, 10 a.m.–4 p.m.; closed Sundays, Mondays, and holidays during the rest of the year; (850) 595-5985, www.historicpensacola.org. Tours are given at 11 a.m. and 1 p.m.

National Museum of Naval Aviation

Radford Boulevard on the U.S. Naval Air Station • (850) 452-3604

Hours - Daily, 9 a.m.–5 p.m.; closed New Year's Day, Thanksgiving, and Christmas

Admission - Free, but donations are appreciated

Appeal by Age Group -

Pre-school ★	Teens ★★★	Over 30 ★★★
Grade school ★★★	Young Adults ★★★	Seniors ★★★

Touring Time - Average 4 hours; minimum 2 hours

Rainy-Day Touring - Recommended

Author's Rating - ★★★; great for history buffs, and fun learning for everyone

Restaurants - Yes

Handicapped access - Yes

Baby stroller rental - No

Pet kennels - No

Private tours - Yes

Alcoholic beverages - Yes

Wheelchair rental - Available at no charge

Lockers - No

Rain check - No

Description and Comments This Naval Air Station has been used by the U.S. Navy and Marine Corps since the turn of the twentieth century, and the museum showcases more than 100 aircraft from the first biplane to the Skylab Command Module. This is one of the world's largest air and space museums, with acres of aircraft parked outside, including planes flown by the Blue Angels. Kids love to strap into cockpit trainers for a pretend test flight, sitting at the controls of a jet trainer. The IMAX theater, with a screen nearly 7 stories tall and 80 feet wide, shows aviation up close. Call (850) 435-2024 for information.

Sam's Fun City

On U.S. Hwy. 29 near "W" Street, Pensacola • (850) 505-0800

Hours - 5p.m.–10 p.m. Friday; 11 a.m.–10 p.m. Saturday; noon– 6 p.m. Sunday

Admission - Free; ticket books start at $6

Appeal by Age Group -

Pre-school ★★★	Teens ★★★	Over 30 ★
Grade school ★★★	Young Adults ★★	Seniors ★

Touring Time - Half a day on average

Rainy-Day Touring - Not recommended

Author's Rating - ★★; theme park fun on a small scale

Restaurant Yes

Alcoholic beverages - No

Handicapped access - Yes

Wheelchair rental - No

Baby stroller rental - No

Lockers - No

Pet kennels - No

Rain check - No

Private tours - No

Description and Comments This new, 20-acre amusement park has something for everyone, from a go-cart track to mini-golf and bumper boats. Old-fashioned rides like the scrambler, the swinger and a Ferris wheel are divided among the park's three "lands," which are Terry Town, Yesterville, and Westerville. Fun for the whole family, and there are plans to expand with a new game arcade set to open in the fall of 2002 and a water park in 2003.

The Zoo

On US 98 about 10 miles east of Gulf Breeze and 15 miles east of Pensacola • (850) 932-2229

Hours - Winter, 9 a.m.–4 p.m.; summer, 9 a.m.–5 p.m.

Admission - $9.95 for adults, $8.95 for senior citizens ages 62 and older, $6.95 for children ages 3–11, free for those younger

Appeal by Age Group -

Pre-school ★★★	Teens ★★★	Over 30 ★★
Grade school ★★★	Young Adults ★★	Seniors ★★

Touring Time - Half a day on average; minimum 2 hours

Rainy-Day Touring - Not recommended

Author's Rating - ★★; fun family afternoon after a morning at the beach

Restaurant Yes

Alcoholic beverages - No

Handicapped access - Yes

Wheelchair rental - Yes

Baby stroller rental - Yes

Lockers - No

Pet kennels - No

Rain check - No

Private tours - No

Description and Comments This 50-acre park is home to more than 750 exotic animals—including white Bengal tigers, gorillas, bears, tigers, rhinos, and zebras—surrounded by botanical gardens. A Safari Line train takes you through a 30-acre wildlife preserve with free-roaming animals. Hand-feed a giraffe or ride Ellie the Elephant when she's not painting or playing music. The farm has a petting zoo and a nursery for newborn animals. Regularly scheduled shows feature birds of prey, elephants, reptiles, and other wildlife.

Family-Friendly Restaurants

Barnhill's Country Buffet

N. Davis Highway at Olive Road, Pensacola • (850) 477-5465

Meals served - Lunch and dinner

Cuisine - American

Entree range - Lunch costs $6.98 adults, $6.44 seniors ages 60 and older, 55 cents times age for children 12 and under; dinner costs $8.83 adults, $8.29 seniors, 55 cents times age for children 12 and under

Kids menu - No, but fried chicken and desserts are popular with the kids

Reservations - Not accepted

Payment - Visa, MC, AmEx, D

Families come for miles around to this buffet, featuring seven tables stacked with fried chicken, fish, ham, roast beef, vegetables, salads, and old-fashioned desserts.

Hopkins' House

900 N. Spring Street, Pensacola • (850) 438-3979

Meals served - Breakfast, lunch, and dinner, Monday–Friday; breakfast and lunch on Saturday and Sunday

Cuisine - Southern

Entree range - Full meals $8.55

Kids menu - No, but kids like the chicken

Reservations - Not accepted

Payment - No credit cards

You might have to wait for a spot in the dining room, but the rocking chairs on the wraparound porch make it easy. Everyone gathers around the large dining tables to eat family style, with platters piled high with freshly cooked vegetables from area farms along with fried chicken, fried fish, or whatever is the special of the day. And everyone cleans up, just like in mom's dining room at home, except here you pay in cash.

Peg Leg Pete's Oyster Bar

1010 Fort Pickens Road, Pensacola Beach • (850) 932-4139

Meals served - Lunch and dinner

Cuisine - American

Entree range - $6–$44.95

Kids menu - Yes

Reservations - Not accepted

Payment - All major credit cards accepted

This casual eatery is fun for everyone, with kid's meals—burgers, corn dogs, grilled cheese, or fried shrimp—served in a beach sand bucket. Grown-ups love the Cajun specialties or the whopping seafood-for-two platter that includes lobster, shrimp, and snow crab. Hands-down favorite is the grouper supreme sandwich, with blackened fish, sauteed veggies, and melted Swiss cheese, with a side of fries. Steaks also are on the menu.

Ft. Walton Beach, Destin, and the Beaches of South Walton

More fabulous sugary sand and emerald waters are the claim to fame for these Southern sea towns—24 miles of powdery beaches, with more than 60% protected by law from development.

The beaches have been voted the safest in the country, with gentle waves and sloping, sandy shallows, and consistently have been named a "favorite family vacation spot" by readers of *Southern Living.* This part of the Panhandle is considered one of the top five shelling destinations in the world—but you have to snorkel (or dive) the off-coast sandbars to find them, spots like Sand Dollar City, a pure white sandbar 200 feet off Destin Beach, that is rich with circular "sea money."

Destin has been called the "world's luckiest fishing village," with the "100 Fathom curve" drawing closer to Destin than to any other spot in Florida. The proximity of the curve creates the speediest deep-water access to the Gulf, and the town has the largest charter boat fleet in Florida—with plenty of captains willing to take your family for a half-day of fishing. And your catches can be cooked for free at some of the harbor restaurants.

"The beaches of South Walton" is the area between Destin and Panama City Beach that includes 26 miles of beaches along Scenic 30-A, and US 98. Among the noted stops is Seaside, famed for its internationally acclaimed, award-winning pastel architecture. Grayton Beach is also here, the oldest community in the area, surrounded by Grayton Beach State Recreation Area, one of the prettiest beaches in Florida (see page 27).

Family Resorts

Radisson Beach Resort

1110 Santa Rosa Boulevard, Ft. Walton Beach • (850) 243-9181 • fax (850) 664-7652 • www.radisson.com • www.beachit@ft-walton-beach.com

The Radisson, formerly a Holiday Inn, is on the ocean with 388 rooms. Guests can request refrigerators, given on a first-come, first-served basis. There are four swimming pools, one that's only a foot deep just for tots, and on the beach are jet skis, kayaks, parasailing, and volleyball. The activities director is there on weekends, organizing free daylong family activities. Kids ages 17 and under stay free with parents. Rates start at $149 in the summer, $89 in the winter.

Sandestin Golf and Tennis Resort

(850) 267-8150 or (800) 277-0800 • fax (850) 267-822
www.sandestin.com.

This oceanfront resort has it all: a marina (with ocean kayaks, Waverunners, ski boats, and more), a health club and spa, golf, tennis, bikes to rent, and its own little "downtown" of more than 30 shops and kiosks. A children's program offers arts and crafts, beach and pool games, bingo, biking, fishing, hiking, scavenger hunts, and storytelling. There's also a teen social night. Accommodations range from a room at the inn (refrigerators and coffeemakers are furnished) to 1- to 4-bedroom villas; rates start at $85 in the winter and $216 in the summer. Sandestin is 8 miles east of Destin on US 98 West.

ON THE WATER

Glass-bottom boats offer underwater viewing, dolphin encounters, crab trapping, bird feeding, and nature cruises from Boogies Dock at the foot of Destin Bridge; 2 US 98E, Destin; (850) 654-7787. $15 adults, $5 ages 12 and under.

Southern Star offers dolphin cruises all year from Harbor Walk Marina at the foot of Destin Bridge; (850) 837-7741. $17 adults, seniors $14, $7 kids.

For snorkeling, Kokomo Snorkeling Headquarters at 500 US 98E in Destin offers daily trips to two locations—one for shelling, one for feeding fish. An instructor gives how-to lessons for ages 4 and older. Cost is $20 per person for a 3-hour trip. (850) 837-9029.

If you want to escape the busy beach and get out on the water with no hassles, settle back on one of the glass-bottom boat tours from the Treasure Island Marina, 3605 Thomas Drive in Panama City Beach. Try to time your tour during an incoming tide to see the most sea life. The friendly, informative guides take you for a 3-hour trip to Shell Island for shell collecting, and to spots where you're likely to see dolphins. Cost is $9.50 for adults, $9 seniors, and $5.50 ages 3 to 1. Phone (850) 234-8944, or visit www.shellislandtours.com.

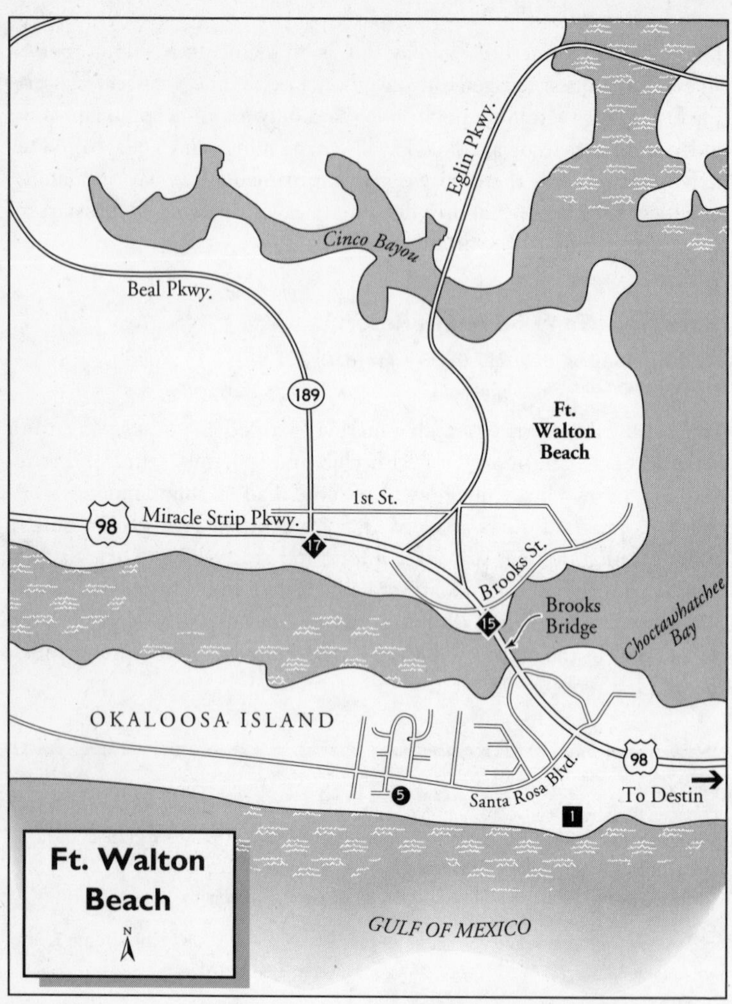

(See the following pages for maps of Destin and the Beaches of South Walton.)

FAMILY RESORTS

1 Radisson Beach Resort
2 Sandestin Golf and Tennis Resort
3 Seaside

ATTRACTIONS

4 Big Kahuna's
5 Gulfarium
6 Morgan's

RESTAURANTS

7 Another Broken Egg Cafe
8 The Back Porch
9 Bud and Alley's
10 Cafe Thirty-A
11 Criolla's
12 The Donut Hole
13 Goatfeathers
14 June's Dunes
15 Old Bay Steamer
16 Picolo and the Red Bar
17 Staff's Seafood Restaurant

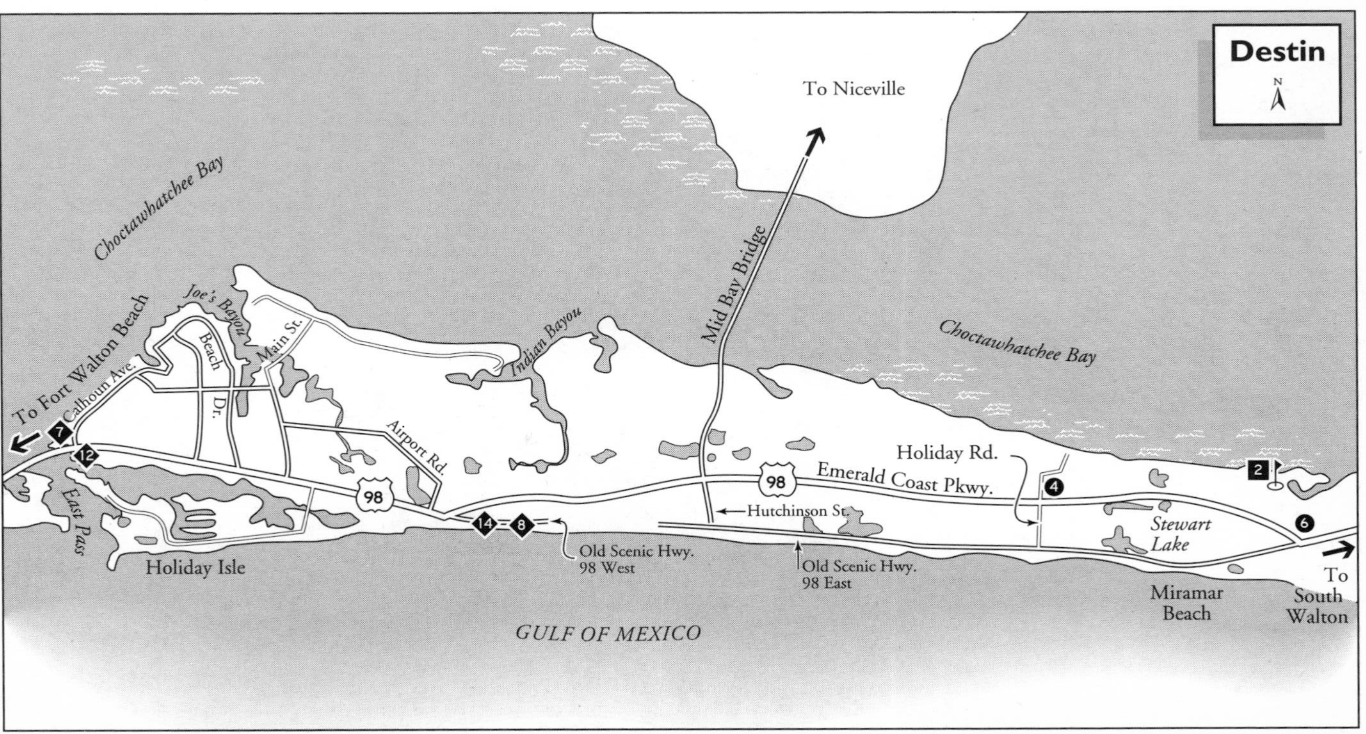

Destin
N
To Niceville
Choctawhatchee Bay
Mid Bay Bridge
Choctawhatchee Bay
To Fort Walton Beach
Calhoun Ave.
Joe's Bayou
Beach Dr.
Main St.
Indian Bayou
Airport Rd.
98
Holiday Rd.
Emerald Coast Pkwy.
Hutchinson St.
East Pass
Holiday Isle
Old Scenic Hwy. 98 West
Old Scenic Hwy. 98 East
Stewart Lake
To South Walton
Miramar Beach
GULF OF MEXICO
2
4
6
7
8
12
14

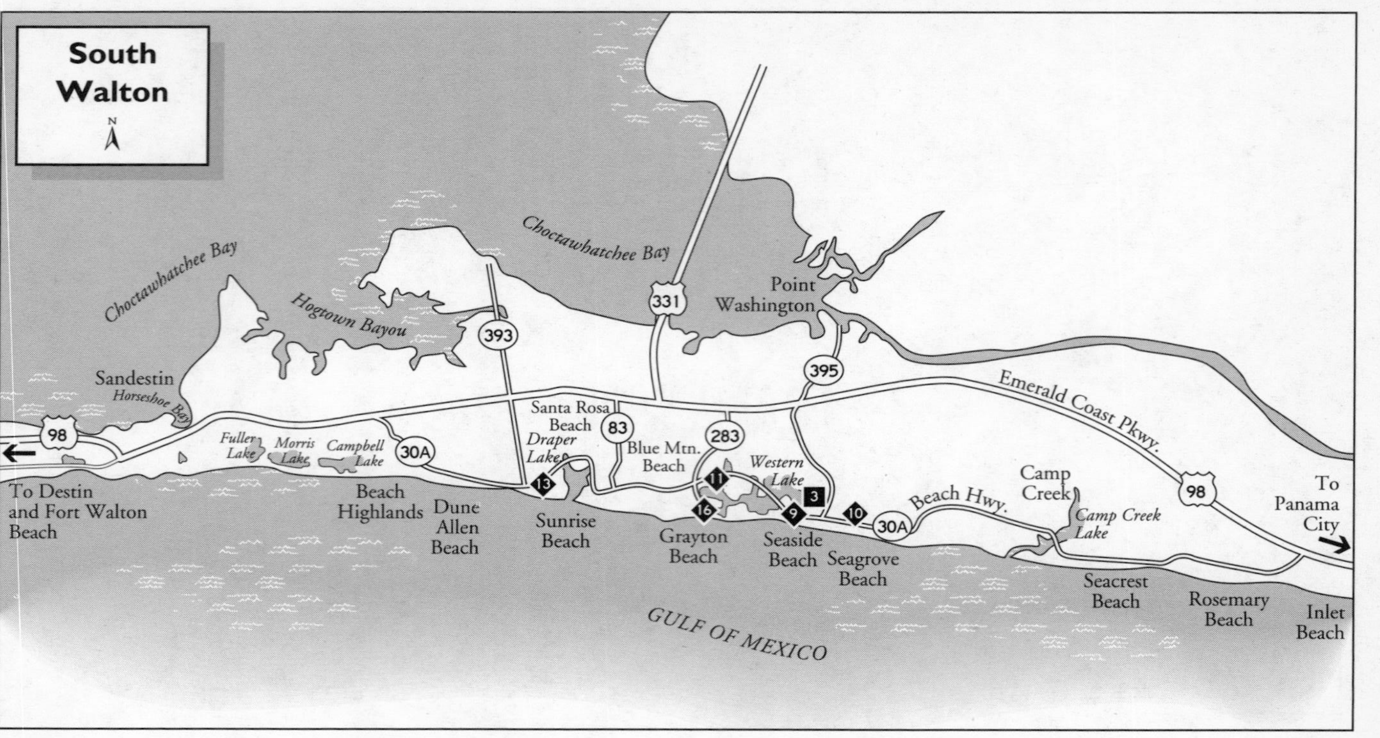
South Walton
N
Choctawhatchee Bay
Hogtown Bayou
Choctawhatchee Bay
Point Washington
Sandestin
Horseshoe Bay
98
393
331
395
Emerald Coast Pkwy.
Santa Rosa Beach
83
283
Fuller Lake
Morris Lake
Campbell Lake
30A
Draper Lake
Blue Mtn. Beach
Western Lake
13
11
16
9
3
10
30A
Beach Hwy.
Camp Creek
Camp Creek Lake
98
To Panama City
To Destin and Fort Walton Beach
Beach Highlands
Dune Allen Beach
Sunrise Beach
Grayton Beach
Seaside Beach
Seagrove Beach
Seacrest Beach
Rosemary Beach
Inlet Beach
GULF OF MEXICO

Seaside

(800) 277-8696 • fax (850) 231-5680 • www.seasidefl.com.

For families looking for a comfortable place at the beach, this small retreat of clapboard cottages is ideal. Town founder Robert Davis spent his boyhood summers here and returned in the 1980s to create a town that would remind him of his own family gatherings. No two homes are alike, but there's a lovely visual harmony to Seaside, thanks to a building code that, among other stipulations, requires each cottage to have a picket fence (and no two identical fences on the same street). The result is a community of more than 200 tasteful cottages in warm colors with the architectural details of the 1920s. All have charming names, like "Jack's Beanstalk," "Savannah Sands," or "Dream Catcher," and many are available for rent.

From the cottages, the beach is a pleasant walk across 30-A, the old coast highway—where traffic slows to 15 mph. Each neighborhood has its own beach and a pavilion that serves as a gateway to the white sand.

You really don't need to ever leave Seaside; the town has a small but sophisticated grocer, good restaurants, and great shopping at galleries, antique shops, and boutiques with casual wear from around the world, even an excellent wine bar. The well-stocked bookstore just steps from the ocean is an amazing find.

There are swimming pools, but most everyone heads for the ocean, more like a big bathtub with the gentle Gulf waves and white sand. Seaside also has tennis courts, croquet, and bikes to rent. One- to six-bedroom cottages, completely and beautifully furnished, rent from $140 per day year-round. Some cottages provide free breakfast. There's also a small motel and bed-and-breakfast. Take Highway US 98 E. to SR 283, turn right. Take SR 283 to SR 30-A, turn left and drive 2 miles.

Attractions

Big Kahuna's

1007 Highway 98 E., Destin • (850) 837-4061

Hours - 10 a.m.–6 p.m seven days a week, except in winter when the park closes

Admission - $29.95 adults; $27.95 under 48", free ages 2 and under.

Appeal by Age Group -

Pre-school ★★★	Teens ★★★	Over 30 ★
Grade school ★★★	Young Adults ★★	Seniors ★

Touring Time - Average 5–6 hours; minimum 2 hours

Rainy-Day Touring - Not recommended

Author's Rating - ★★; something for everyone when you're bored with the beach

Restaurants - Yes
Alcoholic beverages - Beer
Handicapped access - Yes
Wheelchair rental - No
Baby stroller rental - No
Lockers - Yes ($5 plus $5 deposit)
Pet kennels - No
Rain check - No
Private tours - No

Description and Comments If your family wants action, there's plenty in this water park with more than 50 slides and attractions, including "the world's largest tube river" and Bombs Away Bay with real a B-25 bomber. Also miniature golf, arcade games, go-carts, dune buggies, and a Vertical Accelerator that drops 10 stories—but they all cost extra and it adds up quickly.

Gulfarium

On US 98 just east of Ft. Walton Beach • (850) 244-5169

Hours - Daily, 9 a.m.–5 p.m.

Admission - $16 for adults, $14 for senior citizens ages 55 and older, $10 for children ages 4–11

Appeal by Age Group -

Pre-school ★★★	Teens ★★	Over 30 ★★
Grade school ★★★	Young Adults ★★	Seniors ★★

Touring Time - Average 3–4 hours; minimum 2 hours

Rainy-Day Touring - Not recommended

Author's Rating - ★★; fun for a beach diversion

Restaurants - Yes
Alcoholic beverages - No
Handicapped access - Yes
Wheelchair rental - No
Baby stroller rental - No
Lockers - No
Pet kennels - No
Rain check - No
Private tours - No

Description and Comments Opened in 1955, Gulfarium is one of America's original marine parks. The "Living Sea" exhibit is a panorama of undersea life, from a 600-pound gray seal to a 2-ounce clownfish. There are also performances by trained dolphins; sea lion shows; marine life exhibits featuring seals, otters, penguins, and a host of other sea animals.

Morgan's

10406 Emerald Coast Parkway (Silver Sands Factory Stores), Destin • (850) 654-3320

Hours - Different hours for market, bakery, entertainment center, and restaurant

Admission - Free

Appeal by Age Group -

Pre-school ★★★	Teens ★★★	Over 30 ★★★
Grade school ★★★	Young Adults ★★★	Seniors ★★★

Touring Time - Average 2–3 hours; minimum 1½ hours

Rainy-Day Touring - Recommended

Author's Rating - ★★★; perfect rainy day option—parents get to shop, the kids get to play

Restaurants - Yes

Alcoholic beverages - Yes

Handicapped access - Yes

Wheelchair rental - No

Baby stroller rental - No

Lockers - No

Pet kennels - No

Rain check - No

Private tours - No

Description and Comments The third-largest designer outlet center in the United States, this is a favorite place for local families. There are two levels of entertainment and eateries, with more than 160 video games, virtual sports, motion-simulation rides, and a "soft play" maze for little ones. Creehan's Market is an upscale food court with five quick-service restaurants offering everything from pizza to sushi. For sit-down service, Harbor Docks Seafood and Brewery gets rave reviews for its fresh fish and six different beers brewed on the premises.

Family-Friendly Restaurants

Another Broken Egg Cafe

US 98 E Destin • (850) 650-0499

Meals served - Breakfast, lunch, and dinner

Cuisine - American

Entree range - $4.89–9.99

Kids menu - Yes

Reservations - Yes

Payment - All major credit cards accepted

This cozy little eatery specializes in omelets—you name it, they'll make it. And try the grits sweetened with blackberries.

The Back Porch

1740 Old US 98 E., Destin • (850) 837-2022

Meals served - Lunch and dinner

Cuisine - Seafood

Entree range - $9–15 (sandwiches start at $6)

Kids menu - Yes

Reservations - Not accepted

Payment - All major credit cards accepted

This quintessential seafood shack sits near the western boundary of Henderson Beach State Recreation Area, with lovely beach and Gulf views. Fish and burgers are grilled over coals—the local favorite, amberjack, is the house specialty.

Bud and Alley's

Seaside • (850) 231-5900

Meals served - Lunch and dinner

Cuisine - Gourmet American and continental

Entree range - $9–15 lunch; $19–27 dinner

Kids menu - Yes, $7–10

Reservations - Accepted

Payment - Visa, MC

Go early, because this casual Seaside eatery, named after a dog and a cat, gets crowded. Everything is fresh and creatively prepared, from tempura fried soft-shell blue crab to a simple blackened grouper. For kids, it's as basic as noodles with butter and cheese ($4.95) or as sophisticated as chicken breast with fresh grilled vegetables ($6.95).

Cafe Thirty-A

Located on C30-A, between Destin and Panama City (near the town of Seaside) • (850) 231-2166

Meals served - Dinner, closed Sunday

Cuisine - Contemporary, eclectic

Entree range - $21–30

Kids menu - Yes

Reservations - Accepted

Payment - Visa, MC, AmEx, D

Cafe Thirty-A is trendy and upscale, but families are welcome. Go for the rich, fried soft-shell crab if it's on the menu; otherwise, whether it's lamb, fish, or beef, Cafe Thirty-A does a splendid job.

Criolla's

170 E. C30-A, Grayton Beach, near Seaside • (850) 267-1267

Meals served - Dinner

Cuisine - Gourmet, Creole-style

Entree range - $20–28

Kids menu - Yes

Reservations - Accepted

Payment - Visa, MC, AmEx, D

This award-winning restaurant is pricey, but worth a special family night out. You won't be disappointed with any fish, and save room for the from-scratch desserts, like Aunt Irma's banana and pecan beignets. The upscale children's menu offers grilled beef tournedos ($12.95) and grilled fish or shrimp ($8.95).

The Donut Hole

635 US 98E, Destin • (850) 837-8824

Meals served - Open 24 hours

Cuisine - American

Entree range - $4.75–9.50

Kids menu - No

Reservations - No

Payment - Cash only

Who needs a kid's menu when the menu has burgers, shakes, and 28 varieties of donuts. Breakfast is served all day long. Omelet fans will love the Destin omelet, with fresh local crabmeat, peppers, onions, and cheese.

Goatfeathers

3865 W. SR C30-A, between Dune Allen and Blue Mountain Beach • (850) 267-3342

Meals served - Lunch and dinner; closed Wednesdays

Cuisine - Seafood

Entree range - Lunch $5.95–9.95; dinner $8.95–18.95

Kids menu - Yes

Reservations - Accepted

Payment - All major credit cards accepted

The food is hearty, Southern, and fried—and fresh under that crunchy breading. Seafood po' boy sandwiches come with fries or steamed new potatoes; fried scallops, oysters, shrimp, or fish come with coleslaw, hush puppies, and potatoes or vegetables. OK, you can get fish or shrimp grilled, but go for the fried unless you're on fat patrol. The extensive kids menu offers a dozen entrees, from burgers and pizza to fried shrimp, with mini–side orders of applesauce, potatoes, and vegetables.

June's Dunes

1780 Old US 98 E., Destin • (850) 650-0455

Meals served - Breakfast and lunch

Cuisine - American

Entree range - $4–10

Kids menu - No, but there are items on the menu that kids like

Reservations - Not accepted

Payment - No credit cards

This is one of those "junk food" places the locals favor, where you eat beachside on picnic tables. The menu is on a chalkboard and includes hearty breakfast favorites like waffles and biscuits with sausage gravy. Good burgers for lunch. And, yes, June is usually there.

Old Bay Steamer

1310 Highway 98 E, Okaloosa Island (4 miles from Destin Bridge) • (850) 664-2795

Meals served - Dinner

Cuisine - Seafood

Entree range - $10.95–22.95

Kids menu - Yes

Reservations - Not accepted

Payment - Visa, MC, AmEx, DC

Locals don't go for the view (there isn't one), but for enormous platters of steamed seafood. Old Bay's motto: "We don't do fried." Try the royal red shrimp fresh from the Gulf, mussels, crabs, or lobsters, and don't worry about making a mess—just toss your empty shells in a bucket on the table.

Picolo and the Red Bar

70 Hotz Avenue, Grayton Beach • (850) 231-1008

Meals served - Lunch and dinner

Cuisine - Seafood

Entree range - $8–18.95

Kids menu - No, but appetizers include chicken fingers, fish sticks, and pizza bread

Reservations - Not accepted

Payment - Cash only

This casual eatery bustles with activity—a lively bar is just inside the front door, and most of the restaurant seating is on a big screened porch right on the beach. The locals love this place, and it's definitely a lively crowd on the weekends. Try the chicken with lemon caper sauce or the crab cakes.

Staff's Seafood Restaurant

24 Miracle Strip Parkway SE (US 98), Ft. Walton Beach • (850) 243-3482

Meals served - Dinner

Cuisine - Seafood

Entree range - $14.95–27

Kids menu - Yes, 10 and under, $4.95–5.95

Reservations - Not accepted

Payment - All major credit cards accepted

The Staff has been around since 1913, and its delicious home-baked wheat bread has been homemade with Pop Staff's recipe since the 1920s. The seafood gumbo is excellent; another house specialty is the Seafood Skillet, brimming with yellowfin tuna, shrimp, scallops, and crab cooked with plenty of butter and cheese. Plenty of folks go for the $19.95 Florida lobster dinner.

Panama City Beach

If you're looking for nonstop entertainment and action, you can find plenty to do in this high-energy, affordable beach town. You name it, you'll probably find a place to do it here, from bungee jumping and parasailing to jet skiing, wind surfing, even oceanfront minigolf.

The locals boast that the sun shines about 320 days a year, and the "sand is like a bar of Ivory soap—ninety-nine and forty-four one-hundredths percent pure quartz," according to Dr. Stephen P. Leatherman, a.k.a. "Dr. Beach," from the University of Maryland. The pretty beach is, however, lined with hotels, motels, and beach houses.

Be forewarned: This is the beach for high school spring breakers from neighboring states, and it's also full of teenagers in the summertime. And as Panama City beach has grown up, there has not been a lot of thoughtful planning—just more T-shirt shops and more fast-food joints and more little motels crowded along the oceanfront. Still, it's full of energy, and if you don't mind sharing your space with other revelers, this can be a pretty fun place. If you're looking for peace and quiet, head farther east.

Family Resorts

Holiday Inn SunSpree

11127 Front Beach Road, Panama City Beach • (850) 234-1111 or (800) 633-0266
fax (850) 235-0888 • www.holidayinnsunspree.com

This 15-story, 342-room hotel was chosen by Holiday Inn as its Best Family Vacation Hotel in the world. Located smack in the middle of all the Panama City Beach action, every room has a balcony on the ocean, a microwave, coffeemaker, and refrigerator. A children's playground, electronic game room, and a swimming pool with a waterfall make the kids extra happy. And there are free supervised activities in the Kids Splash Around Club, like sand-castle building, raft racing, beach games, pirates'

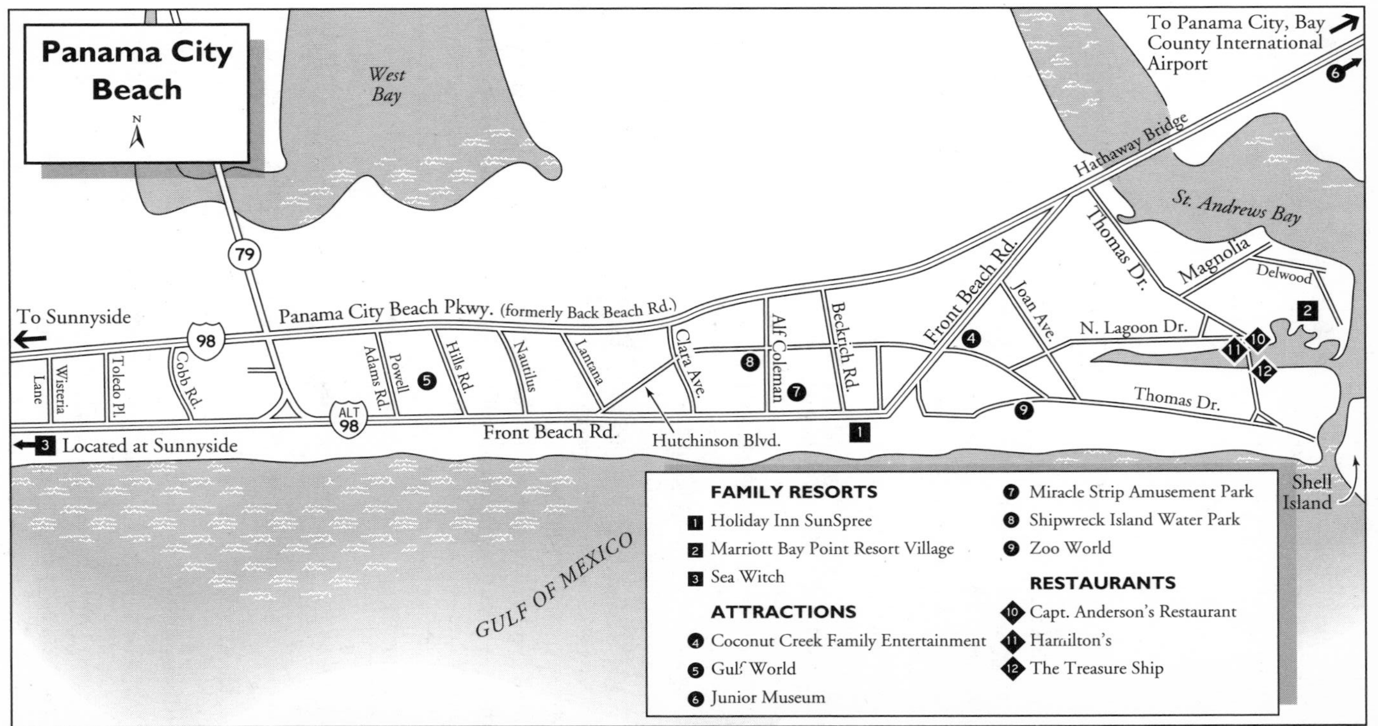
Panama City Beach
N
West Bay
St. Andrews Bay
To Panama City, Bay County International Airport
Hathaway Bridge
Thomas Dr.
Magnolia
Delwood
N. Lagoon Dr.
Joan Ave.
Front Beach Rd.
Beckrich Rd.
Alf Coleman
Clara Ave.
Lantana
Nautilus
Hills Rd.
Powell
Adams Rd.
Cobb Rd.
Toledo Pl.
Wisteria
Lane
79
98
ALT 98
Panama City Beach Pkwy. (formerly Back Beach Rd.)
To Sunnyside
3 Located at Sunnyside
Front Beach Rd.
Hutchinson Blvd.
Thomas Dr.
Shell Island
GULF OF MEXICO
FAMILY RESORTS
1 Holiday Inn SunSpree
2 Marriott Bay Point Resort Village
3 Sea Witch
ATTRACTIONS
4 Coconut Creek Family Entertainment
5 Gulf World
6 Junior Museum
7 Miracle Strip Amusement Park
8 Shipwreck Island Water Park
9 Zoo World
RESTAURANTS
10 Capt. Anderson's Restaurant
11 Hamilton's
12 The Treasure Ship

lunch, storytelling, and a kid's night out with a pizza meal. Children ages 19 and younger stay free with parents, and children ages 12 and younger eat free when accompanied by a dining parent. A human-size dolphin mascot, named Splash, hangs out with the kids and will even tuck them in at bedtime. Rates start at $99 in the winter, $159 in the summer.

Marriott Bay Point Resort Village

4200 Marriott Drive, Panama City Beach • (850) 236-6000 or (800) 874-7105 fax (850) 233-1308 • www.marriottbaypoint.com

Recognized by *Better Homes and Gardens* as one of "America's Favorite Family Resorts," Bay Point sits on 1,100 acres with St. Andrews Bay and the Gulf of Mexico on either side. It's about a five-minute car ride to the ocean, but the resort has plenty to offer, including two golf courses, a dozen tennis courts, and four swimming pools (including one indoors). An original paddle wheeler, the *Island Queen,* takes guests around the Grand Lagoon or on a 7-mile trip to secluded Shell Island. The Village Explorers Kids Camp offers scavenger hunts, sea life exploration, arts and crafts, and beach games for children ages 5–12 every day, 10 a.m.–3 p.m., and Friday and Saturday, 6 p.m.–11p.m. Cost is $40 per child per day. Bay Point has 355 rooms and suites, with coffeemakers and wet bars; rates start at $129 in the winter, $169 in the summer.

Sea Witch

21905 Front Beach Road, Panama City Beach • (800) 322-4571 • fax (850) 233-4971 • www.seawitchmotel.com

This family-oriented motel is a little off the beaten path in Panama City Beach—about 10 minutes away from the crowds on a quiet stretch of beach known as Sunnyside. The Sea Witch is nothing fancy but was designed especially for families with children and features suites with kitchenettes (including coffeemakers), and balconies (ask for a ground-floor unit if you have small children), a laundry, kiddie pool, and ice-cream parlor. A one-bedroom apartment is an affordable $100 during summer months and $60 during the winter.

Attractions

Coconut Creek Family Entertainment

9807 Front Beach Road, Panama City Beach • (850) 234-2625

Hours - Open 9 a.m., closing times vary

Admission - $14 daily special includes unlimited golf, maze, and bumper boats (valid until 5 p.m. the next day); $7 for golf, $7 for maze, $5 for bumper boats

Appeal by Age Group -

Pre-school ★	Teens ★★★★	Over 30 ★★
Grade school ★★★	Young Adults ★★	Seniors ★

Touring Time - Half a day on average; minimum 2–3 hours

Rainy-Day Touring - Not recommended

Author's Rating - ★★; a good beach diversion

Restaurants - No | **Alcoholic beverages -** No
Handicapped access - Yes | **Wheelchair rental -** No
Baby stroller rental - No | **Lockers -** No
Pet kennels - No | **Rain check -** No
Private tours - No

Description and Comments Coconut Creek has two 18-hole miniature golf courses, Grand Maze (a giant human-size maze approximately the length of a football field), Mirror Maze (an indoor sea adventure), bumper boats, and a game room.

Gulf World

15412 Front Beach Road, Panama City Beach • (850) 234-5271

Hours - Open 9 a.m.; last show starts at 4 p.m.

Admission - $19.42 for adults, $13.40 for children ages 5–11

Appeal by Age Group -

Pre-school ★★	Teens ★★	Over 30 ★★
Grade school ★★	Young Adults ★★	Seniors ★★

Touring Time - Average 3 hours; minimum 2 hours

Rainy-Day Touring - Not recommended

Author's Rating - ★★; entertaining and educational

Restaurants - Yes | **Alcoholic beverages -** No
Handicapped access - Yes | **Wheelchair rental -** No
Baby stroller rental - No | **Lockers -** No
Pet kennels - No | **Rain check -** Yes
Private tours - No

Description and Comments This old-fashioned marine park recently completed a $6 million expansion that added dolphin encounters and new theaters. Guest can learn about dolphins and even get in the water with them as part of an educational program at the new Dolphin Stadium. By night, the 2,000-seat theater turns into a laser, fountain, and fireworks show called SplashMagic. The park still has its comic sea lions, parrots, and coral reef. Kids can touch a stingray, see sharks, sea turtles, alligators, and other water creatures.

Junior Museum

1731 Jenks Avenue, Panama City • (850) 769-6128

Hours - Monday–Friday, 10 a.m.–4:30 p.m.; Saturday, 10 a.m.–4 p.m.

Admission - Free (except special exhibits), but donations are appreciated

Appeal by Age Group -

Pre-school ★★★	Teens ★★	Over 30 ★
Grade school ★★★	Young Adults ★★	Seniors ★

Touring Time - Average 2–3 hours; minimum 1 hour

Rainy-Day Touring - Recommended

Author's Rating - ★★★; perfect for your kids for a rainy day—take along a good book and read while they entertain themselves

Restaurants - No

Alcoholic beverages - No

Handicapped access - Yes

Wheelchair rental - No

Baby stroller rental - No

Lockers - No

Pet kennels - No

Rain check - No

Private tours - Yes

Description and Comments Children can experience science, art, and nature through exhibits, concerts, puppet shows, classes, and traveling displays. Young visitors can play Native American games and explore a life-size tepee in the children's room. Chickens and ducks can be fed in the pioneer village. A nature trail twists through three environments common to Northwest Florida—a hardwood swamp, a pine island, and a hardwood hammock. Targeted to children ages 2–14.

Miracle Strip Amusement Park

12001 Front Beach Road, Panama City Beach • (850) 234-5810
www.miraclestrippark.com

Hours - April–June, 10:30 a.m.–5 p.m.; June–Labor Day, until 5:30 p.m.

Admission - $17 per person, under 35" tall free admission; admission for both Miracle Strip and Shipwreck Island (following profile) is $31.50 (above 50"); $5.50 Gate Pass available for carousel and train only

Appeal by Age Group -

Pre-school ★★★	Teens ★★★★	Over 30 ★★
Grade school ★★★★	Young Adults ★★	Seniors ★★

Touring Time - Average 3–4 hours; minimum 2 hours

Rainy-Day Touring - Not recommended

Author's Rating - ★★; it will make your kids happy

Restaurants - Yes	**Alcoholic beverages -** No
Handicapped access - Yes	**Wheelchair rental -** No
Baby stroller rental - No	**Lockers -** No
Pet kennels - No	**Rain check -** No
Private tours - No	

Description and Comments Miracle Strip is a family-oriented park on the beach with more than 30 rides and attractions with a 105-foot-high roller coaster, the 40-foot swinging Sea Dragon, the stomach-turning Shock Wave, kiddie rides, live stage shows, an arcade, and food concessions.

Shipwreck Island Water Park

12000 W. Front Beach Road, Panama City Beach • (850) 234-0368
www.miraclestrippark.com

Hours - April–June, 10:30 a.m.–5 p.m.; June–Labor Day, until 5:30 p.m.

Admission - $18.50 above 50" tall; $22.50 under 50" tall; under 35" tall free; $13 for senior citizens ages 62 and older; admission for both Miracle Strip (preceeding profile) and Shipwreck Island is $31.50 (above 50")

Appeal by Age Group -

Pre-school ★★	Teens ★★★	Over 30 ★
Grade school ★★★	Young Adults ★★	Seniors ★

Touring Time - Average 3–4 hours; minimum 2 hours

Rainy-Day Touring - Not recommended

Author's Rating - ★★; fun if the beach gets boring

Restaurants - No	**Alcoholic beverages -** No
Handicapped access - No	**Wheelchair rental -** No
Baby stroller rental - No	**Lockers -** Yes, $2 plus $1 deposit
Pet kennels - No	**Rain check -** No
Private tours - No	

Description and Comments Next door to Miracle Strip Amusement Park, this ever-expanding water park has six acres of rides and picnic areas. Water rides include the Rapid River Run, the Wave Pool, the Lazy River, and the awesome Tree Top Drop, a free-fall slide. The Tadpole Hole is exclusively for young visitors.

Zoo World

9008 Front Beach Road, Panama City Beach • (850) 230-1243

Hours - Daily, 9–7 p.m. (summer); closes at 5:30 p.m. off season

Admission - In season, $10.95 for adults, $6.95 for children ages 4–11; off-season, $8.95 for adults, $6.50 for children

Appeal by Age Group -

Pre-school ★★	Teens ★★	Over 30 ★
Grade school ★★	Young Adults ★	Seniors ★

Touring Time - Average 2 hours; minimum 1½ hours

Rainy-Day Touring - Not recommended

Author's Rating - ★★; nothing spectacular, but an afternoon's diversion

Restaurants - No

Alcoholic beverages - No

Handicapped access - Yes

Wheelchair rental - Yes

Baby stroller rental - Yes

Lockers - No

Pet kennels - No

Rain check - Yes

Private tours - Yes

Description and Comments This old-fashioned zoo has more than 300 species of tropical animals from around the world—orangutans, big cats, reptiles, and other creatures. There's also a petting zoo with a giraffe feeding platform, walk-through aviary, and bat exhibit.

Family-Friendly Restaurants

Capt. Anderson's Restaurant

5551 N. Lagoon Drive at Thomas Drive, Panama City Beach • (850) 234-2225

Meals served - Dinner, closed Sunday

Cuisine - Seafood

Entree range - $12–40

Kids menu - Yes

Reservations - Not accepted

Payment - All major credit cards accepted

It's fun to watch fishers unload the catch of the day at the marina next door, but come early because this famous, award-winning restaurant gets crowded after the boats come in. Opt for whatever fish is freshest or the seafood platter and you can't go wrong.

Hamilton's

5711 N. Lagoon Drive, Panama City • (850) 234-1255

Meals served - Dinner

Cuisine - Seafood

Entree range - $10–20

Kids menu - Yes

Reservations - Not accepted

Payment - Visa, MC, AmEx, D

Dine right on the lagoon in the air-conditioned dining room. Locals recommend the Florida bay scallops and the Apalachicola oysters. All desserts, salad dressings, sauces, and soups are made fresh from original recipes.

The Treasure Ship

3605 Thomas Drive, Panama City • (850) 234-8881

Meals served - Lunch and dinner

Cuisine - American, Caribbean, seafood

Entree range - Lunch, $5.95–16.95; dinner, $11.95–27.95

Kids menu - Yes

Reservations - Not accepted

Payment - All major credit cards accepted

Hook's Grille is open for lunch, but go for dinner when the "pirates" invade the Treasure Ship dining room to entertain the kids. Try the Calypso Grouper, Cuban loin of pork, or pepper steak Port-au-Prince.

Tallahassee

This is a great little town for walking or a trolley ride, with lush rolling hills, fragrant magnolias in the springtime, ancient oaks, and lovely springs and lakes.

Families will enjoy touring the seat of state government, including the Old Capitol, restored to its 1902 American Renaissance splendor with red-and-white striped awnings and stained-glass dome. Behind it is the New Capitol, where you can view from public galleries the legislature from March through May. The New Capitol's 22nd-floor observatory offers a breathtaking view—clear to the Gulf of Mexico, about 20 miles away, on a cloudless day.

The Old Capitol is open for self-guided tours Monday–Friday, 9 a.m.–4:30 p.m.; Saturdays 10 a.m.–4:30 p.m.; and Sunday, noon–4:30 p.m. The New Capitol is open Monday–Friday, 8 a.m.–5 p.m. Tour times vary. Call (850) 488-6167 for capitol tour reservations. Admission is free to both buildings.

Peek in the Governor's Mansion just north of the capitol, furnished with eighteenth- and nineteenth-century antiques; tours are given when the legislature is in session and at Christmas. For a tour of the Governor's Mansion, call (850) 488-4661.

The Old Town Trolley is free, and you can get on or off at any point between Adams Street Commons, at the corner of Jefferson and Adams streets, and the Governor's Mansion. The trolley runs every twenty minutes Monday–Friday, 7 a.m–6:30 p.m.

Family Resorts

Cabot Lodge North

2735 N. Monroe Street, Tallahassee • (850) 386-8880 • fax (850) 386-4254

You can relax in true Southern style in the rocking chairs on the wraparound porch at this clapboard plantation-style house just north of

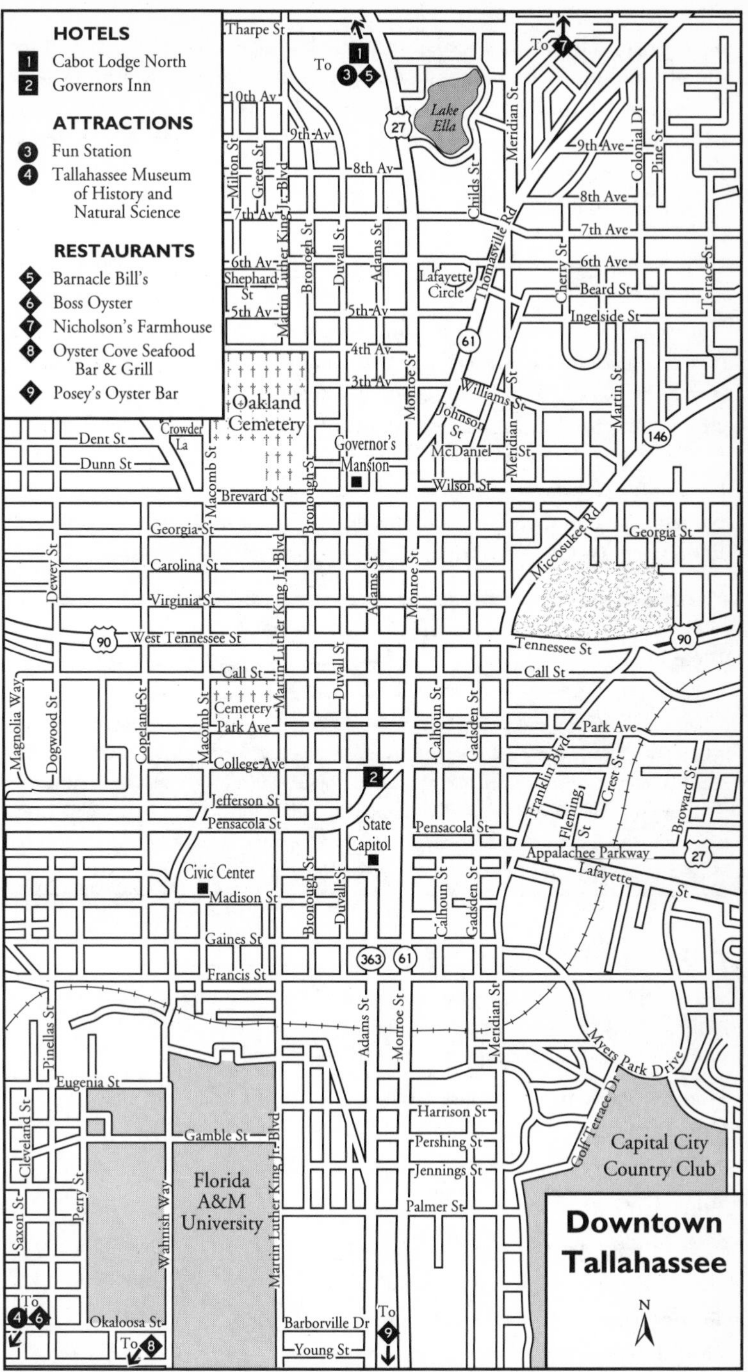
HOTELS
1 Cabot Lodge North
2 Governors Inn
ATTRACTIONS
3 Fun Station
4 Tallahassee Museum of History and Natural Science
RESTAURANTS
5 Barnacle Bill's
6 Boss Oyster
7 Nicholson's Farmhouse
8 Oyster Cove Seafood Bar & Grill
9 Posey's Oyster Bar
Downtown Tallahassee
N
Tharpe St
10th Av
9th Av
8th Av
7th Av
6th Av
5th Av
4th Av
3rd Av
Shephard St
Milton St
Green St
Martin Luther King Jr. Blvd
Bronough St
Duvall St
Adams St
Monroe St
Lake Ella
Childs St
Thomasville Rd
Meridian St
Colonial Dr
Pine St
9th Ave
8th Ave
7th Ave
6th Ave
Beard St
Ingelside St
Cherry St
Terrace St
Lafayette Circle
Williams St
Johnson St
McDaniel St
Wilson St
Martin St
Oakland Cemetery
Governor's Mansion
Crowder La
Dent St
Dunn St
Brevard St
Macomb St
Georgia St
Carolina St
Virginia St
Dewey St
West Tennessee St
Tennessee St
Miccosukee Rd
Call St
Cemetery
Park Ave
College Ave
Jefferson St
Pensacola St
Magnolia Way
Dogwood St
Copeland St
Calhoun St
Gadsden St
Franklin Blvd
Fleming St
Crest St
Broward St
State Capitol
Civic Center
Madison St
Gaines St
Francis St
Appalachee Parkway
Lafayette St
Myers Park Drive
Golf Terrace Dr
Capital City Country Club
Pinellas St
Eugenia St
Gamble St
Cleveland St
Saxon St
Perry St
Wahnish Way
Florida A&M University
Harrison St
Pershing St
Jennings St
Palmer St
Okaloosa St
Barborville Dr
Young St
To
27
61
146
90
363

downtown. The guest rooms are plain but spacious in the two-story motel buildings behind the main house, and there is a swimming pool for warm afternoons. Continental breakfast is free, as are cocktails between 5:30 and 7:30 p.m. Children up to age 13 stay free with parents. Rates start at $72 year-round.

Governors Inn

209 S. Adams Street, Tallahassee, just north of the state capitol • (850) 681-6855 fax (850) 222-3105

The elegant Governor's Inn is right in the historic district, and though it's mostly a place for businesspeople, particularly when the Florida legislature is in session, it's a wonderful respite if you're traveling with teenagers and are in town for touring. There are 40 rooms, some with wood-burning fireplaces, wet bars, and four-poster beds. All rooms have HBO, some have mini-refrigerators and coffeemakers. Continental breakfast is complimentary, and there's free limousine service to and from the airport. Rates start at $129 year-round.

A MOON PIE AND A COLA

In Tallahassee, take time for a break at Bradley's Country Store—now on the National Register of Historic Places—where you'll likely meet one of the Bradley clan, who have run the place since it opened in 1927. Along with Moon Pie and a cola, they also make world-famous sausage—they sell more than 80,000 pounds over the counter every year. Or ask for one of Grandma Mary's seasoned sausage biscuits hot off the griddle. Bradley's is open Monday–Friday, 8 a.m.–6 p.m. and Saturday, 8 a.m.–5 p.m. (closed Sunday). Located on Centerville Road 12 miles north of Tallahassee; (850) 893-1647

Attractions

Fun Station

2821 Sharer Road, Tallahassee, off N. Maine Street • (850) 383-0788

Hours - Monday–Thursday, 10 a.m.–11 p.m.; Friday, 10 a.m.–1 a.m., Saturday, 9 a.m.–1 a.m.; Sunday, 11 a.m.–11 p.m.

Admission - Separate prices for each activity; no standard admission

Appeal by Age Group -

Pre-school ★	Teens ★★★	Over 30 ★
Grade school ★★★	Young Adults ★★★	Seniors ★

Touring Time - Average 3 hours; minimum 1½ hours

Rainy-Day Touring - Not recommended

Author's Rating - ★★; plenty of action for grade schoolers and teenagers

Restaurants - Yes
Handicapped access - Yes
Baby stroller rental - No
Pet kennels - No
Private tours - No
Alcoholic beverages - No
Wheelchair rental - No
Lockers - No
Rain check - No

Description and Comments If your kids are antsy, this entertainment center has two 18-hole minigolf courses, a laser-tag arena, a 10,000-square-foot video arcade, bumper boats, batting cages, and concessions.

A COOL RESORT

If you're looking for a slice of old Florida, away from the beach and the crowds, head to Steinhatchee Landing Resort, 3 miles from the Gulf in the southeast portion of the Panhandle. Opened in 1990, this family- and pet-friendly resort is tucked in a 25-acre habitat of pines, moss oaks, and silver palms on the banks of the Steinhatche River. Abundant wildlife—deer, wild boar, eagles, owls, ducks and turkeys—roam in the surrounding acreage.

Amenities include a petting zoo with goats, duck, and chickens, a playground, a swimming pool, bicycles, tennis, archery, and canoes. Accommodations are Victorian, Georgian, and Cracker-style villas, fully furnished with kitchens. Rates start at $180 in summer, $120 in the winter. You might plan your stay during the Gulf's scallop season (July 1–September 10). With a mask and snorkel in 4 feet of water, it's like an underwater Easter egg hunt for kids.

Steinhatchee is on SR 51, 70 miles east of Gainesville; (352) 498-3513; www.steinhatcheelanding.com.

Tallahassee Museum of History and Natural Science

3945 Museum Drive, Tallahassee • (850) 576-1636

Hours - Monday–Saturday, 9 a.m.–5 p.m.; Sunday, 12:30–5 p.m.
Admission - $6.50 for adults, 46 for seniors, $4.50 for ages 4–15
Appeal by Age Group -

Pre-school ★★	Teens ★★★	Over 30 ★★★
Grade school ★★★	Young Adults ★★★	Seniors ★★★

Touring Time - Average 2 hours; minimum 1½ hours
Rainy-Day Touring - Not recommended
Author's Rating - ★★★; one of the few museum in the country that combines historical buildings, displays of native wildlife, and a beautiful natural setting

Restaurants - Foodstand
Handicapped access - Yes
Baby stroller rental - No
Alcoholic beverages - No
Wheelchair rental - No
Lockers - No

Pet kennels - No
Rain check - No
Private tours - No

Description and Comments History, nature, and wildlife are intertwined at the museum to tell a story about the culture and natural history of the Big Bend. Along a trail through 52 acres of woodlands, you can see alligators, red wolves, Florida panthers, and other animals—the state's only zoological collection solely devoted to native wildlife. A collection of historical buildings, including an original plantation house from the 1840s, a church, and a one-room schoolhouse, illustrate what life was like in a bygone era. The Big Bend Farm is a re-creation of a farm typical of the Big Bend region during the late nineteenth century, with volunteers spinning, weaving, churning butter, and performing other duties on the weekends. The Hands-on Discovery Center allows close-up views of native reptiles.

Family-Friendly Restaurants

Barnacle Bill's

1830 N. Monroe Street, Tallahassee • (850) 385-8734

Meals served - Lunch and dinner
Cuisine - Seafood
Entree range - $9–15.95
Kids menu - Yes
Reservations - Not accepted
Payment - All major credit cards accepted

This well-known restaurant serves about 750 dozen oysters every week, along with seafood grilled, steamed, smoked, and fried.

Boss Oyster

125 Water Street, Apalachicola • (850) 653-9364

Meals served - Lunch and dinner
Cuisine - Seafood
Entree range - $9.95–21.95
Kids menu - Yes
Reservations - Not accepted
Payment - Visa, MC, AmEx, D

Locals recommend Boss Oyster not just for the freshly shucked oysters with more than 30 creative toppings but also for their delicious burgers. It's the best spot on the water in Apalachicola.

Nicholson's Farmhouse

Off SR 12 in Havana (small town located 30 minutes north of Tallahassee) • (850) 539-5931

Meals served - Dinner, Tuesday–Saturday

Cuisine - American

Entree range - $8.95–24.95

Kids menu - Yes

Reservations - Recommended

Payment - Visa, MC, AmEx, D

This is an actual family plantation, built in 1820, and so authentic that they offer boiled peanuts as an appetizer. The food is as Southern as it gets, with beef grown right on the farm and fresh-baked bread.

Oyster Cove Seafood Bar and Grill

Corner of E. Pine and E. Second Streets, St. George Island • (850) 927-2600

Meals served - Dinner

Cuisine - Seafood, American

Entree range - $11.95–22.95

Kids menu - Yes

Reservations - Not necessary

Payment - Visa, MC, AmEx

Locals love the Oyster Cove for its consistently good seafood dishes, though they also go for their "famous" East Bay steak, a rib eye grilled with oysters and Spanish onions. Ask for a window seat for a world-class view of Apalachicola Bay, especially at sunset.

Posey's Oyster Bar

55 Riverside Drive, St. Marks • (850) 925-6172

Meals served - Lunch and dinner

Cuisine - Seafood

Entree range - $10–15

Kids menu - No, but there's pizza, corn dogs, and chicken strips

Reservations - Not accepted

Payment - Visa, MC

Posey's is at the south end of the Tallahassee–St. Marks Historic Rail Trail, the perfect respite after a bicycle ride. The dilapidated eatery has been there for years, serving the freshest Apalachicola oysters. If you don't like raw oysters, try them baked with cheddar cheese, butter, bacon bits, or garlic. Also on the menu are grouper, shrimp, scallops, and clams.

Side Trips

Apalachicola In the 1860s Apalachicola was the third-largest town on the Gulf, when steamboats from Georgia and Alabama carried cotton down the river to the Gulf of Mexico. Sponge fishing also was big business, but by the 1920s shellfish reigned as the most prosperous way to make a living.

Today, 90% of all oysters eaten in Florida are harvested here, and fisherfolk still work the waters. But progress passed Apalachicola by, and today it's a sleepy little fishing town, where most visitors are stopping for the fresh fish or oysters at the little seafood eateries found all over town. We suggest a meal at Boss Oyster, where you can sit right next to the docks and watch the oyster and shrimp boats unloading their day's catch. The food is great; if you're not in the mood for oysters, they also serve delicious burgers. After a satisfying lunch or dinner, you can take a scenic walking tour of some of the more than 200 historic sites; Apalachicola has one of the largest collections of antebellum homes in the state. One of its most famous spots is the Gibson Inn, perfect for a little fancier lunch (but not with little ones). There's not a stop light in the entire town, other than a blinking caution light at the intersection of Market Street and Avenue E downtown.

Cedar Key Not every family will find this quiet little island appealing, but we've included it for families who enjoy history and a very slow pace.

Just 3 miles from the mainland, Cedar Key is like a step back in time. Back in the mid-1800s it was the second-largest city in Florida, when the first major railroad in Florida ran from Fernandina Beach in the northeast to Cedar Key. After the Civil War, pencil making was big business—until the cedar forests were leveled. Today it's merely a haven for fishers.

Stop off at the Cedar Key Historical Museum for brochures that offer self-guided tours of the city. The museum is in an 1870s-era house on Second Street at SR 24; (352) 543-5549. Cycle past the picturesque city docks, one of the most-photographed sites on Florida's west coast, or stop for seafood at any of the Dock Street restaurants.

For families, the waterfront cottages at Mermaids Landing are a good bet, about six blocks from downtown on the bay. The cottages can sleep up to four and include a full kitchen; rates are $60–70. The friendly proprietors will loan you a bike (they keep three there for guests) or help you rent one. And if you don't want to cook dinner, Cooke's Oysters is just down the road, and they'll deliver to your cottage—farm-raised clams, flounder, grouper, oysters, and live blue crabs. Mermaid's Landing is on SR 24 as you come into town; (352) 543-5949. Cedar Key is halfway between Tampa and Tallahassee; to get there from Tallahassee, take US 27 south, then SR 24 into Cedar Key.

Part Two

Northeast Florida

Authentic history lessons and the great outdoors are the two best reasons for families to head to northeast Florida, a region alive with meticulously re-created historic districts, natural springs, lush inland forests, tree-lined rivers, and wide beaches. If you're traveling southward by car, this region offers the first glimpse of the Sunshine State, stretching from the Georgia state line.

Northeast Florida is the spot on the map where intrepid Spanish explorers, determined English settlers, and French homesteaders seeking religious freedom landed—and immediately began to battle over their respective claims. Today, St. Augustine, the oldest continuous European settlement in the United States, is a fascinating melting pot of cultures that influenced the formation of the New World. North of St. Augustine, tiny Amelia Island shows off blocks of old mansions, miles of beaches, and lots of seafood.

But Florida's "First Coast" is also home to Jacksonville, one of the most modern Florida, which swiftly moved into the twenty-first century with a thriving seaport.

Heading southwest from Jacksonville, it looks as though time stood still in the 1930s in lovely old towns like Micanopy, Alachua, and Newberry, where freshwater springs, gentle hills, and forests dot the landscape. Gainesville, home of the very modern University of Florida, manages to retain its small-town charm with architecture dating back to the late 1800s. Just south of Gainesville is Cross Creek, hometown of Pulitzer Prize–winning author Marjorie Kinnan Rawlings, who was attracted to the timeless landscape in the 1920s.

Getting There

By Plane Two airports—Gainesville Regional Airport, (352) 377-4681, and Jacksonville International Airport, (904) 741-2000. Also close by is Daytona International Airport, (386) 248-8030.

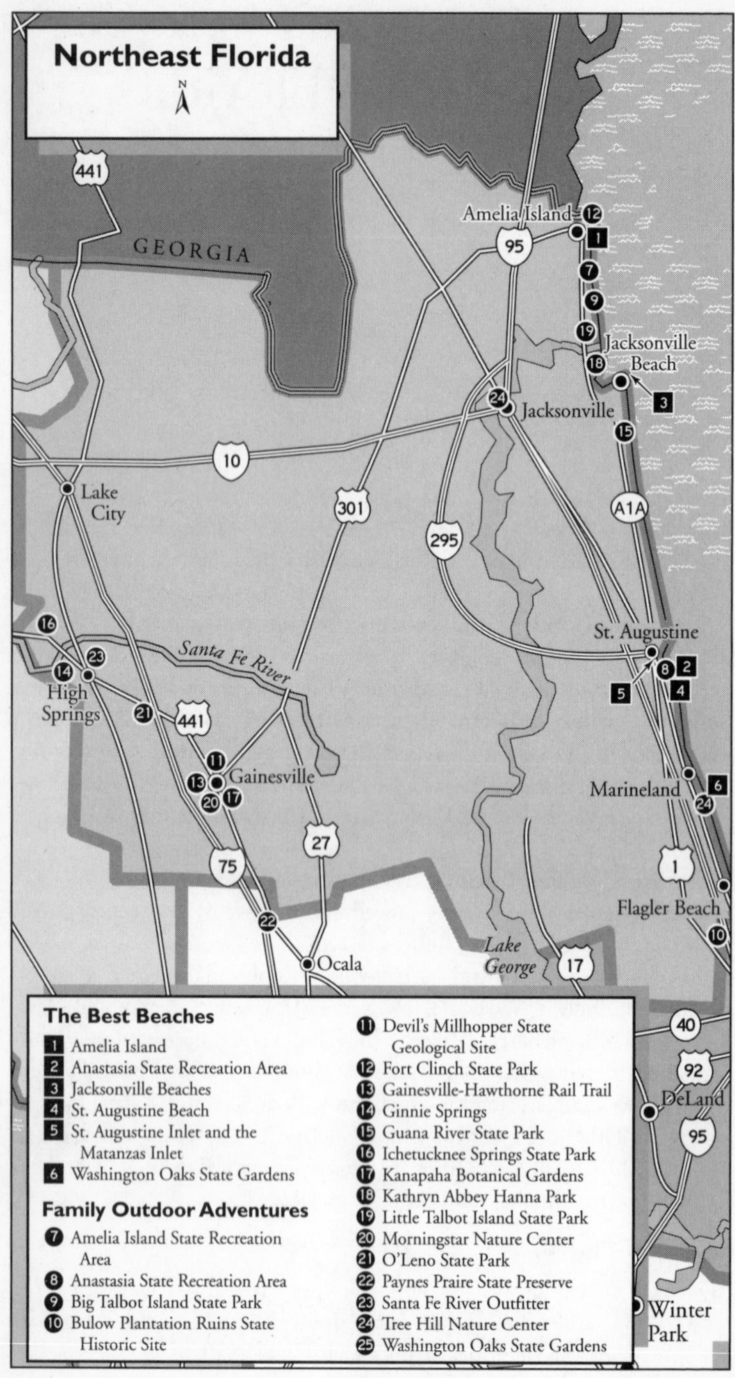
Northeast Florida
N
GEORGIA
441
Amelia Island
95
Jacksonville Beach
Jacksonville
10
Lake City
301
295
A1A
St. Augustine
Santa Fe River
High Springs
441
Gainesville
Marineland
27
75
1
Flagler Beach
Ocala
Lake George
17
40
92
DeLand
95
Winter Park
The Best Beaches
1 Amelia Island
2 Anastasia State Recreation Area
3 Jacksonville Beaches
4 St. Augustine Beach
5 St. Augustine Inlet and the Matanzas Inlet
6 Washington Oaks State Gardens
Family Outdoor Adventures
7 Amelia Island State Recreation Area
8 Anastasia State Recreation Area
9 Big Talbot Island State Park
10 Bulow Plantation Ruins State Historic Site
11 Devil's Millhopper State Geological Site
12 Fort Clinch State Park
13 Gainesville-Hawthorne Rail Trail
14 Ginnie Springs
15 Guana River State Park
16 Ichetucknee Springs State Park
17 Kanapaha Botanical Gardens
18 Kathryn Abbey Hanna Park
19 Little Talbot Island State Park
20 Morningstar Nature Center
21 O'Leno State Park
22 Paynes Prairie State Preserve
23 Santa Fe River Outfitter
24 Tree Hill Nature Center
25 Washington Oaks State Gardens

By Train Amtrak stations are in Lake City, Waldo, Jacksonville, Palatka, and Gainesville; (800) USA-RAIL; www.amtrak.com.

By Car Major roads include US 1, I-10, and I-75. SR A1A South runs along the Atlantic with some beautiful views.

How to Get Information before You Go

Amelia Island Tourist Development Council, 102 Centre Street, Fernandina Beach 32034; (800) 226-3542; www.ameliaisland.org.

Beaches Chamber and Visitors Center, 1101 Beach Boulevard, Jacksonville Beach 32250; (904) 249-3868.

Jacksonville and the Beaches Convention and Visitors Bureau, 201 E. Adams Street, Jacksonville 32202; (800) 733-2668; www.jaxcub.com.

St. Augustine–St. Johns County Chamber of Commerce, 1 Riberia Street, St. Augustine 32084; (904) 829-5681; www.staugustinechamber.com.

St. Johns County Visitors and Convention Bureau, 88 Riberia Street, Suite 400, St. Augustine 32804; (800) OLD-CITY (U.S. & Canada); www.visitoldcity.com.

Alachua County Visitors and Convention Bureau, 30 E. University Avenue, Gainesville 32601; (352) 374-5231; www.visitgainesville.net.

The Best Beaches

♥ **Amelia Island** The island's 13 miles of white sandy beach are among the world's most scenic. A state park and state recreation area offer great access points (see Outdoor Adventures page 76).

♥ **Anastasia State Recreation Area** On Anastasia Boulevard in St. Augustine, this is the perfect beach for families looking for lots of activity. There's a parking lot in front of the high dunes that's big enough to hold 500 cars, but you also can drive right on the hard-packed sand for a 3-mile stretch just to the north of the beach entrance. If you have younger children and want to avoid the cars, take a right as you head over the dunes where no driving is permitted on a half-mile stretch of sand. On the beach there's volleyball, tennis courts, and beach paraphernalia for rent, like bicycles, sailboards, paddleboats, beach chairs, and umbrellas. Just be sure to tell your children to "stop, look, and listen" if you head for the traffic side. Entry fee is $3 per vehicle. You can also camp inland for $16, $20 with electricity; (904) 461-2033.

Jacksonville Beaches Vacationers don't generally head to Jacksonville for a beach vacation, but there are several options about 12 miles from downtown via J. Turner Butler Boulevard. Bustling Jacksonville Beach, the favorite for teens and families, has lifeguards, an oceanfront pavilion with live entertainment, plenty of restaurants, a pier, and nearby hotels. Sleepy Mayport Beach is where you can watch the naval fleet come home to the Mayport Naval Station. The more secluded Atlantic and Neptune

Beaches are where many Jacksonville residents head on the weekends. We recommend the Kathryn Abbey Hanna Park just south of Mayport on SR A1A at 500 Wonderwood Drive—450 acres on the ocean with a great beach, lifeguards, nature trails, picnicking, and freshwater fishing.

St. Augustine Beach About a ten-minute drive from downtown St. Augustine, cross the Bridge of Lions to SR A1A and head south to Dondanville Road. You can park right on the beach. Cost is $5 per car from Memorial Day to Labor Day at official access points. Driving is permitted on this beach, so you'll have to keep a close eye on little ones. Lifeguards are on duty 10 a.m.–5 p.m. There are restaurants nearby, but no bathrooms on the beach; (904) 471-6616.

St. Augustine Inlet and the Matanzas Inlet Just a roadside stop on SR A1A a few miles south of St. Augustine, but shell seekers can park alongside A1A to search for souvenirs at the mouths of the St. Augustine Inlet and the Matanzas Inlet—sand dollars, moon snails, olive and scallop shells, jack-knife clam shells, and angel wings are found in abundance. Restaurants are nearby.

Washington Oaks State Gardens About a 20-minute drive south of St. Augustine on SR A1A is a picturesque, boulder-strewn beach where shorebirds feed at low tide while brown pelicans soar overhead. It's not great for swimming because of the coquina rocks in the surf, but it's lovely for wading and walking or fishing for whiting, bluefish, and pompano. There are no lifeguards. Entry fee is $3.25 per vehicle; (904) 446-6780.

Family Outdoor Adventures

Amelia Island State Recreation Area If you want to take a horseback ride on the beach, this state recreation area has guided rides operated by Seahorse Stables. If your kids are at least 4'6" and 9 years of age, they're tall enough to ride on the beach. The hour-long, 5-mile beach ride is $40. Reservations are a must. The state recreation area has pristine beaches, salt marshes, and coastal maritime forests that provide a glimpse of the original Florida. The 200-acre park also is great for bird-watching, fishing, and hiking. For horseback riding reservations, call Kelly Seahorse Ranch at (904) 491-5166.

Anastasia State Recreation Area This popular beachfront recreation area stretches over 1,800 acres, and for outdoor enthusiasts it's a complete vacation destination with 4 miles of sandy beach, shaded picnic areas with grills, nature trails, windsurfing, sailing, and canoeing on a saltwater lagoon and 139 campsites. The odds are good that you'll hook pompano or whiting in the surf. In the summer there are chairs, beach umbrellas, and surfboards for rent. And bird-watching is good, too; ask for a free brochure as you enter. Campsites in a pretty wooded area are $12–15, and each has a picnic table and grill. The beach is the perfect place to watch the sunset. $3.25 per vehicle; open daily 8 a.m.–6:30 p.m. Located at St. Augustine Beach off SR A1A at SR 3; (904) 461-2033.

Big Talbot Island State Park If you have any anglers in the family, this park is recommended for surf fishing for bluefish and whiting. Kids love to visit the pelicans, ospreys, owls, eagles, and other wild birds recovering from injuries at the nearby BEAKS, Bird Emergency and Kare Sanctuary. It's free and open daily, except Monday, noon–4 p.m.; (904) 251-2473). Photographers also love Big Talbot, with its rock outcroppings and fallen tress that have become bleached and weathered with time. The island's spectacular bluffs, two plantation ruins, and canoe routes through salt marshes add to the experience. $3.25 per car entry fee. 11435 Fort George Road, Fort George, 20 miles east of downtown Jacksonville on SR A1A N.; (904) 251-2320.

Bulow Plantation Ruins State Historic Site A bit off the beaten path, but this is a fun, short hike to a plantation ruins if there's time. The Bulow Plantation was the largest sugar plantation on the East Coast (1,000 acres) and grew sugar cane, cotton, rice, and indigo in the early 1800s. John James Audubon noted the Bulow's hospitality after a stop here on a collecting and painting trip. The plantation was abandoned during the Second Seminole War as John Bulow followed the troops northward. The Seminoles burned "Bulowville" around 1836, along with other plantations in the area. All that is left today are the coquina ruins of the sugar mill, several wells, a springhouse, and the crumbling foundation of the mansion. A scenic, mile-long walking trail leads to the ruins. Picnicking, canoeing, and fishing on Bulow Creek. $2 admission per car. The site is 35 minutes from St. Augustine, 3 miles west of Flagler Beach on SR 100, south on CR 2001; (386) 517-2084.

Devil's Millhopper State Geological Site If you're up for a hike, this giant sinkhole—120 feet deep and 500 feet across—is worth about an hour's visit, with nature trails around its rim, a dozen waterfalls tumbling down its steep slopes, and 232 steps leading to its foundation (remember, you have to climb back up with the kids). Fossilized sharks' teeth, marine shells, and fossilized remains of extinct land animals have been found at the bottom, evidence that the sea once covered the state. It was once said the millhopper that fed bodies to the devil. (A millhopper is the container that fed grain into grist mill grinders in the 1800s.) There's a nice shady area for picnicking. Admission $2 per car. Open April 1–September 30, 9 a.m.–5 p.m. on weekdays and on weekends 9 a.m.–sunset; open 9 a.m.–5 p.m. the rest of the year. 4732 Millhopper Road, 2 miles northwest of Gainesville off SR 232; (386) 462-7905.

Fort Clinch State Park Fort Clinch opened as a state park in the 1930s and is one of the oldest parks in Florida. The fort, though never completed, was occupied by both Union and Confederate troops during the Civil War. The park covers about 1,100 acres, with camping, good swimming (though it gets chilly in winter), surf and pier fishing, hiking, and candlelight tours of the fort. $3.25 per vehicle entry fee. Camping—41 sites are in the woods, 21 are on the beach—costs $12–17. Off SR A1A at Fernandina Beach; (904) 277-7274.

Gainesville-Hawthorne Rail Trail This flat, winding trail is perfect for families; you can bike as little or as long as you like, with 17 miles of asphalt along a scenic railway corridor, designed for walking, cycling, and horseback riding. The trail extends from Gainesville's historic Boulware Springs Park at Paynes Prairie through Lochloosa Wildlife Management Area to the town of Hawthorne. You'll see sinkholes, abundant wildlife including alligators, and osprey nests in some of the dead live oak trees. Head south on CR 331 from University Avenue in Gainesville, and look for Boulware Springs Park sign at 3300 SE 17th Street. The two Hawthorne trailheads are off SE 200 Drive (slightly west of Hawthorne) and off 300 SW Second Avenue; (352) 466-3397.

Ginnie Springs Smaller and far less crowded than the Ichetucknee, the springs are memorable and fun and perfect for tubing or snorkeling in crystal-clear water that stays 72° year-round. There are also a playground and picnic tables. Admission is $8 adults, $4 children ages 7–14. About 30 miles from Gainesville. Take I-75 to Exit 78, go north 5 miles on US 441, turn left on Main Street to County 340, turn right and go 6.5 miles to 7300 NE Ginnie Springs Road, High Springs; (386) 454-7182; www.ginniesprings.com.

Guana River State Park It's believed that Ponce de Leon's first landing and explorations were probably on Guana River lands, and today the places retain a wilderness ambience, with 2,400 acres of hardwood hammock, marshes, pine forests, and beaches. If you want to fish, there are plenty of opportunities, with abundant catches in the Atlantic, Guana River, or Guana Lake. The beach is nice for swimming, but there are no lifeguards. There are 10 miles of dirt bicycle trails, recommended for beginners, with wide paths marked by color codes that can easily be followed except on the north end where the trails leave the park and enter a wildlife management area. Few trails come closer to the Atlantic Ocean. Admission is $3.25 per car. Located off SR A1A near Ponte Vedra Beach, about 20 miles from downtown Jacksonville; (904) 825-5071.

Ichetucknee Springs State Park It's a little like going to Disney World—everyone wants to experience this crystal clear spring, but it gets so crowded that you wonder if it's really worth it. The fun is a

3-hour float in an innertube from the north entrance of the park. However, it's become so popular that park rangers now limit the number of tubers to 750 per day. So if your idea of vacation is solitude, head elsewhere. The least crowded days are Tuesday through Thursday, say the park rangers.

The Ichetucknee River is fed by a series of springs producing 233 million gallons of water daily, so the water is a constant and cool 73° year-round. The north entrance is open from Memorial Day through Labor Day, with a shuttle waiting at the end of the run to take you back to your car. Or if you prefer, it's a 20-minute hike. Cost is $3.25 per car load up to 8 people. Cave-certified scuba divers can explore Blue Hole Spring in the off season for $5 per person.

The park is open year-round from 8 a.m.–sundown for hiking, picnicking, and swimming. Between Labor Day and Memorial Day, you can tube from the south entrance—a 1.5-hour run that costs $4.25 per carload (if the shuttle isn't running). Shuttle is $4.25 per person, children ages 5 and under free.

You cannot rent innertubes in the park, but private roadside vendors rent them—or you can bring one from home. No food, drinks, or pets are allowed on the run. Take I-75 to SR 47 south 12 miles to SR 238, turn right on SR 238, and follow it to the park entrance; (386) 497-2511; www.ichetuckneeriver.com

Kanapaha Botanical Gardens Sixty-two acres of woodlands, meadows, vineyards, and specialized gardens grow in Florida's most diverse and second-largest botanical gardens. Highlights are Florida's largest bamboo grove, the largest herb garden in the Southeast, and the hummingbird and butterfly gardens. There's a shaded picnic area. Hours: Monday, Tuesday, Friday, 9 a.m.–5 p.m.; Wednesday, Saturday, Sunday, 9 a.m.–dusk; closed Thursday. Admission $5 adults, $3 children ages 6–13, free for ages 6 and under. 4625 SW 63rd Boulevard, Gainesville (Exit 75 off I-75); (352) 372-4981.

♥ **Kathryn Abbey Hanna Park** Just about a 10-minute drive from downtown Jacksonville, this 450-acre oceanfront park is a favorite of locals, who take advantage of the beaches, freshwater lakes, and wooded campsites. It offers more than 15 miles of trails for bicycling, with trails for beginners, intermediates, and experts (though it can be sandy and hard to pedal if it's been particularly dry). The bicycling trail, also great for hiking, runs near the Atlantic for about a mile. Entry fee is $1 per person over age 6. The 300 campsites are $19. Exit onto Atlantic Boulevard from I-10 or I-95 onto SR A1A heading north to Mayport. When CR 101 splits to the right and SR A1A turns left to Mayport, continue on 101 for a short distance and turn right at the Hanna Park sign; (904) 249-4700.

Little Talbot Island State Park You can hear the waves at night when you're camping here, near more than 5 miles of wide, unspoiled beaches. Bird-watchers love this park, with its vegetated dunes and undisturbed salt marshes, where river otters, marsh rabbits, and bobcats join the shorebirds. Fishing, too, is excellent—bluefish, striped bass, redfish, flounder, and mullet are often on the line. The beach has bathhouses, a picnic site, an observation deck, and campsites near a salt marsh (bring the mosquito repellent). Admission $3.25 per car; camping is $15.75 March–September ($18 with electricity), $9 October–February ($11 with electricity). Open daily 8 a.m.–sunset. 11435 Fort George Road E., Fort George (15 miles south of Fernandina Beach via SR A1A); (904) 251-2320.

Morningstar Nature Center Every family member can have fun and learn a little here, taking a step back in time and experiencing the life of a farmer 100 years ago. The 278-acre farm is run by the city of Gainesville, with 7 miles of nature trails and boardwalks (more than 130 species of birds and 225 species of wildflowers have been counted). On the premises are a turn-of-the-century schoolhouse, a Florida homestead garden, and a farmhouse built in 1840. Come after noon and the kids can help feed the animals or milk a goat. Admission is free. Saturday is Farm Day and costs; $2 adults, $1 children. There's also an area for picnicking. 3540 E. University Avenue, Gainesville. Open daily, 9 a.m.–5 p.m.; closed Christmas, New Year's Day, and Thanksgiving; (352) 334-2170.

O'Leno State Park Woods that are fun for exploring are the big draw at O'Leno—turkey, deer, even an occasional bobcat can be spotted on the hiking trails. There's also camping, mountain biking, fishing, swimming, canoeing, and horseback riding (no stables) in this 6,000-acre park. The Santa Fe River disappears and flows underground for more than 3 miles in the park before it again becomes a surface stream. There's a great view of the river from a suspension bridge that was built in the 1930s by the Conservation Corps. O'Leno started as a town in the mid-1800s named Keno (after a game of chance), and the name was changed to Leno in 1876. Like many early Florida towns, Leno became a ghost town, and after 1896 was referred to as O'Leno, a variation on the local name for "Old Leno." Admission $3.25 per car. Camping is $10. Take US 441 6 miles north of High Springs (approximately 30 miles northwest of Gainesville on I-75, between exits 79 and 80); (386) 454-1853.

Paynes Prairie State Preserve A flat stretch of prairie that's home to wild horses and a herd of American bison makes this an unusual destination. You can boat, camp, hike, bird-watch, fish, and picnic on this 20,000-acre wildlife sanctuary. Named for a Seminole chief, Paynes Prairie is one of the most significant and historic areas in Florida, with more than 350 kinds of animals living in the freshwater marsh, lakes, pine flatwoods, hammock, scrub, and grasslands, including plenty of reptiles, fish, and amphibians. Trails range from half a mile to 8 miles. A 50-foot-high viewing tower with a telescope gives an awesome view of the prairie. If you fish, you'll need a license. Free ranger-led activities are held October–March. Admission $3.25 per vehicle. Camping is $10. Open daily 8 a.m.–sundown; visitors center open 9 a.m.–5 p.m. US 441, 10 miles south of Gainesville, near Micanopy; (352) 466-3397.

Santa Fe River Pack your own picnic and rent canoes for day trips from 3 to 15 miles—you paddle downstream with the current, local outfitters pick you up in a van and bring you back. Florida wildlife is abundant—egrets, ibis, great blue herons, turtles, deer, fox, raccoons, possums, and more. There are no big boats, as the river is shallow and only 150 feet wide. Real outdoor enthusiasts can also arrange two- to seven-night camping trips (they'll provide all the gear). Santa Fe Canoe Outpost, on US 441 at the Santa Fe River Bridge, 23 miles north of Gainesville in High Springs; (386) 454-2050.

Tree Hill Nature Center If you want to skip a day at the beach but still want to spend some time outdoors, this is a great place, with 40 acres of urban wilderness. There's a self-guided nature walk through wetland vegetation with all kinds of trees—even the woodpecker holes are clearly marked along the paths. A small natural history museum is open Monday–Saturday, 8:30 a.m.–5 p.m. Admission is $1 adults, 50 cents children ages 17 and under. 7152 Lone Star Road, off Arlington Road in Jacksonville, less than ten minutes from downtown; (904) 724-4646.

Washington Oaks State Gardens This small state beach is distinguished by 400 acres of lovely gardens on property that extends from the Atlantic Ocean to the Matanzas River. The park is named after a relative of George Washington who worked the land in the years before the Civil War. The gardens were expanded with azaleas, camellias, and roses when the place was purchased in 1937 by the Young family (the father was chairman of the board of General Electric). The land was donated to the state in 1964 and has a small museum, which details the history of the site. The lush coastal hammock is home to deer, raccoon, bobcat, fox, and opossum. It's a pleasant stop to stretch on the way north or south, with walking trails and good fishing, but swimming isn't recommended because of the rocky shoreline—ocean waves have washed away the sand, exposing coquina rock and creating a picturesque, boulder-strewn beach. At low tide shorebirds feed; limpets and mussels cling to the rocks, and anemones, starfish, and crabs are common in the tidal pools. $3.25 per car entry fee. 6400 N. Ocean Boulevard (on both sides of SR A1A), 2 miles south of Marineland; (904) 446-6780.

A CALENDAR OF FESTIVALS AND EVENTS

February

Hoggetowne Medieval Faire Gainesville. Medieval festival with jousting in period costumes, arts and crafts. (352) 334-2197.

Olustee Battle Festival and Reenactment Lake City. The Battle of Olustee kept the town of Tallahassee from falling into the hands of Union troops during the Civil War, and this reenactment includes more than 2,000 participants. Also parade, arts and crafts. (386) 752-2031.

April

Bausch and Lomb Tennis Championship Amelia Island. Amelia Island Plantation hosts some of the world's leading women tennis players for this nationally televised tournament; (904) 261-6161.

Beaches Festival Weekend Jacksonville Beach. Dancing, sandcastle-building contest, and parade. (904) 249-3972.

Springing the Blues Festival Jacksonville, Beach. Nationally recognized blues fest, kids' games, rides, and arts and crafts. (904) 249-3972.

St. Augustine Easter Parade St. Augustine. Parade of horses and carriages, floats, and marching bands. (904) 829-2992.

May

Isle of Eight Flags Shrimp Festival Fernandina Beach. Celebration of the birthplace of the shrimping industry. (904) 261-3248.

June

Spanish Night Watch 1740s St. Augustine. Torchlight procession through the Spanish Quarter by actors in period dress. Music and pageantry of Colonial times are relived, including daytime history displays. (904) 829-6476; www.staugustinechamber.com.

July

Fourth of July Celebration Flagler Beach. Parade and continuous live entertainment, including games for children, arts and crafts, food, and fireworks. (386) 439-0995.

September

Days in Spain St. Augustine. Celebrating the city's birthday with live entertainment, food, and games. (904) 825-1010.

October

Caribe Carnvial Jacksonville Riverwalk. Performances, art, bands, and authentic Caribbean cuisine. (904) 260-3843.

Colonial Arts and Crafts Festival St. Augustine. Colonial craftspeople display talents and wares, including blacksmithing, spinning, weaving, and music. (904) 829-1711; www.staugustinechamber.com.

November

Jacksonville Jazz Festival Jacksonville. One of the country's largest, with Great American Jazz Piano Competition. (904) 358-6336.

Lincolnville Festival St. Augustine. Jazz, blues, gospel, and soul at a festival that chronicles Lincolnville, one of the oldest black settlements in the United States, once called "Little Africa." (904) 829-1711; www.staugustinechamber.com.

December

British Encampment St. Augustine. Music and pageantry of Colonial times is relived with torchlight procession through the British Quarter by actors in period dress. Also daytime events and living history displays. (904) 829-6476 or (904) 829-6506.

St. Augustine Christmas Parade St. Augustine. Morning parade with floats and Santa arriving in downtown St. Augustine. (904) 829-6476.

Victorian Seaside Christmas Fernandina Beach. Monthlong celebration highlighted by tours of historic homes, The Nutcracker ballet, teddy bear teas, and New Year galas. (800) 2AMELIA, (904) 261-3248; www.aifby.com.

Amelia Island and Fernandina Beach

Beautiful beaches and an unhurried atmosphere are the best reasons for families to head to this quiet little island, just 2.5 miles wide, located 30 miles northeast of Jacksonville. Though small, the island has 13 miles of scenic beaches, and is home to one of the most varied populations of wildlife on the East Coast.

There's plenty of history, too. Though the Timucuan Indians were the first inhabitants as early as 2000 B.C., it's nicknamed the "Isle of Eight Flags" because it's the only site in the United States that's been controlled by eight different governments in its 400 years—France, Spain, England, the Patriots of Amelia Island, the Green Cross of Florida, Mexico, the Confederacy, and the United States.

Despite the military influences, the most lasting impact on the island was the railroad industry. In the late 1800s, Fernandina was developed as a stop to accommodate passengers traveling to Florida for the winter. The island enjoyed its glory days, building grand Victorian summer homes and a luxurious resort on the ocean.

As the rails expanded, Fernandina Beach was bypassed as travelers hurried to Miami; as a result, Amelia Island and the city of Fernandina Beach retained the charm and graciousness of the Victorian era, leaving many historical landmarks and homes for visitors to enjoy, including the Silk Stocking District, a collection of sherbet-hued mansions.

Today, bring along your walking shoes and as you can step back in time in Fernandina Beach, with its historic district and 450 beautifully restored Victorian structures, including one of the state's oldest saloons. There are 50 blocks in all on the National Register of Historic Places. The focal point is Centre Street, with boutiques and art galleries, outdoor cafes and waterfront restaurants. Stop by the visitors bureau near the city docks for information.

Amelia Island also is the birthplace of the modern-day shrimping industry. Local shrimpers invented a method to preserve the freshness of

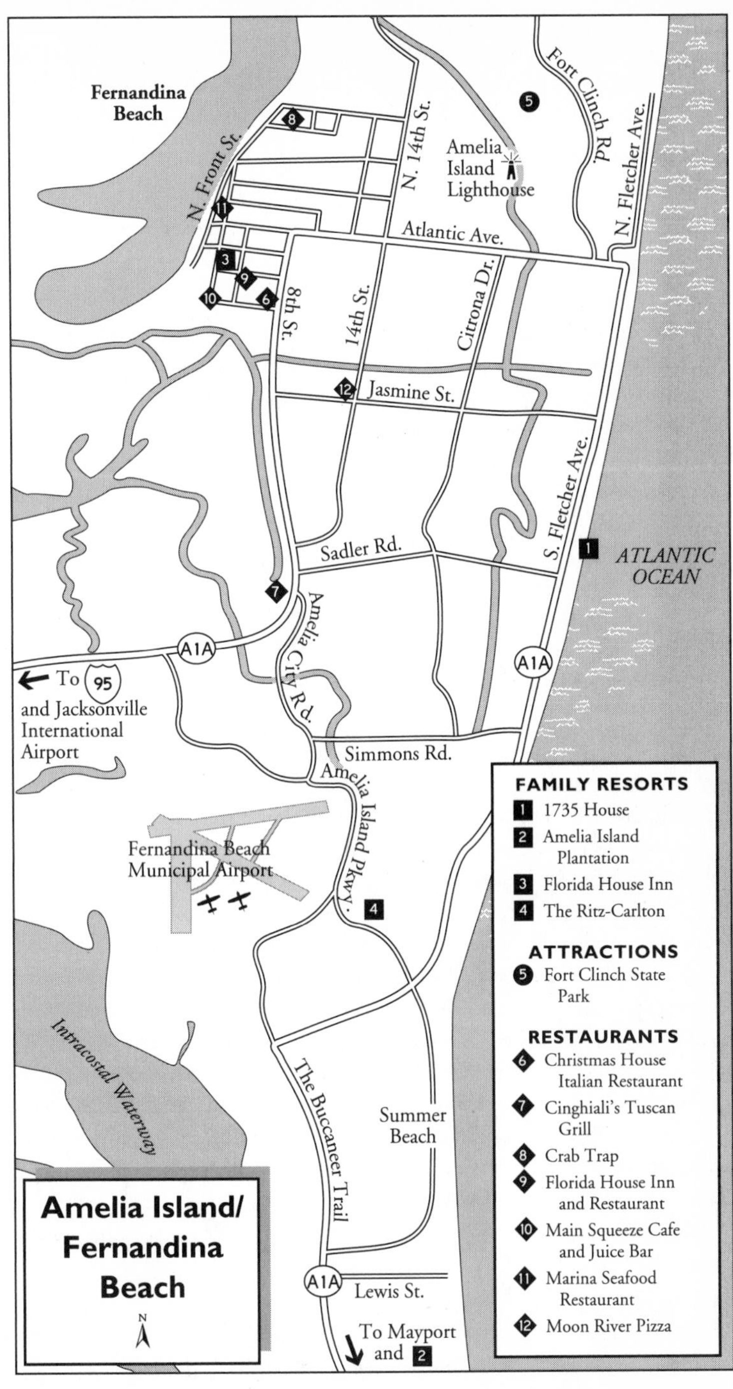

Fernandina Beach
N. Front St.
N. 14th St.
Fort Clinch Rd.
N. Fletcher Ave.
Amelia Island Lighthouse
Atlantic Ave.
8th St.
14th St.
Citrona Dr.
Jasmine St.
S. Fletcher Ave.
Sadler Rd.
ATLANTIC OCEAN
A1A
Amelia City Rd.
To 95 and Jacksonville International Airport
Simmons Rd.
Amelia Island Pkwy.
Fernandina Beach Municipal Airport
Intracostal Waterway
The Buccaneer Trail
Summer Beach
Lewis St.
To Mayport and 2
Amelia Island/ Fernandina Beach
N
FAMILY RESORTS
1 1735 House
2 Amelia Island Plantation
3 Florida House Inn
4 The Ritz-Carlton
ATTRACTIONS
5 Fort Clinch State Park
RESTAURANTS
6 Christmas House Italian Restaurant
7 Cinghiali's Tuscan Grill
8 Crab Trap
9 Florida House Inn and Restaurant
10 Main Squeeze Cafe and Juice Bar
11 Marina Seafood Restaurant
12 Moon River Pizza

the shrimp for shipping around the turn of the century, and the business still is a mainstay for Amelia Island residents. You can watch as shrimp boats unload their bounty, then try the sweet-tasting fresh seafood in local eateries—nearly 1 million tons of shrimp are caught off Amelia Island every year.

SAIL ABOARD AN OLD-FASHIONED SCHOONER

Help hoist the sails or just sit back and relax aboard the *Voyager*, a 100-foot, nineteenth century–style schooner that plies the Cumberland Sound near Amelia Island. The captain and crew will let you pitch in, but don't miss the gorgeous scenery—free-roaming horses grazing on Cumberland Island, the antebellum Fort Clinch, or a beautiful sunset. The schooner moors at Fernandina Harbor Marina at Zachary Court, Amelia Island. Voyage Adventures, (904) 321-1244. Cost is $35, $31 for seniors 65 and older, and $16 for ages 12 and under .

Family Resorts

1735 House

584 S. Fletcher, Fernandina Beach • (904) 261-5878 • fax (904) 261-9200
www.1735house-bb.com

Spend the night on the beach in a lighthouse that sleeps four (one per floor) with circular rooms and wonderful views of the ocean. The lighthouse includes two baths and a kitchen and dining area, and a 360º observation deck. The lighthouse is part of the nautically themed 1735 House that offers five suites (each with decor inspired by Amelia Island's history) in an old house right on the beach. A substantial continental breakfast is served in wooden picnic baskets delivered to your door. The year 1735, by the way, is when Fernandina Beach was discovered by British general James Oglethorpe, who named the island for the daughter of King George II.

If you can't book one of their two lighthouses, the suites are fine; all have private bedrooms with baths and, on the oceanside, a living room that is comfortably furnished with wicker or rattan. Suites can sleep up to six, with built-in bunk beds in an alcove. Three of the suites have kitchens. If you don't have a kitchen, you're welcome to use the inn's; guests can whip up their own lunch or dinner (but you have to clean up).

Children under age 6 stay free in parents' rooms. Seasonal rates: September–March, $216–371; April–August, $186–317.

Amelia Island Plantation

3000 First Coast Highway, Amelia Island • (800) 874-6878 • fax (904) 277-5945
www.aipfl.com

On Amelia Island, across the St. Mary's River from Georgia, this resort overlooks the Atlantic on the east and marshlands on the west. The 1,300-acre resort with 700 rooms, suites, and villas (all with mini-refrigerators and coffeemakers) features miles of beaches, golf and tennis, and an extensive programs for toddlers to teens. Baby-sitting is available for children under age 3.

The staff offers woodland bird tours, an edible plant and wildflower ramble, a paddleboat tour of Red Maple Lake, sunset hikes, crabbing expeditions, a beachside naturalist walk, a turtle talk, a nature bike hike, and more. There are three nature trails at Amelia Island Plantation and a nature center. For information on any of these programs, call the naturalist at (904) 321-5082, ext. 5082. Nature center hikes cost, $7.50 adults, $5 children 4–12.

Kids Camp Amelia offers award-winning nature activities, beach games, swimming, arts and crafts, health and fitness programs, and field trips staffed by recreation majors from colleges and universities around the world. For teenagers, Amelia's Teen Adventures offers deep-sea fishing, sunset sailing, culinary and beauty classes, kayaking, jet ski excursions, volleyball tournaments, bonfires, and DJ-hosted dance-a-thons. Trips to Jacksonville special events, bike hikes, and nature activities with the naturalist are other activities. Just for Kids offers evening programs for children ages 3–10, $25; Wednesday–Saturday March–September; Fridays and Saturdays during fall and winter. Beach bonfires, hay-wagon rides, and pool parties are among planned activities. Recreation on Call offers custom-designed programs for the entire family, such as themed private parties, beach Olympics, hayrides, and bike tours. Also junior golf and tennis clinics, and rainy day programs with indoor events and entertainment. Deep-sea fishing, nature tours—you can even rent a baby jogger.

Rooms start run $135–335; children over age 3 billed at $10 per night.

Florida House Inn

22 S.Third Street (half a block off Centre Street), Fernandina Beach • (800) 258-3301 • (904) 261-3300 • fax (904) 277-3831 • www.floridahouse.com

The funky Florida House Inn is the oldest surviving hotel in the state, opened in 1857 by the Florida Railroad for its passengers. Though it's showing its age a little, it's an adventure, a sort of time travel back to the days of the Civil War. Each of the ten rooms has a private bath (two with claw-foot tubs); six of the rooms have working fireplaces. You can sit on the spacious front porch and watch the world go by, or take a short stroll to Centre Street. At suppertime, the inn is a gathering place for locals and tourists, with family-style seating at long wooden tables and substantial bowls of fresh green beans, corn, mashed potatoes, and fried chicken.

A full-service bar is available. Guests also have access to microwaves, coffeemakers, and refrigerators. Free breakfast. Room rates: $79–179 year-round.

The Ritz-Carlton, Amelia Island

4750 Amelia Island Parkway, Amelia Island • (904) 277-1100 • (800) 627-4688 fax (904) 261-9064 • www.ritzcarlton.com

Poised on a bluff overlooking the Atlantic Ocean, The Ritz-Carlton sprawls over 13 acres of beachfront and includes a mile and a half of white sand beach, indoor and outdoor pools, a recreation center, and children's playground. The posh resort has 449 rooms, including 45 suites (and a maid who comes twice a day). Vacationers familiar with the Ritz-Carlton's impeccable, award-winning service and amenities won't be disappointed at the Amelia Island resort.

The Ritz Kids program is for guests ages 5–12 and is supervised by trained counselors. Programs include physical activities like beach games and water sports as well as creative play—arts and crafts, pastry inventions, and beach sculpturing. Learning sessions include dining etiquette, art appreciation tours, and environmental and nature programs. Enrollment is for full or half days. The resort also offers a Kids Night Out with games, movies, arts and crafts, and a children's menu.

Rates start at $249 in the summer, $200 in the winter.

Attractions

Fort Clinch State Park

2601 Atlantic Avenue, Fernandina Beach • (904) 277-7274

Hours - 8 a.m.–sundown daily

Admission - $3.25 per vehicle (up to 8 people) to enter state park; 50 cents per person (more than 8 people)

Appeal by Age Group -

Pre-school ★★★	Teens ★★★	Over 30 ★★★
Grade school ★★★★	Young Adults ★★★	Seniors ★★★

Touring Time - Average 3–4 hours; minimum 2½ hours

Rainy-Day Touring - Not recommended

Author's Rating - ★★★; a fun way to get some exercise climbing all around the fort and to learn a little history

Restaurants - No

Alcoholic beverages - No

Handicapped access - Yes

Wheelchair rental - No

Baby stroller rental - No

Lockers - No

Pet kennels - No

Rain check - No

Private tours - Yes

Description and Comments Amelia Island's most famous historical site is a must-see for history buffs and something that youngsters especially enjoy. It's most fun when the actors are there, reenacting the daily life of Civil War–era soldiers with infantry demonstrations, marching, and sentry duty. You can even sit on a bunk covered with a straw-filled mattress and get a feeling of what it must have been like for young men to be far from home. Climb the ramparts and look across the sound to Georgia.

There's also fishing from a jetty, the pier, or in the surf—trout, redfish, and sheepshead are abundant. Camping, picnicking, and other activities are available (see Family Outdoor Adventures, page 76).

Family-Friendly Restaurants

Christmas House Italian Restaurant

604 Ash Street, Fernandina Beach • (904) 321-2121

Meals served - Dinner

Cuisine - Italian

Entree range - $12–30

Kids menu - No

Reservations - Suggested

Payment - Visa, MC, AmEx

Decorated year-round for Christmas, and on the 25th of every month they serve turkey with all the trimmings. All kinds of pasta, and the house specialty is farfalle gorgonzola. Kids are welcome to share an entree.

Cinghiale's Tuscan Grill

A1A and Shave Bridge • (904) 277-2336

Meals served - Dinner

Cuisine - Northern Italian

Entree Range: $9.95–$16.95

Kids menu - Yes

Reservations - Yes

Payment - All major credit cards accepted

Lovely view of the intracoastal waterway from the dining room. Try the seafood primavera or the blackened mahi-mahi with roasted red bell pepper cream sauce. Kid's menu includes a petite sirloin.

Crab Trap

31 N. Second Street, Fernandina Beach • (904) 261-4749

Meals served - Dinner 5 p.m.

Cuisine - American, seafood

Entree range - $11.95–23.95

Kids menu - Yes

Reservations - Not accepted

Payment - Visa, MC, AmEx

This is one of the best-known restaurants on the island, but it's closed from October 1 until March. Ask for seafood blackened, broiled, or fried. Also fresh oysters.

Florida House Inn and Restaurant

20 and 22 S. Third Street, Fernandina Beach • (904) 261-3300
www.floridahouse.com

Meals served - Breakfast (inn guests only), lunch, and dinner, closed Mondays, no Sunday dinner

Cuisine - Southern–family style

Entree range - Lunch $6.98; dinner $11.98; Sunday brunch $9.98; (all you can eat)

Kids menu - No, but there are plenty of choices and plenty they'll like, and prices are adjusted according to age; a 5-year-old, for example, eats for $5.00.

Reservations - Accepted for parties of 6 or more

Payment - Visa, MC

Steaming bowls of collards, black-eyed peas, fried chicken, meat loaf, cheese grits, okra and tomatoes—this is true Southern fare, served family style at long tables that encourage everyone to share.

Main Squeeze Cafe and Juice Bar

105 S. 3rd Street, Fernandina Beach • (904) 277-3003

Meals served - Breakfast and lunch Monday–Saturday

Cuisine - Health-conscious Mexican

Entree range - $4.50–5.25

Kids menu - No

Reservations - No

Payment - Visa, MC

Indoor/outdoor cafe and juice bar features Mexican-inspired creations, including nachos, burritos, and quesadillas. Also salads and fruit juices. If you want something special, just ask.

Marina Seafood Restaurant

Centre Street, Fernandina Beach (by the docks on Centre Street) 101 • (904) 261-5310

Meals served - Breakfast, lunch, and dinner

Cuisine - American, seafood

Entree range - $4.55–22.95

Kids menu - Dinner only

Reservations - Not accepted

Payment - Visa, MC, DC

Their cheeseburger has won awards, and customers often ask for the recipe for the homemade shrimp and crab dip.

Moon River Pizza

925 S. 14th Street, Fernandina Beach • (904) 321-3400

Meals served - Lunch and dinner

Cuisine - Pizzas and salads

Entree Range: Pizzas start at $8 and up

Kids menu - No

Reservations - No

Payment - Cash only

If you're craving pizza, this family-owned shop is the place. Calzones, pizzas, and salads comprise the menu, with dough and sauce made fresh daily. They offer 20 different toppings, but we recommend their simple white pizza.

Jacksonville

One of Florida's major urban areas with miles of Atlantic beaches on its eastern border (and the largest city in land area in the lower 48), the waterfront is the big focus in busy Jacksonville. The St. John's River divides the city, with water taxis to carry passengers to Riverwalk and Jacksonville Landing, where families can experience a lively marketplace with street performers, festivals, and concerts. A Skyway monorail gives riders an elevated view of the city.

Though Jacksonville may not be your first choice for a Sunshine State vacation, beyond downtown is another side of Jacksonville, offering hours of family exploration and close encounters with Mother Nature. Just a few miles east is Little Talbot Island State Park, one of the few remaining undeveloped barrier islands in Florida. Big Talbot Island, just north of Little Talbot, offers magnificent views from towering dunes, 3 miles of undeveloped beaches, salt marshes, and a scenic driftwood forest (see page 77).

Family Resorts

Holiday Inn Sunspree

1617 N. First Street, Jacksonville, just east of SR A1A, 1 mile north of US 90 • (904) 249-9071 • fax (904) 241-4321 • www.jaxsunspree.com

"Just look for the humpback whales when you turn the corner," the reservation clerk explained. Humpback whales? They're painted on the front of this family-friendly resort, a giant, colorful 30-by-40-foot mural.

This Sunspree was completely renovated in 1995, and all 143 spacious beachfront rooms have microwaves, refrigerators, and coffeemakers. In-room movies are free, including video games. A hot buffet breakfast is $5.95, and children ages 12 and under eat free at both breakfast and dinner in the resort's restaurant. Free, supervised kid's activities run seven

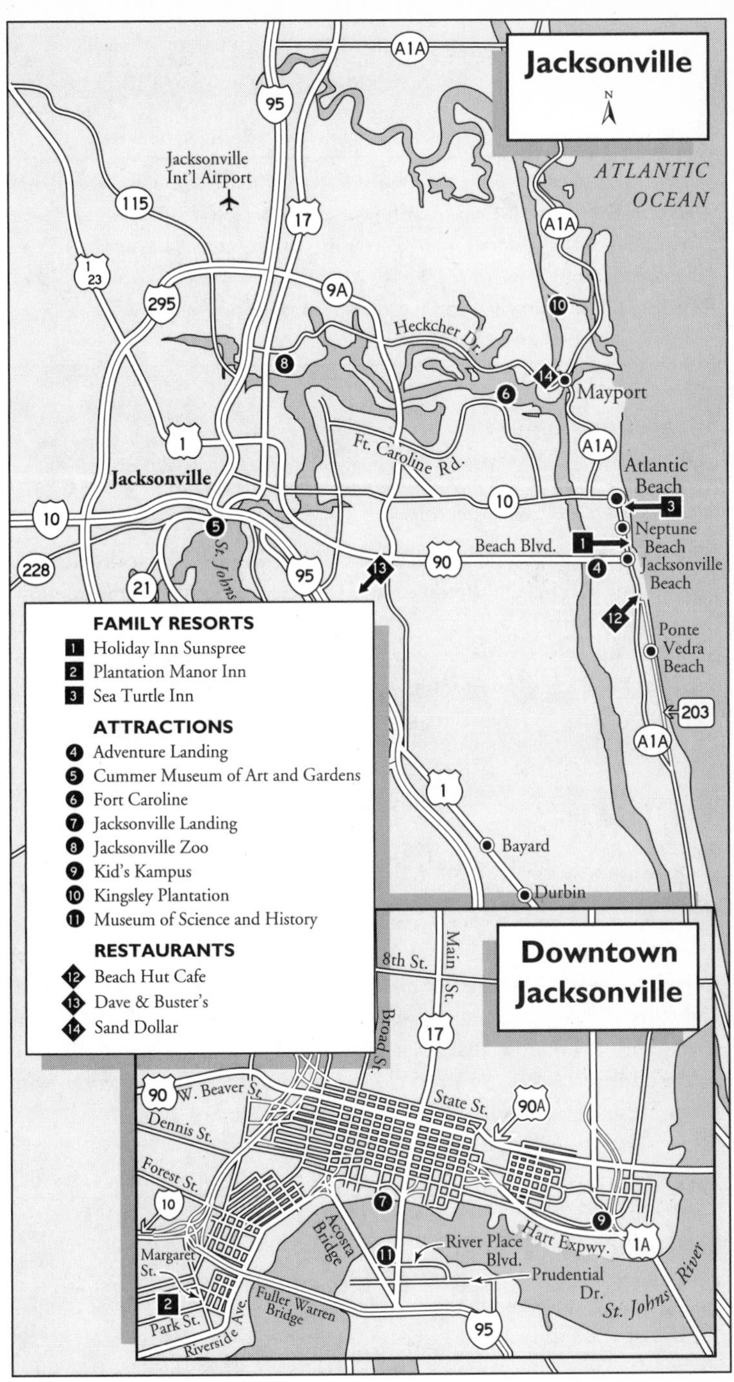
Jacksonville
N
ATLANTIC
OCEAN
A1A
95
17
115
1
23
295
9A
Jacksonville
Int'l Airport
Heckcher Dr.
Mayport
Ft. Caroline Rd.
Jacksonville
Atlantic
Beach
Neptune
Beach
Jacksonville
Beach
Beach Blvd.
10
90
228
21
St. Johns
Ponte
Vedra
Beach
203
Bayard
Durbin
FAMILY RESORTS
1 Holiday Inn Sunspree
2 Plantation Manor Inn
3 Sea Turtle Inn
ATTRACTIONS
4 Adventure Landing
5 Cummer Museum of Art and Gardens
6 Fort Caroline
7 Jacksonville Landing
8 Jacksonville Zoo
9 Kid's Kampus
10 Kingsley Plantation
11 Museum of Science and History
RESTAURANTS
12 Beach Hut Cafe
13 Dave & Buster's
14 Sand Dollar
Downtown
Jacksonville
8th St.
Main St.
Broad St.
W. Beaver St.
State St.
90A
Dennis St.
Forest St.
Hart Expwy.
1A
Acosta Bridge
River Place Blvd.
Prudential Dr.
St. Johns River
Margaret St.
Park St.
Riverside Ave.
Fuller Warren Bridge

days a week from Memorial Day through Labor Day. Rates start at $120 in the summer, $99 in the winter; kids stay free up to age 18.

If You're Driving

Jacksonville can be confusing because the St. John's River bisects the city, so most routes into the area eventually cross one of the city's seven bridges (the Main Street Bridge leads to downtown). I-295 forms a beltway around Jacksonville; I-95 is the north-south highway; and J. Turner Butler Boulevard takes you east (to the beaches) and west. Travelers can also cross the river by way of the St. John's River Ferry, the only public auto ferry operating in Florida.

Plantation Manor Inn

1630 Copeland Street, Jacksonville, just north of Riverside Avenue and less than 1.5 miles south of I-95 Exit 109 (Riverside Avenue) • (904) 384-4630 • fax (904) 387-0960 • www.plantationmanorinn.com

If you're looking for a place to lodge overnight in the historic district, this 1905 home accepts children over age 12. There are nine rooms (all non-smoking, all with TVs) in the three-story house just two blocks from the St. John's River. The inn has a lap pool and spa. Rates start at $135–170, with a $10 charge for children sharing a room, and include breakfast. Complimentary beverages are served, including soft drinks, beer, water, and fruit juice.

Sea Turtle Inn

One Ocean Blvd., Atlantic Beach • (904) 249-7402 or (800) 874-6000
www.seaturtle.com

This 193-room hotel recently had a $6 million facelift, and it's one of the nicest hotels right on the beach, with a big swimming pool a few steps from the ocean. Spacious rooms have refrigerators and coffee makers, and kids stay free (though it's $10 for a rollaway). There's a notable restaurant, Plaintains, that's regularly voted a favorite by locals, and you're also just across the street from Atlantic Beach Town Center, with shopping and restaurants. Rates start at $169.

Attractions

Adventure Landing

4825 Blanding Boulevard, Jacksonville Beach • (904) 77-2803
www.adventurelanding.com

Hours - 10 a.m.– 8 p.m. daily (limited hours off-season)

Admission - Individually priced for each attraction; waterpark is $24.99 (all day), $19.99 (3 hours), $16.99 42" and under

Appeal by Age Group -

Pre-school ★★★	Teens ★★★★	Over 30 ★★
Grade school ★★★★	Young Adults ★★	Seniors ★

Touring Time - Average full afternoon or evening; minimum 2 hours

Rainy-Day Touring - Not recommended

Author's Rating - ★★★; it's not Disney World, but plenty to keep kids busy all day—and plenty of poolside chairs for mom and dad

Restaurants - Yes

Alcoholic beverages - No

Handicapped access - Yes

Wheelchair rental - No

Baby stroller rental - No

Lockers - Yes

Pet kennels - No

Rain check - Yes

Private tours - Yes

Description and Comments Jacksonville's largest amusement park, featuring two miniature golf courses, batting cages, go-cart racing, bumper boats, a laser-tag shooting gallery, and Shipwreck Island, an interactive water park complete with a wave pool, 65-foot-tall Pirate Village with 11 slides, and more than 200 water nozzles. The dollars quickly add up, as all rides and attractions are individually priced.

Cummer Museum of Art and Gardens

829 Riverside Avenue, Jacksonville • (904) 356-6857

Hours - Tuesdays and Thursdays, 10 a.m.–9 p.m.; Wednesdays, Fridays, Saturdays, 10 a.m.–5 p.m.; Sunday, noon–5 p.m. (closed on Monday)

Admission - $6 for adults, $4 for seniors over 62 and military personnel, $3 for students and children over 5, $1 for ages 4 and under

Appeal by Age Group -

Pre-school ★★★	Teens ★★	Over 30 ★★
Grade school ★★★★	Young Adults ★★	Seniors ★★★

Touring Time - Average a half-day; minimum 2 hours

Rainy-Day Touring - Recommended

Author's Rating - ★★; Art Connections is the biggest reason for a family to visit, where kids get a hands-on understanding of art

Restaurants - Small cafe sells snacks,

Alcoholic beverages - No

Handicapped access - Yes

Wheelchair rental - No

Baby stroller rental - No

Lockers - No

Pet kennels - No
Rain check - No
Private tours - Yes

Description and Comments The museum has a decent permanent collection with plenty of Greek and Egyptian works, American impressionist paintings, and lovely Japanese Netsuke ivory carvings. The gardens are another work of art, brilliant with azaleas in the springtime. But the kids are most interested in the child-size, hands-on exhibits in Art Connections.

Fort Caroline

12713 Fort Caroline Road (off Monument Road), Jacksonville • (904) 641-7155

Hours - Daily 9 a.m.–5 p.m.; closed Christmas

Admission - Free

Appeal by Age Group -

Pre-school ★	Teens ★★	Over 30 ★★
Grade school ★★	Young Adults ★★	Seniors ★★

Touring Time - Average 2–3 hours; minimum 2 hours

Rainy-Day Touring - Not recommended

Author's Rating - ★★; a chance to get outdoors and see places where history happened

Restaurants - No
Alcoholic beverages - No
Handicapped access - Yes
Wheelchair rental - No
Baby stroller rental - No
Lockers - No
Pet kennels - No
Rain check - No
Private tours - When rangers are available

Description and Comments Families can explore the area's colonial past at this national memorial, where guided tours of the reconstructed sixteenth-century French fort explain the struggle between European colonial powers for control of Florida. Thirty-minute ranger tours are given on the weekends, followed by fascinating 1½-hour guided nature walks through the Theodore Roosevelt Area. The 2-mile hike along the trail goes into Native American country, inhabited as far back as 500 B.C.

Jacksonville Landing

2 Independent Drive on the St. John's River • (904) 353-1188
www.jacksonvillelanding.com

Hours - Monday–Thursday, 10 a.m.–8 p.m.; Friday–Saturday, 10 a.m.–9 p.m.; Sunday, noon–5:30 p.m.

Admission - Free, but parking is 80 cents an hour after 5 p.m. and all day Saturday and Sunday; merchants will validate parking ticket with $10 purchase

Appeal by Age Group -

Pre-school ★★★	Teens ★★★★	Over 30 ★★★
Grade school ★★★★	Young Adults ★★★	Seniors ★★★

Touring Time - Average 3–4 hours; minimum 2½ hours

Rainy-Day Touring - Recommended

Author's Rating - ★★★, nothing new here, but it's a great place to be if you can't be at the beach. Also fun for late afternoon and early evening entertainment options

Restaurants - Yes

Alcoholic beverages - Yes

Handicapped access - Yes

Wheelchair rental - No

Baby stroller rental - No

Lockers - No

Pet kennels - No

Rain check - No

Private tours - No

Description and Comments There's plenty to keep you occupied, including a 10,000-square foot amusement center called Tilt's Ostrich Landing that features a near-endless selection of video games. There are more than 80 shops and a family-pleasing food court. Special events are often booked, so check if you're planning to be in town.

Water taxis provide a fun family outing, running between Riverwalk and Jacksonville Landing from about 11 a.m. to 10 p.m. Fare is $2 one way or $3 round-trip for adults; children ages 3–10 and seniors over 60 pay $2 one way or $2 round-trip. S. S. Marine Taxi, (904) 733-7782.

Jacksonville Zoo

8605 Zoo Parkway, Jacksonville • (904) 757-4462 • www.jaxzoo.org

Hours - 9 a.m.–5 p.m. daily; closed Thanksgiving and Christmas

Admission - $8 for adults, $6.50 for seniors 65 and over, $5 for children ages 3–12

Appeal by Age Group -

Pre-school ★★★	Teens ★★★	Over 30 ★★
Grade school ★★★	Young Adults ★★	Seniors ★★

Touring Time - Half a day on average; minimum 2 hours

Rainy-Day Touring - Not recommended

Author's Rating - ★★, kids love the wildlife, and especially enjoy the petting zoo of domesticated African animals

Restaurants - Yes
Alcoholic beverages - No
Handicapped access - Yes
Wheelchair rental - Yes
Baby stroller rental - Yes
Lockers - No
Pet kennels - No
Rain check - Varies
Private tours - Yes

Description and Comments The zoo borders the Trout River and includes a petting zoo, an aviary, an 18-acre African veldt exhibit with more than 100 animal species, an elephant pool, a boardwalk, open-air exhibits featuring uncaged animals, an elevated walkway, and a miniature train. The newest addition is the Wild Florida exhibit, with black bears, bald eagles, river otters, and other native species.

There are more than 700 animals on display, with habitats as natural as possible to allow close-up views of animals like lions, ostriches, rhinos, and elephants, side by side.

Kids Campus

410 Gator Bowl Blvd., Jacksonville • (904) 630-KIDS

Hours - Monday–Saturday, 8 a.m.–8 p.m.; Sunday, 10 a.m.–8 p.m.
Admission - Free
Appeal by Age Group -

Pre-school ★★★★	Teens —	Over 30 —
Grade school ★★★★	Young Adults —	Seniors —

Touring Time - 2–4 hours
Rainy-Day Touring - Not recommended
Author's Rating - ★★★★; the next generation of public parks
Restaurants - No
Alcoholic beverages - Yes
Handicapped access - No
Wheelchair rental - No
Baby stroller rental - No
Lockers - No
Pet kennels - No
Rain check - No
Private tours - No

Description and Comments This 10-acre park is geared to 2- to 12-year-olds, with everything from a splash park (with a separate one for toddlers) to small athletic fields with free rental of footballs, soccer balls, Frisbees and more. They even rent bikes with training wheels for little ones to ride through a "safe city" streetscape. A re-creation of a Timucuan village is a highlight. Plenty to keep the kids busy while parents relax—or join in the fun.

Kingsley Plantation

11676 Palmetto Avenue, Fort George Island • (904) 251-3537

Hours - Daily 9 a.m.–5 p.m.; closed Christmas

Admission - Free, but donations are appreciated

Appeal by Age Group -

Pre-school ★	Teens ★★★	Over 30 ★★★
Grade school ★★	Young Adults ★★★	Seniors ★★★

Touring Time - Average 1–2 hours; minimum 1 hour

Rainy-Day Touring - Not recommended

Author's Rating - ★★★; fascinating peek into history; the natural scenery is right out of a picture book, with spectacular views of barrier islands and savannahs

Restaurants - No
Alcoholic beverages - No
Handicapped access - Yes
Wheelchair rental - No
Baby stroller rental - No
Lockers - No
Pet kennels - No
Rain check - No
Private tours - No

Description and Comments Kingsley was built in 1804 on Fort George Island near Jacksonville, and cotton and other crops were cultivated in the eighteenth and nineteenth centuries. It is the oldest plantation in Florida and a State Historic Site that is preserved and interpreted by the National Park Service as part of the Timucuan Ecological and Historic Preserve.

A guided tour of the two-story residence, kitchen house, and barn/carriage house includes a peek at the remains of slave cabins, a reminder of the days when Zebediah Kingsley and his African wife trained slaves.

Museum of Science and History (MOSH)

1025 Museum Circle, Southbank • (904) 396-6674 • www.themosh.org

Hours - Monday–Friday, 10 a.m.–5 p.m.; Saturday, 10 a.m.–6 p.m.; Sunday, 1–6 p.m.

Admission - $6 for adults, $4.50 for seniors, $4 for children ages 3–12, free for ages 3 and under

Appeal by Age Group -

Pre-school ★★★	Teens ★★	Over 30 ★★
Grade school ★★★	Young Adults ★★	Seniors ★★

Touring Time - Average full morning or full afternoon; minimum 2 hours

Rainy-Day Touring - Recommended

Author's Rating - ★★; plenty of fun for a rainy day

Restaurants - No
Alcoholic beverages - No
Handicapped access - Yes
Wheelchair rental - No
Baby stroller rental - No
Lockers - No
Pet kennels - No
Rain check - No
Private tours - Yes

Description and Comments Entertaining, from the 72-pound alligator snapping turtle in the 1,200-gallon aquarium to Kid Zone, with fun science displays and a motion simulator. The interactive exhibits cover local history and one hallway honors pro football's Jacksonville Jaguars. There is also a planetarium.

GO FISH

If you want to try deep-sea fishing, the *King Neptune,* (904) 246-0104, heads out into the Atlantic every morning at 8 from 4378 Ocean Street, a half-mile south of the Mayport Ferry. A trip on the 65-foot, air-conditioned boat costs $45 per person, all bait and tackle included. Reservations are required (but not a fishing license). Children must be 6 or older.

Family-Friendly Restaurants

Beach Hut Cafe

South Beaches Plaza, 1281 S.Third Street, Jacksonville • (904) 249-3516

Meals served - Breakfast and lunch

Cuisine - American—hearty homemade fare

Entree range - $3–5.75

Kids menu - No, but they'll make half sandwiches or a grilled cheese or peanut butter and jelly; just ask for most anything on the menu in a smaller portion

Reservations - Not accepted

Payment - Visa, MC, AmEx, D

Everything is simply delicious and made from scratch. The Downing family runs the Beach Hut, and you'll love the artwork, by children in their son's elementary school class. The Beach Hut has a bit of celebrity status; Ladybird Johnson used to eat there when she came to town, and Andre Agassi still drops by when he's playing tennis in the area.

Dave & Buster's

7025 Salisbury Rd., Jacksonville • (904) 296-1525

Meals served - Lunch and dinner, open 11 a.m.–midnight daily

Cuisine - American

Entree range - $7.95–12.95

Kids menu - Yes

Reservations - No

Payment - All major credit cards accepted

You won't mind the wait (and there's often a line), since Dave & Buster's lets you pass the time with interactive and arcade games, pocket billiards, and shuffleboard. The all-American choices are delicious, from simple burgers to steak and ribs. Also pasta, pizza, and seafood.

Sand Dollar

9716 Heckscher Drive, Jacksonville • (904) 251-2449

Meals served - Lunch and dinner

Cuisine - Seafood

Entree range - Lunch, $4.95–7.95; dinner, $10.95–29

Kids menu - Yes

Reservations - Accepted for parties of six or more

Payment - All major credit cards accepted

A perfect stop after a trip to the Jacksonville Zoo or Kingsley Plantation. Great water views, and outdoor tables on the riverside deck in the summertime. Seafood steamed, fried, or broiled is on the menu, though you can get chicken and burgers. Locals love the cashew grouper served with a lobster-curry sauce.

Side Trips

Ponte Vedra Inn and Club This seaside retreat dates back to 1928, and generations of fiercely loyal families have been returning for decades. The impeccable service, gently sloped white beaches, oversized rooms, luxurious amenities—including two 18-hole golf courses, notable tennis courts, and an award-winning spa—keep pampered guests coming back. Add to that four pools, fishing, sailing, and hiking.

Throughout the year the recreation department conducts numerous children's activities such as bingo, dinner clubs, movies, storytelling, arts and crafts, computer instruction, etiquette classes, and organized games. From June through August there's a summer youth camp for ages 4–12, with youth counselors to direct children in organized games, swimming instruction, beach walks, fishing, boating, tennis, golf, gymnastics, and arts and crafts.

For families, gear and bait are available for fishing in Lake Vedra. Trail rides and lessons are available at nearby Sawgrass Stables. For a day at the beach, bicycles, boogie boards, surfboard, paddleball, volleyball, Frisbees, ocean kayaks, and even sand buckets are for rent.

All rooms have refrigerators, some have kitchenettes. Rates start at $235, with children ages 18 and under free in parents' room. Family packages also are available. 200 Ponte Vedra Boulevard, Ponte Vedra Beach (20 minutes southeast of Jacksonville); (800) 234-7842; fax (904) 285-2111; www.pvresorts.com.

St. Augustine

St. Augustine is not only the oldest city in the United States, but also probably the oldest Florida vacation stopover and a must for families who are looking for a history lesson with proven kid appeal. An odd blend of historical sites and strange museums, St. Augustine has preserved its historical identity and remains the most unchanged of Florida's popular tourist haunts.

We recommend spending a day or two in St. Augustine—longer if you also want to spend some time at the beach, just minutes from the heart of town (see page 76). To get the most out of your stay, settle into one of the local bed-and-breakfasts; it's an easy drive to the beach for a swim or to watch the sunset. The beaches, with tall sand dunes, are less crowded than those farther south.

The city of St. Augustine is a tourist attraction in itself, an amazing composite of the lavish splendor of Florida's early boom years and the honest simplicity of the city's ancient heritage. Narrow streets, warm and intimate, fronted with the worn but enduring homes and courtyards of long-departed garrison populations, blend almost effortlessly with the embellished Spanish Renaissance design of Flagler College, formerly the Ponce de Leon Hotel; the former Alcazar Hotel, now city hall; and modern downtown St. Augustine.

Much of St. Augustine can be enjoyed without admission charges; the city's lovely thoroughfares and aged streets are treasures beyond description and are often more worthwhile than the attractions that charge admission.

The city is busiest in summer, on weekends, and during holiday periods. At many other times of the year you can almost have the place to yourself. Getting oriented is not difficult; stop at the official information center at the corner of San Marco Avenue, SR A1A, and Castillo Drive as you enter the city from the north. The information center has plenty of free maps, brochures, and hotel and restaurant information.

FAMILY RESORTS
1 Carriage Way Bed-and-Breakfast
2 Casa Monica Hotel
3 LaFiesta Oceanside Inn
4 Saragossa Inn
5 Secret Garden
6 St. Francis
ATTRACTIONS
7 Castillo de San Marcos National Monument
8 Colee's Sightseeing Carriage Tours
9 Fountain of Youth National Historic Park
10 Ghostly Walking Tour
11 Lightner Museum
12 Old Jail
13 Oldest Store Museum
14 Oldest Wooden Schoolhouse
15 Potter's Wax Museum
16 Ripley's Believe It Or Not! Museum
17 Spanish Quarter Museum
18 St. Augustine Alligator Farm and Zoological Park
19 St. Augustine Historical Tours
20 St. Augustine Light-house and Museum
21 St. Augustine Scenic Cruises
22 St. Augustine Sight-seeing Trains
RESTAURANTS
23 A1A Ale Works
24 Athena Restaurant
25 Barnacle Bill's
26 Columbia Restaurant
27 Creekside Dinery
28 Fiddler's Green
29 Gypsy Cab Co.
30 Harry's
31 Pizza Garden
32 Salt Water Cowboys
33 Sunset Grille
St. Augustine
San Sebastian River
Matanzas River
Macaris Creek
Maria Sanchez Lake
Bridge of Lions
To the Beach
Ponce de Leon Blvd.
San Marco Ave.
Genoply St.
Milton St.
Douglas Ave.
Dismure St.
May St.
Matanzas Ave.
Dufferin
Magnolia Ave.
Williams St.
Ballard Ave.
Ocean Ave.
Old Mission Rd.
Pine St.
Locust St.
Rhode Ave.
Mulberry St.
Water St.
Castillo Dr.
Spanish St.
Orange St.
Cuna St.
Saragossa St.
Carrera St.
Sevilla St.
Cordova St.
Valencia St.
Avenida Menendez
Hypolita St.
Treasury
Cathedral Pl.
Riberia St.
Artillery Lane
Cadiz St.
Bay St.
Aviles St.
Bridge St.
Weedon St.
Granada St.
St. Francis St.
DeHaven St.
Washington St.
St. George St.
Charlotte St.
Marine St.
Lovet St.
Central Ave.
South St.
Cerro St.
St. Augustine Blvd.
Anastasia Blvd.
A1A N
BUS 1
1
207
5A
214

It's best to take a drive around St. Augustine and get a feel for the city. Be sure to drive up and down the small side streets on both the north and south sides of the plaza (central square). Next take a walking tour that includes the restoration area, much of which is limited exclusively to pedestrian traffic. Don't rush your visit; we recommend taking several short walking tours punctuated with meals, a few hours at the beaches, or maybe a nap at the hotel. You'll encounter many of the paid attractions described in this guidebook on your walks. The sightseeing trains are a good alternative to walking, stopping at several points along the way (you can disembark and jump back on later, as the tours run throughout the day) and giving a good narrated orientation to the city.

Family Resorts

A stay in a bed-and-breakfast is part of the St. Augustine experience. We've found that most innkeepers are full of wonderful information about the city and are willing to share helpful, honest information. Breakfast is always complimentary, from a minimal continental to exquisite culinary creations. There are five in town and one on the ocean that accept children.

Carriage Way Bed-and-Breakfast

70 Cuna Street (between Cordova and Spanish Streets), St. Augustine • (800) 908-9832 • fax (904) 829-2467 • www.carriageway.com

Children ages 8 and older allowed in this 1883 Victorian home with 11 rooms furnished with antiques and reproductions. Full breakfast and bicycles are included. Coffeemakers and cable TV are available in the guest parlor only. Rates are $85–165. Free parking.

Casa Monica Hotel

95 Cordova Street, St. Augustine • (800) 648-1888 • fax (904) 827-0426 www.casamonica.com

This beautiful hotel, built in 1888, was closed for years then reopened as the county courthouse. In the late 1990s hotelier Richard Kessler bought the building to restore it to its original splendor, and it reopened in 1999 after extensive renovation of the marble floors, rare wood detailing, fountains, and art. Listed on the National Register of Historic Places, its five towers and Moorish-Revival–style architecture resemble a medieval European castle. No two of the 138 rooms are alike, but all have cable TV and coffeemakers. The hotel is in walking distance of all the St. Augustine sites, with a pool on the second story deck for after-sightseeing fun. Rates start at $149 and go to $599 for a tower suite.

LaFiesta Oceanside Inn

810 SR A1A Beach Boulevard, St. Augustine Beach • (904) 471-2220 • fax (904) 471-0186 • www.lafiestainn.com

This little motel isn't a historic recommendation, but it's a great place to stay if your family insists on beachside accommodations. Beware, however: Driving is permitted on the beach, so children must be carefully supervised. Independently owned, it has 36 guest rooms (ask for the ground floor if you have small children, since upper-floor oceanside rooms have balconies), some with refrigerators, coffeemakers, and microwaves. The motel's Beach House Cafe serves decent family fare for breakfast and lunch. And there's a miniature golf course right next door. Rates range from $59–139 in the off-season and $99–259 in summer.

Saragossa Inn

34 Saragossa Street (between Orange and Carrera streets), St. Augustine • (904) 808-7384 • fax (904) 808-1203 • www.thesaragossainn.com

Built in 1920, this inn is in a neighborhood a few blocks off the historic district and offers six rooms with private baths, outside entrances, and private decks. Two suites have a microwave, refrigerator, sink, and dining area for large families; three rooms have wetbars. Cable TV and coffeemakers in each room, free parking. Full breakfast in the dining room or in your room. Rates $99–199.

Secret Garden

56½ Charlotte Street (between Cuna and Treasury Streets, St. Augustine) • (904) 829-3678 • www.secretgardeninn.com

This little jewel is tucked away in the heart of the historic district. Three lovely suites, all with private entrances, kitchens, and private decks or patios, are comfortable for a family of four (the sitting room sofa also is a bed). Cable TV in the rooms. Ample breakfast includes cereal, fresh fruit, and pastries with coffee, tea, and juice. Double occupancy rates are $105–145; extra person $10. Free parking.

St. Francis

279 George Street (between St. Francis and Bridge streets), St. Augustine • (904) 824-6068 • fax (904) 810-5525 • www.stfrancisinn.com

Children 10 and older are allowed in the St. Francis, built in 1791, with its courtyards, balconies, and swimming pool; some of the 14 rooms have fireplaces, microwaves, coffeemakers, and refrigerators. Nice extras are the free bicycles and admission to the nearby Oldest House museum. Generous buffet breakfast served each morning. Children under age 10 may be allowed to stay in the cottage, which sleeps four people. Rates are $80–149 weekdays, $189–249 weekends and holidays. Free parking.

Attractions

Castillo de San Marcos National Monument

1 Castillo Drive E., St. Augustine • (904) 829-6506

Hours - Daily 8:45 a.m.–4:45 p.m.; closed Christmas

Admission - $5 for adults, $2 seniors over 61 and children ages 7–16, 6 and under free

Appeal by Age Group -

Pre-school ★★	Teens ★★★	Over 30 ★★★
Grade school ★★★	Young Adults ★★★	Seniors ★★★

Touring Time - Average 1–3 hours; minimum 1 hour

Rainy-Day Touring - Not recommended

Author's Rating - ★★; history comes to life in this oceanfront fort; fun to climb around on the cannon or try out a soldier's bunk

Restaurants - No

Alcoholic beverages - No

Handicapped access - 1st level only

Wheelchair rental - No

Baby stroller rental - No

Lockers - No

Pet kennels - No

Rain check - No

Private tours - Yes

Description and Comments The oldest masonry fort in the continental United States, constructed of native shell stone (coquina) between 1672 and 1695 by the Spanish to guard St. Augustine from pirate raids and from Great Britain during a time when this coastline was an explosive international battleground.

A double drawbridge over a 40-foot moat makes an impressive entrance for this massive coquina fort. You can tour prison cells, the chapel, guard rooms, and more with a self-guided tour map. The staff is quite helpful, and rangers give 30-minute talks several times each day. Kids like the occasional "firing" of the cannon by costumed soldiers during the living history presentation.

Colee's Sightseeing Carriage Tours

Bayfront near entrance to Fort Castillo de San Marcos • (904) 829-2818

Hours - Daily, 10 a.m.–10 p.m.; closed Christmas

Admission - $15 for adults, $7 for children ages 5–11, free for children ages 4 and under

Appeal by Age Group -

Pre-school ★★	Teens ★★	Over 30 ★★
Grade school ★★	Young Adults ★★	Seniors ★★

Touring Time - Average 1 hour; minimum 45 minutes

Rainy-Day Touring - OK since carriage is covered

Author's Rating - ★★; good way to get acclimated; especially nice at sunset; no handicapped access

Restaurants - No

Alcoholic beverages - No

Handicapped access - No

Wheelchair rental - No

Baby stroller rental - No

Lockers - No

Pet kennels - No

Rain check - Yes

Private tours - Yes

Description and Comments This family-owned business has been showing visitors around town since 1877. The quaint carriages are a pleasant, relaxing way to see the sights, especially if your driver knows a little history and likes to chat. They'll also pick you up at some hotels and restaurants for an additional charge.

Fountain of Youth National Archaeological Park

11 Magnolia Avenue at Williams Street, St. Augustine • (904) 829-3168 or (800) 356-8222

Hours - Daily 9 a.m.–5 p.m.; closed Christmas

Admission - $5.75 for adults, $4.75 for seniors ages 60 and over, $2.75 for children ages 6–12, free for children ages 6 and under

Appeal by Age Group -

Pre-school ★	Teens ★	Over 30 ★★
Grade school ★	Young Adults ★	Seniors ★★

Touring Time - Average 1–2 hours; minimum 1 hour

Rainy-Day Touring - Not recommended

Author's Rating - ★; a whole bunch of hype, though the landscaping is beautiful, and it's worth a visit just to sip the awful-tasting water from the famed spring of eternal youth

Restaurants - No

Alcoholic beverages - No

Handicapped access - Yes

Wheelchair rental - No

Baby stroller rental - No

Lockers - No

Pet kennels - No
Rain check - No
Private tours - Yes

Description and Comments This National Archaeological Park gets you out under the trees and close to the water to see the foundations and artifacts of the first St. Augustine mission.

Magnolia Avenue, the street that runs in front of the park, sets the tone for a visit. Also known as "the street of 1,000 arches," it's like a high-ceilinged tunnel formed by magnolia trees. Inside the 4½-acre park, a path leads to the water where legend has it explorer Ponce de Leon drank from the natural springs when he landed in America in 1513.

Along with the famed fountain in the springhouse is a coquina stone cross believed to date from Ponce de Leon's visit. Hold your nose and sip a sample of sulfury springwater.

There are a couple of fairly interesting historical shows. One, the Historical Discovery Globe, is a lighted globe that is viewed in a darkened auditorium and represents the Earth as seen from outer space. As you watch and listen, the first 100 years of Spanish history in the New World are depicted. The other show is in a planetarium with the skies appearing as they did when Ponce de Leon crossed the ocean on his quest.

The park also is the site of an important Indian burial ground. Great history, but a bit of a yawner for youngsters.

Ghostly Walking Tour

Meets every night at the city gate • (888) 461-1009

Hours - Nightly walks begin at 8 p.m.; 9:30 p.m. Friday and Saturday

Admission - $9 per person, free for children under age 6

Appeal by Age Group -

Pre-school ★	Teens ★★★	Over 30 ★★★
Grade school ★★★	Young Adults ★★★	Seniors ★★★

Touring Time - Average 1½ hours; minimum 1 hour

Rainy-Day Touring - Not recommended

Author's Rating - ★★★; fun, especially for teenagers; not much fun for kids under 8

Restaurants - No
Alcoholic beverages - No
Handicapped access - Yes
Wheelchair rental - No
Baby stroller rental - No
Lockers - No
Pet kennels - No
Rain check - Yes
Private tours - Yes

Description and Comments Does Henry Flagler really haunt the hallways of Flagler College? Does a lone soldier still guard a home on St. George Street? Teenagers especially love this tour through the streets by lantern light, with spooky tales of centuries past, legendary stories, and folklore.

Lightner Museum

City Hall Complex, King Street, St. Augustine • (904) 824-2874

Hours - Daily, 9 a.m.–5 p.m.; closed Christmas

Admission - $6 for adults, $4 students 12–18, free for children age 12 and under

Appeal by Age Group -

Pre-school ★	Teens ★★	Over 30 ★★
Grade school ★	Young Adults ★★	Seniors ★★

Touring Time - Average 2–3 hours; minimum 2 hours

Rainy-Day Touring - Recommended

Author's Rating - ★★; opulent displays, but kids get bored easily

Restaurants - No

Alcoholic beverages - No

Handicapped access - Yes

Wheelchair rental - Yes

Baby stroller rental - No

Lockers - No

Pet kennels - No

Rain check - No

Private tours - Yes

Description and Comments Ask the locals about what not to miss in St. Augustine and the Lightner Museum is mentioned time after time. There's obviously a deep sense of civic pride in this not-for-profit museum, and in this instance, the pride is well justified.

The museum is housed in what once was a 300-room hotel, the Alcazar, constructed in 1888 by railway magnate Henry Flagler. Closed in 1930, the hotel was bought in 1947 by Otto C. Lightner of Chicago. Lightner, who died in 1950, donated the building and his collection to the citizens of St. Augustine.

The museum covers three floors and is filled with a vast collection including Tiffany glass, extraordinary music boxes, beautiful furnishings, and other artifacts of the nineteenth century. The hotel's swimming pool, known as the world's largest in 1888, now houses a cafe and antiques shops.

The Old Jail

167 San Marco Avenue, St. Augustine • (904) 829-3800

Hours - Daily 8:30 a.m.–4:30 p.m.; closed Christmas Eve day, Christmas, and Easter

Admission - $5 for adults, $4 for children ages 6–12 (*Note:* Special tickets can be purchased at the Old Jail for admission into St. Augustine Historical Tours, the Old Jail, and the Florida Heritage Museum all located at 167 San Marco Avenue. Tickets are $25 for adults and $19 for children ages 6–12.)

Appeal by Age Group -

Pre-school ★	Teens ★★	Over 30 ★
Grade school ★★	Young Adults ★	Seniors ★

Touring Time - Average 1–2 hours; minimum 1 hour

Rainy-Day Touring - Recommended

Author's Rating - ★; kids like to check out the cells and the weapons

Restaurants - No
Alcoholic beverages - No
Handicapped access - No
Wheelchair rental - No
Baby stroller rental - No
Lockers - No
Pet kennels - No
Rain check - No
Private tours - No

Description and Comments Fun tours are given by costumed guides playing Sheriff Joe Perry and his wife, Lulu, in this attraction that epitomizes small-town jails of the Deep South in the late 1800s through about 1940. Spartan, austere, cramped, and hot pretty well sum up the centerpiece of the attraction, but there's a neat collection of manacles, knives, small arms, and other weapons and memorabilia. You get to clamber up and down the stairs and gawk at the cellblocks, bunks, steel tables, and other trappings of prisoner life.

The Oldest House

14 St. Francis Street at Charlotte Street, St. Augustine • (904) 824-2872

Hours - Daily, 9 a.m.–5 p.m.; closed Christmas. Tours depart on the hour and half-hour, with the last tour leaving at 4:30 p.m.

Admission - $5 for adults, $4.50 for seniors 55 and over, $3 for students, free for children ages 6 and under, $12 for families; AAA discount

Appeal by Age Group -

Pre-school ★	Teens ★★	Over 30 ★★
Grade school ★★	Young Adults ★★	Seniors ★★

Touring Time - Average 1–2 hours; minimum 1 hour

Rainy-Day Touring - Recommended

Author's Rating - ★; not much there to interest kids

Restaurants - No
Alcoholic beverages - No
Handicapped access - (See below)
Wheelchair rental - No
Baby stroller rental - No
Lockers - No
Pet kennels - No
Rain check - No
Private tours - No

Description and Comments The Oldest House is one of the "must" stops for history buffs. There's been a house on this site since the seventeenth century, but the first one probably was burned by the British in 1702. Today, the Gonzales-Alvarez House is there, where Tomas Gonzales lived from about 1727 to 1763. The Alvarez family bought the house at an auction in 1790. The downstairs furniture is Spanish, most of it is more than 200 years old. The oldest piece—a credenza—dates back more than 500 years. Only the first floor is wheelchair accessible, but nonambulatory guests are admitted free, and a video of the second floor is available.

Oldest Store Museum

4 Artillery Lane between St. George and Aviles Streets, St. Augustine • (904) 829-9729

Hours - Monday–Saturday, 10 a.m.–4 p.m.; Sunday, 12–4 p.m.; closed Christmas

Admission - $6 for adults, $5.50 for seniors, $2.50 for children ages 6–12, free for children age 5 and under

Appeal by Age Group -

Pre-school ★	Teens ★★	Over 30 ★★
Grade school ★★	Young Adults ★★	Seniors ★★

Touring Time - Average 1 hour; minimum 45 minutes

Rainy-Day Touring - Recommended

Author's Rating - ★; grown-ups, not kids, get a kick out of browsing

Restaurants - No
Alcoholic beverages - No
Handicapped access - Yes
Wheelchair rental - No
Baby stroller rental - No
Lockers - No
Pet kennels - No
Rain check - No
Private tours - Yes

Description and Comments This is a museum with a variety of antiques in a general store kind of setting, but hardly an authentic historical interpretation of the actual oldest stores in the city. The place contains more than 100,000 items, everything from a steam-driven tractor to 1890s-era bathing suits. Guided tours are available.

Oldest Wooden Schoolhouse

14 St. George Street between Orange and Cuna Streets, St. Augustine • (904) 824-0192

Hours - Daily, 9 a.m.–5 p.m.

Admission - $2.75 for adults, $2.25 for seniors 55 and over, $1.75 for children ages 6–12

Appeal by Age Group -

Pre-school ★	Teens ★★	Over 30 ★★
Grade school ★★	Young Adults ★★	Seniors ★★

Touring Time - Average 15 minutes; minimum 10 minutes

Rainy-Day Touring - Recommended

Author's Rating - ★; don't spend the money unless you're an education buff, or unless you want your kids to know how good they've got it now

Restaurants - No

Alcoholic beverages - No

Handicapped access - Yes

Wheelchair rental - No

Baby stroller rental - No

Lockers - No

Pet kennels - No

Rain check - No

Private tours - Yes

Description and Comments Unless you're a real student of this sort of thing, so to speak, a stroll through the Oldest Wooden Schoolhouse will take less than 15 minutes. This schoolhouse, constructed of red cedar and cypress joined by wooden pegs and handmade nails, was built before the American Revolution. A backyard kitchen contains cooking utensils used during colonial times. It is the oldest wooden structure in St. Augustine and is entirely original.

This is a fun history lesson that doesn't take too much time. And it makes kids appreciate modern-day classroom wonders, like computers and air conditioning. The classroom is re-created today using animatronics of pupils and a teacher, with a dunce and "dungeon" for unruly children. The last class attended school here in 1864.

Potter's Wax Museum

17 King Street between Aviles and St. George Streets, St. Augustine • (904) 829-9056

Hours - Summer, 9 a.m.–9 p.m.; winter, 9 a.m.–5 p.m.; closed Christmas

Admission - $6.95 for adults, $5.95 for seniors 55 and older, $3.75 for children ages 6–12

Appeal by Age Group -

Pre-school ★	Teens ★★	Over 30 ★
Grade school ★★	Young Adults ★★	Seniors ★

Touring Time - Average 1–2 hours; minimum 1 hour
Rainy-Day Touring - Recommended
Author's Rating - ★; peek in the windows, and only go in if you must see more

Restaurants - No
Alcoholic beverages - No
Handicapped access - Yes
Wheelchair rental - No
Baby stroller rental - No
Lockers - No
Pet kennels - No
Rain check - No
Private tours - Yes

Description and Comments Not the most sophisticated wax dummies you'll find nowadays, but kids like this sort of thing (though you can get a fairly good idea of the place just by looking in the front windows where they show much of the process to passers-by). There is a guided tour, and kids seem to especially like the torture section that focuses on the Spanish Inquisition. Also see Ulysses S. Grant, Thomas Jefferson, Louis Pasteur, and Leonardo da Vinci—more than 170 in all, including religious leaders, poets, composers, artists, authors, explorers, philosophers, kings, and presidents.

Ripley's Believe It Or Not! Museum

19 San Marco Avenue at Castillo Drive, St. Augustine • (904) 824-1606

Hours - Daily, 9 a.m.–8 p.m.
Admission - $9.95 for adults, $5.95 for children ages 5–12, $7.95 for seniors age 55 and over (discounts for AAA, military, residents)
Appeal by Age Group -

Pre-school ★	Teens ★★★	Over 30 ★★
Grade school ★★★	Young Adults ★★★	Seniors ★★

Touring Time - Average 2–3 hours; minimum 1 hour
Rainy-Day Touring - Recommended
Author's Rating - ★★★; full of fun, fascinating stuff; teenagers can spend hours here

Restaurants - No
Alcoholic beverages - No
Handicapped access - No
Wheelchair rental - Yes
Baby stroller rental - No
Lockers - No
Pet kennels - No
Rain check - No
Private tours - No

Description and Comments People are fascinated by weird things, and the *Ripley's Believe It or Not!* Museum is the height of weirdness. We can bet you won't find such a collection of oddities anywhere else in the world (except at another branch of this museum).

Where else can you find paintings on ordinary potato chips, a genuine shrunken head from Ecuador, or the disciples at the Last Supper sculpted of pecans? There are plenty of exhibits like those representing genuine oddities produced by man or natural mishap, all of them fascinating.

The museum is in a building that is interesting in its own right. It's the old Castle Warden, built in 1888 by an associate of Henry Flagler, the railroad company official who was so influential in the development here and elsewhere in Florida.

Spanish Quarter Museum

Entrance at the Triay House on St. George Street • (904) 825-6830

Hours - Daily, 9 a.m.–5:30 p.m.

Admission - $6.50 for adults, $5.50 for seniors age 62 and older, $4 for children ages 6–18, free for age 5 and under

Appeal by Age Group -

Pre-school ★★	Teens ★★★	Over 30 ★★★
Grade school ★★★	Young Adults ★★★	Seniors ★★★

Touring Time - Average 2–3 hours; minimum 2 hours

Rainy-Day Touring - Not recommended

Author's Rating - ★★★; children of all ages can find something interesting in this little area that really brings history to life

Restaurants - No

Alcoholic beverages - No

Handicapped access - Yes

Wheelchair rental - No

Baby stroller rental - No

Lockers - No

Pet kennels - No

Rain check - No

Private tours - Yes

Description and Comments This restored part of old St. Augustine, operated by the state of Florida, shows how life was lived in the 1740s. If you're interested in the old city you won't want to miss this part of St. Augustine. It's a favorite stop for school-age children and even holds the attention of teenagers because of the demonstrations by lace- and net-makers, spinners, blacksmiths, weavers, and woodworkers, all showing how the work was done in the eighteenth century. Today there are six restored and reconstructed houses and a blacksmith shop.

St. Augustine Alligator Farm and Zoological Park

SR A1A S., St. Augustine • (904) 824-3337

Hours - Daily, 9 a.m.–5 p.m.

Admission - $14.25 for adults, $8.50 for children ages 3–10 (AAA, military, and senior discounts offered)

Appeal by Age Group -

Pre-school ★★★	Teens ★★★	Over 30 ★★★
Grade school ★★★	Young Adults ★★★	Seniors ★★★

Touring Time - Average 2–4 hours; minimum 2 hours

Rainy-Day Touring - Not recommended

Author's Rating - ★★★; the way attractions used to be—low key, clean, fun, and uncrowded

Restaurants - Yes

Alcoholic beverages - Yes

Handicapped access - Yes

Wheelchair rental - Yes

Baby stroller rental - No

Lockers - No

Pet kennels - No

Rain check - Yes

Private tours - No

Description and Comments Florida has no shortage of alligator shows and exhibits, but we think the St. Augustine Alligator Farm is the best. It claims to be the oldest and the largest, too, and we have no reason to dispute either superlative.

Founded in 1893, this attraction really is a piece of old Florida that has aged gracefully. There is cool shade everywhere, even in the small parking lot, and beautiful boardwalks through the wetlands. The park's rookery is especially neat in the spring, when the wading birds hatch and you can see the newborns in their nests. The presence of the alligators keeps out such predators as raccoons and snakes, so birds find the swampy lagoon area to be an ideal nesting place. Be sure to check out the three rare albino alligators that recently were added to the collection of crocodilians. Only 30 of these creatures are estimated living in the world

Children also can feed an ostrich or pet a pot-bellied pig in the small petting zoo. The 20-minute-long alligator and reptile shows throughout the day are educational and quite entertaining in an old-fashioned sort of way.

St. Augustine Historical Tours

167 San Marco Avenue at Williams Street, St. Augustine • (904) 829-3800

Hours - 8:30 a.m.–4:30 p.m. daily

Admission - $15 per person, free for children age 5 and under *(Note:* Special tickets can be purchased at the Old Jail for admission into St. Augustine Historical Tours, the Old Jail, and the Florida Heritage Museum all located at 167 San Marco Avenue. Tickets are $25 for adults and $19 for children ages 6–12.)

Appeal by Age Group -

Pre-school ★★	Teens ★★★	Over 30 ★★★
Grade school ★★	Young Adults ★★★	Seniors ★★★

Touring Time - Average 2–4 hours; minimum 2 hours

Rainy-Day Touring - OK since cars are covered

Author's Rating - ★★★; relaxing way to see the city; no handicapped access

Restaurants - No

Alcoholic beverages - No

Handicapped access - No

Wheelchair rental - No

Baby stroller rental - No

Lockers - No

Pet kennels - No

Rain check - No

Private tours - No

Description and Comments The trolleys stop at several points throughout the city, and riders can disembark, visit an attraction, then catch the next trolley about 20 minutes later. The narrated tour is an interesting overview of the city.

St. Augustine Lighthouse and Museum

81 Lighthouse Avenue, St. Augustine • (904) 829-0745

Hours - Daily, 9 a.m.–6 p.m.

Admission - $6.50 for adults, $5.50 for seniors over 55, $4 for children ages 7–11, free for children under age 7

Appeal by Age Group - Children under 7 years must be 48" to climb tower

Pre-school ★★	Teens ★★	Over 30 ★★
Grade school ★★	Young Adults ★★	Seniors ★★

Touring Time - Average 1–2 hours; minimum 1 hour

Rainy-Day Touring - Recommended

Author's Rating - ★★; it's fun to climb the winding stairs, and the view is definitely worth the climb. Kids under 7 who meet the 48" height requirement still might not make it up to the top, and the steep staircase can be a little forbidding on the way down

Restaurants - No

Alcoholic beverages - No

Handicapped access - 1st floor only

Wheelchair rental - No

Baby stroller rental - No

Lockers - No

Pet kennels - No

Rain check - No

Private tours - No

Description and Comments This is the site of Florida's first lighthouse, and today's lighthouse is an active aid to navigation, with a beam that can be seen for 19 nautical miles. The tower is 165 feet tall with 219 steps that can be climbed for a panoramic view of St. Augustine and the beaches.

The Spanish erected a wooden watchtower here in 1565, and in 1824 the tower officially became Florida's first lighthouse. By 1870 erosion threatened the tower, and the current light tower replaced the original in 1875. A lightkeeper's house was added, and lightkeepers and their families lived and worked on the site until 1955.

St. Augustine Scenic Cruises

Depart from Municipal Marina, just south of the Bridge of Lions, St. Augustine • (800) 542-8316

Hours - Schedules change, so call for hours, but generally, daily departures are at 11 a.m., 1 p.m., 2:45 p.m., and 4:30 p.m. except Christmas, with additional tours Labor Day–October 15 and April 1–May 14 at 6:15 p.m. and May 15–Labor Day at 6:45 and 8:30 p.m.

Admission - $10.50 for adults, $7.50 for ages 13–18, $5 for children ages 4–12, free for ages 3 and under, $9 for seniors age 60 and older

Appeal by Age Group -

Pre-school ★★	Teens ★★	Over 30 ★★
Grade school ★★	Young Adults ★★	Seniors ★★★

Touring Time - Average 1½ hours; minimum 1½ hours

Rainy-Day Touring - Not recommended

Author's Rating - ★★; kids love to get out on the water, and these 75-minute cruises are just right

Restaurants - No

Alcoholic beverages - Yes

Handicapped access - Yes

Wheelchair rental - No

Baby stroller rental - No

Lockers - No

Pet kennels - No

Rain check - Yes

Private tours - Yes

Description and Comments Owned by the Usina family since the turn of the century, this is a great way to get out on the beautiful bay without piloting your own craft. Kids can watch for frolicking dolphins and shorebirds. Rest rooms on board.

St. Augustine Sightseeing Trains

170 San Marco Avenue, St. Augustine • (904) 829-6545

Hours - Daily, 8:30 a.m.–5 p.m., with departures every 15–20 minutes

Admission - $12 for adults, $5 for children age 6–12, free for ages 6 and under

Appeal by Age Group -

Pre-school ★★	Teens ★★	Over 30 ★★★
Grade school ★★	Young Adults ★★	Seniors ★★

Touring Time - Average 2–4 hours; minimum 2 hours

Rainy-Day Touring - Yes (trains are covered to protect from rain)

Author's Rating - ★★★; both the train and the trolley (see St. Augustine Historical Tours) give the same tour, and the cost is the same, so take whichever arrives first; small step to board but wheelchairs accommodated

Restaurants - No

Alcoholic beverages - No

Handicapped access - Yes

Wheelchair rental - No

Baby stroller rental - No

Lockers - No

Pet kennels - No

Rain check - No

Private tours - No

Description and Comments A great way to relax and avoid the traffic on the narrow streets of St. Augustine—plus get a quick and fairly interesting history lesson that covers 500 years. Tickets include stop-off privileges at attractions.

SEA LOVE MARINA

If your family wants to try deep-sea fishing, contact Sea Love Marina, 250 Vilano Road, St. Augustine (800) 940-FISH. Seasickness can be a problem with all ages, so choose a day with relatively calm seas, and book a half-day trip to start (though full-day and overnight trips are available). Fishing sounds much more fun than it generally is after about 30 minutes at sea. And a boatload of anglers isn't turning around just because your 6-year-old wants to go home. But there's a good chance of landing snapper, grouper, porgies, and even a shark. Fishing tackle and bait are provided, but you must bring your own food and beverages (they'll put it on ice for you).

Family-Friendly Restaurants

A1A Ale Works

1 King Street, St. Augustine • (904) 829-2977

Meals served - Lunch and dinner

Cuisine - New World (described as a "fusion of culinary influences that includes the regional dishes of Florida, Cuba, the Caribbean, and Latin America") and microbrewery

Entree range - $6.95–19.95

Kids menu - Yes

Reservations - Not accepted

Payment - All major credit cards accepted

No red meat on the menu—try the trio of bonito, sweet potato, and yucca chips, or the snapper burger with mango ketchup. Great microbrewed beers and homemade root beer for the kids. Noisy enough for families to feel right at home. Outdoor seating on a balcony overlooking the bay.

Athena Restaurant

14 Cathedral Place, St. Augustine • (904) 823-9076

Meals served - Breakfast, lunch, and dinner

Cuisine - Greek, American

Entree range - $3–15.95

Kids menu - Yes

Reservations - Not necessary

Payment - Visa, MC

Breakfast is served anytime at this wonderful little diner right in the middle of historic St. Augustine. With a 12-page menu, there's something for everyone. Traditional Greek souvlaki, moussaka, and lamb kebabs, but also gourmet burgers.

Barnacle Bill's

14 Castillo Drive, St. Augustine • (904) 824-3663

Meals served - Lunch and dinner

Cuisine - Seafood, chicken, and steaks

Entree range - $6–16

Kids menu - Yes

Reservations - Not accepted

Payment - Visa, MC, AmEx, D

Barnacle Bills serves traditional seafood, and locals recommend the fried shrimp.

Columbia Restaurant

98 St. George Street, St. Augustine • (904) 824-3341

Meals served - Lunch and dinner

Cuisine - Spanish, Cuban, continental

Entree range - Lunch, $5–15; dinner, $11–20

Kids menu - Yes

Reservations - Recommended for evenings only

Payment - All major credit cards accepted

This boisterous and beautiful Spanish restaurant is an integral part of the St. Augustine experience. Try arroz con pollo (yellow rice and chicken), black bean soup, or their authentic paella. Sunday brunch is especially crowded.

Creekside Dinery

160 Nix Boat Yard Road (off US 1) • (904) 829-6113

Meals served - Dinner

Cuisine - Old-fashioned Florida

Entree range - $8–14

Kids menu - Yes

Reservations - Not accepted

Payment - Visa, MC, AmEx, D

You may have a wait for a table, but even that is pleasant on the vine-covered front porch. Fresh fish baked on an oak plank and pan-broiled shrimp are favorites. Also barbecue and Aunt Ada's Florida-style fried chicken.

Fiddler's Green

2750 Anahma Boulevard, Vilano Beach • (904) 824-8897

Meals served - Dinner

Cuisine - Traditional seafood

Entree range - $8.99–17.99

Kids menu - Yes, $4–6

Reservations - Recommended (not accepted on Saturday)

Payment - All major credit cards accepted

This popular eatery is right on the ocean and serves fresh fish and shellfish, but you'll find steaks and chicken, too. The specialty is crispy fried coconut shrimp.

Gypsy Cab Co.

828 Anastasia Boulevard, St. Augustine • (904) 824-8244 • www.gypsycab.com

Meals served - Lunch and dinner

Cuisine - American

Entree range - $6.25–22.99

Kids menu - Yes

Reservations - Recommended, but accepted only for parties of 6 or more on the weekends

Payment - All major credit cards accepted

Portions are huge, so share with the kids. There's something for everyone on the eclectic menu, featuring fish, chicken, even a tofu-veggie saute. The weekend wait can be long, so go for lunch, not dinner, if you have antsy youngsters.

Harry's

46 Avenida Menendez, St. Augustine • (904) 824-7765

Meals served - Lunch and dinner

Cuisine - New Orleans–inspired seafood, pastas, steak, and chicken

Entree range - $7.45–22.95

Kids menu - Yes

Reservations - Not accepted

Payment - All major credit cards accepted

A favorite of the locals, with dining al fresco in the lovely garden. Jambalaya, etouffee, and red beans and rice are on the menu.

Pizza Garden

21 Hypolita Street, St. Augustine • (904) 825-4877

Meals served - Lunch and dinner

Cuisine - Pizza, salads, and sandwiches

Entree range - $1.95–16.95

Kids menu - No, but pizza slices are popular with the kids

Reservations - Not accepted

Payment - All major credit cards accepted

Great pizza, just $1.95 a slice—a whole vegetarian pie is $14.95. Calzones are tasty, and the salads are ample. Located in the heart of old St. Augustine, with outdoor tables in a fenced courtyard.

Salt Water Cowboys

299 Dondanville Road, St. Augustine Beach • (904) 471-2332

Meals served - Dinner

Cuisine - Seafood

Entree range - $6.99–15.99

Kids menu - No, but kids like the fried shrimp and chicken

Reservations - Not accepted

Payment - All major credit cards accepted

Lines get long in the summer at this rustic, tin-roofed eatery built out over a saltwater marsh. But kids love to look at the stuffed animals, like raccoons and possums, that decorate the place. The house specialty is soft-shell crab. Plenty of seafood, including a delicious redfish chowder that the locals recommend.

Sunset Grille

421 Beach Boulevard, St. Augustine Beach • (904) 471-5555

Meals served - Lunch and dinner

Cuisine - American

Entree range - $4.50–17.95

Kids menu - Yes

Reservations - Not accepted

Payment - All major credit cards accepted

Seafood, steaks, and decent omelets are served at this little restaurant across the street from the beach, but locals go for the cheeseburgers. You can even order from the walk-up window and dine at a picnic table or in the open-air lounge.

Side Trips

Fort Matanzas Built by the Spanish between 1740 and 1742 to protect St. Augustine, Fort Matanzas is now part of a 298-acre park. A free ferry takes you to the fort on Rattlesnake Island in the Matanzas River. (Matanzas means "slaughter" in Spanish, so named for a battle that took place in 1565 near here.) Park rangers give free tours, and you can explore the living quarters and observation deck, hiking trails, and beach. About 11 miles south of St. Augustine on SR A1A; (904) 471-0116.

Marineland Opened in 1938, this small, old-fashioned marine park has struggled in recent years to keep its doors open. One popular offering is a dolphin encounter for $120 that allows participants to don a wetsuit and get in the water with the mammals. You must be at least 50 inches tall.

The dolphins, sea lions, and penguins still perform daily, and a morning or afternoon is plenty of time to see it all. Admission is $14 adults, $9 ages 3–11, free for ages 2 and under. 9600 Ocean Boulevard, Marineland (18 miles south of St. Augustine); (904) 460-1275; www.marineland.net.

Gainesville and Environs

Heading southwest from Jacksonville, you'll discover off-the-beaten path adventures along the quiet rural routes leading to Gainesville, home of the University of Florida. Unless you're visiting the college campus or have a special interest in history or architecture, you might bypass this quaint little town. The town's Northeast Historic District, listed on the National Register of Historic Places, is a 63-block area of 290 buildings that reflect Florida architectural styles from 1880 through the 1920s, worth a stroll if your family enjoys historic architecture. Step back in time and see what Florida was like in the 1800s with a visit to nearby Micanopy, 13 miles south of Gainesville, or High Springs, an old railroad town to the north. Though there are no beaches or theme parks, this part of the Sunshine State is for families who love to be outdoors. There are excellent camping, canoeing, fishing, hiking, and bicycling opportunities, including sections of the Florida Trail, which links one end of Florida to the other.

Family Resorts

Doubletree

1714 SW 34th St., Gainesville • (352) 371-3600 • fax (352)384-3455

Across the street from the University of Florida campus, this 248-room hotel is one of the nicest in the area, and though it's mostly a convention hotel, families visiting UF students will enjoy the proximity. Rooms are spacious and there's an Olympic-size pool and fitness center. The 2-Bits Lounge is often full of families cheering on sports team on the large-screen TV, or playing a game of billiards. Rates start at $99, with kids under 18 staying for free.

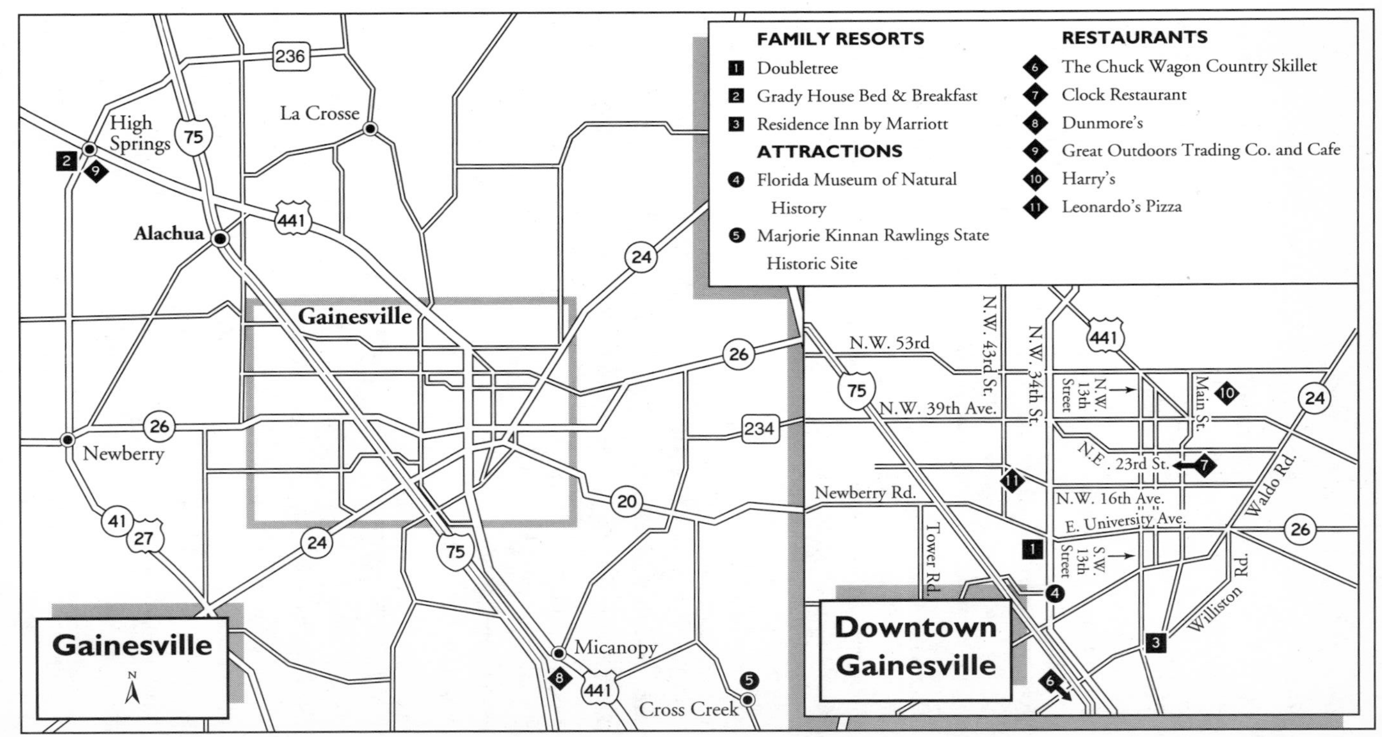

FAMILY RESORTS
1 Doubletree
2 Grady House Bed & Breakfast
3 Residence Inn by Marriott
ATTRACTIONS
4 Florida Museum of Natural History
5 Marjorie Kinnan Rawlings State Historic Site
RESTAURANTS
6 The Chuck Wagon Country Skillet
7 Clock Restaurant
8 Dunmore's
9 Great Outdoors Trading Co. and Cafe
10 Harry's
11 Leonardo's Pizza
Gainesville
High Springs
La Crosse
Alachua
Newberry
Micanopy
Cross Creek
Downtown Gainesville
N.W. 53rd
N.W. 43rd St.
N.W. 34th St.
N.W. 39th Ave.
N.W. 13th Street
S.W. 13th Street
Main St.
N.E. 23rd St.
N.W. 16th Ave.
E. University Ave.
Newberry Rd.
Tower Rd.
Waldo Rd.
Williston Rd.

Grady House Bed & Breakfast

420 NW 1St Ave., High Springs • (386) 454-2206 • www.gradyhouse.com

The little town of High Springs is a perfect locale for a stay in this part of Florida, just minutes from Gainesville, Ichetucknee Springs, Ginnie Springs, O'Leno State Park and other destinations. The lovingly restored Grady House, built in the 1890s, welcomes kids 8 and older. For extra space, ask for the Green Room with its adjoining parlor. Rates start at $85 and include a delicious breakfast.

Residence Inn by Marriott

4001 SW 13th Street, Gainesville • I-75 exit 74, 2 miles northeast on SR 331, north on US 441 • (352) 371-2101 • fax (352) 371-2101

There's plenty of room to spread out, with 80 roomy suites each with a living room with a sofabed, bedroom, and fully equipped kitchen. For entertainment you and your kids can enjoy volleyball, basketball, and a swimming pool. Rates start at $104 year-round. Free buffet-style breakfast.

Attractions

Florida Museum of Natural History Education and Exhibition Center

SW 34th Street and Hull Road (Powell Hall), Gainesville • (352) 846-2000

Hours - Monday–Saturday, 10 a.m.–5 p.m.; Sunday, 1–5 p.m.; closed Thanksgiving and Christmas

Admission - Free

Appeal by Age Group -

Pre-school ★	Teens ★★★	Over 30 ★★★
Grade school ★★★	Young Adults ★★★	Seniors ★★★

Touring Time - Average 2 hours; minimum 1 hour

Rainy-Day Touring - Recommended

Author's Rating - ★★★; great fun for everyone in the family

Restaurants - No

Alcoholic beverages - No

Handicapped access - No

Wheelchair rental - No

Baby stroller rental - No

Lockers - No

Pet kennels - No

Rain check - No

Private tours - No

Description and Comments Rated among the top 10 natural history museums in the United States, the Florida Museum of Natural History is built in the style of a Mayan temple, with much of it underground. Exhibit subjects vary from paleontology and animal life to cultural diversity and computers. You can venture into a man-made cave populated by rattlesnakes, opossum, bats, barn owls, wood rats, raccoons, and other Florida wildlife. Also, see the skeleton of a sloth that roamed Florida nine million years ago.

Marjorie Kinnan Rawlings State Historic Site

On CR 325, in Cross Creek, 21 miles southeast of Gainesville • (352) 466-3672

Hours - Guided tours Thursday–Sunday, 10 a.m., 11 a.m., and every hour from 1 to 4 p.m. on a first-come, first-served basis; tours are not available in August and September; closed Thanksgiving, Christmas, and New Year's

Admission - $4 for adults, $3 for children ages 6–12, free for children ages 5 and under

Appeal by Age Group -

Pre-school ★	Teens ★★★	Over 30 ★★★
Grade school ★★	Young Adults ★★★	Seniors ★★★

Touring Time - Average 2 hours; minimum 1 hour

Rainy-Day Touring - Not recommended

Author's Rating - ★★★; we love this old farmhouse nestled in the shade of an orange grove and the nostalgic ambience that lingers—Rawlings's car is still parked in the driveway, for instance

Restaurants - No

Alcoholic beverages - No

Handicapped access - No

Wheelchair rental - No

Baby stroller rental - No

Lockers - No

Pet kennels - No

Rain check - No

Private tours - Yes

Description and Comments This is truly a step back in time. Rawlings' turn-of-the-century home is on a country road, still far from civilization, and the gardens and house look much the same today as they did in the 1920s when she recorded her impressions in the award-winning *Cross Creek*—even her table, chair, and typewriter are still there on the screened porch. Only 10 people per tour; first-come, first-served. But there's a quarter-mile hammock trail if you have to wait, as well as a playground and picnic tables.

Family-Friendly Restaurants

The Chuck Wagon Country Skillet

3483 SW Williston Road, Gainesville • (352) 336-5677

Meals served - Breakfast, lunch, and dinner Sunday–Thursday, 6 a.m.–9 p.m.; Friday–Saturday, 6 a.m.–10 p.m.

Cuisine - Southern

Entree range - Lunch, $5.50–6.50; dinner, $5.50–11; breakfast, $4–7

Kids menu - Yes

Reservations - Not accepted

Payment - Visa, MC, AmEx

This clean, cozy eatery has some great all-you-can-eat specials for around $6. Real Florida foods, like fried green tomatoes, catfish, pot roast, and cornbread fill the menu. Kids love the fried cinnamon apples at breakfast.

Clock Restaurant

2010 N. Main Street, Gainesville • (352) 375-1411

Meals served - Breakfast, lunch, and dinner (open 24 hours)

Cuisine - American

Entree range - $4–10

Kids menu - Yes

Reservations - Not necessary

Payment - All major credit cards accepted

Good ol' diner food, and anything on the menu can be ordered 24 hours a day.

Dunmore's Burgers

U.S. Hwy. 441, Micanopy • (352) 466-0057

Meals served - Lunch, dinner

Cuisine - American

Entree range - $3–6

Kids menu - No

Reservations - No, walk-up window only

Payment - Cash only

This is one of those "best-kept" secrets, run by Mary and Chester Dunmore (he used to be the mayor). In tiny Micanopy, this is the place for a true Southern delight: fried chicken and hush puppies. Meals are cooked to order, so plan to wait. There are burgers on the hand-written menu, but go for the chicken with sweet tea; find a shady tree and have a picnic.

Great Outdoors Trading Co. and Cafe

65 N. Main Street, High Springs • (386) 454-2900

Meals served - Breakfast, lunch, and dinner

Cuisine - Gourmet

Entree range - $4.95–14.95

Kids menu - No, but the grilled cheese sandwich ($4.75) and the pasta dishes are popular with children. Half orders are available for some dishes.

Reservations - Priority seating available

Payment - All major credit cards accepted

This eatery serves everything from vegetarian dishes to steaks, with excellent homemade desserts. The gift shop is stocked with nifty souvenirs.

Harry's

110 Southeast First St., Gainesville • (352) 372-1555

Meals served - Lunch and dinner

Cuisine - American

Entree range - $12–15

Kids menu - Everything from fish to soup to burgers

Reservations - No

Payment - All major credit cards accepted

In downtown Gainesville, you can sit on the patio or inside at this New Orleans-themed eatery. Try a Cajun specialty like jambalaya.

Leonardo's Pizza

4131 NW 16th Boulevard, Gainesville • (352) 376-2001

Meals served - Lunch and dinner

Cuisine - Italian

Entree range - $6–22.50

Kids menu - No, but special-priced pizza slices are available to children until 5 p.m. And the whole family can share a pizza.

Reservations - Not accepted

Payment - All major credit cards accepted

The house specialty is the Big Leo, a 14" deep-dish, Chicago-style pizza that weighs "at least 5 pounds."

Part Three

Central East Florida

Sand, surf, space shuttles, the Speedway—and don't forget the seafood. Central East Florida, stretching down the coast, with the tiny resort town of Ormond Beach at the north and burgeoning Ft. Pierce at the south, has plenty to satisfy a family.

But when most vacationers think of Central East Florida, they think of Daytona Beach, one of the most popular destinations in America. More than 8 million worldwide visitors come to the area each year, mainly because of location. The beaches are, of course, the closest to Walt Disney World and other Central Florida attractions, but Central East Florida has some star attractions of its own, including wide, sweeping beaches and the Daytona International Speedway, known as the world center of car racing.

Early automotive pioneers once raced horseless carriages on the hard-packed sands of the Daytona-area beaches, and today vacationers still drive along most of the 23-mile-long shore from Ormond Beach south to Ponce Inlet.

The beach and the Speedway may lure first-time visitors to the area, but hidden treasures keep them coming back, like Blue Spring State Park, with a natural spring that's a winter home for manatees; Spruce Creek Preserve, with natural sightseeing trips on pontoon boats; and Ponce de Leon Lighthouse, still a beacon in the night.

Drive a little farther south from Daytona and you'll be on the Space Coast, where the biggest draw is the Kennedy Space Center Visitor Complex. You can look at real missiles, see the actual launch pads for the space shuttle, and watch as the International Space Station is being completed. Real space hardware, combined with kid-friendly, hands-on exhibits, make this a fun and painless lesson in science and U.S. history. The Kennedy Space Center Visitor Complex is located adjacent to Merritt Island National Wildlife Refuge.

The refuge is a very different experience, where giant sea turtles lay their eggs in the sand in the late winter and early spring, and gators bask in the sun (sometimes in the middle of the road). We recommend a stop here.

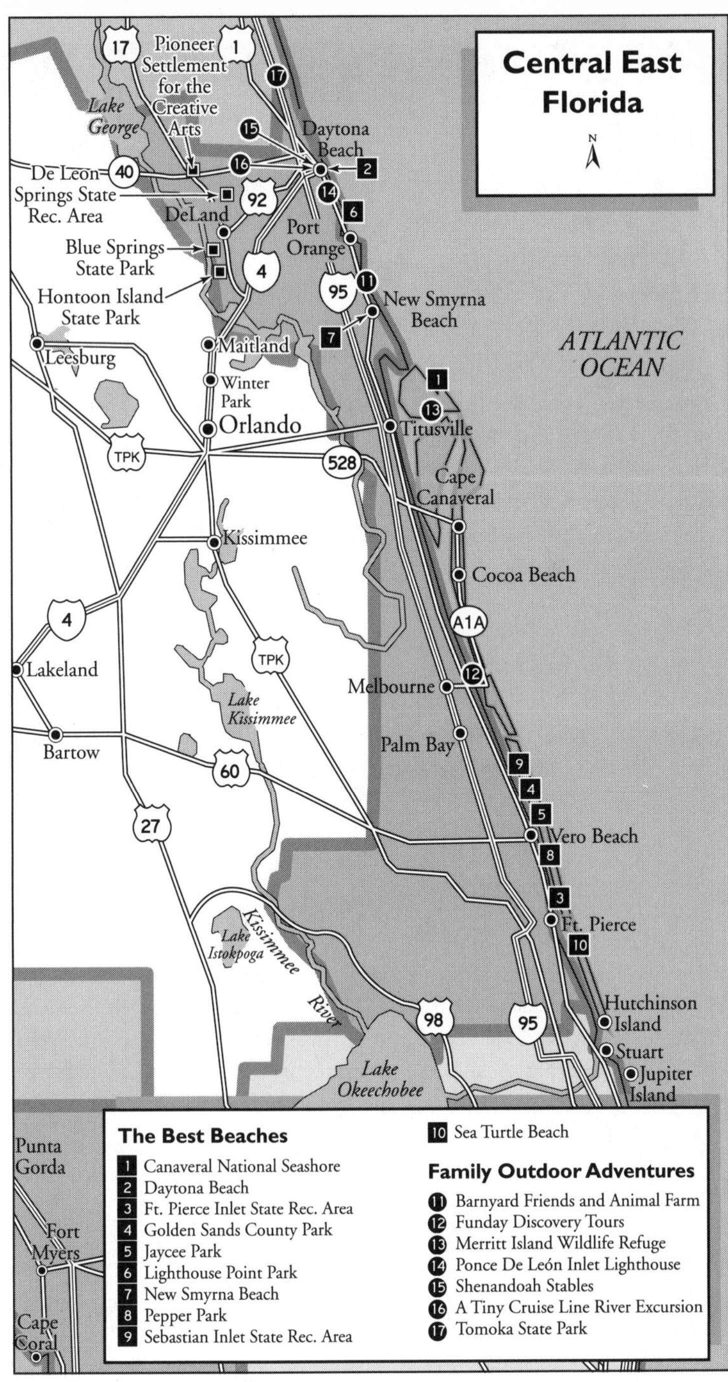
Central East Florida
N
ATLANTIC OCEAN
Pioneer Settlement for the Creative Arts
Lake George
Daytona Beach
De Leon Springs State Rec. Area
DeLand
Port Orange
Blue Springs State Park
Hontoon Island State Park
New Smyrna Beach
Leesburg
Maitland
Winter Park
Orlando
Titusville
Cape Canaveral
Kissimmee
Cocoa Beach
Lakeland
Melbourne
Lake Kissimmee
Palm Bay
Bartow
Vero Beach
Ft. Pierce
Lake Istokpoga
Kissimmee River
Hutchinson Island
Stuart
Jupiter Island
Lake Okeechobee
Punta Gorda
Fort Myers
Cape Coral
The Best Beaches
1 Canaveral National Seashore
2 Daytona Beach
3 Ft. Pierce Inlet State Rec. Area
4 Golden Sands County Park
5 Jaycee Park
6 Lighthouse Point Park
7 New Smyrna Beach
8 Pepper Park
9 Sebastian Inlet State Rec. Area
10 Sea Turtle Beach
Family Outdoor Adventures
11 Barnyard Friends and Animal Farm
12 Funday Discovery Tours
13 Merritt Island Wildlife Refuge
14 Ponce De León Inlet Lighthouse
15 Shenandoah Stables
16 A Tiny Cruise Line River Excursion
17 Tomoka State Park

A CALENDAR OF FESTIVALS AND EVENTS

January

Blue Spring Manatee Festival Blue Spring State Park and Volusia County Fairgrounds host the event, which features endangered-species exhibits. The site often changes, call the park at (386) 775-3663 for more information.

February

Speedweeks Daytona. Includes the Rolex 24 and the Daytona 500. Daytona International Speedway; (386) 254-2700.

Grant Seafood Festival south of Melbourne. This is where thousands of seafood lovers come together for a weekend of indulgence. (321) 723-8687; www.grantseafoodfestival.com.

Jambalaya Jam Wickham Park Pavilion, Melbourne. Cajun food and live entertainment. (321) 633-4028.

March

Valiant Air Command Air Show Tico Airport, Titusville. (321) 268-1941.

April

Indian River Festival Sandpoint Park, Titusville. With artists, boat races, children's activities, and midway rides. (321) 267-3036.

Hands down, the prettiest beach in Central East Florida is Canaveral National Seashore, where there are no miniature golf courses, no bikes or boogie boards for rent—nothing but sand and sea.

Farther south is the Treasure Coast, named for the treasures in the Spanish galleons that sank offshore. This area is less congested than the Daytona and Space Coast areas; the main cities are Sebastian and Vero Beach. Sebastian has great saltwater fishing, but the entire Indian River area is known for its citrus trees and beautiful beaches—more than 40 miles edging cobalt-blue ocean waters.

Getting There

By Plane Daytona Beach International Airport, (386) 248-8069; Arthur Dunn Air Park, (321) 267-8780; Melbourne International Airport, (407) 723-6227; Merritt Island Airport, (407) 453-2222; Space Coast Regional Airport, (321) 267-8780; Vero Beach Municipal Airport, (561) 770-2708.

By Train Amtrak goes to Deland; (800) USA-RAIL; www.amtrak.com.

May

Seafest Port Canaveral. Although there are rides and entertainment to keep the kids happy, the big draw is the fresh seafood: fish, shrimp, scallops, crabs, crawfish, lobster, and other local specialties. Don't forget the trimmings; there's plenty of corn-on-the-cob, hush puppies, and coleslaw to go around. Nonseafood items include barbecue, gyros, and fajitas. The event takes place on Port Canaveral at the lot adjacent to Terminal 5, with easy access from I-95. Adults: $3 in advance, $5 at the gate. Seniors: $2 in advance, $3 at the gate. Children ages 10 and under get in free. (407) 459-2200.

July

Pepsi 400 Daytona International Speedway. Held annually the first Saturday of July. (386) 254-2700.

August

Fais Do-Do Cajun Festival and Craft Show Cocoa. Arts, crafts, Cajun food, and music at Burton Smith Park. (321) 632-7445.

September

Pro-Am Surf Festival Lori Wilson Park, Cocoa Beach. Annual surfing contest benefitting the National Kidney Association. (321) 868-1123.

By Car Major roads include I-95 (north-south) and I-4 (east-west). Other major roads include SR 40, which connects to I-75, US 1, US 92, and A1A that runs along the coastline.

How to Get Information before You Go

Daytona Beach Area Convention and Visitors Bureau, 126 E. Orange Avenue, Daytona Beach 32114; (904) 255-0415 (Florida), (800) 854-1234 (U.S. & Canada); www.daytonabeach.com.

Cocoa Beach Area Chamber of Commerce–Convention and Visitors Bureau, 400 Fortenberry Road, Merritt Island 32952; (321) 459-2200; www.cocoabeachchamber.com.

New Smyrna Beach Resort Area, serving New Smyrna Beach, Edgewater, and Oak Hill, 115 Canal Street, New Smyrna Beach 32168; (800) 541-9621; www.newsmyrnabeachonline.com.

Florida's Space Coast Office of Tourism, 8810 Astronaut Boulevard, No. 102, Cape Canaveral 32920; (800) USA-1969 (U.S. & Canada); www.space-coast.com.

Okeechobee County Tourist Development Council, 55 S. Parrot Avenue, Okeechobee 34974; (800) 871-4403 (U.S. & Canada); www.tourism.okeechobee.com.

Tourist Council: Vero Beach–Indian River County Chamber of Commerce, 1216 21st Street, P.O. Box 2947, Vero Beach 32960; (561) 567-3491; 800-338-2678 ext. 802; www.vero-beach.Fl.us/chamber/main/html.

St. Lucie County Tourist Bureau, 2300 Virginia Avenue, Ft. Pierce 34982; (800) 344-TGIF (U.S. & Canada); www.visitstluciefla.com.

TURTLE MOUND

A 40-foot-high heap of oyster shells... remnants of a hearty seafood dinner? Actually, historians believe Timucuan Indians created the mound between A.D. 600 and 1200 but are unsure why it was created. Some speculate it was used as a barrier during poor weather, others suggest it served as a lookout point. It is visible 7 miles out to sea and historically was used as a navigational device by early sailors.

You'll find the mound at the northern corner of Canaveral National Seashore on US A1A, once there take the quarter-mile wooden pathway to the top of the mound for a view of the ocean and Mosquito Lagoon. The lagoon is an estuary, a "cradle to the ocean" where saltwater meets and mixes with freshwater. Snook, sea turtles, blue crabs, dolphins, and manatees live in these waters. The mound is open daily during daylight hours—the mosquitoes in the evening can be lethal. For more information: District Ranger's Office, Canaveral National Seashore, 308 Julia Street, Titusville 32796; (904)428-3384.

The Best Beaches

♥ **Canaveral National Seashore** No driving on the beach, no condos, no high-rise hotels, no neon... this beach is deliberately undeveloped, so be sure to bring drinking water and snacks. But what this area north of Kennedy Space Center does have is more than 25 miles of beautiful beaches where wildlife is abundant. You may spot alligators (not in the ocean), turtles, and birds in this pristine place where more than 310 species of birds and 1,045 species of plants make their home. Apollo Beach is at the north end of the seashore, and Playalinda Beach is at the south end. Playalinda and Apollo both have lifeguards on duty from May 1 to September 30. Klondike Beach, in the middle, is accessible only by foot, bicycle, or horseback; it's worth the walk to Klondike just for the seashells. The north end of the beach offers some great trails; check out Castle Windy. Turtle Mound at the north end also is a must; the 40-foot-tall mound of shells offers a great view of the ocean and nearby lagoon. The south end of the beach is great for birdwatching. In the midst of all this wilderness, civilization is not far away: space shuttle launch pads also are in full view from the south end of the beach.

Both Apollo and Playalinda beaches have parking areas and rest rooms (although no running water), but there are no snack bar areas so take water and food. Also, there are very few lifeguards in the summer, usually only one at each boardwalk. The seashore is open daylight hours, except when the road is closed because of NASA activities. For more information on the seashore, call the district ranger's office at (321) 267-1110.

Daytona Beach Look both ways before you cross the... beach? Cars can cruise on most of this wide—500 feet at low tide—beach of firmly packed sand from an hour before sunrise and an hour after sundown, at a cost of $5 per vehicle. Cars move slowly, but you still need to warn your children to "stop, look, and listen." But a welcome change is a 1-mile, vehicle-free beach area in front of Daytona Beach's Boardwalk and the Pier. This area begins at US 92 (International Speedway Blvd.) and ends at SR 430. Day guests can park in a new garage ($1 per half-hour, $5 per day) at the Ocean Center arena. From this parking garage, you can take a tram to several stops along the beach. The parking garage is located at 101 N. Atlantic Avenue.

At the beach you'll find floats, umbrellas, beach cruiser bicycles, and motorbikes available for rent, and vendors sell everything from hot dogs to beach towels and T-shirts. Lifeguards regularly patrol the beach. For entertainment, the band shell, constructed of coquina rock in 1937, offers free weekly concerts in the summer.

Daytona Beach has been given the name World's Most Famous Beach, but infamous may be more like it. Why? The beach and its related activities attract auto enthusiasts, motorcyclists, and spring breakers—all are given a bad rap as rowdy vacationers. Although these crowds are usually harmless, you may want to look for another vacation destination if you have small children and are looking for a little peace and quiet. This is especially true in the early spring when many of the special events are held.

NO CARS ALLOWED

In addition to the 1-mile zone of vehicle-free beach in front of the Pier, there is a small piece of Daytona Beach oceanfront that does not allow traffic—south of the pier between Emilia Avenue and Beach Street is considered a "natural conservation zone" with no cars. So if you have particularly young children, this may be a good spot to consider. You're still only a short distance from the center of the action.

New Smyrna Beach is about 50/50—vehicles are permitted on about half the beach, from Smyrna Dunes Park on the north to 27th Avenue on the south. South of 27th Avenue is considered a natural conservation zone with less development and no vehicles.

Ft. Pierce Inlet State Recreation Area Two pretty beaches and a coastal hammock at the southernmost end of North Hutchinson Island have a picnic area, rest rooms, and playground. We don't recommend swimming at Inlet Beach because the waters are swift, and that means unsafe swimming. But the ocean side, known as North Beach or Jetty Park, is protected from waves by its jetty, so it's safe for even small children, and lifeguards are on duty. Adjacent Jack Island on the Intracoastal Waterway is open to foot traffic only. You can take a footbridge from the recreation area over to the island and explore several miles of nature trails, where you can expect to see plenty of birds and butterflies. Open daily, 8 a.m.–sunset; admission is $3.25 per car. Located 4 miles east of Ft. Pierce via the North Causeway; (561) 468-3985.

Golden Sands County Park This small park and nearby Treasure Shores Park are excellent for families: both have well-maintained playgrounds, picnic shelters with grills, and lifeguards on the beach. The two parks are in Indian River Shores, just north of Vero Beach.

Jaycee Park There are lifeguards, a playground, plenty of shade trees, and a spot for picnicking. Located off A1A at Mango Road in Vero Beach.

Lighthouse Point Park Many families travel south to this park, named for the nearby lighthouse still in use, to escape Daytona's packed beaches around the pier. The park features a picnic area, nature trails, and a marina. To the south, the beach is especially beautiful and peaceful and the waves are gentle—perfect for young swimmers, but there are no lifeguards. Driving is allowed on this beach. Admission is $3.50 per vehicle, up to 8 people per vehicle; $1 per person beyond 8 people. Hours are 6 a.m.–9 p.m. daily. The park is located at the south end of Atlantic Avenue in Daytona Beach; (386) 756-7488.

New Smyrna Beach This is actually 13 miles of beach and a small town just south of Daytona where Central Floridians often escape. A wooden walkway stretches more than a mile over the dunes at Smyrna Dunes Park at the north end of Peninsula Avenue. Canaveral National Seashore marks the southern tip. It's a little less hectic and less developed than nearby Daytona. Teenagers love Daytona; New Smyrna is more family oriented. The ocean is considered extra safe here because of rock ledges offshore that protect against undercurrents. Vehicles are permitted on New Smyrna Beach between Sand Dunes Park and 27th Avenue ($5 per car). Though traffic moves slowly, it's important for your children to "stop, look, and listen." There are lifeguards and rest rooms.

Pepper Park Spreading from the bayfront to the ocean, the park has a nice beach with lifeguards, bathhouses, and tennis and basketball courts (though they're getting a bit worn). On the bay, you can fish, hike, canoe, and picnic—there are two boat docks and six fishing piers. The park is open daily from dawn to dusk. In the park is the UDT-SEAL Museum (phone (561) 595-5845) that tells about the Underwater Demolition Teams (UDT) and the navy's Sea Air and Land (SEAL) program. Admission is $4 adults, $1.50 children ages 5–12, free for preschoolers. The museum is open Tuesday–Saturday, 10 a.m.–4 p.m.; Sunday, noon–4 p.m.; and January–April, Monday, 10 a.m.–4 p.m. Located on A1A in north Ft. Pierce.

Sebastian Inlet State Recreation Area This popular park is a favorite with surfers and is a premier saltwater fishing location of Florida's east coast, where lucky anglers hook snook, redfish, bluefish, and Spanish mackerel from the jetties and bridge catwalks. There's no driving on the beach, which has lifeguards and a decent, protected snorkeling area (you can rent gear there). A lot of anglers bunk down at the 51 campsites that overlook the inlet; the nightly rate is $18.70, $20.84 with electricity. For reservations, call (321) 984-4852. The fee to enter the recreation area is $3.25 per car. If you need to rent fishing gear, call (321) 768-6621; $3 per hour, $9.50 for 4.5 hours, $15 all day.

Special activities include nighttime walks to see loggerhead turtles in June and July. The McLarty Treasure Museum (call (561) 589-2147), showcasing treasures from a 1715 shipwreck, is 2 miles south of the Sebastian Inlet Bridge. The museum is open daily, 10 a.m.–4 p.m.; admission is $1, free for kids ages 6 and under. Sebastian Inlet State Recreation Area is located on A1A in Melbourne Beach; (321) 984-4852.

Sea Turtle Beach Plenty of family activities are available on the well-maintained, half-mile-long stretch of sand at Jensen Beach, including food and beach concessions (you can rent floats and boogie boards), volleyball, and a picnic area. The beach is open daily, 8 a.m.–8 p.m., with lifeguards on duty. Located at the intersection of Jensen Beach Causeway and A1A.

DO YOU WANNA SURF?

Surfer Lou Maresca swears he can have your kid surfing in just four short lessons. Maresca runs his Surf School in the Ft. Pierce Inlet area, where waves are easy for beginners, and starts with children as young as 8. If you want to try surfing on your own, he rents equipment. Cost is $60 for a 1½-hour lesson, $100 for a full day, or $180 for two days. All you need are a bathing suit, towel, and sunscreen. His weeklong summer camps are popular, too. You can reach Lou at (561) 231-1044 or at his website: www.surfschoolcamp.com.

Family Outdoor Adventures

Barnyard Friends and Animal Farm Out in the rural farm country of New Smyrna Beach, Donna and Terry Sanders welcome children through the gates, then let them have a hands-on experience with dozens of animals that city kids might never get to touch—pigs, ponies, ducks, goats, rabbits. More than 200 animals are all hand-raised and hand-fed, which makes them gentle enough to be around the children. Tours last 2 hours and are $5; tours are available Friday and Saturday at 10 a.m., Sunday at noon and 2 p.m. Located at 505 Samsula Drive; (386) 428-0983; www.volusia.com/barnyardfriends.

Funday Discovery Tours If you think your kids are up to a half-day on the water, Funday offers excellent environmental tours to places like Merritt Island, a desolate rookery island, and other sanctuaries. Tours, starting at $30, originate at both the Melbourne Marina and Sebastian Inlet Marina. Open daily, 8 a.m.–6 p.m.; (321) 725-0796; www.fundaytours.com.

Merritt Island Wildlife Refuge This 40-mile-long, 7-mile-wide stretch of land was set aside in the 1950s as a buffer zone for the nearby National Aeronautics and Space Administration (NASA) activities. In cooperation with NASA, the U.S. Fish and Wildlife Service has managed the refuge since 1963, a safe haven for more endangered or threatened animals than any other area of the continental United States. The animals include sea turtles, West Indian manatees, southern bald eagles, wood storks, peregrine falcons, eastern indigo snakes, and Florida scrub jays. Some of the more commonly seen wildlife includes laughing gulls, royal terns, snowy egrets, great blue herons, and turkey vultures. The numbers are amazing—year-round residents include 310 species of birds, 25 species of mammals, 117 species of fish, and 65 species of amphibians and reptiles. Admission is free; the refuge is open daily, dawn to dusk. The visitor center on SR 402 provides great brochures to help you find your way around, with many pamphlets available on spotting animals. The center is open Monday–Friday, 8 a.m.–4:30 p.m.; Saturday–Sunday, 9 a.m.–5 p.m. The center is closed Sundays from April through October and on federal holidays. From I-95, take Exit 80 and head east; cross over US 1, and the refuge is 4 miles ahead on the right; (321) 861-0667.

Ponce De León Inlet Lighthouse It's a challenge to climb all 203 spiraling steps, but the sweeping view of Daytona and New Smyrna Beach is worth the trek. Built in 1887, this 175-foot-high working lighthouse is Florida's tallest, the second tallest in the U.S., and is designated a National Historic Landmark. Little ones may find the climb too difficult and frightening, but there's plenty to explore on the grounds: All seven original buildings still stand, including the lightkeeper's restored house. This is a fun spot for a picnic, with resident cats and a small playground. Admission is $4, $1 ages 11 and under. Located about 3 miles south of Daytona Beach, at 4931 S. Peninsula Drive, Ponce Inlet; (386) 761-1821. Open 10 a.m.–5 p.m. daily, with extended summer hours.

Shenandoah Stables Make reservations for a family ride along one of the many country trails. For beginners, lessons are offered on ponies and horses. Hour-long guided tours cost $20 per person. Open daily, 10 a.m.–4 p.m., by appointment. 1759 Tomoka Farms Road, Daytona Beach; (386) 257-1444.

A Tiny Cruise Line River Excursion Themed boat tours take families on short excursions, for instance out on the Halifax River to see dolphins, manatees, and other wildlife. Cost for a 1-hour tour is $10 for adults, $6.50 ages 12 and under. The 2-hour morning cruise costs $15 for adults, $8 ages 12 and under. 425 South Beach Street; (386) 226-2343.

Tomoka State Park Tomoka State Park was once the site of the Timucuan Indian village, at the junction of the Tomoka and Halifax rivers. After Florida was acquired from Spain by the British in 1763, the area was used to plant indigo, rice, and sugarcane in what became the Mount Oswald Plantation. Today, Tomoka is back to its original condition. This 1,540-acre park is filled with beautiful oaks and offers camping, fishing, canoeing, nature trails, and picnic areas to its visitors. There are 100 campsites; cost is $12. Canoe rentals are available for a 13-mile trip down the beautiful Tomoka River. (The canoe trail starts at SR 40, 1 mile west of I-95.) Also on the property is the Fred Dana Marsh Museum and Visitor Center. Park hours: daily, 8 a.m.–dusk. Museum hours: 9 a.m.–4:30 p.m. For further information, contact Tomoka State Park, 2099 North Beach Street, Ormond Beach 32174; (386) 676-4050.

Trail Tips

- If your schedule allows, hike the trails—on the Hoeck Drive there aren't many places for vehicles to pull aside to soak in the scenery. Also, several roads, which are only accessible by foot, branch off the drive. The trails are easy for the young and old to maneuver, and hiking allows you to get closer to the marshes that provide feeding and resting habitat for the many birds in the area.
- If you'd like to get more out of the hike, Canaveral National Seashore Rangers offer ranger walks to teach about beach vegetation, sand dunes, and marine life. Call (321) 267-1110 for more information on these one- to 2-hour hikes.
- The cool-weather months, October–April, are usually the best times of year for bird-watching. The best times of day are early morning and late afternoon.
- Don't forget insect repellent!

Self-Guided Drives and Hikes

Canaveral National Seashore and its neighbor to the south, Merritt Island National Wildlife Refuge, are often lumped together (and therefore confused) because of their location and because they are both government-managed areas. If you are planning a trip to this area, stop at either visitors center; the guides are extremely helpful and will assist you in sorting out your travel options.

Canaveral National Seashore

Castle Windy Beginning at Parking Area 3, this 1-mile round-trip trail crosses the island from the beach to Mosquito Lagoon. Don't attempt to hike here during the summer; there's a reason this pool of water is called Mosquito Lagoon. For more information contact District Ranger's Office, Canaveral National Seashore, 308 Julia Street, Titusville 32796; (321) 267-3036; www.nbbd.com/godo/ns.

Max Hoeck Creek Wildlife Drive A 4.3-mile auto tour that follows a railroad bed through marshland. Begin at Canaveral National Seashore Visitors Center, off CR 402; end at Playalinda Beach Road. Estimated time: 20 minutes.

Merritt Island National Wildlife Refuge

Black Point Wildlife Drive A 6-mile self-guided auto tour that takes motorists on a sand and shell road through pine woods and marshlands. This drive is located off SR 406 north of Titusville. Estimated time: 30–60 minutes.

Cruickshank Trail Named after famous wildlife photographer, writer, and naturalist Allan Cruickshank, this trail leaves from stop Number 8 along Black Point Wildlife Drive. Closed to vehicles, this 5-mile trail circles a water marsh and is a great place to bird-watch. Estimated time: 2–3 hours.

Oak Hammock A half-mile trail through the trees, with a portion of the trail on a boardwalk. The trail is located three-quarters of a mile west of Merritt Island National Wildlife Refuge Visitor Center. Estimated time: 15 minutes. For more information on these trails or Merritt Island National Wildlife Refuge: P.O. Box 6504, Titusville 32782; (407) 861-0667.

SEA TURTLES

Endangered sea turtles are often spotted along this part of the East Coast; in fact, the area is the largest sea turtle nesting area in the United States.

From May through August, the giants lumber ashore to lay their eggs—about 100 round, white, leathery eggs in each nest. If the eggs survive, they begin to hatch in about 60 days, and the tiny turtles try to make it to the ocean (though raccoons, ghost crabs, and birds create quite an obstacle course).

Once they make it past the surf, they swim to a region of the Atlantic Ocean known as the Sargassum Sea, a large area of seaweed that drifts with the ocean currents. Here the hatchlings feed on seaweed and tiny animals. When they reach adolescence, many turtles return to the inshore waters of the Florida coastline.

It's important never to disturb a turtle nest, and if you encounter turtles on a beach, turn off flashlights and car lights and don't interfere with the turtle's activities—if a sea turtle is disturbed, it will not nest.

Guided nighttime turtle watches are great educational fun for children. They take place in June and July at several places along the East Coast, notably at Canaveral National Seashore.

Daytona

Daytona was built on speed; in the early 1900s this stretch of firmly packed sand served as a natural racetrack for roadsters. It all started in 1902 in Ormond Beach just north of Daytona, a playground for the wealthy where oil billionaire John D. Rockefeller and other members of high society spent winters. Ransom E. Olds, father of the Oldsmobile, was a fellow vacationer, and in 1902 he spent the winter at the Ormond Hotel. Legend claims that one day Olds drove his roadster, "the Pirate," an incredible 50 mph down the beach. Olds soon challenged one of his friends to race, the first-known competitive automobile race.

Although most people want to leave traffic behind on a vacation, many vacationers flock to Daytona Beach to be in the heart of auto action. Today, vehicles are still allowed to cruise the sand (at a law-abiding speed of 10 mph), but the real racing takes places just miles away from the beach at the Daytona International Speedway. In mid-February race enthusiasts take over the beach for the Daytona 500, followed by leather-clad cyclists for Bike Week. And finally, college students eager to release midterm-exam stresses pile in their cars and head to Daytona's beaches in March for spring break.

Daytona Beach has tried to change its raucous image, but for families looking for a quiet vacation, we suggest checking out the areas north and south of Daytona Beach, such as Ormond Beach, Ponce Inlet, or Daytona Beach Shores. Or visit the Daytona area during the winter months when it's relatively quiet. If, however, your family is looking for an action-packed vacation, rev up your motor and head to Daytona Beach.

Family Resorts

Breakers Beach Motel

27 S. Ocean Avenue, Daytona Beach • (800) 441-8459

When you're this close to the action, you don't need a big chain hotel to

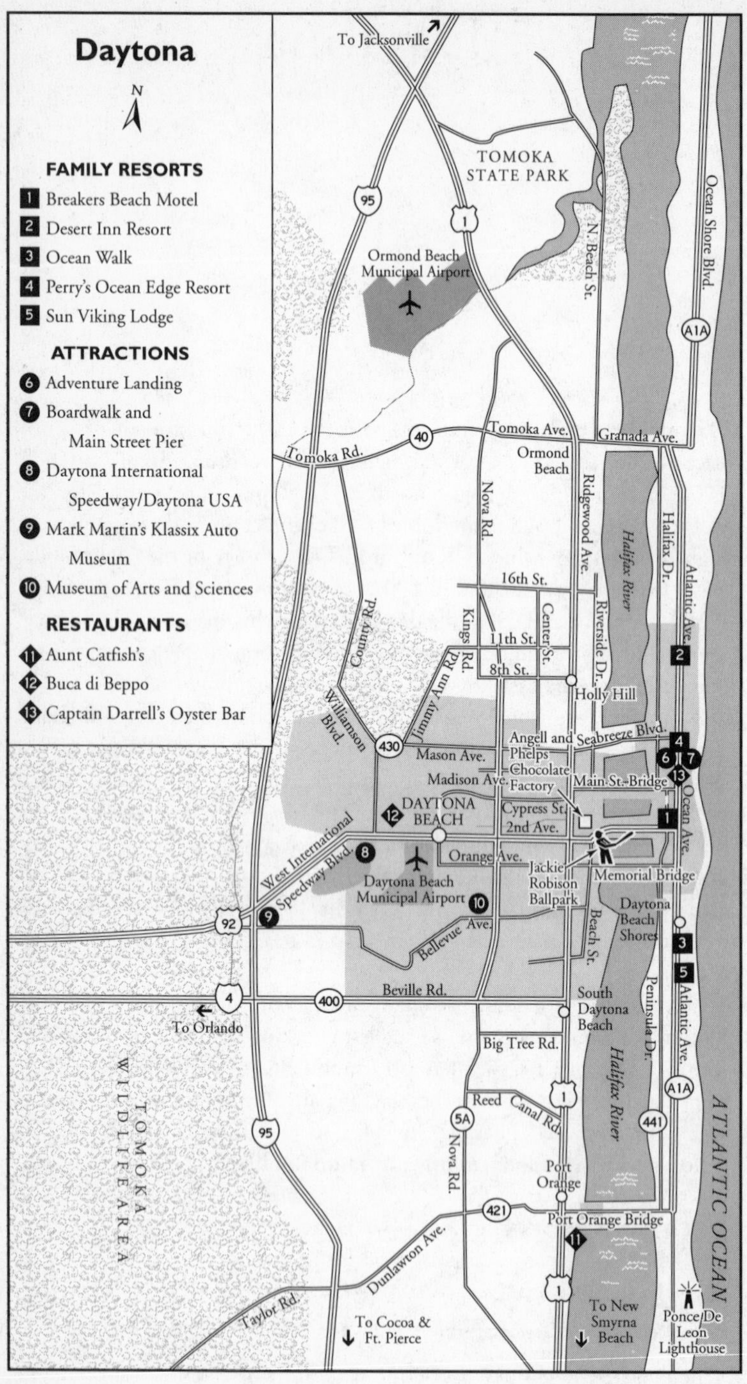
Daytona
N
FAMILY RESORTS
1 Breakers Beach Motel
2 Desert Inn Resort
3 Ocean Walk
4 Perry's Ocean Edge Resort
5 Sun Viking Lodge
ATTRACTIONS
6 Adventure Landing
7 Boardwalk and Main Street Pier
8 Daytona International Speedway/Daytona USA
9 Mark Martin's Klassix Auto Museum
10 Museum of Arts and Sciences
RESTAURANTS
11 Aunt Catfish's
12 Buca di Beppo
13 Captain Darrell's Oyster Bar
To Jacksonville
TOMOKA STATE PARK
Ormond Beach Municipal Airport
N. Beach St.
Ocean Shore Blvd.
A1A
Tomoka Ave.
Granada Ave.
Tomoka Rd.
Ormond Beach
Nova Rd.
Ridgewood Ave.
Halifax River
Halifax Dr.
Atlantic Ave.
16th St.
County Rd.
Kings Rd.
Center St.
Riverside Dr.
11th St.
8th St.
Jimmy Ann Rd.
Williamson Blvd.
Holly Hill
Angell and Seabreeze Blvd.
Mason Ave.
Phelps Chocolate Factory
Madison Ave.
Main St. Bridge
Ocean Ave.
DAYTONA BEACH
Cypress St.
2nd Ave.
West International Speedway Blvd.
Orange Ave.
Jackie Robison Ballpark
Memorial Bridge
Daytona Beach Municipal Airport
Daytona Beach Shores
Bellevue Ave.
Beach St.
Beville Rd.
To Orlando
South Daytona Beach
Peninsula Dr.
Atlantic Ave.
Big Tree Rd.
TOMOKA WILDLIFE AREA
Reed Canal Rd.
Halifax River
ATLANTIC OCEAN
Nova Rd.
Port Orange
Port Orange Bridge
Dunlawton Ave.
Taylor Rd.
To Cocoa & Ft. Pierce
To New Smyrna Beach
Ponce De Leon Lighthouse

provide activities to entertain your family. There are just 23 rooms, and you couldn't ask for a better location; park your car at Breakers and walk to everything, including the Boardwalk, the Main Street Fishing Pier, shops, and restaurants. If you don't plan to stray from the motel, there's enough here to keep you happy. This unadorned motel has suites, oceanfront efficiencies (they include full kitchens), and regular rooms (all have microwaves and refrigerators). Coffeemakers are provided upon request. Enjoy the heated pool and the ocean deck, or cook up your catch of the day on the gas grills near the picnic tables. Your pet is welcome here, too. Rover and the whole family can expect special attention here. Rates in January begin at $70, in May they begin at $100. For special events, prices increase to $140 and up.

Desert Inn Resort

900 N. Atlantic Avenue, Daytona Beach • (800) 826-1711 or (3886) 258-6555

This family-friendly resort features 200 deluxe rooms and suites, with kitchenettes with microwaves in some rooms. The resort also has a kiddie pool, a children's playground, guest laundry, three game rooms, and Aladdin's Mini Theater (where movies are shown for all ages). Children under age 18 stay free. Rates start at $59 during winter and $69 during summer.

Ocean Walk

300 N. Atlantic Ave., Daytona Beach • (800) 649-3566 • www.oceanwalkresort.com

In the heart of Daytona Beach, families can spread out in one- and two-bedroom units in this luxurious new condo resort. All have full kitchens, washers and dryers, and beautiful furnishing. The grounds include a waterslide pool and lazy river with an island putting green. A full-time activities director will keep the kids busy. Rates starts at $159 in the winter, $199 in the summer.

Perry's Ocean Edge Resort

2209 S. Atlantic Avenue, Daytona Beach Shores • (386) 255-0581

There are plenty of activities for kids and adults in this unassuming little place. The staff is friendly; the rooms are big (75% have ocean views), and there's a mini-refrigerator in every room—some even have full kitchens. A grocery store is directly across the street. The indoor pool has a retractable roof, and there are two outdoor pools and a kiddie pool, a nine-hole putting green, video game room, and a bar. And best of all, fresh donuts are served in the lobby for free every morning.

The resort is family owned and operated. Rates start at $71 during winter and $91 during summer.

Sun Viking Lodge

2411 S. Atlantic Avenue, Daytona Beach Shores • (800) 847-4469 or (904) 252-6252

A pool with a waterslide, two game rooms, a kiddie pool, and a playground . . . not enough? There are also supervised kids' activities from beach volleyball to Twister, horseshoes, and more at this 91-unit hotel. Most rooms here have fully equipped kitchens, and there's also a barbecue area, a fitness center and sauna, and coin-operated laundry facilities. For more privacy, ask about their one-, two-, and three-bedroom cottages. Rates start at $69–99 in the winter (oceanfront) and $102–159 in the summer.

Attractions

Adventure Landing

601 Earl Street, Daytona (321) 258-0071 • www.adventurelanding.com

Hours - Dry park attractions open daily, 10 a.m.–midnight, waterpark hours are seasonal, call for more information

Admission - Waterpark: $20 for adults, $16.99 for people under 42" tall, free for children 3 and under with adult admission; evening hours: 4–8 p.m., $12.99 for all age groups. Go-kart track: single seat go-karts $6, double-seat go-karts $8, drivers must be 56" or taller and a licensed driver, riders must be 36" or taller. Miniature golf: 18 holes $6; 27 holes $7; $3 and $4 respectively for ages 5 and under; game tokens 25 cents each

Appeal by Age Group -

Pre-school ★★	Teens ★★★★	Over 30 ★★
Grade school ★★★★	Young Adults ★★★★	Seniors ★★

Touring Time - Average full afternoon or evening; minimum 2 hours

Rainy day touring Not recommended

Author's Ratings ★★★, you may be able to find these activities at home, but their familiarity will keep kids happy

Restaurants - Yes

Alcoholic beverages - Yes

Handicapped access - Yes

Wheelchair rental - No

Baby stroller rental - No

Lockers - Yes

Pet kennels - No

Rain check - Yes

Private tours - No

Description and Comments There's a little bit of everything at this amusement park, including an arcade, a two-story go-kart track, three miniature golf courses, a five-acre waterpark with 12 slides, a lazy river, and more. Your best bet may be to stop by for an evening or afternoon.

Boardwalk & Main Street Pie

Ocean Avenue (Off A1A), Daytona Beach • (386) 253-1212

Hours - Daily, 6 a.m.–11 p.m. daily (extended hours in summer)

Admission - To fishing end of pier: $3.50, $2.50 12 and under ($5 with pole rental), $1 for spectators; Skylift admission $3, Space Needle $2 (both rides $4)

Appeal by Age Group -

Pre-school ★★	Teens ★★	Over 30 ★★
Grade school ★★	Young Adults ★★	Seniors ★★★

Touring Time - Minimum 1 hour

Rainy-Day Touring - Not recommended

Author's Rating - ★; old Florida kitsch

Restaurants - Yes

Alcoholic beverages - Yes

Handicapped access - Yes

Wheelchair rental - No

Baby stroller rental - No

Lockers - No

Pet kennels - No

Rain check - No

Private tours - No

Description and Comments This low-tech boardwalk and pier looks like a movie set from the '60s, a bit worn on the edges. We don't recommend this after dark (the crowd is often raucous), but kids get a kick out of fishing off the 1,000-foot-long pier, or taking a ride out over the water on the gondola Sky Lift, or up in the 18-story-high Space Needle. The good news is no cars are allowed, so you can stroll and play arcade games, munch on junk food, and re-live another era.

Daytona International Speedway/Daytona USA

1802 W. International Speedway Boulevard, Daytona Beach • (386) 253-7223 for tickets for races • (386) 254-2700 for general information

Hours - Daily, 9 a.m.–7 p.m.

Admission - Tram is $7 per person, children ages 5 and under get in free with a paying adult; Daytona USA costs $20 for adults, $17 for senior citizens ages 60 and older, $14 for children 6–12, under age 6 get in free

Appeal by Age Group -

Pre-school ★	Teens ★★★	Over 30 ★★
Grade school ★★★	Young Adults ★★	Seniors ★

Touring Time - Average 2½ hours; minimum 1 hour

Rainy-Day Touring - Recommended

Author's Rating - ★★★; live vicariously—you can design and test a stock car

Restaurants - Yes
Alcoholic beverages - Yes
Handicapped access - Yes
Wheelchair rental - No
Baby stroller rental - No
Lockers - No
Pet kennels - No
Rain check - No
Private tours - Yes

Description and Comments The Speedway hosts eight weekends of racing a year, including NASCAR, stock car, sports car, and motorcycle races. Guests also can catch vehicle testing scheduled throughout the year. But for race car enthusiasts, the only time to visit Daytona is during Speedweeks, a two-week-long event at Daytona International Speedway. Speedweeks begins the first weekend in February. More than 160,000 attend the Daytona 500 each year, the culmination of Speedweeks, to fully absorb the speed, sights, and sounds of racing. (The Daytona 500 lasts about 5 hours, and may be a little too long for young children.) Racing is one of the country's fastest-growing spectator sports, and it's fans are a faithful bunch. For some, watching from the grandstand is not enough; they watch the races from their recreational vehicle parked in the middle of the track—it's as close as anyone can get without taking the wheel.

If you don't plan your vacation around a race, there are still ways to get your motor fix at the Speedway. Two attractions let visitors become drivers for a day. One attraction, a 30-minute tram tour, takes you on the Speedway's high-banked, 2.5-mile tri-oval course and a 3.5-mile road course. You'll also see the infield, pit, and garage areas. These tours depart daily, every half-hour, 9:30 a.m.–4:30 p.m., weather and track schedule permitting.

Interactive Daytona USA is the other big draw at the Speedway. Daytona USA has an admittance fee separate from the tram. Guests enter the building through a replica of the raceway's famous twin tunnels...just the first of many exhibits that put race car enthusiasts in the driver's seat. Visitors can change tires in a timed pit stop competition, broadcast a race, talk to drivers through video monitors, test their knowledge in an auto trivia game, and computer design and test their own stock car. Real race cars are also on display. Your kids will enjoy the interactive exhibits, but both children and parents must see the Daytona 500 Thunder Round Sound film. The film stars NASCAR's most famous drivers in a 14-minute documentary of a day in the life of a race-car driver. Wake up with the drivers, learn their superstitions, and watch as they prepare for the big race. As guests leave the theater, they step into Victory Lane where the winning car from the latest Daytona 500 is on display.

For those who can't get enough speed, there's the Richard Petty Driving Experience ticket for $106 (which includes admission to Daytona USA). Climb into the front seat of a stock car with a professional instructor at the wheel for three laps on the 2.5-mile trial. You must be a licensed driver to ride in the car. This experience is not always available, so call ahead for more information.

FREE . . . OR ALMOST FREE

Angell and Phelps Chocolate Factory Take a guided tour of this Daytona Beach original, established in 1924, and watch as more than a hundred kinds of candies are made. Of course, there are free samples. Open Monday–Friday, 9:30 a.m.–5:30 p.m.; Saturday, 9–5. Thirty-minute tours available at 10 and 11 a.m. and 1, 2, and 3 p.m., Monday–Friday. Located at 154 South Beach Street; (386) 252-6531 or (800) 969-2634.

Sun Glow Fishing Pier If you've never taken the kids fishing, this is a great place to start. This is where the old-timers like to hang out, and you can rent poles for $2 per hour or $5.25 for the whole day and just relax. It costs $4.50 to get out on the pier. Located on A1A south of Dunlawton Bridge in Daytona Beach Shores; (386) 756-4219.

Mark Martin's Klassix Auto Museum

2909 W. International Speedway Boulevard, Daytona • (386) 252-3800 or (800) 881-8975 • www.klassixauto.com

Hours - Daily, 9 a.m.–6 p.m.

Admission - $8.50 for adults, $4.25 for children ages 7–12, $8 seniors ages 65 and older

Appeal by Age Group -

Pre-school ★	Teens ★★★	Over 30 ★★
Grade school ★★	Young Adults ★★★	Seniors ★★★

Touring Time - Average 1½ hours; minimum 1 hour

Rainy-Day Touring - Recommended

Author's Rating - ★★; especially fun for car buffs

Restaurants - Ice cream parlor

Alcoholic beverages - No

Handicapped access - Yes

Wheelchair rental - No

Baby stroller rental - No

Lockers - No

Pet kennels - No

Rain check - No

Private tours - Yes

Description and Comments Dramatic sets tell the story of the automobile's place in U.S. history. The tour begins in the 1950s at a drive-in restaurant, complete with roller-skating carhops. With retro being the rage these days, both you and your kids will feel right at home in the 1970s display. The Corvette display features one of each model from 1953 to the present. Cars of NASCAR Winston Cup Series champions Richard Petty and Dale Earnhardt are also on display, as well as Tom Cruise's car from the movie *Days of Thunder* and a collection of antique motorcycles. If the classic cars leave you feeling a little nostalgic, visit the 1950s-style soda fountain. One last dose of the "good old days" for parents, one scoop of ice cream for the kids.

PLAY BALL

Jackie Robinson Ballpark This baseball stadium is home to the Daytona Cubs, the Chicago Cubs' Class A affiliate in the Florida State League. There are no records of when the stadium was built, but it's the oldest minor league stadium in use. In 1946 Robinson played his first spring training game with the Brooklyn Dodgers' farm team, the Montreal Royals, here. In honor of Robinson, a bronze statue was erected at the entrance of this 4,500-seat ballpark. Games are played April–September. Make a day of it—visit the farmer's market held every Saturday morning on City Island near the ballpark for great deals on produce, plants, fruits, and seafood. Located at 105 E. Orange Avenue at City Island Parkway. For ticket information call (386) 257-3172.

Museum of Arts and Sciences

1040 Museum Boulevard, Daytona • (386) 255-0285 • www.moas.org

Hours - Tuesday–Friday, 9 a.m.–4 p.m.; Saturday–Sunday, noon–5 p.m.; closed Monday. Planetarium shows: Tuesday–Friday, 2 p.m.; Saturday–Sunday, 1 p.m. and 3 p.m.

Admission - $7 for adults, $2 for children ages 6 and over; planetarium, additional $5 per person

Appeal by Age Group -

Pre-school ★★	Teens ★★	Over 30 ★★★
Grade school ★★★	Young Adults ★★★	Seniors ★★★★

Touring Time - Average 2 hours; minimum 1 hour

Rainy-Day Touring - Recommended

Author's Rating - ★★★; where else can kids see a sloth skeleton?

Restaurants - No

Alcoholic beverages - No

Handicapped access - Yes

Wheelchair rental - No

Baby stroller rental - No

Lockers - No

Pet Kennels - No

Rain Check - No

Private tours - Yes

Description and Comments Traditional museums may be a snore for young children, but this museum has a little something for everyone. Centered on the 60-acre Tuscawilla Preserve, the museum has five wings: The Main Gallery; a Science Gallery (exhibits here change every few weeks); the Dow Gallery of American Art; the Prehistory of Florida Wing—the favorite for children—including a 13-foot tall skeleton of a 130,000-year-old giant ground sloth and other cool fossils; and the Cuban Art Gallery, considered the finest example of modern Cuban art in the free world. There's also a small planetarium in the museum.

Nature trails through the scenic Tuscawilla Preserve and the "window in the forest" interpretive center give children an up-close view of nearby coastal hammock environments.

Family-Friendly Restaurants

Aunt Catfish's

4009 Halifax Drive (west end of Port Orange Bridge), Port Orange • (386) 767-4768

Meals served - Lunch and dinner

Cuisine - "Down South River Cookin'"

Entree range - $6.99–26.99

Kids menu - Yes

Reservations - Priority seating and call-ahead seating

Payment - Visa, MC, AmEx, D

Seafood, anything you could want: shrimp, lobster, crabs, scallops, oysters, and fish, and any way you want it: Cajun, fried, broiled, grilled, or baked. And since there's one in every family, picky eaters can choose from chicken and beef dishes. Wash it down with an ice-cold glass of sweet tea or freshly squeezed lemonade. With special menus for early birds, seniors, and children, this restaurant aims to please. And the kids menu is exotic compared to the standard fare: they can choose from fried shark bites (tell them it's chicken) to pork back ribs and fried shrimp. When your kids arrive, they'll be greeted with crayons to entertain them before their meal; they're given a balloon as they leave. In the summer, lounge on the dock and listen to the bands.

Buca di Bepo

2514 W. International Speedway Blvd., Daytona • (386) 253-6523

Meals served - Dinner daily, lunch on Saturday, Sunday

Cuisine - Italian

Entree range - $6.95–20.95

Kids menu - Yes

Reservations - Accepted

Payment - All major credit cards accepted

When you're hungry after a day at the beach, this is the place to bring a crowd for gargantuan servings of pasta, pizza, and more. If possible, save room for tiramisu, but it's enough for a four to share.

Captain Darrell's Oyster Bar

13 Boardwalk, Daytona • (386) 255-5822

Meals served - Lunch and dinner

Cuisine - Seafood

Entree range - $4–15

Kids menu - No

Reservations - Not accepted

Payment - Cash only

Seafood is plentiful, but Darrell's also pleases the picky with staples such as hamburgers and chicken. The highlight—a go-cart track on the roof.

Side Trips

Blue Spring We make an annual pilgrimage to Blue Spring every January or February to see the lumbering manatees who take refuge in the 72° water, one of the few places you can observe them in their native habitat, and it's not unusual to see 25 or more of them on a January morning. About 121 million gallons of water flow from Blue Spring's boil, making snorkeling fun in the summertime, when you'll see lots of catfish, gar, tilapia, and largemouth bass. A frame house built in the 1800s is now the visitors center, restored to look as it did back when farmers sent their crops to Jacksonville by steamboat. There's also picnicking, camping on 51 sites ($14) and canoe rentals. The park opens daily at 8 a.m. and closes at sunset year-round. $4 per vehicle entry fee. I-4 East from Orlando and follow the signs; 2 miles west of Orange City off I-4 and US 17; (386) 775-3663.

DeLeon Springs State Recreation Area This beautiful spring looks like a swimming pool, with concrete sides and a restaurant just steps away. Canoes and kayaks are for rent, and a nearby nature trail helps you work up an appetite. Plan your visit around breakfast at the Old Spanish Mill and Griddle House, once an old stone waterhouse and now a restaurant with specially built tables with big griddles in the middle. You order pitchers of batter and little bowls of fresh fruit and make your own all-you-can-eat flapjacks for $6 a person. The kids love it. If it's cool outdoors, ask for a seat on the screened porch—it's a perfect way to spend the morning. Go early, the lines get long, although reservations are accepted for parties of 10 or more. Open daily, weekends at 8 a.m., weekdays at 9 a.m. $4 a carload to enter the park. 601 Ponce de Leon Boulevard, DeLeon Springs. Park, (904) 985-4212; restaurant, (386) 985-5644.

Hontoon Island State Park You can only get there by boat, and a daily ferry will take you across the St. John's River to this little island that's a sanctuary for bald eagles. There's great fishing, and you can camp in primitive cabins (shared bathhouses) for $20–25, or in tents for $8–10. Open daily, 8 a.m.–sunset year-round. West of DeLand 6 miles, off SR 44; (386) 736-5309.

Pioneer Settlement for the Creative Arts The 25-acre settlement gives children a chance to experience Florida like it was in the early 1900s—a blacksmith shop, woodwright shop, pottery shed, and post-and-beam barn have on-going demonstrations, and kids can try churning butter, dipping wax candles, spinning wool, and more. Open year-round, except for major holidays; Monday–Friday, 9 a.m.–4 p.m.; Saturday, 9 a.m.–2 p.m. Admission ($3 adults, $2 children ages 5–12, free for kids ages 4 and under) includes a guided tour. Barberville is about 25 miles west of Daytona, 1 block west of the intersection of SR 40 and US 17, about 15 miles north of DeLand; (386) 749-2959.

The Space Coast: Cocoa Beach, Titusville, and Cape Canaveral

In the 1940s the federal government selected Cape Canaveral as a long-range testing site. Cape Canaveral had "the right stuff": sparsely populated land, a climate conducive to year-round launches, and proximity to the ocean, allowing over-the-water launches. Once a small, mostly rural area, Cape Canaveral boomed in the 1950s, as missile contractors began moving to the area. In 1958, NASA began operations at Cape Canaveral, and three years later it launched the first American, Alan Shepherd, into space. But NASA had greater ambitions—to send humans to the moon.

Soon, NASA developed the Apollo program and the Saturn V rocket. As the Mercury and Gemini programs were undertaken in the 1960s, a launch complex designed specifically for the Saturn V took shape—this was the birth of the Kennedy Space Center. In 1969, Neil Armstrong, Buzz Aldrin, and Michael Collins began their trip to the moon from the Kennedy Space Center. Through the years, this site has undergone many changes, including space shuttle missions. Today, it's the only space shuttle launch site in the world. With dozens of interactive displays, it's an enriching stop for families—you can even climb around the shuttle *Explorer.*

Not only does the Space Coast have command of the air but it also dominates the sea. Cape Canaveral is home to Florida's fastest-growing cruise port. The cruise lines that operate out of this area include Carnival Cruise Lines, Disney Cruise Line, Cape Canaveral Cruise Line, and Royal Caribbean Cruise Lines. Natural coral and artificial reefs attract numerous fish, making this area one of the major commercial fishing ports in Florida. Trawlers supply Central Florida with hours-old seafood, but charter boats and boat rentals can be your ticket to a home-cooked fresh fish dinner. Mackerel, sailfish, marlin, wahoo, tuna, and more can be found in these waters.

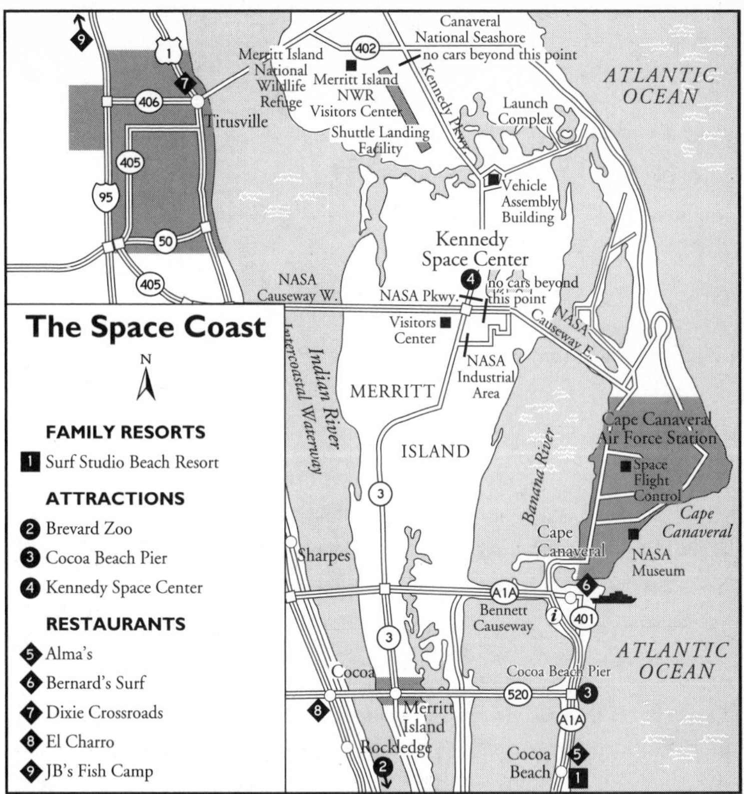

Family Resorts

Surf Studio Beach Resort

1801 S. Atlantic Avenue, Cocoa Beach • (321) 783-7100 • fax (321) 783-2695

If you're planning a visit to the space center, or just want a comfortable spot to watch a rocket launch, this friendly little beachfront resort is perfect. Owned and operated by the same family for 50 years, Surf Studio has 11 ground-floor "cottages," most with full kitchens and separate bedrooms and living rooms. All units have coffeemakers, TVs, microwaves, and VCRs available. There's a swimming pool and deck with a grill. Rates are $80–140 per night in the winter and $85–150 in the summer. Pets, too, are allowed for an additional $20 per night. You're just minutes from the Kennedy Space Center.

Attractions

Brevard Zoo

8225 N. Wickham Road, Melbourne • (321) 254-3002 • www.brevardzoo.org

Hours - Daily, 10 a.m.–5 p.m; closed Thanksgiving and Christmas

Admission - $7 for adults, $7 for seniors ages 60 and older, $5 for children ages 2–12

Appeal by Age Group -

Pre-school ★★★	Teens ★★★	Over 30 ★★★
Grade school ★★★	Young Adults ★★★	Seniors ★★★

Touring Time - Half a day on average; minimum 3 hours

Rainy-Day Touring - Not recommended

Author's Rating - ★★; fun entertainment for a cool or cloudy day

Restaurants - Yes

Alcoholic beverages - No

Handicapped access - Yes

Wheelchair rental - Yes

Baby stroller rental - Yes

Lockers - No

Pet kennels - No

Rain check - No

Private tours - No

Description and Comments Shaded boardwalks lead past species of animals indigenous to Latin America, Florida, and Australia—more than 400 in all, representing 109 species. You'll see myriad animals, including alligators and crocodiles, giant anteaters, marmosets, a jaguar, eagles, river otters, kangaroos, and kookaburras. The Australia exhibit features a free-flight aviary with cockatoos, lorikeets, and cockatiels.

An interactive area called the Animal Study Zone allows children and adults to walk into the mouth of a full-size replica of a right whale or dig for dinosaur bones. You can compare your jumping skills to that of a cricket or a frog and see if you can outrun an alligator or zebra. Nearby, Animal Encounters gives kids a chance to pet chickens, goats, and pot-bellied pigs. There's also a minitrain and an animal-themed playground.

New to the zoo is the Wetlands Outpost, a pavilion leading to the wetlands that have recently been enhanced. Checkout the Outpost for good views and boat trips though the wetlands.

Kennedy Space Center

Kennedy Space Center (located off SR 405, NASA Parkway) • (321) 449-4400 or in Florida (800) KSC-INFO • www.kennedyspacecenter.com

Hours - Daily, 9 a.m.–dusk; closed Christmas

Admission - Kennedy Space Center Visitor Complex tour into restricted areas, visitor complex exhibits, and any of the IMAX movies; $26 for adults, $16 for children ages 3–11

Appeal by Age Group -

Pre-school ★★	Teens ★★★★	Over 30 ★★★★
Grade school ★★★★	Young Adults ★★★★	Seniors ★★★★

Touring Time - Average 4 hours, plus 40 minutes for each IMAX; minimum 2 hours

Rainy-Day Touring - Recommended

Author's Rating - ★★★★; a "must-see" attraction

Restaurants - Yes

Alcoholic beverages - Yes

Handicapped access - Yes

Wheelchair rental - Yes

Baby stroller rental - Yes

Lockers - No

Pet kennels - Yes

Rain check - No

Private tours - Yes

Description and Comments As you approach the Visitor Complex, you'll see the Astronaut Memorial, a stunning, $6.4 million monument to the 14 astronauts who have died during missions. Their names are etched in black granite panels that rotate above a mirrored steel structure. A computer controls the granite so that it rises and sets with the sun. You can't miss the full-scale model of the space shuttle *Explorer* that you can actually board. Nearby, the Rocket Garden shows rockets from each stage of the U.S. exploration program.

The newest attraction is Mad Mission to Mars: 2025, a virtual theater attraction with 3-D computer animation that gives a fun and educational look at space travel. And schedule your visit to include an Astronaut Encounter, an opportunity to meet a real astronaut every day of the year as they tell their stories and answer questions.

In the Exploration in the New Millennium exhibit, you'll have the opportunity to touch a piece of Mars, and in the Early Space Exploration Museum, you'll see artifacts from the Gemini and Mercury programs.

As part of the bus tour into the restricted areas of KSC, you'll head to the Launch Complex 39 Observation Gantry, a 60-foot tower that puts you less than a half-mile away from space shuttle launch pad 39A. The 2-hour bus tour also includes the Apollo–Saturn V Center that celebrates the U.S. mission to the moon. Here you can participate in hands-on displays and see a real Saturn V rocket—the most powerful rocket ever built. Its sheer size is impressive: 363 feet long and 6.2 million pounds.

You'll also pass the Vehicle Assembly Building, one of the largest buildings in the world, and the Crawler, which transports space shuttles to the launch pad.

The Visitor Complex offers back-to-back IMAX theaters, each with 70-foot-wide screens that put you in space with an extraordinary sound system. There are two films, each 45 minutes long—*Space Station,* a film that captures seven shuttle crews and two resident station crews as they transform the International Space Station into a scientific research outpost, and *The Dream Is Alive,* with footage captured by astronauts and narrated by Walter Cronkite.

If you have space buffs in the family and your schedule is flexible, plan your visit around a launch date. Call (800) KSC-INFO or (321) 452-2121 for current shuttle launch information, which is always subject to change. And if you're traveling to the coast on the day of a launch, allow plenty of time for bumper-to-bumper traffic.

MORE FOR SPACE BUFFS

The U.S. Astronaut Hall of Fame and Space Camp takes guests back to the early days of the U.S. space program, featuring Mercury and Gemini astronauts. The memorabilia include artifacts, rare video, and personal mementos. Guests can board a full-scale space shuttle orbiter mock up for an interactive trip to the future, land the space shuttle Columbia, or float weightless while trying to repair Skylab. Hours: in summer, daily, 9 a.m.–7 p.m.; till 5 p.m. in winter. Admission: $13.95 adults, $12.95 seniors, $9.95 for ages 6–12. 6225 Vectorspace Boulevard, Titusville 32780; (321) 269-6100; www.astronauts.org.

The Hall of Fame is also home to the **U.S. Space Camp,** where kids are put through astronaut training, and math and science studies are encouraged. If your youngsters are really interested in the space program, sign them up for the five-day space camp where kids can train like real astronauts. The camp includes building and launching model rockets, constructing a space station, trying out a microgravity trainer and space walk simulator, and sampling freeze-dried astronaut meals. Call (321) 267-3184 for camp schedules and further information.

Astronaut Memorial Planetarium and Observatory is recognized as one of the best planetariums in the world. 1519 Clearlake Road, Cocoa 32922; (321) 634-3732; brevard.cc.fl.us/~planet.

Valiant Air Command Warbird Museum has preserved vintage World War II and postwar aircraft. Open daily, 10 a.m.–6 p.m.; closed Thanksgiving, Christmas, and New Year's Day. Admission is $9 for adults, $8 for military or seniors, $5 for children ages 3–12. 6600 Tico Road, Titusville 32780; (321) 268-1941; www.vacwarbirds.org.

Family-Friendly Restaurants

Alma's

306 N. Orlando Avenue, Cocoa Beach • (321) 783-1981

Meals served - Dinner

Cuisine - Italian

Entree range - $8.95–22

Kids menu - Yes

Reservations - Accepted

Payment - All major credit cards accepted

We have friends who dined at this mom-and-pop eatery back in the 1960s and recently returned to find the same friendly service and hearty portions of authentic Italian cuisine. An order of their delicious spaghetti and meatballs is enough to feed two. It's been around for generations for a good reason—service with a smile, fair prices, and comfort food.

Bernard's Surf

2 S. Atlantic Avenue, Cocoa Beach • (321) 783-2401 • 628 Glen Cheek Drive, Cape Canaveral • (321) 783-8732

Meals served - Lunch and dinner

Cuisine - American, seafood

Entree range - $4.95–10.95 (raw bar); $9.95–15.95 (bar and grill); $15–50 (fine dining area)

Kids menu - Yes

Reservations - Recommended for dinner

Payment - All major credit cards accepted

This longtime favorite is divided into three parts: a raw bar (Rusty's), a bar and grill (Fischer's), and a formal dining room (Bernard's). The restaurant opened in 1948 with Bernard Fischer serving fish caught by his fleet of boats. His nephew now runs the restaurant. It's most fun to head for Rusty's for a casual meal with the kids.

Dixie Crossroads

1475 Garden Street, Titusville. Exit 80 off I-95 E., go 2 miles • (321) 268-5000

Meals served - Lunch and dinner

Cuisine - Seafood

Entree range - $5.95–18.95

Kids menu - Yes

Reservations - Accepted

Payment - All major credit cards accepted; no checks

Although this is a large restaurant (with a seating capacity of more than 400), they don't compromise on quality. Crossroads will only offer seafood items from local waters; their policy guarantees freshness and lower prices. Usually, about six local seafood items are offered—caught by fisherman in the area fishing exclusively for the restaurant. One of the most popular items is the rock shrimp, and the Crossroads goes through about 1,000 pounds a day. The Indian River mullet is also very popular. The dishes aren't fancy—most of the seafood is broiled, steamed, fried, and sometimes smoked, but it's always good, fresh, and inexpensive. Entrees are served with all the fixins, including shrimp or vegetable soup, salad or starch, and their famous corn fritters. The kids menu is small, but there is a fenced-in play area adjoining the restaurant—perfect for restless little ones.

El Charro

1916 Florida Ave., Coca Village • (321) 639-1004

Meals served - Lunch and dinner, closed Sundays

Cuisine - Mexican

Entree range - $4–10

Kids menu - Yes

Reservations - Accepted

Payment - All major credit cards

This is where the locals head for home-style Mexican dinners, icy margaritas, sangria, and Bohemia beer, all served by a friendly wait staff that treats everyone like family. For a real south-of-the-border experience, skip the ordinary (but delicious) tacos and nachos and try something that's not on every menu: "chilaquiles" made with tart tomatillos, homemade pork tamales, or "pechugas gratinada," a cheesy casserole with chicken, bell peppers, onion, and tomato. Deep-fried beef or chicken flautas are a house specialty, topped with guacamole. A generous helping of beans and rice accompanies each dish. No matter what time of day, a siesta is in order after this food fest.

JB's Fish Camp

859 Pompano Avenue, New Smyrna Beach • (386) 427-5747

Meals served - Lunch and dinner

Cuisine - Seafood

Entree Range: $5–15

Kids menu - No

Reservations - No

Payment - All major credit cards

First-time diners may think twice about eating at JB's, but don't let the dirt parking lot, picnic tables, or unairconditioned dining room fool you. Don't bother with the fried foods, instead order different types of seafood by the quarter or half-pound and share (the spiced rock shrimp is wonderful) or order the blackened fish.

FREE . . . OR ALMOST FREE IN COCOA BEACH

Ron Jon Surf Shop Dude, visitors have to see this amazing surfer's paradise. Purchase your beachwear here, but the store also carries in-line skates, surfboards, and diving equipment. Equipment such as boogie boards and beach bikes are also available for rent. Open daily, 24 hours. Admission is free. Handicapped-accessible facilities. Located at 4151 N. Atlantic Avenue, between Dixie and Hernando, one block from the beach on 520 and A1A; (321) 799-8888; www.ronjons.com.

Cocoa Beach Pier Shop, play in the arcade, eat ice cream in the parlor, or dine in any of the three restaurants—all on an 800-foot pier overlooking the Atlantic Ocean. Oh, we almost forgot—you can fish here, too. 401 Meade Avenue, Cocoa Beach; (321) 783-7549.

Vero Beach

Vero is the ideal spot for a quiet family getaway. Orlando may have the theme parks, and Miami the club scene, but Vero is famous for what it doesn't have: smog, traffic, congestion, and long lines. Indian River County and St. Lucie County to the south make up Florida's Treasure Coast, named for the treasure-laden Spanish galleons that sank offshore.

Indian River County is known for its oranges and grapefruit, and for first-rate saltwater fishing. The beaches are beautiful, and Vero Beach itself is known as a premier resort community with excellent shopping and award-winning restaurants.

Family Resorts

Aquarius Oceanfront Resort (South Beach Location)

1526 Ocean Drive, Vero Beach • (561) 231-5218

One of the resort's brochures, says "the Aquarius is a great place to stay and do nothing." And when you're staying on the beach, there's no better time for you and your family to kick back and do nothing. The deck area has lighted tiki huts, barbecues, shuffleboard courts, and heated swimming pools. Each room has a full kitchen. Oceanview rates May–December start at $80 for a standard room (two double beds); December–January, $90; February–April, $100.

Disney Vacation Club Vero Beach

9250 Island Grove Terrace, Vero Beach • (800) 359-8000 • www.dvcresorts.com

Although this resort is officially part of Disney's "vacation ownership program," you can book a room here if you're not a member. The resort is perfect in typical Disney fashion, and AAA agrees. The resort received the prestigious 4 Diamond Award from AAA in 1995, its first year of

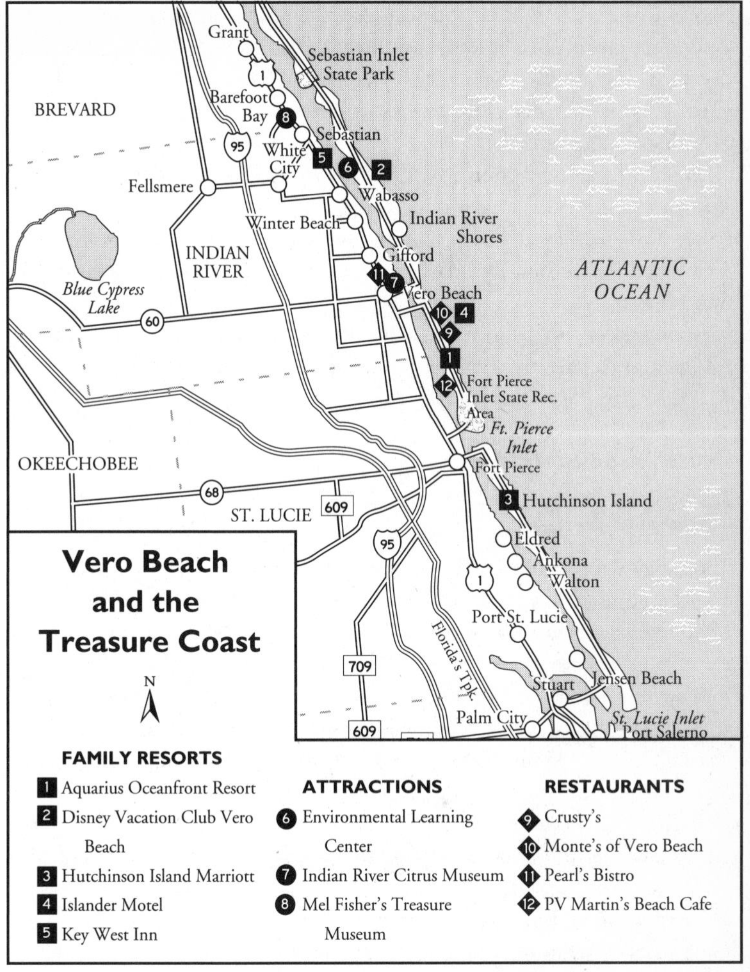

operation. All 115 rooms in the inn overlook a garden or the ocean, and there are 60 vacation villas.

The beautiful resort has two restaurants, a pool bar and grill, an ocean view lounge, a general store, a kids camp, a nine-hole minigolf course, a croquet lawn, a themed pool with a spiral slide, and an exercise facility. The kids camp, 2DC (a.k.a. Disney Discovery Club), is for children ages 3–14. On half-day adventures, your kids will be taken to area attractions such as the Environmental Learning Center or Adam's Ranch, a 20,000-acre working cattle ranch. Evening programs range from Surf and Turf

Sports Camp, where your kids can test their skills in archery and lawn games, ice cream socials, and campfires (they include marshmallows and campfire sing-alongs...you may be tempted to crash the party, and that's OK). Cost is $25 per child for resort guests; $20 per child for Disney Vacation Club members.

There are plenty of coordinated outdoor excursions for the whole family, from sunset river cruises to oceanside campfires. In June and July the resort hosts turtle watches in conjunction with the Department of Environmental Protection, Florida Marine Conservation, and Sebastian Inlet State Park.

Rooms sleep up to four and all have either a full kitchen or mini-refrigerator, microwave, and coffeemaker. June–December rates start at $205, January–May they start at $295.

Hutchinson Island Marriott

555 NE Ocean Boulevard, Stuart • (561) 225-3700 or (800) 775-5936
www.flortidatreasures.com

Tucked away on Hutchinson Island, Hutchinson Island Marriott Resort is edged on one side by the ocean and by the Indian River on the other. The resort stretches across 200 acres, with 298 rooms and suites (all with refrigerators and coffeemakers, some with wet bars), three nearby golf courses, four swimming pools, 13 tennis courts, and a marina with guided fishing trips. On the beach, you can rent sailboats, kayaks, and Waverunners, or go parasailing. The Kolius Sailing School offers lessons during peak season, and there are year-round guided eco-tours to explore the area's natural surroundings. The resort has its own boat, the *Island Princess,* that holds up to 149 passengers and offers an enjoyable nature cruise into the wilds of the St. Lucie Inlet Park, an uninhabited wildlife refuge.

The Pineapple Bunch Kids Camp offers everything from bike hikes to nature walks, swimming, and arts and crafts for ages 4–12. Cost is $25, including lunch. Kids Night Out for ages 4–12 is every Saturday, 6–9 p.m., for $18, including dinner. There are also special activities planned for teenagers, like movie nights, fishing trips, and rollerblading parties. Room rates start at $109 in the summer, $199 in the winter.

Islander Inn

3101 Ocean Drive, Vero Beach • (800) 952-5886 or (561) 231-4431

Enjoy the convenience of being about a two-minute walk from the beach without paying on-the-beach prices. Although there are no ocean views, the motel overlooks Humiston Park, which provides direct access to the beach. There are only 16 rooms, all recently refurbished, which means personal attention for each guest. Each room has a snack-size refrigerator (efficiencies include two-burner stoves and microwaves); several have private decks. Every room overlooks the courtyard or pool. Rent a bike to cruise the neighborhood, or head to the beach with a novel from the motel's lending library of about 30 books. You can even have a cookout at the public barbecue area. Rates range from $99–124 in the peak season, $59–94 in off-season (April 15–December 23).

Key West Inn

1580 US 1, Sebastian • (561) 388-8588 or (800) 833-0555 • www.keywestinn.net

Although this hotel chain thrives in Alabama, Georgia, Mississippi, and Tennessee, it's right at home in Florida. You'll get the charm of Key West, complete with tropical colors, lattice porches and waterfront views—without the lengthy drives to the southernmost Key. Suites, kitchenettes, and efficiencies are available, as well as kids' suites. There are coffeemakers in each room, and there's a complimentary breakfast bar. Rates vary only about $10 between season, but range from $79–154 depending on the type of accommodations you're looking for, from standard rooms to rooms with lofts that overlook the marina.

Attractions

Environmental Learning Center

255 Live Oak Drive, Vero Beach • (561) 589-5050

Hours - Weekdays, 9 a.m.–4 p.m.; Saturday 9 a.m.–4 p.m.; closed Sunday

Admission - Free

Appeal by Age Group -

Pre-school ★★	Teens ★★★	Over 30 ★★★★
Grade school ★★★★	Young Adults ★★★	Seniors ★★★★

Touring Time - Average 2 hours; minimum 1½ hours

Rainy-Day Touring - OK for indoors but not for outdoor part

Author's Rating - ★★★; lots of first-person learning

Restaurants - Picnic area

Alcoholic beverages - No

Handicapped access - Yes

Wheelchair rental - No

Baby stroller rental - No

Lockers - No

Pet kennels - No

Rain check - No

Private tours - Yes

Description and Comments Wet labs and dry labs? Bring back bad memories of chemistry class? Don't be alarmed, you and your kids will get a huge kick out of the Environmental Learning Center (ELC) located on Wabasso Island in Indian River County. The center encourages guests to become familiar with their surroundings and teaches visitors to respect and appreciate nature. The center also teaches us to preserve our national treasures. Although it is a learning center, there are no lectures here . . . but your whole family will learn valuable information about the environment.

Visit the wet lab, home of the fish and snakes. In the dry lab, you'll find computers that take you through the center's grounds. Hands-on exhibit areas let you pick up skeletons, shells, and other remnants of marine life. You can even slide them under a microscope for a closer look. The outdoor laboratory is just as impressive. Visit the butterfly gazebo or stroll the grounds to look at the trees and flowers—everything is labeled.

The center is a private, not-for-profit organization and is staffed by a wonderful group of volunteers. Hour-long guided tours through the center's trails allow you to get to know your guide. One very popular volunteer is Lee, a 95-year-old woman who knows her nature. Guided walking tours are offered Saturday at 1:30 p.m. and other times, but guests are free to explore the area on their own.

If you're planning your vacation in the Vero area and your family is into the outdoors, call ahead for an ELC program schedule. Special programs let you talk to a "sharkologist" or track dolphins in the Indian River Lagoon. The cost of the programs is usually $3–4. Guests must preregister for these programs and can do so by calling the main number.

PLAY BALL

Dodgertown is the Los Angeles Dodgers' spring-training headquarters, where you can watch your favorite players in the intimate setting of Holman Stadium. Exhibition games are from March to early April; the Vero Beach Dodgers regular season games are from mid-April to early September. Located at 3901 26th Street (take I-95 to SR 60; go east to Vero Beach; turn left on 43rd Avenue and follow the signs); (561) 569-4900; for ticket information (561) 569-6858.

Indian River Citrus Museum

2140 4th Ave., Vero Beach • (561) 770-2263

Hours - 10 a.m.–4 p.m. Tuesday–Friday

Admission - Donation of $1 adults, 50 cents children

Appeal by Age Group -

Pre-school ★	Teens ★★	Over 30 ★★
Grade school ★★	Young Adults ★★	Seniors ★★

Touring Time - Minimum an hour

Rainy-Day Touring - Recommended

Author's Rating - ★★; a little history lesson never hurt anyone

Restaurants - No **Alcoholic beverages -** No

Handicapped access - Yes **Wheelchair rental -** No

Baby stroller rental - No **Lockers -** No

Pet kennels - No **Rain check -** No

Private tours - No

Description and Comments If it's raining, this museum is a brief diversion, showcasing how Florida's citrus industry got its start in Indian River County. Displays take you back to the days when citrus crate labels were works of art. It won't hold the kid's attention for too long, but it's intriguing to check out the old photographs, antiques, farm tools, and memorabilia that stretch back to the 1800s. Might come in handy for a school report.

MCKEE BOTANICAL GARDEN'S COMEBACK

Once a blooming beauty, this botanical garden was neglected in the 1970s after theme parks entered the tourism scene. The competition forced McKee to close its doors in 1976, despite the historical significance of the site. Landscape architect William Lyman Phillips, of the esteemed firm of Frederick Law Olmsted, designed the garden in 1932, and it became home to an amazing collection of water lilies and orchids. In 1995, the Indian River Land Trust purchased the property and began the garden's revival. It's now on the National Register of Historic Places and features ponds filled with water lilies, along with palms, ferns, and more. For more information, call (561) 794-0601.

Mel Fisher's Treasure Museum

N. US 1, Sebastian • (561) 589-9874

Hours - Monday–Saturday, 10 a.m.–5 p.m.; Sunday, noon–5 p.m.

Admission - \$5 for adults, \$4 for seniors 55 and older, \$1.50 for children ages 6–12, free for children ages 5 and under

Appeal by Age Group -

Pre-school ★★	Teens ★★★	Over 30 ★★★
Grade school ★★★★	Young Adults ★★★	Seniors ★★★★

Touring Time - Average 1½ hours; minimum 1 hour

Rainy-Day Touring - Recommended

Author's Rating - ★★★; great fun to see all the stuff Mel dredged up

Restaurants - No **Alcoholic beverages -** No

Handicapped access - Yes
Wheelchair rental - No
Baby stroller rental - No
Lockers - No
Pet kennels - No
Rain check - No
Private tours - Yes

Description and Comments Visitors can actually pick up a $250,000 gold bar from the ship *Atochia,* found off of Key West by Fisher in 1985.

Family-Friendly Restaurants

Crusty's

1050 Easterlily Lane (off Ocean Drive), Vero Beach • (561) 231-4728

Meals served - Lunch and dinner

Cuisine - American, seafood, Italian

Entree range - $9.95–23.95

Kids menu - No, but the menu has items (pizza, hamburgers, hot dogs) that kids love

Reservations - Not accepted

Payment - All major credit cards accepted

You can almost dip your toes in the ocean at Crusty's, just steps from the Atlantic. The view is lovely, and the homemade soup is filling after a day spent playing at the beach. The blackened and mesquite-style fresh fish is in great demand, and there's a raw bar if you're eating light.

Monte's of Vero Beach

1517 S. Ocean Drive, Vero Beach • (561) 231-6612

Meals served - Dinner

Cuisine - Italian, American

Entree range - $7.95–36

Kids menu - No

Reservations - Strongly recommended

Payment - All major credit cards accepted

We were intrigued when we discovered that former Dodger manager Tommy Lasorda frequented this restaurant during his days at spring training camps in Vero Beach. If anyone knows Italian food, it's Tommy. But when asked if the restaurant was family-friendly, the reply was, "Let's put it this way. We don't have high-chairs. We don't cater to children, but they are welcome . . . especially if they are well-behaved." Kids . . . consider yourselves warned. This is not a place for young children, but if you're the parents of teenagers you all may enjoy a great, authentic Italian meal.

Pearl's Bistro

56 Royal Palm Boulevard, Vero Beach • (561) 778-2950

Meals served - Lunch and dinner

Cuisine - Island-style seafood

Entree range - Lunch $5.25–7.25; dinner $10.95–19.95

Kids menu - No, but the menu has items for kids such as chicken fingers and pasta

Reservations - Suggested for dinner; accepted at lunch for 5 or more

Payment - Visa, MC, AmEx

Authentic Caribbean food, like Jamaican jerk shrimp, coconut fried shrimp, and a barbecued Key West–style dolphin steak, is served in this tiny restaurant tucked away in a strip mall.

PV Martin's Beach Cafe

5150 N. A1A, N. Hutchinson Island • (561) 465-7300
www.pcpalm.com/sites/pvmartins

Meals served - Dinner and Sunday brunch

Cuisine - Seafood

Entree range - $13.95–34.95

Kids menu - Yes

Reservations - Suggested

Payment - All major credit cards accepted

Their delicate Indian River crab cakes and fresh Florida pompano are popular creations. Families can fill up at the evening buffets, with bargain nights on Wednesday and Thursday, seafood on Mondays and Fridays.

Side Trips

Club Med Sandpiper, Port St. Lucie On the banks of the St. Lucie River in Port St. Lucie (about 45 minutes south of Vero Beach), Club Med operates one of its extravagant family resorts exclusively for members. It's more like a country club, catering to active families who want to sail, golf, play tennis, water ski. Activities really are nonstop here, even for the little ones—starting at four months old in the Baby Club.

This Club Med is noted for its golf program; there are two 18-hole golf courses and a golf academy with access to a Jack Nicklaus course as well as two PGA courses. But kids give the high marks to the circus workshop that teaches juggling, trampoline jumping, and tightrope-walking tricks. And you can take your pick from four swimming pools (one just for the kids), nine Plexipave tennis courts, and a fitness center. There are 664 rooms (all with mini-refrigerators), three restaurants, a central bar, theater, and disco. A free shuttle whisks you to the Atlantic Ocean, 20 minutes away.

The vacation costs approximately $1,000–1,500 per adult, $400–900 per child ages 4–11, and $280–500 per child ages 2–3, per week, depending on the season. This rate includes three meals daily including beer and wine, supervised kids' club activities, sailing, water polo, tennis, and much more (although golfing fees are extra). Along with these costs, there is also a membership fee when you book the reservation ($55 per adult, $25 per child under 12). For parents who want to leave the decision-making to others while on vacation, this may be the place for you. Club Med—Sandpiper, 3500 SE Morningside Boulevard, Port St. Lucie 34952; (561) 398-5100 or (800) 258-2633.

Part Four

Orlando, Walt Disney World, and Beyond

Mention Central Florida and the first notion that comes to mind is Walt Disney World. Though the center of the Sunshine State encompasses everything from the solitude and beauty of Ocala National Forest to the frenzy of the Central Florida attractions, most families flock to the world's number-one vacation destination to experience one thing: Disney.

But there's another side to Central Florida that families can enjoy—one of the country's largest national forests; more than 1,000 lakes and rivers for canoeing, kayaking, swimming, snorkeling, tubing, and skiing; and the largest rodeo in the Southeast.

When Walt Disney flew over the area and selected 28,000 acres on which to build his theme park, he jump-started a multibillion-dollar tourism industry and forever changed the face of sleepy Central Florida. Truth is, the attractions got their start way before Walt, back in the 1930s when Richard Pope bought 200 acres along the shores of Lake Eloise near Winter Haven and created a water-themed park called Cypress Gardens, with daily ski shows. Today, Walt Disney World, Universal Studios Florida, SeaWorld, and other attractions vie for the time (and dollars) of millions of vacationers.

New theme parks, hotels, and restaurants continue to open at an astounding pace—there are now more than 100,000 hotel rooms and dozens of man-made attractions that lure vacationers from around the world.

Beyond the glitz of the themed attractions, there are little towns such as Winter Park, where you can wander amid the world's most extensive collection of Tiffany glass in the Morse Museum of American Art; and Kissimmee, where camping, horseback riding, bass fishing, and the rodeo take precedence. The ocean may be miles away, but the lakes in Central Florida offer adventures from canoe rides to airboat treks through alligator country. Or you can traverse the St. John's River, the state's longest navigable waterway, by pontoon or on guided boat tours.

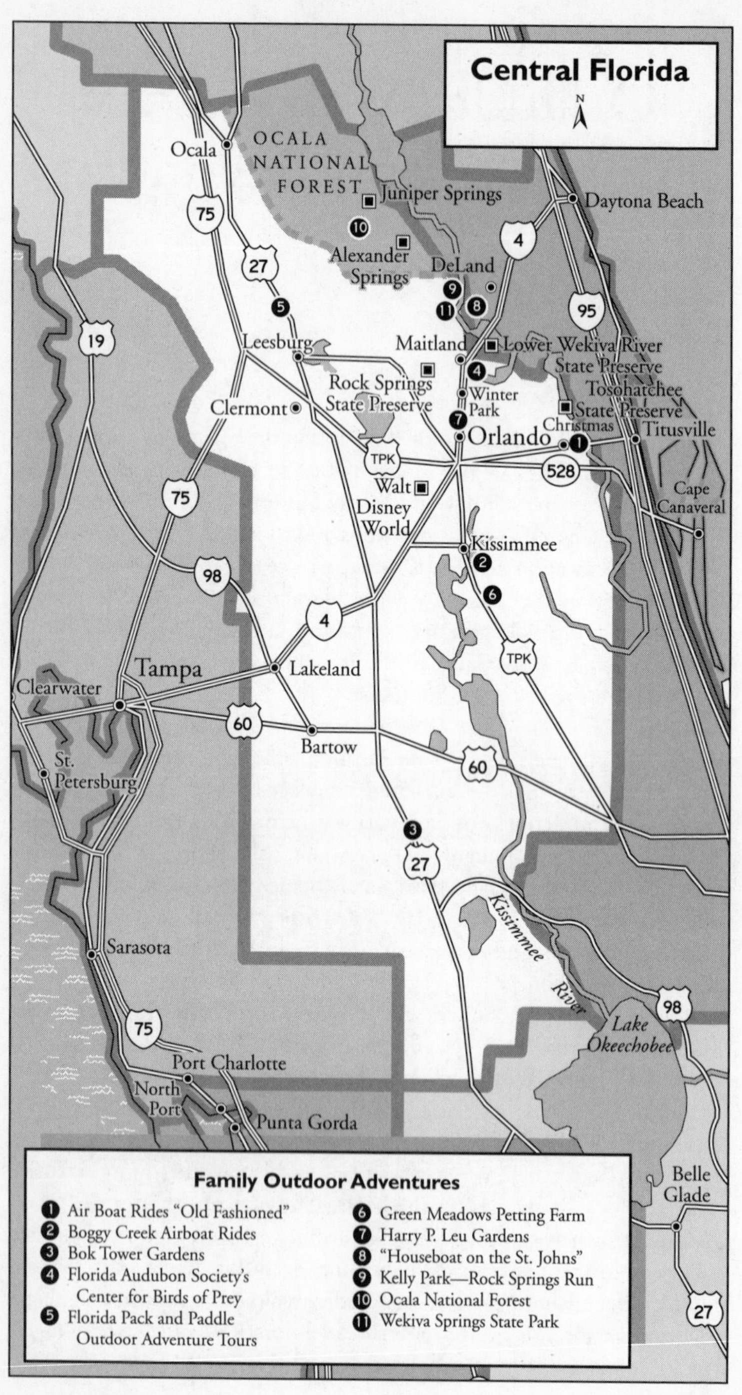
Central Florida
N
Ocala
OCALA
NATIONAL
FOREST
Juniper Springs
Daytona Beach
75
27
4
Alexander
Springs
DeLand
95
19
Leesburg
Maitland
Lower Wekiva River
State Preserve
Rock Springs
State Preserve
Winter
Park
Tosohatchee
State Preserve
Clermont
Christmas
Titusville
Orlando
TPK
528
Walt
Disney
World
Cape
Canaveral
75
Kissimmee
98
4
TPK
Tampa
Lakeland
Clearwater
60
Bartow
St.
Petersburg
60
27
Kissimmee
River
Sarasota
98
Lake
Okeechobee
75
Port Charlotte
North
Port
Punta Gorda
Belle
Glade
27
Family Outdoor Adventures
1 Air Boat Rides "Old Fashioned"
2 Boggy Creek Airboat Rides
3 Bok Tower Gardens
4 Florida Audubon Society's Center for Birds of Prey
5 Florida Pack and Paddle Outdoor Adventure Tours
6 Green Meadows Petting Farm
7 Harry P. Leu Gardens
8 "Houseboat on the St. Johns"
9 Kelly Park—Rock Springs Run
10 Ocala National Forest
11 Wekiva Springs State Park

To get "lost" in nature, visit Central Florida's northern boundary, a national forest administered by two ranger districts. Covering 378,178 acres , Ocala National Forest is divided into three recreation areas linked by a 65-mile-long trail. You can hike, fish, camp, snorkel, swim, and canoe.

Getting There

By Plane Two airports service Central Florida. Orlando International Airport is 7 miles south of Orlando; (407) 825-2001. Orlando-Sanford Airport is 2 miles east of Sanford; (407) 322-7771.

By Train Amtrak has four Central Florida stations: Sanford, downtown Winter Park, downtown Orlando, and Kissimmee. Daily trains originate in New York, Washington D.C., Tampa, and Miami; (800) USA-RAIL.

By Car Orlando is approximately in the center of the state, midway between Jacksonville and Miami. Major highways include I-4, which runs from Daytona Beach in the east to St. Petersburg on the west coast, through downtown Orlando and past the attractions; I-10, which enters the state at the southwest tip in Pensacola and extends to Jacksonville in the northeast; I-75, which enters Florida just south of Valdosta, Georgia, and runs south to Naples and then east to Ft. Lauderdale; I-95, which enters the state just north of Jacksonville and extends south to Miami; and the Florida Turnpike, which connects with I-75 south of Ocala, extending southeast through Orlando and continuing to Miami.

How to Get Information before You Go

Central Florida Visitors and Convention Bureau, P.O. Box 61, Cypress Gardens 33884; (800) 828-7655 (U.S. & Canada); www.cfdc.org/tourism.

Kissimmee–St. Cloud Convention and Visitors Bureau, 1925 E. Irlo Bronson Highway, Kissimmee 34744; (800) 327-9159 (U.S. & Canada); (800) 333-5477 (worldwide); www.floridakiss.com.

Lake County Convention and Visitors Bureau, 20763 US 27, Groveland 34736; (352) 429-3673 or (800) 798-1071 (U.S. only); www.lakecountyfl.com.

Orlando-Orange County Convention and Visitors Bureau, 6700 Forum Drive, Suite 100, Orlando 32821-8087; (800) 551-0181 (U.S. & Canada); www.toorlando.com. The bureau also has an office that's staffed and offers plenty of brochures and maps for area attractions at 8445 International Drive (in the Mercado Shopping Village). Also ask for the Magicard, for discounts of 10–50% on restaurants, attractions, car rentals, and more. They also sell discount tickets to many attractions (not Disney) at the International Drive location.

The Walt Disney Travel Company Walt Disney World Vacations Brochure, Walt Disney World, P.O. Box 10,000, Lake Buena Vista 32830-1000; (407) 934-7639 or (800) 327-2996; www.disneyworld.com.

Seminole County Convention and Visitors Bureau—Tourist Development Council, 105 International Parkway, Heathrow 32746; (407) 665-2900, or (800) 800-7832 (U.S. & Canada); www.visitseminole.com.

SHOULD YOU RENT A CAR?

More than a dozen rental car companies have fleets in Orlando, so shop for the best rates if you decide to rent. Mears Motor Transportation Service (call (407) 423-5566 or 422-4561) operates handicapped-accessible, air-conditioned shuttles that run from the baggage claim level at Orlando International Airport to area hotels, and they operate around the clock. Round-trip cost is about $25 per adult to the hotels near the attractions, $23 to downtown. Children ages 5–11 ride for $19 ($16 for downtown); children age 4 and under ride free. If you're here to see the big three—Disney, Universal, SeaWorld—many hotels offer a bus to the major attractions, so you can save on car rental. Transportation across Disney property is free if you're a Disney resort guest. International Drive offers efficient trolleys, called I-Ride, to carry you from one end of that street to the other, (407) 248-9590; www.mearstransportation.com). If you have small children, it's often convenient to have a car so you can return to your hotel on your own schedule.

Time of Year to Visit

If there is any way you can swing it, avoid the hot, crowded summer months. Try to go in October, November (except Thanksgiving), early December, January, February, March, or April (except Easter). If your kids are preschoolers, don't even think about going during the summer. If you have children of various ages and the school-age kids are good students, take the older ones out of school so you can visit during the cooler, less-congested off-season. Arrange special study assignments relating to the many educational aspects of Walt Disney World. If your school-age students cannot afford to miss any school, take your vacation as soon as the school year ends in late May or early June.

A Few Words of Advice

No matter how much diversity you'll find in Central Florida, the one reason most families come is to visit the theme parks. Walt Disney World in particular is a mammoth place, and it's tough to keep up a frantic pace for more than a day or two with kids in tow. Be sure to break up the days you spend in the theme park; sleep in some mornings, or take a day off and try an outdoor adventure. Your vacation will be much more memorable if it's not all about seeing every single attraction.

If Disney is tops on your to-do list, be sure you start with the Magic Kingdom, where most of the legendary characters and attractions are. But if you have teenagers looking for thrill rides, you might consider a day "riding the movies" at Universal Studios Florida or a roller-coaster or day trip to Busch Gardens in nearby Tampa.

Waiting Line Strategies

Central Florida is the land of long lines—plan on cooling your heels in the Magic Kingdom, Disney-MGM Studios, Epcot, Disney's Animal Kingdom, Universal, and SeaWorld, especially if you visit during peak seasons, including spring break, summertime, or Christmas. Even the water park slides have substantial lines. Children hold up better through the day if you minimize the time they have to spend in lines. Here are some ways to reduce stress on little ones:

Disney's FASTPASS System With this system, you can obtain a free FASTPASS ticket near the entrance to the most popular rides in all four Disney parks. The ticket designates a time to return and skip the regular line.

Line Games Watch for, and count, theme park characters, especially at Disney. Play a simple guessing game like 20 Questions. And if you're waiting in the holding area of a theater attraction, pull out a pen and some paper for a game of tic-tac-toe or hangman.

Last-Minute Entry Some shows accommodate a large number of people at one time—the *Liberty Belle* Riverboat in the Magic Kingdom, for example. The boat holds about 450, usually more than are waiting in line. So grab a snack, sit in the shade, and wait until the boat arrives and loading is well under way before you board.

At large capacity theater shows like *Terminator 2 3-D* at Universal Studios Florida, ask the entrance greeter how long it will be until guests are admitted. If it's 15 minutes or more, take a rest room break or have a snack, and return to the attraction just before the show starts.

The Hail-Mary Pass Certain lines are configured in such a way as to allow you and your smaller children to pass under the rail to join your partner just before actual boarding or entry. Take your child to rest, cool off, or go to the bathroom while another adult does the waiting. Other guests usually are understanding unless you try to pass older children or more than one adult under the rail.

Switching Off (also known as the Baby Swap) Disney, Universal, and SeaWorld all have rides with minimum height or age requirements, but couples with children too small or too young don't have to forgo these attractions or take turns riding separately. Take advantage of "switching off" or "the baby swap." To switch off, there must be at least two adults. Everybody waits in line together, adults and children. When you reach the ride attendant, say you want to switch off. The greeter will allow everyone to enter the attraction; when you reach the loading area, one adult will ride while the other stays with the kids. Then the riding adult disembarks and takes responsibility for the children while the other adult rides.

A third adult in the party can ride twice, once with each of the switching-off adults, so they do not have to experience the attraction alone.

Last-Minute Cold Feet If your child gets cold feet at the last minute, you can usually arrange with the loading attendant for a switch off.

Lost Children

Lost children do not usually pose much of a problem. All theme park employees are schooled in how to handle the situation should they encounter it. If you lose a child in any of the parks, report the situation to an employee, and then check in at Guest Services near the theme park's main entrance. Paging systems are not used in any of the parks, but in an emergency an "all points bulletin" can be issued throughout the park(s) via internal communications.

We suggest that children under age 8 be color-coded by dressing them in purple T-shirts or equally distinctive attire. It is also a good idea to sew a label into each child's shirt that states his or her name, your name, and the name of your hotel. The same thing can be accomplished less elegantly by writing the information on a strip of masking tape: hotel security professionals suggest the information be printed in small letters and the tape be affixed to the outside of the child's shirt 5 inches or so below the armpit.

Family Outdoor Adventures

Air Boat Rides "Old Fashion" See wild critters on this 90-minute private guided tour on real airboats on the St. John's River. 7 days a week, 24 hours a day. Adults $32; children age 12 and under $17. 24004 Sisler Avenue, Christmas; (407) 568-4307.

Boggy Creek Airboat Rides Half-hour ride covers 10 miles of wetlands and creeks with plenty of wildlife. U.S. Coast Guard–approved. Open daily, 9 a.m.–dusk. Adults $17.95; children age 12 and under $12.95. Nightly gator tours from 9–10 p.m. $25 all ages. 3702 Big Bass Road, Kissimmee; (407) 344-9550.

Bok Tower Gardens This is an incredibly beautiful setting, with a 57-bell carillon tower as its centerpiece, surrounded by 157 acres of gardens and nature trails. Bok Tower is listed in the National Register of Historic Places, dedicated to the American people by Edward Bok, a Dutch immigrant. There are daily bell serenades from the 205-foot "singing tower," which has been called one of the world's great carillons. The gardens are located on Iron Mountain, the Florida peninsula's highest point at 295 feet. Open daily, 8 a.m.–6 p.m. (last admission at 5 p.m.). Adults $6; children ages 5–12 $2; under 5 free. North of Lake Wales 3 miles, off CR17A (Burns Avenue) and Tower Boulevard, Lake Wales; (863) 676-1408.

Florida Audubon Society's Center for Birds of Prey Located just outside Seminole County, the Center for Birds of Prey is noted as the leading raptor rehabilitation center on the Eastern Seaboard. Thousands of birds—bald eagles and other raptors—have been released since 1979 after rehabilitation at the center. Birds that can't be released are housed at a lakeside aviary. Requested entry donations are $5 for adults; $4 for children ages 6–15. 1101 Maitland Way, Maitland; (407) 644-0190.

Florida Pack and Paddle Outdoor Adventure Tours This is the only full-service outdoor tour company in Central Florida that takes families canoeing, camping, and hiking to some of the best natural attractions in the area—Wekiva River, Ichetucknee Springs, the Suwannee, and Peace Rivers. They provide everything, including food, camping equipment, and guides. Trips can be as short as half a day or as long as six days; one-day trips start with a continental breakfast, a lunch, and a "farewell toast" at 4 p.m. The best time to go is spring or fall when there's a nice breeze. Overnight trips are recommended for kids 8 and older; the half-day canoe tours are recommended for kids 6 and older. 11025 SE Highway 192, Summerfield. Call (800) 297-8811 for rental rates and reservations.

Green Meadows Petting Farm For some people, this is as close to a real farm as they'll ever get. Milk a cow; feed the goats; pet a pig; ride a pony. Guided tours last 2 hours and end with a tractor-drawn hay ride. Daily, 9:30 a.m.–4 p.m. (farm closes at 5:30 p.m.); $15 per person, $13 Florida residents, free for children age 2 and under. 1368 S. Poinciana Boulevard, Kissimmee, 5 miles south of US 192; (407) 846-0770.

Harry P. Leu Gardens Camellias, palms, roses, and orchids are showcased in these magnificent gardens that include the Leu House Museum, a turn-of-the-century Florida farmhouse that's open for tours. Open daily, 9 a.m.–6 p.m.; closed Christmas. Adults $4, students (K–12) $1. 1920 N. Forest Avenue, Orlando; (407) 246-2620.

Houseboat on the St. John's Adventurous families can cruise the scenic St. John's River on a houseboat, for rent from the Hontoon Landing Marina. The boats sleep six to ten and are furnished with gas grills, cooking and eating utensils, linens, and even a microwave. Rentals start at $595 a day or $975 for a weekend (Friday–Sunday), and you're free to cruise as far south as Lake Monroe or as far north as Palatka. If you're planning a day or two on the boat, we recommend heading to Silver Glen Spring, about a 5½-hour ride, where you can anchor overnight and swim in the crystal-clear water. There's plenty of great fishing along the way. It takes no special training to operate a houseboat; most renters have never driven a houseboat, say the folks at Hontoon Landing. Just be sure to bring along mosquito repellent, especially in the summertime. Hontoon Landing Resort and Marina, 2317 River Ridge Road, DeLand 32720; (904) 734-2474 or (800) 248-2474; www.hontoon.com.

Kelly Park–Rock Springs Run This old park just north of Orlando has been a favorite of Central Floridians for generations. Bring an inner tube or snorkel and while away the day in the icy (72° year-round) water. Tubers, by the way, have right of way, but it's great fun and easy to snorkel along the 1.5-mile-long spring run with a sandy bottom and plenty of fish and turtles for viewing (no fishing allowed)—best in early morning, late afternoon, and weekdays, when the crowds haven't scared away the fish. Picnicking and camping available ($10, $18 with electric). Admission is $1 per person. Take I-4 to Exit 51, then west on Highway 46 and follow the signs to Kelly Park–Rock Springs Run; (407) 889-4179.

Ocala National Forest This 400,000-acre refuge for wildlife has a quartet of untamed springs, winding streams, and natural lakes that brighten one of the oldest national forests east of the Mississippi. There are also numerous hiking and horseback trails; perfect for families is the Juniper Nature Trail, complete with signs describing the fauna and ecology.

1. **Alexander Springs** This is the place for excellent swimming and snorkeling—the springs pumps out 76 million gallons of 72° water each day—also picnicking, canoe rentals, and camping ($15 site). Take US 441 to the intersection of SR 19 at Eustis; turn right at the overpass and follow SR 19 to SR 445. Turn right and follow the signs to the recreation area; (352) 669-3522.
2. **Silver Glen Springs** This spring is known for its thick grass beds, white sand bottom, and plenty of fish, like largemouth bass and striped bass in the spring. Beware, boat traffic on the half-mile spring run is especially heavy on the weekends. No fishing rentals. On SR 19 about 6 miles north of the SR 19–SR 40 intersection; (352) 685-2799.
3. **Salt Springs** There are three spring boils to snorkel around and a 5-mile run that leads to Lake George. There are gators along the way, so be especially careful during springtime mating season—and always leave the water if you spot one. On SR 19 in the town of Salt Springs; (352) 685-2048.
4. **Juniper Springs** This spring has a popular campground ($14 for tent camping, $16 for RV camping—no electricity) where you can't make reservations—it's first come, first served. The springs pump out 20 million gallons every day, ideal for swimming. There's also excellent canoeing on the 7-mile spring run. On SR 40 just west of SR 19; (352) 625-3147.

Wekiva Springs State Park The Wekiva River meanders 25 miles north of Orlando, a gin-clear ribbon of water fed by springs. Flat and gentle currents make it perfect for first-time canoers. The best backwoods canoeing starts on the north part of the river near Sanford. There's also biking over 8 miles of trail primarily intended for horseback riding (and the rolling terrain is prime habitat for black bears). This lush park contains almost 6,900 acres of wild scenery, with a main spring that pumps out 42 million gallons of water each day. Canoe rentals, walking trails, and camping are available. Admission is $4 per car. Located 15 miles northwest of Orlando (take I-4 to Exit 49 and follow the signs); (407) 884-2009.

Bicycling Central Florida

Rail Trails

General James A. Van Fleet Trail in the Green Swamp, Clermont Travel 29 miles from Mabel to Polk City through the Green Swamp, which is home to many varieties of wildlife and plant life. Trailheads at Green Pond and Mabel; (352) 394-2280.

♥ **West Orange Trail, Orlando** This paved trail is 19 miles from the Lake County line into Apopka. You can rent bikes and rollerblades from West Orange Trail Bikes & Blades Co. at 17914 SR 438 in Winter Garden located at the very western end of the West Orange Trail; (407) 877-0600.

Withlacoochee State Trail, Clermont With trailheads at Citrus Springs and SR 50, this 46-mile paved trail from Dunellon to Trilby passes through the Withlacoochee State Forest, Fort Cooper State Park, and rural areas. Forest, sandhill, and wetlands, with gopher tortoises, bobcats, deer, and turkeys; (352) 394-2280.

Mountain Biking

Lower Wekiva State Preserve A mile of trail and many miles of old logging trams (horseback riders share this trail). Off SR 46 near the Wekiva River; (407) 330-6725.

Orlando Wilderness Park Also near Christmas, this park offers 15–20 miles of easy, scenic riding, with spectacular bird life (especially in winter). The park is open from February 1 to September 30, dawn to dusk; (407) 568-1706.

Rock Springs State Preserve Off SR 46 in Lake County, where you can wander park roads and logging trams. Take plenty of water if you're riding in the summer—it's hot in the pine flats. Hunting is allowed in the fall, so call ahead; (407) 330-6725.

Tosohatchee State Reserve Near Christmas in East Orange County, on all roads in the park and on the orange-blazed trail (the white-blazed

A CALENDAR OF FESTIVALS AND EVENTS

January

Walt Disney World Marathon Families run the 5-K; some teenagers run the marathon. Open to physically challenged. (407) 824-4321.

Zora Neale Hurston Festival of Arts and Humanities Highlights the life and works of one of America's most celebrated collectors and interpreters of Southern and rural African-American culture through theatrical performances, educational programs, and art exhibits. Free; (407) 647-3307.

The Battle of Townsend's Plantation and Civil War Festival Step back into the Civil War era and experience plantation life through blacksmithing, butter churning, and can grinding demonstrations. The event, located at Renniger's Antique Center in Mount Dora, culminates with daily Civil War battle reenactments and a dress ball. Admission is $5 for adults, $1 for children age 12 and under; (407) 422-5560.

Indy 200 at Walt Disney World This 200-lap, 200-mile main event caps three days of exciting activities on the Walt Disney World Speedway as part of the Indy Racing league championship series events that lead to the Indianapolis 500. Tickets are available that provide admission and grandstand seating for all three days; (407) 839-3900.

Walt Disney World Festival of the Masters One of the South's largest juried art shows at Downtown Disney Marketplace the second weekend in November. Free; (407) 824-4321.

February

Silver Spurs Rodeo Legendary bull riders and cowboys have been competing since 1944 in this rodeo, the largest in the eastern United States and one of the top 20 in the country. Always the third week in February. Silver Spurs Arena, 1875 Irlo Bronson Memorial Highway (US 192) in Kissimmee. $10–17 for reserved seating; (407) 847-5118.

Florida Strawberry Festival It's berry picking time, and this fest features the sweetest berries in shortcakes, shakes, and other imaginative culinary creations. Also arts and crafts, country music, and amusement rides during the 11-day celebration. Plant City, I-4 West of Orlando; (813) 752-9194.

Cypress Gardens' Spring Lights Through April, more than 4 million twinkling lights magically transform the park's rolling terrain into a glowing, glistening fantasy land of whimsical garden creatures. Fanciful animated light sculptures include frogs, jungle plants, butterflies, sunflowers, swans, and other sequential and stationary light pieces. Boasts the world's tallest floral arrangement featuring an assortment of spring flowers in a kaleidoscope of color. Regular Cypress Gardens admission; (863) 324-2111.

International Carillon Festival at Bok Tower Gardens This annual event features guest performers from England, Australia, the University of California at Berkeley, and the University of Kansas. Other events include recitals, a special moonlight recital, lectures, exhibits, organ recitals, and choral concerts. Regular Bok Tower Gardens admission (adults $6, children ages 5–12 $2); (863) 676-1408.

Spring Training for the Houston Astros and Atlanta Braves Astros games through March or early April at Osceola County Stadium, 1000 Bill Beck Boulevard, Kissimmee; (407) 933-5400. The Braves practice at Disney's Wide World of Sports through April; (407) 363-6600.

March

Kissimmee Bluegrass Festival Major bluegrass and gospel entertainers from all across the United States perform in this four-day fest. Always the first weekend in March at the Silver Spurs Arena; (800) 473-7773.

Central Florida Fair Runs for 11 days in early March, at the Central Florida Fairgrounds, 4603 W. Colonial Drive; (407) 295-3247. Rides, shows, 4H and livestock exhibits, a petting zoo, and plenty of junk food.

Winter Park Sidewalk Art Festival Downtown Winter Park, showcases artists and artisans from all over the United States. Also, hands-on art activities for children. Always the third day of the third month, and runs for three days. (407) 644-8281.

Cypress Gardens Spring Flower Festival Through May, spring blooms with a unique award-winning display that features 24 larger-than-life floral topiaries—graceful swans, butterflies, peacocks, tropical fish, and a 19-foot Easter bunny. The only festival of its kind in the world, the event also includes 30,000 floral bed annuals. Regular Cypress Gardens admission; (863) 324-2111.

Mardi Gras at Universal Studios Florida The event redefines the spirit, soul, and sizzle that have made the world's biggest party an international legend. From top entertainment to float-filled, spectacular parades and food that slams its style home, Universal's backlot streets explode into a moving, pulsating street party. Mardi Gras is included in regular admission price; (407) 363-8000.

May

Epcot International Flower and Garden Festival Through June, more than 30 million blooms are showcased in Future World and World Showcase, including topiary and other Disney specialties. The month-long festival also includes free demonstrations and seminars. Regular Epcot admission; (407) 824-4321.

A CALENDAR OF FESTIVALS AND EVENTS *(continued)*

July

Independence Day The Fourth of July brings expanded fireworks to the Magic Kingdom at Walt Disney World; also fireworks at Disney-MGM Studios, Epcot, and SeaWorld.

Lake Eola Picnic in the Park Lake Eola celebrates the Fourth of July with games, activities, entertainment, and fireworks. This event has been held for more than 20 years. Free; (407) 246-2827.

October

Night of Joy The Magic Kingdom is home to this festival of contemporary Christian music featuring top artists. Teenagers flock to this event, and tickets go fast. Not included with regular admission. Call for exact dates; (407) 824-4321.

Halloween Horror Nights Universal Studios throws the best Halloween party in Central Florida, a 14-night event that showcases Universal's theatrical talents when monsters emerge to spook the masses. The famous Universal backlot is transformed into a maze of mystery with haunted houses, special shows, and hundreds of roaming monsters, mutants, and misfits. Teenagers love it; may be too intense for youngsters under age 10. Adults $42 ($59 includes after-hours party), children ages 3–9 $34 ($51 includes after-hours party); (407) 363-8000.

Mickey's Not-So-Scary Halloween Party Magic Kingdom, Walt Disney World Resort. This is the perfect party for little ones, complete with the Disney characters decked out in Halloween costumes. Not included with theme park admission. Tickets are cheaper if purchased in advance; (407) 824-4321.

Ghouls Night Out at Silver Springs Safe trick or treating for the entire family with games, magic shows, and decorated places to gather candy and other goodies. Also a Creepy Crawly Cruise and Creature Feature Show. Regular Silver Springs admission; (352) 236-2121.

Silver Spurs Rodeo Legendary bull riders and cowboys have been competing since 1944 in the rodeo. Ranked in the Professional Rodeo Cowboys Association's top 2%, the event draws 25,000 spectators and the world's top rodeo athletes for 6 days each February and October. Admission is $10-17 for reserved seating; (407) 847-5118.

Cypress Gardens' Halloween Party A safe and fun Halloween at Ghostly Gardens. Separate admission ticket required; (863) 324-2111.

Walt Disney World Teddy Bear and Doll Convention This popular convention features doll and teddy bear designers from all over the world. Some events are open to public at Epcot. (407) 824-4321.

November

Epcot International Food and Wine Festival This monthlong festival gets bigger and better every year, with wines from around the world poured from booths around World Showcase. Also appetizer-size portions of international cuisine. Free seminars and special dinners are held throughout the month. (407) 824-4321.

Cypress Gardens' Chrysanthemum Festival The largest display of its kind in the world, the festival features more than 3 million brilliant blooms in magnificent arches, "poodle" baskets, and various other arrangements. With a 35-foot cascading waterfall as its centerpiece, the annual mum festival also includes mum-filled gazebos and acres of flowering mum beds. Regular Cypress Park admission; (863) 324-2111.

Cypress Gardens Annual Poinsettia Festival and Garden of Lights Late November through mid-January there are more than 400,000 dazzling lights depicting children's favorite characters from the *Wizard of Oz, Cinderella,* and *Alladin,* plus 40,000 poinsettia blooms showcased at Cypress Gardens. Strolling carolers and a special music production are part of the event. Regular Cypress Park admission; (863) 324-2111.

Epcot Holidays around the World Through December, this holiday tradition features the Lights of Winter, a daily tree-lighting ceremony, *Holiday Illuminations,* themed storytellers, and special atmosphere entertainment. The highlighted event is the Candlelight Processional, featuring a celebrity narrator accompanied by a 450-voice choir and a 50-piece orchestra. Regular park admission; (407) 824-4321.

December

Harlem Globetrotters Holiday Series The famous Globetrotters show off at this annual event. Disney's Wide World of Sports complex; (407) 363-6600.

Holidays at Walt Disney World All the Disney theme parks and resorts are decked out, and special shows are presented throughout the month. Highlights includes Mickey's Very Merry Christmas Party on weekends in the Magic Kingdom and the Candlelight Procession at Epcot. Ticket prices vary; (407) 824-4321 (call (407) W-DISNEY for holiday packages). Candlelight Procession is free with Epcot admission.

Walt Disney World New Year's Eve Celebration New Year's Eve is celebrated in all three theme parks with special entertainment and fireworks, at Downtown Disney Pleasure Island, and at many of the Disney restaurants in the resorts. Also there are special parties for children at some Disney child-care centers in the resorts; (407) 824-4321.

trails are for hikers only). Plenty of wildlife. There's hunting in the fall, so call first to find out if there's a hunt scheduled; (407) 568-5893.

Orlando Magicard

This free card offers savings of 10–50% at 73 establishments, including attractions, accommodations, restaurants, shops, rental car companies, and more. To get a Magicard before you leave home, visit www.go2orlando.com, or call (800) 255-5786.

Walt Disney World

Walt Disney World encompasses 43 square miles, an area twice as large as Manhattan Island, or roughly the size of Boston. There are four theme parks, three water theme parks, a shopping, dining, and entertainment district, a competitive sports complex, several golf courses, hotels and campgrounds, more than 400 places to eat, four large interconnected lakes, and a complete transportation system consisting of four-lane highways, elevated monorails, and a system of canals.

If you are selecting among the tourist attractions in Florida, the question is not whether to visit Walt Disney World but how your family can see the best of the various Disney offerings with some economy of time, effort, and money.

Make no mistake, there is nothing on earth quite like Walt Disney World. Incredible in its scope, genius, beauty, and imagination, it is a joy and wonder for people of all ages. A fantasy, a dream, and a vision all rolled into one, it transcends simple entertainment, making us children and adventurers, freeing us for an hour or a day to live the dreams of our past, present, and future.

While dreams of visiting Walt Disney World are tantamount to Nirvana for a three-year-old and dear enough to melt the heart of any parent, the reality of actually taking that three-year-old (particularly during the summer) is usually a lot closer to agony than to ecstasy.

Most small children are about as picky about rides as they are about what they eat, and many preschoolers are intimidated by the friendly Disney characters. Few humans (of any age), moreover, are mentally and physically equipped to march all day in a throng of 50,000 people, not to mention the unrelenting Florida Sunday. Finally, would you be surprised to learn that almost 60% of preschoolers said the thing they like most about their Walt Disney World vacation was the hotel swimming pool?

When contemplating a Disney vacation with small children, anticipation is the name of the game. Here are some things you need to consider:

Age Although the color and festivity of Walt Disney World excite children of all ages, and while there are specific attractions that delight toddlers and preschoolers, the Disney entertainment mix is generally oriented to older kids and adults. We believe children need to be fairly mature 7-year-olds to appreciate the Magic Kingdom and a year or two older to get much out of Epcot or the Disney-MGM Studios.

Building Naps and Rest into Your Itinerary The Disney parks are huge, so don't try to see everything in one day. Tour in the early morning and return to your hotel around 11:30 a.m. for lunch, a swim, and a nice nap. Just be sure to hold on to your theme park tickets and have your hand stamped if you want to return later in the day.

Where to Stay The time and hassle involved in commuting to and from the theme parks will be somewhat lessened if you can afford to stay in Walt Disney World. But even if you lodge outside of Disney, it is imperative that you get small children out of the parks each day for a few hours to rest and recuperate.

Be in Touch with Your Feelings While we acknowledge that a Walt Disney World vacation seems like a major capital investment, remember that having fun is not necessarily the same thing as seeing everything. When you or your children start getting tired or irritable, call time out and regroup. Trust your instincts. What would really feel best right now? Another ride, a rest break with some ice cream, going back to the room for a nap?

The way to protect your investment is to stay happy and have a good time, whatever that takes. You do not have to meet a quota for experiencing a certain number of attractions or watching parades or anything else. It's your vacation; you can do what you want.

Building Endurance Though most children are active, their normal play habits usually do not condition them for the exertion, particularly the walking, required to tour a Disney theme park. We recommend initiating a program of family walks four to six weeks before your trip to get in shape.

Be Flexible Having a game plan does not mean forgoing spontaneity or sticking rigidly to the itinerary. Once again, listen to your intuition. Alter the plan if the situation warrants. Any day at Walt Disney World includes some surprises, so be prepared to roll with the punches.

Things You Forgot or Things You Ran Out Of Rain gear, diapers, diaper pins, formula, film, aspirin, topical sunburn treatments, and other sundries are for sale at all major theme parks and at Typhoon Lagoon, Blizzard Beach, River Country, and Pleasure Island. For some reason rain gear is a bargain, but most other items are pretty high priced. Ask for goods you do not see displayed; some are stored behind the counter.

Infants and Toddlers at Theme Parks The Magic Kingdom, Epcot, Disney-MGM Studios, and Disney's Animal Kingdom all have special centralized facilities for the care of infants and toddlers. Everything necessary for changing diapers, preparing formulas, warming bottles and food, and so on is available in ample quantity. A broad selection of baby supplies is for sale, and there are even rockers and special chairs for nursing mothers. In the Magic Kingdom, Baby Care is located next to the Crystal Palace at the end of Main Street. At Epcot, Baby Care is located to the right of Test Track in Future World. At Disney-MGM Studios, Baby Care is located in the Guest Services Building to the left of the entrance. At Disney's Animal Kingdom, it's next to the Creature Comforts shop in Safari Village. Dads are welcome at the centers. Also, changing tables have been placed in several men's rooms in the major theme parks.

Strollers Strollers are available for a modest rental fee at all three major theme parks, and the rental covers the entire day. If you rent a stroller at the Magic Kingdom and later decide to go to Epcot, Disney-MGM Studios, or Disney's Animal Kingdom, turn in your Magic Kingdom stroller and hang on to your rental receipt. When you arrive at the next park present your receipt. You will be issued another stroller without additional charge.

If you elect to go to your hotel for lunch, a swim, or a nap, and intend to return to the park, do not turn in your rental stroller. Simply park it near an attraction located close to the entrance, marking the stroller with something personal like a bandanna. When you come back after your break, your stroller will be right there waiting for you.

You can bring your own stroller, but only collapsible models are permitted on the Disney monorails and buses.

Lost Parents Always choose a meeting place in case you get separated; the guest relations office is a good place. Point out to your children that Disney employees wear name tags and tell them to go to one of the employees if they are lost.

10 Tips for an Optimum Disney Visit

1. Do your homework before you go. *The Unofficial Guide to Walt Disney World* offers touring plans, including one for families.
2. Let your children help with the planning—everyone can choose favorites that can be worked into the itinerary.
3. In spite of all your planning, be flexible once you arrive.
4. If you're planning to spend more than a couple of days at Disney, spring for a multiday pass. You'll save a few bucks and have the flexibility to move between the theme parks. Some passes even include admission to the water parks.

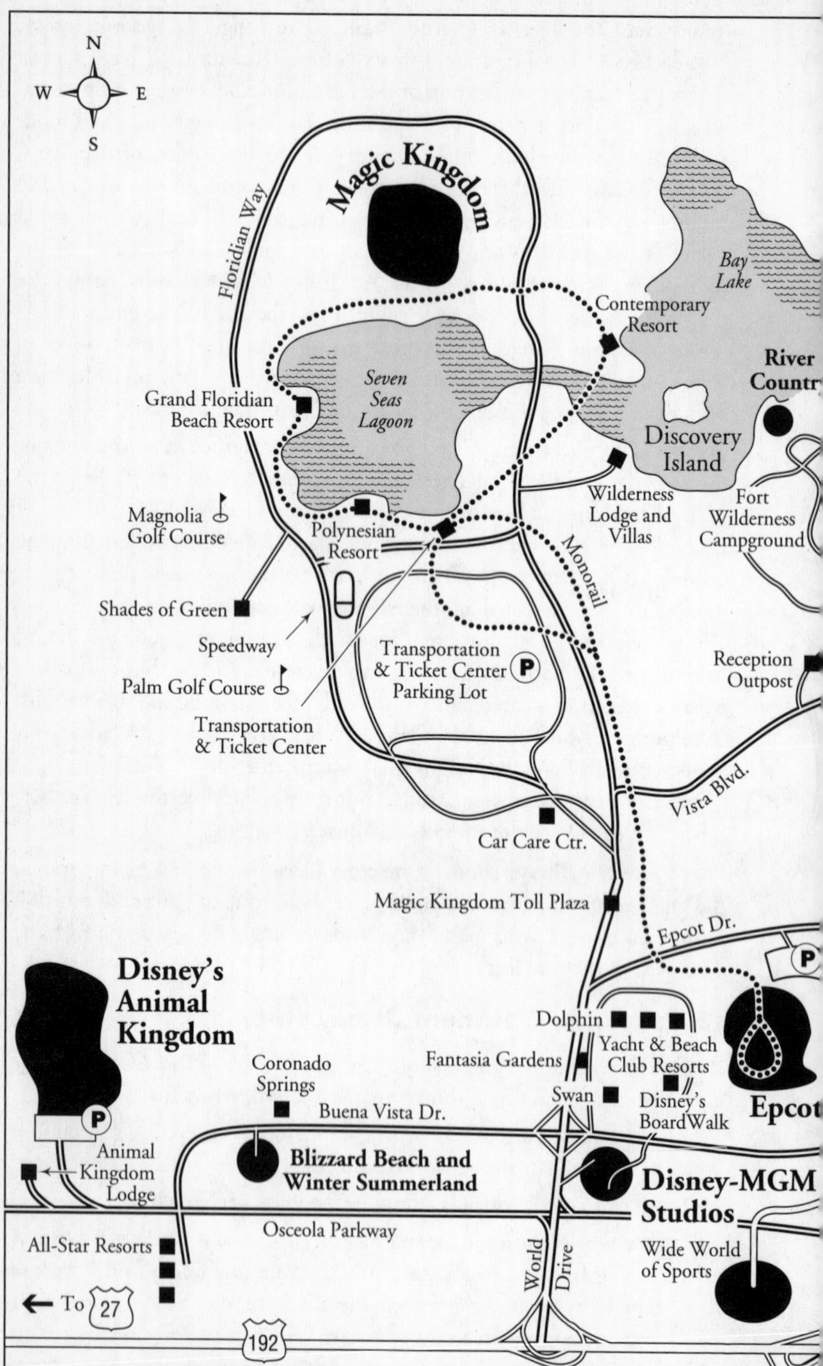
N
W
E
S
Magic Kingdom
Floridian Way
Bay Lake
Contemporary Resort
Seven Seas Lagoon
Grand Floridian Beach Resort
River Countr
Discovery Island
Wilderness Lodge and Villas
Fort Wilderness Campground
Magnolia Golf Course
Polynesian Resort
Monorail
Shades of Green
Speedway
Transportation & Ticket Center Parking Lot
P
Palm Golf Course
Transportation & Ticket Center
Reception Outpost
Vista Blvd.
Car Care Ctr.
Magic Kingdom Toll Plaza
Epcot Dr.
Disney's Animal Kingdom
Dolphin
Yacht & Beach Club Resorts
Fantasia Gardens
Coronado Springs
Swan
Disney's BoardWalk
Epcot
Buena Vista Dr.
Animal Kingdom Lodge
Blizzard Beach and Winter Summerland
Disney-MGM Studios
Osceola Parkway
All-Star Resorts
World Drive
Wide World of Sports
To 27
192

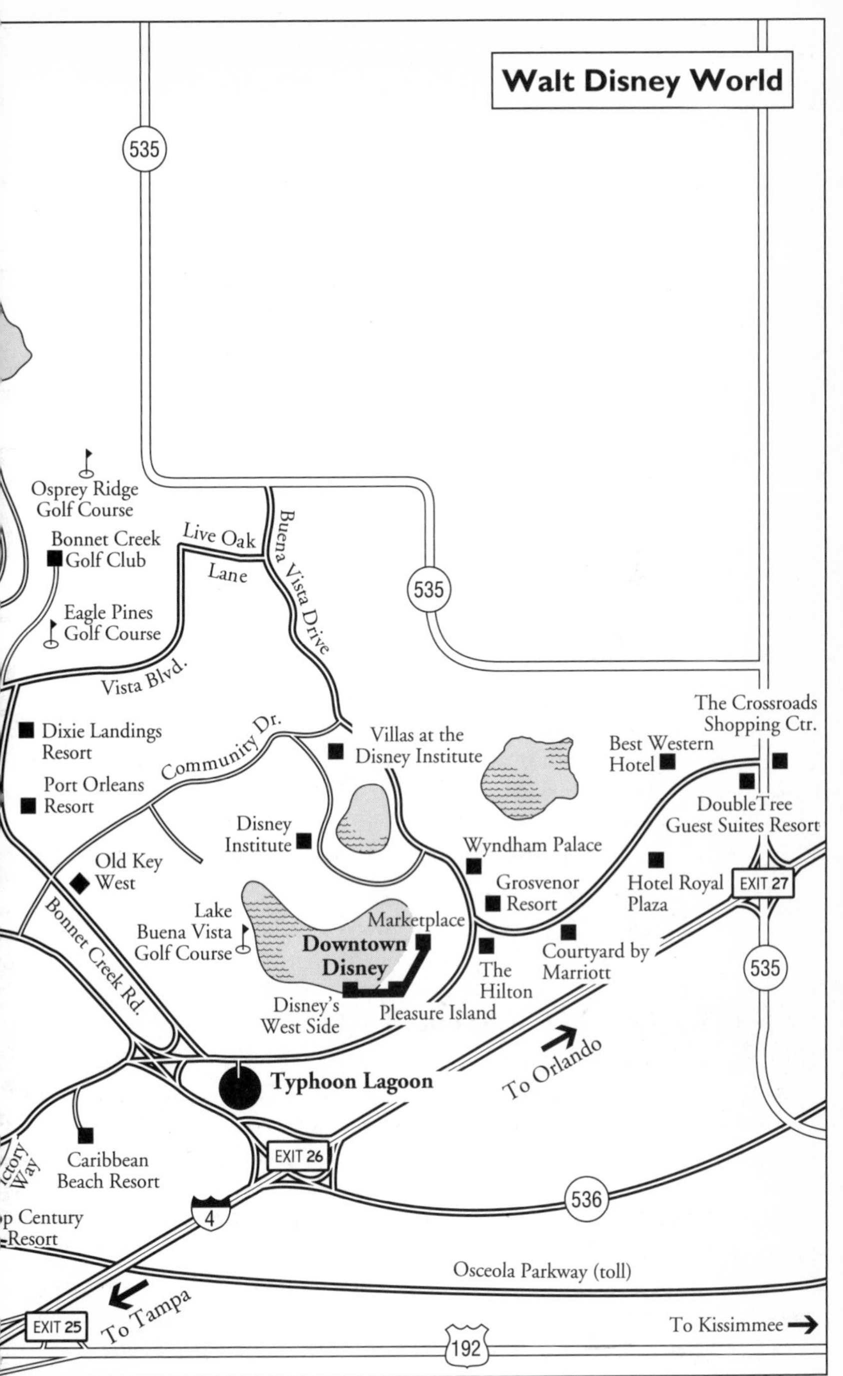

Walt Disney World
535
535
535
Osprey Ridge Golf Course
Bonnet Creek Golf Club
Eagle Pines Golf Course
Live Oak Lane
Buena Vista Drive
Vista Blvd.
Dixie Landings Resort
Port Orleans Resort
Community Dr.
Villas at the Disney Institute
Disney Institute
Old Key West
Bonnet Creek Rd.
Lake Buena Vista Golf Course
Marketplace
Downtown Disney
Disney's West Side
Pleasure Island
The Crossroads Shopping Ctr.
Best Western Hotel
DoubleTree Guest Suites Resort
Wyndham Palace
Grosvenor Resort
Hotel Royal Plaza
EXIT 27
Courtyard by Marriott
The Hilton
Typhoon Lagoon
To Orlando
Caribbean Beach Resort
EXIT 26
536
4
Osceola Parkway (toll)
To Tampa
EXIT 25
192
To Kissimmee

5. Start your day early—arrive at the parks at least 30 minutes before the scheduled opening and plan a break in the middle of the day, returning to your hotel for a swim or a nap, then back to the theme parks for the evening. Also, mix and match parks if you have a multiday pass; if you spent the morning in the Magic Kingdom, head to Epcot for dinner and fireworks.
6. Split up—let dad do the thrill rides with an older child while mom spends time in Fantasyland with younger siblings. If you have at least two teenagers, they can take off on their own, as the park is very safe. Just be sure to pick a meeting place, and advise them not to lose track of time.
7. If your budget is tight but you don't want to miss out on the themed restaurants, book lunch instead of dinner. Portions are generally huge, so you also can share meals. The top family choices in each park: Crystal Palace in the Magic Kingdom, 50s Prime Time Cafe at the Disney-MGM Studios, Italy or Mexico in World Showcase at Epcot, and Tusker House in Disney's Animal Kingdom.
8. Don't try to see it all. Enjoy what you can, and save some attractions for another visit.
9. Take a break from the theme parks. Even if you don't leave Disney property, you can play at one of the water parks or take an afternoon to visit Downtown Disney. The LEGO Imagination Center at the Downtown Disney Marketplace, for instance, keeps kids happy for hours; it's free; and there are benches for mom and dad.
10. Wait until it's time to go home to buy souvenirs. The kids will see so many things they want, and you won't waste money if they wait and anticipate one really special keepsake.

Should You Take Your Kids out of School?

If your children are good students, take them out of school so you can visit during the cooler, less-congested off-season. Arrange special study assignments relating to the many educational aspects of Walt Disney World. If your school-age students cannot afford to miss any school, take your vacation as soon as the school year ends in late May or early June. Nothing, repeat, nothing, will enhance your Walt Disney World vacation as much as avoiding summer months and holiday periods.

A week spent with family can be as enriching as classroom time. Use travel time for an impromptu geography lesson, using the destination maps in the back of the airline's in-flight magazine or a road map in your car, for instance. Epcot in particular offers opportunities for learning and having fun: the trip through the greenhouse in The Land, a visit to a coral reef in The Living Seas, a film journey to Canada or Japan in World Showcase. At the Disney-MGM Studios, there are great lessons in special effects (Indiana Jones Epic Stunt Spectacular), in animation (the Animation Tour) and sound effects (ABC Sound Studio). Your kids will experience science, technology, history, and geography, not just read about it.

Should You Book a Room at Disney?

Luxury accommodations can be found both in and out of Walt Disney World. Budget lodging, however, is another story. Room rates start at about $100 in Walt Disney World and range to more than $500. Outside Walt Disney World, rooms go for as low as $45.

There are specific privileges and amenities available to guests staying at a Walt Disney World resort:

Convenience Decreased commuting time made possible by proximity to the theme parks and easy access to the Walt Disney World bus, boat, and monorail transportation system. This is especially advantageous if you stay in one of the hotels connected by the monorail or by boat service. If you plan to use a car, however, dozens of hotels just outside Walt Disney World are a within a five- to ten-minute commute to the theme parks.

Baby-sitting and Childcare Alternatives A number of alternatives for baby-sitting, child care, and special children's programs are offered to Disney resort guests. Several of the resort hotels offer themed child care centers where potty-trained children ages 3–12 can be dropped off during the evening while adults go out. In-room baby-sitting is offered by Kinder-Care, (407) 827-5444.

Guaranteed Theme Park Admissions On days of unusually heavy attendance, Walt Disney World resort guests are guaranteed admission to the theme parks. (In practice, however, no guest is ever turned away until a theme park's parking lot is full.)

Children Sharing a Room with Their Parents There is no extra charge per night for children under 18 sharing a room with their parents (but that's also the case in many non-Disney hotels).

Free Parking. Walt Disney World resort guests with cars do not have to pay for parking in the theme park lots ($7 a day).

A Handful of Favorite Disney Resorts

Every Disney hotel is geared to families, and here are some of our favorites in a variety of price ranges. To book a room, call (407) W-DISNEY. Be sure to ask about seasonal specials or discount rates. Guests 17 and under stay free in their parents' room.

Disney's All-Star Resorts

Disney's best value has ample storage space and room for four in the room (luggage fits under the beds, for example), a food court for finicky eaters, and big swimming pools. Rates start at $77.

Disney's Animal Kingdom Lodge

Built in the middle of a 33-acre savannah filled with more than 100 animals and 100 birds, this 1,293-room resort is designed like an African village, with thatched ceilings and panoramic views of the animals. Most balconies overlook a giraffe, zebra, wildebeests, and other exotic animals roaming the spacious wildlife reserve, sometimes as close as 30 feet away. Restaurants offer African-inspired cuisine. Rates start at $194.

FAVORITE DISNEY EATS

There are more than 400 places to dine at Walt Disney World Resort, from quick service to fancy, award-winning restaurants. Every Disney restaurant offers a children's menu, with meals for about $5 at the quick-service restaurants, $7 at the sit-down restaurants. For families, we've chosen a few:

Best casual family dining Spoodles at Disney's Boardwalk Resort and Boma at Disney's Animal Kingdon Lodge

Great fresh pasta Alfredo's at Italy in World Showcase, Epcot

Tacos, burritos, and authentic Mexican goodies Mexico in World Showcase, Epcot

Best quick service in the Magic Kingdom Cosmic Ray's Starlight Cafe in New Tomorrowland, Magic Kingdom

Most entertaining Sci-Fi Dine-In Theater at Disney-MGM Studios; a seat next to the aquarium at Coral Reef in the Living Seas pavilion in Future World, Epcot; or a Disney character meal

Best all-around California Grill at Disney's Contemporary Resort

World's best milk shakes The peanut-butter-and-jelly shake at 50's Prime Time at the Disney-MGM Studios

Best family fun Hoop-Dee-Doo Musical Revue at Disney's Fort Wilderness Resort and Campground

Best hot dogs Sunset Market Ranch at Disney-MGM Studios

Best all-you-can-eat Whispering Canyon Cafe, where the food is served family style at your table, with plenty of meat and veggies. The staff encourages the kids to run around the room on stick ponies and indulge in plenty of other nonsense.

Disney's BoardWalk

A short stroll to Epcot and a boat ride to the Disney-MGM Studios, this fanciful resort was inspired by turn-of-the-century seaside resorts and includes tons of fun on a real boardwalk, from midway games to street musicians. There are plenty of free activities to keep the whole family entertained, and bicycles built for four (plus a front seat for kids too short to pedal) that you can take for a spin around the lake. Some of the accommodations are part of the Disney Vacation Club, with full kitchens and living rooms. Rates start at $319.

Disney's Polynesian Resort

Great for families because it's just across the Seven Seas Lagoon from the Magic Kingdom, a short monorail or boat ride away. Also, the hotel's Neverland Club gets the highest marks of any child-care service at Disney, with characters, Disney movies, and great kid food during the evening hours (a perfect way for mom and dad to carve out some quiet time). Rates start at $194.

Disney's Pop Century Resort

Temporarily closed as of press time, this 5,760-room resort is themed with pop icons—larger-than-life yo-yos, rollerblades, bowling pins, and more—to characterize each decade of the 20th century. Located adjacent to Disney's Wide World of Sports complex near Victory Way. Opening is set for early 2003 with rates comparable to All-Star Resort.

Disney's Port Orleans Resorts

This resort has one of the highest "guest satisfaction" ratings of any Disney hotel. Friendly service, spacious grounds, bicycling paths, two themed swimming pools, boats to rent, a playground, and even fishing at the Ol' Fishin' Hole. You can park near your room. Rates start at $133.

Disney Vacation Club Villas

If you want room to spread out, consider the Disney Vacation Club Villas, which are available to the public if members have not reserved them all. There are four choices, each with condo-like accommodations with one-, two- and three-bedroom units: Beach Club Villas and Disney's Yacht and Beach Club Resort; BoardWalk Villas; Villas at Disney's Wilderness Lodge; and Old Key West. Rates start in the $250 range for a one-bedroom unit complete with living room, VCR, full kitchen, and washer and dryer.

Disney's Yacht and Beach Club Resorts

This resort offers large rooms for four or five, walking distance to Epcot, and a boat ride to the Disney-MGM Studios, the best swimming pool at any Disney resort. Rates start at $194.

NEED A NIGHT OUT?

If you want to escape for a special evening alone with your spouse, Disney offers child care clubs at some hotels or in-room baby-sitting through Kinder-Care (call (407) 827-5444). Even if you're not staying in a Disney hotel, some of the clubs will take your child if you are having dinner at that Disney resort; just call ahead to check availability. Clubs operate afternoons and evenings. All require reservations.

Childcare Clubs

Hotel	Name of Program	Ages	Phone
BoardWalk Inn & Villas	Harbor Club	4–12	(407) 939-6301
Contemporary Resort	Mouseketeer Clubhouse	4–12	(407) 824-3038
Disney's Beach Club Resort	Sandcastle Club	4–12	(407) 934-8000
Grand Floridian Beach Resort	Mouseketeer Club	4–12	(407) 824-2985
The Hilton	All About Kids	4–12	(800) 728-6506
Polynesian Resort	NeverLand Club	4–12	(407) 939-3463
Wilderness Lodge Resort	Cub's Den	4–12	(407) 824-1083
Wyndham Palace	All about Kids	All	(407) 827-2727

Wilderness Cabins at Disney's Fort Wilderness Resort and Campground

These new log-cabin-like homes sleep six, and you're in the middle of peace and quiet. You can cook your own meals in the kitchen, and there's a private deck for dining under the pine trees. Rates start at $304.

Save Money with a Disney Club Card

Anyone can be a member of the club by calling (800) 49-DISNEY and paying $39.95 for a year's membership. Membership entitles you to variable discounts on Disney lodging and a 3–5% discount on theme park tickets, among other things. If you work for a large company or organization, ask your personnel department if the Magic Kingdom Club benefit is provided; it's often offered as a benefit by employers, credit unions, and organizations.

Lodging discounts are based on time of year. You must have your card in hand when making hotel reservations. Book your room at least four months in advance for the best possibility of getting the hotel of your choice.

The card also is worth a 10% discount in the Disney Store nationwide and even in the catalog. With kids, this can add up to big savings.

Magic Kingdom

The Magic Kingdom–Transportation and Ticket Center parking lot opens about 2 hours before the park's official opening time for the general public. After paying the parking fee, you board a tram for the Transportation and Ticket Center, where you can take either a monorail or a ferry to the entrance of the Magic Kingdom.

Entering Main Street, be sure to pick up a guide map at City Hall if you haven't been given one; it lists all attractions, shops, and eating places, as well as information about first aid, baby care, and entertainment for the day.

Main Street ends at a central hub, from which branch the entrances to five other sections of the Magic Kingdom: Adventureland, Frontierland, Liberty Square, Fantasyland, and Tomorrowland, in clockwise order. Mickey's Toontown Fair is wedged between Fantasyland and Tomorrowland and does not connect to the central hub.

Cinderella Castle is the entrance to Fantasyland and the focal landmark and visual center of the Magic Kingdom. It's a great place to meet if your family decides to split up for any reason or an emergency meeting place if you are accidentally separated.

Only five rides in the Magic Kingdom have age or height requirements: Splash Mountain, Space Mountain, Alien Encounter, Tomorrowland Speedway, and Big Thunder Mountain Railroad.

Avoid lines by taking advantage of FASTPASS, for Big Thunder Mountain Railroad, Buzz Lightyear's Space Ranger Spin, The Haunted Mansion, Jungle Cruise, The Many Adventures of Winnie the Pooh, Peter Pan's Flight, Space Mountain, Splash Mountain. To get a FASTPASS, insert your park ticket in the turnstile for a free FASTPASS ticket with your designated ride time.

FRIGHT-POTENTIAL CHART

On the following pages we have assigned a fright potential rating to each ride in the theme park.

A = not frightening in any way

B = scares some preschoolers

C = frightens many preschoolers

D = scares many children age 10 and under

F = potentially frightening to all ages

SMALL CHILD FRIGHT POTENTIAL

What It Is:	Fright Potential Rating
MAGIC KINGDOM	
Adventureland	
Enchanted Tiki Room: *Under New Management*	
Audio-Animatronic Pacific Island musical theater show	B
Jungle Cruise	
Outdoor safari-themed boat ride adventure	B
Magic Carpets of Aladdin	
A kid-friendly spin on elevated "carpets"	A
Pirates of the Caribbean	
Indoor pirate-themed adventure boat ride	C
Swiss Family Treehouse	
Outdoor walk-through treehouse	A
Fantasyland	
Ariel's Grotto	
Interactive fountain and character greeting area	A
Cinderella's Golden Carrousel	
Merry-go-round	A
Dumbo the Flying Elephant	
Disneyfied midway ride	A
It's a Small World	
World brotherhood–themed indoor boat ride	A
Mad Tea Party	
Midway-type spinning ride	B
The Many Adventures of Winnie the Pooh	
A ride through storybook pages	A
Mickey's Philharmagic Orchestra	
3-D movie starring Disney Character's	NA
Peter Pan's Flight	
Indoor fantasy adventure	B
Snow White's Scary Adventures	
Disney version of a spook-house track ride	C
Frontierland	
Big Thunder Mountain Railroad	
Tame Western mining-themed roller coaster	C
Country Bear Jamboree	
Audio-animatronic country hoe-down theater show	A
Diamond Horseshoe Saloon Revue	
Live Western song-and-dance show	A

AND ATTRACTION RATINGS: Magic Kingdom

Author's Rating	Pre-school	Grade School	Teens	Young Adults	Over 30	Senior Citizens
★★★½	★★★½	★★★★	★★★	★★★	★★★	★★★
★★★	★★★½	★★★½	★★½	★★★	★★★	★★★
★★	★★★	★★★	★★	★★	★★	★★
★★★★★	★★★	★★★★★	★★★★	★★★★	★★★★½	★★★★½
★★★	★★★	★★★½	★★★	★★★	★★★	★★★
★★★	★★★★★	★★★★	★★	★	★	★
★★★	★★★★	★★½	—	—	—	—
★★★	★★★★★	★★★★	★½	★½	★½	★½
★★★	★★★½	★★★	★★½	★★½	★★½	★★★
★★	★★★★	★★★★	★★★★	★★★	★★	★★
★★★	★★★★	★★★	★★	★	★	★★
	Ratings unavailable because attraction had not opened as of press time.					
★★★★	★★★½	★★★½	★★★½	★★★½	★★★½	★★★½
★★½	★	★★½	★★	★★½	★★½	★★½
★★★★	★★★	★★★★	★★★★	★★★★	★★★★	★★★
★★★	★★★½	★★★	★★½	★★★	★★★	★★★
★★★	★★	★★★	★★	★★★½	★★★½	★★★½

SMALL CHILD FRIGHT POTENTIAL

What It Is:	Fright Potential Rating
MAGIC KINGDOM *(continued)*	
Frontierland (continued)	
Frontierland Shootin' Arcade	
Electronic shooting gallery	A
Splash Mountain	
Indoor-outdoor water-flume adventure ride	D
Tom Sawyer Island and Fort Sam Clemens	
Outdoor walk-through exhibit and rustic playground	A
Liberty Square	
The Hall of Presidents	
Audio-animatronic historical theater presentation	A
The Haunted Mansion	
Haunted-house dark ride	C
***Liberty Belle* Riverboat**	
Hutdoor scenic boat ride	A
Mike Fink Keelboats	
Outdoor scenic boat ride	A
Main Street, USA (Entrance)	
Walt Disney World Railroad	
Scenic railroad ride around perimeter of the Magic Kingdom; also transportation to Frontierland and Mickey's Toontown Fair	A
Mickey's Toontown Fair	
Barnstormer at Goofy's Wiseacres Farm	
Small roller coaster	B
Donald's Boat	
Interactive fountain and playground	A
Mickey's Country House and Judges Tent	
Walk-through tour of Mickey's House	A
Minnie's Country House	
Walk-through exhibit	A
Toontown Hall of Fame	
Character-greeting venue	A
Alien Encounter: *The Extra TERRORestrial*	
Theater-in-the-round sci-fi horror show	F

AND ATTRACTION RATINGS: Magic Kingdom

Author's Rating	Pre-school	Grade School	Teens	Young Adults	Over 30	Senior Citizens
★½	★★★	★★★	★★★	★★	★★	★★
★★★★★	†	★★★★★	★★★★★	★★★★★	★★★★★	★★★½
★★★	★★★★★	★★★★★	★★	★★	★★	★★
★★★	★	★★½	★★★	★★★½	★★★★	★★★★
★★★★	★★★½	★★★★★	★★★★	★★★★	★★★★	★★★★
★★★½	★★★	★★½	★★★	★★★	★★★	★★★
★★	★★★½	★★★	★★★	★★★	★★★	★★★
★★½	★★★★	★★★	★★½	★★★	★★★½	★★★½
★★	★★★★	★★★	★★½	★★½	★★½	★★
★★½	★★★★	★★½	★	★½	★½	★½
★★★	★★★½	★★★	★★½	★★½	★★½	★★½
★★	★★★	★★★	★★½	★★½	★★½	★★½
★★	★★★★	★★★★	★★	★★	★★	★★
★★★	—	★★★½	★★★★	★★★★	★★★★	★★★

† Many preschoolers are too short to meet the height requirements and others are visually intimidated by watching the ride from standing in line. Of those preschoolers who actually ride, most give the attraction high marks (3–5 stars).

SMALL CHILD FRIGHT POTENTIAL

What It Is:	Fright Potential Rating
MAGIC KINGDOM *(continued)*	
Tomorrowland	
Astro Orbiter	
Buck Rogers–style rockets revolving around a central axis	B
Buzz Lightyear's Space Ranger Spin	
Whimsical space travel–themed indoor ride	A
Space Mountain	
Roller coaster in the dark	F
The Timekeeper	
Time travel movie adventure	B
Tomorrowland Indy Speedway	
Drive-'em-yourself miniature cars	A
Tomorrowland Transit Authority	
Scenic tour of Tomorrowland	A
Walt Disney's Carousel of Progress	
Audio-animatronic theater production	A

NOT TO BE MISSED AT THE MAGIC KINGDOM

Adventureland	Pirates of the Caribbean
Frontierland	Big Thunder Mountain Railroad
	Splash Mountain
Liberty Square	The Haunted Mansion
Tomorrowland	Space Mountain
Special Events	SpectroMagic evening parade
If your kids are under age 6	
Adventureland	Jungle Cruise
Fantasyland	Dumbo, the Flying Elephant
	It's a Small World
Frontierland	*Country Bear Jamboree*
	Tom Sawyer Island
Mickey's Toontown Fair	All attractions geared to youngsters
Special Events	3 p.m. parade
Tomorrowland	Astro Orbiter
	Tomorrowland Speedway

AND ATTRACTION RATINGS: Magic Kingdom

Author's Rating	Pre-school	Grade School	Teens	Young Adults	Over 30	Senior Citizens
★★	★★★★	★★★	★★½	★★½	★★	★
★★★★	★★★★	★★★★	★★★	★★	★	★
★★★★	†	★★★★★	★★★★★	★★★★½	★★★★	†
★★★★	★★	★★★½	★★★½	★★★½	★★★★	★★★★
★	★★★★	★★★	★	½	½	½
★★★	★★★½	★★★	★★½	★★½	★★½	★★★
★★★	★★	★★★	★★★	★★★	★★★	★★★★

WHERE CAN YOU FIND THE DISNEY CHARACTERS?

Consult the daily entertainment schedule for each park. You'll always find them in Toontown Fair in the Magic Kingdom, Camp Minnie-Mickey at Disney's Animal Kingdom, and along Mickey Avenue at the Disney-MGM Studios. Epcot isn't always a sure thing, but characters often are in World Showcase countries—Pinocchio in Germany, Belle and the Beast in France, Mary Poppins or Winnie the Pooh in the United Kingdom, Aladdin and Jasmine in Morocco. If you spring for one of the Disney character meals, you're guaranteed a stop at your table by the characters. The meals are in select restaurants in the theme parks and Disney resorts, with an abundance of food and plenty of time to mingle with the characters. For information and reservations, call (407) 939-3463 (WDW-DINE).

† Some preschoolers loved Space Mountain, others were frightened. The sample size of senior citizens who experienced this ride was too small to develop an accurate rating.

Epcot

Though this theme park is more of an adult place than the Magic Kingdom, our children love to spend a day here. For starters, there are few lines and plenty of interactive attractions—even the entertainers, many performing outdoors in World Showcase, do their best to involve willing youngsters. And it always seems less crowded than the other theme parks.

Disney has combined two vastly different areas—Future World and World Showcase—into a one-of-a-kind theme park, with all the attractions oriented toward education, inspiration, or corporate imagery. Epcot is more than twice the physical size of the Magic Kingdom or Disney-MGM Studios, and it takes a considerable amount of walking from attraction to attraction. The size and scope mean one can't really see the whole place in a day without skipping an attraction or two and giving other areas a cursory glance. Choose to linger over or skim through, based on your personal interests.

As in the other theme parks, we have identified several attractions in Epcot as "not to be missed." But part of the enjoyment of a place like Epcot is that there is something for everyone. No doubt there will be quite a variety of opinions in your family as to which attraction is "best." Disney FASTPASSes are available to cut time waiting in line at *Honey I Shrunk the Audience,* Living with the Land, Maelstrom, and Test Track.

Future World

This is the first area you encounter, and everything, including the bountiful landscaping, is clean and sparkling to the point of asepsis and seemingly bigger than life. Pavilions dedicated to man's past, present, and future technological accomplishments form the perimeter of the Future World area, with Spaceship Earth and its flanking Innoventions East and West standing prominently front and center.

World Showcase

This is the second theme area of Epcot, situated around picturesque World Showcase Lagoon. It is an ongoing World's Fair, with the cuisine, culture, history, and architecture of almost a dozen countries permanently on display in individual national pavilions. The pavilions are spaced along a promenade a little more than a mile long, which circles the impressive 40-acre lagoon.

While most adults enjoy World Showcase, some children find it boring. Disney has added a craft booth at each country, called Kidcot, with hands-on activities, such as painting with watercolors in Paris or learning Arabic lettering in Morocco. And there's also live entertainment to keep kids amused, from colorful dancing dragons in China to participatory street theater in Italy.

Passport Kits are available for about $10 in most Epcot retail shops. Each kit contains a blank passport and stamps for all the World Showcase countries. As the kids accompany their folks to each country, they tear out the appropriate stamp and stick it on the passport. The kit also contains some basic information on the respective countries, as well as a Mickey Mouse button.

NOT TO BE MISSED AT EPCOT

Future World	Body Wars (great for kids over 7, but may cause vertigo)
	Cranium Command
	Honey, I Shrunk the Audience (can frighten kids age 6 and younger)
	Living with the Land
	Spaceship Earth
	Test Track (kids must be 40 inches tall to ride)
World Showcase	The American Adventure
	IllumiNations

Disney-MGM Studios

Disney-MGM Studios is about the same size as the Magic Kingdom and about half as large as Epcot. Unlike the other parks, however, Disney-MGM Studios is a working motion picture and television production facility. This means, among other things, that about half the entire studio area is controlled access, with guests permitted only on tours accompanied by guides or restricted to observation walkways.

There's a definite kid appeal with shows based on films like *Beauty and the Beast, The Little Mermaid, Indiana Jones,* and Jim Henson's *Muppets.* This park is not nearly as overwhelming as the Magic Kingdom or Epcot. It's easy to see the park in a single day. The FASTPASS system is available for Indiana Jones Epic Stunt Spectacular, *Jim Henson's Muppet Vision 3-D,* Rock 'n' Roller Coaster Starring Aerosmith, Star Tours, Twilight Zone Tower of Terror, *Who Wants to Be a Millionaire?,* and Voyage *of the Little Mermaid.*

SMALL CHILD FRIGHT POTENTIAL

What It Is:	Fright Potential Rating
EPCOT	
Global Neighborhood	
Interactive communications playground	A
Innoventions	
Multifaceted attraction featuring static and hands-on exhibits relating to products and technologies of the near future	A
The Living Seas	
An underwater ride beneath a huge saltwater aquarium and a number of exhibits and displays dealing with oceanography, ocean ecology, and sea life	A
Spaceship Earth	
Educational dark ride through past, present, and future	A
Imagination Pavilion	
Honey, I Shrunk the Audience	
3-D film with special effects	C
Journey into Imagination with Figment	
Dark fantasy adventure ride	A
Test Track Ride	
Racetrack simulator ride	C
The Land Pavilion	
Circle of Life Theater	
Film exploring man's relationship with his environment	A
Food Rocks	
Audio-animatronic theater show about food and nutrition	A
Living with the Land	
An indoor boat ride adventure through the past, present, and future of U.S. farming and agriculture	A
Wonders of Life Pavilion	
Body Wars	
Flight-simulator ride through the human body	C
Cranium Command	
Audio-animatronic theater show about the brain	A
Fitness Fairgrounds	
Much of the pavilion's interior is devoted to an assortment of visitor participation exhibits, where guests can test their senses in a fun house, receive computer-generated health analyses of lifestyles, work out on electronically sophisticated exercise equipment, and watch a video presentation called Goofy about Health (starring who else?)	A
The Making of Me	
Humorous movie about human conception and birth	A

AND ATTRACTION RATINGS: Epcot

Author's Rating	Pre-school	Grade School	Teens	Young Adults	Over 30	Senior Citizens
★★½	★★	★★★½	★★★½	★★★½	★★½	★★½
★★★½	★½	★★★½	★★★★	★★★½	★★★	★★★
★★★½	★★★	★★★	★★★	★★★★	★★★★	★★★★
★★★★	★★★	★★★★	★★★½	★★★★	★★★★	★★★★
★★★★½	★★★	★★★★½	★★★★½	★★★★½	★★★★½	★★★★
★★½	★★	★★	★★	★★★	★★★	★★★
★★★★½	★★★½	★★★★½	★★★★½	★★★★½	★★★★	★★★★
★★★½	★★½	★★★	★★½	★★★	★★★	★★★
★★½	★★★	★★★	★★½	★★★	★★★	★★★
★★★★	★★½	★★★	★★★½	★★★★	★★★★	★★★★
★★★★	★★★	★★★★	★★★★	★★★★	★★★½	★★½
★★★★½	★★	★★★★	★★★★	★★★★½	★★★★½	★★★★½
★★	★★	★★★	★★★	★★	★★	★★
★★★	★½	★★★½	★★½	★★★	★★★	★★★

SMALL CHILD FRIGHT POTENTIAL

What It Is:	Fright Potential Rating
EPCOT *(continued)*	
The "Mom, I Can't Believe It's Disney" Fountain	
Combination fountain and shower	A
Universe of Energy Pavilion: Ellen's Energy Adventure	
Combination ride/theater presentation about energy	B
World Showcase	
The American Adventure	
Patriotic mixed-media and Audio-animatronic theater presentation on U.S. history	A
El Río del Tiempo	
Indoor scenic boat ride	A
Impressions de France	
Film essay on the French people and country	A
Maelstrom	
Indoor adventure boat ride	B
O Canada	
Film essay on the Canadian people and country	A
Wonders of China	
Film about the Chinese people and country	A

THE DREAMS OF MICKEY MOUSE

***Fantasmic!* at Disney-MGM Studios** Modeled after the wildly successful *Fantasmic!* at Disneyland, this Florida nighttime water spectacle features 50 performers and combines lasers, special effects, animation, and dancing waters synchronized to the melodies of Disney classics.

The 25-minute show is staged in a new, 6,900-seat amphitheater behind The Twilight Zone Tower of Terror off Sunset Boulevard. Encircling a newly created waterway and island, the theater can accommodate another 3,000 standing guests. *Fantasmic!* takes guests inside the dreams of Mickey Mouse—dancing water, shooting comets, animated fountains, swirling stars, balls of fire, and other special effects.

The theater is packed most nights, so arrive early—or make a dinner reservation at the nearby Hollywood Brown Derby or at Mama Melrose's Ristorante Italiano. The *Fantasmic!* dinner package allows diners to enter a reserved area 30 minutes before showtime.

AND ATTRACTION RATINGS: Epcot

Author's Rating	Pre-school	Grade School	Teens	Young Adults	Over 30	Senior Citizens
★★★★	★★★★★	★★★★★	★★★★	★★★★	★★★★	★★★★★
★★★★	★★★	★★★★	★★★½	★★★★	★★★★	★★★★
★★★★	★★	★★★	★★★	★★★★	★★★★½	★★★★★
★★	★★	★★	★½	★★	★★	★★½
★★★½	★½	★★½	★★★	★★★★	★★★★	★★★★
★★★	★★★½	★★★½	★★★	★★★	★★★	★★★
★★★½	★★	★★½	★★★	★★★½	★★★★	★★★
★★★	★★	★★½	★★★	★★★½	★★★★	★★★★

NOT TO BE MISSED AT THE DISNEY-MGM STUDIOS

Disney-MGM Studios Backlot Tour
Indiana Jones Epic Stunt Spectacular
Jim Henson's *Muppet Vision 3-D* (a little loud at end for toddlers)
The Magic of Disney Animation
One Man's Dream
Rock 'n' Roller Coaster Starring Aerosmith not for the youngest; height requirement)
Star Tours (not for kids under 5 or anyone prone to motion sickness)
The Twilight Zone Tower of Terror (not for kids under 5, and there's a height requirement)
Voyage of the Little Mermaid

If your kids are under age 6, add:
Beauty and the Beast Live on Stage
Honey, I Shrunk the Kids Movie Set Adventure

SMALL CHILD FRIGHT POTENTIAL

What It Is:	Fright Potential Rating
DISNEY-MGM STUDIOS	
Backlot Theater	
Live musical, usually based on a Disney film	A
Disney-MGM Studios Backlot Tour	
Combination tram/walking tour of modern film production	C
Fantasmic!	
Mixed-media nighttime spectacular	A
The Great Movie Ride	
Movie history indoor adventure ride	C
***Honey, I Shrunk the Kids* Movie Set Adventure**	
Small but elaborate playground	A
Indiana Jones Epic Stunt Spectacular	
Movie-stunt demonstration and action show	B
Jim Henson's *Muppet Vision 3-D*	
3-D movie starring the Muppets	B
The Magic of Disney Animation	
Walking tour of the Disney Animation Studio	A
New York Street Backlot	
Walk-through backlot movie set	A
Playhouse Disney—Live on Stage	
Music, songs, stories of friendship	A
Rock 'n' Roller Coaster Starring Aerosmith	
Rock music–themed roller coaster	F
Sounds Dangerous	
Audience-participation show demonstrating sound effects	A
Star Tours	
Indoor space-flight simulation ride	C
Theater of the Stars	
Live musical, usually featuring Disney characters	A
The Twilight Zone Tower of Terror	
Sci-fi–themed indoor thrill ride	F
Voyage of the Little Mermaid	
Musical stage show featuring characters from *The Little Mermaid*	A
Walt Disney: One Man's Dream	
Homage to Disney	A
Who Wants to Be a Millionaire?—Play It	
Theme park version of TV game show	A

ATTRACTION RATINGS: MGM Studios

Author's Rating	Pre-school	Grade School	Teens	Young Adults	Over 30	Senior Citizens
★★★	★½	★★★	★★★	★★★	★★★	★★★
★★★★	★★★	★★★★	★★★★	★★★★	★★★★	★★★
★★★★★	★★★★	★★★★★	★★★★½	★★★★½	★★★★½	★★★★½
★★★½	★★½	★★★½	★★★½	★★★★	★★★★	★★★★
★★½	★★★★½	★★★½	★★	★★½	★★★	★★½
★★★★	★★★	★★★★	★★★★	★★★★	★★★★	★★★★
★★★★½	★★★★½	★★★★★	★★★★½	★★★★½	★★★★½	★★★★½
★★★★	★★★	★★★	★★★	★★★★	★★★★	★★★
★★★	★½	★★★	★★★	★★★	★★★	★★★
★★★	★★★★	★★★	★	★	★	★
★★★★★	★	★★★	★★★★★	★★★★★	★★★★	★★★★
★★★	★★½	★★★½	★★★	★★★	★★★	★★★★
★★★★	★★★★	★★★★	★★★★	★★★★	★★★★	★★★★
★★★★	★★★★	★★★★	★★★	★★★★	★★★★	★★★★
★★★★★	★★★	★★★★★	★★★★★	★★★★★	★★★★★	★★★★½
★★★★	★★★★	★★★★	★★★½	★★★★	★★★★	★★★★
★★★★	★★	★★★	★★	★★★★	★★★★	★★★★
★★★★	★★	★★★★	★★★★	★★★★	★★★★	★★★★

WHAT'S NEXT?

The blockbuster Disney attraction everyone's anticipating is Mission: SPACE, scheduled to open in late 2002 at Epcot Future World. Offering a one-of-a-kind "astronaut-like" experience, riders will be launched into a simulated space adventure, from a pulse-racing lift-off to weightlessness in outer space. NASA astronauts and scientists are advising the creative team, which is crafting a story set decades in the future at the International Space Training Center, where guests will encounter simulated challenges faced by real astronauts. The all-new attraction is on the park's east side, next to Test Track.

Disney's Animal Kingdom

Disney's storytelling techniques have nearly been perfected in this fourth theme park at Walt Disney World. Every inch of the park tells a tale about animals—real, imaginary, and extinct. And if animals are the stars, then incredible landscaping with its lush flora, winding streams, meandering paths, and exotic setting, gets credit for best supporting actor. This giant park—500 acres—is remarkably beautiful.

Don't let the numbers fool you—this park can comfortably be seen in a day, because nearly 25% of the park (110 acres) is "Africa," where wild animals roam. They get the space; but you get a wild, 20-minute safari adventure.

You park your car and board a tram for the entrance. Be sure to pick up a guide map and entertainment schedule; this is also the place for package pick-up, Guest Services, lockers, rest rooms, and kennels. There is an ATM, and wheelchairs and strollers can be rented in Garden Gate Gifts shop. You also can buy film here, but there are no cameras, camcorders, or binoculars for rent at this park. A giant Rainforest Cafe, open for breakfast, lunch, and dinner, is just to the left of the entrance, accessible from both inside and outside the theme park.

Much like Main Street, USA, sets the scene in the Magic Kingdom, Disney's Animal Kingdom starts "decompressing" visitors in The Oasis, a tropical garden filled with real animals like tiny deer, anteaters, kangaroos, and a two-toed sloth. Birds, including scarlet ibis, hyacinth macaws, and African spoonbills, can be seen in the trees and in the streams and waterfalls.

Immediately past The Oasis is Safari Village, the park's "hub" to the other lands. The buildings are covered in brilliantly colored animal designs, with clever wood carvings from Bali protruding from above doors and windows, and on corners. But most visitors are more amazed by the giant Tree of Life, more than 14 stories high, with nearly 350 animal forms hand-carved into its massive trunk. Live animals, too, live at the base, like otters, ring-tailed lemurs, and red kangaroos.

From Safari Village, you can choose Africa and the Kilimanjaro Safaris ride; Chester and Hester's Dino-Rama, a new mini-land with a family coaster, a spinning dinosaur ride, and arcade games; DinoLand, USA, and the thrill ride Dinosaur; Asia and the thrilling Kali River Rapids; Conservation Station, for a backstage look at the animals and conservation messages; or Camp Minnie-Mickey if your kids need a dose of Disney characters. Use the FASTPASS on Dinosaur, *It's Tough to Be a Bug,* Kali River Rapids, Kilimanjaro Safaris, and Primeval Whirl.

NOT TO BE MISSED AT DISNEY'S ANIMAL KINGDOM

Africa	Kilimanjaro Safaris
Asia	Kali River Rapids
Camp Minnie-Mickey	*Festival of the Lion King*
DinoLand, U.S.A.	Dinosaur
Safari Village	*It's Tough to Be a Bug!*

The Disney Water Theme Parks

There are two water theme parks to choose from at Walt Disney World, plus two more independent area water parks. Typhoon Lagoon is the most diversified of the splash pads, while Blizzard Beach takes the grand prize for the most slides and the most bizarre theme.

Before you go Call (407) 824-4321 the night before you go for opening times. For a day at the water parks consider the following:

- Visit on weekdays, when the parks are less crowded. We recommend Monday or Tuesday, when most tourists are visiting the theme parks; Fridays are also a good bet since people traveling by car often use this day to start home.
- Go early in the morning or late in the afternoon. Don't wait for the Disney bus if you have your own car, and arrive 30 minutes before park opening. The parks often close by 11 a.m. when they are filled to capacity, and they don't open again until guests pack up in the afternoon. There can be long waits—up to 30 minutes—for some slides.
- The perfect time to go is after an afternoon storm, when the park has been closed due to bad weather. When the parks reopen after the inclement weather has passed, you can almost have a whole park to yourself. Evenings are great, too, when special lighting after dusk makes Typhoon Lagoon and Blizzard Beach enchanting places to be, and crowds are definitely lighter.
- Wear your bathing suit under your clothes, and wear shoes. Take your own towel and sunscreen.

SMALL CHILD FRIGHT POTENTIAL

What It Is:	Fright Potential Rating
DISNEY'S ANIMAL KINGDOM	
DinoLand, USA	
Dinosaur	
Motion-simulator dark ride to rescue a dinosaur from extinction	C
Primeval Whorl	
Spinning "time machines"	A
TriceraTop Spin	
Kiddie roller coaster	B
Africa	
Conservation Station	
You can observe animal care and experience 7 exhibits: among them an interactive video of endangered animal information, interactive video kiosks that connect to world-famous biologists and conservationists, and the Affection Section, where you can touch small animals	A
Kilimanjaro Safaris	
Truck ride through an African wildlife reservation	A
Pangani Forest Exploration Trail	
Area filled with East African wildlife; come face to face with western lowland gorillas and hippos in an underwater viewing area	A
Wildlife Express	
Scenic railroad ride to Conservation Station (see next entry)	A
Asia	
Flights of Wonder at the Caravan Stage	
Stadium show about birds	A
Kali River Rapids	
Whitewater raft ride through dense rainforest with raging cataracts, log jams, and other dangers	C
Maharaja Jungle Trek	
Walk-through zoological exhibit of Asian animals including Komodo dragons, Malayan tapirs, Bengal tigers, Blackbuck antelope, and Asian deer; concludes with an aviary	A
Safari Village	
The Boneyard	
Giant playground with fake dinosaur bones for unearthing, sliding, and crawling	A
Camp Minnie-Mickey's *Festival of the Lion King*	
Outdoor theater-in-the-round stage show based on the animated film *The Lion King*	A

ATTRACTION RATINGS: Animal Kingdom

Author's Rating	Pre-school	Grade School	Teens	Young Adults	Over 30	Senior Citizens
★★★★½	†	★★★★½	★★★★½	★★★★½	★★★★½	★★★½
★★★	★★★	★★★½	★★★½	★★★	★★★	★★
★★★	★★★	★★★★	★★	★★	★★	★★
★★★	★★½	★★	★½	★★½	★★½	★★½
★★★★★	★★★★	★★★★★	★★★★½	★★★★½	★★★★½	★★★★★
★★★	★★½	★★★	★★½	★★★	★★★	★★★
★★	★★★	★★★	★½	★★½	★★½	★★½
★★★★	★★★★	★★★★	★★★½	★★★★	★★★★	★★★★
★★★½	★★★★	★★★★	★★★★	★★★½	★★★½	★★★
★★★★	★★	★★★½	★★★	★★★½	★★★★	★★★★
★★★½	★★★★½	★★★★½	—	—	—	—
★★★★	★★★★	★★★★½	★★★★	★★★★	★★★★	★★★★

† Many preschoolers are too short to meet the height requirements and others are visually intimidated by watching the ride from standing in line.

SMALL CHILD FRIGHT POTENTIAL

What It Is:	Fright Potential Rating
DISNEY'S ANIMAL KINGDOM ***(continued)***	
Safari Village (continued)	
Camp Minnie-Mickey's ***Pocahontas and Her Forest Friends at Grandmother Willow's Grove***	
Conservation-themed stage show	A
It's Tough to Be a Bug	
Theater attraction in the Tree of Life combining 3-D images, Audio-animatronics and special effects.	C
Theater in the Wild's ***Tarzan Rocks!***	
Open venue for live stage shows (venue changes periodically)	A

- Since wallets and purses just get in the way, lock them in the trunk or leave them in the hotel. Carry enough cash for the day and a Disney resort ID (if you have one) in a plastic bag. It's relatively safe to leave stuff at your chair instead of renting a locker—just be sure it's well concealed.
- Don't bring personal gear (fins, masks, rafts, etc.)—it's not allowed. You can rent towels, or buy bathing suits or sunscreen. Tubes and personal flotation devices are free (you need a credit card or driver's license as a deposit, held until the equipment is returned).
- Head straight for the most popular slides and ride them first thing in the morning, before the crowd has time to build up.
- You can take a picnic, but no glass containers or alcoholic beverages.
- If your children are young, choose a base spot near the children's swimming area in all three parks. There are shelters for those who prefer shade and even a few hammocks. There are also picnic tables.

Blizzard Beach

This is Disney's second and most exotic water adventure park, and like Typhoon Lagoon, it arrived with its own legend. This time, as the story goes, an optimistic entrepreneur tried to open a ski resort in Florida during a particularly savage winter. But alas, the snow melted, the palm trees grew back, and all that remained of the ski resort was its Alpine lodge, the ski lift, and of course, the mountain. Plunging off the mountain are ski slopes and bobsled runs transformed into water slides. Visitors to Blizzard Beach catch the thaw in midcycle—with dripping icicles and

ATTRACTION RATINGS: Animal Kingdom

Author's Rating	Pre-school	Grade School	Teens	Young Adults	Over 30	Senior Citizens
★★½	★★★½	★★★½	★★★	★★★½	★★★	★★★
★★★★	★★½	★★★★★	★★★★★	★★★★	★★★★	★★★★
★★½	★★★	★★★★	★★★	★★★	★★★	★★★

patches of snow here and there. The melting snow has formed a large lagoon (the wave pool), fed by gushing mountain streams.

Blizzard Beach is distinguished by its landscaping and by the attention paid to detailing its theme. There are 17 slides in all, among them Summit Plummet, the world's longest, fastest speed slide, which begins with a 120-foot free fall, and the Teamboat Springs bobsled run, 1,200 feet long. If you are going primarily for the slides, you will have about 2 hours in the early morning to enjoy them before the waiting becomes completely intolerable during busy times of the year.

A ski lift carries guests to the top of the mountain (you can also walk up) where they choose from three rides—Summit Plummet, the Slush Gusher, and Teamboat Springs. For all other slides, you walk to the top. If you are among the first in the park, the ski lift is fun and provides a bird's-eye view of the park. After riding it once to satisfy your curiosity, however, you are better off taking the stairs to the top of the mountain.

A wave pool and a float creek circle the park. The children's areas, Tike's Peak and Ski Patrol Training Camp, are creatively designed, nicely isolated from the rest of the park, and visually interesting, with attractions like Frozen Pipe Springs, where your kids can take a trip through a frozen pipe and drop down into 8 feet of water.

Quick-service restaurants, rest rooms, shops, as well as tube, towel, and locker rentals are located in the ski resort's now-converted base area.

Admission is about $32 a day for adults; $25 for children ages 3–9; free for children under age 3.

Typhoon Lagoon

Typhoon Lagoon is comparable in size to Blizzard Beach. Nine water slides and streams, some as long as 400 feet, drop from the top of a 100-foot-high man-made mountain. An "aftermath of a typhoon" theme imparts an added adventure touch to the wet rides.

Beautifully landscaped, Typhoon Lagoon is entered through a misty rain forest that emerges in a ramshackle tropical town, where concessions and services are located. Disney special effects make every ride an odyssey, as swimmers encounter bat caves, lagoons and pools, spinning rocks, dinosaur bone formations, and countless other imponderables.

Like Blizzard Beach, Typhoon Lagoon is costly, about $32 a day for adults and $25 for children ages 3–9; free for children under age 3. If you enjoy all the features of Typhoon Lagoon, the admission cost is a fair value. If you are going primarily for the slides, you will have only two early morning hours to enjoy the slides before the wait becomes prohibitive during busy seasons.

Ketchakiddee Creek, for those under 4 feet tall features geysers, tame slides, bubble jets, and fountains. For the older and more adventurous there are two speed slides, three corkscrew body slides, and three tube rapids rides (plus one children's rapids ride) plopping off Mount Mayday. A scenic, 2,100-foot stream floats tubers through a hidden grotto and rain forest.

Two attractions, the surf pool and Shark Reef, are unique. The wave pool is the world's largest inland surf facility, with waves up to 6 feet in a lagoon large enough to "encompass an ocean liner." Shark Reef is a salt-water snorkeling pool, where guests can swim around with a multitude of real fish.

Shark Reef is a great opportunity for youngsters to try snorkeling in a controlled environment. We recommend doing the reef early in the day, even first thing, if you have young children. Guests are grouped into impromptu classes for a briefing, then launched together. You're not allowed to paddle about aimlessly, but must swim more or less directly across the reef.

If you don't want to swim with fish, you can avail yourself of an underwater viewing chamber, accessible any time.

Elsewhere in the World

Downtown Disney

This is the most fun for free at Disney. Besides shopping and restaurants, what's here for families? Kids can splash for an entire afternoon in the interactive water fountains (be sure to take along a bathing suit or a change of clothes), and we love the new LEGO Imagination Center, with fabulous designs made from the tiny plastic blocks, like a life-size dragon in the lagoon and the snoring man on the park bench just outside the door. There are plenty of LEGOs for kids to play with on tables inside the store and just outside in a expansive play area, with plenty of benches for mom and dad to rest and places for restless teenagers to explore nearby. Also, Disney's Once Upon a Toy store has plenty of toys—and hands-on examining is encouraged.

Encompassing three areas—the Marketplace, Pleasure Island, and West Side—Downtown Disney is the place to shop, dine, and play away from the theme parks—nearly a dozen restaurants, 24 movie theater screens, and more than 50 shops and stores. The world's largest Disney character shop, World of Disney, is one-stop shopping for souvenirs. Some of the most fun restaurants in Central Florida are here—Rainforest Cafe, Planet Hollywood, House of Blues, Wolfgang Puck, to name a few. During the winter holidays, from late November to early January, Disney builds an outdoor ice-skating rink, a real novelty in 80° weather.

DisneyQuest

DisneyQuest is a five-story, indoor interactive theme park at Downtown Disney West Side that combines Disney's creativity with technology, including virtual reality and real-time 3-D. There are activities for every age group in four zones: Explore Zone with virtual reality attractions; Score Zone that tests game-playing skills; Create Zone, a studio for artistic self-expression and invention; and the Replay Zone, a favorite for youngsters with retro midway games and high-tech bumper cars.

The latest attraction is Pirates of the Caribbean: Battle for Buccaneer Gold, where a crew of four boards a "ship" to enter a 3-D world of plundered towns, fortress islands, and erupting volcanoes for an action-packed, five-minute experience.

DisneyQuest is open daily from 10:30 a.m.–midnight. Admission is $29 plus tax, $23 for ages 3–9, free for children under age 3. All children age 9 and under must be accompanied by an adult.

Cirque du Soleil

Recognized throughout the world for its astounding shows, Cirque du Soleil has a permanent home at Downtown Disney's West Side for the theatrical, spellbinding "La Nouba," presented twice nightly Wednesday through Sunday. This extraordinary show wows audiences with surreal sets, theatrical lighting, and high-energy choreography. More than 60 artists from around the world, including gymnasts, acrobats, dancers, and clowns, weave a story of life and high drama during each 90-minute performance. It's definitely worth the $68 ticket ($40 ages 3–9).

Miniature Golf

First, Fantasia Gardens: We actually found it a little frustrating and too difficult for amateur golfers. But then we discovered there are two courses, and we were on the tougher approach-and-putt course with serious sand traps and water hazards. The other course is easier, themed after Disney's animated film Fantasia, and kids (and nongolfing parents) actually have a chance to hit the hole without picking up the ball and putting it in. So pick the one that suits your game. The two, 18-hole courses are on Epcot Resorts Boulevard, directly across from the Walt Disney World Dolphin hotel; (407) 560-8760.

Disney's Winter Summerland offers two 18-hole courses near Blizzard Beach water park. Both courses are loaded with interactive gadgets, like the snowman who squirts you with water when a golf ball passes beneath him. Fun for families ready for a break from the theme parks.

Disney Cruise Line

You can combine a Disney World vacation with a cruise, or just sail on one of two ships, the *Disney Magic* and the *Disney Wonder.*

When families board the ship, a camp counselor creates an itinerary for each child and offers a tour of the Oceaneer Adventure kids areas. Oceaneer's Club is for ages 3–8, and Oceaneer's Lab is for ages 9–12. Parents whose children choose to participate in supervised activities are given a pager so they can enjoy the ship's adult areas knowing their children can reach them.

The *Disney Magic* and *Disney Wonder* have the largest number of children's counselors of any ships at sea—up to 50. Activities are divided by age and start at 9 every morning and don't stop until 1 a.m. There's also a club just for teens, and private in-cabin baby-sitting for children under 3.

The ships are designed to offer activities and areas for all ages, including an adults-only spa, a sports club, four restaurants, a movie theater and a theater for Broadway-style shows, a nightclub for families, and a nighttime entertainment district for adults.

If your cruise starts at Disney World, one key will open both your hotel room and your onboard stateroom. Three- and four-day cruises sail to Nassau in the Bahamas; seven-day cruises offer ports in the Caribbean. Both ships stop at Castaway Cay, Disney's private Bahamian Island. For information, call (407) 566-7000.

Disney's Wide World of Sports

This 200-acre, multimillion-dollar sports complex hosts more than 30 types of sporting events, from baseball and basketball to tennis and aerobics. It's the home of the Amateur Athletic Union, the spring training home of the Atlanta Braves, and the training site of the Tampa Bay Buccaneers football team, and hosts the Harlem Globetrotters basketball showteam.

When at Disney, check to see if there's an event you might like to watch; tickets to premium events like an Atlanta Braves game can be purchased through TicketMaster, (407) 839-3900. If you want to take a chance and see what's going on or take a self-guided tour through the complex, tickets are $10 for adults; $9 for children ages 3–9.

Universal Orlando

Universal Orlando Resort

1000 Universal Studios Plaza, Orlando; (407) 363-8000 or (800) U-ESCAPE
www.uescape.com

Operating daily, 9 a.m.–9 p.m., with extended hours during peak seasons, Universal Studios opened its doors to the public in June 1990. At that time the single theme park was almost four times the size of Disney-MGM Studios (Disney-MGM has expanded somewhat subsequently), with much more of the total facility accessible to the visiting public. Over the last decade, the resort has grown dramatically, adding a second theme park named Islands of Adventure, three hotels, and an entertainment district. Like its sister facility in Hollywood, Universal Orlando is spacious, beautifully landscaped, meticulously clean, and delightfully varied in its entertainment offerings.

Where Universal Studios Hollywood is essentially a tram tour with built-in surprises and several extra-large theaters, the Florida parks have lots of exciting, innovative rides, and individual shows on movie making. While many of the rides represent prototypical state-of-the-art technology and live up to their advance billing in terms of excitement, creativity, uniqueness, and special effects, they unfortunately lack the capacity to handle the number of guests who frequent major Florida tourist attractions. If a ride has great appeal but can accommodate only a small number of guests per ride or per hour, long lines will form. It is not unusual for the wait to exceed 75 minutes for the Spiderman ride, and 50 minutes for the Dueling Dragons roller coaster.

Happily, most of the shows and theater performances are in good-size theaters, which accommodate large numbers of people. Since most performances run continuously, waits usually do not exceed the performance time of the show (40–50 minutes). Many stage shows are multisegmented, with the audience moving to three or more staging areas during the course of the presentation.

Universal Studios has the greatest appeal for teenagers. We found it difficult to spend a day in the park with a teenager and a toddler without splitting up for most of the day. And for little ones, there's just not much to see and do. Still, if there's a teenager in your family, they're going to want to ride the coasters at Islands of Adventure and see Kongfrontation, Back to the Future, *Terminator 2 3-D,* and Jaws. Stretching between the two theme parks is Universal CityWalk, a 30-acre entertainment district.

Universal Orlando now features three hotels: Portofino Bay Hotel, with a Mediterranean theme; Hard Rock Hotel, with a cache of cool rock 'n' roll memorabilia; and the newest, Royal Pacific Resort, opening in fall 2002. All are just a short (and free) boat taxi ride from CityWalk and the theme parks. Rates start at $159.

A great advantage for resort guests is the new Universal ExpressPass. If you're staying in a Universal hotel, you simply show your room keycard to be directed to an "express line" for almost every ride and attraction in the two parks. (The system is also available to non-resort guests who buy theme park tickets—but they must receive an Express Pass for a single ride or attraction, and can only get another Express Pass after visiting the attraction or after 2 hours have passed.)

FRIGHT POTENTIAL CHART

On the following pages we have assigned a fright potential rating to each ride in the theme park.

A = not frightening in any way

B = scares some preschoolers

C = frightens many preschoolers

D = scares many children age 10 and under

F = potentially frightening to all ages.

Islands of Adventure

This theme park expanded Universal's offerings, and it features the best collection of roller coasters and thrill rides of any Central Florida attraction. Many of the rides have characters for inspiration—The Cat in the Hat, Spider-Man, Popeye, The Incredible Hulk, and the dinosaurs of Jurassic Park.

The park is configured with five islands, each with rides, attractions, shows, and restaurants: Seuss Landing, Toon Lagoon, Marvel Super Hero Island, The Lost Continent, and Jurassic Park.

SMALL CHILD FRIGHT POTENTIAL

What It Is:	Fright Potential Rating
UNIVERSAL STUDIOS FLORIDA	
Animal Planet Live!	
Special animals take center stage	A
Back to the Future...The Ride	
Flight-simulator thrill ride	D
Beetlejuice's Graveyard Revue	
Rock-and-roll stage show	A
A Day in the Park with Barney	
Live character stage show	A
E.T. Adventure	
Indoor adventure ride based on the movie *E.T.*	B
Fievel's Playland	
Children's play area with water slide	A
The Gory Gruesome and Grotesque Horror Make-up Show	
Theater presentation on the art of makeup	B
Jaws	
Adventure boat ride	D
Earthquake—The Big One	
Combination theater presentation and adventure ride	D
Kongfrontation	
Indoor adventure ride featuring King Kong	D
Lucy: A Tribute	
Walk-through tribute to Lucille Ball	A
Men in Black Alien Attack	
Interactive video game experience	C
Nickelodeon Studios Tour and Gamelab	
Behind-the-scenes guided tour	A
Set Streets	
Elaborate outdoor sets for making films	A
Terminator 2 3-D	
3-D thriller mixed-media presentation	D
Twister...Ride It Out	
Wind, rain, and the world's largest indoor tornado	D
Woody Woodpecker's Kid Zone	
Woody Woodpecker and Curious George interactive play area	A
Woody Woodpecker Nuthouse Coaster	
Kid-sized roller coaster	A
Wild, Wild, Wild West Stunt Show	
Stunt show with a Western theme	A

ATTRACTION RATINGS: Universal Studios

Author's Rating	Pre-school	Grade School	Teens	Young Adults	Over 30	Senior Citizens
★★★★	★★★★	★★★★	★★★	★★★	★★★★	★★★★
★★★★★	—	★★★★★	★★★★★	★★★★★	★★★★	★★½
★★½	★★	★★½	★★★	★½	★★	★★½
★★★★	★★★★	★★★	★★	★★½	★★★	★★★
★★★★	★★★★½	★★★★½	★★★★	★★★★	★★★★	★★★★
★★★★	★★★★	★★★★	—	—	—	—
★★★½	★★★	★★★★	★★★★	★★★½	★★★½	★★★½
★★★★½	★★★★	★★★★★	★★★★★	★★★★★	★★★★★	★★★★½
★★★★	★★★	★★★★★	★★★★★	★★★★½	★★★★½	★★★★½
★★★★	★★★½	★★★★★	★★★★★	★★★★	★★★★	★★★★
★★★	★	★	★★	★★★	★★★	★★★
★★★★	★★	★★★★	★★★★	★★★★	★★★	★★
★★★	★★½	★★★	★★★	★★★	★★	★★
★★★	★★★	★	★★	★★	★★★	★★★
★★★★★	★★★	★★★★½	★★★★★	★★★★	★★★★	★★★★
★★	★	★★	★★★	★★	★★	★★
★★★★	★★★★	★★★	★	★	★	★
★★★	★★★★	★★★★	★	★	★	★
★★★½	★★★★½	★★★★★	★★★★½	★★★★	★★★★	★★★★

SMALL CHILD FRIGHT POTENTIAL

What It Is:	Fright Potential Rating
UNIVERSAL STUDIOS FLORIDA ISLANDS OF ADVENTURE	
Jurassic Park	
Jurassic Park River Adventure	
Close-up look at dinosaurs, an 85-foot plunge	D
Pteranodon Flyers	
Slow glide on the back of a dino high above Jurassic Park	A
Triceratops Encounter	
Learn about these dinosaurs with life-like robotics	A
Jurassic Park Discovery Center	
Entertaining, educational exhibits	A
Camp Jurassic	
Interactive play area	A
The Lost Continent	
Dueling Dragons	
Two coasters speed toward each other at nearly 60 m.p.h.	F
The Eighth Voyage of Sinbad	
Stunt show with flames, fireworks	B
Poseidon's Fury: Escape from the Lost City	
Multi-media stage show	C
Flying Unicorn	
Kiddie coaster	B
Marvel Super Hero Island	
Doctor Doom's Fearfall	
Plummet from 200-foot towers of steel	F
The Amazing Adventures of Spider-Man	
High-speed moving simulators, 3-D special effects	D
Incredible Hulk Coaster	
State-of-the-art coaster; zero to 40 in 2 seconds	F
Storm Force Accelatron	
Spinning kiddie ride	C
Seuss Landing	
The Cat in the Hat	
Ride through scenes from the Dr. Seuss storybook	A
Caro-Seuss-el	
A fanciful merry-go-round of Dr. Seuss characters	A

ATTRACTION RATINGS: Universal Studios

Author's Rating	Pre-school	Grade School	Teens	Young Adults	Over 30	Senior Citizens
★★★★	★	★★★★	★★★★	★★★★	★★★	★★
★★	★★★	★★	★	★★	★★	★★
★★	★★	★★	★	★★	★★	★★
★★	★	★	★	★★	★★	★
★★★	★★★★	★★★	★	★	★	★
★★★★	★★★★	★★★★	★★★★	★★★★	★★★	★★
★★	★★	★★	★	★★	★★	★★
★★	★★	★★	★	★★	★★	★★
★★★	★★★	★★★★	★	★	★	★
★★	—	★★	★★★	★★★	★★	★
★★★★★	★★	★★★★	★★★★★	★★★★★	★★★★★	★★★★
★★★★★	—	★★★★★	★★★★★	★★★★★	★★★★	★★★★
★★	★★★	★★★	★	★	★	★
★★★	★★★★	★★★★	★★	★★	★★	★★
★★★	★★★★	★★★★	★	★	★	★

SMALL CHILD FRIGHT POTENTIAL

What It Is:	Fright Potential Rating
UNIVERSAL STUDIOS FLORIDA ISLANDS OF ADVENTURE *(continued)*	
Seuss Landing (continued)	
If I Ran the Zoo	
Interactive playland	A
One Fish Two Fish Red Fish Blue Fish	
Squirting water and fish-shaped cars	A
Toon Lagoon	
Dudley Do-Right's Ripsaw Falls	
Flume ride with a 75-foot drop	C
Popeye & Bluto's Bilge-Rat Barges	
A very wet river rapids raft ride	C
Me Ship, *The Olive*	
Interactive playland	A

Universal Studios CityWalk

CityWalk, a 30-acre entertainment district, stretches between the two theme parks. After parking in the garage, you must walk through CityWalk to reach either of the two Universal theme parks.

Perhaps CityWalk's biggest claims to fame are Emeril's Restaurant Orlando by famed Chef Emeril Lagasse, and Jimmy Buffett's Margaritaville, where the musician has been know to drop by for an impromptu concert. Other eateries include Hard Rock Cafe (next door is a Hard Rock Live concert venue), NBA City, Bob Marley—A Tribute to Freedom, Motown Cafe, NASCAR Cafe, Pat O'Brien's, and Latin Quarter.

A 20-screen, Universal Cineplex draws crowds on weekends and rainy days. Shopping is limited but fun, with about a dozen specialty shops carrying everything from cigars to surf and beach wear.

Children are welcome in most of the restaurants, but Emeril's, for instance, does not have a children's menu. Most restaurants are open for lunch and dinner. Shops open at 10 a.m. daily, and many are open until midnight. CityWalk Party Pass $8.95, $12 with movie pass.

ATTRACTION RATINGS: Universal Studios

Author's Rating	Pre-school	Grade School	Teens	Young Adults	Over 30	Senior Citizens
★★★	★★★★	★★★★	★	★	★	★
★★★	★★★★	★★★	★★	★★	★	★
★★★	★★	★★★	★★★	★★	★	★
★★	★★	★★★	★★★	★★	★	★
★★	★★★	★★	★	★	★	★

BREEZE PAST THE LONG LINES

If you can afford it, Universal Studios offers a guided tour of the top attractions for $120 per person. An employee meets your family and escorts you to the front of the line at major attractions. Theme park tickets are $49.75 (adult) and $40.95 (children ages 3–9), so you're spending about $70 not to stand in interminably long lines. It's a great way to experience the best of the park in a few hours. Just be aware that many of the attractions on the tour are not suitable for children under 6.

Orlando beyond the Major Theme Parks

Family Resorts

Central Florida has more than 100,000 hotel rooms, from budget hotels to lavish suites. Because the area is such a family destination, many resort hotels in all price ranges offer family-oriented amenities such as children's programs, in-room baby-sitting, themed swimming pools, all-you-can-eat dining, kids-eat-free programs, and shuttles to the attractions. Most allow kids to stay free.

We have listed toll-free numbers for chain hotels and advice for choosing a hotel in the Introduction on page 21 and some Disney favorites on pages 189–192. For a comprehensive listing of Central Florida hotels, call Orlando and Orange City Convention and Visitors Bureau (800) 643-9492 and ask for a free accommodations guide. Also, the Kissimmee–St. Cloud Convention and Visitors Bureau has a reservation system; call (800) 333-KISS for free assistance in booking a reservation in hotels, motels, condos, villas, private homes, and campgrounds. Phone lines are open 24 hours a day. Hotels located on US 192 are close to the Disney theme parks; we caution you to stick with the chain hotels in this area unless someone you trust can vouch for a particular lodging.

The following are a few tried-and-true favorites with exceptional children's programs.

Embassy Suites Lake Buena Vista Resort

8100 Lake Avenue, Lake Buena Vista • (407) 239-1144 • (800) EMBASSY • fax (407) 239-1718 • www.embassysuites.com

Every accommodation in this pretty hotel is a suite with a living room and bedroom, complete with microwave, coffeemaker, mini-refrigerator, even an iron and hair dryer. The 280 suites can sleep up to six and kids age 18 and under stay free, with some suites offering safety components and precautions for families traveling with small children—electrical outlet covers, corner guards, microwave latches, and no glass objects. The resort is minutes from Disney on a free shuttle.

A breakfast buffet, including some items cooked to order, is free every morning and there's a free morning newspaper on weekdays. There's an indoor-outdoor swimming pool; a fitness center; tennis, basketball, and sand volleyball courts; and a fitness trail. Poolside family games take place all day. Rates start at $119.

Gaylord Palms

6000 W. Osceola Parkway, Kissimmee • (407) 586-0315 • fax (407) 586-0397
www.gaylordpalms.com

Just minutes from Disney World, this striking resort features a four-acre, glass-covered atrium with restaurants, shopping, and even a replica of Castillo de San Marcos—the historic Spanish fort in St. Augustine—as part of the resort's Florida theming. Guest rooms are subtly themed, too, to three Florida locales: St. Augustine, Key West, and the Everglades.

The children's program, La Petite Kids' Station, is one of the best, most organized we've encountered, operated by La Petite Academy. The spacious play area offers supervised activities from indoor wall climbing to arcade games and arts and crafts. Programs are open to kids ages 3–14 on a drop-in, hourly basis.

The resort also features two swimming areas, including a family pool with an octopus water slide. Parents can indulge at the beautiful Canyon Ranch SpaClub.

Rates start at $250, with children 18 and under staying free. All rooms are equipped with refrigerators, stocked daily with complimentary water and orange juice.

Holiday Inn Sunspree Resort Lake Buena Vista

13351 State Road 535 • (407) 239-4500 or 800-FON-MAXX • fax (407) 239-7713
www.kidsuites.com

Sunspree is a concept Holiday Inn created to cater specifically to families, and the Lake Buena Vista hotel's Kidsuites make even teenagers happy, with separate kid-themed bedrooms, like a space capsule, a circus tent, or a treehouse. The bedroom-playhouse sleeps three or four and has a TV, phone, and VCR. Oh, and a Super Nintendo is a standard amenity.

At check-in, there's even a separate desk for youngsters, where they receive a bag of goodies to start the vacation, including tokens for the hotel's video arcade, coloring gear, and a toy. Every room has a small refrigerator, microwave, and coffeemaker, and kids eat free in the hotel's buffet restaurant. There are two pools and a bar. Camp Holiday has free

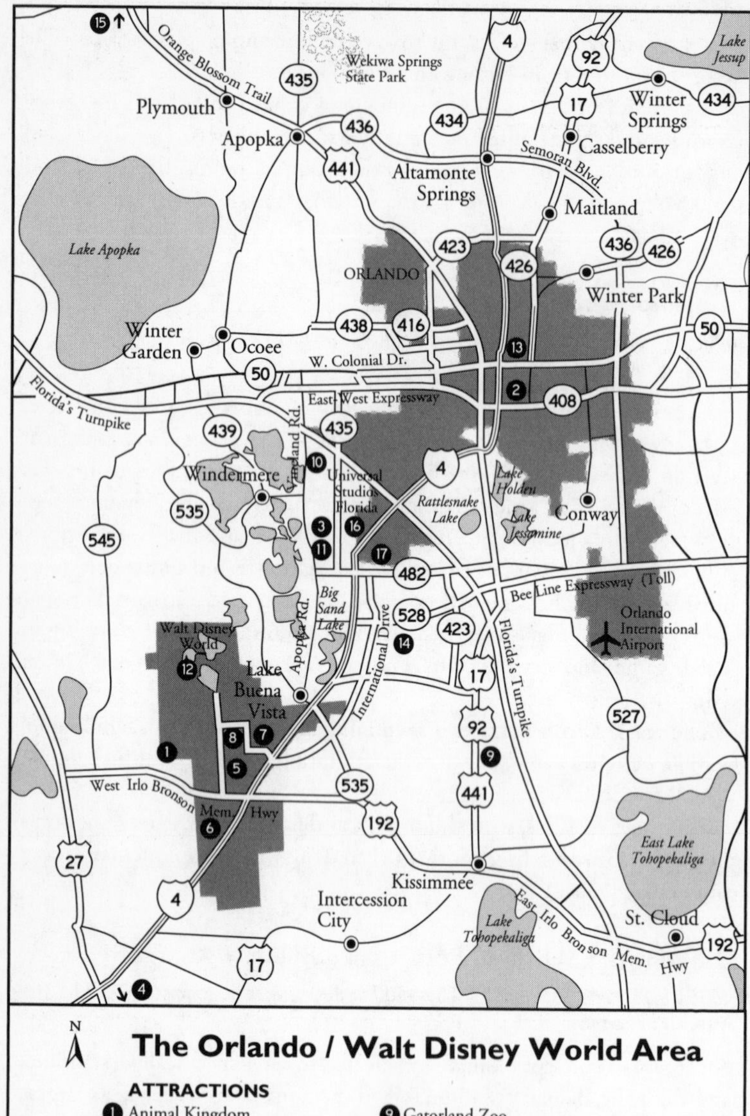

N

The Orlando / Walt Disney World Area

ATTRACTIONS

1. Animal Kingdom
2. Church Street Station
3. CityWalk
4. Cypress Gardens
5. Disney MGM Studios
6. Disney's Wide World of Sports
7. Downtown Disney / Pleasure Island / Disney's West Side
8. Epcot
9. Gatorland Zoo
10. Holy Land Experience
11. Islands of Adventure
12. Magic Kingdom
13. Orlando Science Center
14. SeaWorld of Orlando and Discovery Cove
15. Silver Springs
16. Universal Studios Florida
17. Wet 'n' Wild

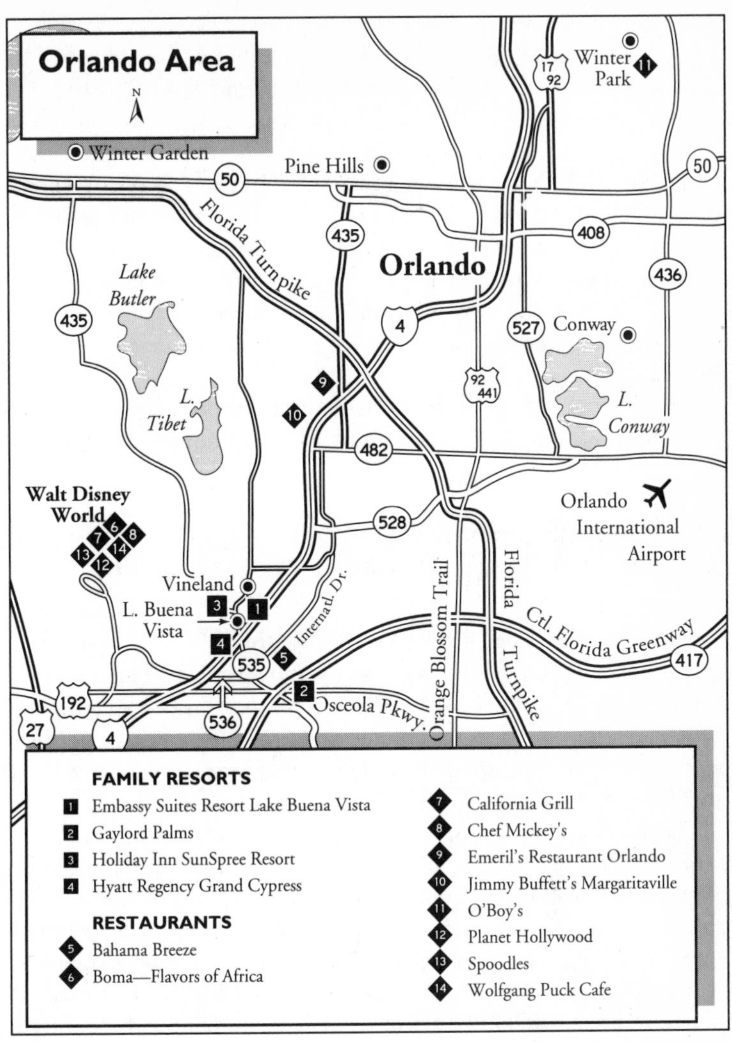

Orlando Area
N
Winter Garden
Pine Hills
Winter Park
Orlando
Florida Turnpike
Lake Butler
L. Tibet
Conway
L. Conway
Walt Disney World
Vineland
L. Buena Vista
Internatl. Dr.
Orange Blossom Trail
Florida Turnpike
Orlando International Airport
Ctl. Florida Greenway
Osceola Pkwy.
FAMILY RESORTS
1 Embassy Suites Resort Lake Buena Vista
2 Gaylord Palms
3 Holiday Inn SunSpree Resort
4 Hyatt Regency Grand Cypress
RESTAURANTS
5 Bahama Breeze
6 Boma—Flavors of Africa
7 California Grill
8 Chef Mickey's
9 Emeril's Restaurant Orlando
10 Jimmy Buffett's Margaritaville
11 O'Boy's
12 Planet Hollywood
13 Spoodles
14 Wolfgang Puck Cafe

daily activities for ages 3–12, from kids karaoke to coloring contests. The Castle Movie Theater plays kid movies all day long. From 5 to 10 p.m., there are activities at Max's Magic Castle for a nominal fee, including bingo games, movies, and clown and magic shows. The CyberArcade located right off the lobby has eight stations for Internet access and more than 30 CD-ROMS as well as video games. And Max the Raccoon will even tuck your little ones in at night.

The hotel stocks baby food and disposable diapers and offers free diaper pails, high chairs, cribs, and childproof outlets. To facilitate parents leaving the hotel, beepers can be rented at $5 for 6 hours, with a refundable deposit.

Rates start at $69 for a standard room off-season and $101 during peak season; children age 19 and under stay free with parents. Kidsuites start at $159.

Hyatt Regency Grand Cypress

One Grand Cypress Boulevard, Orlando • (407) 239-1234 • fax (407) 239-3837
www.hyatt.com

This deluxe, 750-room hotel, just 3 miles from Disney, is part of a sprawling, 1,500-acre resort that offers golf, tennis, horseback riding, a nature area and Audubon walk, and watercraft to rent for exploring the hotel's 21-acre lake. The beautifully landscaped, 800,000-gallon free-form swimming pool covers more than half an acre, with 12 waterfalls and a 115-foot water slide.

The hotel's Camp Hyatt Grand Cypress is for children ages 5–13, with supervised activities such as bike tours, scavenger hunts, video game tournaments, and paddle boat rides. Camp Hyatt operates weekends year-round (9 a.m.–4 p.m. and 6–10 p.m.), with weekday programs (9 a.m.–4 p.m.) from Memorial Day to Labor Day. Supervision for children under 5 years old is available Monday–Thursday, 8 a.m.–10 p.m., and on Friday and Saturday until 11 p.m. Cost is $7 an hour and the service requires reservations 24 hours in advance.

Room rates start at $235, with children 18 and under staying free; families can reserve a second room for their children at half the rate of the parent's room (subject to availability). Suites start at $675. Refrigerators are available upon request. There are several bars in the resort.

Attractions

Cypress Gardens

Cypress Gardens (off US 27, 22 miles south of I-4 between Orlando and Tampa)
(863) 324-2111 • www.cypressgardens.com

Hours - Daily, 9:30 a.m.–5:30 p.m.

Admission - $34.95 for adults, $19.95 for children ages 6–17, free for ages 5 and under (call or check website for special unadvertised deals)

Appeal by Age Group -

Pre-school ★★★★	Teens ★★★	Over 30 ★★★★
Grade school ★★★★	Young Adults ★★★★	Seniors ★★★★★

Touring Time - Average 5 hours; minimum 4 hours

Rainy-Day Touring - Not recommended

Author's Rating of Major Features -

Birdwalk Aviary	★★	Nature's Way Zoo	★★★
Carousel Cove	★★★★	Original Gardens	★★★★
Cypress Junction	★★	Pontoon Lake Cruise	★★★
Cypress Roots	★★	Wacky Water Park	★★★
Flora Dome	★	Water Ski Show	★★★★
Gator Gulch	★	Wings of Wonder	★★★
Island in the Sky	★★		

Restaurants - Yes

Alcoholic beverages - Yes

Handicapped access - Yes

Wheelchair rental - Yes

Baby stroller rental - Yes

Lockers - Yes

Pet kennels - Yes

Rain check - No

Private tours - No

Description and Comments This is another off-the-beaten path, nostalgic vacation spot, and many parents can remember a stop to see the Southern belles posing against flowered backdrops and the impressive water skiers skimming past the cypress knees and magnolia blossoms.

It's all still there today, but the 200-acre park has added impressive new exhibits to appeal to a whole new generation. Still, there are no big crowds, and the place has a sense of plantation charm and natural beauty. It's a great family place, with room to wander and plenty of fun things to see and do.

There are more than 8,000 varieties of plants from 90 countries, and the Original Gardens look spectacular year-round: brilliantly colored bougainvillea and roses in the winter and spring; hibiscus, jasmine, and birds of paradise in the summer; camellias in the fall. If your trip happens to be in late November or early December, it's worth a stop to see the Chrysanthemum Festival, with more than 2.5 million blooms all over the park.

The legendary water ski shows continue, still as impressive, still featuring the park's four-tier human pyramid, as well as huge stunt kites that soar as high as 50 feet above the water. Be sure to bring you own swimwear so you don't miss out on the giant Slip 'n' Slide or the monstrous Titanic Slide.

Among other highlights are the Island in the Sky, a revolving platform that rises 15 stories for a spectacular view of the gardens; Nature's Way, wildlife sanctuary with dozens of animals in their natural habitats; Wings of Wonder butterfly conservatory; Cypress Junction, an elaborate model railroad with up to 20 trains moving at one time; Cypress Roots, a museum of park memorabilia; and Carousel Cove, with eight kiddie rides and arcade games (and it's never very crowded). And don't forget to leave time for a Pontoon Lake Cruise on scenic Lake Eloise (about $6).

The New Wacky Water Park includes six flumes and a huge kiddie pool. It's open from April through September. Special entertainment changes throughout the year.

Discovery Cove

6000 Discovery Cove Way, Orlando 32821 • (877) 4-DISCOVERY

Hours - Open daily from 9 a.m.–5:30 p.m.

Admission - March 1–April 30: all-inclusive $199, without dolphin swim $119, trainer for a day $389. May 1–Dec. 31: all-inclusive $219, without dolphin swim $119, trainer for a day $389. Includes a seven-day pass to SeaWorld Orlando

Appeal by Age Group -

Pre-school ★★★★	Teens ★★★★★	Over 30 ★★★★★
Grade school ★★★★★	Young Adults ★★★★★	Seniors ★★★★★

Touring Time - Average 7 hours; minimum 5 hours

Rainy-Day Touring - Not recommended

Author's Rating of Major Features -

Aviary	★★★	Ray Lagoon	★★★★
Coral Reef	★★★★	Tropical River	★★★
Dolphin Lagoon	★★★★★		

Restaurants - Yes

Handicapped access - Yes

Baby stroller rental - No

Pet kennels - No

Private tours - Yes

Alcoholic beverages - Yes

Wheelchair rental - Yes (special beach wheelchairs)

Lockers - Yes

Rain check - No

Description and Comments Discovery Cove is a "soft adventure" at SeaWorld Orlando, where families can take a break from the mega parks to swim with dolphins, snorkel with tropical fish, and just plain relax on a sandy beach without driving 50 miles to the Atlantic Ocean. The park requires reservations and is limited to 1,000 guests a day. You pay for that privilege, but the experience is worth it.

The park is manageably small—30 acres—and beautifully landscaped, with four main attractions: the Dolphin Lagoon, swimming with stingrays, snorkeling with 4,000 tropical fish, and a 100-foot-long aviary filled with birds.

A large pool with waterfalls is for swimming, and Tropical River, a freshwater winding river encircles the park, with a gentle current to coax along snorkelers and swimmers.

Visitors check in at a concierge desk and a personal guide takes them for a walking tour and overview of the park. The entire day is designed to be very laid-back and relaxing, with the Dolphin Lagoon the only timed part of the day. Otherwise, you're free to swim, sleep, eat and play on the sandy beaches. A word of caution: Bring water socks or rubber pool shoes, as the sand gets scorching hot in the middle of the day.

The highlight, of course, is the dolphins, and children must be age 6 or older to get in the water with the mammals. The program starts with a 30-minute orientation for groups up of to eight swimmers, then swimmers wade into Dolphin Lagoon for a shallow water introduction. Next, three guests at a time go with the trainer into deeper water to swim, snorkel, or hang onto a dorsal fin for a high-speed ride. If you're nervous, you can stay in the shallow water and just cradle a dolphin in your arms.

The Ray Lagoon inhabitants are harmless—no barbs, and it's a startling experience to snorkel amidst dozens of sleek southern and cownose rays, some up to 4 feet in diameter. If you hold out a hand, they will take a finger in their mouths (they have no teeth).

The Coral Reef is designed with underwater shipwrecks and grottos and more than 75 species of tropical fish. Barracudas and sharks are just inches from snorkelers, separated by acrylic glass.

The free-flight aviary is a treat for tropical-bird lovers with more than 30 species and hundreds of birds, from tiny thrushes and starlings to big, brightly colored parrots. But if you have any fear or dislike of birds, do not enter—they're friendly enough to perch on heads, arms, and hands.

You need to be comfortable in the water, but not an exceptional swimmer to enjoy Discovery Cove, as everyone must wear a personal flotation device in the Dolphin Lagoon, the Coral Reef, and Tropical River. There also is an abundance of lifeguards. If you wear sunscreen, Discovery Cove offers one that is safe for the animal habitats, and it is the only sunscreen you can wear there. Wetsuits also are offered, but the water temperature is 78–85° year-round.

After a visit to the mega theme parks, Discovery Cove is a welcome diversion, where the longest line is for the free lunch. The admission covers beach umbrellas, lounges, towels, wetsuits, lockers, snorkel gear, and lunch.

Gatorland Zoo

14501 S. Orange Blossom Trail, Kissimmee • (407) 855-5496 • www.gatorland.com

Hours - Daily, 9 a.m.–dusk

Admission - $19.95 for adults, $8.50 for children ages 3–12, free for age 3 and under

Appeal by Age Group -

Pre-school ★★★½	Teens ★★★★	Over 30 ★★★½
Grade school ★★★★	Young Adults ★★★½	Seniors ★★★½

Touring Time - Average 3 hours; minimum 1½ hour

Rainy-Day Touring - Some of the exhibit is under cover

Author's Rating of Major Features -

Gator Jumparoo	★★★	Lily's Pad Water Fountain Park	★★★
Gator Wrestlin' Cracker-Style	★★★	Swamp Walk	★★
Jungle Crocs	★★★	Upclose Animal Encounters	★★★

Restaurants - Yes
Alcoholic beverages - No
Handicapped access - Yes
Wheelchair rental - Yes
Baby stroller rental - Yes
Lockers - No
Pet kennels - No
Rain check - No
Private tours - No

Description and Comments A kitschy roadside attraction, but the kids really love to see the alligators leap as high as 5 feet from the water and snatch the whole chickens in Gator Jumparoo, one of three daily shows at this old-fashioned attraction.

The 70-acre park opened in 1949, and the trademark gaping gator jaws at the entrance were put in place back in 1962. The jaws lead to a boardwalk spanning a seven-acre lake filled with dozens of the critters.

Gator Wrestlin' Cracker-Style demonstrates how Florida cowboys used to go one-on-one with the reptiles. Snakes of Florida features venomous and nonvenomous snakes native to the state.

Covered walkways lead past monkeys, goats, deer, bears, and wild birds. At the far end of the park is a 2,000-foot-long walkway through an ancient cypress swamp and a ten-acre breeding marsh with a three-level observation tower that offers a great view of gators and thousands of bird's nests.

Holy Land Experience

4655 Vineland Road, Orlando • (866) 872-4659

Hours - 9 a.m.–5 p.m. Monday–Thursday; 9 a.m.–6 p.m. Friday and Saturday, noon–6 p.m. Sunday; closed Thanksgiving and Christmas Day

Admission - 22, $17 ages 4-12

Appeal by Age Group -

Pre-school ★	Teens ★★	Over 30 ★★★
Grade school ★★	Young Adults ★★	Seniors ★★★

Touring Time - Average 3 hours

Rainy-Day Touring - Not Recommended

Author's Rating of Major Features -

Calvary's Garden Tomb Musicals	★★	Shofar Auditorim Musical Dramas	★★
The Seed of Promise	★★	Wilderness Tabernacle	★★★

Restaurants - Yes

Alcoholic beverages - No

Handicapped access - Yes

Wheelchair rental - Yes

Baby stroller rental - Yes

Lockers - No

Pet kennels - No

Rain check - No

Private tours - No

Description and Comments The Holy Land Experience isn't for everyone, but it is a peaceful retreat and a fascinating look at places recorded in the Bible. From the moment you pass through the gates of the "Walled City," the architecture transports you to Jerusalem, circa 1450 B.C. to A.D. 66, with replicas of Calvary's garden tomb, the Qumran Caves (where the Dead Sea Scrolls were found in 1947), the Wilderness Tabernacle, the Temple of the Great King, and the Plaza of the Nations. Throughout the day, live shows are staged, showing, for instance, ancient Jewish rituals in the Wilderness Tabernacle or the resurrection of Jesus. The Christian message is subtle but obvious. The park is the creation of Zion's Hope, a Christian ministry headquartered in Orlando.

Orlando Science Center

777 E. Princeton Street, Orlando • (407) 514-2000 • www.osc.org

Hours - Tuesday–Thursday, 9 a.m.–5 p.m.; Friday and Saturday, 9 a.m.–9 p.m.; Sunday, noon–5 p.m.; closed Monday

Admission - $9.50 for adults, $8.50 for senior citizens; $6.75 for children ages 3–11; additional for films, planetarium shows $2–6, combo tickets available

Appeal by Age Group -

Pre-school ★★★	Teens ★★★	Over 30 ★★
Grade school ★★★★	Young Adults ★★★	Seniors ★★

Touring Time - Average 4 hours; minimum 2 hours

Rainy-Day Touring - Recommended

Author's Rating - ★★★★; this new science center keeps kids entertained for hours, and there's plenty for adults to do, too

Restaurant Yes	**Alcoholic beverages -** No
Handicapped access - Yes	**Wheelchair rental -** Yes
Baby stroller rental - Yes	**Lockers -** No
Pet kennels - No	**Rain check -** No
Private tours - No	

Description and Comments Though the nearby beaches and world-famous attractions bring families to Central Florida, this jewel is worth a stop in Orlando proper. Where else can you build a bridge, fire a laser, and touch an alligator all in one day?

A good place to start is on the ground floor (one story down from the entrance), where children ages 8 and under—no parents allowed—let their imaginations run free in Kids Town. They can explore the root system of a tree by crawling though an underground tunnel, build with blocks at the construction site, and shop in the miniature stores. Parents have to wait for their youngsters (there are benches just inside the entryway), so in families with older children parents should split up, or let teenagers take off by themselves to explore the other exhibits.

The number of exhibits can be overwhelming—there are ten interactive exhibition halls on four floors, so take a few moments to study a guide map. We've found that it's easy to spend more than an hour in one area, so if you're on a tight schedule, be sure to visit your top choices first.

Make time during your visit to experience a show in the CineDome (separate admission), with an eight-story domed screen that immerses you in the image—traveling to the depths of a live volcano, swimming with a great white shark, racing through the human blood stream. The breathtaking cinematography on the giant screen creates a memorable experience for all ages, though the images are so large that they may at first be overwhelming for small children; ask them to close their eyes for a few moments. The films run about 30–40 minutes, so we don't really recommend the CineDome for children under 5 unless they have an appropriate attention span. The seating is quite steep, and you have to climb the stairs and exit at the rear of the darkened theater if you must leave during the show.

The Orlando Science Center is a perfect rainy day solution. Even parking is covered, with a new 600-space garage that's connected to the building by a glass walkway.

SeaWorld Orlando

7007 SeaWorld Drive, Orlando 32809 • (407) 351-3600 • www.seaworld.com

Hours - Open daily at 9 a.m., closing time varies by season

Admission - $49.95 for adults, $40.95 for children ages 3–9, free for age 2 and under; $7 for parking

Appeal by Age Group -

Pre-school ★★★★★	Teens ★★★★	Over 30 ★★★★★
Grade school ★★★★★	Young Adults ★★★★	Seniors ★★★★★

Touring Time - Average 6 hours; minimum 4 hours

Rainy-Day Touring - Not recommended

Author's Rating of Major Features -

Kraken	★★★★★	Manatees: The Last Generation?	★★★★
Journey to Atlantis	★★★★	Pacific Point Preserve	★★★★
Intensity Ski Show	★★★★	Clyde and Seamore	★★★★
Wild Arctic	★★★★	Key West Dolphin Fest	★★★★
Shamu Adventure	★★★★	Cirque de la Mer	★★★
Terrors of the Deep	★★★★½	Pets Ahoy!	★★★
Shamu's Happy Harbor	★★★★		
Penguin Encounter	★★★★½		

Restaurants - Yes

Handicapped access - Yes

Baby stroller rental - Yes

Pet kennels - Yes

Private tours - Yes

Alcoholic beverages - Yes

Wheelchair rental - Yes

Lockers - Yes

Rain check - No

Description and Comments Some families come to Central Florida with the idea that Walt Disney World is it. Their minds are closed to the suggestion that they visit any other attractions because they feel that any other place would pale by comparison.

If you've only got time to see one attraction other than Disney, this is the place we recommend. Over the last seven years, SeaWorld has added more then 20 new shows and attractions, and the park admirably combines entertainment, education, research, and conservation to create a fascinating experience, with hands-on, close-up encounters with hundreds of marine mammals. Not to mention the longest, fastest, steepest roller coaster in Orlando, Kraken—a real draw for teens.

The park is open every day of the year, and you should allow at least 6 hours to see the shows and exhibits—a great plan is to arrive at midday and stay later into the evening when temperatures are cooler and there are nighttime fireworks and laser shows.

As with all major attractions, start the tour by studying a map of SeaWorld and a schedule of the day's shows. A great way to steal a little time: Make a left when you enter the park and start your day in Key West at SeaWorld, where the kids can pet the dolphins or stingrays while you strategize a game plan for the day.

Unless you want to head straight for the two thrill rides—Kraken or Journey to Atlantis—the Dolphin Fest in the Key West area is as good a place as any to start the day. While you're waiting for the show to start, you can observe (and sometimes feed) the dolphins, turtles, stingrays, and other species indigenous to the Florida Keys. The biggest crowd is always around Dolphin Cove, where everyone tries to pet the mammals when they emerge for a breath of air or some food.

Except for Kraken, Journey to Atlantis, and Wild Arctic, SeaWorld primarily features open-air theater shows or walk-through exhibits, so you will spend a lot less time waiting in line at SeaWorld than you would in the same length visit at a Disney park. Just check show times and be at the theater about 15 minutes early—there's plenty of seating, and even if you're a few minutes late you won't miss much (with one exception, the Seal and Otter Show).

When you plan the day, notice that Shamu Stadium is all the way across the ground from the Key West at SeaWorld area, and the park is big enough to recommend seeing shows in some order. Rent strollers for little ones since there's quite a bit of walking. Wheelchairs can move around easily.

Aside from Dolphin Fest, there are three other big daytime shows: the Shamu Adventure, Clyde and Seamore, and the Intensity Ski Show. When you arrive, develop your touring itinerary around these four shows. One of the first things you will notice as you check out the performance times is that the shows are scheduled in a way that make it almost impossible to see the productions back to back in sequence. With a park map and show times, you can plan a logical excursion.

If you're visiting on a tight schedule, the only "don't miss" is the Shamu Adventure. Where else can children stand inches away from Shamu, the 8,000-pound killer whale, and be splashed by his wake? Keep in mind that Shamu's antics can really soak your clothes, so if it's chilly, you may want to sit a few rows back from the splash zone, especially with toddlers.

Older kids really like Terrors of the Deep, with a moving sidewalk that passes through a 9-foot-high acrylic tube at the bottom of a 600,000-gallon aquarium with sharks, moray eels, and barracudas swimming alongside and overhead.

The only real waits we encountered—up to an hour in the peak summer season—were for the Kraken roller coaster, Journey to Atlantis water-coaster thrill ride, and Wild Arctic, a fast-paced flight simulator. For Wild Arctic, you can bypass the ride and walk into a superb exhibit of live beluga whales, walruses, harbor seals, and polar bears. (The line is much shorter.)

Small children especially enjoy *Pets Ahoy!*, a silly show starring a cast of pets adopted from animal shelters—12 dogs, 18 cats, and cameo appearances by a pony and three 50-pound pot-bellied pigs.

If you're exhausted from all the walking but the kids still have energy to burn, make a stop at Shamu's Happy Harbor, a three-acre play area near Shamu Stadium with dozens of special places for little ones to explore and shade for parents to relax. There's an arcade next door for older kids.

It's worth keeping the kids up late to see Rockin' Nights, the park's evening extravaganza starring Shamu in a nighttime show with theatrical effects (and plenty of kid-pleasing splashes) and the largest theatrical fireworks and laser show in the United States.

If you've got a child who's age 10 or older and interested in marine life, visit SeaWorld's new Discovery Cove, an interactive park that offers a Swim with Dolphins program and a Swim with Tropical Fish and Manta Rays program where you don a wet suit and interact with the animals. Also at Discovery Cove are a bird aviary and a nature trail where you're guaranteed to catch a glimpse of small animals such as anteaters and porcupines. For the day it's $219 per person ($229 March through June), which includes one meal and a seven-day pass to SeaWorld. Reservations are required; (877)-4-DISCOVERY.

Special behind-the-scenes tours at SeaWorld include Trainer for a Day, ranked one of the best animal adventures in the world for $389; a False Killer Whale Interaction Program where guests get in the water with the animals for $200; and Animal Care Experience, a full day with SeaWorld marine mammal experts for $389. You must be at least 13 years old to participate in any of the programs. Call (407) 351-3600 ext. 3384 for more information.

Silver Springs

5656 E. Silver Springs Boulevard, Silver Springs • (352) 236-2121
www.silversprings.com

Hours - Daily, 10 a.m.–5 p.m., with longer hours during summer and select holidays

Admission - $31.95 for adults, $28.99 Seniors 55 and older, $22.99 for children ages 3–10, free for age 2 and under

Appeal by Age Group -

Pre-school ★★★	Teens ★★	Over 30 ★★★★
Grade school ★★★★	Young Adults ★★★	Seniors ★★★★

Touring Time - Average 5 hours; minimum 3 hours

Rainy-Day Touring - Not recommended

Author's Rating of Major Features -

Alligator and Crocodile Encounter	★★	Jeep Safari	★★
		Jungle Cruise	★★★
Birds of Prey	★★	Kids Ahoy!	★★★
Birds of the Rainforest	★★	Lost River Voyage	★★★★
Creature Feature	★★	Reptiles of the World	★
Doolittle's Petting Zoo	★★	A Touch of Garlits	★★★½
Florida Natives	★★	World of Bears	★★
Glass-Bottom Boats	★★★★		

Restaurants - Yes

Alcoholic beverages - Yes

Handicapped access - Yes

Wheelchair rental - Yes

Baby stroller rental - Yes

Lockers - No

Pet kennels - Free

Rain check - Yes

Private tours - No

Description and Comments This delightful park, though constantly changing, is like a pleasant step back in time. Billed as "Florida's Original Attraction," Silver Springs is a 350-acre nature park surrounding the headwaters of the beautiful Silver River.

For families who have been coming to Florida for years, the attraction is almost a tradition. Each generation is ceremoniously exposed ("This is where your grandma brought me when I was your age"). Chances are if you enjoyed it as a kid, you'll enjoy watching your own children experience this piece of old Florida. If you've never been before, be forewarned—the animals are real; there are no nifty mechanical fish; and the boats are not on a track. If plastic and glitter are what you want, keep heading south.

The hallmark of Silver Springs is a tour of the natural springs in the glass-bottom boats. More than half a billion gallons of water bubble out of the ground each day, forming a crystal-clear lagoon in the midst of a luxurious tropical jungle. Wildlife abounds both above and below the water, but it is the diverse aquatic life seen through the glass that captivates most visitors. The boat ride, relaxed and unhurried, is informatively narrated by the driver of the boat. The boats are covered top and side, providing protection from sun and rain. Boats depart every few minutes and the waiting area is under cover with a substantial amount of seating available.

Also at Silver Springs are a Jeep Safari through 35 acres of Florida backwoods, lots of live animal shows, reptile shows, and a kids' playground.

Wet 'n' Wild

6200 International Drive, Orlando 32819 • (407) 351-WILD • www.wetnwild.com

Hours - Daily, 10 a.m.–5 p.m., with extended hours in peak seasons

Admission - $30 for adults, $16.98 for seniors 55 and older, $24.95 for children ages 3–9, free for ages 3 and under (admission does not include tube or towel rentals)

Appeal by Age Group -

Pre-school ★★★★	Teens ★★★★★	Over 30 ★★★★
Grade school ★★★★	Young Adults ★★★★★	Seniors ★★

Touring Time - Average 5 hours; minimum 3 hours

Rainy-Day Touring - Not recommended

Author's Rating - ★★★★; it's not themed or as aesthetically pleasing as the Disney water parks, but the rides are awesome, and there are more than you'll find anywhere else. Just be prepared for the crowds

Restaurants - Yes

Alcoholic beverages - Yes

Handicapped access - Limited

Wheelchair rental - No

Baby stroller rental - No

Lockers - Yes

Pet kennels - No

Rain check - No

Private tours - No

Description and Comments Before Disney started building water parks, this was the place to cool off in Central Florida. Universal Orlando recently acquired the park, so it's been spiffed up substantially. Conveniently located on 25 acres on International Drive, Wet 'n Wild still offers more rides than any other water park, and teenagers in particular can make a day of it.

Wet 'n' Wild doesn't offer the themed ambience of the Disney water parks, but in over 20 years the rides have gotten higher, faster, and more popular—waits for a 60-second splashdown can be up to 20 minutes. But thrill-ride enthusiasts swear that patience pays off for rides like the Fuji Flyer, which sends four passengers plunging down six stories through 450 feet of banked curves, or the Black Hole, which propels riders through 600 feet of twisting, turning, watery darkness.

Of course, there are tamer rides, like the Bubba Tub or Raging Rapids that the whole family can experience together. And for children under 48 inches tall (or under age 10), Kids Park features miniature versions of the park's most popular attractions along with water-oriented playground equipment.

All the rides have a symbol that denotes who will enjoy the ride most: a green square denotes rides for supervised toddlers, youngsters, seniors, or handicapped guests; a gold circle for experienced riders, beginning swimmers, supervised children, and partially handicapped guests; a diamond, aggressive ride action, strong swimming skills needed, or both; and a triangle for high thrills or deep-water action.

Though the park employs an army of certified lifeguards, we recommend constant vigil for children under 10 and non-swimmers. The park gets quite crowded during peak seasons, and it can be a major headache just keeping up with little ones.

Pools are heated on chillier days. The fast food is mediocre, but you're allowed to bring along a picnic (but no alcoholic beverages). And don't forget the sunscreen. The Florida sun can be brutal, especially when you're waiting in those long lines.

International Drive

International Drive, or "I-Drive," is the epicenter of Central Florida's tourism business. This is where you'll find most of the factory outlet stores, many hotel chains, and just about any fast-food restaurant your imagination can dream up.

If you're staying on I-Drive, there are myriad small attractions that are great for rainy days, or if you're short on time or have overspent the budget for the premier parks. Here are four we recommend for families:

WonderWorks, in the distinctive "upside-down" building at 9067 International Drive, is an interactive playground where you can experience earthquakes and hurricanes, swim with sharks, put yourself inside a huge bubble, design and ride a roller coaster, or play in the world's largest laser tag arena. The owners visited science centers all over the world, then re-created the best of the best. Hours are 9 a.m.–midnight daily; cost is $15.95, $11.95 ages 4–12. (407) 352-0411; www.wonderworksonline.com.

Ripley's Believe It or Not is just plain fun, filled to the rafters with oddities like shrunken heads, unusual animals, and animals made of matchsticks. Ripley's is at 8201 International Drive. Hours are 9 a.m.–1 a.m. daily; cost is $14.95, $9.95 ages 4 to 12; (407) 363-4418.

Vans Skateboard Park is the place to go if you've got a kid who's jonesin' for a little skateboard time. The mack daddy skatepark features 61,000 square feet of indoor and outdoor skating with riding areas and obstacles. Highlights include the "Dough Boy," an above-ground bowl, and a 40-foot competition-size vertical ramp. Grown-ups can hang out on the mezzanine viewing area. At Festival Bay, 5220 International Drive, Orlando; (407) 351-3881; www.vans.com.

Dinner Shows

Most of the families we know are usually exhausted at the end of the vacation day. However, if you're looking for a special night out, consider these entertaining dinner shows. The food isn't memorable, but there's plenty of it, and the entertainment is fun for the whole family.

Medieval Times Dinner and Tournament 4510 N. Irlo Bronson Highway (US 192), Kissimmee; (800) 229-8300. This cavernous dining hall takes you back to the days of knights, chivalry, and regal feasts with a banquet in an eleventh-century-style castle—cheer for your knight on horseback jousting and sword fighting. The four-course meal—chicken, ribs, bread, potatoes, soup, and dessert—isn't served with silverware; you dine just like in the olden days—eating with your hands. Adults, $44; children ages 3–11, $28. Shows nightly, 8 p.m.

Hoop-de-Doo Revue Disney's Fort Wilderness Campground and Resort; (407) 939-3463. Even sophisticated New Yorkers end up hooping and hollering at this long-running show in Pioneer Hall. The revue plays three times nightly (5, 7:15, and 9:30 p.m.) with all-you-can-eat ribs and fried chicken. Adults, $47.80; children ages 3–11, $24.81. This one books up fast, so call early for reservations.

Aloha! Polynesian Luau SeaWorld; (407) 363-2200. 2 hours of authentic island entertainment and a four-course meal, including fresh fruit, sweet and sour chicken, white fish, and smoked pork loin. Adults, $37.95; children ages 8–12, $27.95; ages 3-7, $16.95. Showtime: 5:30 and 8:15 p.m.

Polynesian Luau Disney's Polynesian Resort; (407) 939-3463. Another Disney show that's been around forever, featuring authentic island dancing in a pretty outdoor setting. Dine on Hawaiian roasted chicken, seafood, and fruit salad. Seatings nightly at 5:15 and 8 p.m. Adults, $47.80; children ages 3–11, $24.81.

Arabian Nights Dinner Attraction 6225 W. Irlo Bronson Highway (US 192); (407) 239-9223. Equestrian performance featuring more than 60 horses, including white Lipizzans, and great riders. The highlight is a high-speed chariot race re-created from the film *Ben Hur*. Dine on prime rib or vegetable lasagna; for children, it's chicken fingers and mashed potatoes. Adults, $44; children ages 3–11, $27. Showtimes: Sunday–Thursday 7:30 p.m., Friday–Saturday 8:30 p.m.

Family-Friendly Restaurants

Central Florida, though not a culinary capital, has more than 2,000 restaurants, many of them familiar chains geared to serving families who patronize the attractions. If you're looking for ethnic cuisine, dozens of Asian restaurants are clustered around Mills Avenue at Colonial Drive in Orlando, where Korean, Vietnamese, and Chinese cuisines have turned storefronts into a culinary tour of the Far East. Local families frequent many of the little restaurants, and children are most welcome.

The following are a few favorites, from chains to mom-and-pop places, all catering to families.

Bahama Breeze

8849 International Drive, Orlando • (407) 248-2499

Meals served - Dinner

Cuisine - American with Caribbean twist

Entree range - $8.95–16.95

Kids menu - Yes

Reservations - Not accepted

Payment - All major credit cards accepted

This chain eatery (brought to you by the creators of Red Lobster and Olive Garden) is casual and noisy enough for families to have fun. Try the conch chowder or conch fritters for a pretty authentic taste of the Caribbean. Kids love the sweet piña colada bread pudding.

Boma—Flavors of Africa

Disney's Animal Kingdom Lodge • (407) WDW-DINE

Meals served - Breakfast and dinner

Cuisine - African

Entree range - Breakfast, $14.99, $7.99 ages 3–11; dinner $21.99, $8.99 ages 3–11

Kids menu - Yes

Reservations - Necessary

Payment - All major credit cards accepted

Boma gets raves from local families, who enjoy the expansive "cooking station" concept and the unusual setting of this Disney restaurant. There's an array of choices, and many of the dinner creations are African-inspired, including delicious soups and sauces for meats. But there's also simple fare for kids. After dinner, take a stroll and check out the animals, from giraffes to wildebeests, on the savannah.

California Grill

Disney's Contemporary Resort • (407) WDW-DINE

Meals served - Dinner

Cuisine - New American

Entree range - $19.50–28.50

Kids menu - Yes

Reservations - Priority seating recommended

Payment - All major credit cards accepted

If you splurge for just one meal, make this the place, high atop Disney's Contemporary Resort with a spectacular view of the Magic Kingdom's nightly fireworks. The simple, sophisticated food, too, is stellar, voted "The Best Meal in America" by *USA Today.* Start with a brick oven-baked flatbread or sushi.

Chef Mickey's

Disney's Contemporary Resort • (407) WDW-DINE

Meals served - Breakfast and dinner

Cuisine - New American

Entree range - Breakfast, $15.99, $8.99 ages 3–11; dinner, $21.99, $9.99 children

Kids menu - Yes

Reservations - Not accepted

Payment - All major credit cards accepted

If your kids want an audience with the Big Cheese, this is the easiest way to do it. Mickey Mouse and friends are there for each meal, and make a point to stop at every table. The food is served buffet style, with delicious choices for grown-ups, including prime rib and pasta with shrimp. Kids love their very own dessert bar.

Emeril's Restaurant Orlando

Universal Studios CityWalk • (407) 224-2424

Meals served - Lunch and dinner

Cuisine - New Orleans contemporary

Entree range - Lunch $18.50–25; Dinner $20–40.

Kids menu - No

Reservations - Yes

Payment - All major credit cards accepted

Emeril's Restaurant Orlando is a mecca for fans of the flamboyant chef. It's high-calorie, New Orleans-style cooking, giant plates heaped with fish and meats. Entrees are big enough to share, so if you're taking the kids, look for something they will like. Much of the food is heavily sauced; we love the simple grilled rib eye steak with garlic mashed potatoes. Save room for the banana cream pie.

Jimmy Buffett's Margaritaville

Universal Studios CityWalk • (407) 224-2155

Meals served - Lunch and dinner

Cuisine - American/Caribbean

Entree range - \$8.95–19.95

Kids menu - Yes

Reservations - No

Payment - All major credit cards accepted

If you're a parrothead, stop for a cheeseburger and introduce the kids to Jimmy Buffett's music, always blaring with giant-screen videos to match. The food's fun, like the conch fritters or Buffet's favorite (so they say), Margaritaville shrimp and bowtie pasta.

O'Boy's Barbeque

610 W. Morse Blvd., Winter Park • (407) 478-6269

Meals served - Lunch and dinner

Cuisine - Barbeque

Entree range - \$5.95–12.95

Kids menu - Yes

Reservations - Not accepted

Payment - All major credit cards accepted

This friendly Winter Park eatery is a favorite for families because you can dine outdoors in a pretty "back yard," and no one seems to mind if kids run free. Also serving some of Central Florida's best 'cue.

Rainforest Cafe

1800 E. Lake Buena Vista Drive, Lake Buena Vista • (407) 933-2800

Meals served - Lunch and dinner

Cuisine - Multiethnic

Entree range - \$10–40

Kids menu - Yes

Reservations - Not accepted

Payment - All major credit cards accepted; also, Disney room charges and Disney packages

You can't miss this place, just look for the smoking volcano at Downtown Disney Marketplace. The wait for a table can be painfully long, but they give you a pager so you can wander in the shops to keep the kids entertained. Everyone goes to see the enormous fish tanks, jungle-size butterflies, cascading waterfalls, thunder, lightning, and animated gorillas. The food sounds better than it tastes and portions are huge, so plan on sharing entrees like the Rasta Pasta (bow-tie pasta in a cream sauce with chicken and spinach) or a thick sandwich. By the way, Rainforest won't buy beef raised on deforested land, and all the fish is line caught. They give free tours for children if you call ahead.

Spoodles

Disney's BoardWalk Resort • (407) WDW-DINE

Meals served - Breakfast, lunch, and dinner

Cuisine - Mediterranean

Entree range - Breakfast, $12.95, $8.95 ages 3–11; lunch, $10–17; dinner, $14–32

Kids menu - Yes

Reservations - Priority seating recommended

Payment - All major credit cards accepted

The open kitchen and big wooden tables create the ambience of a casual Mediterranean eatery. It's a great place for the thin-crust pizzas or plates of interesting food like Moroccan-spiced tuna with fennel, lemon, chives, and spiced olive oil, or crispy calamari. Kids love the macaroni and cheese. Breakfast is a tasty, all-you-can-eat buy.

Wolfgang Puck Cafe

Downtown Disney West Side • (407) 938-9653

Meals served - Lunch and dinner

Cuisine - Contemporary

Entree range - $6.95-11.95 lunch; $9.95-19.95 dinner

Kids menu - Yes

Reservations - Upstairs dining room only

Payment - All major credit cards accepted

Puck's menu has something for everyone. Try the best-selling Chinois Chicken Salad, or the delicious crab cakes. For families, the Wolfgang Puck Express, next door to the main dining room, is a good bet offering Puck's famous pizzas, soups, and salads. Be forewarned, the place is packed most nights.

Side Trips

Kissimmee/Osceola County Walt Disney World dramatically changed this quiet burg that's home to cattle farmers and real-life cowboys. Kissimmee is the town closest to the front door of Walt Disney World, just 10 miles to the east, and today it's most noted for dozens of big hotels, tiny motels, souvenir shops, fast-food restaurants, and more that are packed side by side on US 192, a road that stretches from downtown Kissimmee through the main entrance to Walt Disney World.

But there's much more to Kissimmee and Osceola County, and for families who want to step outside the man-made attractions and connect with nature, the area is known for fishing, canoeing, boating, and airboating (see Family Outdoor Adventures, page 174). Lake Tohopekaliga near downtown Kissimmee has a waterfront park with a 3-mile stretch that's perfect for strolling or bike riding. And for the real thing, visit the Silver Spurs Arena in February or October for one of the top rodeos in the nation, with bull and bronco riding, steer wrestling, and barrel racing. For tickets, call (407) 67-RODEO, two months before the event.

Winter Park This charming town just north of Orlando on I-4 has two fun family recommendations: the Scenic Boat Tour, a relaxing, 1-hour cruise through the lakes and canals of this historic little burg, and the Morse Museum of American Art, showcasing the rarest collection of Tiffany glass in the world. The boat tour leaves the dock on East Morse Boulevard at Interlachen Avenue daily (except Christmas) from 10 a.m.–4 p.m. Cost is $6, $3 ages 2–11. (407) 644-4056. The Morse Museum at 445 Park Ave. N. is open 9:30 a.m.–4 p.m. Tuesday–Saturday, 1–4 p.m. Sunday. Cost is $3, $1 ages 12 and under. (407) 645-5311.

Forever Florida Just minutes from Disney World, experience a wilderness adventure that combines a 2-hour tour of the 1,500-acre working Crescent J. Ranch and nine Florida ecosystems in a 3,200-acre nature preserve. It's Florida *au naturel,* with deer, alligators, herds of cattle, and flocks of sandhill cranes, and the best way to take it all in is the guided Cracker Coach Tour in an elevated swamp buggy. The first tour of the morning leaves at 9 a.m., and we recommend this one to both avoid the heat and to improve your odds for sighting wildlife. After the tour, kids can feed calves and goats at the petting zoo, or take a pony ride. $28, $18 ages 5-12. Open daily (except Easter, Thanksgiving, and Christmas) at 8 a.m., with tours at 9, noon, and 3 p.m. 4755 N. Kenansville Rd., St. Cloud. (888) 957-9794; www.foreverflorida.com.

Mount Dora Scenic Railway For a real change of scenery, take a side trip to Mount Dora, about 30 minutes northwest of Orlando, and hop a ride on the rails. Weekdays, you'll board the Dora Doodlebug, a 1920s-style, 48-passenger motorcar built to run forward and backward during its 8-mile trek past local landmarks, with a friendly conductor telling tales about the New England–style town. Seatbacks flip to face forward as the train reverses directions. On weekends, the ride is on the Cannonball, the only steam-operated train in Florida running on standard track. Nicknamed "Florida's Movie Train," the Cannonball was featured in *Rosewood,* the miniseries *North and South* and *O Brother, Where Art Thou?* After the train ride, kids can let off their own steam in nearby Gilbert Park (Liberty Avenue and Tremain) on a huge wooden play fort. Cost for the Doodlebug is $10, $6 ages 12 and under. Cannonball is $16, $8 ages 12 and under. The station is at Alexander Street and Third Avenue in Mount Dora; (800) 625-4307. Call for schedules.

Part Five

Central West Florida

Convenient beaches and plenty of man-made attractions, from Busch Gardens to the Florida Aquarium, make Central West Florida a popular destination for active families.

For great oceanfront fun, head just south to Clearwater or St. Petersburg, with 28 miles of beaches on the bustling peninsula across the bay from Tampa. Added bonuses are glorious sunsets (which you miss on the Atlantic coast of Florida). These beaches, by the way, boast an annual average of 361 days of sunshine and an average water temperature of 75°, making nearly every day a good one for shelling, sunning, and swimming. Also, many of these beaches, including Fort Desoto, St. Pete Beach, Treasure Island, Honeymoon Island, and others, received special recognition for environmental quality and safety by the Clean Beaches Council.

Away from the ocean, there's more Florida wilderness and gentle, rolling hills, with glimpses of small-town America in Citrus, Hernando, and Pasco counties.

This also is a sports fan's mecca, with pro football, soccer, baseball, and hockey teams in Tampa (see page 281). Because of the beautiful weather, many baseball teams conduct their spring training camps in this region, a real treat for kids when the players are more relaxed and willing to please their fans, and the venues are often small and intimate. The Yankees venue is particularly special, a miniature replica of Yankee Stadium in the Bronx.

The area offers rich ethnic diversity, from the Greek seaside village of Tarpon Springs to the Cuban enclave of Ybor City. Your family can have a real culinary adventure—from baklava from Greek bakeries to paella at the legendary Columbia restaurant in Ybor City. In addition to great food, all these ethnic groups have a story to tell, and by visiting their neighborhoods your family can learn about their cultures—see the centuries-old sponge industry in Tarpon Springs or historic cigar factories in Ybor City. And St. Petersburg is overflowing with wonderful cultural activities, including the noted Dali Museum that attracts thousands of vacationers each year.

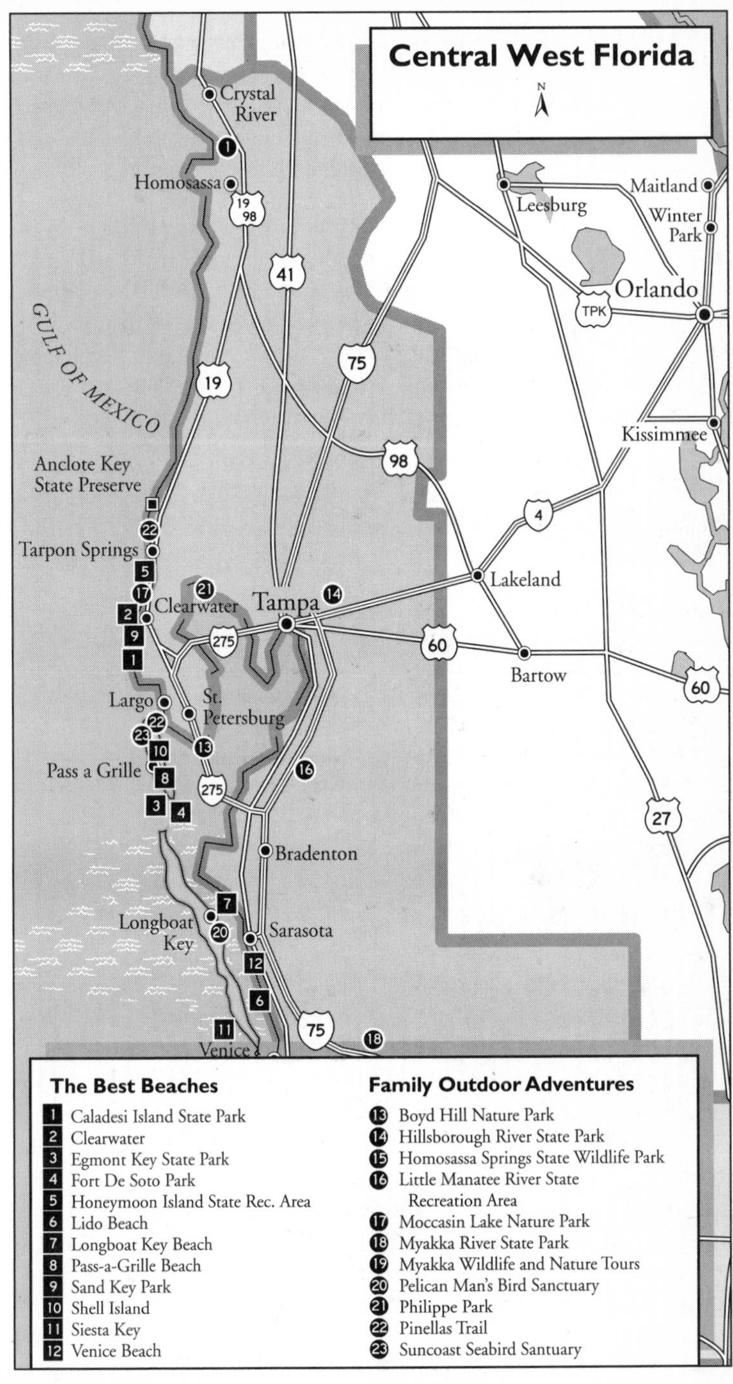
Central West Florida
N
Crystal River
Homosassa
Leesburg
Maitland
Winter Park
Orlando
GULF OF MEXICO
Kissimmee
Anclote Key State Preserve
Tarpon Springs
Lakeland
Clearwater
Tampa
Bartow
Largo
St. Petersburg
Pass a Grille
Bradenton
Longboat Key
Sarasota
Venice
The Best Beaches
1 Caladesi Island State Park
2 Clearwater
3 Egmont Key State Park
4 Fort De Soto Park
5 Honeymoon Island State Rec. Area
6 Lido Beach
7 Longboat Key Beach
8 Pass-a-Grille Beach
9 Sand Key Park
10 Shell Island
11 Siesta Key
12 Venice Beach
Family Outdoor Adventures
13 Boyd Hill Nature Park
14 Hillsborough River State Park
15 Homosassa Springs State Wildlife Park
16 Little Manatee River State Recreation Area
17 Moccasin Lake Nature Park
18 Myakka River State Park
19 Myakka Wildlife and Nature Tours
20 Pelican Man's Bird Sanctuary
21 Philippe Park
22 Pinellas Trail
23 Suncoast Seabird Santuary

A little farther south along the coast is Sarasota, where the pace slows down a notch. A fine arts community thrives here, as do beautiful beaches of pure white sand and blue waters. The city once was the home of John Ringling and his world-famous Ringling Bros. Circus; today, the legacy is on display at the John and Mable Ringling Museum of Art.

Getting There

By Plane Hernando County Airport, 40 miles north of Tampa, (352) 754-4061; St. Petersburg–Clearwater International Airport, 7 miles southeast of Clearwater, (727) 453-7800; Sarasota-Bradenton International Airport, 3 miles north of Sarasota, (941) 359-5200; Tampa International Airport, 5 miles west of downtown Tampa, (813) 870-8700; and Venice Municipal Airport, half a mile south of Venice, (945) 485-9293.

By Train Amtrak offers services to Tampa, St. Petersburg, and Sarasota; (800) USA-RAIL, www.amtrak.com.

By Car St. Petersburg–Clearwater is accessible from I-75, I-275, I-4, US 19, and SR 60.

How to Get Information before You Go

St. Petersburg–Clearwater Area Convention and Visitors Bureau, 14450 46th Street, N. Clearwater 34622; (727) 464-7200; www.floridasbeach.com. The website allows you to preview and book accommodations in the area.

Sarasota Convention and Visitors Bureau, 655 N. Tamiami Trail, Sarasota 34236; (941) 957-1877 or (800) 522-9799; www.sarasotafl.org.

Tampa-Hillsborough Convention and Visitors Association, 400 N. Tampa Street, Suite 1010, Tampa 33602; (813) 223-2752 or (800) 44-TAMPA; www.gotampa.com.

The Best Beaches

♥ **Caladesi Island State Park** Discover a 600-acre barrier reef that looks like it did in the 1500s. Caladesi is in the Gulf of Mexico, off the coast of Dunedin north of Clearwater Beach. After a ferry ride to the island you'll find 3 miles of beautiful undeveloped beaches edged in sea grass and palmettos. A self-guided nature trail winds through the interior of the island, thick with live oak hammocks and a ridge of virgin pine flatwood. The beach side of Caladesi is on the Gulf of Mexico, and the bay side of Caladesi is a mangrove swamp, home to many wading birds and shorebirds. Boardwalks on the beach provide access from the beaches (no lifeguards) to the concession stand, playground, bathhouses, and picnic areas while protecting the dunes and sea oats. Ferry service runs every hour from Honeymoon Island to Caladesi; cost is $7 for adults, $3.50 for children ages 4–12. Open 10 a.m.–4:30 p.m. Call the ferry at (727) 734-5263 for more information.

♥ **Clearwater** Clearwater Beach, known for its wide and long beaches, is one of the most popular west coast beaches. The more populated areas of this 3-mile beach are in the south end where there are many hotels; families visiting for the day may like the quieter north end. There are lifeguards all along the beach. At sunset, Pier 60, at the intersection of Causeway and Gulfview Boulevards, offers a sunset celebration patterned after Key West's popular Mallory Square festival, with craftspeople, artists, and entertainers performing nightly 2 hours before and after sunset. For kids, adjacent Pier 60 Park has a terrific covered playground

Ample parking for the beach can be found off Gulfview Avenue, on the street from 15th to 27th Avenues, and on 1st and 8th Avenues. For family members with disabilities, Clearwater offers two beach wheelchairs that feature all-terrain-type tires. Pier 60; (727) 462-6936.

♥ **Egmont Key State Park** This 440-acre island has everything: a fort from the Spanish American War, a long beach for swimming and shelling, and nature trails. It's also home to the only manned lighthouse in the United States. Several boats offer snorkeling excursions to this island—the fort is sliding into the ocean, providing a new reef. Take sunscreen, water, and a picnic if you plan to stay, because there are no facilities here except a rest room, and there are no lifeguards. Egmont is located at the mouth of Tampa Bay, southwest of Fort DeSoto Beach, and is only accessible by boat. Hubbard's Sea Adventures, (727) 358-6577, offers trips out of St. Pete; $35 for adults, $25 for children ages 12 and under. *Cortez Lady* offers trips from Bradenton; cost is $20 for adults, $10 for children ages 15 and under, and $15 for seniors. For reservations (required two days in advance) call (941) 794-1223.

Fort DeSoto Park Five barrier islands create the 900 acres of Fort DeSoto Park, home to 7 miles of picturesque, undeveloped beaches. Mullet Key is the largest island and the site of Fort DeSoto, an artillery installation built in 1898 to protect Tampa Bay during the Spanish American War. The war ended before construction was finished and the fort's cannons were never fired. Hiking trails take you to the fort, now listed in the National Register of Historic Places.

Fort DeSoto has 235 campsites on the water, surrounded by giant oaks, palms, cactus, sea grape shrubs, and sea oats. The prettiest, most secluded areas are on the north and east ends of the park. Facilities include beaches with lifeguards for swimming (though there are swift currents in parts), a boat ramp, a large playground, a concession stand, rest rooms, showers, picnic areas, and 4 miles of bicycle and in-line skating trails. There are also two piers, where the fishing is terrific. Call (727) 864-3345 for rod rentals; $4.75 for 4 hours, $8.50 for 8 hours. Entrance to the park is free; it is open sunrise to sunset, and the sunsets are spectacular. Camping is $24–34 per night (same price with or without electricity). Fort DeSoto Park is located southwest of St. Petersburg, 3500 Pinellas Bayway S., Tierra Verde; campgrounds, (727) 582-2267.

Honeymoon Island State Recreation Area Once named Hog Island, this island was renamed in 1939 when a developer constructed 50 palm-thatched honeymoon bungalows for use by couples chosen through a contest sponsored by Northern department stores. The developer's dream was interrupted by history—Pearl Harbor—and the site was recommissioned as a rest and recreation site for exhausted workers during World War II.

Now, visitors can see one of the few remaining South Florida virgin slash pine stands along the island's northern loop trail, a nesting site for osprey. Mangrove swamps, seagrass beds, salt marshes, tidal flats, and sand dunes are among other natural habitats, home to more than 208 species of plants and many shorebirds. The beaches aren't the greatest for swimming, but shelling is good, and the ocean here has a bounty of flounder, snook, trout, redfish, snapper, whiting, sheepshead, and tarpon.

Facilities include picnic pavilions, bathhouses, and a park concession building. Not only is this beach family friendly, with lifeguards patrolling on weekends, but four-legged friends are welcome, too, with an area of the beach designated for pets. Admission is $4 per vehicle. The park is open 8 a.m.–sunset. Accessible by Dunedin Causeway, Honeymoon Island State Recreation Area is at the west end of SR 586, north of Dunedin, which is just north of Clearwater; (727) 469-5942.

Lido Beach At the north end of Lido Beach, you'll discover a pristine strip of white sand, accented by towering Australian pines. In the middle of Lido is a public beach with a swimming pool, a playground, and shops. Nature trails wind through the south end of the key in South Lido Park, where there are volleyball courts and picnic areas. Lifeguards are on duty year-round, and the beach can get crowded at times because parking is plentiful. The beach is located just off Sarasota.

Longboat Key Beach This "Rolls Royce of Islands" stretches about 10 miles north from St. Armands Key, located between the waters of the Gulf of Mexico and Sarasota Bay. Enjoy the beach or explore the upscale island by bike or on inline skates on a 10-mile bike path that meanders beside the Gulf of Mexico. Public access beaches (but with no lifeguards or rest rooms) are at 3037 and 3100 Gulf of Mexico Drive. Parking is limited, but after you fight for a spot you'll enjoy a desolate beach.

♥ **Pass-a-Grille Beach** This tiny beach community is near St. Petersburg Beach on the southern tip of Long Key. Facilities include showers, dressing rooms, a snack bar, and a picnic area, but no lifeguards. Take the bridge spanning the opening of Boca Ciega Bay to get here. Day visitors can park on Eighth Avenue, with access to the public beach; (727) 367-2735.

Sand Key Park This beautifully landscaped park and wide beach area is great for swimming, with lifeguards on duty. Facilities include showers, picnic areas, grills, and playground equipment. The park is located at the northern end of Belleair Beach on Gulf Boulevard. Drive to the southernmost tip of Clearwater Beach, then over the Clearwater Pass Bridge to get to here. Open 7 a.m.–sunset; free entrance, metered parking; (727) 588-4852.

Shell Island Hunt for seashells or observe rare and endangered shorebirds on Shell Island. Remember to take water and snacks; there are no facilities here. Many boats offer sightseeing packages that take you out to the island for sunbathing; the packages often include dolphin watching. Shell Island is located just south of St. Petersburg. You must catch a ferry (there are no bridges to the island) at Merry Pier to Shell Island. One service, Shell Island Shuttle, provides ferry shuttles from Merry Pier at Pass a Grille to Shell Island. Cost is $9.50 for adults, $5.50 for ages 12 and under. Call (800) 227-0132 for more information on the shuttle.

♥ **Siesta Key** Siesta Key is said to have some of the whitest, finest sand in the world. Not only is the beach beautiful, but it is also family-oriented, with playgrounds for kids. Near the playgrounds in the middle of the key, you'll also find volleyball nets, tennis courts, showers, rest rooms, concession stands, and picnic areas. Lifeguards are here year-round. All these features, in addition to ample parking, make this beach one of the most popular (and populated) beaches in Sarasota County. Siesta Key is connected to the mainland by two bridges and can be reached by 948 Beach Road, west of the Midnight Pass Road intersection.

Venice Beach This beach is known as the "Fossilized Shark Tooth Capital of the World"; the title alone is bound to impress your kids. You'll love it too, because the beaches are rarely crowded. There are lifeguards at the Venice Public Beach daily 10 a.m.–4:15 p.m. and rest rooms with showers. Cast your line at the Venice fishing pier, or visit Grinder, the resident dolphin, in the Venice jetties. Venice, bordered by the Intracoastal Waterway, is laced with canals and natural waterways—bearing a resemblance to its Italian counterpart. Public access and parking are great. Located at the south end of Sarasota.

Family Outdoor Adventures

Boyd Hill Nature Park Ask for a butterfly checklist when you enter the park to help you spot the 22 different kinds of butterflies that have been identified here. In addition to these beautiful creatures, you'll experience

Florida's diverse ecosystem in this 245-acre park. On a small nearby island, you'll find the gopher tortoise; in the willow marsh, look for lizards on the trees; in the swamp woodlands, box turtles will be hiding on the forest floor; and in the pine flatwoods, the trees provide a canopy for blue jays and cardinals. You'll also find flying squirrels, possums, raccoons, snakes, and gators. More than 3 miles of trails and boardwalks lead visitors through these areas. There are also picnic areas and a playground. Admission is $2 for adults and $1 for children ages 3–17. Open daily, 9 a.m.–5 p.m.; from April to October, hours are extended to 8 p.m. on Tuesday and Thursday. Closed on Thanksgiving and Christmas. 1101 Country Club Way S., St. Petersburg; (727) 893-7326.

Hillsborough River State Park History blends with nature in this 3,000-acre park, home of Fort Foster, built on the banks of the Hillsborough River during the Second Seminole War. The fort and the bridge it protected have been reconstructed on the original site. Park Service volunteers, often dressed in replica outfits, greet visitors. Call ahead for dates of monthly tours. Admission is $2 for adults, $1 for children ages 7–12.

You can also hike along 8 miles of nature trails through live oaks, sabal palms, hickory, and magnolias bordering the scenic Hillsborough River. There are 106 sites for camping; cost is $13. The park is open daily, 8 a.m.–sunset; $3.25 per car. Located 6 miles southwest of Zephyrhills at 15402 US 301 N.; (813) 987-6771.

Homosassa Springs State Wildlife Park The centerpiece of this 166-acre park is a huge spring from which millions of gallons of fresh, clear water bubble every hour. You can walk through an underwater observatory to view manatees and fish in this spring that's home to 10,000 fish (someone must be counting). Wildlife you'll see includes a Florida black bear, bobcats, alligators, and wild birds. Educational programs are offered on West Indian manatees, alligators, crocodiles, Florida snakes, and other wildlife. Boat tours are provided daily. The park is open daily 9 a.m.–5:30 p.m. (Ticket counter closes at 4 p.m.) Admission is $7.95 for adults, $4.95 ages 3–12. Homosassa Springs is 75 miles north of Tampa on US 19; call (352) 628-5343 or 628-2311 for recorded information.

Little Manatee River State Recreation Area The Little Manatee has been designated an Outstanding Florida Water, and it flows for 4.5 miles through this 1,638-acre recreation area. Canoeing is especially popular, with a rich river hammock along the banks and many birds that make their permanent or migratory homes here. A 6.5-mile hiking trail meanders through the north side of the area. There are 30 campsites for $10. Little Manatee is located 4 miles south of Sun City in Hillsborough County, off US 301 on Lightfoot Road, Wimauma; (813) 671-5005.

Moccasin Lake Nature Park This park is an odd combination, part nature park and part energy education center. The grounds include more than 51 acres of laurel, live oaks, and wildflowers. Alligators, bald eagles, barn owls, flying squirrels, and snapping turtles live here, and chances are you'll spot some of these animals on the mile-long nature trail that winds through forests and wetlands to the five-acre Moccasin Lake. Once you reach the lake, you can climb the 30-foot observation pier that extends over the lake for a better view of marine life. Often, you'll see the eyes of an alligator peering from the water. At the Interpretive Center, you'll find wildlife exhibits, live native reptiles and fish, and solar and wind power exhibits. The energy exhibits show how the park produces a portion of its energy, and the building itself is an example of energy conservation with its passive cooling design and wood stove heating system. Open Tuesday–Friday, 9 a.m.–5 p.m.; Saturday and Sunday, 10 a.m.–6 p.m. Closed on Mondays. Cost is $2 for adults, $1 ages 3–12. 2750 Park Trail Lane, Clearwater; (727) 462-6024.

Myakka River State Park To get a good look at these 29,000 acres of wilderness, explore some of the 38 miles of hiking trails through dry prairie, pine flatwoods, and small wetlands. You may see cottontail rabbits, deer, bobcat, red-shouldered hawks, and other wildlife. There are also 14 miles of vehicle/bike trails. Although swimming is not allowed, fishing is very popular here, and rental boats and bicycles ($4 an hour)—including tandems ($7 an hour)—are available. The 12-mile-long Myakka River is perfect for canoe rides. On these and airboat tours, you're likely to spot alligators, some of the largest in the state. A guide said this park is on a par with the Everglades for wildlife viewing. On Saturdays at 9 a.m. rangers provide guided walks, and on Sundays at 9 a.m. there are birding programs.

But the best way to experience Myakka is to camp. Cabins, constructed with the trunks of cabbage palms and chinked with tar and sawdust, were built in the 1930s by members of the Civilian Conservation Corps. A few modern conveniences have been added over the years. Each cabin now has air conditioning and heat, an electric stove, a refrigerator, and a bathroom with a shower. They are also furnished with two double beds, a sofa bed, a dining table with chairs, linens, and kitchen utensils. Cost is $61 a night. You can also camp in tents here for $11–15. Reservations are needed; some dates are booked for months in advance. Myakka is just north of Sarasota on SR 72. Stop at the park office for good area maps. Admission is $4 per vehicle or $1 per person (bike- or walk-in). Call (941) 361-6511 for more information.

Myakka Wildlife and Nature Tours Board the "World's Largest Airboat," the 70-passenger Gator Gal, for a wild ride on Myakka Lake. Your

A CALENDAR OF FESTIVALS AND EVENTS

Year-round

Sunsets at Pier 60 A year-around street festival featuring local performers and artisans held for 2 hours before and 2 hours after sunset. Admission is free. Clearwater beach just south of Hilton resort; (727) 449-1036.

January

Epiphany Tarpon Springs. A daylong Greek Orthodox religious celebration that includes a dive for a cross in Spring Bayou, releasing a white dove of peace, Greek foods, music, and dancing. (727) 942-5628.

A Celtic Celebration/Scottish and Irish Festival Dundein at our Lady of Lourdes Church near Highland Park. Watch Highland and Scottish dancers, Celtic show dogs, and more at this annual event. (727) 733-3606.

March

Gasparilla Invasion Tampa. This celebration, started in 1904, begins when a pirate ship with more than 500 pirates sails into Tampa Bay to capture the city. They lead a parade into Ybor City, and crowds line the streets waiting for the trinkets and booty to be thrown. The parade is named after pirate Jose Gaspar, who took refuge on Florida's west coast. (813) 876-1747.

Plant City Strawberry Festival Plant City, just east of Tampa, is home to this annual fruit fest, with just-picked berries piled high on shortcake, and other delicious strawberry-inspired fare. Top-name musical entertainment and arts and crafts round out the event. (813) 752-9194.

Sailor Circus Sarasota. Sarasota County schoolchildren, from 3rd to 12th grades, perform remarkable circus acts. The circus celebrated its 50th anniversary in 1998. (941) 361-6350.

guide will describe the lake and wildlife, and point out the alligators. Trips are at 10 a.m., 11:30 a.m., 1 p.m., and 2:30 p.m. daily.

If you'd rather see the wildlife by land, take the Tram Safari Land Tour that travels off paved roads into remote areas of subtropical forests and marshlands. Your guide explains the plants, animals, and birds, along with the history of area. Trips are daily at 1 p.m. and 2:30 p.m.

Boat and tram tours leave from the Boat Basin located 3 miles inside main entrance of Myakka River State Park; bear left at the Y in the road. Fare for each tour is $7 per adult, $4 for ages 6–12, 5 and under free. In recent years the tours have been affected by drought in the summer, so call (941) 365-0100 to ensure that the tours are available.

Sarasota Medieval Fair Sarasota. The grounds of Ringling are turned into a medieval village. Search for pirate treasures, gather for high tea, even learn to belly dance. (941) 355-5101.

April

Highland Games Dunedin. This celebration of Scottish Heritage, includes highland dancing, bagpipe and drumming, and athletic events. Highlander Park; (727) 733-6240.

Florida Heritage Festival Bradenton. Activities take place all month and include a Children's Parade with floats designed and built by children, a Seafood Fest, an Easter Egg Hunt, and an incredibly fun Plastic Bottle Boat Regatta—boats that float on plastic bottles and have only paddles for propulsion. (941) 747-1998.

May

Taste of Tarpon Springs Food and Art Fest Tarpon Springs. The best in Greek food from the area's finest eateries, plus entertainment, arts, and kids activities. (727) 937-6109.

Fun 'n' Sun Night Parade Clearwater. Enjoy bands, floats, animals, at Cleveland Street; starts at 7:30 p.m. (727) 562-4804.

June

Kid's Week Clearwater Beach. Special events specifically designed for kids include arts and crafts, beach activities, a fishing tournament, and magic shows. (727) 562-4800.

Pelican Man's Bird Sanctuary Dale Shields, the "Pelican Man," created this rescue center in 1988, and today more than 200 permanently injured birds make their home here. The staff and volunteers have rescued, rehabilitated, and released thousands of pelicans and birds. Open daily, 10 a.m.–5 p.m.; closed major holidays. Admission is free but donations are accepted. The sanctuary is next to Mote Marina on City Island just south of Longboat Key, 1708 Ken Thompson Parkway, City Island; (941) 388-4444.

Philippe Park This archaeological site was once occupied by Indians, and a sizable ceremonial mound from its first inhabitants is still here, now on the National Register of Historic Places. The park, which overlooks old

A CALENDAR OF FESTIVALS AND EVENTS *(continued)*

July

Tampa's Official Independence Day at Curtis Hixon Park. Featuring live music from national recording artists, a children's area with a snow play area and snowman building, fun, and fireworks.

September

Taste of the Beaches Treasure Island. An outdoor gathering of the area's finest eateries vending their specialty foods; a carnival-like atmosphere offers games, music, and fireworks. Located on Pinellas County Beach; (727) 360-6957.

October

John's Pass Fall Grouper Fest and Art Show Medeira Beach. This weekend festival usually attracts more than 100,000 visitors to one of the largest seafood festivals in the state. Sample fish, crab, and lobster here. (813) 391-1341.

Guavaween Tampa. This Latin-style Halloween features family activities and entertainment during the day and a parade and street party at night. Admission free for daytime activities, $5 for evening events. (888) 293-4770 or (813) 621-7121.

Tampa Bay, was named for Count Odet Philippe, a Frenchman credited with introducing the first grapefruit trees to the New World. Facilities include a boat ramp, picnic areas, a ball field, grills, and playground facilities. Open 7 a.m.–sunset. Located on Philippe Parkway/SR 590, Safety Harbor (at the edge of Tampa Bay on the eastern tip of the Clearwater area); (727) 669-1947.

Pinellas Trail This trail is part of the Rails-to-Trails Conservancy program that converts abandoned railroad tracks into recreation trails, and it's one of the most popular urban trails in the United States. This 34-mile paved trail begins (or ends) in the south end of St. Petersburg and meanders to the north at the sponge docks in Tarpon Springs. As your family bikes, rollerblades, or walks the trail, you'll pass many coastal towns and cities along the way. Near the trail, you'll also find restaurants, campgrounds, and motels…and most importantly, bathrooms. Park in

Clearwater Cup International Yacht Races Clearwater. The Clearwater Yacht Club hosts this event, which draws nearly 100 racing yachts from around the world. (727) 447-6000.

Clearwater Jazz Holiday Clearwater. Dizzy Gillespie, Count Basie Orchestra, Spyro Gyra, and more—this festival has seen it all since its beginning 20 years ago. Free admission; (727) 461-5200.

November

St. Petersburg Times Festival of Reading Eckerd College, St. Petersburg. At this festival, adults may enjoy the panels that feature well-known authors, while the junior writers in the family can check out the workshops, storytellers, and more. (727) 892-2358; www.festivalofreading.com.

Festival of Tress At this celebration of holiday tradition, volunteers provide decorated trees, vignettes, and continuous live entertainment. Harborview Center, 300 Cleveland Street, Clearwater.

December

Lighted Boat Parade St. Petersburg. The pier is the focal point where boats of all sizes show their Christmas spirit. (727) 893-7494.

downtown Tarpon Springs, near the trail north of Curlew Road, or at Azalea Park in St. Petersburg below 22nd Avenue North. There is also on-street and small public lot parking near the trail for its entire length. Open during daylight hours. Pinellas County Parks; (727) 464-3347.

Suncoast Seabird Sanctuary Suncoast is an unusual site—cages cover an acre site along the beach at one of the largest wild bird hospitals in the United States, devoted to the rescue, repair, and release of sick or injured birds. You'll find 500 land and seabirds at the sanctuary compound at any one time; about 20 arrive daily. The sanctuary also breeds permanently disabled birds and releases the offspring into the wild. Educational programs are presented monthly, and guided tours and lectures are offered every Wednesday and Sunday at 2 p.m. Open daily, 9 a.m.–dusk. Donations requested. 18328 Gulf Boulevard, Indian Shores Beach, just north of St. Petersburg Beach; (727) 391-6211.

Tampa

This city on Hillsborough River began as a small American Indian fishing village. Native tribes called the village by the bay "Tanpa," which loosely translated means "land by the water." Hernando de Soto and other explorers put the town on the map in 1539 during their searches for gold; after being illegibly written on the maps of early explorers, the name of the area became Tampa.

In the 1880s Don Vicente Martinez Ybor, a cigar manufacturer and Cuban exile, moved his business from Key West to an area east of Tampa, which is now known as Ybor City (pronounced "EE-bore"). Cigar makers were attracted to Florida because of the large number of skilled workers, mainly Spaniards and Cubans from Havana. At its peak, the cigar industry boasted 200 factories and 12,000 workers.

A lot has changed since the days of cigar factories and fishing villages. Cigars are still produced in Tampa—about 500 million a year, but machines have taken over what was once done by hand. Now, many vacant cigar factories are being transformed into shops and restaurants. Although many of the factories are no longer in operation, the strong Latin community these workers created is still present in Ybor City.

For the most part, the cigar industry has been replaced by tourism. Tampa is an ideal port for the cruise industry. Currently, Carnival Cruise Line's *Tropicale* and *Sensation* sail from Port Tampa. But the number-one reason families visit Tampa is for Busch Gardens, the second most popular attraction in the state behind Walt Disney World. Roller-coaster enthusiasts and animal lovers already know that Busch Gardens is a don't-miss experience, but there are plenty of other attractions to occupy you. Because of the warm weather, families can enjoy many outdoor activities, including golf and tennis. The city is home to more than 1,000 public and private courts. Or bring your rollerblades; your whole family can skate or bike on Bayshore Boulevard, the "World's Longest Continuous Sidewalk."

Family Resorts

Doubletree Guest Suites

11310 30th Street • (813) 971-7690 or (800) 222-TREE

If you're looking for a family-friendly hotel near Busch Gardens, the Doubletree Guest Suites has 129 one-bedroom suites, with queen-size beds and a sofa bed in the living room. Each unit has a refrigerator, microwave, coffeemaker, and wet bar. There's a swimming pool. Breakfast is free, and so is the shuttle to Busch Gardens. Rates start at $109 in the summer, $124 in the winter.

Holiday Inn Tampa

2701 E. Fowler Avenue • (813) 971-4701 or (800) 206-2747

Another option for the Busch Gardens area is the Holdiay Inn Tampa. After a $12.5 million renovation, this Holiday Inn now features Kidsuites, a room within the adult guestroom that has single bunk beds, kid-sized furniture, and even their own TV, VCR, and Super Nintendo (great if your kids are missing the comforts of home). The hotel even has a pirate ship pool with those ever-popular water cannons. There aren't refrigerators or microwaves in the room, but kids under 12 eat free with an adult at the restaurant. Rates begin at $140 in the summer, $125 in the winter.

Saddlebrook

5700 Saddlebrook Way, Tampa • (813) 973-1111 or (800) 729-8383 • fax (813) 973-4504 • www.saddlebrookresort.com

This swanky, 480-acre resort, 12 miles north of Tampa, is probably best known for the two 18-hole golf courses designed by golf legend Arnold Palmer. In fact, the Arnold Palmer Golf Academy World Headquarters is here. Take part in the half-day academy, or take individual lessons. Two-, three-, and five-day programs are also available. For tennis buffs, there are 45 courts, including two grass courts. There also are Harry Hopman–Saddlebrook International Tennis clinics for individual and group lessons.

For kids ages 13–17, there are junior golf and tennis programs. There is also the S'kids Club for ages 4–12 with themed activities every day from 9 a.m. until 4 p.m. Cost is $40 a day plus $5 for lunch. Half-days are $20.

There are an impressive fitness center and spa, basketball and volleyball courts, and a pool just for water sports like water volleyball and basketball, with 25-meter racing lanes. There are two more pools for relaxing, and you can go bass fishing in privately stocked resort lakes.

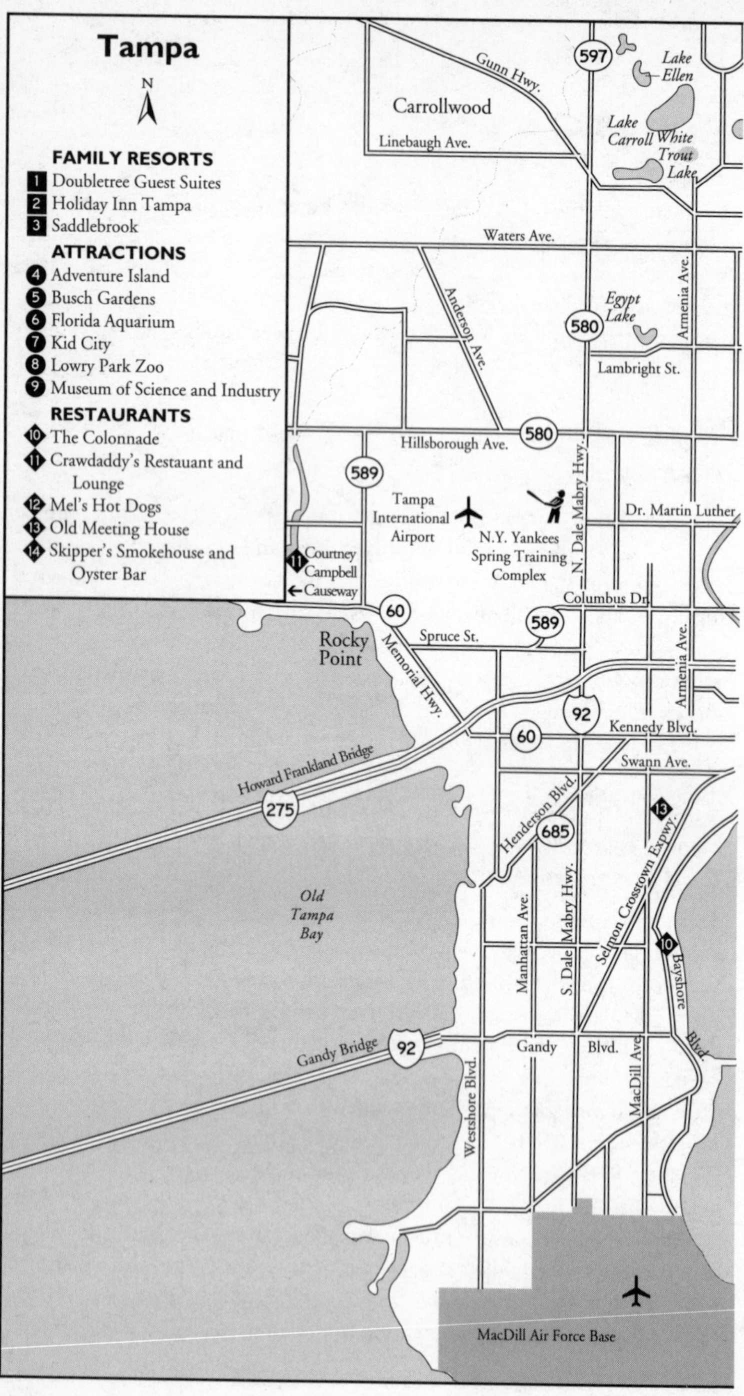

Tampa
N
FAMILY RESORTS
1 Doubletree Guest Suites
2 Holiday Inn Tampa
3 Saddlebrook
ATTRACTIONS
4 Adventure Island
5 Busch Gardens
6 Florida Aquarium
7 Kid City
8 Lowry Park Zoo
9 Museum of Science and Industry
RESTAURANTS
10 The Colonnade
11 Crawdaddy's Restaurant and Lounge
12 Mel's Hot Dogs
13 Old Meeting House
14 Skipper's Smokehouse and Oyster Bar
Gunn Hwy.
597
Lake Ellen
Carrollwood
Lake Carroll
White Trout Lake
Linebaugh Ave.
Waters Ave.
Anderson Ave.
Egypt Lake
580
Armenia Ave.
Lambright St.
Hillsborough Ave.
589
Tampa International Airport
N.Y. Yankees Spring Training Complex
N. Dale Mabry Hwy.
Dr. Martin Luther
Courtney Campbell Causeway
Columbus Dr.
60
Rocky Point
Memorial Hwy.
Spruce St.
92
Kennedy Blvd.
Swann Ave.
Howard Frankland Bridge
275
Henderson Blvd.
685
Old Tampa Bay
Manhattan Ave.
S. Dale Mabry Hwy.
Selmon Crosstown Expwy.
Bayshore Blvd.
Gandy Bridge
Gandy Blvd.
Westshore Blvd.
MacDill Ave.
MacDill Air Force Base

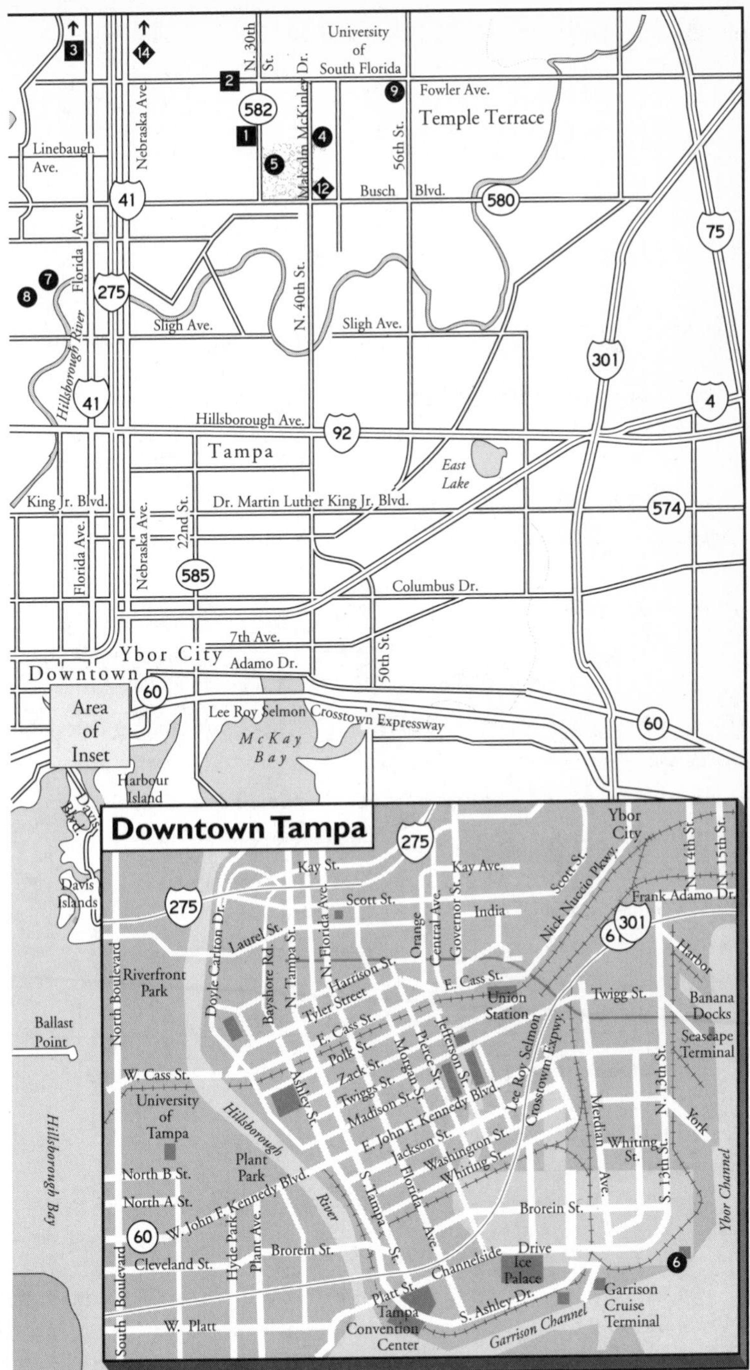

University of South Florida
Fowler Ave.
Temple Terrace
N. 30th St.
Malcolm McKinley Dr.
56th St.
Nebraska Ave.
Linebaugh Ave.
Busch Blvd.
Florida Ave.
Hillsborough River
Sligh Ave.
N. 40th St.
Sligh Ave.
Hillsborough Ave.
Tampa
East Lake
King Jr. Blvd.
Dr. Martin Luther King Jr. Blvd.
22nd St.
Columbus Dr.
7th Ave.
Ybor City
Adamo Dr.
50th St.
Downtown
Area of Inset
Lee Roy Selmon Crosstown Expressway
McKay Bay
Harbour Island
Davis Blvd.
Davis Islands
Ballast Point
Hillsborough Bay
Downtown Tampa
Kay St.
Kay Ave.
Scott St.
India
Laurel St.
Doyle Carlton Dr.
Bayshore Rd.
N. Tampa St.
N. Florida Ave.
Orange
Central Ave.
Governor St.
Scott St.
Nick Nuccio Pkwy.
Frank Adamo Dr.
N. 14th St.
N. 15th St.
Harbor
North Boulevard
Riverfront Park
Harrison St.
Tyler Street
E. Cass St.
Union Station
Twigg St.
Banana Docks
Seascape Terminal
E. Cass St.
Polk St.
Zack St.
Twiggs St.
Madison St.
Morgan St.
Pierce St.
Jefferson St.
E. John F. Kennedy Blvd.
Lee Roy Selmon Crosstown Expwy.
Ashley St.
W. Cass St.
University of Tampa
Hillsborough River
Jackson St.
Washington St.
Whiting St.
Meridian Ave.
Whiting St.
N. 13th St.
S. 13th St.
York
Ybor Channel
Plant Park
North B St.
North A St.
W. John F. Kennedy Blvd.
S. Tampa St.
Florida Ave.
Brorein St.
Hyde Park Ave.
Plant Ave.
Brorein St.
Cleveland St.
South Boulevard
Channelside Drive
Ice Palace
Platt St.
Tampa Convention Center
S. Ashley Dr.
Garrison Channel
Garrison Cruise Terminal
W. Platt

Saddlebrook has 165 one-bedroom and 247 two-bedroom villas with living rooms and fully equipped kitchens. In each cluster of 50 villas, there are laundry facilities and ice machines. There are also 131 hotel rooms, and many have patios or balconies. Deluxe guest rooms start at $187 per person and go to $327; one-bedroom suites range from $217 per person to $352; and two-bedroom suites range from $180 per person to $287. Some rooms have coffeemakers and refrigerators or mini-bars. Golf green and tennis court fees are additional.

Busch Gardens

Busch Gardens Tampa Bay

Busch Boulevard, Tampa • (800) 4-ADVENTURE or (813) 987-5082 or 987-5171
www.buschgardens.com

Hours - Open 365 days a year, hours vary daily; call ahead.

Admission - $49.95 for adults, $40.95 for children ages 3–9. Parking $7–8.

Appeal by Age Group -

Pre-school ★★	Teens ★★★★★	Over 30 ★★★
Grade school ★★★★★	Young Adults ★★★★	Seniors ★★

Touring Time - Average a whole day (6–8 hours); minimum a half-day

Rainy-Day Touring - Not recommended

Author's Rating - ★★★★; does anyone have some Pepto-Bismol?

Restaurants - Yes

Alcoholic beverages - Yes

Handicapped access - Yes

Wheelchair rental - Yes

Baby stroller rental - Yes

Lockers - Yes

Pet kennels - Yes (free)

Rain check - No guarantees

Private tours - For large groups, arranged in advance

One of the top five theme parks in Florida, Busch Gardens features gravity-defying roller coasters that coexist with beautiful zoo animals. More than 3,000 animals representing more than 320 species make it one of the nation's top zoos.

Theming is turn-of-the-century Africa, with 10 separate regions in the park—more than 10,000 exotic plants and authentic costuming set the mood.

The park covers 335 acres, so take it easy and board the sky ride, the monorail (that goes in a circle and will end where you started), or the Trans-Veldt Railroad for an informative overview of the theme park.

The Ten Areas

Morocco This is the first area guests encounter and consists mostly of shops and eateries, with snake charmers and roving sheiks performing in the streets. There are three theaters with impressive live shows: the Moroccan Palace Theater, the Marrakesh Theater, and the Tangiers Theater, but we recommend saving the shows for later in the day when the hot sun and lines for attractions can be unbearable.

In Morocco you'll find bank machines, bathrooms, a lost and found, and lockers. It's a great place to pick up your souvenirs and your last snack (we like the cherry turnovers at Boujad Bakery) as you head for home. The most important thing about Morocco is that it can lead you to Gwazi, Busch Garden's newest coaster.

Nairobi Adjacent to Morocco is Nairobi, featuring an ample variety of small animal exhibits in an African, thatched-hut village setting. The walkways are a bit of a maze, making it difficult to see the exhibits systematically without backtracking.

Nairobi includes Myombe Reserve: The Great Ape Domain, a sophisticated three-acre habitat housing western lowland gorillas and chimpanzees. Nairobi's Field Station animal nursery, petting zoo, elephant habitat, and Aldabra tortoise habitat offer up-close encounters with animals. Reptilian environments for crocodiles, alligators, and turtles are sites in Nairobi for daily presentations. And Nocturnal Mountain illustrates the behaviors of nighttime creatures.

Serengeti Plain Bordering Nairobi to the right (on the park's map) is the Serengeti Plain, an ideal place to start in the early morning when the animals are most active. Nearly 800 free-roaming African animals, including hippos, giraffes, antelopes, camels, Nile crocodiles, flamingos, and ostriches can be found in these 80 lushly landscaped acres. This is a breeding ground for several endangered species, including the black rhino.

You can see this area from the monorail, steam locomotive, Sky Ride, or promenade. The monorail allows the most unhindered view but is slow loading; take the monorail if you're there first thing, or wait and ride it during the hour before dusk. The Sky Ride passes over the Serengeti, but it's a one-way trip to the Congo and also may have long lines. The steam train connects Nairobi with the Congo and Stanleyville, and passes through the Serengeti Plain. It's a nice way to get a ground-view perspective of the Serengeti wildlife, and it takes you close to many animals who are far away and difficult to see from the monorail and Sky Ride. Since the train can carry a large number of guests and loads pretty fast, it can be enjoyed almost any time of day without long waits in line.

The highlight in this area is the animal exhibit Edge of Africa, which puts you in the heart of the veldt. The barriers between guests and the animals are natural and mostly hidden. The Edge of Africa begins at a welcome center that posts daily recordings of animal sightings and their diets. Close to the entrance, you'll spot a meerkat habitat. As you move on, you'll discover a "Masai village" that a nomadic African tribe has vacated—once you see the lions and hyenas, you'll know why. You are just inches away from these animals.

Farther into the exhibit, you'll see a crocodile nest and a hippopotamus pool from an underwater viewing area. Next, step into a vulture habitat, a giraffe feeding area, and a spring that is home to flamingos, turtles, and fish.

To add to the fantasy throughout the expedition, you'll spot signs of a research outpost hinting at civilization: scientific instruments, recording devices, abandoned vehicles, and more. Roaming safari guides offer guests talks about the animals and the ecosystem. Guidebooks are also available to help with animal identification.

To get a special look at Edge of Africa, try the Serengeti Safari (separate fee). Board a safari-themed flatbed truck that puts guests even closer to giraffes, zebras, ostriches, and rhinos. This tour lasts about a half-hour and is offered several times throughout the day.

Crown Colony Overlooking the Serengeti, this is the place to get a bite to eat at the park's only table-service restaurant, the Crown Colony. Akbar's Adventure Tour, a simulator attraction starring comedian Martin Short, is located here. There's also the Clydesdale Hamlet, home to the massive Clydesdale horses that Busch Garden's parent company, Anheuser-Busch, owns.

Egypt Egypt is the newest area of Busch Gardens, on seven acres tucked behind the Crown Colony. The highlight is Montu, the Southeast's longest (4,000 feet) and tallest inverted roller coaster, with speeds that exceed 60 miles per hour. This three-minute ride features a dropout platform that leaves your feet dangling (the cars are attached to ride below the track instead of riding on it), and the ride turns you upside down a total of seven times. Egypt also offers a tour through a replica of King Tut's Tomb as it appeared during the actual excavation in the 1920s and the Egypt Sand Dig area for young archaeologists.

Timbuktu Timbuktu is sandwiched between the Serengeti Plain and the Congo with a walkway connecting it to Nairobi. Arranged in a large square reminiscent of an African market or bazaar, Timbuktu offers the Scorpion, a small roller coaster that's a good "beginner coaster" with one inversion. The Dolphins of the Deep show is here, as well as the German Das Festhaus restaurant with live entertainment and skill and arcade games for all ages.

Congo If your heart can take it, head over to the Congo for another roller coaster. Kumba, the Southeast's largest and fastest steel roller coaster, features a camelback weightless maneuver, a spiraling cobra roll (upside down, right side up, upside down), and a 135-foot drop. Nearby is the Congo River Rapids, complete with rapids, standing waves, geysers, caverns, and waterfalls—fun for the whole family (and refreshing on a hot Florida day). Don't miss the Python corkscrew roller coaster, old-fashioned by today's standards, with a short, twisting-turning ride featuring the G-force thrill of a corkscrewing double helix.

For those who don't meet the height requirements for the wild rides, try the Ubanga-Banga Bumper Cars.

Claw Island is a beautifully executed exhibition of Bengal tigers, the perfect showcase for the big cats. The exhibit can be viewed from all sides as well as from a bridge passing over the tigers' lagoon. The cats, large, sleek, and ample in number, are usually on the move, providing a colorful spectacle for visitors.

Stanleyville Moving out of the Congo past the terminus of the Sky Ride, a trail leads to Stanleyville, more spacious and roomier than other regions but lacking distinctive identity and atmosphere. The two water rides in Stanleyville—the Stanley Falls Log Flume and the Tanganyika Tidal Wave—are guaranteed to cool you off on a hot summer afternoon. Beware, many bystanders on a bridge near the tidal wave get drenched as the boats splash down into the pool. You'll also find a habitat for warthogs and orangutans, and see snakes, insects, and reptiles in Stanleyville. Orchid Canyon provides a boardwalk tour of numerous species of these flowers.

Bird Gardens Across the bridge from Stanleyville is Bird Gardens. Teenagers won't appreciate this part of the park, but it's a nice place to take a breather from the long lines and hustle of the park, with exotic birds and birds of prey—and complimentary beer samplings from parent company Anheuser-Busch for guests 21 and older. Lory Landing allows bird lovers to feed nectar to colorful lorikeets (a type of parakeet). The Birds of Prey show is here, as well as a koala habitat that draws big crowds. Guests also can see the television production of *Jack Hanna's Animal Adventures.*

Land of the Dragons This adventure play area lets kids let expend some energy while parents take a break. Dumphrey, a friendly, costumed dragon, makes appearances, and youngsters are invited to climb a three-story treehouse with towers and stairways that create a maze. Other activities include a rope climb, a ball crawl, an outdoor theater showing *A Dragon's Tale,* and various children's rides. Real dragons are here, too—a Komodo dragon and rhino iguana, for example.

RATINGS OF BUSCH GARDENS' MAJOR FEATURES

What It Is:	Author's Rating
Akbar's Adventure Tours	
Motion simulator attraction starring Martin Short as Akbar, guiding riders on a comical simulated journey across Egypt. Children must be at least 42" tall to ride.	★★★
Congo River Rapids	
A fast-moving white water journey accentuated with water jets and falls. Children must be at least 2 years old or 39" tall to ride.	★★★½
Edge of Africa	
15-acre, self-guided walk through a safari habitat	★★★★
Egypt Sand Dig	
Playground for kids to dig for treasure.	★★★
Gwazi	
Largest dueling wooden roller coaster (choose the lion or the tiger trains) in the Southeast. Although there are no inversions, Gwazi reaches a height of 90 feet, and there are six "flybys" when the two trains dive at each other. Children must be at least 48" tall to ride.	★★★★
King Tut's Tomb	
A tour through a replica of King Tut's Tomb.	★★★
Kumba	
The Southeast's largest and fastest steel roller coaster, with a 108-foot vertical loop—a spiraling maneuver that creates 3 seconds of weightlessness. Children must be at least 54" tall to ride.	★★★★★
Land of the Dragons	
A special land for youngsters, with kiddie rides and a three-story treehouse to climb. Sorry mom, dad, and siblings, if you're taller than 56", you're not allowed in.	★★★★
Monorail	
Air-conditioned transportation above the safari.	★★★
Montu	
One of the top-rated inverted roller coasters in the world and the largest of its kind in the southeastern United States. Children must be at least 54" tall to ride.	★★★★★
Myombe Reserve: The Great Ape Domain	
Western lowland gorillas and chimps in a three-acre natural habitat.	★★★★
Python	
One of Busch's original coasters. Children must be at least 48" tall to ride.	★★★

Pre-Rating	Grade School	Teens	Young Adults	Over 30	Senior Citizens
★★	★★★	★★★	★★	★★	★★
★★★	★★★★½	★★★★½	★★★★	★★★★	★★★½
★★★	★★★★	★★★★	★★★★	★★★★	★★★★
★★★★	★★★	★	★	★	★
—	★★★★	★★★★★	★★★★★	★★★★★	★★
★	★★★	★★★	★★★	★★★	★★★
—	★★★★	★★★★★	★★★★★	★★★★	★★
★★★★★	★★★★½	—	—	—	—
★★★	★★★	★★★	★★★	★★★	★★★
—	★★★	★★★★★	★★★★★	★★★★	★★
★★★★	★★★★	★★★★	★★★★	★★★★	★★★★
—	★★★	★★★★	★★★	★★★	★★

RATINGS OF BUSCH GARDENS' FEATURES *(continued)*

What It Is:	Author's Rating
Rhino Rally	
Safari "competition" with a raging river thrill ride.	★★★
Scorpion	
A looping, spiraling coaster with speeds up to 45 mph. Children must be at least 42" tall to ride.	★★★★
The Serengeti Plain	
Hundreds of free-roaming animals on a 60-acre veldt.	★★★★
Serengeti Railway	
An open-sided train ride with stops in Stanleyville, Nairobi, and the Serengeti Plain. The train has recently been rerouted so you can see even more wildlife.	★★
Serengeti Safari	
A truck ride onto the Serengeti Plain. Children must be at least 5 years old to ride.	★★★½
Skyride	
Open gondolas that glide over the Serengeti Plain. Tighten the shoelaces, hold on to your hats, and get a grip on your glasses.	★★★
Stanley Falls Log Flume	
A water flume ride with a 40' drop. Children must be at least 46" tall to ride.	★★★½
Tanganyika Tidal Wave	
A water ride that starts out serene, then ends with a 55-foot dive that creates a massive wave of water that soaks both riders and spectators. Children must be at least 48" tall to ride.	★★★★
World Rhythms on Ice	
36-minute dance performance on ice, highlighting seven countries.	★★★

Tips for Touring the Park

It requires hustle to see Busch Gardens Florida in one day. Personal taste and family ages will serve to eliminate some exhibits or rides. Our recommendation is to plan your tour in advance and work out some objectives and compromises that will keep everybody reasonably happy. Alternatively, split your family (let teenagers take off, for example) and gather everyone back together at an appointed time for a show or to share a meal.

We talked to parents of grade school children who allowed the kids a specific number of rides, following the completion of which the parents

Pre-Rating	Grade School	Teens	Young Adults	Over 30	Senior Citizens
★★★	★★★★	★★★	★★★	★★★	★★★
—	★★★★½	★★★★½	★★★★½	★★★½	★★
★★★★	★★★★	★★★★	★★★★	★★★★	★★★★
★★★	★★★	★★	★★	★★	★★
—	★★★½	★★★	★★★	★★★	★★
★★★★	★★★★	★★	★★★	★★★	★★★
—	★★★★	★★★★½	★★★★	★★★★	★★★
—	★★★★½	★★★★½	★★★★	★★★★	★★★★
★★	★★	★★	★★	★★★	★★★

orchestrated the remainder of the tour. Other parents planned the kids rides around the live entertainment schedule, placing the children safely in line, then attending a performance or a nearby show while the youngsters waited and rode.

The single most effective strategy for efficient touring and avoiding long waits in line is to arrive at the park a little before 9 a.m. (gates usually open by 9:30 a.m.). Park, then purchase your admission pass and be at the turnstile ready to roll when the attraction opens. The same four rides you can experience in a single hour in the early morning will require more than 3 hours of your time after 11:30 a.m. Have breakfast before you arrive. Do not waste your most wait-free touring time sitting in a restaurant.

Most of the live shows play in large amphitheaters, so save shows and walk-through zoological exhibits for after 11:30 a.m., when the lines for rides grow long.

BUSCH GARDENS BASICS

ROLLER COASTERS: Number of Inversions

Montu: 7 | Kumba: 6 | Python: 2 | Scorpion: 1

WATER RIDES: Level of Wetness, 3 Meaning "Soaked"

Stanley Falls: 1 | Congo River Rapids: 2 | Tidal Wave: 3

LONGEST LINES

Montu, Congo River Rapids, Gwazi, and Kumba

Attractions beyond Busch Gardens

Adventure Island

1001 McKinley Drive, Tampa, adjacent to Busch Gardens • (813) 987-5660

Hours - 10 a.m.–5 p.m., varies seasonally (February 26–March 31, Saturday and Sunday; April 1–September 4, daily; September 9–October 29, Saturday and Sunday)

Admission -$27.95 for adults, $25.95 for children ages 3–9; parking $5

Appeal by Age Group -

Pre-school ★★	Teens ★★★	Over 30 ★★
Grade school ★★★★	Young Adults ★★	Seniors ★

Touring Time - Average a whole day (6–8 hours); minimum half a day

Rainy-Day Touring - Not recommended

Author's Rating - ★★; works well with any vacation plan: a day at Busch, and a day at the water park

Restaurants - Yes

Alcoholic beverages - Yes

Handicapped access - Yes

Wheelchair rental - No

Baby stroller rental - No

Lockers - Yes

Pet kennels - No

Rain check - By request

Private tours - No

Description and Comments This 25-acre water park is owned by Busch Gardens and offers acres of twists and turns with 18 attractions. Water slides are plentiful, and everything is supervised—they generally have 50 lifeguards watching the pools at all times. There are also a championship volleyball complex, a game arcade, and outdoor cafes. Lockers, showers, and changing areas are located near the park's entrance. Adventure Island offers something for all ages.

For Daredevils: Calypso Coaster, spiraling down an open flume, and Aruba Tuba, winding through open and closed portions of a twisting slide, are for one or two riders, and both end with a splash in Rambling Bayou. The Caribbean Corkscrew is a four-story slide through a 240-foot translucent tube. KeyWest Rapids is a six-story-high twisting, extrawide water slide. The Water Moccasin is a steep slide that twirls riders down triple-linked tubes. Everglides is a 35-foot drop on a water sled that travels down a 72-foot slide, then hydroplanes as far as 100 feet. The Runaway Rapids takes you to the peak of a 34-foot mountain, where there are five separate water flumes to choose from, including three twirling water slides down 300 feet, and two shorter runs of 200 feet. If you are looking for speed, check out Tampa Typhoon, a 76-foot, near-free-fall drop. It's one of the park's most thrilling attractions. The Gulf Scream shoots riders down a 210-foot sliding surface and lands you in a splash pool at speeds more than 25 mph.

The whole family can enjoy Wahoo Run, as up to five riders slide down six stories of more than 600 feet of turns and curves in and out of tunnels.

For younger visitors, a little excitement goes a long way: Rambling Bayou inner-tube ride floats through scenic surroundings—fogs, mists, and monsoons. Splash Attack, a 12-level tree house attraction for the whole family, includes twisting slides, cascading waterfalls, controllable water jets, and rope climbs—more than 50 elements that guarantee a good time. The different levels of the tree house are connected by bridges, cargo nets, and web crawl tunnels. After climbing to the top, guests must slide their way down nearly 500 feet of open flumes and closed tubes. Every few minutes, 1,000 gallons of water splash down from a water tower bucket 40 feet in the air. Paradise Lagoon is a giant swimming pool with cascading waterfalls, jumping platforms, cannonball slides, translucent water tubes, and a hand rope walk. At Endless Surf, a 17,000-square-foot wave pool provides waves of up to 5 feet for body surfing.

For the littlest tadpoles: Fabian's Funport includes a small wave pool and stars Fabian, Adventure Island's amphibious costumed character. There also is an arcade room. Picnicking is permitted in the park, and there are tables throughout.

Florida Aquarium

701 Channelside Drive, Tampa • (813) 273-4000 • www.flaquarium.net

Hours - Daily, 9:30 a.m.–5 p.m.

Admission - $15 for adults, $10 for children ages 3–12, $12 seniors 60 and over

Appeal by Age Group -

Pre-school ★★★	Teens ★★	Over 30 ★★★
Grade school ★★★★	Young Adults ★★	Seniors ★★★★

Touring Time - Average 3 hours; minimum 2 hours

Rainy-Day Touring - Perfect

Author's Rating - ★★★; kids love the shark exhibit

Restaurants - Yes

Alcoholic beverages - Yes

Handicapped access - Yes

Wheelchair rental - Yes

Baby stroller rental - Yes

Lockers - Yes

Pet kennels - No

Rain check - No

Private tours - Yes

Description and Comments This distinctive, glass-domed attraction has more than a million gallons water filled with living things. Located along downtown Tampa's waterfront, the three-story aquarium features five galleries: Florida Bays and Beaches, Florida Coral Reefs, Florida Sea Hunt, No Bone Zone, and the Wetlands Gallery. In all, more than 4,300 plants and animals representing 550 species native to Florida are represented.

The Florida Aquarium is designed in somewhat of a chronological order; something like "a day in the life of a drop of water."

The adventure begins in the Wetlands, where water travels through rivers, streams, marshes, and other freshwater areas. You'll see shallow tanks of water filled with fish. The environment is very natural, with grass marshes, cypress swamps, bogs, and more. You'll also spot more than a dozen birds wading or hiding in more than 1,000 indigenous trees and shrubs. Alligators hide in the grass marshes, otters play in the rivers, and in the hammocks you may see a great horned owl. You'll see vampire bats, tarantulas, and poison dart frogs in the aquarium's new "Frights of the Forest" exhibit. Frights features hands-on activities, including spotting scopes, where you can view a bee stinger, a bed-bug moth, and a human louse.

Next, move on to Bays and Beaches, where bonnet head sharks, mullet, and snook coexist with spiny lobsters and a 144-pound jewfish.

Following Bays and Beaches, check out the aquarium's newest exhibit, No Bone Zone. The highlight is the "S.C.U.M" touch tank, where you can get your hands on sea stars, crustaceans, urchins, mollusks, and other invertebrates. Nearby is a second tank, Terrific Pacific, with IndoPacific corals and invertebrates—and all of the invertebrates on display were farm raised or confiscated from illegal shipments. Some of the exhibits within No Bone Zone include "Ocean Architects"—a display featuring shells from around the world, a crawl area where kids can pretend that they're a hermit crab and try on a few shells for size. There's also "No Bones X-ray," where actual x-rays compare vertebrates with invertebrates.

In Florida Coral Reefs, you get a view of the ocean usually reserved for experienced divers—60 feet under the sea to the deep dark waters where coral reefs grow. First you'll encounter grouper, moray eel, and parrotfish. Deeper, you'll encounter a 43-foot-wide, 14-foot-tall panoramic window that offers a spectacular view along the reef face, with its multicolored fish, wandering sharks, and coral colonies. This large coral reef exhibit holds 500,000 gallons of water, with more than 1,200 fish and shellfish. Twenty-minute dive shows in the Coral Reef Gallery feature a diver speaking with the audience from the 50,000-gallon exhibit. While you're here, check out Dragons Down Under to see the Australian sea dragon, a unique creature whose body resembles a seahorse, yet leaf-like appendages extending from their heads and bodies make them resemble seaweed. Shows are at 11 a.m., 1 p.m., and 3 p.m.

The final exhibit area is the Sea Hunt area, out in the deep water. The jellyfish exhibit is especially beautiful, with special lighting to "electrify" the jellies. The shark exhibit is just around the corner, with more than 30 species of sharks and rays concentrated in a 130,000-gallon tank and a 5,000-gallon touch pool. Rubber mats are placed right next to the tank's glass so your kids can get as close as they can to the sea life. You'll also find huge sea turtles (one weighs 252 pounds), jellyfish, and stingrays.

You can take a break from the water exhibits at Explore a Shore, where children of all ages can climb among mangrove tree roots, dig for buried shells, crawl through coral caves, and touch live sea creatures in a pool with everything from sea stars to anemones to horseshoe crabs.

In addition to seeing aquatic life, you can visit a lab where water testing and experiments are performed. Wonderful photography accompanies many of the exhibits. The aquarium is also a great architectural beauty, with many open ceilings and glass walls that let you soak in the city skyline or view a huge cruise ship in the nearby port.

Explore the museum on your own, or rent audio wands ($2) for a 1½-hour tour. Animal identification cards are also available (you may need them more than your kids). Special tours include a 20-minute behind the scenes tour, offered three times a day. Guides explain the animals, where water comes from, and more. The tours are free; the information desk on the main level can give you information.

Call ahead for events and workshops. There are also special music series, ocean sleep-overs, and kid's fishing clinics.

Kid City: Children's Museum of Tampa

7550 North Boulevard, Tampa 33604, next to Lowry Park Zoo • (813) 935-8441

Hours - Monday–Friday, 9 a.m.–5:30 p.m.; Saturday, 10 a.m.–5:30 p.m.; Sunday, noon–5:30 p.m.

Admission - $4 for everyone ages 2 and older; free parking

Appeal by Age Group -

Pre-school ★★★★	Teens ★★	Over 30 —
Grade school ★★★★	Young Adults —	Seniors —

Touring Time - Average 2 hours; minimum 1 hour

Rainy-Day Touring - Recommended

Author's Rating - ★★★; a fun side trip from the Lowry Park Zoo for little ones

Restaurants - No

Handicapped access - No

Baby stroller rental - Yes

Pet kennels - No

Private tours - No

Alcoholic beverages - No

Wheelchair rental - No

Lockers - No

Rain check - No

Description and Comments The coolest thing about this museum is the kid-size village with more than 22 buildings designed to represent Tampa. Your kids can visit NationsBank, shop at Publix, serve as a judge at the courthouse, or stop by for a burger at McDonald's. Museum facilitators interact with the children to make the city lifelike. The museum is geared to ages 2–12, and displays and programs are built to help children with self-esteem and confidence.

Lowry Park Zoo

7530 North Boulevard, Tampa • (813) 932-0245 or 935-8552
www.lowryparkzoo.com

Hours - Daily, 9:30 a.m.–5 p.m.

Admission - $9.50 for adults, $5.95 for children ages 3–11, $8.50 for seniors ages 50 and older

Appeal by Age Group -

Pre-school ★★★★	Teens ★★	Over 30 ★★★
Grade school ★★★★	Young Adults ★★	Seniors ★★★

Touring Time - Average 3½ hours; minimum 2 hours

Rainy-Day Touring - Not recommended

Author's Rating - ★★★; enjoy your day without feeling the stress of waiting in long theme park lines

Restaurants - Yes

Alcoholic beverages - No

Handicapped access - Yes

Wheelchair rental - Yes

Baby stroller rental - Yes

Lockers - No

Pet kennels - No

Rain check - Yes

Private tours - Arranged in advance

Description and Comments Lowry Park Zoo is rated as one of the top three midsize zoos in the country. Animals roam freely across much of the zoo's 41 acres, controlled by natural barriers. The zoo features more than 1,500 animals of 375 different species and includes a manatee hospital. Check the show schedule when you arrive for special attractions such as the Meet a Keeper experience to learn more about care and feeding for these animals. Areas include:

- *Asian Domain,* featuring animals from around the world, including bears, tigers, chimpanzees, and an extremely rare Indian rhinoceros.
- *Birds of Prey Show,* with owls, hawks, eagles, and falcons.
- *Children's Petting Zoo,* with sheep, goats, pot-bellied pigs, turtles, and more.
- *Florida Manatee and Aquatic Center,* with 200,000 gallons of water reserved for native fish, reptiles, and manatees. Twin observation pools get you close to the water, as a taped narrative explains manatees and the preservation efforts taken to protect them. Behind the scenes, manatees are treated at the zoo's manatee hospital. There are both fresh- and saltwater exhibits here, too, where otters, sharks, eels, fish, and other animals play.
- *Free Flight Aviary,* with more than 50 fine-feathered subtropical species. At nearby Lorikeet Landing, you can find parrot-ike Lorikeets.
- At the *Harrell Discovery Center* and *Saunders Conservation Theater,* you'll see poison arrow frogs, tarantulas, emperor scorpions, and other wonders.
- *Native Florida Wildlife Center,* a special sanctuary for native Floridians, including alligators, panthers, bears, red wolves, birds, and plains bison.
- *Primate World,* home to more than a dozen different species, from chimpanzees to woolly monkeys.
- *The Reptile Encounter* is sure to score big points with your kids, featuring all the slimy things some parents hate: snakes, alligators, lizards, and frogs. After the show, your children get to touch some of the creatures.
- *Wallaroo Station* is the newest expansion of the zoo, with kangaroos you can pet and feed, kookaburras, cockatoos, and other wildlife from "down under." Also a small water play park.

Museum of Science and Industry

4801 E. Fowler Avenue, Tampa • (813) 987-6100 or (800) 995-6674 (995-MOSI)
www.mosi.org

Hours - Open at 9 a.m. 365 days a year, closing hours seasonal

Admission - $15.95 for adults, $13.95 for seniors, $11.95 ages 2–13, free for ages 2 and under. MOSIMAX movie is additional, but combination tickets can be purchased. Free parking. Visit the website for an online coupon

Appeal by Age Group -

Pre-school ★★★	Teens ★★★	Over 30 ★★★★
Grade school ★★★★	Young Adults ★★★	Seniors ★★★★

Touring Time - Average 4–5 hours; minimum 3 hours

Rainy-Day Touring - Recommended

Author's Rating - ★★★★; an incredible museum, great for rainy days

Restaurants - Yes

Alcoholic beverages - No

Handicapped access - Yes

Wheelchair rental - Yes

Baby stroller rental - No

Lockers - No

Pet kennels - No

Rain check - No

Private tours - Arranged in advance

Description and Comments MOSI's (rhymes with Rosie's) philosophy is "hands-on, minds-on." It's the largest science center (254,000 square feet on a 65-acre campus) in the southeastern United States, with three floors and more than 450 hands-on displays.

Starting in the lobby, you'll see the massive bones of diplodocus dinosaurs, reaching three stories high. Begin your tour in the Focus Gallery, where exhibits are rotated. The highlight is Kids in Charge, designed for children ages 5 and under to explore science concepts with an adult. There are vehicles to drive, structures to climb, animals to ride, discovery boxes to explore, and more.

Take the ramp to the second floor to EarthWorks, where you can experience the 74-mph hurricane-like winds in the Gulf Coast Hurricane. You also can view ice age fossils in the Florida Fossil Gallery or pedal a bike to create enough energy to turn on a light.

Cross the bridge to the west wing to MOSI's "backyard," Welcome to Our Place on the Planet: An Exhibition on Florida. An ordinary backyard serves as the backdrop for science that takes place in our own backyards. For instance, a giant Tower of Trash illustrates solid waste disposal, and a palmetto bug insectarium lets you look closely at the creepy crawlies.

Next, experience the 5,500-square-foot Amazing You exhibit that explores the human body, from DNA cells to organs to individuals. Themes include How We Work, Wellness—How We Keep Ourselves Going, and Taking Care of Ourselves When Things Go Wrong. Highlights include the Miracle of Life theater, which explains human development from conception to birth (a live birth is shown). The bike course monitors heart rate, time, speed, and the physiological changes that occur when exercising. A video operating room creates the illusion of a real operation, and a wheelchair allows guests to experience the challenges of being mobility impaired.

The next exhibit, Our Place in the Universe, includes a flight simulator that takes you to the outer limits of Earth. The main focus is flight, space exploration, and astronomy in this 5,000-square-foot exhibit. On the east wing of the third floor, you'll find the GTE Challenger Learning Center, a living memorial to the crew of the Challenger. Guests can assume roles of astronauts and engineers at 12 different work stations. Nearby is the Saunders Planetarium, which hosts family shows throughout the day and on weekends. There are also "star parties" weather permitting, on Saturday nights.

Schedule your visit around a film in MOSIMAX, a 353-seat IMAX theater that projects movies with a 180° fisheye lens onto an 82-foot-high curved dome screen. Different films are featured, often nature-based.

The Back Woods lets you head outdoors and showcases conservation efforts on several miles of trails. Signs identify plant life, and cassette players are available for an audio tour. There is also the BioWorks Butterfly Garden with 175 butterflies representing 9 species. There may also be special traveling exhibits on hand during your visit.

At MOSI's Mining Company, their retail store, you can pan for gold or select a geode and have it cracked before your eyes, revealing the crystals inside.

TAMPA SPORTS

If you'd like to catch a game while you're vacationing, here are numbers to call for schedules for sports teams:

Baseball New York Yankees Minor League, Legends Field, (813) 875-7753; New York Yankees Spring Training, (813) 875-7753

Football National Football League's Tampa Bay Buccaneers, Raymond James Stadium, (813) 879-2827

Hockey Tampa Bay Lightning, Ice Palace, (813) 301-6500

Soccer Major Soccer League's Tampa Bay Mutiny, Raymond James Stadium, (813) 386-2000

Family-Friendly Restaurants

The Colonnade

3401 Bayshore Boulevard, Tampa • (813) 839-7558

Meals served - Lunch and dinner

Cuisine - Seafood

Entree range - Lunch, $5.99–8.99; dinner, $8.99–18.99

Kids menu - Yes

Reservations - Not accepted

Payment - All major credit cards accepted

The Colonnade is a favorite for the locals. The grouper is a popular item, prepared seven different ways. Unusual appetizers include wild Florida gator and fried green tomatoes.

Crawdaddy's Restaurant and Lounge

2500 Rocky Point Drive, Tampa • (813) 281-0407

Meals served - Dinner

Cuisine - American, seafood

Entree range - $12.95–29.95

Kids menu - Yes

Reservations - Accepted

Payment - All major credit cards accepted

Don't let the clothesline, shack house, and junked truck in the yard scare you—good ol' New Orleans cuisine awaits your family. Try the jalapeno crab cakes or the etouffee.

Mel's Hot Dogs

4136 E. Busch Boulevard, Tampa • (813) 985-8000

Meals served - Lunch and dinner

Cuisine - American

Entree range - $5–8

Kids menu - Yes

Reservations - Not accepted

Payment - No credit cards

Try the special, an all-beef hot dog served on a poppy seed bun with mustard, onions, sauerkraut, relish, and a pickle. The Chicago is another favorite, with mustard, onions, relish, pickle, tomatoes, celery salt, and hot peppers. Other items on the menu include veggie burgers, chicken sandwiches, bratwurst, and corn dogs.

Old Meeting House

901 S. Howard Avenue, Tampa's Hyde Park district • (813) 251-1754

Meals served - Breakfast, lunch, and dinner

Cuisine - American diner

Entree range - $4.50–10

Kids menu - Yes

Reservations - No

Payment - Cash only

While everyone's going retro, the Old Meeting House has kept hungry guests coming back by staying exactly the same as when it opened in 1947. In fact, the one and only pair of hands that made the ice cream back then is still churning today. His name is Harold, and he has created more than 40 flavors (although only about 10 are available at one time), including brownie ice cream, Cherry Seinfeld, and more. After you fill up, visit nearby Hyde Park Village, a unique shopping area.

Skipper's Smokehouse Restaurant and Oyster Bar

At the corner of Skipper Road and Nebraska Avenue, Tampa • (813) 971-0666
www.skipperssmokehouse.com

Meals served - Lunch and dinner

Cuisine - Seafood

Entree Range: $4.99–14.99

Kids menu - Yes

Reservations - No

Payment - Major credit cards accepted

This cracker-style shack with a rusty tin roof just feels right—and the locals agree. Nestled in an island atmosphere (some liken it to Gilligan's Island) Skipper's offers unusual Caribbean- and Louisiana-flavored treats, including black bean gator chili, grilled gator kabob, alligator ribs, mudbugs, and fried gator tails. After dinner, visit the "Skipper Dome"—not a high-ticket venue, but a stage shaded by tall oaks. Over the years, the Skipper Dome has hosted an eclectic group of musicians, including the best in blues, zydeco, roots rock, and reggae. The Skipper Dome is separate from the Smokehouse, but the cover charge is usually only a few bucks for most shows and kids 10 and under are admitted free.

Side Trips

Dinosaur World, Plant City Little tykes enamored with dinosaurs will be enchanted with this roadside attraction that's just off I-4 between Tampa and Orlando. Not realistic enough to be scary, these life-size creatures of fiberglass, steel, and concrete don't move, they just pose in the swampy grove, 150 in all, awaiting their next young visitor. Admission $9.75, $7.75 ages 3–12. 5145 Harvey Tew Road, Plant City; (813) 717-9865; www.dinoworld.net.

Tarpon Springs The music, sights, and sounds make Tarpon Springs feel like a village on the Mediterranean. The heritage is Greek, and the language is still spoken here by many of the residents.

Tarpon Springs was known as "America's Sponge Capital" at the turn of the century, after a man named John Cocoris brought Greek sponge divers from Key West to settle this area because of the rich and sizable sponge beds in the Gulf of Mexico. In the 1930s and 1940s the industry prospered, until bacteria destroyed most of the sponge beds in the 1940s.

Today tourism and fishing make Tarpon Springs vibrant, and a recent $2.5 million streetscape renovation has rejuvenated this historic center. Walk along Dodecanese Boulevard among the heaps of harvested sponges (you can still buy them in the shops), and sample some of the authentic Greek cuisine at one of the many restaurants—we recommend the family-run Pappas Restaurant at 10 Dodecanese. The old Sponge Exchange has been converted into a shopping and dining district featuring Greek foods and handicrafts.

To learn more about the sponge diving and the Greek community, visit the free Sponge-O-Rama museum housed in an old sponge factory. A half-hour film is shown, and many tools, diving suits, and other equipment used by early divers are on display. 510 Dodecanese Boulevard, Tarpon Springs; (727) 937-6105.

Weeki Wachee We imagine that most parents who visited Florida when they were young have fond memories of the amazing mermaids at Weeki Wachee. Today, children are still amazed by their ability to perform 12 feet under water.

The mermaid show has been a Weeki Wachee trademark of long-running distinction. You watch from a spacious theater that's partially built into the ground and facing a bank of large plate glass windows. As the show begins, visitors find themselves peering into the depths of the dazzling Weeki Wachee Spring, alive with verdant flora and brimming with marine life. Against the incomparable background a graceful and lively water ballet is performed. The performance is well paced and the mermaids are indeed lovely, combining music, elaborate props, imaginative costuming, and a little melodrama for a visually rich experience.

Seating is tiered, providing a good view from anywhere in the theater, and the sound system is clear and audible.

Outdoor attractions include a narrated Wilderness River Cruise to a refuge where injured birds are nursed back to health. Young children will enjoy the Animal Forest Petting Zoo where they can touch the llamas, goats, and other small animals.

Weeki Wachee is about a 3-hour experience. And it's fun even in the rain. Admission is $16 for adults; $12 for children ages 3–10. Weeki Wachee is open year-round 10 a.m.–4 p.m. The park is located at US 19 and SR 50, 20 miles south of Homosassa (north of Tampa); (352) 596-2062.

Ybor City Ybor City, once a cigar-making center, today is a quaint suburb of Tampa, with cobblestone streets and Spanish-tiled buildings that remain from the early 1900s when Cuban, Spanish, German, Italian, and Jewish immigrants called it home.

For families, it's an interesting place to take a stroll or stop for lunch, particularly if you've spent the morning at the nearby Florida Aquarium. A tour through the Ybor City State Museum at 1818 E. 9th Avenue (call (813) 247-6323) gives a quick history. It is open 9 a.m.–5 p.m daily, and the cost is $2. You can also stop by the Ybor City Chamber of Commerce at 1800 E. 9th Avenue (call (813) 248-3712) for a self-guided walking tour map. Ybor Square at 8th Avenue and 13th Street showcases arts and crafts and specialty shops; you can still watch cigars being rolled here at Tampa Rico Cigars.

We recommend a meal at the original Columbia restaurant, in the same location since 1905 and known as "America's Oldest Spanish Restaurant."

The Columbia has been under the same ownership for 90 years, run by the fourth generation of its founder, Casimiro Hernandez Sr. It's a huge place, spanning an entire city block in the heart of Ybor City—11 rooms seat 1,660 people.

Lunch and dinner are served, and there is a children's menu. The Columbia is at 2117 E. 7th Avenue, between 22nd and 21st streets; (813) 248-4961.

St. Petersburg and Clearwater

Start in Tampa and cross Florida's first suspension bridge, the Sunshine Skyway, that spans Tampa Bay. This 4-mile-long bridge, modeled after the Bretonne (or Brotonne) Bridge over the Seine river in France, is one of the longest cable-stayed bridges in the Western Hemisphere. Constructed in 1987 at a cost of $244 million, it soars 183 feet above Tampa Bay, and at night it is especially beautiful when the cables are lit. Once you pay the $1 toll to cross the bridge, you'll find yourself in the St. Petersburg–Clearwater region.

Wonderful weather and amazing art welcome families here. Bordered on the east by Tampa Bay and on the west by the Gulf of Mexico, this area boasts 35 miles of white sand, with a diverse ecosystem that includes amber sea oats, stands of pine, cypress, and mangrove hammocks.

Downtown St. Petersburg is home to the museum district, which includes Florida International Museum, Salvador Dali Museum, Museum of Fine Arts, Museum of History, Great Explorations, and the Pier.

It all adds up to a great place for families to visit.

Family Resorts

Best Western Sea Stone Resort

445 Hamden Drive, Clearwater Beach • (727) 441-1722 • fax (727) 461-1680

Take your pick of a room on the bay or the ocean. There are 44 one-bedroom suites with kitchens overlooking Clearwater Harbor and 65 hotel rooms facing the Gulf.

In addition to comfortable rooms with coffeemakers and refrigerators, you'll find a heated pool, private dock, sundeck, marina, restaurant, and guest laundry. Each suite has a microwave.

Rates start at $99 for a room and $149 for a suite year-round.

Don CeSar

This beautiful pink palace on the beach opened in 1928, and architect-builder Thomas J. Rowe named it after his favorite opera character. Many celebrities have enjoyed the splendid hotel, including F. Scott Fitzgerald, Babe Ruth, Lou Gehrig, and presidents George Bush, Jimmy Carter, and Bill Clinton.

Through the years, the hotel has seen many changes, most notably when it was used as a military hospital during World War II. Today, it's on the National Register of Historic Places, recently refurbished with Italian crystal chandeliers, French furniture, and French and Italian marble.

Don't let the luxury be intimidating: the Don is a great family respite, with countless activities and friendly service. There are 275 rooms with ocean views, including 43 suites and two penthouses. You'll find a fitness center and spa, two heated swimming pools, tennis courts on the beach, and water-sport rentals including aquabikes, Waverunners, sailboats, and kayaks. Standard rooms start at $184 in the summer and are a little higher in the winter. Each room has a mini-bar, some rooms include microwave, refrigerator, and coffeemaker.

For children ages 4–12, there are arts and crafts and other activities led by retired schoolteachers who live in the area. There is also a nighttime pizza parlor.

Just a short stroll from the hotel (or an even shorter ride in resort-provided transportation) is the Don CeSar Beach House, a resort with 70 condominium-style suites. Each condo has a fully equipped kitchen, beach or gulf views, private balconies, and washers and dryers. Guests here share all hotel privileges. Condo rates run from $209 to $620. 3400 Gulf Boulevard, St. Petersburg Beach; (800) 282-1116 or (727) 360-1881; fax: (727) 363-0600; www.doncesar.com.

Sheraton Sand Key

1160 Gulf Blvd., Clearwater Beach • (800) 325-3535 • fax (727) 596-8488
www.beachandsand.com

This 375-room hotel has been spiffed up with a new pool and spa, though the big draw is still the gorgeous stretch of white sand where most of the activities are centered. And you're just across the street from the Shoppes of Sand Key, a boardwalk with 30 shops, restaurants, and other activities.

The Sheraton Kids Camp operates Monday–Friday 9 a.m.–2 p.m., with supervised activities from beachcombing to visits to area attractions. Cost is $18 for the day. For fun on your own, there's windsurfing, kayaking, sailing, snorkeling, volleyball, and lighted tennis courts. From May

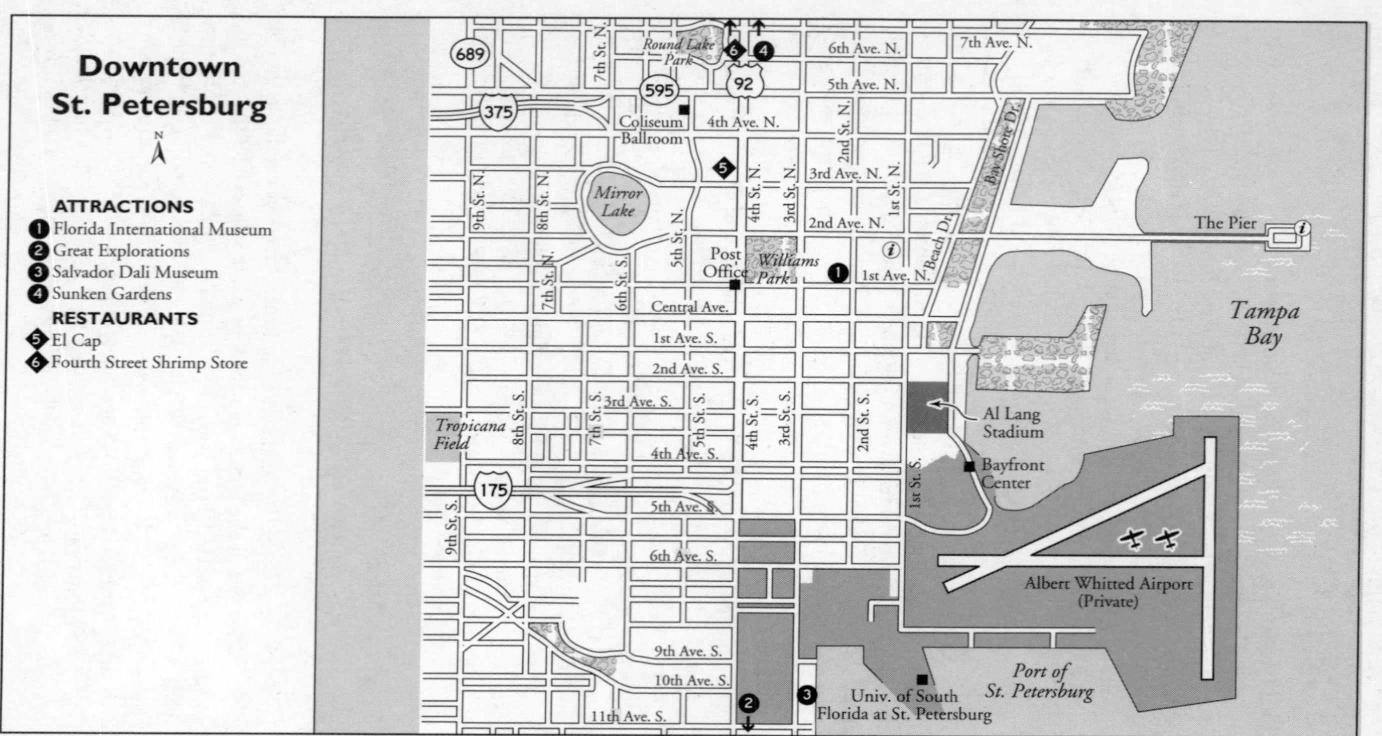

Downtown St. Petersburg
N
ATTRACTIONS
1 Florida International Museum
2 Great Explorations
3 Salvador Dali Museum
4 Sunken Gardens
RESTAURANTS
5 El Cap
6 Fourth Street Shrimp Store
689
375
595
92
175
Round Lake Park
Coliseum Ballroom
Mirror Lake
Post Office
Williams Park
Tropicana Field
The Pier
Tampa Bay
Al Lang Stadium
Bayfront Center
Albert Whitted Airport (Private)
Port of St. Petersburg
Univ. of South Florida at St. Petersburg
7th Ave. N.
6th Ave. N.
5th Ave. N.
4th Ave. N.
3rd Ave. N.
2nd Ave. N.
1st Ave. N.
Central Ave.
1st Ave. S.
2nd Ave. S.
3rd Ave. S.
4th Ave. S.
5th Ave. S.
6th Ave. S.
9th Ave. S.
10th Ave. S.
11th Ave. S.
9th St. N.
8th St. N.
7th St. N.
5th St. N.
4th St. N.
3rd St. N.
2nd St. N.
1st St. N.
9th St. S.
8th St. S.
7th St. S.
6th St. S.
5th St. S.
4th St. S.
3rd St. S.
2nd St. S.
1st St. S.
Bay Shore Dr.
Beach Dr.

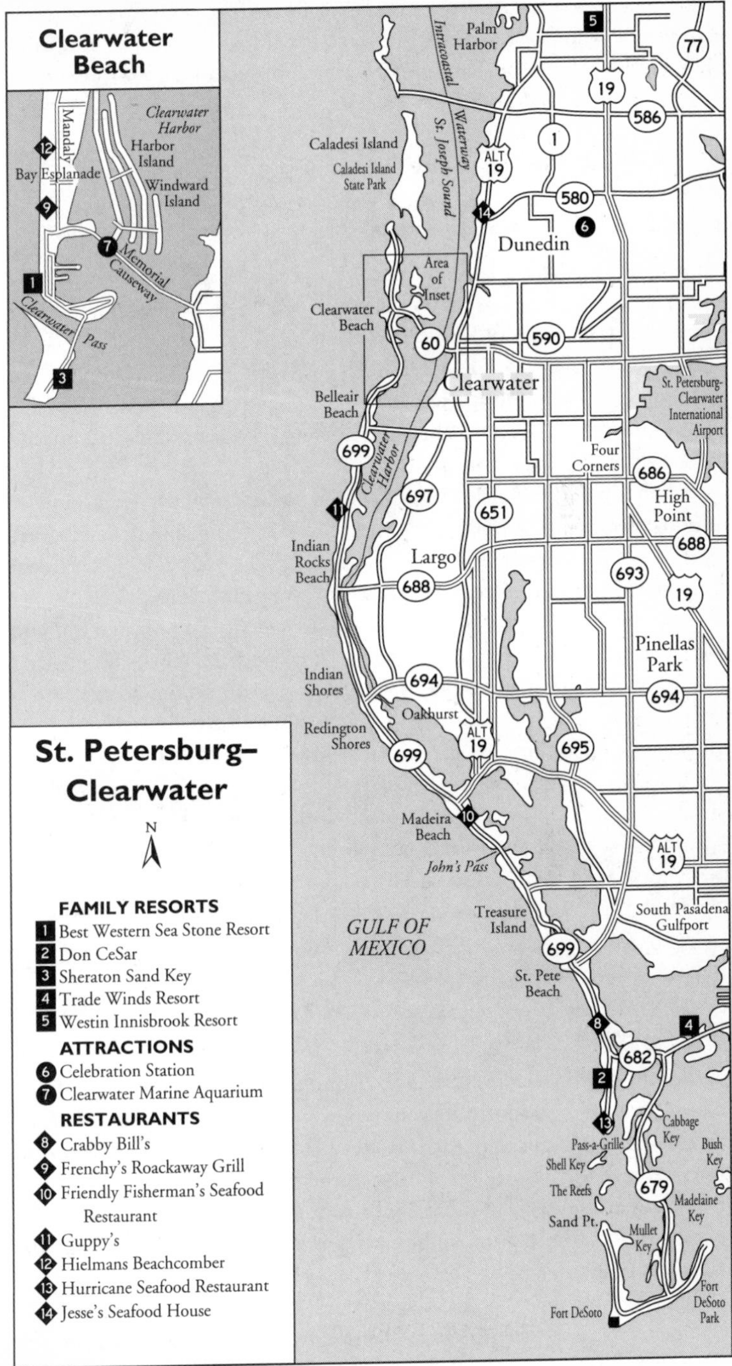
Clearwater Beach
Mandaly
Clearwater Harbor
Harbor Island
Bay Esplanade
Windward Island
Memorial Causeway
Clearwater Pass
St. Petersburg–Clearwater
N
FAMILY RESORTS
1 Best Western Sea Stone Resort
2 Don CeSar
3 Sheraton Sand Key
4 Trade Winds Resort
5 Westin Innisbrook Resort
ATTRACTIONS
6 Celebration Station
7 Clearwater Marine Aquarium
RESTAURANTS
8 Crabby Bill's
9 Frenchy's Roackaway Grill
10 Friendly Fisherman's Seafood Restaurant
11 Guppy's
12 Hielmans Beachcomber
13 Hurricane Seafood Restaurant
14 Jesse's Seafood House
Palm Harbor
Intracoastal Waterway
St. Joseph Sound
Caladesi Island
Caladesi Island State Park
Dunedin
Area of Inset
Clearwater Beach
Clearwater
Belleair Beach
Clearwater Harbor
St. Petersburg-Clearwater International Airport
Four Corners
High Point
Largo
Indian Rocks Beach
Pinellas Park
Indian Shores
Oakhurst
Redington Shores
Madeira Beach
John's Pass
GULF OF MEXICO
Treasure Island
South Pasadena
Gulfport
St. Pete Beach
Pass-a-Grille
Shell Key
Cabbage Key
Bush Key
The Reefs
Sand Pt.
Mullet Key
Madelaine Key
Fort DeSoto
Fort DeSoto Park
77
19
586
1
ALT 19
580
590
60
699
686
697
651
688
693
694
695
682
679

to June, you might catch a glimpse of the giant Loggerhead turtles as they lumber ashore on the resort's 10 acres of private beach to lay their eggs. Rates start at $140.

TradeWinds Resort, Island Grand

5500 Gulf Boulevard, St. Petersburg Beach • (800) 237-0707 or (727) 367-6461 fax (727) 562-1222 • www.tradewindsresort.com

Your family will get a kick out of riding gondolas to your room in this resort with meandering waterways that are used as byways, cutting through the 18 beautifully landscaped acres.

The resort offers the KONK club—Kids Only, No Kidding, where children ages 4–11 can finger paint, make puppets, and collect seashells. There are pajama parties and Indian powwows, and kids get in the kitchen to make their own desserts.

For children ages 7–11, there are beach parties, pool parties, and dive-in movies in the swimming pool. Ages 12–17 can in-line skate, participate in fun runs, play minigolf, and snorkel. The activities are offered year-round; some are free, and others charge a nominal fee.

The resort's 577 guest rooms include refrigerators, coffeemakers, and toasters; suites have living rooms and fully equipped kitchens. The Island Grand is right on the ocean and also has five swimming pools, a fitness center, tennis courts, racquet sports, and water sports rentals. And for those who are familiar with the Trade Winds Island Grand but want to try something new, the hotel has two other properties within walking distance: The Sandpiper and the Sirata Beach Resort. These resorts are a little less expensive than the Island Grand, and guests at one hotel are welcome to use the facilities at any of the hotels. Rates start at $199 in the winter, $169 in the summer.

The Westin Innisbrook Resort

36750 US Highway 19 N., Palm Harbor • (800) 456-2000 • (727) 942-2000 www.westin-innisbrook.com

Kids will love the Loch Ness, a $3.4 million monster pool (one of six) complete with a 15-foot waterfall, two water slides, and two sand beach areas. And if you can drag them from the monster, there's a whole world to explore at this resort. Try fishing in the stocked lakes, filled with catfish, bass, and bluegill (fishing equipment is available). Or you can rent bikes, explore the nature trails, play miniature golf, or check out the recreation center complete with a kids' play area filled with swings, slides, a climbing fort, and the Loch Ness Pool. While the kids are busy, mom and dad can golf (there are four championship golf courses) play tennis (eleven courts, seven lit for night play), or use the indoor racquetball courts. You never have to leave the 1,000 acre property—but if you're a beach bum at heart, there's even a complimentary shuttle to the beach.

There are 700 guestrooms clustered among 28 lodges. Rates range from $119–175 for standard guestrooms in the summer, and in the winter rates can run about $209. Suites with kitchenettes are available. If you're traveling in the summer, ask about their summer getaway packages that often include free junior golf.

HASLAM'S BOOK STORE

Before you head to the beach, hit Haslam's Book Store for some great summer reads. Haslam's, located near Tropicana Field and the downtown museums, opened in 1933 and has become the largest independently owned bookstore in the Southeast. Browse the new, used, and unusual books—there are more than 300,000 in all in every category imaginable. 2025 Central Avenue; (727) 822-8616; www.haslams.com.

Attractions

Celebration Station

24546 US 19 N., Clearwater • (727) 791-1799

Hours - Sunday–Thursday, noon–9 p.m.; Friday, noon–midnight; Saturday, 10 a.m.–midnight; hours vary during peak season

Admission - Free; each activity is a separate fee

Appeal by Age Group -

Pre-school ★★★	Teens ★★★	Over 30 ★
Grade school ★★★	Young Adults ★	Seniors ★

Touring Time - Average 4 hours; minimum 2 hours

Rainy-Day Touring - Not recommended

Author's Rating - ★★; all the stuff kids love

Restaurants - Yes

Handicapped access - Yes

Baby stroller rental - No

Pet kennels - No

Private tours - No

Alcoholic beverages - No

Wheelchair rental - No

Lockers - No

Rain check - No

Description and Comments This minitheme park includes go-carts, bumper boats, minigolf, batting cages, and a two-story arcade. If the kids get hungry, pizza is available.

Clearwater Marine Aquarium

249 Windward Passage, Clearwater • (727) 441-1790 or (888) 239-9414
www.cmaquarium.org

Hours - Monday–Friday, 9 a.m.–5 p.m., Saturday, 9 a.m.–4 p.m., Sunday, 11 a.m.–4 p.m.

Admission - $8.75 for adults, $6.25 for children ages 3–11, free for children under age 3

Appeal by Age Group -

Pre-school ★★★	Teens ★★★	Over 30 ★★★
Grade school ★★★★	Young Adults ★★★	Seniors ★★★★

Touring Time - Average 2 hours; minimum 1 hour

Rainy-Day Touring - Recommended

Author's Rating - ★★★; a chance to see some serious work with marine life

Restaurants - No

Alcoholic beverages - No

Handicapped access - Yes

Wheelchair rental - Yes

Baby stroller rental - Yes

Lockers - No

Pet kennels - No

Rain check - No

Private tours - Yes

Description and Comments This nonprofit center rescues, rehabilitates, and releases injured and sick marine mammals, including whales, dolphins, otters, and sea turtles. Handicapped animals are given a permanent home here.

Part of the aquarium's mission is to educate the public and foster conservation, so there are many interactive displays including Stingray Beach, where you can touch stingrays, hermit crabs, snails, and starfish. There is also the Mangrove Seagrass Tank, a 55,000-gallon aquarium with a fish-eye view of more than 100 species of Florida fish and invertebrates, including trout, grouper, snook, snapper, and sharks. You can also visit dolphins or sea turtles being readied for release back to the wild. A special Day with a Dolphin program takes kids 8–10 behind the scenes.

If you have a child with physical or mental challenges, the aquarium has a program called Full Circle for children 4–16. Children's needs are assessed, then the aquarium's daily animal caretaking and training activities are used as therapy sessions. For instance, a child with a physical disability may work to develop motor skills by putting fish in a bucket, giving hand signals to the dolphin, holding and dropping fish into a dolphin's mouth, and more. Intensive one- and two-week programs are available. For more information call (727) 441-1790, ext. 21.

The aquarium is on an island in Clearwater Bay, accessible by the Memorial Causeway.

St. Pete Trolleys

If you want to make a day of the wonderful museums in St. Petersburg, jump on the teal-colored trolley that runs through downtown St. Petersburg and includes stops at the Pier, Museum of History, Museum of Fine Arts, the Renaissance Vinoy Resort, Florida International Museum, Salvadore Dali Museum, Great Explorations Museum, Bayfront Hilton Hotel, and Beach Drive. Stops are marked by special pink Looper signs. The cost is a reasonable 50 cents. The trolley runs daily, 10 a.m.–4:30 p.m., every half-hour on the hour; (727) 821-6164.

Florida International Museum

100 Second Street N • (727) 822-3693 or 824-6734 or (800) 777-9882
www.floridamuseum.org

Hours - Monday–Saturday, 10 a.m. to 5 p.m., Sunday noon–5 p.m., last tour starts at 4 p.m.

Admission - $12 for adults, $11 for seniors 65 and older, $6 for students. Admission includes an audio guided tour, two theater presentations, and access to the galleries

Appeal by Age Group -

Pre-school ★	Teens ★★★★	Over 30 ★★★★
Grade school ★★★	Young Adults ★★★★★	Seniors ★★★★

Touring Time - Average 2 hours; minimum 1 hour

Rainy-Day Touring - Recommended

Author's Rating - ★★★★, first-class; if they are featuring an exhibit you have some interest in, it's definitely worth a visit

Restaurants - No
Alcoholic beverages - No
Handicapped access - Yes
Wheelchair rental - Yes
Baby stroller rental - No
Lockers - No
Pet kennels - No
Rain check - No
Private tours - No

Description and Comments Once a museum devoted to housing one blockbuster exhibit each year, the Florida International Museum now is home to the largest collection of private Kennedy artifacts in the world and is an affiliate of the Smithsonian museum. The many galleries re-create times and places lodged in our minds—from Kennedy's PT109 days to the Oval Office. You'll see china from Air Force One, Kennedy's rocking chair, an Oleg Cassini dress of Jaqueline Kennedy's, and much more.

Great Explorations: The Hands-On Museum

The Pier, Third Floor, 800 Second Avenue NE • (727) 821-8992
www.greatexplorations.org

Hours - Monday–Saturday, 10 a.m.–8 p.m.; Sunday, 11 a.m.–6 p.m.

Admission - $4 for adults, free for children ages 2 and under

Appeal by Age Group -

Pre-school ★★★★	Teens ★	Over 30 ★
Grade school ★★★	Young Adults ★	Seniors ★

Touring Time - Average 2 hours; minimum 1½ hours

Rainy-Day Touring - Recommended

Author's Rating - ★★; make a pit stop here if you have little ones

Restaurants - No

Alcoholic beverages - No

Handicapped access - Yes

Wheelchair rental - No

Baby stroller rental - No

Lockers - No

Pet kennels - No

Rain check - No

Private tours - For 10 or more kids

Description and Comments Great Explorations caters to the younger crowd, which is encouraged to touch, move, and explore. This not-for-profit museum focuses on art, science, and health, with exhibits like the 55-foot-long Touch Tunnel for kids to crawl, slide, wriggle, or slink through. At the Body Shop, children can measure fitness levels and nutrition awareness. Touch- or audio-activated equipment allows you to create your own masterpiece at the Light Strokes exhibit in Phenomenal Arts. Explore Galore is filled with hands-on activities, a pint-size fire engine, and slides to keep your 2–6-year-olds happy. Squeamish people, stand back; the Exchange features snakes, spiders, and scorpions. The Experimental Gallery showcases prototype exhibits on their way to the science center and other children's museums around the world.

Kids also will enjoy playing doctor in the veterinary office, where they can adopt stuffed pets and perform an examination, complete with shots and blood pressure. Kids can even view x-rays on a light table. Also, Sssnakes, Ssspiders, & Ssscorpions gives children a closer look at the creepy critters. Adults will be pleasantly surprised by this museum. You'll find yourself testing your strength at the grip machines or even attempting a pull-up on the bar when no one is looking.

Salvador Dali Museum

1000 Third Street, St. Petersburg • (727) 823-3767 • www.daliweb.com

Hours - Monday–Saturday, 9:30 a.m.–5:30 p.m. (open until 8 p.m. Thursday); Sunday, noon–5:30 p.m.

Admission - $10 for adults, $7 for seniors, $5 for students with college ID, free for ages 10 and under; free parking; Thursday 5–8 p.m. admission is $5 adults, $3.50 seniors, $2.50 students

Appeal by Age Group -

Pre-school ★	Teens ★★	Over 30 ★★★★
Grade school ★	Young Adults ★★★★★	Seniors ★★★★

Touring Time - Average 2 hours; minimum 1 hour

Rainy-Day Touring - Recommended

Author's Rating - ★★★★; incredible, pack a lunch to enjoy near the harbor after your visit

Restaurants - No

Alcoholic beverages - No

Handicapped access - Yes

Wheelchair rental - Yes

Baby stroller rental - No

Lockers - No

Pet kennels - No

Rain check - No

Private tours - No

Description and Comments Dali is more than melting clocks. True, his *Persistence of Memory* (1931) is still one of the best-known surrealist works. But although Dali is best known for his Surrealist period (1929–40), this collection spanning 1914–70 affords guests the opportunity to view the scope of his artistic ability and style. It's the world's largest collection of his work, valued at more than $125 million, housed in a renovated waterfront warehouse situated on Bayboro Harbor.

The collection includes 95 oils, 100 watercolors and drawings, nearly 1,300 graphics, plus sculptures, objets d'art, photographs, documents, and an extensive archival library. For a chronological tour, enter the exhibit and walk clockwise.

Of the 18 of his "master works," 6 are in this museum. They include *Hallucinogenic Toreador* and *Discovery of America by Christopher Columbus,* and they are stunning. The docent tours are recommended, revealing amazing hidden elements in Dali's paintings.

If you think all of this art is too high-brow for your kids, think again. Teenagers love Dali's craziness, and it's a perfect opportunity to introduce them to twentieth-century art. The museum's programs include Junior Docents and Soapbox Docents Day, where fourth- and fifth-graders get to explain Dali's works from a youngster's view. Also, there are Dali Days for Kids, which are summer art workshops open to children ages 6–12.

TAKE ME OUT TO THE BALL GAME

Baseball spring training sites:

- The Baltimore Orioles and the St. Louis Cardinals play at Al Lang Stadium in St. Pete, (727) 825-3137.
- You'll find the Philadelphia Phillies in Jack Russell Stadium in Clearwater, (727) 442-8496.
- Toronto Blue Jays play at Grant Field in Dunedin, (727) 733-9302.
- Pittsburgh Pirates are at McKechnie Field in Bradenton, (941) 748-4610; off-season (941-747-3031.

Sunken Gardens

1825 Fourth Street N., St. Petersburg • (727) 551-3100 • www.stpete.org/sunken.htm

Hours - Wednesday–Sunday, 10 a.m.–4 p.m; closed Monday and Tuesday.

Admission - $7 for adults, $3 for children ages 3–12, $5 for seniors

Appeal by Age Group -

Pre-school ★★	Teens ★★	Over 30 ★★★
Grade school ★★★	Young Adults ★★	Seniors ★★★

Touring Time - Average 2 hours; minimum 2 hours

Rainy-Day Touring - Not recommended

Author's Rating - ★; the orchids here are phenomenal

Restaurants - Snack bar

Alcoholic beverages - Yes

Handicapped access - Yes

Wheelchair rental - Yes

Baby stroller rental - Yes

Lockers - No

Pet kennels - Can keep in office

Rain check - Yes

Private tours - Arranged in advance

Description and Comments An original roadside attraction that once boasted of its alligator wrestling show, Sunken Gardens has now become a true botanical garden after being purchased by the city of St. Petersburg.

Change is good—the acquisition resulted in an addition of 6,000 plants and a butterfly garden, as well as greatly reduced ticket prices. You'll also find an exotic collection of more then 50,000 tropical plants and flowers, including more than 200 species blooming year-round at the six-acre garden. A walk-through aviary features tropical birds of all types, and thousands of rare, fragrant orchids are found in the Orchid Arbor.

On the Water

Here are three fun trips we can recommend from the Clearwater Beach Marina:

Captain Memo's Pirate Cruise Board the candy-apple red *Pirate's Ransom* for a swashbuckling adventure your kids won't forget. This full-size reproduction of a 70-foot buccaneer pirate ship holds up to 125 passengers for a trip into the Gulf of Mexico. The crew insists that everyone participate in dancing, treasure hunts, dolphin sightings, and water-pistol battles.

Captain Memo sails several times a day, depending on the season; call ahead for specific information on times. Admission is $28 in daylight and $30 nightly for adults, $22 for seniors 65 and older and children ages 13–17, $18 for children ages 3–12. The boat anchors at the Clearwater City Marina, Dock No. 3, at the end of US 60 on Clearwater Beach; (727) 446-2587; www.pirateflorida.com. (Reserve tickets online and receive a discount.)

Dolphin Encounter "Dolphin Sighting Is Guaranteed or Another Trip FREE," reads the brochure. And the friendly crew on the double-decker *Clearwater Express* will help you spot the playful mammals on the 1½-hour trip into the Gulf of Mexico, with a lovely view of the shoreline along Clearwater and Caladesi Island. Food is provided to feed the birds.

You can board the 125-passenger boat at the west end of Clearwater Beach Marina, across from the Pier 60 parking lot. Cruises leave daily at 11 a.m., 1 p.m., 3 p.m., and 5 p.m (no 11 a.m. trip on Sunday). Admission is $13 for adults, $7.50 for children ages 4–12. Reservations are recommended; (727) 442-7433.

ST. PETERSBURG PIER

The quarter-mile-long St. Petersburg Pier in Tampa Bay features an inverted five-story pyramid housing a festival marketplace with shops, restaurants, an aquarium, and a large observation area. The Columbia restaurant (of Ybor City fame) is also here but without the charm and character of the original restaurant—probably not necessary when you are surrounded by ocean views. On the second floor there is an aquarium, and on the fifth floor an observation deck. Rentals include skates, boats, and bikes. Miniature golf is also nearby. Family-oriented cruises and Duck Tours of Tampa bay (aboard a WWII amphibious vessel) depart from here as well. The Pier shops and restaurants are open daily, 10 a.m.–11 p.m. 800 Second Avenue, St. Petersburg; (727) 821-6164; www.stpete-pier.com.

Sea Screamer If you want to have a little fun out on the water, the 72-foot *Sea Screamer* races up to 40 mph, and the dolphins love to dive in the wake created by the boat. Cruises are about an hour long, and tickets are available at the dock 30 minutes before each of the four daily cruises at noon, 2 p.m., 4 p.m., and 6 p.m. The boat runs every day with a monthlong break from mid-January to mid-February. Admission is $13.50 for adults, $9 for children ages 5–12, free for children ages 4 and under. Cruises take off from the Clearwater Beach Marina at the end of US 60 on Clearwater Beach; (727) 447-7200 or 398-9612.

Family-Friendly Restaurants

Crabby Bill's

401 Gulf Boulevard, Indian Rocks Beach • (727) 595-4825

Meals served - Lunch and dinner

Cuisine - Florida-style seafood, American

Entree range - $5–24.95

Kids menu - Yes

Reservations - Accepted only for parties of 15 or more

Payment - Visa, MC, AmEx

This family owned and operated restaurant serves up good, cheap food in a no-frills environment. We love the Maryland-style crab cakes. Other favorites include shrimp, oysters, oyster stew, and catfish.

El Cap

3500 Fourth Street N., St. Petersburg • (727) 521-1314

Meals served - Lunch and dinner

Cuisine - American

Entree range - $2.60–5.95

Kids menu - No, but the menu has hamburgers and other items for kids

Reservations - Not accepted

Payment - Accepts all major credit cards

Locals and members of major league baseball teams hang out here, and their memorabilia hangs on the walls. The food is simple, with delicious burgers that have been voted the best in the Tampa Bay area.

Fourth Street Shrimp Store

1006 Fourth Street N., St. Petersburg • (727) 822-0325

Meals served - Lunch and dinner

Cuisine - Seafood, American

Entree range - $4–20
Kids menu - No, but the menu has hamburgers and other items for kids
Reservations - Not necessary
Payment - Visa, MC
Family friendly, and the seafood is excellent.

Frenchy's Rockaway Grill

7 Rockaway Street, Clearwater Beach • (727) 446-4844

Meals served - Lunch and dinner
Cuisine - American, seafood
Entree range - $8.95–18.95
Kids menu - Yes
Reservations - Not accepted
Payment - Visa, MC, AmEx
Try the Caribbean jerk grouper sandwich or the Rockaway shrimp primavera.

Friendly Fisherman's Seafood Restaurant

150 128th Avenue E., Madeira Beach • (727) 391-6025

Meals served - Breakfast, lunch, and dinner
Cuisine - Seafood, American
Entree range - $1.99–5.99, breakfast; $3.95–8.95, lunch; $8.95–24.95, dinner
Kids menu - Yes
Reservations - Not accepted
Payment - Visa, MC, AmEx, D
If you just caught a fish, they'll clean it and cook it for you . . . if not, you'll still enjoy the fresh seafood. The fresh grouper and seafood platter are their most popular creations. After dinner, there's plenty nearby to keep the family happy. The Friendly Fisherman is located in John's Pass Village and Boardwalk, where you can rent jet skis or sign up for a cruise.

Guppy's

1701 Gulf Boulevard, Indian Rocks Beach • (727) 593-2032

Meals served - Lunch and dinner
Cuisine - Seafood
Entree range - $7–22
Kids menu - Yes
Reservations - Only for parties of six or more

Payment - All major credit cards accepted

This casual oceanfront restaurant was voted "best seafood" by the locals.

Heilmans Beachcomber

447 Mandalay Avenue, Clearwater Beach • (727) 442-4144

Meals served - Lunch and dinner
Cuisine - American
Entree range - Lunch, $6.95–12.95; dinner, $11.95–25.95
Kids menu - Yes
Reservations - They almost insist on it
Payment - All major credit cards accepted

The seafood is fresh, but for a down-home dinner, try their Back-to-the-Farm chicken, sauteed in a Dutch oven skillet and served with potatoes, gravy, vegetable of the day, soup of the day, coleslaw, and fresh bread.

Hurricane Seafood Restaurant

807 Gulf Way, St. Petersburg Beach • (727) 360-9558

Meals served - Breakfast, lunch, and dinner
Cuisine - Seafood
Entree range - $2.50–9.99 breakfast, $3.15–22 lunch and dinner
Kids menu - Yes
Reservations - Not accepted
Payment - Visa, MC, AmEx, D

The food is good here, but the sunsets are even better. The Hurricane is located just across from the beach with unobstructed, breathtaking views of the ocean from certain seating areas. You can eat on any level of this three-story restaurant, but each level seats separately (so if the wait is long downstairs, head for another level to check on wait times).

Jesse's Seafood House

345 Causeway Boulevard, Dunedin • (727) 736-2611

Meals served - Lunch and dinner
Cuisine - Seafood, American
Entree range - $7.95–26.95
Kids menu - Yes
Reservations - Accepted for parties of ten or more
Payment - Visa, MC, AmEx, D

This family-oriented restaurant offers a diverse menu and reasonable prices, on the waterfront.

Sarasota

After you've conquered all the museums and roller coasters, expect the pace to slow down some here. Many families come here to relax on the beautiful barrier islands, with white sand, blue-green ocean, and 35 miles of beaches.

The area is refined and sophisticated, with upscale shopping and gourmet restaurants on St. Armand's Circle, as well as high-priced oceanfront resorts. Sarasota is a great supporter of the arts; when you're planning your stay, call the 24-hour ArtsLine, a service of the local newspaper, (941) 953-4636 ext. 6000, for the latest area events. Please note area code changes. From January 1–March 31 2003 both (941) and (239) will apply; after Macrh 31, 2003, (239) will be used for most of Sarasota proper.

Family Resorts

Colony Beach and Tennis Resort

1620 Gulf of Mexico Drive, Longboat Key • (800) 4-COLONY or (941) 383-6464
fax (941) 383-7549 • www.colonybeachresort.com

The Colony comes highly recommended, from tennis buffs, beach bums, and folks who love good food.

There are 235 comfortable, tasteful accommodations, ranging from one-bedroom suites (with microwave, refrigerator, and coffeemaker) to private two- and three-bedroom houses on the ocean. Each has a living room, dining area, bedrooms, and a kitchen with a dishwasher, refrigerator, and microwave.

If you love tennis, it doesn't get much better than this: 21 courts with an ocean breeze, and programs for all ages and ability levels—the pro will even work with your whole family. They start young here, with a tiny tots tennis program for children under age 6.

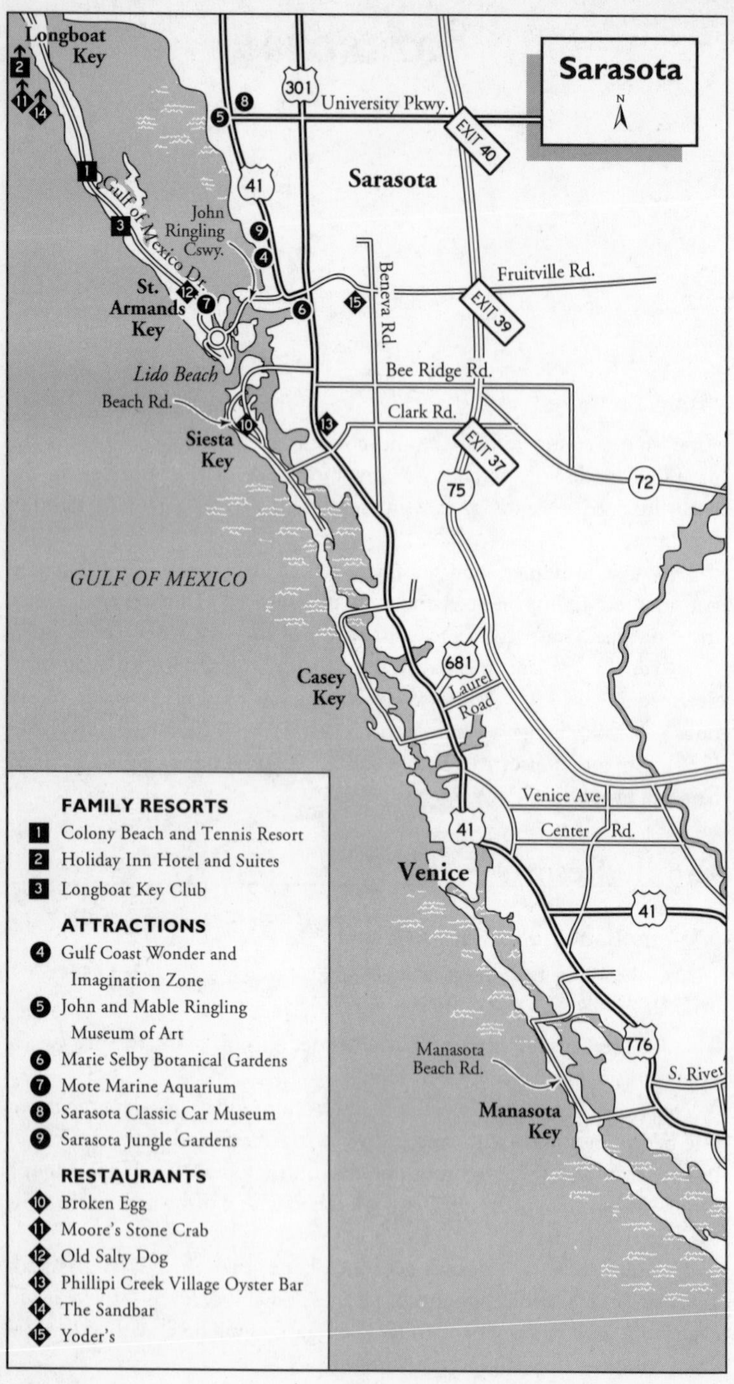

Sarasota
N
Longboat Key
University Pkwy.
EXIT 40
301
41
Sarasota
Gulf of Mexico Dr.
John Ringling Cswy.
Beneva Rd.
Fruitville Rd.
EXIT 39
St. Armands Key
Lido Beach
Bee Ridge Rd.
Beach Rd.
Clark Rd.
Siesta Key
EXIT 37
75
72
GULF OF MEXICO
681
Casey Key
Laurel Road
Venice Ave.
41
Center Rd.
Venice
41
Manasota Beach Rd.
776
S. River
Manasota Key
FAMILY RESORTS
1 Colony Beach and Tennis Resort
2 Holiday Inn Hotel and Suites
3 Longboat Key Club
ATTRACTIONS
4 Gulf Coast Wonder and Imagination Zone
5 John and Mable Ringling Museum of Art
6 Marie Selby Botanical Gardens
7 Mote Marine Aquarium
8 Sarasota Classic Car Museum
9 Sarasota Jungle Gardens
RESTAURANTS
10 Broken Egg
11 Moore's Stone Crab
12 Old Salty Dog
13 Phillipi Creek Village Oyster Bar
14 The Sandbar
15 Yoder's

There are also a swimming pool (with a poolside bar), a fitness center with aerobics classes, and beach activities.

Free and supervised children's programs are offered for two age groups: Kinder Kamp for ages 3–6 and Kids Klub for ages 7–12. Activities include bowling, skating, fishing, movies, minigolf, and field trips to the Mote Marine Laboratory or Ringling Circus Museum. The only cost is admission to attractions on field trips. The programs run from Memorial Day weekend through Labor Day weekend, Monday–Saturday, 9 a.m.–noon and 1–4 p.m. Evening programs are also offered. For children under age 3 or for nonprogram hours, nannies are available.

The resort's award-winning Colony Dining Room is worth a mention, with a chef who serves healthful creations that use almost no cream, butter, salt, or fat. Tastebuds, the resort's market, can stock your room's fridge before your family arrives.

Rates range from $195 (May–September) to $395 (February–April, and near the Christmas holiday).

Holiday Inn Hotel and Suites

4949 Gulf of Mexico Drive, Longboat Key • (941) 383-3771 • fax (941) 383-7871 www.hilongboat.com

A recent renovation spruced up this popular oceanfront resort with its own private beach, outdoor pool, heated indoor pool, kiddie pool, lighted tennis courts, a putting green, and fitness center. There's a Pizza Hut right on the property as well as other restaurants. There is a bar located in a one of the restaurants as well as one poolside. There are 146 rooms in the three-story hotel, including suites and Kidsuites, specially decorated for children. All rooms have coffeemakers and mini-refrigerators. Suites have microwaves. Rates start at $189 in the summer, $239 in the winter, and kids up to age 17 stay free with parents.

Longboat Key Club

301 Gulf of Mexico Drive, Longboat Key 34228 • (941) 383-8821 or (800) 237-8821 • fax (941) 383-5396 • www.longboatkeyclub.com

This crème de la crème resort covers the southern tip of Longboat Key. Mobil and AAA have lavished Longboat Key Club with their coveted stars and diamonds, and golf aficionados rate it among the best in the United States.

Guests are pampered in the 232 rooms, ranging from standard quarters to deluxe two-bedroom suites. Every room has a refrigerator and coffeemaker, and the suites include washers and dryers. Some rooms include a wet bar.

There are two golf courses on the 410-acre resort and 38 tennis courts, with clinics and private lessons available. The swimming pool overlooks the Gulf of Mexico, with 9 miles of private beach with water sport rentals—aqua cycles, boogie boards, kayaks, Hobie Cats, and aqua cats—on site.

The resort has a 9.5-mile path for biking, jogging, and rollerblading that runs the length of Longboat Key. (You can rent rollerblades on nearby St. Armands Circle, and the resort rents bicycles.) The fitness center has personal trainers at your service.

For children ages 5–12, the Kids Club is open from Memorial Day weekend through Labor Day weekend, Monday–Saturday, 9:30 a.m.–3 p.m. The cost of $25 a day includes lunch. Field trips are part of the fun, to the Mote Marine Aquarium and Ringling Circus Museum. Bowling, skating, minigolf, and beach games are free.

Kids as young as 4 can take part in tennis clinics. Private golf lessons for children 7 and older can also be arranged. Rates start at $195 in the summer, $225 in the winter.

Attractions

Gulf Coast Wonder & Imagination Zone (GWIZ)

1001 Boulevard of the Arts, Sarsota • (941) 906-1851 • www.gwiz.org

Hours - Tuesday–Saturday, 10 a.m.–5 p.m., Sunday 1–5 p.m.

Admission - $7 for adults, $6 for seniors, and $5 for children. Free the first Wednesday of each month, 5–8 p.m

Appeal by Age Group -

Pre-school ★★★	Teens ★★	Over 30 ★★
Grade school ★★★★	Young Adults ★★	Seniors ★★★

Touring Time - Average 2½ hours; minimum 2 hours

Rainy-Day Touring - Recommended

Author's Rating - ★★★; great place to get out of the sun

Restaurants - Yes **Alcoholic beverages -** No

Handicapped access - Yes **Wheelchair rental -** No

Baby stroller rental - No **Lockers -** No

Pet kennels - No **Rain check -** No

Private tours - No

Description and Comments Learn about sound, electricity—even create your own exhibit! This museum guarantees hands-on fun, and invites you to dig for fossils, climb inside a giant bubble, pet animals, and more. If young ones are looking to blow off steam, there's a beautiful playground area (completely made of recycled materials), and picnickers are welcome.

John and Mable Ringling Museum of Art

5401 Bayshore Drive, Sarasota • (941) 359-5700 • www.ringling.org

Hours - Daily, 10 a.m.–5:30 p.m., except holidays

Admission - $15 for adults, $12 for senior citizens 55 and older, free for children under age 12. The art museum is free on Saturdays except the weekend of the Medieval Fair

Appeal by Age Group -

Pre-school ★	Teens ★★★	Over 30 ★★★
Grade school ★★★	Young Adults ★★★	Seniors ★★★★

Touring Time - Average 3 hours; minimum 1½ hours

Rainy-Day Touring - Recommended

Author's Rating - ★★; great for rainy days; kids especially enjoy the circus museum

Restaurants - Yes

Alcoholic beverages - Yes

Handicapped access - Yes

Wheelchair rental - Yes

Baby stroller rental - No

Lockers - Yes

Pet kennels - No

Rain check - No

Private tours - For 10 or more

Description and Comments The Ringling Museums of Sarasota consist of John and Mable Ringling Museum of Art, the John Ringling Mansion, known as Ca' d'Zan, the Museum of the Circus, the Asolo Theater, and 86 acres of gardens and grounds. The museums are owned and operated by the state of Florida.

The building that houses the celebrated Ringling Museum of Art is as grand as the priceless art that graces its walls. An enormous, detailed duplication of a classic Italian villa of the fifteenth century, the museum's external facade is plain and inauspicious. Stepping through the entrance into the internal courtyard with its reflection pool, graceful statuary, and manicured formal gardens, you're launched on an instantaneous odyssey in time and beauty. The gardens are surrounded on three sides by long rows of the delicately rounded arches of the museum's colonnades and on the fourth side by a Roman bridge from which a gigantic bronze cast of Michelangelo's David surveys a profusion of columns, doorways, bronze and stone sculptures, fountains, pools, and Italian oil pots. Staggering in its proportions, the garden court is likewise overwhelming in its splendor, the loveliness of the whole seeming to be so much more than simply the sum of its individual treasures.

The Museum of Art consists of 20 galleries in the original building plus a contemporary art gallery that is an extension of the museum's south wing.

The Ringling art collection is extensive, with more than 250 paintings and other objects of art on display, one of the world's largest collections of Baroque, Italian, and Flemish Renaissance and Old Master paintings.

Several hundred yards west of the museum, on Sarasota Bay, is Ca' d'Zan, the Ringling residence. Patterned after the Doge's Palace in Venice, the 32-room mansion was built at a cost of $1.5 million in the 1920s. You can tour the residence on your own or take a narrated tour (the narrated version might be a little slow for young children and teenagers).

The Museum of the Circus is a short walk north of the art museum and houses a fantastic collection of circus memorabilia. The major part of the museum is devoted to the American circus with emphasis on the development of *The Greatest Show on Earth.* The crown jewel of the museum is the circus "backyard," a full-scale re-creation of the circus back lot in the heyday of *The Greatest Show on Earth.*

The Asolo Theater is a 200-seat, horseshoe-shaped playhouse for opera, classical, and modern plays, and a year-round program of films, lectures, concerts, and recitals.

Marie Selby Botanical Gardens

811 S. Palm Avenue, Sarasota • (941) 366-5731 or 366-5730 • www.selby.org

Hours - Daily, 10 a.m.–5 p.m.

Admission - $10 for adults, $5 for children ages 6–11

Appeal by Age Group -

Pre-school ★	Teens ★	Over 30 ★★★
Grade school ★★	Young Adults ★★	Seniors ★★★★

Touring Time - Average 3 hours; minimum 1½ hour

Rainy-Day Touring - Not recommended

Author's Rating - ★★★★; beautiful orchids

Restaurants - Yes

Alcoholic beverages - No

Handicapped access - Yes

Wheelchair rental - Yes

Baby stroller rental - No

Lockers - No

Pet kennels - No

Rain check - Yes

Private tours - Yes

Description and Comments Reconnect with nature at the Marie Selby Botanical Gardens. What began as a pastime for amateur horticulturist Marie Selby has grown into an internationally known center for botanical research and conservation.

The focus is on tropical plants, with an emphasis on epiphytic plants, commonly known as "air plants," like orchids, pineapples, and ferns. The garden's 6,000 orchids are stunning.

You'll find yourself immersed in more than 20,000 colorful plants on nine acres, many collected in the wild on scientific expeditions.

The Tropical Display House has the most concentrated collection of epiphytic plants in the United States in a rainforest setting. Torch ginger from Indonesia, colorful bromeliads from the Amazon, the vanilla orchid from Mexico, and others thrive in this fragrant greenhouse. There are collections of ferns, hibiscus, Banyan trees, cacti, wildflowers, cycads, bromeliads, and bamboo.

Children are attracted to the Koi Pond, filled with white, orange, and golden Japanese carp swimming among the water lilies.

The Tropical Food Gardens feature pineapples, papayas, plantains, bananas, and sugar cane, and the Butterfly Garden is especially fun.

Selby offers several half-day summer classes where children can participate in painting, nature printing, and canopy climbing. There are also Children's Days offered three times a year, free of charge: Spring Celebration Day with an egg hunt and a parade, Summer Children's Day, and a Christmas Holly Day. Greenhouse tours available daily; no reservations are required. Garden tour is self-guided although arrangements can be made for a personal tour.

Mote Marine Aquarium

600 Ken Thompson Parkway, Sarasota (between Lido and Longboat Keys)
(800) 691-MOTE or (941) 388-2451 • www.mote.org

Hours - Daily, 10 a.m.–5 p.m.

Admission - $12 for adults, $8 for children ages 4–12

Appeal by Age Group -

Pre-school ★★★	Teens ★★★	Over 30 ★★★
Grade school ★★★	Young Adults ★★★	Seniors ★★★

Touring Time - Average 2 hours; minimum 1½ hours

Rainy-Day Touring - Recommended

Author's Rating - ★★★; just the right size to be fun

Restaurants - Yes

Alcoholic beverages - No

Handicapped access - Yes

Wheelchair rental - Yes

Baby stroller rental - No

Lockers - No

Pet kennels - No

Rain check - No

Private tours - Arranged in advance

Description and Comments Sharks are the kid magnet here, along with sea turtles, seahorses, fishes, and all sorts of cool sea life for kids to learn about. They can reach in and touch the horseshoe crabs, stingrays, and sea urchins.

As you wander through the aquarium, photos and text explain the serious research happening here every day, and now guests can peek into the aquarium's research labs to find more scientists hard at work. The latest exhibits, including Fish in Disguise and How the Puffer Got Its Puff, illustrate how fish find food and protection.

A short walk from the aquarium is the Marine Mammal Visitor Center, home to the manatees born in captivity at the Miami Seaquarium, now permanent residents at Mote. Sick and injured marine mammals recover here, and you can view their 52,000-gallon home through windows and on TV monitors. Injured sea turtles are rehabilitated nearby.

If your children really want a night to remember, plan your trip so they participate in the Mote overnight programs. They'll learn about shark tagging, shark teeth, and more. When bedtime arrives, they snuggle up next to the shark tank. There's also Moonlight with the Manatees, an overnight with resident manatees Hugh and Buffett, and Twilight with the Turtles. Contact the education division at (941) 388-4441 ext. 229 for information on these programs. The cost is $40 for children ages 7–12.

Sarasota Classic Car Museum

5500 N. Tamiami Trail, Sarasota • (941) 355-6228

Hours - Daily, 9 a.m.–6 p.m.

Admission - $8.50 for adults, $7.65 for seniors 65 and older, $4 for ages 6–12, free for ages 6 and under

Appeal by Age Group -

Pre-school ★★	Teens ★★	Over 30 ★★★
Grade school ★★	Young Adults ★★★	Seniors ★★★★

Touring Time - Average 1½ hours; minimum 1 hour

Rainy-Day Touring - Recommended

Author's Rating - ★★; car buffs will enjoy the museum; kids love the music room and arcade

Restaurants - Ice cream shop

Alcoholic beverages - No

Handicapped access - Yes

Wheelchair rental - Yes

Baby stroller rental - Yes

Lockers - No

Pet kennels - No

Rain check - No

Private tours - Yes, also music tours

Description and Comments In the late 1990s, this museum was totally overhauled and dozens of cars were added to the collection of classic and antique cars. The collection includes several celebrated vintage models of

Rolls-Royce and Pierce Arrows, rare antiques such as the 1930 Ruxton and the 1948 Tucker, and, wonderfully, the cars of almost everyone's youth, from Model A's to '57 Fords to '63 VWs.

A second room of football-field dimensions displays one of the world's largest collection of mechanical musical devices, everything from hurdy-gurdies to player pianos to calliopes. Access is by guided tour only, and the guide demonstrates many of the fascinating devices. The size of the collection is mind boggling, but not more so than the inventiveness of the antique machines.

Supplementing the two main museums is an extensive collection of antique penny arcade pieces that you can play.

Sarasota Jungle Gardens

3701 Bayshore Road, Sarasota • (941) 355-5305 or 355-1112
www.sarasotajunglegardens.com

Hours - Daily, 9 a.m.–5 p.m.

Admission - $10 for adults, $9 for seniors 62 and older, $6 for children ages 3–12

Appeal by Age Group -

Pre-school ★★★	Teens ★★	Over 30 ★★
Grade school ★★★	Young Adults ★★	Seniors ★★

Touring Time - Average 2 hours; minimum 1 hour

Rainy-Day Touring - Not recommended

Author's Rating - ★★; old-fashioned fun

Restaurants - Snack bar, picnic area

Alcoholic beverages - No

Handicapped access - Yes

Wheelchair rental - Yes

Baby stroller rental - Yes

Lockers - No

Pet kennels - No

Rain check - Yes

Private tours - Arranged in advance

Description and Comments Practically tucked away in a Sarasota residential area, Sarasota Jungle Gardens is an artful blend of beauty, education, and showmanship. Central to the attraction is the Jungle Garden, a series of beautiful winding trails spread over 10 acres of sparkling lakes, luxurious vegetation, and sunny greens. Exotic birds and animals, many of them uncaged, inhabit the garden and add to its grace. The garden itself is an interesting combination of manicured, planned landscapes and naturally occurring tropical hammock, all integrated so skillfully that you can pass from one to the other and never sense the transition. Macaws, cockatoos, flamingos, and peacocks lend living color to the garden while leopards, monkeys, and otters add a touch of excitement. Shady resting spots are plentiful along the trails.

Two shows are offered several times each day in a roofed amphitheater. A colorful platoon of feathery performers work through a fascinating, well-paced, and imaginative routine in the bird show. And snakes and alligators are the stars in the reptile show, a straightforward and understandable presentation. Each show lasts about 25 minutes.

Smaller exhibits consist of a nice petting zoo and playground, and a sculptural oddity called the Gardens of Christ. This latter, tucked away next to the reptile show, consists of eight hand-carved religious dioramas depicting the life of Christ.

ALBRITTON FRUIT COMPANY TROLLEY TOUR

Get to know Florida's history by touring 1,000 acres of citrus groves, plus fruit-packing and juicing facilities. You'll even see how the juice is squeezed and bottled. After the tour, stop by the original grove store, which opened in 1948. Tours are available at 10 a.m. and 3 p.m. on Thursdays only; call for reservations. 5947 Clark Center Avenue, (941) 925-0013.

Family-Friendly Restaurants

Broken Egg

210 Avenida Madera, Sarasota • (941) 346-2750

Meals served - Breakfast and lunch

Cuisine - Creative American

Entree Range - $3–12

Kids menu - Yes

Reservations - No

Payment - Major credit cards

Stop by the Broken Egg, where you can dine inside or out, on the way to the beach. Fill up on their giant pancakes (at 8 ounces, one covers the plate) and you won't need lunch.

Moore's Stone Crab

800 Broadway, Long Boat Key • (941) 383-1748

Meals served - Lunch and dinner

Cuisine - Seafood, American

Entree range - $6–42

Kids menu - Yes

Reservations - Not accepted

Payment - Visa, MC, AmEx, D

Their boats work the traps each day from October 15 to May 15 to bring in the freshest crabs around. A day's catch runs from 500 to 600 pounds of claws. During a season, close to 50,000 pounds of stone crab claws are served. They're the best!

Old Salty Dog

1601 Ken Thompson Parkway, Sarasota • (941) 388-4311

Meals served - Lunch and dinner

Cuisine - American, seafood

Entree range - $4–10

Kids menu - Yes

Reservations - Not accepted

Payment - Visa, MC

Service is fast, it's casual, and you can sit outside on the waterfront. Everyone goes for the fried grouper sandwich, and the burgers are great, too.

Phillipi Creek Village Oyster Bar

5353 S. Tamiami Trail, Sarasota • (941) 925-4444

Meals served - Lunch and dinner

Cuisine - Local and northern seafood

Entree range - $4.95–29.95

Kids menu - Yes

Reservations - Not accepted

Payment - Visa, MC, AmEx

They're known for their blackened charbroiled grouper.

The Sandbar

100 Spring Avenue, Ana Maria • (941) 778-0444

Meals served - Lunch and dinner

Cuisine - American, seafood

Entree range - $7–22

Kids menu - Yes

Reservations - Preferred seating available

Payment - All major credit cards accepted

The menu is diverse, from pasta and salads to beef, chicken, and seafood. Try the fresh fish, conch fritters, and conch chowder.

Yoder's

3434 Bahia Vista, Sarasota • (941) 366-8817

Meals served - Breakfast, lunch, and dinner

Cuisine - Amish

Entree range - $5.95–14

Kids menu - Yes

Reservations - Not accepted

Payment - No credit cards

Stop here for breakfast, lunch, or dinner—you can't go wrong with Yoder's Amish home cooking. It's the type of place that serves the daily specials locals look forward to—especially Thursday's scalloped potatoes with ham and Friday's cabbage rolls. Don't leave without trying the pie, made fresh every morning. Choose from chocolate peanut butter, coconut cream, chocolate, raspberry cream, fresh strawberry, Key lime, pumpkin, blueberry, and more. On Thanksgiving Day they sell close to 2,000 pies. There's also wonderful banana bread.

SHOPPING AT ST. ARMAND'S CIRCLE

This world-renowned center of more than 150 fine shops, galleries, and gourmet restaurants combines lush landscaping, courtyards, patios, and contemporary architecture to create a great shopping adventure—more than just your average trip to the mall. St. Armand's Key; (941) 388-1554.

Part Six

Southwest Florida

Southwest Florida has been referred to as an "ecological Disneyland," and it's the only zone in which we recommend bringing a pair of binoculars. This part of the Sunshine State, known as the "gateway to the Everglades," is paradise for families seeking fresh air, sunshine, and the great outdoors.

The southwest coast offers miles and miles of beaches famous for rare shells, and the calm, shallow waters of the Gulf of Mexico. Families particularly enjoy the gently sloping sands of Ft. Myers Beach on Estero Island, often called the "world's safest beach," with sugary white sand for sculpting sand castles and numerous public parks with plenty of amenities.

Off the coast, Sanibel and Captiva islands are popular for excellent shelling and beaches. On the lush island of Sanibel, where all the buildings must be lower than the tallest palm, the sites are best seen by cycling along Periwinkle Way's canopy of whispering pines and expansive banyans.

Heading south, families enjoy the pristine shores of Naples and Ten Thousand Islands, where myriad boat and ferry services from Marco Island, largest of the Ten Thousand Islands, will take you on a journey through the ancient mangroves and marshes. The wildest Florida frontier, the Everglades, reaches up into Southwest Florida.

If waterfront is a prerequisite for your family's vacation, Southwest Florida is the place.

Getting There

By Plane Three airports serve Southwest Florida, Charlotte County Airport, 3 miles southeast of Punta Gorda, (888) 7000-2232; Naples Municipal Airport, 2 miles northeast of Naples, (941) 643-0733; and Southwest Florida International Airport, 10 miles southeast of Ft. Myers, (239) 768-1000.

By Train Amtrak makes stops in Port Charlotte, Ft. Myers, and Naples; (800) USA-RAIL, www.amtrak.com.

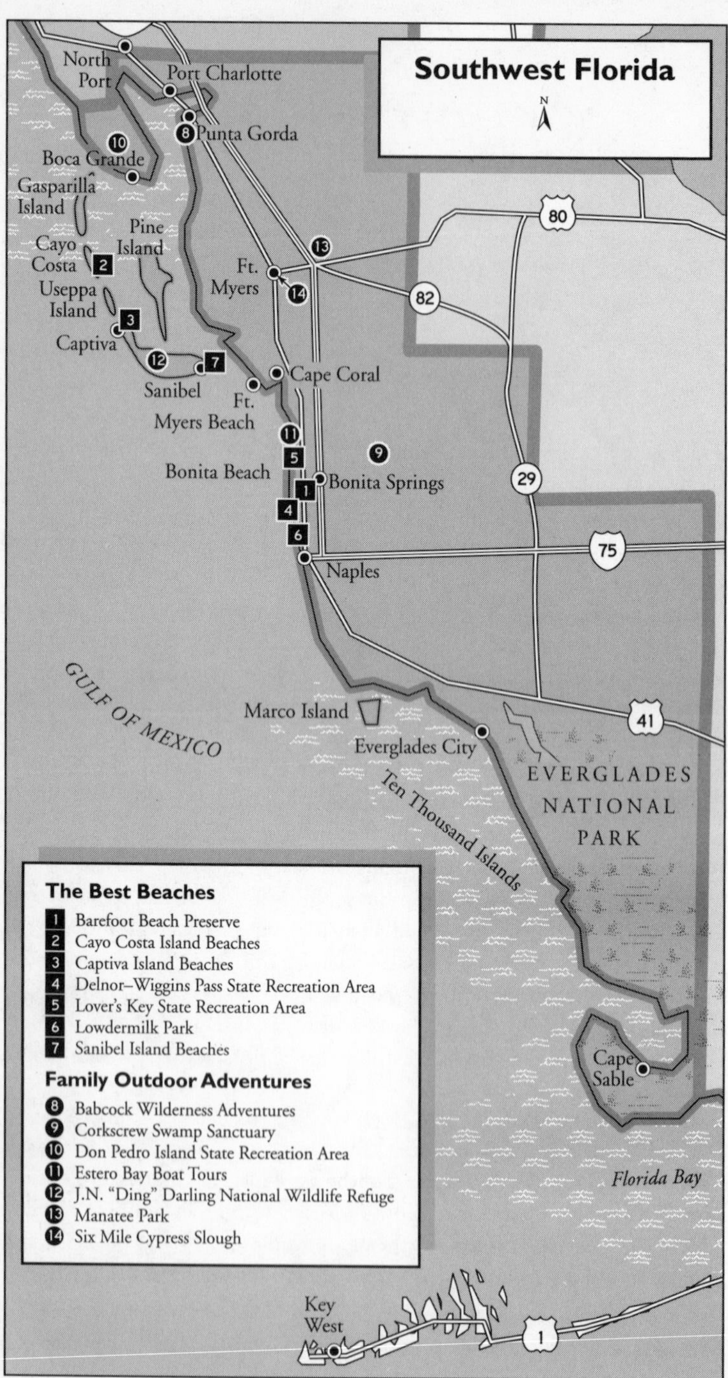
Southwest Florida
N
North Port
Port Charlotte
Punta Gorda
Boca Grande
Gasparilla Island
Pine Island
Cayo Costa
Useppa Island
Captiva
Sanibel
Ft. Myers
Ft. Myers Beach
Cape Coral
Bonita Beach
Bonita Springs
Naples
Marco Island
Everglades City
Ten Thousand Islands
GULF OF MEXICO
EVERGLADES NATIONAL PARK
Cape Sable
Florida Bay
Key West
80
82
29
75
41
1
The Best Beaches
1 Barefoot Beach Preserve
2 Cayo Costa Island Beaches
3 Captiva Island Beaches
4 Delnor–Wiggins Pass State Recreation Area
5 Lover's Key State Recreation Area
6 Lowdermilk Park
7 Sanibel Island Beaches
Family Outdoor Adventures
8 Babcock Wilderness Adventures
9 Corkscrew Swamp Sanctuary
10 Don Pedro Island State Recreation Area
11 Estero Bay Boat Tours
12 J.N. "Ding" Darling National Wildlife Refuge
13 Manatee Park
14 Six Mile Cypress Slough

By Car Both I-75 and US 41 run north-south, US 80 and US 41 go to the beaches.

How to Get Information before You Go

Lee Island Coast Visitor and Convention Bureau–Tourist Development Council, 2180 W. First Street, Suite 100, Ft. Myers 33901; (800) 237-6444; www.leeislandcoast.com.

Marco Island and the Everglades Convention and Visitors Bureau, 1102 N. Collier Boulevard, Marco Island 33937; (800) 788-marco; www.marco-island-florida.com.

Naples Area Tourism Bureau, P.O. Box 10129, Naples 33941; (800) 605-7878 or (941) 263-3666; www.visit-naples.com.

The Best Beaches

Barefoot Beach Preserve, North Naples There's not much here but the sand, the sea, and wide-open spaces—no lifeguards, but rest rooms, concessions, and nature trails. Barefoot Beach is open 8 a.m.–sundown. Location is at the intersection of Hickory Boulevard and Bonita Beach Road, north of Naples.

Cayo Costa Island Beaches You can choose just about any beach on these three islands for some of the world's best seashell collecting. Read more in the Island Hopping section on page 321.

Captiva These beaches have some of the best shelling in the world, and they're also excellent for swimming. For a list of specific beaches, see page 324.

♥ **Delnor-Wiggins Pass State Recreation Area** This 166-acre preserve is on a narrow barrier island, separated from mainland Naples by mangrove swamps and tidal creeks. It's the perfect setting for all-day family fun, with lifeguards, a boat launch, barbecue grills and picnic tables in the shade, and showers. Native gopher tortoises, manatees, dolphins, osprey, and a wide variety of wading birds are commonly seen; a lookout station provides a view of the beach, and woods. From June to August, there's a Sea Turtle Beach Walk Program at 9 a.m. every Friday and other ranger programs throughout the year, from native plant walks to talks on marine mammals and beach habitats. To make reservations for any programs, call (941) 597-6196. Hours are 8 a.m.–sundown; admission is $4 per car for 2–8 people. Located 6 miles south of Bonita Springs, off CR 901, off US 41.

Lover's Key State Recreation Area Accessible by tram or footpath, Lover's Key is just south of Ft. Myers Beach. The recreation area recently expanded, merging with the Carl. E. Johnson Park next door to create a relaxing and fun beachfront park. There are nearly 3 miles of pristine beach (no lifeguards), reachable by tram or footpath from a paved parking lot. With the expansion, there are rest rooms, canoe and kayak rentals, and a beach concession. Several short nature walks are marked near the beach on this 712-acre expanse. And the shelling is great if you get there early enough. The park is open daily 8 a.m.–sunset; admission is $2–4 per vehicle. On CR 865 between Ft. Myers Beach and Bonita Beach; (941) 463-4588.

Lowdermilk Park in Naples is a favorite of the locals, with 1,000 feet of beach, lifeguards, a playground, shady picnic spots, sand volleyball, showers, and rest rooms. Special attractions are the duck ponds and complimentary sand chairs for wheelchair-bound beachgoers. Location is at Gulf Shore and Banyan Boulevards neighboring Old Naples. Parking is metered. The park is open daily from dawn to dusk.

Sanibel These beaches also have some of the best shelling in the world and are excellent for swimming. For a list of specific beaches, see page 324.

How to Get Out on the Water

The southwest beaches are among the best in Florida, but to really take full advantage of all the area has to offer, we recommend some time on the water. Even toddlers enjoy a boat ride, though airboats may be too noisy for younger children. Be sure children under age 6 are wearing life jackets and safely seated. There are several ways to get on the water, depending on your family's tolerance level for the confines of a boat:

- A tour boat to the off-coast islands can be a short jaunt of 1–2 hours.
- Airboat tours, though noisy, explore the natural beauty and ecosystems of the Ten Thousand Islands and the inland back-country waters around the Everglades.
- Hobie Cats, Sunfishes, aquabikes, windsurfers, or sailboats are especially fun for teenagers.
- You can charter a boat with a personal guide.
- You can canoe or kayak along rivers.

Best Shelling

Southwest Florida is known for shelling, with nearly 300 varieties washing up on the beaches. Where are the best spots to find a perfect specimen? We talked with Captain Mike Fuery, author of *New Florida Shelling Guide,* who says the easiest shelling is on Cayo Costa or North Captiva, both only accessible by boat.

If you haven't got a boat, he recommends Blind Pass between Sanibel and Captiva, or Bowman's Beach smack in the middle of Sanibel. Gasparilla Island is another good spot. If you're looking for shark's teeth, Manasota Key is the place, he says.

Nearly all the beaches on Sanibel and Captiva offer decent shelling but nowhere to park. And if you're on a good shelling beach with parking, like Lighthouse Beach, it's probably going to get crowded. Fuery recommends traveling the two islands by bicycle and stopping whenever the urge strikes. The best time of day is early morning, around 7 a.m., finishing by 10 when the sun starts to scorch. Shelling is best after a storm.

Though shelling is great year-round, he loves the summertime when he can introduce kids to the joys of snorkeling for shells in 2–3 feet of water. "It opens a whole new world," says Fuery.

Family Outdoor Adventures

Babcock Wilderness Adventures Get a real Florida experience on this 90-minute swamp buggy tour of the Crescent B Ranch. Or if you're an off-road cyclist, Babcock recently added guided off-road biking tours for both novice and experienced bikers. Experienced guides point out alligators, panthers, American bison, native birds, wild turkeys, snakes, and other animals. Cost is $17.95 for adults, $10 for ages 3–12. Reservations required. November–May, 9 a.m.–3 p.m.; mornings tours only June–October. No handicap access. 8000 SR 31, Punta Gorda; (800) 500-5583; www.babcockwildnerness.com.

Corkscrew Swamp Sanctuary This is mecca for bird-watchers, an 11,000-acre natural preserve maintained by the National Audubon Society. A 2-mile boardwalk trail takes you past the world's largest remaining stand of virgin bald cypress. Some of the trees are more than 700 years old, soaring 13 stories. You might also see native wildlife, including alligators, bobcats, and otters, and you'll always be entertained by a symphony of birds and frogs. Corkscrew is the nesting site for the largest colony of wood storks in the United States. There are picnic tables and a small welcome center; hours are 7 a.m.–5 p.m. from December through April; 8 a.m.–5 p.m. from May through November. Admission is $8 for adults, $5.50 for students with ID, $3.50 for minors. 375 Sanctuary Road, about 20 miles north of Naples and 14 miles west of Immokalee; (941) 348-9151.

Don Pedro Island State Recreation Area, Cape Haze You can only get here by private (or chartered) boat, but the shelling and swimming are worth the adventure. There's nothing man-made here except picnic tables, so come prepared. For more information call the ranger's office on Boca Grande at (941) 964-0375.

Estero Bay Boat Tours If your family is vacationing at Ft. Myers beach, this is a nice way to get back to nature, with an expert guide to help you spot dolphin, manatee, birds, and other Florida wildlife in the state's first aquatic preserve. Tours depart three times a day, at 10:30 a.m., 1:30 p.m.,

A CALENDAR OF FESTIVALS AND EVENTS

February

Seafood Festival Everglades City. Seafood, arts and crafts. (941) 695-3941.

Edison Festival of Light Ft. Myers. One of the area's biggest and most celebrated annual events commemorates the birthday of the area's most famous winter resident, inventor Thomas Edison. The Edison Festival of Light features weeks of events, including a spectacular nighttime parade through downtown Ft. Myers, gala ball, fashion show, 5-K race, and crafts show. (941) 334-2229; www.edisonfestival.org.

Swamp Buggy Races Naples. Held at the Mile o' Mud arena at Florida Sports Park, this is one of Naples's most popular and unusual events. Races take place three times a year (January, March, and October). (941) 774-2701; www.swampbuggy.com.

March

Annual Sanibel Shell Fair Sanibel Island. In celebration of one of the finest shelling areas in the United States, this annual show features shell displays and crafts with prizes awarded. (941) 472-1080.

Ft. Myers Beach Lions Club Shrimp Festival Ft. Myers. This festival celebrates Ft. Myers Beach as home of one of the nation's largest shrimp fleets with runs, a dance, a parade, a shrimp boil, and an arts and crafts show. (941) 466-4228.

Swamp Buggy Races Naples. Held at the Mile o' Mud arena at Florida Sports Park, this is one of Naples's most popular and unusual events. Races take place three times a year (January, March, and October). (941) 774-2701; www.swampbuggy.com.

July

Ft. Myers Beach Fourth of July A family Fourth of July celebration at the pier on Ft. Myers Beach offers various special events, including entertainment, a children's fishing tournament, and spectacular fireworks. (941) 463-2588.

An All-American Fourth of July Celebration Naples. Games and activities at Cambier Park and a fireworks display off Naples Pier are followed by two days of arts and crafts, shows, and music. (941) 434-3883.

September

Clamming with the Natives Marco Island. Trek to the northwest tip of the island and don your swimsuit to discover the famous south quahog clam. Wade out at low tide to waist deep and feel around with your toes. Find the pointed end of the shell, reach out and grab it. You'll only need one of these giant clams to fill a large bowl of chowder. (800) 788-MARCO.

October

Bear Fair Naples Teddy Bear Museum. Doll and teddy bear artisans, pony rides, live entertainment, and a flea market. Fee for games and rides only. (941) 598-2711.

Swamp Buggy Races Naples. Held at the Mile o' Mud arena at Florida Sports Park, this is one of Naples's most popular and unusual events. Races take place three times a year (January, March, and October). (941) 774-2701; www.swampbuggy.com.

November

Ft. Myers Beach Sand Sculpting Festival. Expert sand sculptors from around the world gather to create incredible works of art on the beach. (941) 454-7500.

Festival of Lights Naples. More than 30 professional and local entertainment groups, and a spectacular view of a quarter of a million white Italian lights decorating trees and shops in the area. (941) 649-6707.

Old Florida Festival Collier County Museum, Naples. One day of music, Seminole War reenactments, history camps, and traditional arts and craft. (941) 774-8476.

December

Edison-Ford Winter Estates Holiday House Ft. Myers. The sounds of Christmas fill the air at the neighboring Thomas Edison and Henry Ford winter homes as the houses and surrounding grounds are dressed up for a week of festivities. (941) 461-2687.

Christmas Luminary Trail Open House Sanibel-Captiva Islands. A 3-mile walking tour on Periwinkle Way through displays of beautifully decorated businesses. The shops along the way offer refreshments. (941) 472-1080.

Christmas Boat Parade Ft. Myers. This nighttime parade featuring beautifully decorated boats of all kinds begins at the docks of the Pink Shell Beach Resort on Ft. Myers Beach. (239) 454-7500.

and in the evening (2 hours before sunset), last for 2 hours, and are recommended for all ages; cost is $15 for adults, $10 for children ages 12 and under. The launching point is 5 miles north of Bonita Beach Road, off US 41 at the end of Coconut Road, Bonita Springs; (941) 992-2200.

♥ **J. N. "Ding" Darling National Wildlife Refuge** This 5,000-acre wildlife refuge on the southern end of Sanibel Island is part swamp, part prairie, crisscrossed with elevated boardwalks, hiking trails, and streams. More than 290 bird species and 50 types of reptiles live in the spongy shallows—roseate spoonbills, raccoons, and otter are often spotted. You can stay in your car and take the 5-mile scenic drive, but the best way to see it is on foot, by bicycle, or in a canoe.

Even inexperienced boaters can maneuver a canoe through the shallows and mangroves, where you may even see an occasional manatee.

First-timers might want to take the 2-hour tram tour narrated by a naturalist. You can catch the tram at the Tarpon Bay Recreation Center at the north end of Tarpon Bay Road. Cost is $10 for adults, $5 for ages 12 and under; call (941) 472-8900 for tour times.

The best time to visit, when you'll see the most wildlife, is just after sunrise or late afternoon. Gates open half an hour after sunrise and close about half an hour before sunset. Admission is $5 per vehicle. The visitors center is open daily, 9 a.m.–4 p.m.; (941) 472-1100. Darling, by the way, was a Pulitzer Prize–winning cartoonist and a conservationist.

For more back-to-nature fun, visit the Sanibel-Captiva Conservation Center with nature trails and interpretive tours; (941) 472-2329. Also, Care and Rehabilitation of Wildlife (CROW), where kids can see rescued animals offers a tour at 11 a.m., Monday–Friday; (941) 472-3644. Both centers are nearby.

Manatee Park You can observe the endangered West Indian manatee in its natural habitat from three observation decks in the park from November through March. Naturalists are there to answer questions, and you can rent kayaks for $8 an hour from 8 a.m. to 8 p.m. to cruise the Orange River. To find out if the manatees are there, call (941) 694-3537 for updates. Parking is 75 cents an hour, $3 maximum. SR 80, 1.5 miles east of I-75, Ft. Myers.

Six Mile Cypress Slough ("Slew") Take a stroll with your family on this mile-long boardwalk through a 2,200-acre wetlands ecosystem to see subtropical ferns, wild ferns, wild orchids, and birds such as herons, storks, spoonbills, and egrets. Admission is free, and the park is open 8 a.m.–8 p.m. daily, with guided tours at 9:30 a.m on alternating days. Parking is 75 cents an hour or $3 a day. Located at Parkways and Penzance Boulevard, Ft. Myers; (941) 432-2004.

Island Hopping

This part of Florida has dozens of little islands just off the coast, everything from uninhabited beaches to seaside resorts.

Cabbage Key

Built on top of an ancient Calusa Indian shell mound, rustic Cabbage Key Restaurant, Bar, and Inn is about all you find on this 100-acre island, accessible only by boat. The rustic watering hole was built in 1938 by the children of mystery novelist Mary Roberts Rinehart.

Julia Roberts has dined here, as well as Sean Connery, and it's rumored that Jimmy Buffett wrote "Cheeseburger in Paradise" after a burger at the Cabbage Key Inn. You can eat on the screened porch or have a drink in Mrs. Rinehart's library, plastered with $1 bills left by former guests—it's estimated that there's more than $40,000 on the walls. There are six rooms at the inn, but the rooms are just down the hall from the bar and restaurant, and the noise level makes it nearly impossible to sleep—we definitely don't recommend this for families. But do book a lunch trip with Captiva Cruises at South Seas Plantation; cost is $27.50 for adults, $15 for children ages 4–12 (lunch is additional). The cruises leave at 10:30 a.m. and return at 3:30 p.m; (941) 472-5300.

Cayo Costa

South of Gasparilla Island and Boca Grande Pass, Cayo Costa is 2,225 acres—one of the largest undeveloped barrier islands in Florida, with Cayo Costa State Park occupying most of the island.

You can only get there by private boat or ferry, but the journey is worth it: miles of beaches, acres of pine forest, oak palm hammocks, mangrove swamps, and a spectacular display of bird life. Shelling is especially good during the winter months. There are 12 cabins for rent and tent camping, but no drinking water or electricity. In the fall, park rangers lead guided beach walks; in the summer, rangers offer morning programs about sea turtles; (941) 964-0375. Cayo Costa is directly south of Boca Grande. January–April Captiva Cruises out of the South Seas Plantation on Captiva Island offers a daily cruise to Cayo Costa. $35 for adults, $17.50 for ages 12 and under; (941) 472-5300.

Tropic Star Nature Cruises provides year-round transportation to Cayo Costa and other islands daily at 9:30 a.m., returning at 4 p.m. $20 for adults, $15 for children ages 11 and under; (941) 283-0015.

Gasparilla Island

Gasparilla Island is a fun day trip for families, with pretty beaches and a historic lighthouse. The island is named for notorious pirate Jose Gaspar, and it's said that his treasure still is buried on the island. But today Gasparilla is most famous for the tarpon that run here in spring and summer, and since the early 1900s the rich and famous have come to the island to fish. Many fourth- and fifth-generation families still live on the island as fishing and sightseeing guides.

For a fun family beach, try Gasparilla Island State Recreation Area, where there are summertime turtle walks with park rangers in the morning and beach nature walks and shelling walks in the fall and winter; (941) 964-0375.

You can also explore the town of Boca Grande by bike, on a 6.5-mile bike path (13 miles round-trip) that follows the trail of the original Seaboard Airline Railroad and passes the historic Boca Grande Railroad Depot. The rail-trail is well maintained, the terrain is flat, and there's always a ocean breeze—a perfect ride for families. Beware, traffic does cross at some points, so caution energetic children to stop at all road crossings. To get to the trail, take the toll bridge to Gasparilla Island and downtown Boca Grande. From Park Avenue, turn right onto First Street and left onto Gulf Boulevard. The bike path is on the opposite side of the road. Bikes are for rent at Island Bike 'n Beach, 333 Park Avenue, for $7 an hour; (941) 964-0711. The shop is open Monday–Saturday, 9 a.m.–6 p.m., and on Sunday 9 a.m.–5 p.m.

There is expensive lodging at the Gasparilla Inn, but the hotel doesn't offer much for kids.

To get there by car, take I-75 to Exit 32, then west to the end of Toledo Blade Boulevard. Right onto SR 776, left on SR 771 to Placida and the Boca Grande Causeway. There are also boat trips from Pine and Captiva Islands.

Palm Island Resort on Knight Island

Escape where your kids are free to roam: a barrier island that's only accessible by ferry. No cars are allowed at Palm Island.

If you're looking for a laid-back, beach-only environment, Palm Island has one- to three-bedroom villas (160 in all), with screened porches, full kitchens, and washers and dryers. Kids under age 6 stay free; ages 6 and over $15. Cribs and high chairs can be rented for a nominal fee. There are five pools, eleven tennis courts, an island store, a full-service marina with boat rentals, two playgrounds, and a nature center. We recommend taking your own groceries or for a dinner out, take the ferry over to Johnny Leverock's Seafood House in Cape Haze.

The upscale resort covers 2.5 miles of a 7-mile island, surrounded by abundant wildlife. Shelling is bountiful on the beach—you can stroll to the end of the island where a pass connects the Intracoastal Waterway to the Gulf of Mexico (and where dolphins love to frolic).

Families can fish, snorkel, bicycle, canoe, go kayaking, or just read a good book. Every day of the week there are morning and afternoon nature activities, from family bicycle tours to kid fishing and canoe nature tours. Kids ages 6–12 are kept busy at the Kids Club, open daily from 10:30 a.m.–3 p.m.; cost is $25, $10 for ages 2–4. There are also teen activities planned Monday–Saturday, from teen canoe tours to pool parties. Call ahead—children's programs are seasonal.

Villas start at $200 in the summer, $310 in the winter. Palm Island Resort, 7092 Placida Road, Cape Haze; (941) 697-4800 or (800) 824-5412.

Pine Island

Just east of Sanibel, Pine Island, the largest island off the west coast of Florida, is dotted with tiny fishing villages. Today it's mostly residential and agricultural, with mangoes, guavas, and other fruit harvested. Contact Gulf Coast Kayak Company trips for guided tours of local natural areas, including the Matlacha Aquatic Preserve. Cost is $35 per person; (941) 283-1125. Or take a day trip on Tropic Star Nature Cruise out of Four Winds Marina at Bokeelia on the north end of Pine Island. Tropic Star heads to Cabbage Key, Cayo Costa, and other islands daily at 9:30 a.m., returning at 4 p.m. You can bring a picnic or have lunch at Cabbage Key; $25 for adults, $15 for children ages 11 and under; (941) 283-0015.

Useppa Island

Millionaire Barron G. Collier bought this island in 1906, and it's been the refuge of the rich and famous ever since. Today it's a chichi island country club. Captiva Cruises takes day guests over for a 2-hour stay with lunch at the Collier Inn, but you can't stay the night unless you're a member or know a member of this private vacation club. If your children are teenagers you'll enjoy the day trip, catching a glimpse of the lifestyles of the rich and famous. Captiva Cruises depart from the South Seas Plantation on Captiva Island. $27.50 for adults, $15 for children ages 12 and under; (941) 472-5300.

Sanibel and Captiva

Residents of these two beautiful islands fiercely protect their precious community—no live shelling, garbage, or pollution is allowed. Nature lovers and beach enthusiasts flock here, with miles of undisturbed land and beaches littered with countless seashells. The best things are free, particularly the beaches, perfect for small children because the waves are gentle and the water along the shoreline is shallow.

Bicycling

Sanibel is great for safe and easy bicycling, with wide, paved paths along most of the major roads, including the entire length of Periwinkle Way and along Sanibel-Captiva Road to Blind Pass. Bikes can be rented at several places along Periwinkle Way. Don't forget: helmets are required for all children under the age of 16 in the state of Florida.

One place to rent a bike is from Finnimore's Cycle Shop, open daily, 9 a.m.–5 p.m. 2352 Periwinkle Way; (941) 472-5577. You can also rent from Bike Route, open daily 9 a.m.–5 p.m., except Sunday. 14530 Palm Ridge Road; (941) 472-1955.

Best Beaches

- Eastern point around Sanibel Lighthouse, with a fishing pier.
- Gulfside City Park at the end of Algiers Land, off Casa Ybel Road.
- Tarpon Bay Road Beach, at the south end of Tarpon Bay Road.
- Bowman's Beach to the north on Bowman's beach Road—most secluded and shelly beach; 75 cents an hour to park.
- Turner Beach at Blind Pass between Sanibel and Captiva—the place to watch the sunset.

On the Water

A trip out on the ocean is a great way to experience this part of Florida, but be sure to consider your family's stamina as you plan an excursion on

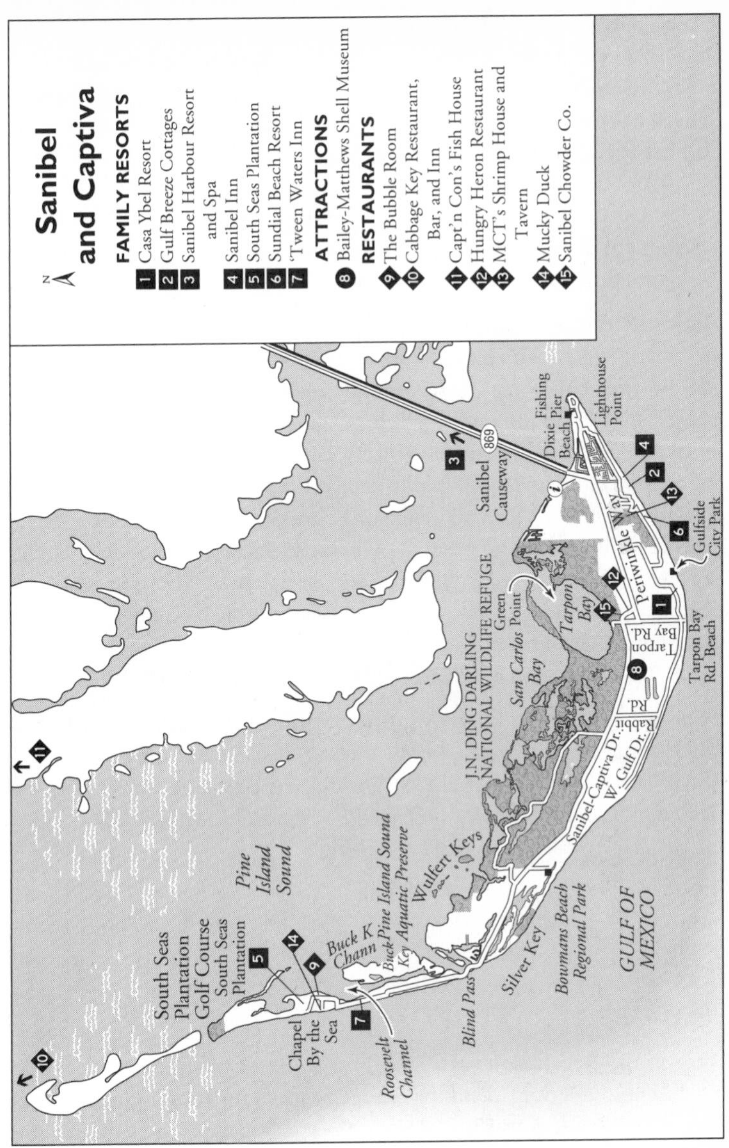

the water; many cruises are too long for most children, departing in the morning and not returning until midafternoon. We've included both long and short trips in this list of recommendations. And don't forget hats and sunscreen, and to take along snacks and water.

Canoe Adventures Highly recommended by the locals, guide Mark "Bird" Westall formerly was the mayor of Sanibel, and now he leads excellent environmental tours, three that are appropriate for children. One heads for The J. N. "Ding" Darling Wildlife Refuge, a second to the Sanibel River, and a third to Buck Key. You can reach Westall at (941) 472-5218, and he'll discuss the best trip for your family. If your kids are under age 6, he recommends a 1½-hour tour ($30 for adults, $10 for children up to age 18); for kids over age 6, he suggests a 2½–3-hour trip ($35 for adults, $15 for kids up to age 18).

Captiva Cruises Captiva Cruises are a popular way to get out on the water. You will be with a crowd of other folks, but it's still a reliable, enjoyable way to see the Gulf Coast islands. Cruises to Cabbage Key and Useppa islands are $27.50 for adults, $15 for children ages 12 and under. Cruises to Boca Grande and Cayo Costa islands are $35 for adults, $17.50 for children ages 12 and under. Dolphin-watch cruises depart every day at 4 p.m., $20 for adults, $10 for children ages 12 and under. Sunset cruises depart daily according to sunset times; $17.50 for adults, $10 for children ages 12 and under. There are two daily shelling cruises on Tuesday, Thursday, and Saturday: one from 9 a.m.–noon and a second from 1–4 p.m.; cost is $35 for adults, $17.50 for children ages 12 and under. All cruises depart from South Seas Plantation on Captiva; (941) 472-5300.

Mike Fuery's Tours Fuery, who has written a book about shelling in these parts, offers private, 3-hour shelling charters to North Captiva or Cayo Costa Islands. Cost is $180 for up to 4 people. Departure time is 7:30 a.m. Call him at (941) 466-3649 to schedule a trip.

Shell Seekers This service works out of the bayside of South Seas Plantation on Captiva and offers a 3-hour excursion to Cayo Costa, north of Captiva, for seashell hunts. They depart at 9 a.m. and 1 p.m. every day January–April, and if you can make the early trip, you'll find more treasures. Cost is $35 for adults, $17.50 for children ages 4–11; (941) 472-5111.

Tarpon Bay Recreation Area This is the easiest way to see the spectacular "Ding" Darling Wildlife Refuge, with tram tours, guided canoe tours, and kayak trips through the refuge. Tram tours are 2 hours long and cost $8 for adults, $4 for children ages 12 and under. The 1½-hour canoe and kayak guided trips, departing at 9:30 a.m., are $25 per person. If you're an early riser and more experienced, there's a 2½-hour trip that departs every morning at 7:30 for $40 per person. Located inside the J. N. "Ding" Darling Wildlife Refuge, 900 Tarpon Bay Road, Sanibel; (941) 472-8900.

Tropic Star Nature Cruise The Tropic Star is like a taxi service to the islands—you get dropped off and they come back for you, like clockwork, at specified times. The boats depart from Four Winds Marina at Bokeelia on the north end of Pine Island, east of Sanibel and Captiva, and offer cruises to Cabbage Key, Cayo Costa, and other islands daily at 9:30 a.m., returning at 4 p.m. You can bring a picnic if you're headed to Cayo Costa or the other beaches, or have lunch at Cabbage Key. Cost is $25 for adults, $15 for children ages 11 and under; (941) 283-0015.

Wildside Adventures McCarthy's Marina on Captiva is home to Wildside, where you can take your pick of kayaking, sailing, and hiking tours with a guide, many trips as short as 2 hours. A 2-hour day trip or a 2-hour moonlight trip in kayaks is $35 or $45 for adults, $25 or $35 for teens, $20 or $30 for children. The hour-long sunset kayak trip is $45 for adults, $35 for teens, $25 for children. 15041 Captiva Drive, Captiva; (941) 395-2925.

Family Resorts

Casa Ybel Resort

2255 W. Gulf Drive, Sanibel Island • (800) 276-ISLE • fax: (941) 472-2109
www.casaybelresort.com

Inspired by a turn-of-the-century home, Casa Ybel has 141 one- and two-bedroom suites with fully equipped kitchens (and a barbecue grill just outside your back door). To make it just like home, there's pizza delivery and a VCR, with videotapes for rent at the front desk.

An expansive beachfront terrace has a swimming pool with a water slide, a children's pool, and a playground; elsewhere on the 23-acre resort are six tennis courts, and at the beach there's sailing, windsurfing, kayaking, and, of course, shell hunting.

The Casa Kids Club is for ages 3–12, Monday, Tuesday, and Thursday 10 a.m.–1 p.m. The recreation staff offers activities like Beachmania morning, focusing on shelling and the beach environment; Shipwrecked on Sanibel, a morning of high-seas adventure and treasure hunting; and Earthly Encounter, a back-to-nature adventure outdoors. Other activities include face painting, pool games, lizard hunts, and a sea life excursion conducted on the water by a marine biologist. The Casa Kids Club is $12–15; Kids Night Out is $20; other activities charge a nominal fee.

Families can join in the Beach Discovery Walk to learn about the island's shells or in classes to make beach bags, sand candles, and other crafts. Bikes can be rented for family excursions on the island. Rates start at $240 in the summer, $400 in the winter.

Gulf Breeze Cottages

1081 Shell Basket Lane, Sanibel Island • (239) 472-1626 • fax (239) 472-4664 www.gbreeze.com

If your family wants to escape the crowds and isn't looking for supervised kids program, we suggest Gulf Breeze Cottages, tucked away at the end of a private street on Sanibel. When we last called, the proprietor was out on the beach, shelling at low tide, portable phone in hand.

They have efficiencies and one- and two-bedroom apartments with kitchens, including microwave, coffeemaker, linens, and dishes. All apartments are nonsmoking and start at $115 from May to December, $215 from December to May.

Sanibel Harbour Resort and Spa

17260 Harbour Point Drive, Ft. Myers • (800) 767-7777 • fax (239) 466-2150 www.sanibel-resort.com

Nestled on a private peninsula overlooking Sanibel and Captiva islands, this 80-acre oceanfront resort recently was named one of the country's Top 10 family beach resorts by *Family Circle* magazine. It's the kind of place where parents can be pampered in the spa (with more than 60 different services) while kids participate in the Kids Klub for ages 5–12, Monday–Sunday 10 a.m.–4 p.m. Each day has a different theme, like Space Exploration Day, Pirate Invasion Day, and Nature Day. Cost is $34 a day, including lunch and prizes. The fun continues Friday and Saturday, 6–8 p.m. ($20 for the evening).

There are sand castle–building contests, pool games, bingo, picnics, pirate's treasure hunts, finger painting, nature hikes, and more. The resort also has a family game room with chess, checkers, Monopoly, and other board games. Amenities include four swimming pools, tennis, kayaks, and a fleet of sailboats and Waverunners to rent. The whole family can kayak through the mangroves on a trail designed for beginners. The staff also can arrange wilderness tours by boat or swamp buggy, including dolphin sightseeing cruises and "just for beginners" family fishing cruises.

There are 240 rooms (with coffeemakers and mini-bars) and 80 condominiums. Room rates start at $159 in the summer and $299 in the winter; children under age 18 stay free in room with parents. Two-bedroom, two-bath condominiums start at $249 in the summer, $469 in the winter.

Sanibel Inn

937 E. Gulf Drive • (800) 965-7772 or (239) 472-3181 • fax (239) 472-5234 www.ssrc.com

The Sanibel Inn is a "little big resort" with commendable kids programs. Sitting amid 500 palm trees and eight acres of tropical gardens, the resort offers activities like a nature-themed Mad Hatter Tea Party and programs held in the resort's butterfly- and bird-attracting bromeliad gardens. Families can participate in weekly educational activities for all ages, like Beach Discovery, Sanibel Shell Safari, or Dolphin Watch. Younger children can learn about nature in fun activities such as How Does Your Garden Grow? and Bugs Don't Bug Me. An evening kids camp is held twice a week, with dinner included.

The resort offers canoe, kayak, tennis, and bicycle rentals.There are two bars: one poolside and one in the four star restaurant.

Every room includes a refrigerator, coffeemaker, and microwave, but the two bedroom–two bath suites that include a washer and dryer and a complete kitchen are perfect for families. And all the balconies and patios are screened. Rates start at $315 February–April, $175 May–December.

South Seas Resort

Captiva Island • (800) CAPTIVA or (941) 472-5111 • fax (941) 472-7533
www.southseas.com

Located at the northern tip of Captiva Island, South Seas Resort is more like a small town than a resort, spread out on 330 acres with its own trolley transportation system. There are more than 600 accommodations, from hotel rooms (all with coffeemakers and refrigerators) to beach homes and cottages.

The resort's wildlife is abundant: Loggerhead turtles nest on the South Seas beach from May to September; dolphins play year-round in the waters surrounding the resort; and in the winter months, manatees often seek the warmth of the resort's harbor. More than 100 species of migratory and nesting birds are found at South Seas Plantation.

South Seas Resort offers a wide range of family activities, including nature excursions, the Fun Factory for ages 3–10 and teen activities. Family activities include arts and crafts with local shells, family fishing fun, bingo, and crab races. A full-time naturalist conducts complimentary programs including Birds of Captiva, Shells of Captiva, Manatee Awareness, and Plantation Exploration. Canoe trips, kayak excursions, and wild refuge trips also are available.

The Fun Factory is packed with themed activities geared toward recreation, the environment, and education. Specially trained counselors lead beach walks, skits, scavenger hunts, even language learning. Lunches are themed, too: turkey melt "pop tarts" and make your own tomato soup. Themes teach about Florida's ecological treasures. Cost is $22 per half day or evening, including lunch, snack, or dinner, or $40 for a whole day.

Tennis, biking, golf, and water sports all are available at South Seas Resort. Rates start at $385 in the winter, $240 in the summer. Children 16 and under stay free.

Sundial Beach Resort

1451 Middle Gulf Drive, Sanibel • (941) 472-4151 or (800) 237-4184 • fax (941) 472-8892 • www.sundialresort.com

Kids will love this resort's Environmental Coastal Observatory (ECO), the first of its kind to be housed in a resort in the United States. The ECO center has a 450-gallon touch tank with sea creatures that kids can pick up and examine, like a fighting conch or a horseshoe crab. (Beware, there's also a hermit crab adoption center, so you'll likely end up with a new pet.)

The award-winning family resort is on 33 acres with 270 rooms, including two-bedroom suites, all with fully equipped kitchens and screened balconies or patios. There are five swimming pools, tennis, and a fitness center. Bicycles and jogging strollers can be rented, as well as catamarans, sea kayaks, and boogie boards for water fun.

Kids ages 4–11 will love the Fun Factory, packed with themed activities geared toward recreation, the environment, and education. Specially trained counselors lead beach walks, skits, scavenger hunts, even language learning. Lunches are themed, too: turkey melt "pop tarts" and make-your-own tomato soup, for instance. All themes teach about Florida's ecological treasures. Cost is $22 per half-day or evening session, including lunch, snack, or dinner, or $40 for the whole day. Several teen programs are offered as well, such as aerobics, island sightseeing tours, bike-blade excursions, and crafts like decorating T-shirts. The Crocodial's Pen Pal Club pairs children with previous guest pen pals. Parents are invited to participate in any of the activities.

After a long day, kids can wind down with the Sun-Dial-a-Story line, a two-minute, prerecorded children's story, free to guests, with a new story every day.

The resort offers daily programs, including shell lectures and nature beach walks with a trained guide to find rare birds, shells, and animals.

All suites have full kitchens, including dishwasher and microwave, and living area. Suites start at $189 in the summer, $395 in the winter.

'Tween Waters Inn

15951 Captiva Road, Captiva Island • (941) 472-5161 • fax (941) 472-5161 www.tween-waters.com

On the narrowest piece of Captiva, this historic inn was the place you'd find pioneer conservationist J. N. "Ding" Darling in the 1920s. Today it's nearly as quaint, and natural, though new condos have just been built to replace some of the old cottages. The resort is across the street from the placid Gulf of Mexico. (Though drivers on the island are mostly considerate, caution your youngsters about crossing the two-lane highway.)

This is an ideal resort for a family that's not looking for structured kids and family programs—there are none except for the Kids for Sail sailing school for ages 8 and older. The day program teaches the fundamentals of navigation from 9 a.m.–noon; cost is $50. There are plenty of outdoor activities without the hustle and bustle of a large resort: The beach is lovely, uncrowded, and great for shelling, and they have canoe, kayak, and bike rentals. The swimming pool is adequate, and the tennis, shuffleboard, and bocce ball courts are never too busy.

'Tween Waters has 137 rooms, suites, and cottages on 13 acres with a full-service marina. And this is one of the few hotels that allows your pet to stay ($15 a day). The Disney Channel is free in every room. And if you want a baby-sitter for the evening, the front desk will help you find one. Each room has a refrigerator and coffeemaker. Some rooms have a wet bar. Rates start at $175 in the summer and $195 in the winter.

Attractions

Bailey-Matthews Shell Museum

3075 Sanibel-Captiva Road, Sanibel Island • (941) 395-2233

Hours - Tuesday–Sunday, 10 a.m.–4 p.m.

Admission - $5 for adults, $3 for children ages 8–16, free for ages 8 and under

Appeal by Age Group -

Pre-school ★	Teens ★★	Over 30 ★★★
Grade school ★★★	Young Adults ★★★	Seniors ★★★

Touring Time - Average 2 hours; minimum 1 hour

Rainy-Day Touring - Recommended

Author's Rating - ★★★; educational and fun

Restaurants - No

Alcoholic beverages - No

Handicapped access - Yes

Wheelchair rental - No

Baby stroller rental - No

Lockers - No

Pet kennels - No

Rain check - No

Private tours - No

Description and Comments Visitors can see how nature has created shells with a breathtaking variety of colors, patterns, and shapes in this museum devoted entirely to shells of the world. The centerpiece is a six-foot revolving planet surrounded by shells from geographic regions from around the world. You can hear the sounds of the Florida Everglades while walking through the Kingdom of the Landshells, learn about the relationship between shells and the web of life in the habitat exhibits, and discover why shells wash ashore in abundance on Sanibel and Captiva.

A play area for children has hands-on displays and a live shell tank, offering a chance to become familiar with these extraordinary creatures from under the sea. Kids 17 and younger get to choose two free shells to take home.

Family-Friendly Restaurants

The Bubble Room

15001 Captiva Road • (941) 472-5558

Meals served - Lunch and dinner

Cuisine - Steak, seafood

Entree range - Lunch $6–14; dinner $19–29

Kids menu - Yes

Reservations - Not accepted

Payment - All major credit cards accepted

Kids love this garish place, packed with toys, movie stills, and all sorts of fun-to-look-at junk. Though the food is not haute cuisine, there's plenty of it, so consider sharing a plate. Kids eat for $4–10 at lunch, $6–10 at dinner.

Cabbage Key Restaurant, Bar, and Inn

Located on Cabbage Key Island • (941) 283-2278

Meals served - Breakfast, lunch, and dinner

Cuisine - Seafood, American

Entree range - $10–19.95

Kids menu - No, but the cheeseburgers, hot dogs, and other items appeal to kids

Reservations - Required for dinner

Payment - Visa, MC

You have to take a boat to reach the Cabbage Key Restaurant, but it's truly a piece of old Florida and worth the trip. The seafood is good, and the cheeseburgers are perfect—you'll understand why Jimmy Buffett wrote "Cheeseburger in Paradise" after a visit to this watering hole.

Capt'n Con's Fish House

8421 Main Street, Bokeelia (on Pine Island) • (941) 283-4300

Meals served - Breakfast, lunch, and dinner

Cuisine - American, seafood

Entree range - $4.50–19.95

Kids menu - Yes

Reservations - Accepted for parties of 10 or more

Payment - All major credit cards accepted

Try the seafood chowder and the grouper prepared any way you like.

Hungry Heron Restaurant

2330 Palm Ridge Road, Sanibel • (941) 395-2300

Meals served - Lunch and dinner

Cuisine - American

Entree range - $8.95–21.95

Kids menu - Yes

Reservations - Preferred seating available

Payment - All major credit cards accepted

Try the homemade sweet potato chips. Sandwiches are huge, so you can share. The restaurant has big-screen TVs and often pops in a cartoon video for the kids.

McT's Shrimp House and Tavern

1523 Periwinkle Way, Sanibel • (941) 472-3161

Meals served - Dinner

Cuisine - Seafood

Entree range - $12–46

Kids menu - Yes

Reservations - Not accepted

Payment - All major credit cards accepted

This is casual seafood dining, and if you're among the first 100 to show up between 5 and 6 p.m., you get the early-bird special for $8.95 (your choice of six dishes). They also serve a good prime rib and barbecue, along with fresh seafood, including the requisite all-you-can-eat shrimp and crab platters.

Mucky Duck

11546 Andy Rosse Lane, Sanibel • (941) 472-3434

Meals served - Lunch and dinner

Cuisine - American

Entree range - $11–29

Kids menu - Yes

Reservations - Not accepted

Payment - All major credit cards accepted

Owners are impromptu comedians who keep the kids laughing. And the Mucky Duck is right on the water so it's a great place to watch the sunset. Locals recommend the grouper sandwich. There's no smoking anywhere in this restaurant.

Sanibel Chowder Co.

2075 Periwinkle Way, Sanibel Island • (941) 472-2525

Meals served - Breakfast, lunch, and dinner

Cuisine - American

Entree range - $4.95–14.95

Kids menu - Yes

Reservations - Accepted

Payment - Visa, MC, AmEx, D

Great breakfast. The restaurant is located in a small shopping center, so you can shop and eat at the same time. And if the kids finish first, there's a children's playground in front of the restaurant so parents can watch children from inside.

Ft. Myers and Ft. Myers Beach

The Caloosahatchee River is a pretty backdrop for the historic city of Ft. Myers, long considered an ideal spot for winter homes. Thomas Edison, for instance, lived here on his 14-acre winter estate, laboratory, and botanical garden beside the Caloosahatchee, which today is a fun stop for families on their way to the beach. Ft. Myers Beach is really an adjacent barrier island, Estero Island, about 30 minutes from downtown, where families flock year-round. It's also the gateway to the two most popular Gulf Coast islands, Sanibel and Captiva.

SHELL FACTORY

After admiring all the shells on the beach, lots of kids like to spend some of their souvenir money on a beauty from the Shell Factory, 2787 N. Tamiami Trail in North Ft. Myers (call (800) 282-5805). This giant showroom claims to have the world's largest collection—more than 5 million—and they're for sale, some as cheap as a nickel or a handful for 25 cents. This place has been around for 60 years. Open 10 a.m.–9 p.m. everyday.

Family Resorts

Best Western Pink Shell Beach Resort

275 Estero Boulevard, Ft. Myers Beach • (800) 952-6574 • fax (941) 481-4947
www.pinkshell.com

This hotel really targets families, with a reputation for some of the most fun activities on Ft. Myers Beach. Situated on 12 acres between the Gulf and the mangroves of Estero Bay, the Pink Shell has 209 efficiencies, suites, cottages, and beach villas. Microwaves, refrigerators, and coffee-makers are in every room. There are three swimming pools and a children's wading

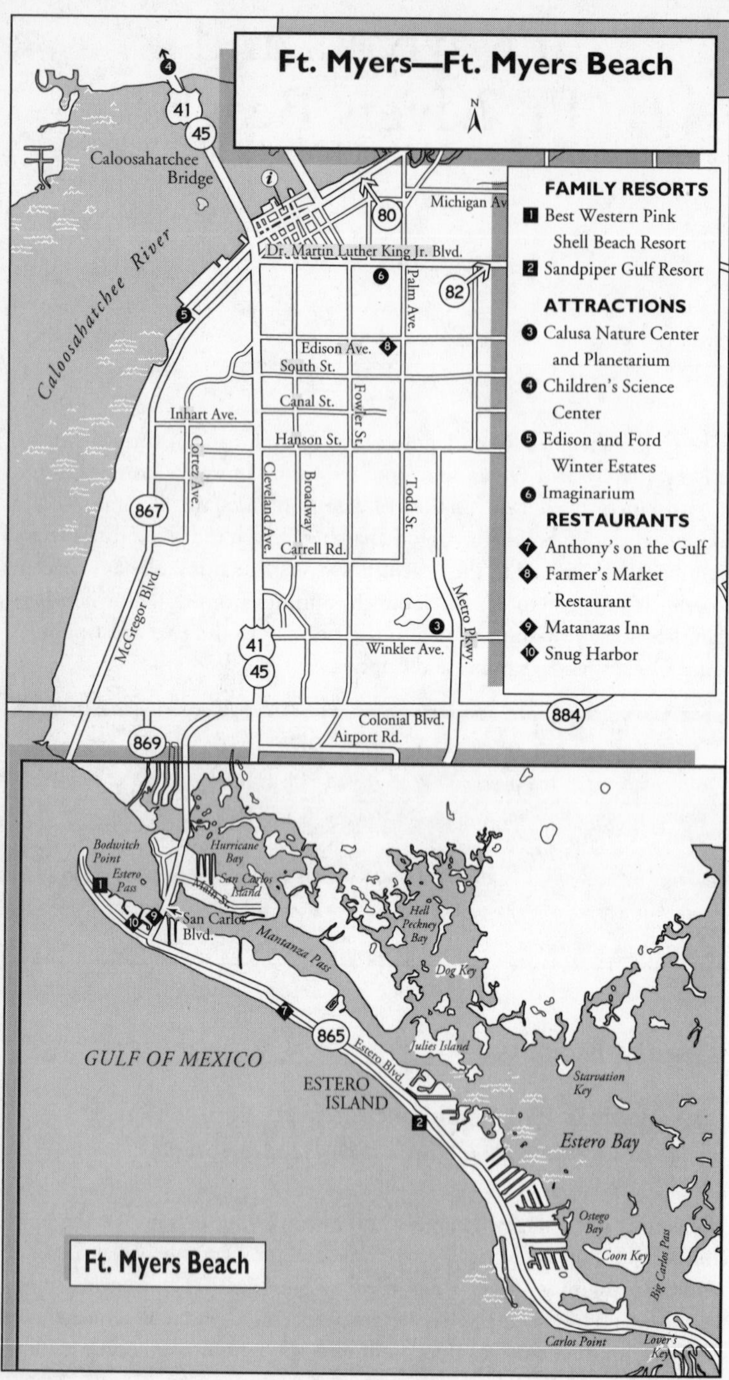

Ft. Myers—Ft. Myers Beach
N
FAMILY RESORTS
1 Best Western Pink Shell Beach Resort
2 Sandpiper Gulf Resort
ATTRACTIONS
3 Calusa Nature Center and Planetarium
4 Children's Science Center
5 Edison and Ford Winter Estates
6 Imaginarium
RESTAURANTS
7 Anthony's on the Gulf
8 Farmer's Market Restaurant
9 Matanazas Inn
10 Snug Harbor
Caloosahatchee Bridge
Caloosahatchee River
Michigan Av
Dr. Martin Luther King Jr. Blvd.
Palm Ave.
Edison Ave.
South St.
Canal St.
Inhart Ave.
Hanson St.
Fowler St.
Cortez Ave.
Cleveland Ave.
Broadway
Todd St.
Carrell Rd.
McGregor Blvd.
Metro Pkwy.
Winkler Ave.
Colonial Blvd.
Airport Rd.
41
45
80
82
867
869
884
865
Bodwitch Point
Estero Pass
Hurricane Bay
San Carlos Island
Main St.
San Carlos Blvd.
Mantanza Pass
Hell Peckney Bay
Dog Key
Julies Island
GULF OF MEXICO
ESTERO ISLAND
Estero Blvd.
Starvation Key
Estero Bay
Ostego Bay
Coon Key
Big Carlos Pass
Carlos Point
Lover's Key
Ft. Myers Beach

pool, tennis and volleyball, bike rentals, boat tours, even a fishing pier on the bay side. Grills and picnic tables are scattered throughout the resort for impromptu picnics.

Teenagers have plenty to do here, with nighttime pool parties, scavenger hunts, casino night, and other supervised fun. Kids 4–11 will love the Fun Factory, packed with themed activities geared toward recreation, the environment, and education. Specially trained counselors lead beach walks, skits, scavenger hunts, even language learning. All themes teach about Florida's ecological treasures. Cost is $22 per half-day or evening session, including lunch, snack or dinner, or $40 for the whole day.

This hotel encourages family togetherness in the afternoons, with activities like family volleyball, sand sculpting, and face painting, and a chance to make kitschy crafts like sand dollar night-lights and tie-dyed T-shirts. Rates start at $149 in summer and $259 in winter, and they warmly welcome your youngsters with a check-in gift.

Sandpiper Gulf Resort

5550 Estero Boulevard, Ft. Myers Beach • (941) 463-5721 • fax (941) 765-0039 ext. 299 • www.sandpipergulfresort.com

Though it's nothing fancy, we've included this affordable, family-oriented hotel because it's right on the beach and offers 63 spacious efficiency apartments with furnished kitchens, a living area that converts for sleeping, and a large bedroom with two double beds and a generous closet. Every apartment has a balcony overlooking one of the two swimming pools or the Gulf. There also are laundry facilities. It's the kind of place that brews a pot of coffee every morning in the front office so guests can stop by for a cup.

Families with smaller children might prefer the ground floor courtyard apartments. All apartments are for up to six people and start at $79–141.

Attractions

Calusa Nature Center and Planetarium

3450 Ortiz Avenue, Ft. Myers • (941) 275-3435 • www.calusanature.com

Hours - Monday–Saturday, 9 a.m.–5 p.m.; Sunday, 11 a.m.–4 p.m.

Admission - $5 for adults (museum), $3 (planetarium); $3 for children ages 3–12 (museum), $2 (planetarium)

Appeal by Age Group -

Pre-school ★★	Teens ★★	Over 30 ★★
Grade school ★★	Young Adults ★★	Seniors ★★

Touring Time - Average 3–4 hours; minimum 2 hours

Rainy-Day Touring - Recommended for museum and planetarium only

Author's Rating - ★★★; plenty of wildlife and outdoor fun

Restaurants - No
Alcoholic beverages - No
Handicapped access - Yes
Wheelchair rental - No
Baby stroller rental - No
Lockers - No
Pet kennels - No
Rain check - No
Private tours - Yes

Description and Comments Tour Florida's native environment on a rustic 2-mile-long boardwalk through acres of cypress forest and wetlands, including an Audubon aviary and children's natural history museum, live reptile exhibit, and a 400-gallon freshwater aquarium. Wildlife includes alligators, birds, and snakes. The planetarium shows change frequently.

The Children's Science Center

2915 NE Pine Island Road, Cape Coral • (941) 997-0012

Hours - Monday–Friday, 9:30 a.m.–4:30 p.m.; Saturday and Sunday, noon–5 p.m.

Admission - $4 for adults, $2 for children ages 2–16

Appeal by Age Group -

Pre-school ★★	Teens ★★	Over 30 ★★
Grade school ★★★	Young Adults ★★	Seniors ★★

Touring Time - Average 2–3 hours; minimum 1 hour

Rainy-Day Touring - Recommended

Author's Rating - ★★; good rainy day fun, or afternoon entertainment after a morning at the beach

Restaurants - No
Alcoholic beverages - No
Handicapped access - Yes
Wheelchair rental - No
Baby stroller rental - No
Lockers - No
Pet kennels - No
Rain check - No
Private tours - Yes

Description and Comments A 1940s house has been converted into a center with hands-on exhibits on electricity, optical illusions, dinosaurs, the solar system, and more. Outdoors there are nature walks, a science park, and an iguana garden. The center offers telescope viewing January–April, and there also are live reptiles on display.

SKATE OF THE ART

Too rainy, too cold, too sunburned for another beach day? Head for the Fort Myers Skatium where everyone can burn up energy on the ice and in-line rinks, along with laser tag, indoor soccer, and volleyball. Skating prices range from $4 to $5; skate rentals are $3 (for groups). Hours vary. The Skatium is at 2250 Broadway in downtown Ft. Myers; (941) 461-3145.

Behind the Skatium is the Sanctuary Skate Park, a $500,000 outdoor skate park with 20 pieces of equipment for skateboarding and in-line skating. Sessions are $7 for non-members and last 2 hours; $2 per helmet, wrist pad, or knee pad. (Protective gear is required.) Open 7 days a week; (941) 337-5297.

If you just want to watch the action on ice, the new Florida Everblades' hockey team plays in the TECO Arena on Everblades Parkway, Estero; (941) 948-7825.

Edison and Ford Winter Estates

2350 McGregor Boulevard, Ft. Myers • (941) 334-3614

Hours - Monday–Saturday, 9 a.m.–5:30 p.m.; Sunday, noon–5:30 p.m.; tours end at 4 pm. sharp; closed Thanksgiving and Christmas

Admission - $12 for adults, $6 for children ages 6–12

Appeal by Age Group -

Pre-school ★	Teens ★★½	Over 30 ★★★
Grade school ★★	Young Adults ★★★	Seniors ★★★

Touring Time - Average 2–3 hours; minimum 1½ hours

Rainy-Day Touring - Recommended except for grounds

Author's Rating - ★★★; authentic and educational

Restaurants - No
Alcoholic beverages - No
Handicapped access - Yes
Wheelchair rental - Yes
Baby stroller rental - Yes
Lockers - No
Pet kennels - No
Rain check - Yes
Private tours - Yes

Description and Comments The Edison and Ford Winter Estates afford a pleasant change of pace and an interesting history lesson for school-age children, especially on a rainy day. Educational and relaxing, the Edison home personifies at once the sleepy elegance of the Old South and the dynamic genius of America's premier inventor. Henry Ford lived next door, and his home also is still furnished as it was in the 1920s.

The 90-minute tour takes you through both homes, but Edison's is the most elaborate part of the tour; you can see the first modern swimming pool in Florida, Edison's laboratory, a guest house, grounds and gardens, and a museum. Quick-paced, guided tours depart every 30 minutes. No unguided touring is permitted, but you can browse in the museum, loaded with Edison's inventions, possessions, and artifacts, at the completion of the tour.

The many dimensions of the inventive and often zany Edison create a sense of curiosity and expectation, and as you proceed through the home, you quickly realize this is not just another old Southern house; it's like stumbling into the magical lair of H. G. Wells. Even the landscaping is part of the Edison story, much of it transplanted by the inventor from all over the world.

Imaginarium

2000 Cranford Avenue, Ft. Myers • (941) 337-3332

Hours - Monday–Saturday, 10 a.m.–5 p.m.; Sunday 12–5 p.m.

Admission - $7 for adults, $4 for children ages 3–12, $6.50 for senior citizens 65 and older

Appeal by Age Group -

Pre-school ★★★	Teens ★★	Over 30 ★★
Grade school ★★★	Young Adults ★★	Seniors ★★

Touring Time - Average 2–3 hours; minimum 2 hours

Rainy-Day Touring - Recommended

Author's Rating - ★★★; perfect for a rainy day

Restaurants - Yes

Alcoholic beverages - No

Handicapped access - Yes

Wheelchair rental - Yes

Baby stroller rental - Yes

Lockers - No

Pet kennels - No

Rain check - No

Private tours - Yes

Description and Comments Your kids can touch absolutely everything in this sensory attraction, located in the old city water plant. They can stand in a Florida thunderstorm without getting wet, watch an eel slither through the coral in a 900-gallon aquarium, or feel the force of a hurricane. Outside there's a touch tank with live conchs and other sea critters, and a butterfly habitat.

Family-Friendly Restaurants

Anthony's on the Gulf

3040 Estero Boulevard, Ft. Myers Beach • (941) 463-2600

Meals served - Lunch and dinner

Cuisine - Seafood, Italian

Entree range - $6.95–22

Kids menu - Yes

Reservations - Not accepted

Payment - Visa, MC, AmEx, D

Try any of the daily specials. Anthony's also features a "light" menu if you're counting calories.

Farmers Market Restaurant

2736 Edison Avenue • (941) 334-1687

Meals served - Breakfast, lunch, and dinner

Cuisine - Southern

Entree range - $5–11

Kids menu - No, and no special portions either

Reservations - Not accepted

Payment - No credit cards

This eatery is right next door to the Farmers Market, so there are plenty of fresh tomatoes, green beans, and other veggies. Smoked beef, pork barbecue, and country-fried steak are favorites.

Matanzas Inn

416 Crescent Street, Ft. Myers Beach • (941) 463-3838

Meals served - Lunch and dinner

Cuisine - American, seafood

Entree range - $4–17

Kids menu - Yes

Reservations - Not accepted

Payment - All major credit cards accepted

Try the gator tail or the conch chowder. Fish any way you like it is a good bet, and they cook up some interesting seafood specials.

Snug Harbor

645 San Carlos Boulevard, Ft. Myers Beach • (941) 463-4343

Meals served - Lunch and dinner

Cuisine - American, seafood

Entree range - $6–22

Kids menu - Yes

Reservations - Accepted for groups of 4 or more

Payment - Visa, MC, AmEx, D

Seafood doesn't get any fresher, as Sung Harbor has its own fishing fleet. Their most popular creation is Grouper Popeye, steamed fish with spinach in a lemon-butter sauce.

Naples

Naples is working hard to shake its image as a winter-only retreat for the wealthy and retired, and is reaching out for families and eco-tourists, taking advantage of its proximity to the Everglades, the barrier islands, and the cypress swamps. It's both sophisticated and serene, with world-class shopping and galleries just minutes from the Everglades wilderness. And the city is fringed with beautiful beaches.

FUN AND FREE

A fabulous place to watch the sunset is the 1,000-foot-long Naples Pier, listed on the National Register of Historic Places. The pier and adjacent beach make a great multigenerational gathering spot all day long for fishing, swimming, walking, and just relaxing. There's a bait shop, snack bar, rest rooms, and showers, with concessions open from 7:30 a.m. until 6 p.m. Parking is metered, and it's sometimes tough to find a spot.

Family Resorts

Naples Beach Hotel

851 Gulfshore Blvd. N., Naples • (800) 237-7600 • fax (239) 261-7380
www.naplesbeachhotel.com

For three generations, the Watkins family has cared for this beachfront resort, and returning guests say they come back for the personal attention. All 318 rooms recently were renovated to the tune of $2.5 million, including 41 suites (with microwaves and refrigerators) and 22 kitchenette efficiencies.

There's an 18-hole golf course on the 125-acre resort, as well as tennis courts, a spa, and Olympic-sized pool. While mom and dad are on the golf course or at the spa, kids can hang out at the Beach Clubber 4 Kids,

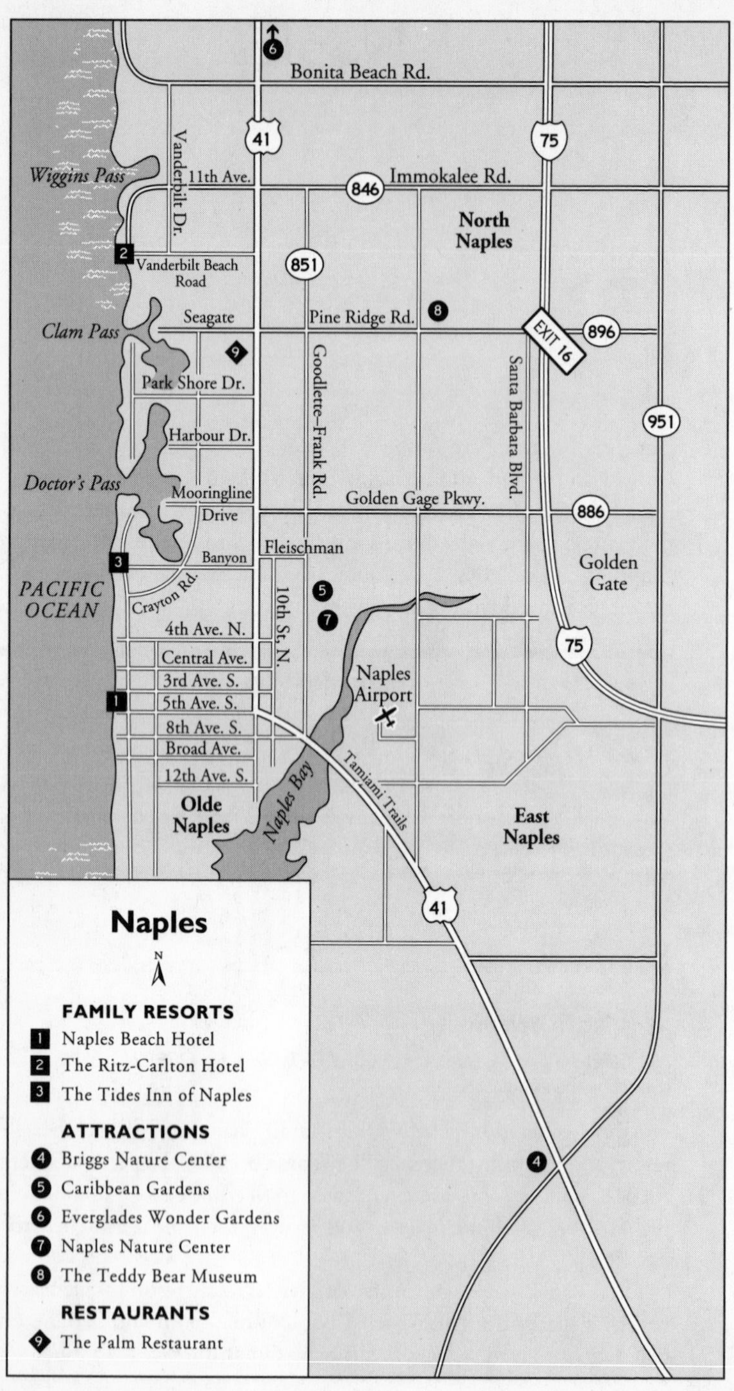
Bonita Beach Rd.
41
75
Vanderbilt Dr.
Wiggins Pass
11th Ave.
846
Immokalee Rd.
North
Naples
2
Vanderbilt Beach
Road
851
Seagate
Pine Ridge Rd.
Clam Pass
EXIT 16
896
Park Shore Dr.
Goodlette–Frank Rd.
Santa Barbara Blvd.
951
Harbour Dr.
Doctor's Pass
Mooringline
Drive
Golden Gage Pkwy.
886
Fleischman
Banyon
Golden
Gate
PACIFIC
OCEAN
Crayton Rd.
4th Ave. N.
10th St. N.
Central Ave.
3rd Ave. S.
5th Ave. S.
8th Ave. S.
Broad Ave.
12th Ave. S.
Naples
Airport
Tamiami Trails
Naples Bay
Olde
Naples
East
Naples
Naples
N
FAMILY RESORTS
1 Naples Beach Hotel
2 The Ritz-Carlton Hotel
3 The Tides Inn of Naples
ATTRACTIONS
4 Briggs Nature Center
5 Caribbean Gardens
6 Everglades Wonder Gardens
7 Naples Nature Center
8 The Teddy Bear Museum
RESTAURANTS
9 The Palm Restaurant

with supervised recreation including movies and games. Economical family packages start at $374 for two nights and include a full breakfast buffet (for two adults, two kids) and free Beach Clubber membership.

The Ritz-Carlton Hotel, Naples

280 Vanderbilt Beach Road, Naples • (239) 598-3300 • fax (239) 598-6667
www.ritzcarlton.com

This fine hotel has five stars and five diamonds from Mobil Travel Guide and AAA, respectively, and travel magazine readers consistently vote it No. 1 in glossy publications like *Condé Nast Traveler, Travel and Leisure,* and *Gourmet.* So you can bet on impeccable service and luxury. What may surprise you is the friendliness and helpfulness of the folks who run the place.

The Ritz-Carlton Naples has 20 acres on the ocean, with 463 rooms and suites, all with a lovely view of the Gulf of Mexico. Each room has a refrigerator and an honor bar. Microwaves and coffeemakers can be requested for an additional charge. If you're traveling with young children and heights make you nervous, ask for one of the 11 rooms that doesn't have a private balcony. The hotel will also help childproof your room with socket covers, night lights, and corner protectors.

Every possible luxury is at your fingertips, and if it's not, just ask—there's even a waiter to bring you drinks on the beach. A swimming pool, water sports, tennis, nearby golf, a fitness center…parents are quite content, but not having nearly so much fun as the Ritz Kids. The program, for kids ages 5–12, includes beach walks, pastry making, arts and crafts, and scavenger hunts. It is offered every day from 9 a.m.–4 p.m. with lunch ($45); Friday and Saturday evenings from 6–9 p.m. with dinner ($45).

Planned family activities during peak seasons include the Ritz-Carlton Nature Walk, a Family Carnival with games and prizes, and trips to nearby attractions like Caribbean Gardens. Rates start at $225 in the summer and $490 in the winter.

The Ritz-Carlton offers one of the AAA Audubon Natural Florida Journeys: three days and two nights at the hotel, including an excursion through the Everglades National Park and a side trip to Everglades City, then on to the Ten Thousand Islands environmental preserve for an airboat ride, and the Fakahatchee Strand State Preserve, a park that has the largest concentration and variety of orchids in North America. For reservations and information, call a local AAA office.

The Tides Inn of Naples

1801 Gulf Shore Boulevard N., Naples • (941) 262-6196 or (800) 438-8763
fax (941) 262-3055

For summertime, you can't beat the rates at this spotless, charming motel that offers 35 rooms, efficiencies, and one-bedroom apartments. The inn is right on the beach, on the edge of Naples's Millionaires Row. Every room has a screened balcony or patio looking out to a lushly landscaped courtyard, swimming pool, and the beach. Rates include a continental breakfast and start at $70, $135 for a one-bedroom apartment; children under age 11 stay free, over age 11 for $10.

Attractions

Briggs Nature Center

401 Shell Island Road (off SR 951, 6 miles north of Marco Island) • (941) 775-8569 or (941) 775-7566

Hours - Monday–Saturday, 9 a.m.–4:30 p.m., year-round

Admission - Free except for boardwalk; $4 for adults, $2 for children ages 3–12. Admission is good for both the Briggs Nature Center and Naples Nature Center if visited within two weeks

Appeal by Age Group -

Pre-school ★★	Teens ★★★	Over 30 ★★★
Grade school ★★★★	Young Adults ★★★	Seniors ★★★

Touring Time - Average 3–4 hours; minimum 1 hour

Rainy-Day Touring - Not recommended

Author's Rating - ★★★; real nature

Restaurants - No

Alcoholic beverages - No

Handicapped access - Yes

Wheelchair rental - Yes

Baby stroller rental - No

Lockers - No

Pet kennels - No

Rain check - No

Private tours - By canoe and boat

Caribbean Gardens

1590 Goodlette-Frank Road, Naples • (941) 262-5409

Hours - Daily, 9:30 a.m.–5:30 p.m.; closed Thanksgiving, Christmas, and Easter Sunday.

Admission - $14.95 for adults, $9.95 for children ages 4–15, free for ages 3 and under; annual membership available

Appeal by Age Group -

Pre-school ★★★	Teens ★★★½	Over 30 ★★★★
Grade school ★★★	Young Adults ★★★½	Seniors ★★★½

Touring Time - Average 4 hours; minimum 2 hours
Rainy-Day Touring - Not recommended
Author's Rating - ★★★; family-owned and a piece of the real Florida

Restaurants - Yes	**Alcoholic beverages -** No
Handicapped access - Yes	**Wheelchair rental -** Yes
Baby stroller rental - Yes	**Lockers -** No
Pet kennels - No	**Rain check -** Yes
Private tours - Yes	

Description and Comments Some parents may remember this attraction as Jungle Larry's African Safari Park, where "Jungle Larry, Friend of the Beasts" (a.k.a. Colonel Lawrence Tetzlaff) raised his private collection of animals on a 52-acre site surrounded by the sprawling suburbs of Naples. He opened his animal park to the public in 1969 (though Caribbean Gardens, under different owners, had operated since 1954).

The colonel died in 1984, and his two sons, Tim and David, now run the place and have changed the name back to the simpler Caribbean Gardens. Many of Jungle Larry's animals are still around, and the collection has expanded to more than 200 animals, ranging from rare golden tigers to graceful impala antelope, with the most exotic and unusual showcased in Safari Canyon. Though it's not a state-of-the-art operation (many of the large animals, for example, are in cages), you can tell that the animals are well cared for.

Visitors can ask questions in the Meet the Keeper series, which takes place at select animal exhibits throughout the day. There's a chance to hold or touch small mammals and reptiles in the Scales and Tails show. At different points throughout the park, solar-powered ZooKey audio sites offer insights and knowledge. Hundreds of gators glide through Alligator Bay, where you can watch mealtime.

The Primate Expedition Cruise glides past islands where monkeys, lemurs, and apes live in natural habitats. There are also elephant rides and a petting farm. Coolers and picnic lunches are welcome.

It doesn't have the the glitz and glamour of a major animal theme park but it's great fun for families.

Everglades Wonder Gardens

27180 Old US 41, Bonita Springs • (941) 992-2591

Hours - Daily, 9 a.m.–5 p.m.

Admission - $12 for adults, $6 for children ages 3–12

Appeal by Age Group -

Pre-school ★★★½	Teens ★★	Over 30 ★★★½
Grade school ★★★½	Young Adults ★★	Seniors ★★★½

Rainy-Day Touring - Not recommended

Author's Rating - ★★; we enjoy these enduring attractions that take us back to childhood

Restaurants - Yes
Alcoholic beverages - No
Handicapped access - Yes
Wheelchair rental - No
Baby stroller rental - No
Lockers - No
Pet kennels - No
Rain check - No
Private tours - Yes

Description and Comments Did you ever wonder what Florida was like in the early days of tourism? Happily, there is a time warp situated in Bonita Springs, 18 miles south of Ft. Myers and 10 miles north of Naples, that will let you see how it was in the "old days."

The attraction hasn't changed much since the 1930s, and the gardens are actually an old-fashioned zoo featuring Florida wildlife including bears, otters, deer, wading birds, birds of prey, the Florida panther, and endangered Everglades crocodiles. But the animals, reptiles, and birds are zippy and healthy as well as plentiful and representative of Florida fauna. And the gardens are rather quaint, evoking nostalgic thoughts of the days when tourism was on a smaller scale and less plastic.

The attraction is appealing to all ages if you try not to make comparisons with Busch Gardens or Disney World. There are no shows except for alligator feedings and otters who perform throughout the day.

Naples Nature Center

14th Avenue N. (off Goodlette-Frank Road) • (941) 262-0304

Hours - Year-round, Monday–Saturday, 9 a.m.–4:30 p.m.

Admission - $7.50 for adults, $2 for children ages 3–12. Admission is good for both the Naples Nature Center and Briggs Nature Center if visited within two weeks

Appeal by Age Group -

Pre-school ★★	Teens ★★★	Over 30 ★★★
Grade school ★★★★	Young Adults ★★★	Seniors ★★★

Touring Time - Average 3 hours; minimum 1 hour

Rainy-Day Touring - Recommended

Author's Rating - ★★★; hands-on learning about our natural world

Restaurants - No
Alcoholic beverages - No
Handicapped access - Yes
Wheelchair rental - No
Baby stroller rental - No
Lockers - No

Pet kennels - No **Rain check** - No

Private tours - Yes

Description and Comments These two nature centers are part of the Conservancy, a nonprofit organization dedicated to the preservation of Southwest Florida's fragile ecosystem. At the Briggs Nature Center, located on 12,700 acres in the Rookery Bay National Estuarine Research Reserve, you'll find a butterfly garden, an interpretive center where you can meet some estuary residents including fish and snakes, and a half-mile boardwalk through the reserve. Briggs is also the launching point for canoe and boat rides in Rookery Bay and for guided bird-watching and shelling on Key Island in the bay. Dolphins often breach the water and follow the boat, with egrets guarding the shoreline, and pelicans diving for mouthfuls of fish. Children must be 6 or older to go along on the afternoon shelling trip to Key Island. Cost is $35 per person; (941) 775-8569.

Briggs also offers Just for Kids programs, from an overnight camp to study nocturnal animals to a fun lesson in meteorology.

The Naples Nature Center in the heart of Naples, includes the Conservancy Museum of Natural History, where kids can touch a snake, count an alligator's teeth, and explore Southwest Florida's underwater world; a wildlife rehabilitation center where recuperating patients like owls, eagles, and hawks are on display; guided trail walks; guided electric boat tours through a mangrove forest; and canoe and kayak rentals for exploring the Gordon River.

The Teddy Bear Museum

2511 Pine Ridge Road, Naples, 2 miles west of I-75 (Exit 16) • (941) 598-2711

Hours - Wednesday–Saturday, 10 a.m.–5 p.m.; Sunday, 1–5 p.m.; closed Monday and Tuesday

Admission - Nonprofit; requested donations $7 for adults, $5 for seniors ages 60 and older, $3 for children ages 4–12

Appeal by Age Group -

Pre-school ★★★	Teens ★★	Over 30 ★★
Grade school ★★★	Young Adults ★★	Seniors ★★

Touring Time - Average 1 hour; minimum 30 minutes

Rainy-Day Touring - Recommended

Author's Rating - ★★; "beary" fun for little ones on a rainy afternoon

Restaurants - No **Alcoholic beverages** - No

Handicapped access - Yes **Wheelchair rental** - No

Baby stroller rental - No **Lockers** - No

Pet kennels - No **Rain check** - No
Private tours - Yes

Description and Comments This one-of-a-kind museum is extra fun for kids who love their stuffed bears. There are more than 3,500 teddy bears and "bearaphenalia" from around the world, miniature to giant, crystal to mohair. There's a reading "libeary" with books about bears and a replica of the Three Bears' house that kids love to explore. Saturday morning is storytime.

Family-Friendly Restaurants

The Tropical Palm Cafe

754 Neapolitan Way, Naples • (941) 649-6333

Meals served - Lunch and dinner
Cuisine - American
Entree range - $6–22
Kids menu - Yes
Reservations - Accepted
Payment - Visa, MC, D

The locals frequent this casual eatery for its home-cooked meals and reasonable prices. The menu is old-fashioned and diverse, from hot roast beef sandwiches to fresh sauteed catch of the day.

Marco Island

Just south of Naples, Marco Island is the largest of the Ten Thousand Islands, once the domain of the fierce Calusa Indians. It's been developed considerably over the past 30 years, with high-rises now lining the 3.5-mile-long, sugar-white beach. Families appreciate the informal, low-key ambience.

The Best Public Beach

Tigertail Public Beach on the northern end of Marco Island stretches 1.5 miles with a sandbar, known as Sand Dollar Island, that creates a shallow lagoon for young swimmers. There are rest rooms, showers, a children's playground, and volleyball nets. You can get impromptu windsurfing lessons or rent a pontoon boat for nature and shelling tours. They also rent cabanas, chairs, umbrellas, and other toys. And there's a beach restaurant serving hot dogs and sandwiches from 10 a.m. to 4 p.m. Parking is $3. The park is on Hernando Drive and is open daily dawn to dusk; (941) 353-0404.

Marco Island Trolley Tours

Kids can learn a little history from the humorous drivers on this casual tour of the island. You can jump on and off as often as you like as the trolley takes you past some of the earliest sites of cultural contact between Europeans and Native Americans. There are 11 historical markers, including the Cushing Archaeological site where 3,500-year-old Native American artifacts were unearthed. You'll also see burial mounds of the Calusa Indians who settled this island more than 6,000 years ago. Park at the Chamber of Commerce near the island's north bridge on Collier Boulevard. Cost is $16 for adults, $7 for children under age 12; (941) 394-1600.

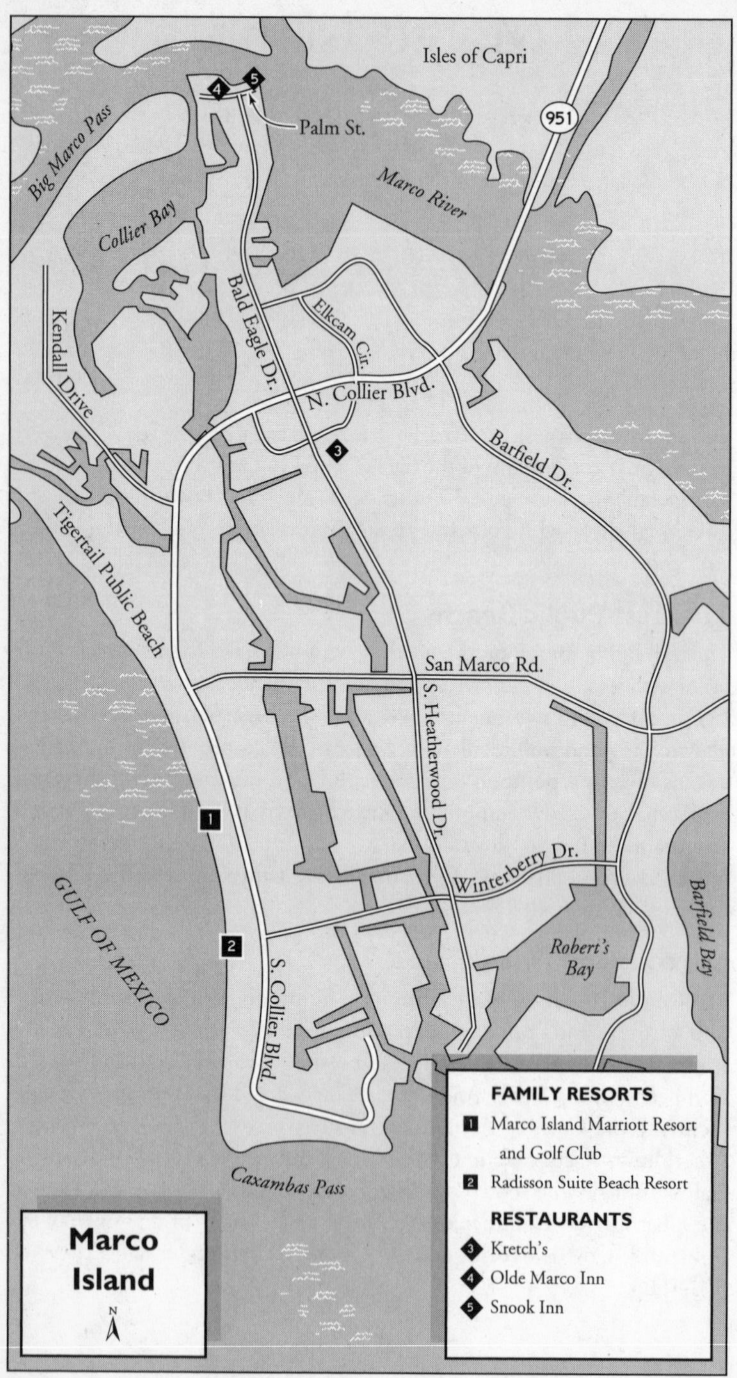
Isles of Capri
951
Palm St.
Big Marco Pass
Marco River
Collier Bay
Bald Eagle Dr.
Elkcam Cir.
Kendall Drive
N. Collier Blvd.
Barfield Dr.
Tigertail Public Beach
San Marco Rd.
S. Heatherwood Dr.
Winterberry Dr.
GULF OF MEXICO
Robert's Bay
Barfield Bay
S. Collier Blvd.
Caxambas Pass
Marco Island
N
FAMILY RESORTS
1 Marco Island Marriott Resort and Golf Club
2 Radisson Suite Beach Resort
RESTAURANTS
3 Kretch's
4 Olde Marco Inn
5 Snook Inn

Family Resorts

Marco Island Marriott Resort and Golf Club

400 S. Collier Boulevard, Marco Island • (941) 394-2511 or (800) 438-4373 fax (941) 642-2672 • www.marriottresort.com

You might be on a tropical island, but it sure isn't deserted. This hotel offers 18 holes of golf, tennis, three swimming pools, water sports, and nearby eco-tourism adventures. The award-winning Kids Klub provides themed activities 10 a.m.–3 p.m. for ages 5–12. The hotel schedules field trips in the summertime to the Everglades for $35 per child. There are also movies and pizza available for children and many free children's activities.

The resort has 724 rooms and 62 suites, and every room has a microwave, coffeemaker, refrigerator, toaster, iron, and ironing board. Rates start at $189 in the summer, $245 in the winter.

Radisson Suite Beach Resort

600 S. Collier Boulevard, Marco Island • (941) 394-4100 or (800) 333-3333 (U.S. & Canada) • fax (941) 394-0419 • www.radisson.com

The Radisson starts with a special registration just for kids, and welcomes 3–10-year-olds to the Fun Factory, a supervised program with games, arts and crafts, and other activities. The hotel is so kid friendly that it's created three human-size mascots: Scooter the turtle, Bubbles the dolphin, and Toby the manatee.

The Fun Factory is packed with themed activities geared toward recreation, the environment, and education for ages 4–11. Specially trained counselors lead beach walks, skits, scavenger hunts, even language learning. All themes teach about Florida's ecological treasures. Cost is $22 per half-day or evening session, including lunch, snack, or dinner, or $40 for the whole day.

On the beach there are boogie boards, aquabikes, and personal watercraft for rent. The hotel also has a swimming pool, a tiki bar, two tennis courts, a basketball court, and a game room.

The Radisson has 267 accommodations, ranging from a room to one- and two-bedroom units. Rooms have microwaves, coffeemakers, and refrigerators; the others have fully equipped kitchens. Free breakfast for children under age 12. Rates start at $179 per night in summer and $239 per night in winter. Pizza Hut delivers.

Family-Friendly Restaurants

Kretch's

527 Bald Eagle Drive, Marco Island • (941) 394-3433

Meals served - Lunch, Monday–Friday; dinner, Monday–Saturday

Cuisine - Seafood and Mexican

Entree range - Lunch, $7–12.25; dinner, $7–24

Kids menu - Yes

Reservations - Recommended in the winter

Payment - Visa, MC, D

Decadent sauces accompany the fresh seafood, or you can go local with great grilled fish. The prime rib is also recommended. "Mexican Friday" lunches are popular, with cheap spicy eats like tacos and burritos.

Olde Marco Inn

100 Palm Street, Marco Island • (941) 394-3131

Meals served - Dinner

Cuisine - American

Entree range - $12.95–25.95

Kids menu - No, but kids meals are half price

Reservations - Accepted

Payment - All major credit cards accepted

Though it's a little pricey, the locals favor Olde Marco for fresh seafood and an interesting selection of international dishes from Wiener schnitzel and sauerbraten to crisp roast duckling and veal Madagascar. Kids love their Southern fried chicken with honey.

Snook Inn

1215 Bald Eagle Drive, Marco Island • (941) 394-3313

Meals served - Lunch and dinner

Cuisine - Seafood

Entree range - $9–27

Kids menu - Yes

Reservations - Not accepted

Payment - All major credit cards accepted

On the Marco River, the inn has myriad seafood choices, all fresh and prepared every way imaginable. You can even bring your own catch and they'll cook it for you with all the trimmings for $13. Save room for a slice of the Sara Lee Milky Way Pie.

Everglades City

This is the place to come for airboat rides and jungle boat tours, and it is the only entrance to Everglades National Park on the west coast of Florida. The historical centerpiece of Everglades City is the Rod and Gun Club, a grand Southern lodge built in 1840 by fur traders that's now a 17-room inn with a restaurant where we recommend a stop for lunch. The club has a wide veranda where families can sit in the same surroundings that once hosted millionaires and dignitaries such as President Franklin D. Roosevelt.

On the Water

The following are some ways to get out on the water:

Everglades National Park Boat Tours This tour docks in the Everglades National Park on the Chokoloskee Causeway, SR 29. There are 1½-hour guided tours with a naturalist through the Ten Thousand Islands starting every 30 minutes, 9 a.m.–4:30 p.m. every day. Cost is $16 for adults, $8 for children ages 6–12, free for ages 5 and under. Canoe rentals are also available; (941) 695-2591 or (800) 445-7724.

North American Canoe Tours The Harraden family operates tours from December–March. Canoe rentals are $25 a day; kayak rentals start at $45 a day. Guides also are available from $40 to $400 a day (lunch included). 107 Camelia Street, Everglades City; (941) 695-4666; www.evergladesadventures.com.

Jungle Erv's Airboat World Jungle Erv's is another old-time airboat ride, open daily 9 a.m.–5 p.m. The boats depart every hour from 11 a.m. until 4 p.m. Large airboat tours lasting half an hour are $17.50 for adults, $8 for children under age 10. Private hour-long rides in smaller airboats are $30 for adults, $20 for children under age 10. Safari rides on pontoon boats are $17.50 for adults, $8 for children under age 10. A package price covers all three excursions at $40 for adults and $30 for children. Located in Everglades City just 2 miles south of US 41 on SR 29; (941) 695-2805.

Wooten's Everglades Adventures Wooten's started offering airboat rides in 1953 and today is one of the oldest companies offering excursions. They're open every day from 9 a.m. until 4:30 p.m. Airboat and swamp buggy rides are $16; a trip through their animal sanctuary is $8, and you'll see more than 350 alligators, crocodiles, panthers, jaguars, sea turtles, otters, and snakes. Private airboat tours are $35 per person. Since airboats are not allowed in Everglades National Park or other nearby federal preserves, Wooten's traverses the nearby areas. Wooten's is on US 41; (941) 695-2781.

A Word about Airboat Rides

These noisy, motorized contraptions are illegal inside the national park. And though the excursions may not be ecologically correct—the boats are big, extremely noisy, and some say, destructive to the environment—a ride on one sure is fun.

Your driver will often try to locate some alligators, usually small specimens 2–3 feet in length.

Airboats are so incredibly loud that customers are given wads of cotton to stuff in their ears. You need them. Very small children may be frightened by the noise.

Family-Friendly Restaurants

Rod and Gun Club

200 Broadway, Everglades City • (941) 695-2101

Meals served - Lunch and dinner

Cuisine - American

Entree range - $7–30

Reservations - Not necessary

Payment - No credit cards

This 130-year-old historic lodge caters mostly to fishermen, but kids are awed by the wildlife "trophies"—giant tarpon, turtles, wild hogs, bears, and more—displayed all over the place. The movie *Gone Fishin'* with Joe Pesci and Danny Glover was filmed here. The restaurant is a great stop after a day in the Everglades, with fresh seafood (there's always grouper on the menu, and Southern-fried is the best), lobster salad, stone crabs, and frog legs. The tart Key lime pie is the real thing.

Everglades National Park

To many people who have never been here—or have only driven through—the Everglades may seem to be nothing to get excited about. It looks like just a broad expanse of grass, water, and trees.

In other words, just another swamp.

They're wrong. The Everglades is, in fact, the last remaining subtropical wilderness in the United States. This huge expanse of water, sawgrass, clumps of trees called "hammocks," and pockets of tropical jungle also is an unparalleled wildlife sanctuary containing an astounding variety of mammals, reptiles, birds, and fish. Our advice: Folks who enjoy the outdoors and thrill to seeing wildlife in its natural environment should put the Everglades on their "A" list during a visit to South Florida.

Admittedly, the Everglades doesn't look like very much when viewed through a car window: seemingly endless expanses of grass and water fade into the distance, with only an occasional clump of trees to break the monotony.

I Spy

To help your children understand just how much wildlife there is in the Everglades, try playing a game to see how many animals your kids can spot. At first there may not be many, until you point out they're hidden in the grass, trees, and water. Point out what happens when an insect gets caught in a silvery spider web, or look for tiny, colorful snails on tree branches and leaves. Observe turtles as they climb slowly over rocks, past busy ants and beetles. There is myriad life all around.

These apparently empty spaces, however, are deceiving. The landscape is teeming with life and activity. The Everglades is a complex, evolving ecosystem that is the result of a unique combination of climate, topography, and vegetation. To experience the Everglades—and to find out what's so special about it—you've got to get out of your car.

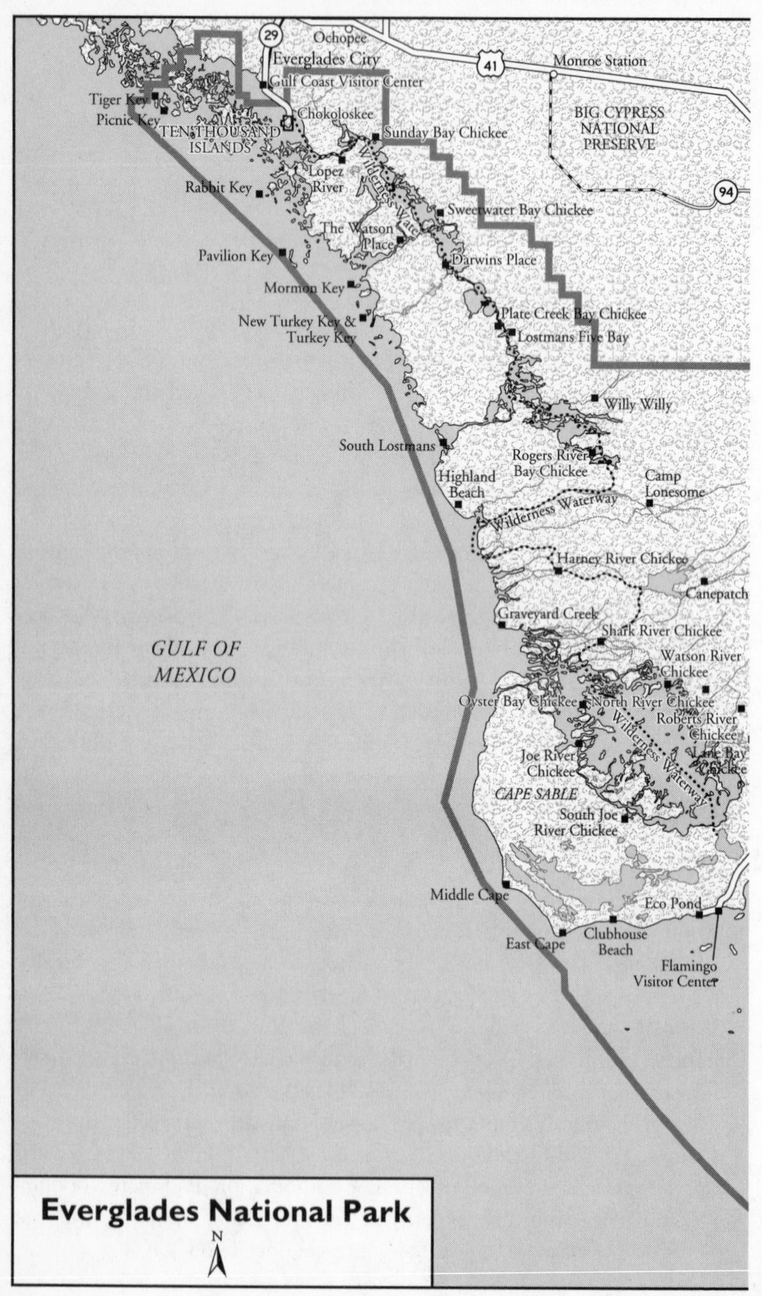

29
Ochopee
Everglades City
41
Monroe Station
Gulf Coast Visitor Center
Tiger Key
Picnic Key
Chokoloskee
TEN THOUSAND ISLANDS
Sunday Bay Chickee
BIG CYPRESS NATIONAL PRESERVE
Lopez River
Rabbit Key
Wilderness Waterway
94
Sweetwater Bay Chickee
The Watson Place
Pavilion Key
Darwins Place
Mormon Key
New Turkey Key & Turkey Key
Plate Creek Bay Chickee
Lostmans Five Bay
Willy Willy
South Lostmans
Rogers River Bay Chickee
Highland Beach
Camp Lonesome
Wilderness Waterway
Harney River Chickee
Canepatch
Graveyard Creek
Shark River Chickee
GULF OF MEXICO
Watson River Chickee
Oyster Bay Chickee
North River Chickee
Roberts River Chickee
Wilderness Waterway
Joe River Chickee
Lane Bay Chickee
CAPE SABLE
South Joe River Chickee
Middle Cape
Eco Pond
East Cape
Clubhouse Beach
Flamingo Visitor Center
Everglades National Park
N

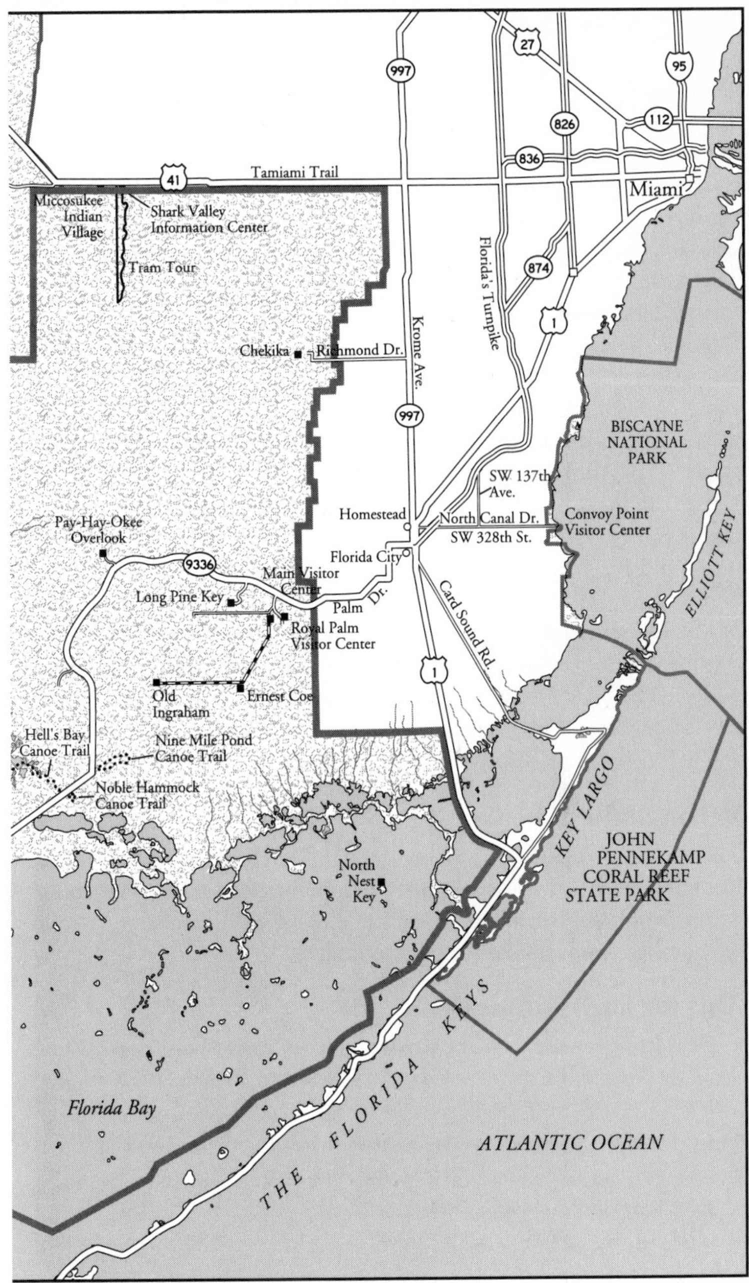

27
997
95
826
112
836
41
Tamiami Trail
Miami
Miccosukee Indian Village
Shark Valley Information Center
Tram Tour
874
Florida's Turnpike
Krome Ave.
1
Chekika
Richmond Dr.
997
BISCAYNE NATIONAL PARK
SW 137th Ave.
Homestead
North Canal Dr.
SW 328th St.
Convoy Point Visitor Center
ELLIOTT KEY
Pay-Hay-Okee Overlook
9336
Florida City
Main Visitor Center
Long Pine Key
Palm Dr.
Royal Palm Visitor Center
Card Sound Rd.
1
Old Ingraham
Ernest Coe
Hell's Bay Canoe Trail
Nine Mile Pond Canoe Trail
Noble Hammock Canoe Trail
KEY LARGO
JOHN PENNEKAMP CORAL REEF STATE PARK
North Nest Key
Florida Bay
THE FLORIDA KEYS
ATLANTIC OCEAN

To appreciate the Everglades, it also helps to understand what's going on here. This huge expanse of grass and water is, in fact, a vast, slow-moving, shallow river that's flowing over land nearly as flat as a pool table. For eons, the overflow of Lake Okeechobee to the north has moved slowly south over this land into Florida Bay, nourishing millions of acres of sawgrass as the water ebbs and flows throughout the year.

The Everglades used to encompass everything south of Lake Okeechobee—including Miami—but encroaching civilization has pushed its perimeter back until today the Everglades is only a fraction of its former size. Today's Everglades National Park makes up about one-seventh of what's left of the Everglades, and it's the only portion of the ecosystem that's federally protected.

While the Everglades is subtle and doesn't easily give up its charms to short-term visitors, day-trippers still gain an appreciation of the area and enjoy a rewarding visit—at least during the winter months, when the mosquito population is down; we don't recommend visiting the Everglades from April through October when mosquitoes and other biting insects can make a visit unbearable. But even in the winter, insect repellent is essential. Another reason to visit in the winter is that you'll see more wildlife. Winter is the dry season, and a vast array of animals and birds congregate near the remaining water.

The varied habitats provide some of the finest wildlife viewing on the continent, best seen by hiking, biking, canoeing, or taking a guided tram or boat. There are at least 14 endangered species living here, including the Florida panther, southern bald eagle, West Indian manatee, wood stork, and peregrine falcon. More than 400 bird species have been identified.

When Should We Go?

The best time to visit is November through March, when it's dry and the low water levels attract wading birds and their predators. The wet season is June to November, when the mosquitoes are peskier, migratory birds are not there, and wildlife is harder to find.

Tips for an Optimum Visit

- Don't forget mosquito repellent, hats, and sunscreen. Mosquitoes and biting flies can be severe during the summer months, so wear long-sleeved clothing and avoid grassy areas and shady places where mosquitoes can hide.
- Get out of the car, even if it's just for a walk, or your kids will get bored.
- Bring binoculars or rent them at the visitors center. While you're there, pick up guide books that explain the natural beauty.
- Take a boat ride with a guide.
- Take the tram tour.

- Better yet, rent a bike in cool weather (else the mosquitoes can be unbearable).
- Take bottles of water and snacks along.
- Stop at the Royal Palm Visitor Center, where there are plenty of hands-on activities.
- Never approach an alligator closer than 15 feet; they can easily outrun you. And do not feed alligators or any other wild animal. Elevated boardwalks, like Anhinga Trail, offer good opportunities to view gators from a safe distance. Never try to catch baby gators (which are undeniably cute) because mother gators are extremely protective of their young.

Everglades City

The Everglades City entrance is best if you're planning to explore the park by boat. The visitors center is open daily 8:30 a.m.–4:30 p.m., staffed intermittently during the summer. Entrance fee to the park is $8.

Daily boat tours into the mangrove estuary and Ten Thousand Islands offer views of a unique environment and its wildlife. Schedules, tickets, and information are available at the visitors center or by calling (941) 695-3311.

You can rent canoes and kayaks and venture into Chokoloskee Bay for a mosquito-free experience and a chance to glimpse wildlife; canoes can be rented at the visitors center.

Shark Valley

If a day trip to Shark Valley is your only visit to the Everglades, our advice is to take the 2-hour, motorized tram that leaves from the Shark Valley parking lot daily, on the hour, from 9 a.m. to 4 p.m. The cost is $11 for adults, $10 for seniors, and $6 for children under age 12. Entrance fee to the park is $8 per car. Plan to arrive early because the parking lot is small and this is a popular visitor destination. To reserve a spot, call (305) 221-8455 or (305) 221-8776.

Soon after the open-air tram leaves the visitors center, you'll discover what all the excitement is about as you view an incredible number of birds, alligators resting beside the narrow road, and a beautiful landscape. Well-informed and enthusiastic guides do a good job of explaining the unique topography and pointing out the unusual fauna. The tram stops often to let visitors view and photograph the wildlife and terrain.

The tram follows a 15-mile paved loop road. At the halfway point, visitors disembark at an observation tower for one of the best views in south Florida: a 360°, 18-mile panorama of the Everglades. Rest rooms, vending machines, and water fountains are also available at the 20-minute stop.

Rental Bikes and Binoculars

Another option when visiting Shark Valley is to rent a bicycle at the visitors center. Single-speed bikes rent for $4.75 an hour between 8:30 a.m.

and 3 p.m.; bikes must be returned by 4 p.m. And remember to bring binoculars when you visit; if you forget, rent a pair at the visitors center; (305) 221-8455.

An Indian Village

The Miccosukee Indians are descendants of Seminole Indians who retreated into the Everglades to escape forced resettlement during the nineteenth century. They lived on hammocks in open-sided "chickees"—thatched-roof huts built from cypress—and hunted and fished the Everglades by canoe. They also learned how to handle alligators.

At the Miccosukee Indian Village on Route SR 41 a mile or so west of the Shark Valley entrance to the Everglades National Park, alligators are the stars of the show—and if this is your only opportunity to visit the Everglades, this is your chance to see an alligator do more than snooze in the sun. Alligator wrestling exhibitions are offered at 11 a.m. and 12:30, 1:30, 2:30, and 3 p.m.; admission to the attraction is $5 for adults and $3.50 for children ages 4–12. Airboat rides are $10 per person, daily, 8:30 a.m.–5 p.m. For more information call (305) 223-8380.

In addition to seeing Miccosukee Indians put a live gator through its paces, you'll get a peek at Miccosukee culture and life on a tour of the "village" (a small collection of open-air chickees and alligator pens) and a small museum. Lots of crafts and tacky souvenirs also are offered for sale.

The Royal Palm Visitor Center

Another option, for day-trippers to Everglades National Park and folks who want to spend a few days in the Everglades, starts south of Miami near Florida City at the Royal Palm Visitor Center, located at the park's main entrance. To get there, take SR 9336 from US 1 at Homestead for 10 miles to the gate.

While this entrance is a longer drive for most visitors, it's worth the time and effort. You can pick up free brochures, view educational displays, obtain information on boat tours and canoe rentals, and get a map to the many trails that intersect with the 38-mile main road that leads to Flamingo.

While it's a stretch for day-trippers, Flamingo is the park's largest visitor complex, featuring a motel, restaurant, a small grocery store, campgrounds, boat tours, a marina, and a visitors center; (305) 242-7700.

Flamingo

The end of the road is the village of Flamingo, which offers boat rides on Florida Bay, canoe rentals, birding cruises, backcountry boat excursions, a restaurant, a marina, and the only overnight sleeping facilities in the park (outside of camping). If you've got the time and interest, it's a great place for an extended visit.

If you stay the night, plan to take a sunset cruise on the *Bald Eagle,* a large pontoon boat that cruises Florida Bay for 90 minutes several times a day. The views of the bay, dense mangrove forests, and the shoreline are spectacular.

The sight-seeing tour of the bay is $12 for adults, $6 for children ages 6–12. Other services visitors can use to explore the Flamingo area include canoe rentals and bike rentals; (941) 695-3101.

Easy Walks

The two-lane road also serves as the jumping-off point for short walking explorations into the Everglades. This end of the park, by the way, is a better destination for families who prefer walking and exploring on their own over a guided tram tour.

Anhinga Trail, which begins just behind the Royal Palm Visitor Center, is a half-mile long, about 30 minutes round-trip. It is named for a large black fishing bird. Children especially enjoy this trail, but remind them that the animals will be frightened by loud noises and will go into hiding if alarmed. A paved road leads to the boardwalk through the sawgrass marsh, where you might spot alligators, turtles, river otters, herons, and egrets.

Gumbo Limbo Trail, 3 miles from Flamingo entrance and right next to Anhinga Trail, is named for the gumbo limbo tree. Less than a half-mile, it takes 30 minutes round-trip through a shaded and junglelike hammock of royal palms, gumbo limbo trees, lush ferns, and orchids. You'll encounter lots of mosquitoes, lizards, snails, tree frogs, and birds, as well as orchids, ferns, and bromeliads.

Pa-Hay-Okee Trail, 11 miles from the main entrance, is a perfect family trail. A quarter-mile-long boardwalk with interpretive signs, a walk takes only 15–30 minutes round-trip. An observation tower at the end of the boardwalk offers a great view of the Everglades.

Mahogany Hammock Trail, 18 miles from the main entrance, has an elevated boardwalk and a half-mile trail, 30 minutes round-trip through subtropical hardwood forest with the largest living mahogany tree in the United States. This trail is lush and junglelike—owls, frogs, insects, small birds, and bald eagles may be sighted.

West Lake Trail, 29 miles from main entrance is a quarter-mile-long boardwalk, less than 30 minutes round-trip, through a forest of red, white, black, and buttonwood mangroves beside a brackish lake. This mangrove forest is a birthplace for sea life such as shrimp, spiny lobsters, stone crabs, snapper, and mullet. You'll see ducks in winter, alligators, and wading birds. Interpretive signs are placed along the way.

Ranger programs are available year-round, but schedules are limited in summer months. Call ahead for current schedules; (305) 242-7730. Admission to Everglades National Park is $10 per vehicle, $5 bike or on foot. The following tours are included in the park admission:

- **Glade Glimpses**, a walking tour on Anhinga Trail pointing out flora and fauna and a discussion of issues affecting the Everglades; daily, 1:30 p.m.
- **Anhinga Ambles,** a walk held daily on the Anhinga Trail at 10:30 a.m. and 1:30 and 4 p.m.
- **Slough Slog** in Shark Valley, an occasional program that involves wading through the muck and stopping at an alligator hole. Lace-up shoes and long pants are required; (305) 221-8776.

Family Resorts

Flamingo Lodge, Marina, and Outpost Resort

1 Flamingo Lodge Highway, Flamingo • (941) 695-3101 • fax (941) 695-3921
www.flamingolodge.com

Flamingo Lodge is 38 miles inside the main entrance of Everglades National Park, and you can't get any closer to wildlife than this and still have air conditioning. It's the only resort in the park, and it's a great place for families who don't mind roughing it in rustic accommodations. There are 24 cottages, a swimming pool, a restaurant that is open November to May, a quick-service restaurant offering pizzas and sandwiches year-round, and a small grocery store nearby. Cottages have small kitchens with dishes and flatware and a coffeemaker (but no TV). There are no organized kids programs, but it's a great place to create your own fun, with everything from binoculars to fishing poles for rent. You can ask for a guided tour on Florida Bay and the backcountry, in either a canoe or motorboat. Beware, the horseflies are vicious; take lots of insect repellent.

Rooms start at $59 in the summer, $95 in winter (December 15–March 31); cottages at $99 in the summer, $135 in winter.

Houseboat Rentals

At Flamingo Lodge Marina you can step on board with just your food and drinking water and cruise the Everglades without worrying about being home by dark. No boating experience is necessary, as the boats cruise up to only 6 mph. There are two types available: a 40-foot pontoon with a head, shower bathroom, and small kitchen for $275 a night in May, September, and October (not air-conditioned), or an air-conditioned Gibson fiberglass boat that sleeps six with a head, shower, and electric stove for $525 for two nights in May, September, and October, $575 November–April; (941) 695-3101; www.flamingolodge.com.

Part Seven

Southeast Florida

Most families travel to South Florida for the miles of clean ocean beaches, the sophistication of Palm Beach and Miami, and the laid-back ambience of the Florida Keys.

Starting just south of Fort Pierce, families can spend the day on miles of wide beaches, many with unusual geographical phenomena, like Blowing Rock Preserve on Jupiter Island, where the surging waves at high tide erupt through the blowholes, sending plumes of water high into the air. And there are tales of sunken treasure in the shallow waters off Hutchinson Island, where everyone likes to look for the gold, silver, gems, and artifacts from a ten-ship Spanish fleet that was sunk during a 1715 hurricane.

Farther south, Palm Beach County, best known as a playground for the rich and famous, offers plenty of family-oriented activities, from historical sightseeing to exploring Indian culture to man-made attractions like Lion Country Safari.

On down the coast, Greater Ft. Lauderdale is known as the "Venice of America," with 300 miles of navigable inland waterways and 40,000 resident yachts. Families can enjoy water taxi rides to various entertainment venues or stroll along the meandering Riverwalk to many downtown cultural sites.

For families looking for a balance of peace and quiet and high-energy action, Miami offers the best of both worlds, from the serenity of the magnificent Fairchild Tropical Gardens to the delightful, flamingo-colored Bayside Marketplace—and a little of everything in between. Parrot Jungle, Monkey Jungle, the Seaquarium, MetroZoo...there's no shortage of family-friendly activities in this world-class city.

From there it's south to the Florida Keys. With parks and special attractions all along the way as you island hop down to Key West along scenic US 1. Swim with dolphins, camp beside the ocean, and soak in the ambience of this tiny chain of islands.

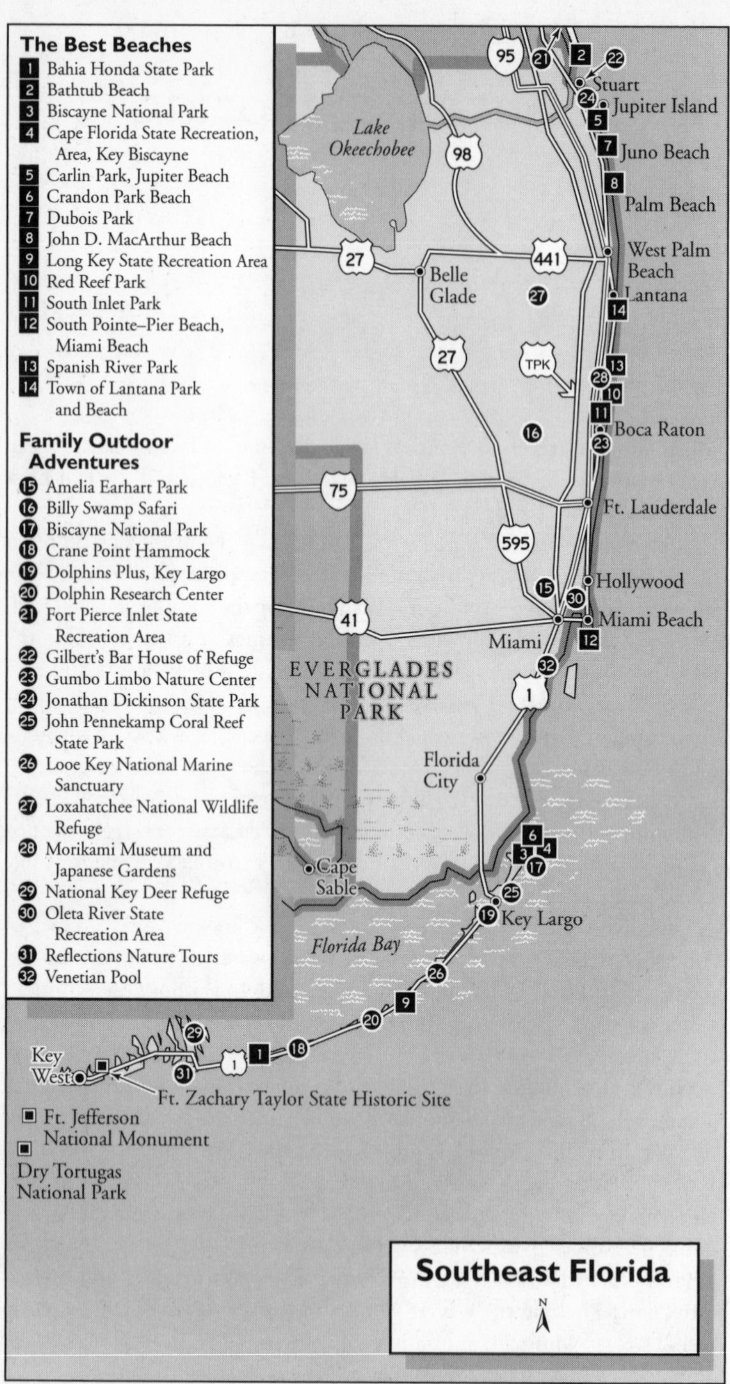
The Best Beaches
1 Bahia Honda State Park
2 Bathtub Beach
3 Biscayne National Park
4 Cape Florida State Recreation, Area, Key Biscayne
5 Carlin Park, Jupiter Beach
6 Crandon Park Beach
7 Dubois Park
8 John D. MacArthur Beach
9 Long Key State Recreation Area
10 Red Reef Park
11 South Inlet Park
12 South Pointe–Pier Beach, Miami Beach
13 Spanish River Park
14 Town of Lantana Park and Beach
Family Outdoor Adventures
15 Amelia Earhart Park
16 Billy Swamp Safari
17 Biscayne National Park
18 Crane Point Hammock
19 Dolphins Plus, Key Largo
20 Dolphin Research Center
21 Fort Pierce Inlet State Recreation Area
22 Gilbert's Bar House of Refuge
23 Gumbo Limbo Nature Center
24 Jonathan Dickinson State Park
25 John Pennekamp Coral Reef State Park
26 Looe Key National Marine Sanctuary
27 Loxahatchee National Wildlife Refuge
28 Morikami Museum and Japanese Gardens
29 National Key Deer Refuge
30 Oleta River State Recreation Area
31 Reflections Nature Tours
32 Venetian Pool
Lake Okeechobee
Stuart
Jupiter Island
Juno Beach
Palm Beach
West Palm Beach
Lantana
Belle Glade
Boca Raton
Ft. Lauderdale
Hollywood
Miami Beach
Miami
EVERGLADES NATIONAL PARK
Florida City
Cape Sable
Key Largo
Florida Bay
Key West
Ft. Zachary Taylor State Historic Site
Ft. Jefferson National Monument
Dry Tortugas National Park
95
98
27
441
TPK
75
595
41
1
Southeast Florida
N

Getting There

By Plane Palm Beach International Airport, (561) 471-7400, 3 miles west of West Palm Beach; Ft. Lauderdale–Hollywood International Airport, 4 miles south of Ft. Lauderdale, (954) 359-6100; Miami International Airport, 5 miles northwest of Miami, (305) 876-7077; Key West International Airport, southeast corner of the island, (305) 296-7223; Marathon Airport, Marathon at mile marker (MM) 52, (305) 743-2155. Witham Field, a mile southeast of Sturat (561) 287-6636.

By Train Amtrak makes several stops in South Florida, including West Palm Beach, Ft. Lauderdale, and Miami; (800) USA-RAIL; www.amtrak.com.

By Car I-95 runs north-south all the way from Maine to Miami; from the northwest, I-75 leads to Miami; from Central Florida, the Florida Turnpike is convenient.

How to Get Information before You Go

Palm Beach County Convention and Visitors Bureau, 1555 Palm Beach Lakes Boulevard, Suite 204, West Palm Beach 33401; (561) 223-3000 or (800) 833-5733 (U.S. & Canada); www.palmbeachfl.com.

Greater Ft. Lauderdale Convention and Visitors Bureau, 1850 Eller Drive, Suite 303, Ft. Lauderdale 33316; (954) 765-4466 or (800) 22-SUNNY (U.S. & Canada); www.sunny.org.

Greater Miami and the Beaches Hotel Association, 407 Lincoln Road, Suite 10G, Miami Beach 33139; (305) 531-3553 or (800) SEE-MIAMI; www.gmbha.org.

Greater Miami Convention and Visitors Bureau, 701 Brickell Avenue, Suite 2700, Miami 33131; (305) 539-3000 or (800) 933-8448 (Florida & U.S.); www.tropicoolmiami.com.

The Florida Keys and Key West, P.O. Box 866, Key West 33041-0866; (305) 296-1552 or (800) FLA-KEYS (U.S. & Canada); www.fla-keys.com.

The Best Beaches

Bahia Honda State Park Powdery, white sand is a surprise in the Florida Keys. This 524-acre park also has excellent swimming in Florida Bay (but no lifeguards) and is a great spot for hiking, birdwatching, and snorkeling. The crowds can be unbearable; last year more than 400,000 day visitors stopped at Bahia Honda. It's Florida's southernmost state park and has a natural environment found nowhere else in the continental United States, hosting many plants and animals of Caribbean origin and several rare and unusual plants, like the endangered small-flowered lily thorn. It's pretty tough to get one of the 80 spots in three popular campgrounds ($19) or one of the eight cabins, complete with linens, kitchenettes, and cooking utensils—so book early. 36850 Overseas Highway, MM 37.5, Big Pine Key; for reservations call (305) 872-2353; for other information call (305) 872-3897.

♥ **Bathtub Beach** Located on Hutchinson Island, this beach has reef-protected swimming for children, and dune and river walks perfect for barefoot exploring. There are showers and rest rooms, and lifeguards are on duty in peak seasons. The park is open dawn to dusk. To get there, cross the Intracoastal Waterway on Ocean Boulevard and turn right onto Mac-Arthur Boulevard. The beach is about 1 mile ahead.

♥ **Biscayne National Park** The nation's largest aquatic park, Biscayne is the nearest place to Miami with reefs close enough to the surface for snorkelers to enjoy. Unlike scuba diving, which requires participants to be certified before they can dive, the requirements for snorkeling are minimal. You only need the ability to swim and a desire to see this subtropical paradise with brilliantly colored tropical fish. If you don't want to get wet, take the glass-bottom boat ride.

Snorkeling trips last 3 hours (2 hours travel, 1 hour exploring the reef) and leave daily at 1:30 p.m., weather permitting; the cost is $35 per person and includes all the equipment you need. The Convoy Visitor Center, the only part of the park accessible by car, is about 25 miles south of Miami and 6 miles east of US 1 and Homestead. From the Florida Turnpike, take SW 328th Street to the park entrance on the left; call (305) 230-1100 to make reservations.

♥ **Cape Florida State Recreation Area, Key Biscayne** This beach is less crowded than Miami Beach, with 5 miles of sand and more of a laid-back family atmosphere. It's a great place for picnics, with plenty of tables in the shade. To get there, take Rickenbacker Causeway ($1 toll). Head for the southern tip of Key Biscayne. There's a lighthouse to explore (the oldest building in South Florida); bikes, sailboats, kayaks, jet skis, and water toys are for rent. Lifeguards are on duty. There's even a restaurant serving delicious Cuban food. Admission is $4 per car; open daily, 8 a.m.–sunset. Cape Florida State Recreation Area, 1200 Crandon Boulevard; (305) 361-5811.

Carlin Park, Jupiter Beach. Carlin is a good family beach, with hard-packed sand for walking and a park with barbecue grills and picnic tables. Lifeguards are on duty. Enter off AIA at 1375 Jupiter Beach Road just north of SR 706; (561) 966-6600.

♥ **Crandon Park Beach** Popular with families, Crandon has 4 miless of beach shaded by palms and sea grapes, with restaurants nearby and plenty of parking ($4 per vehicle). An offshore sandbar protects swimmers from crashing surf, and lifeguards are on patrol. 4000 N. Crandon Park Boulevard, Key Biscayne; (305) 361-5421.

Dubois Park Dubois is located where Jupiter Inlet meets the ocean. The park is perfect for families, with shallow waters for young swimmers, a short fishing pier, and barbecue grills and picnic tables under the shade trees. There are lifeguards on weekends and holidays only. The Dubois Pioneer Home is still there, open to the public. The park is about a mile south of the junction of US 1 and A1A on DuBois Road; (561) 966-6600.

♥ **John D. MacArthur Beach** This state park covers much of Singer Island, a barrier island just north of Palm Beach. A long stretch of white sand is great for walking and swimming; shell collecting and snorkeling are popular. There are no lifeguards. William T. Kirby Nature Center is open Wednesday–Sunday, 9 a.m.–5 p.m; $3.25 per car. Located just under 3 miles south of the intersection of US 1 and PGA Boulevard on A1A; (561) 624-6950.

Long Key State Recreation Area This park offers canoe rentals, camping, and another excuse to get out of the car and unwind. Two nature trails on boardwalks offer views of mangrove forests and tropical hammocks. Long Key is in the Middle Keys, with 60 campsites ($17) on the water. Guided nature walks and lecture programs are conducted by park rangers. Dogs on leashes are allowed off the beach. The park is at MM 67.5, Long Key; (305) 664-4815.

♥ **Red Reef Park** Go early in the morning to beat the crowds (the park opens at 8 a.m.) to this 67-acre oceanfront park in Boca Raton, where your kids can try snorkeling around the rocks and reefs just off the beach in about 2–6 feet of water. Lifeguards are there year-round, and there's room for swimming away from the snorkelers. The small picnic area has grills, tables, and rest rooms. 1400 N. Florida A1A, a half-mile north of Palmetto Park Road; (800) 833-5733.

South Inlet Park The protected swimming area with lifeguards is nice for younger children; there's also a beach boardwalk, picnic tables, barbecue grills, rest rooms, and outdoor showers. Parking is $10. A1A between Ponce de Leon and DeSoto Roads (Boca Inlet); (561) 966-6600.

South Pointe–Pier Beach, Miami Beach This 10-mile-long strip of sand has plenty of nice public beaches that have lifeguards, rest rooms, and metered parking. It can get pretty crowded, but as you head north the crowds thin out. For a nice stroll, there's a 1.5-mile wooden boardwalk from 21st to 46th Streets; (800) 933-8448.

Spanish River Park This is the pride of Boca Raton and a great family spot on the ocean—there's even a grassy area for picnics (with five covered shelters) that includes grills, rest rooms, and a 40-foot observation tower. Lifeguards are on duty. Tunnels under A1A lead to nature trails. North Ocean Boulevard (A1A), 2 miles north of Palmetto Park Road, Boca Raton.

Town of Lantana Park and Beach Stop here for swimming, fishing, snorkeling, and sunbathing, with a lifeguard on duty. There are picnic tables, a restaurant, volleyball, and a children's area. Parking is metered, with a spacious lot. The park is located at Ocean Avenue and A1A in the town of Lantana; (561) 966-6600.

Family Outdoor Adventures

Amelia Earhart Park You can bring a picnic and spend the day at this kid-friendly park, complete with playground, a private island for kids to swing to and tunnel around, and a big red barn full of cows, geese, and goats, even ponies that kids can ride. Try horseshoes or watch sugarcane processing and other old-fashioned activities. Parking is $4. Open daily, 9 a.m.–sunset. 401 E. 65th Street, Hialeah; (305) 685-8389. Take I-95 north from Miami to the NW 103rd Street exit; go west on East Fourth Avenue and turn right.

Billy Swamp Safari. Eco-tours to the land where the legendary Seminoles retreated from the Seminole Wars and settled on the edge of the Everglades. Choose from an hour-long swamp buggy tour ($20 for adults, $18 for seniors, $10 for children ages 6–12) or an airboat ride ($12 per person); both operate daily. You also can visit an Indian village and hear alligator and snake lectures ($8 adult, $4 children). If you want to spend the night, the Seminole Camping Village on the edge of the Everglades has native-style "chickees," or thatched huts, that can comfortably sleep two adults for $40 each and a child (free). Billy Swamp Safari is between Naples and Ft. Lauderdale off I-75 (Exit 14, then north 19 miles to the park entrance); (800) 949-6101.

Biscayne National Park The nation's largest aquatic park covers 181,500 acres of underwater reefs and islands and is the closest coral reef snorkeling to Miami. Clear blue water, a bright yellow sun, dark green woodlands, coral reefs, and islands combine to create a subtropical paradise only an hour or so from hectic Miami. Unlike most parks, however, Biscayne is dominated by water—and to enjoy it requires renting a canoe or taking a boat excursion. The top attraction for most folks is snorkeling the coral reefs, or you can view them by glass-bottom boat if you prefer. You'll see brilliantly colored tropical fish such as stoplight parrotfish and finger garlic sponge, drenched in sunlight. A reef explorer outfitted in mask, snorkel, flippers, and a life vest can spend hours drifting lazily in the water above the reefs while watching a procession of astounding marine life.

Because the park is almost completely underwater, visitors are at the mercy of the weather; tours and canoe rentals are sometimes canceled in windy conditions. If the air is cold, snorkelers can rent wet suits. Boat schedules change seasonally, so it's always a good idea to call first. The park is open daily, 8 a.m.–5 p.m. Glass-bottom boat tours are $22 for adults, $14 for children under age 12; snorkeling is $32 per person, and you need reservations; canoe rentals are $10 an hour. The Convoy Point

Visitor Center, the only part of the park accessible by car, is about 25 miles south of Miami and 6 miles east of US 1 and Homestead. 9700 SW 328th Street, Homestead (east end of 328th Street); (305) 230-1100.

Crane Point Hammock, Marathon Situated on 63 acres, this park is one of the most important ecological, historical, and archaeological sites in the Keys. The area contains evidence of pre-Columbian and prehistoric Bahamian artifacts and was once the site of an entire Indian village. Lots of prehistoric Indian artifacts and historic structures have been unearthed. See shipwreck gold and ancient pottery in the museum. Open Monday–Saturday, 9 a.m.–5 p.m., and Sunday, noon–5 p.m. Admission is $7.50 for adults, $4 for students, free for ages 6 and under. Mile marker 50, Marathon; (305) 743-9100.

Dolphins Plus, Key Largo Visitors get to do more than just swim with the dolphins here. A special marine orientation program includes a 1½-hour swim seminar that gives a general awareness of the plight of dolphins. You get to swim with the mammals, then participate in a question-and-answer session with researchers. Children must be at least 7 years old to participate in the swim. Cost is $100. Corrine Place, MM 99, Key Largo; (305) 451-1993.

Dolphin Research Center You can touch, play, and swim with dolphins here, but the main goal of the center is to educate the public. About 15 dolphins swim in a 90,000-square-foot coral natural saltwater tide pool carved out of the shoreline. Guided tours are $15 for adults, $12.50 for seniors over 55, and $10 for children ages 4–12; ages 3 and under get in free. To swim with the dolphins, children must be at least 5 years old and those under 13 must be accompanied by a paying adult. Cost is $135; reservations are taken the first day of the month for the following month (reservations for July can be made starting June 1, for instance). And it's pretty difficult to get one of the prized spots to swim with the mammals. Mile marker 59, Grassy Key; (305) 289-1121.

Fort Pierce Inlet State Recreation Area There's an interesting variety of natural Florida in this 340-acre park on the north shore of Fort Pierce inlet: Atlantic beach, dunes, and coastal hammock, and adjacent Jack Island on the Intracoastal Waterway is a bird-watcher's paradise. You can swim, surf, picnic, and hike on Jack Island trails. Admission is $3.25 per vehicle, and the park is open dawn to dusk. Located 4 miles east of Fort Pierce via North Causeway; (561) 468-3985.

Gibert's Bar House of Refuge Built in 1875 as a haven for shipwrecked sailors, the refuge is the last remaining in a chain of rescue stations established by the Coast Guard in the nineteenth century. Today, the site includes a boathouse, early life-saving equipment, model ships, and an aquarium. The family can enjoy an easy bicycle ride from the refuge to

Elliott Museum (825 NE Ocean Boulevard, Stuart; (561) 225-1961). Built by inventor Harmon Parker, the museum features American memorabilia and an assortment of strange inventions, like the knot-tying machine and the quadricycle, a forerunner of the automobile. Kids will especially enjoy the scale model of an old-fashioned circus and the baseball memorabilia from Ty Cobb, Babe Ruth, and many others. Open Tuesday–Saturday, 10 a.m.–4 p.m. Admission is $6 for adults (Elliot Museum); (refuge) $4 adults, $2 for children ages 7–13. 301 SE MacArthur Boulevard, Stuart; (561) 225-1875.

Gumbo Limbo Nature Center This 20-acre outdoor nature preserve and indoor learning center (named for an indigenous hardwood tree) is one of the few surviving coastal hammocks in South Florida. You can walk through on a ⅓-mile boardwalk that ends at a 40-foot observation tower for pretty views of the Atlantic Ocean and much of Boca Raton. Another trail leads to the oceanside dunes where sea turtles nest from mid-April to September and the center conducts turtle-watching tours. Admission is free. Open Monday–Saturday, 9 a.m.–4 p.m., and Sunday, noon–4 p.m. 1801 N. Ocean Boulevard, Boca Raton; (561) 338-1473.

Jonathan Dickinson State Park This popular camping park spreads over 11,300 acres on the mangrove-lined Loxahatchee River, Florida's only designated national wild and scenic river and one of the few remaining jungle rivers in America. You can rent cabins here for $65–$85, or camp (135 sites) for $14–16.

There are four different scenic nature and bike trails, and you can rent canoes or take a guided boat tour from the park's concession stand. Canoes are $6 an hour, for rent seven days a week. The Loxahatchee River Adventure is a narrated tour on a 35-foot pontoon boat that cruises up the river with a stop at Trapper Nelson's Site, a former zoo and home to "the Wildman of Loxahatchee," an outdoorsman who lived here in the 1930s. The 2-hour tour is $10 for adults, $5 for ages 6 and older. The park is open dawn to dusk for day hikers, bikers, and walkers; admission is $3.25 per vehicle. The location is 2 miles south of Stuart on US 1; (561) 746-1466 for cabin and boat reservations or (561) 546-2771 for camping reservations.

John Pennekamp Coral Reef State Park The 78 miles of living coral reef in this park is only a small portion of one of the most beautiful reef systems in the world. But because it's all underwater, the best way to see it is snorkeling or diving. Pennekamp is the first undersea preserve in the United States and a sanctuary for 55 species of coral and more than 650 species of fish.

First-time snorkelers, especially children, will not believe their eyes when they get their first glimpse of the underwater world. After a 30-

minute boat ride to the reef, it's over the side for up-close views of a fantastic array of aquatic life. The boat crew gives plenty of coaching to novices and a 10-minute minicourse on how to snorkel. The fee includes rental of a mask, flipper, and snorkel (and you get to keep the snorkel). All snorkelers must wear inflatable life vests, which are provided. Snorkeling tours are $26 for adults, $21 for children ages 17 and under; rental for (required) equipment is $5. Tour times are 9 a.m., noon, and 3 p.m.

If swimming with the fishes doesn't appeal or nonswimmers are in your family, take a 2½-hour glass-bottom boat tour. Cost is $18 for adults, $10 for children ages 11 and under. For reservations, call (305) 451-1621.

Other facilities in the park include hiking trails, a small swimming beach, an aquarium, canoe rentals, and a visitors center featuring ecological displays of Keys flora and fauna. There are 47 campsites, but be prepared for the heat and mosquitoes. Cost is $19. Nature walks and campfire lectures by camp rangers are held. The park is open daily from 8 a.m. to 5 p.m.; admission is $4 per vehicle. Mile marker 102.5, Key Largo; (305) 451-1202.

Looe Key National Marine Sanctuary This 5-square-mile area of submerged reef 6 miles southwest of Big Pine Key is considered the best reef in the Keys for snorkeling, diving, fishing, and boating. Its gin-clear waters reveal underwater sights such as brain coral, tall coral pillars rising toward the surface, and other interesting formations. Make arrangements to visit at any dive shop; prices vary. MM 27.5, Looe Key; (305) 292-0311.

Loxahatchee National Wildlife Refuge This federal preserve has great hiking trails and some of the state's best bird-watching plus a wide variety of reptiles, mammals, and waterfowl. An easy, half-mile boardwalk is near the visitors center; just beyond the boardwalk is a series of loops that let you choose a hike from 1 to 10 miles. Admission is $5 per vehicle; open daily 6 a.m.–6 p.m; visitors center open 9 a.m.–4 p.m., closed Monday and Tuesday in summer. On US 441 and Lee Road, West Palm Beach, between SR 804 (Boynton Beach Boulevard) and SR 806 (Atlantic Avenue); (561) 734-8303.

Morikami Museum and Japanese Gardens This serene spot dates back to 1905 and was once one of the most successful pineapple plantations in South Florida; it was owned by George Sukeji Morikami. Morikami gave the 200-acre gardens, dedicated to the preservation of Japanese culture, to Palm Beach County in 1977. It's a living history lesson for youngsters as they stroll through tranquil pine forests, past Japanese-style gardens, bonsai collections, reflective lakes, and waterfalls. There's a nice spot for picnics and a museum celebrating traditional and modern Japanese culture. Entrance to the gardens is always free; museum admission is $8 for adults, $7 for seniors ages 65 and older, $5 for students and children ages

6–18. Museum hours are daily, 10 a.m.–5 p.m.; closed Monday and major holidays. 4000 Morikami Park Road, Delray Beach; (561) 495-0233; www.morikami.org.

National Key Deer Refuge Come early in the morning or near sunset to watch the tiny deer come out to graze on 2,300 acres. Stand quietly near the Blue Hole, where alligators, birds, and turtles hang out. A nature preserve, called Watson's Hammock, and the Great White Heron Refuge are also part of the park. Open sunrise to sunset. Mile marker 30.5, Big Pine Key; (305) 872-2239.

Oleta River State Recreation Area This park is virtually surrounded by high-rises, but visitors can rent canoes and explore the quiet waters that surround the 854-acre park—and possibly sight a manatee. Admission to the park is $4 per car (up to 8 people); canoe and paddleboat rentals are $12 for the first hour and $25 for half a day. One-person kayaks rent for $8 for the first hour and $30 for half a day. A $25 deposit and a driver's license are also required. Boat rentals are available weekdays 10 a.m.–5 p.m. and weekends 8 a.m.–5 p.m; (305) 947-0302. The park is located off Sunny Isles Boulevard between Miami Beach and the mainland (North Miami Beach); (305) 919-1846.

Reflections Nature Tours Specializing since 1991 on kayak trips to the Keys' backcountry. No experience is necessary to paddle the calm, shallow waters in stable, easy-to-paddle sea kayaks on tours that emphasize seeing wildlife. On the trip you'll view birds, animals, and marine life in Great White Heron Wildlife Refuge and Everglades National Park; snorkeling is another popular option on the tours. Trips are $50 per person, and last about four hours; a guide, equipment, instruction, and a light lunch are provided. Reflections is based on Big Pine Key and offers several different tours. For more information or to make a reservation, call (305) 872-4668 or e-mail Emilygraves@aol.com.

Venetian Pool Take a break from the beach and spend a day at historic Venetian Pool, a spring-fed, Venetian-style lagoon. Originally excavated to supply limestone for early Coral Gables homes, this large coral rock outdoor pool offers a tropical lagoon-like setting, with caves, waterfalls, and stone bridges. The pool is open Tuesday–Friday, 11 a.m.–4:30 p.m., closed Monday (with extended hours in the summer). Admission is $8 for adults, $4.50 for children 12 and under; children 36 months or younger not permitted. A cafe offers a full luncheon menu, including pizza by the slice, hot dogs, burgers, and more. 2701 DeSoto Boulevard, Coral Gables; (305) 460-5356; www.venetianpool.com.

Shopping

Though shopping isn't necessarily an activity of choice for vacationing families, the diversity of outstanding choices in South Florida makes it worth noting:

Bayside Marketplace, downtown Miami Like a UN carnival with stores. The lower level is teeming with stalls offering ethnic wares and cute, if largely useless, merchandise. National chains like the Gap and the Limited are here, as well as the Disney Store. There's waterfront dining with a backdrop of yachts, sailboats, and cruise ships, and lots of free entertainment, like jugglers and singers. It's safe, clean, and there's plenty of parking. Open Monday–Thursday, 10 a.m.–10 p.m., Friday and Saturday, 10 a.m.–11 p.m., and Sunday, 11 a.m.–9 p.m. 401 Biscayne Boulevard; (305) 577-3344.

CocoWalk, Coconut Grove Resembling a big Mediterranean birthday cake, CocoWalk is Miami's most comprehensive shopping and entertainment complex, smack in the middle of the Grove. The two-level mall contains everything the Generation X mall rat craves: music, tapas, loud bands, a multiscreen cinema, and a Gap. There's also a good bookstore. The place is packed most nights, but that's part of the fun. The shops open at 11 a.m. every day and close at 10 p.m. during the week, midnight on Friday and Saturday. The restaurants and nightclubs stay open until 3 a.m. 3015 Grand Avenue, Coconut Grove; (305) 444-0777

Las Olas Boulevard, Ft. Lauderdale Las Olas is a charming avenue lined by gas lamps and divided by a wide, landscaped median of flowers and towering shade trees. Fashion boutiques, art galleries, world-class cuisine, sidewalk cafes, and jazz houses line both sides; you can take a horse-drawn carriage from one end to the other, stretching from the beach on the east to the Museum of Art on the west.

Lincoln Road Mall, Miami Beach The place to see and be seen on Miami Beach. The 10-block area has hundreds of one-of-a-kind shops, galleries, restaurants, and performance art spaces—you can find everything from a $35,000 glass sculpture to a $5 T-shirt. Let the kids bring their rollerblades, and dine at one of the many restaurants with outdoor tables; enjoy an after-dinner drink while the kids burn some energy. (305) 672-1270.

Sawgrass Mills, Sunrise A mecca for off-price shoppers, one of the world's largest outlet malls with more than 400 shops and kiosks—2.5 million square feet covering 50 acres. Just about every name retailer has a discount place here. Open Monday–Saturday, 10 a.m.–9:30 p.m., and

A CALENDAR OF FESTIVALS AND EVENTS

January

Oshagatsu: Japanese New Year Delray Beach. A family-oriented celebration of the New Year in Japanese style. Activities include card-making and calligraphy, hanetsuki (Japanese badminton), fuku warai (a blindfold game), and pounding rice cakes, as well as demonstrations, food, and craft booths. The Morikami Museum and Japanese Gardens; (561) 495-0233.

Annual Redland Natural Arts Festival Homestead. Salutes South Florida's pioneer spirit with handmade arts and crafts. Features wildlife and educational exhibits, pony rides, face painting, sand art, and entertainment, plus Thai, Greek, Cuban, German, and Oriental food. Fruit and Spice Park, 24801 SW 187th Avenue; (305) 247-5727.

Annual Homestead Championship Rodeo Action-packed fun for the whole family featuring seven championship rodeo events. Harris Field, US 1 and SW 312th Street, Homestead; (305) 247-2332.

Art Deco Weekend Festival Ocean Drive (Art Deco District, Miami Beach). A seven-block-long festival featuring art, music, and food. (305) 672-2014.

February

Palm Beach Renaissance Festival Lake Worth. A re-creation of a sixteenth-century English village with live entertainment, contact joust, human chess match, a royal court, theaters, food and drink, games and rides, crafts, and much, much more. Fun for the whole family! For location call (800) 676-7333.

Palm Beach Seafood Festival West Palm Beach. Arts and crafts, kiddie rides, stone crabs, lobster, and more. Currie Park; (561) 832-6397.

Black Heritage Month Celebration Various locations throughout Dade County. A monthlong celebration that includes theater, music, poetry, art exhibits, and a street festival. (305) 672-1270.

Coconut Grove Art Festival Bayshore Drive (Coconut Grove). The largest event of its kind in the United States, with more than 300 visual artists attracting nearly 1 million visitors. (305) 447-0401.

Civil War Days Key West. Fort tours and Civil War reenactments. Fort Zachary Taylor, Key West; (305) 292-6850.

March

Grand Prix of Miami Downtown Miami. South Florida's premier auto racing event. (305) 230-7223.

Carnival Miami–Calle Ocho Festival Miami. The nation's largest Hispanic festival in the spirit of Rio, culminating in a 23-block street party featuring dance, food, costumed revelers, and top Latin entertainers. Orange Bowl Stadium, SW 8th Street (Little Havana); (305) 644-8888.

Italian Renaissance Festival Coconut Grove. This four-day event recreates a Renaissance marketplace with colorful pageantry, period costumes, music, jugglers, and jesters. Vizcaya Museum and Gardens; (305) 250-9132.

Key West Conch Shell Blowing Contest Hear music played on the shells of creatures from which Key Westers take their name. Key West; (800) 527-8539.

April

Kidsfest Boca Raton. Special event for children featuring arts and crafts, historical reenactors, continuous entertainment, museum exhibits, games, rides, and food. Children's Museum; (561) 368-6875.

Spring Fling Boca Raton. Games, arts and crafts, food, walkabout entertainment, picture taking, rides, contests, sweet treats, and face painting make for a special day of fun. Mizner Park; (561) 393-7806.

Children's Day Delray Beach. The traditional Japanese celebration of "Kokomo-no-hi" (Children's Day) offers plenty of hands-on activities, and exciting demonstrations including carp-streamer making, fish printing, origami (paper folding), story telling, Japanese hopscotch, relay races, chopstick lessons, martial arts, and more. Morikami Museum and Japanese Gardens; (561) 495-0233.

Seven Mile Bridge Run Marathon. Annual foot race limited to 1,500 participants. (305) 743-8513.

Conch Republic Independence Celebration Key West. Parades, parties, and fun commemorate the founding of the Conch Republic. (305) 296-0213.

May

The Great Sunrise Balloon Race and Festival Homestead. A celebration featuring balloon races, live entertainment, amusement rides, skydiving, arts and crafts, and food. Harris Field; (305) 273-3052.

June

Miami-Bahamas Goombay Festival Downtown Coconut Grove. The largest black heritage celebration in the United States is a celebration of the city's Bahamian heritage. Features live entertainment, a continuous limbo line, food, arts and crafts, and the Royal Bahamas Police Marching Band. (305) 372-9966.

A CALENDAR OF FESTIVALS AND EVENTS *(continued)*

July

America's Birthday Bash Downtown Miami. One of South Florida's largest multicultural extravaganzas attracts more than 100,000 revelers. Entertainment features Latin headliners, rock and roll superstars, jazz, Big Band sounds, and folk artists. Features fireworks, a laser show, a petting zoo, arts and crafts, amusement rides, and international foods. Bayfront Park's Amphitheater, 301 N. Biscayne Boulevard; (305) 358-7550.

Winter in July West Palm Beach. Snow in the heat of summer! The snow brought in to Dreher Park allows for many winter activities like building snowmen. Also, meet hundreds of animals from Florida, Central and South America, Asia, and Australia, including American bald eagles. Enjoy live music, storytellers, and animal encounters. Palm Beach Zoo at Dreher Park; (561) 533-0887.

Everglades Music and Crafts Festival Festival focusing on the many facets of American Indian heritage along with an international array of arts and crafts, music, and food celebrating the many ethnic cultures of Greater Miami and the beaches. Alligator wrestling, airboat rides, and more, all in the Miccosukee Indian Village, 30 miles west of Miami on SW 8th Street; (305) 223-8380.

Underwater Music Festival Looe Key Marine Sanctuary. Music is piped underwater for divers and snorkelers during this day-long fest. (305) 872-2411.

August

Miami Reggae Festival A celebration of Dade County's rich Caribbean influences that highlights international and local musicians. $10 advance tickets, $15 day of the show, children under 12 admitted free. T and T Amphitheater, 410 Biscayne Boulevard (downtown Miami); (305) 891-2944.

October

Boo at the Zoo West Palm Beach. Families can enjoy a fun and safe Halloween celebration while experiencing the zoo after hours. Lit-up tropical gardens and themed decorations provide the perfect setting for close-up nocturnal animal encounters, scary storytelling, and related activities. Palm Beach Zoo at Dreher Park; (561) 533-0887.

West Indian Carnival Extravaganza Miami Beach. Festival featuring arts and crafts and Calypso, soca, and reggae music, as well as a colorful parade down Washington Avenue. 15th Street and Washington to South Pointe Park (Art Deco District). Free.

Goombay Festival Key West. A street fair in Bahama Village. (305) 293-8898.

November

Winternational Thanksgiving Day Parade North Miami. This fun family event has been the only live Thanksgiving morning parade south of Orlando for many years. Spectators from neighboring communities come to watch the 75 parade units, which include floats, marching bands, clowns, horses, celebrities, and, of course, Santa Claus. NE 125th Street at NE 6th Avenue; (305) 893-6511 ext. 2227.

December

International Kwanzaa Celebration Various locations throughout Dade County. Entertainment, dances, and food to celebrate African heritage. Admission fee; (305) 531-3442.

Annual Indian Arts Festival American Indian artisans from all over the continental Americas gather in the unique setting of the Miccosukee Indian Village for a week of activities. Features colorful costumed dancers, along with alligator wrestling, airboat rides, and a wide array of authentic Indian crafts and foods. Miccosukee Indian Village, 30 miles west of Miami on SW 8th Street; (305) 223-8380.

Orange Bowl Parade Downtown Miami. One of the world's largest, most colorful nighttime parades features enhanced, state-of-the-art floats with hydraulic and animation technology. Complementing the floats are the nation's top marching bands, huge balloons, clowns, antique cars, and more. Along Biscayne Boulevard; (305) 371-4600.

King Mango Strut Downtown Coconut Grove. A spoof of the Orange Bowl parade with zany floats and marching bands. Free; (305) 444-7270.

Big Orange New Year's Eve Celebration, Downtown Miami. The largest New Year's Eve event south of Times Square features musical entertainment, family activities, a variety of ethnic foods, a laser and fireworks extravaganza, and the 400-foot ascent of the 35-foot neon Big Orange to the top of the Hotel Inter-Continental. Bayfront Park, 301 N. Biscayne Boulevard; (305) 447-1224.

Sunday, 11 a.m.–8 p.m. 12801 W. Sunrise Boulevard, Sunrise (exits are clearly marked on I-95); (954) 846-2300.

Swap Shop, Ft. Lauderdale It's a real circus—literally, with elephants and a man on a flying trapeze. Leave the swanky shops and head to the world's largest flea market, with a small circus, amusement rides, a giant video arcade, even drive-in movies after dark. There are a whopping 2,000 vendors on 75 acres. Open daily 9 a.m.–5:30 p.m. 3291 W. Sunrise Boulevard; (954) 791-7927.

Worth Avenue, Palm Beach Even if you can only afford to window shop, a stroll down this chichi street is a pleasant diversion. Stretching for four blocks from South Ocean Boulevard to Coconut Row, this Mediterranean-inspired street is one of the world's most exclusive shopping districts. More than 200 shops, restaurants, and art galleries line the avenue. Tiffany's, Cartier, Ralph Lauren, Hermes, Chanel, St. John, Escada, Gucci…the list goes on.

Turtle Time

This part of the Florida coast is prime for turtle nesting, and from June to July the Marine Life Center of Juno Beach offers free guided expeditions to turtle egg-laying strictly by reservation. Environmentalists recommend these group tours with a guide to minimize disturbance of the turtles; (561) 627-8280.

Palm Beach and Boca Raton

Like a slender strand of pearls, the island of Palm Beach stretches down the coastline, with an eye-popping tour of some of the world's most expensive mansions as you drive along A1A. The town enjoys its high-brow image and strives to keep it; there's a law, for instance, that prohibits jogging without a shirt. And don't even think about washing your car—you have to go across the bridge to West Palm Beach for that sort of everyday activity. Still, it's great fun for families to soak in all the ambience, then head for the beaches (pages 367–370) and attractions.

South of Palm Beach is Boca Raton, where polo and tennis are the favorite ways to while away the time in this upscale resort town. Much of Boca's handsome, 1920s Spanish-style architecture is the work of architect Addison Mizner.

Family Resorts

The Breakers

One South County Road, Palm Beach • (561) 655-6611 or (800) BREAKERS
fax (561) 655-6654 • www.thebreakers.com

Few destinations offer children's programs that are certified by children themselves. The Breakers established a Kids Advisory Board made up of local children ages 5–12 that makes recommendations to the resort; they came up with the Coconut Crew Camp with activities for 3- to 12-year-olds, including swimming, horseshoes, arts and crafts, seashell hunts, and nature walks.

Built in 1896, the Breakers is a 572-room, Italian Renaissance–style hotel in the heart of Palm Beach on 140 oceanfront acres. Listed on the National Register of Historic Places, the landmark hotel has two golf courses, tennis courts, half a mile of private beach, a fitness center, and an extensive program of family and children's activities. A playground

Palm Beach and Boca Raton
N
FAMILY RESORTS
1 The Breakers
2 Four Seasons Ocean Grand
3 Palm Beach Hawaiian Ocean Inn
4 Radisson Palm Beach Shores
ATTRACTIONS
5 Children's Museum of Boca Raton at Singing Pines
6 Dreher Park Zoo
7 Knollwood Groves
8 Lion Country Safari
9 Sports Immortals Museum
RESTAURANTS
10 Baja Cafe
11 Crab Pot
12 Mississippi Sweet's BBQ
13 Prezzo
14 Sailfish Marina Restaurant
15 Tom's Place
16 Wilt Chamberlains's
Jupiter
Florida Turnpike
Donald Ross Rd.
Juno Beach
Hood Rd.
Bee Line Hwy
Intracoastal Waterway
PGA Blvd.
Palm Beach Gardens
N. Palm Beach
Northlake Blvd.
Ocean Blvd.
Singer Island
Lake Park
Blue Heron Blvd.
Riviera Beach
Palm Beach Shores
45th St.
8th St.
Lake Mangonia
West Palm Beach
Military Blvd.
Clear Lake
Broadway
Palm Beach
Belvedere Rd.
Haverhill
Southern Blvd.
West Palm Beach Canal
Palm Beach International Airport
Forest Hill Blvd.
Greenacres City
Palm Springs
Loxahatchee Wildlife Refuge
Jog Rd.
Palm Beach Co. Park Airport
Osborne Lake
Lake Worth
S. Palm Beach
Atlantis
Hypoluxo Rd.
Lantana
Range Line Rd.
Congress Ave.
Manalpan
Boynton Beach
Ocean Ridge
Briny Breezes
Woolbright Rd.
Gulfstream
Florida Turnpike
Atlantic Ave.
Delray Beach
Military Trail
ATLANTIC OCEAN
Clint Moore Rd.
Highland Beach
Morikami Gardens
Jog Rd.
Boca Raton Municipal Airport
Boca Raton
706
95
809
811
702
710
A1A
704
7
98
1
812
804
441
806
798
808

on the beach includes a jungle gym, slides, swings, and a miniature railroad station.

From June through August, the daylong Coconut Crew Summer Camp is for ages 6–12, with environmental activities, seaside activities, and outdoor recreational sports. Weekly themes include culinary, etiquette, and money management. Cost is $65 a day, or $300 a week, which includes lunch.

Teenagers can sign up for in-line skating, snorkeling, biking, golf, tennis, scuba, and more. Prices to participate depend on the activity.

Families can visit the Activities Center and play video games, pinball, board games, puzzles, and cards, or watch movies or read.

Renovations at the Breakers added soundproofing to most of the 572 rooms. Also, at check-in, if you have children under age 4, housekeeping will childproof the room with electrical outlet covers, door guards, and other safety devices.

Rates start at $270 in the summer, $420 in the winter; children ages 17 and under stay free with parent. And if your kids would rather bunk on the floor, the hotel has sleeping bags for children under age 10. All rooms have a wet bar, hair dryer, and iron; refrigerators can be requested.

A Bike Is Best

The most fun way to gawk at the mansions along the ocean in Palm Beach is on a bicycle, pedaling the Lake Trail that runs the length of the island—10 miles—along the Intracoastal Waterway. You'll even spot some wildlife along the way. You're sharing the trail with walkers, joggers, and rollerbladers, and it gets a little crowded on the weekends. If you need to rent a bike, stop at Palm Beach Bicycle Trail, 223 Sunrise Avenue; (561) 659-4583. Cost is $8 an hour, $16 for half a day, $20 for 24 hours, and $59 a week. To get to Lake Trail, exit I-95 at Okeechobee Boulevard and head east across the bridge. Turn left on A1A and go past Flagler Museum. Park anywhere it's legal. Ride toward the Intracoastal Waterway until coming to the asphalt path.

Four Seasons Ocean Grand

2800 S. Ocean Boulevard, Palm Beach • (561) 582-2800 • fax (561) 586-2690
www.fourseasons.com

Four Seasons may be elegant and upscale, but it's one fancy resort where children are welcome with open arms. Their complimentary Kids for All Seasons program offers some of the most elaborate ideas we can imagine: a "Fifties Night" with costumes and live entertainment, a "Kitchen Day" with chef's hats and aprons, rolling pastry, making icing and strawberry sauce. Children must be age 3 or older to participate in the programs, which run daily from 9 a.m.–noon.

The only charge is for the themed Kids Dinner Club, with dinner and an evening of entertainment—a sea life show, a wild animal show, or a Hawaiian luau, for instance. Cost is $40 and hours are 6–9 p.m. However, if parents are dining in one of the resort's two restaurants, the child care fee is waived.

The playroom is packed with puzzles, videos, buckets and pails, crayons, bean bags, and period costumes. And if you can time your visit around Easter, don't miss the Fabergé egg hunt—six real (yes, real) Fabergé eggs are hidden on the grounds for lucky kids to uncover.

The oceanfront resort has 210 rooms and suites, tennis courts, a swimming pool, and a health club and spa. Each room has a refrigerator, and microwaves can be requested. Rates start at $275 in the summer, $375 in the winter.

Palm Beach Hawaiian Ocean Inn

3550 S. Ocean Boulevard (A1A), Palm Beach • (561) 582-5631
www.lodging/hawaiianocean.com/destinations/palm-beaches/

This nostalgic little motel is tucked among the new high rises in chichi Palm Beach, directly on the ocean. You can't stay anywhere for less and have a friendlier experience. The inn has 35 spotless efficiency, suites, and deluxe rooms, all centered around a grassy courtyard and swimming pool. Single rooms start at $75 in the summer, a two-room combo for $135; in the winter rooms start at $135, a two-room combo for $210, and children 17 and under stay free. Some rooms have a refrigerator, coffeemaker, and stove or microwave.

Radisson Palm Beach Shores

181 Ocean Ave., Palm Beach Shores • (561) 863-4000 • fax (561) 845-3245
www.radisson.com/palmbeachfl

There's space to spread out in this family-friendly, 257-room resort, right on the ocean. Accommodations are comfortable two-room suites that include a refrigerator, coffeemaker, microwave, two color TVs, and a Nintendo games console.

Resort activities seem endless, from bike rentals, tennis, and volleyball to water sports—jet skis, kayaks, snorkeling, and more. Or just relax on the uncrowded stretch of private beach or by the pool while the kids are at the Beach Buddies Kids Club for an hour or all day. Kids 3–12 can go on field trips, take boat rides, play dress-up, or just hang out with counselors. Cost is $25 for a half day. Room rates start at $180.

Attractions

Children's Museum of Boca Raton at Singing Pines

498 Crawford Boulevard, Boca Raton • (561) 368-6875

Hours - May–October, Tuesday–Saturday, noon–4 p.m.

Admission - $3 per person

Appeal by Age Group -

Pre-school ★★	Teens —	Over 30 —
Grade school ★★	Young Adults —	Seniors —

Touring Time - Average 2–3 hours; minimum 1 hour

Rainy-Day Touring - Recommended

Author's Rating - ★★; more rainy day diversions; recommended for children ages 2–8

Restaurants - No

Alcoholic beverages - No

Handicapped access - Yes

Wheelchair rental - No

Baby stroller rental - No

Lockers - No

Pet kennels - No

Rain check - No

Private tours - Yes

Description and Comments The Children's Museum is a small, hands-on museum for children between the ages of 2 and 8. It specializes in programs that highlight arts and culture, history, and the humanities. Five exhibitions change throughout the year, such as the Pioneer Kitchen, the NationsBank KidCents Mini-Bank, and the Collections Room.

The museum is located in Singing Pines, one of the oldest wood structures in Boca Raton, and is nestled in a garden that highlights native plants and shrubs.

Dreher Park Zoo

1301 Summit Boulevard, West Palm Beach (east of I-95 between Southern and Forest Hill Boulevards) • (561) 533-0887

Hours - Daily, 9 a.m.–5 p.m.; closed Thanksgiving

Admission - $7.50 for adults, $6 for senior citizens, $5 for children ages 3–12

Appeal by Age Group -

Pre-school ★★★	Teens ★★	Over 30 ★★
Grade school ★★★	Young Adults ★★	Seniors ★★

Touring Time - Average 2–3 hours; minimum 2 hours

Rainy-Day Touring - Not recommended

Author's Rating - ★★; it's a zoo

Restaurants - Yes
Alcoholic beverages - No
Handicapped access - Yes
Wheelchair rental - Yes
Baby stroller rental - Yes
Lockers - No
Pet kennels - No
Rain check - No
Private tours - Yes

Description and Comments Animals from Florida, Central and South America, Asia, and Australia call 22-acre Dreher Park home, with more than 400 exotic and domestic inhabitants. The zoo is working to preserve several species, including the Komodo dragon, the Bengal tiger, jaguar, lemur, cotton top tamarin, golden lion tamarin, and Florida panther. There are also a boardwalk nature trail and an animal encounter area that youngsters enjoy.

Knollwood Groves

8053 Lawrence Road, Lake Worth • (561) 734-4800

Hours - Daily, 8:30 a.m.–5:30 p.m.; closed Sunday and holidays from May to October

Admission - Groves are free; $1 for wagon train tour; alligator show $6 adults, $4 children

Appeal by Age Group -

Pre-school ★★	Teens ★★	Over 30 ★★
Grade school ★★★★	Young Adults ★★	Seniors ★★

Touring Time - Average 1½ hours; minimum 1 hour

Rainy-Day Touring - Not recommended

Author's Rating - ★★; a living history lesson

Restaurants - No
Alcoholic beverages - No
Handicapped access - Yes
Wheelchair rental - No
Baby stroller rental - No
Lockers - No
Pet kennels - No
Rain check - No
Private tours - Yes

Description and Comments Knollwood Groves is another pre-Disney attraction that's a wonderful, old-fashioned adventure. The orange and grapefruit trees were planted in the 1930s, and they still harvest the trees—during the season they'll start your tour with a walk through the packing house.

For kids the real fun begins when Martin Two-Feather, a Blackfoot Indian transplanted from northern Montana, cranks up an old McCormick tractor that pulls a wooden wagon through the groves and through a five-acre Florida hammock (you may even spot an alligator or two). For more than an hour he talks about the birds, trees, alligators, and the Native Americans who first settled the area. The tour stops at Hallpatee Indian Village, where Martin shows off his gator wrestling. The kids love it.

Knollwood Groves started these tours back in the 1950s, and owner Barbara Dwyer is quite proud of the fact that little has changed.

Lion Country Safari

Southern Boulevard West (SR 80), 18 miles west of I-95 Exit 50 in West Palm Beach (561) 793-1084 • www.lioncountrysafari.com

Hours - Daily, 9:30 a.m.–5:30 p.m.

Admission - $17 adults, $13 children ages 3–9, $15 seniors

Appeal by Age Group -

Pre-school ★★★★	Teens ★★★★	Over 30 ★★★★
Grade school ★★★★	Young Adults ★★★★	Seniors ★★★★

Touring Time - Average 3–5 hours; minimum 2 hours

Rainy-Day Touring - OK, but not recommended

Author's Rating - ★★★★; the safari is marvelous

Restaurants - Yes

Alcoholic beverages - No

Handicapped access - Yes

Wheelchair rental - Yes

Baby stroller rental - Yes

Lockers - No

Pet kennels - Yes

Rain check - Yes

Private tours - Yes

Description and Comments Lion Country Safari, opened in 1967, was North America's first "cageless zoo." Today you can drive your car through more than 4 miles of wilderness and see more than 1,200 animals from around the world all roaming free—giraffes, rhinos, zebras, ostriches, and lions among them.

The park covers 500 acres; besides the safari, there is Safari World, a walk-through animal exhibit area, with macaws, monkeys, tortoises, alligators, pythons, and other exotic animals. Safari World also includes rides, games, and restaurants. The *Safari Queen* is a jungle cruise past islands of birds and spider monkeys. There's also a petting zoo, minigolf, and a recently added free-flight lory feeding aviary.

Sports Immortals Museum

6830 N. Federal Highway, Boca Raton • (561) 997-2575

Hours - Monday–Friday, 10 a.m.–6 p.m.; Saturday, 10 a.m.–5 p.m.; closed Sunday

Admission - Ground floor, free; 2nd floor, $5 for adults, $3 for children ages 12 and under

Appeal by Age Group -

Pre-school ★	Teens ★★★	Over 30 ★★★
Grade school ★★★	Young Adults ★★★	Seniors ★★★

Touring Time - Average 1½ hours; minimum 1 hour

Rainy-Day Touring - Recommended

Author's Rating - ★★★; a perfect place for sports fans to spend a rainy afternoon

Restaurants - No

Alcoholic beverages - No

Handicapped access - Yes

Wheelchair rental - No

Baby stroller rental - No

Lockers - No

Pet kennels - No

Rain check - No

Private tours - Yes

Description and Comments This museum showcases the largest sports memorabilia collection in the world—1 million pieces at last count—from Ty Cobb's spikes to Muhammad Ali's championship belt. They don't play favorites in this wide array of collectibles, recognized by the Smithsonian Institution as "absolutely the most outstanding single collection of sports."

Part of the museum offers interactive games against famous athletes—you can race a car with Mario Andretti, box Muhammad Ali, hit a Nolan Ryan fast ball, try to strike out Babe Ruth, or kick the winning field goal at the Super Bowl.

Family-Friendly Restaurants

Baja Cafe

201 NW First Avenue, Boca Raton • (561) 394-5449

Meals served - Lunch and dinner

Cuisine - Mexican, American

Entree range - $4–18

Kids menu - Yes

Reservations - Accepted for parties of 10 or more

Payment - Cash only

The blackened mahimahi tacos are sensational, but plenty of folks order the giant half-pound burger with the works.

Crab Pot

386 E. Blue Heron Boulevard, Riviera Beach • (561) 844-2722

Meals served - Lunch and dinner

Cuisine - Seafood

Entree range - Lunch, \$5–12; dinner, \$8–34

Kids menu - Yes

Reservations - Not accepted

Payment - Visa, MC, AmEx

The crabs come from wherever they're freshest: hard shell crabs from the East Coast, stone crab claws from Florida waters. Every sort of crab except Dungeness is on the menu. Order it with Baltimore-style seasoning or garlic. The locals who get tired of crab go for the fresh dolphin and grouper.

Mississippi Sweet's BBQ

2399 N. Federal Highway, Boca Raton • (561) 394-6779

Meals served - Lunch and dinner

Cuisine - Barbecue

Entree range - \$6–14

Kids menu - No, but lots of kids order the chicken fingers and ribs

Reservations - Not accepted

Payment - Visa, MC

Waitresses at this nine-table restaurant seem to know most of the customers by name. Take your pick of beef or pork ribs, and save room for one of their homemade desserts.

Prezzo

7820 Glades Road, Boca Raton • (561) 451-2800

Meals served - Lunch and dinner

Cuisine - Northern Italian

Entree range - Lunch, \$6.95–12.95; dinner, \$9.95–24.95

Kids menu - No, but pizza and pasta are highly requested by kids

Reservations - Accepted for parties of 5 or more

Payment - All major credit cards accepted

Trendy pizzas—oak-grilled chicken, roasted eggplant, shrimp are among toppings—pastas, soups, salads are offered here. For a little variety try the veal meat loaf or the Dijon and herb-crumb-crusted chicken breast.

Sailfish Marina Restaurant

90 Lake Drive, Palm Beach Shores (at Sailfish Marina) • (561) 842-8449

Meals served - Breakfast, lunch, and dinner

Cuisine - Seafood

Entree range - $4–22

Kids menu - Yes

Reservations - Not accepted

Payment - Visa, MC, AmEx

The delicious chowders—spicy conch and New England clam—are homemade, the fish as fresh as can be. Locals recommend old-fashioned fried fish and chips with a splash of vinegar.

Tom's Place

7251 N. Federal Highway, Boca Raton • (561) 997-0920

Meals served - Lunch and dinner

Cuisine - Barbecue

Entree range - $6–23 (sandwiches $4–6)

Kids menu - Yes

Reservations - Not accepted

Payment - Visa, MC, AmEx

Owners Tom and Helen Wright serve perfectly grilled meats with homemade sauce. There's also fish on the menu. Kids love Helen's mashed potatoes and rice with gravy. Grown-ups go for the collard greens and black-eyed peas. Nothing fancy, and families feel right at home.

Wilt Chamberlain's

8903 W. Glades Road, Boca Raton • (561) 488-8881

Meals served - Lunch and dinner

Cuisine - American

Entree range - $8.99–22.99

Kids menu - Yes

Reservations - Not accepted

Payment - All major credit cards accepted

Another "eatertainment" spot, with a 50-game arcade, 45 TV sets, and four jumbo TVs. If you order Wilt's clubhouse sandwich, share. The burgers, pastas, and ribs are the best-sellers.

Side Trips

Lake Okeechobee A 45-minute drive west on US 441 from Palm Beach takes you into the heart of sugarcane country and to Lake Okeechobee, the second-largest freshwater lake in the country, covering more than 700 square miles in five counties. The lake, only about 12 feet deep, is famous for its bass and speckled perch. You can also walk, bike, or rollerblade along the Lake Okeechobee Scenic Trail, a 140-mile-long trek along a 35-foot levee encircling the lake. There are parks along the way and several marked entrances.

The first burg you'll drive through is Belle Glade, and you can see the huge farms that produce much of Florida's fresh produce—sugarcane, sweet corn, green beans, lettuce, carrots, radishes, and rice. If you want to sample some fresh-picked produce, it's usually on the menu at Linda's, 232 South Main Street; (561) 996-0300. The locals head here for baked chicken and dressing, smoked turkey, turnip and collard greens, black-eyed peas and rice, yams, potato salad, and more. You won't leave hungry, and a complete dinner is just $5.57. And they don't mind if you share your plate with the kids.

Farther west on Lake Okeechobee is the town of Clewiston, where sugar is the major crop—300,000 acres worth. Another pleasant lunch stop is at the pretty Clewiston Inn. The inn is operated by the U.S. Sugar Corporation, so you might go straight for the fresh-baked desserts: Key lime pie, peanut butter pie, toffee mousse cake, or banana chocolate chip cake. Also on the sumptuous Friday buffet are catfish, barbecued chicken, green beans, corn, peas, broccoli—whatever's fresh and available—for $8.95. Kids eat for half price, or they can opt for grilled cheese, peanut-butter-and-jelly sandwiches, or other kid-friendly favorites. Clewiston Inn is at 108 Royal Purple Palm Avenue; (800) 749-4466.

Big Cypress Seminole Reservation, 30 miles south of Clewiston on CR 61, is home of the Ah-Tah-Thi-Ki (Ah-TAW-thi-key) Museum. In the Seminole language, Ah-Tah-Thi-Ki means "to learn," and the museum tells the story of the Seminole Indians—their customs, language, and rich culture. The 60-acre site is in the heart of the Big Cypress Seminole Reservation, and you can walk nature trails, watch traditional dances performed at the ceremonial grounds, and see exhibitions of quilting, open-fire cooking, chickee hut construction, fishing, and hunting. A folklore theater tells the story of Seminole beliefs and legends. Open Tuesday–Sunday, 9 a.m.–5 p.m. Admission is $6 for adults, $4 for seniors, $4 for children ages 6–12. For more information, call (863) 902-1113.

Greater Ft. Lauderdale

Beaches that run for 23 miles, culture, history, shopping—Ft. Lauderdale has it all, but it's still probably best known as the ultimate spring break destination. It's also known for balmy weather—it even records the hours of sunshine, averaging 3,000 hours of sunny skies each year.

The expansive Riverwalk in Greater Ft. Lauderdale and the cafe-trimmed Broadwalk in neighboring Hollywood are two of the newest destinations, providing plenty of family fun.

On the Water

Greater Ft. Lauderdale, laced with 300 miles of waterways, is nicknamed the "Venice of America." Here are a few of the best ways to get out on the water:

Water Taxi Who needs a car? You can take the enjoyable water taxi almost anywhere you want to go in Ft. Lauderdale, gliding along the New River and the Intracoastal Waterway in an open-sided, canopied boat. Trips start daily at 10 a.m. and run until late night, with at least 70 stops along the Intracoastal. Cost is $4 one way, or you can buy a pass for $5 to ride all day; (954) 467-6677; www.watertaxi.com.

Jungle Queen Take a sightseeing cruise on a double-decker sternwheeler that has been cruising the Intracoastal and New River for more than 60 years. The narrated, 3-hour cruises depart daily at 10 a.m. and 2 p.m. with a stop at Jungle Queen Indian Village to watch alligator wrestling and meet Seminole Indians. Cost is $13 for adults, $9 for children ages 2–10. Evenings, there's an all-you-can eat barbecue dinner cruise, with sing-alongs of family favorites. Cost is $30 for adults, $16 for ages 10 and under. 801 Seabreeze Boulevard (Bahia Mar Yachting Center); (954) 462-5596.; www.junglequeen.com.

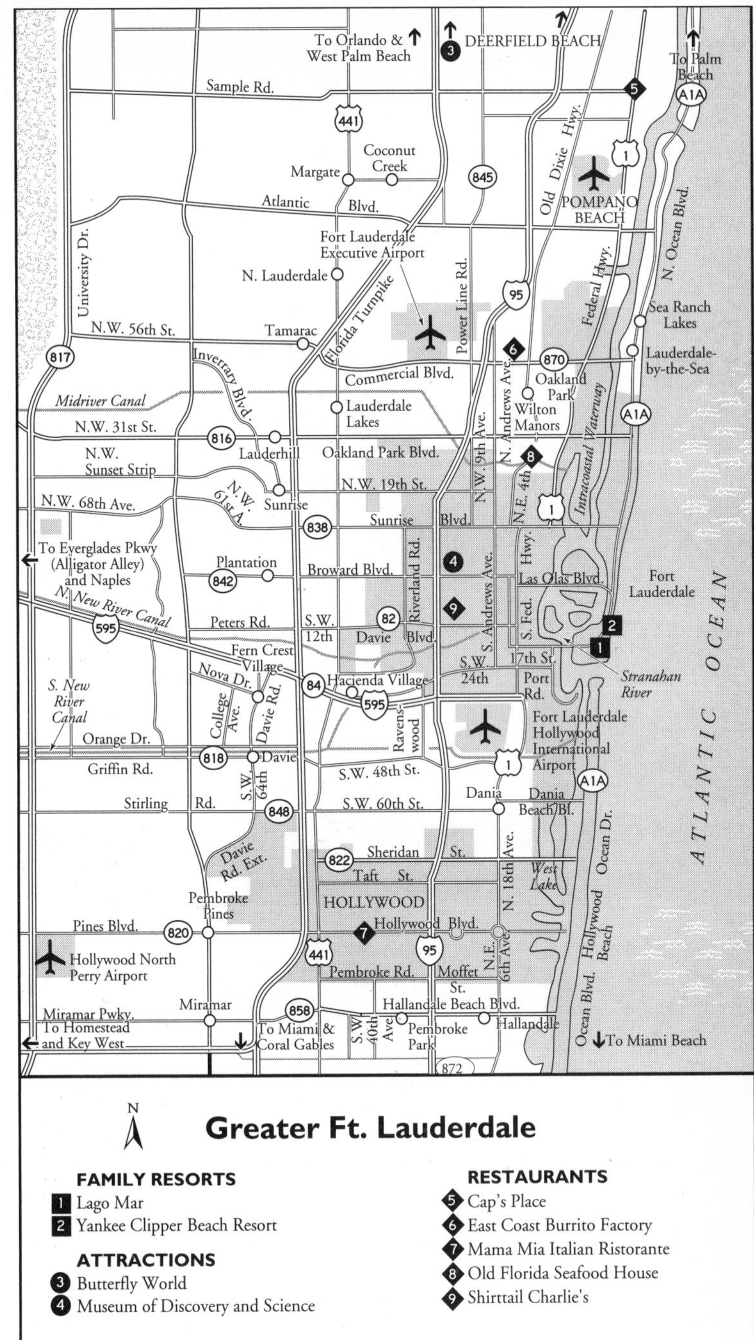

Greater Ft. Lauderdale

FAMILY RESORTS

1 Lago Mar
2 Yankee Clipper Beach Resort

ATTRACTIONS

3 Butterfly World
4 Museum of Discovery and Science

RESTAURANTS

5 Cap's Place
6 East Coast Burrito Factory
7 Mama Mia Italian Ristorante
8 Old Florida Seafood House
9 Shirttail Charlie's

Family Resorts

Lago Mar

1700 S. Ocean Lane, Ft. Lauderdale • (954) 523-6511 or (877) 524-6627 • fax (954) LAGOMAR • www.lagomar.com

Many parents vacationing at Lago Mar spent holidays here when they were youngsters, and now they're bringing their own children to this oceanfront resort, under the same family ownership for the past 37 years. Lago Mar is between Lake Mayan and the Atlantic Ocean, so there's a cozy island feel to the sprawling resort that features two swimming pools, four tennis courts, a fitness center, minigolf, and an old-fashioned kids' playground with swings, monkey bars, and a merry-go-round. The Ft. Lauderdale water taxi pulls right up to its private dock.

Families don't book vacations here for the kid programs, rather they talk about the cordial staff, the good food in the four restaurants, and the safe and comfortable surroundings. The only time there are planned activities are the holidays—Easter, Thanksgiving, and Christmas—because so many families return each year that a party is in order. During the holidays, kids ages 5–12 are kept busy with free activities and special events, and parents are encouraged to join in the fun.

The resort has 138 suites with microwaves, coffeemakers, and refrigerators or full kitchens. There's also a guest laundry. Rates start at $120 in the summer, $205 in the winter.

Yankee Clipper Beach Resort

1140 Seabreeze Boulevard (A1A), Ft. Lauderdale, on A1A just south of Bahia Mar Marina • (954) 524-5551 • fax (954) 523-5376 • www.sheratonclipper.com

This popular Sheraton is right in the center of the action on Ft. Lauderdale Beach, with 502 rooms, some with wet bars, all with refrigerators, coffeemakers, ironing boards, and hair dryers. There are three swimming pools, tennis courts, and a fitness center. Movies and arts and crafts are available for children. Rates start at $119 in the summer, $159 in the winter, with kids up to age 17 staying free with parents. .

RIDE 'EM COWBOYS

All the Florida cowboys aren't in Kissimmee—you can visit a five-star rodeo the fourth weekend of every month in Davie, at 4271 Davie Road (covered arena). The clowns and bull riders start the action at 8 p.m. on Fridays and Saturdays. Cost is $12 for adults, $5 for children ages 3–12; (954) 389-5311.

Attractions

Butterfly World

3600 W. Sample Road, Coconut Creek (10 minutes north of Ft. Lauderdale) • (954) 977-4400 • www.butteflyworld.com

Hours - Monday–Saturday, 9 a.m.–5 p.m.; Sunday, 1–5 p.m.; closed Thanksgiving and Christmas

Admission - $14 for adults, $9.95 for children ages 4–12

Appeal by Age Group -

Pre-school ★★★	Teens ★★★	Over 30 ★★★
Grade school ★★★	Young Adults ★★★	Seniors ★★★

Touring Time - Average 2–3 hours; minimum 1½ hours

Rainy-Day Touring - Not recommended

Author's Rating - ★★★; friendly butterflies will light on your head, and the colors are awesome. Between 4,000 and 5,000 butterflies inhabit three acres of gardens and waterfalls

Restaurants - Yes

Alcoholic beverages - No

Handicapped access - Yes

Wheelchair rental - Call ahead

Baby stroller rental - No

Lockers - No

Pet kennels - No

Rain check - Yes

Private tours - Yes

Description and Comments Thousands of live butterflies from all over the world—up to 5,000 on a warm afternoon—flit from blossom to blossom in this three-acre tropical garden, the largest butterfly educational and breeding facility in the world.

Four large aviaries are home to the butterflies that represent dozens of species, with orchids and other flowers creating a lovely setting. A hummingbird aviary includes birds from Peru, Surinam, and the United States.

Museum of Discovery and Science

401 SW Second Street, Ft. Lauderdale • (954) 467-6637 • www.mods.org

Hours - Monday–Saturday, 10 a.m.–5 p.m.; Sunday, noon–6 p.m.; closed Christmas

Admission - $14 for adults, $13 for senior citizens, $12 for children ages 3–12; includes one IMAX film

Appeal by Age Group -

Pre-school ★★★	Teens ★★★	Over 30 ★★
Grade school ★★★	Young Adults ★★	Seniors ★★

Touring Time - Average 2½–3 hours; minimum 2 hours
Rainy-Day Touring - Recommended
Author's Rating - ★★; a rainy day option
Restaurants - Yes
Alcoholic beverages - No
Handicapped access - Yes
Wheelchair rental - Yes
Baby stroller rental - No
Lockers - No
Pet kennels - No
Rain check - No
Private tours - No

Description and Comments Don't tell your kids it's a museum, they'll think it's just a really cool place to spend a rainy afternoon, with eight kid-friendly exhibits including Gizmo City, Florida EcoScapes, Kid-Science, Space Base, Choose Health, Sound, Great Gravity Clock, and the Explore Zone. There's also a five-story 3-D IMAX theater.

WALK THIS WAY

Riverfront or oceanfront, take your pick for a great place to stroll close to the water. Renovated at a cost of $26 million, Riverwalk Arts and Entertainment District in downtown Ft. Lauderdale is a 1.5-mile-long park that spans the north and south banks of the New River. Tropical landscaping and winding walkways link attractions, restaurants, and shops. Among the things to do and see: the historic Stranahan House, the Museum of Discovery and Science, and the shops in nearby Las Olas Riverfront dining and shopping complex. To get there from I-95, exit east on Broward Boulevard and continue east to SW 5th Avenue and turn right to municipal parking. From US 1, take Broward Boulevard West to SW 5th Avenue.

In Hollywood, the family-oriented, oceanfront Broadwalk is the place to hang out; no cars, just bikes, rollerblades, and strollers, with dozens of shops and outdoor cafes along the 2.5-mile paved walkway. The closest parking is on Johnson Street off A1A.

Family-Friendly Restaurants

Cap's Place

2765 NE 28th Court, Lighthouse Point (Ft. Lauderdale, Pompano area)
(954) 941-0418

Meals served - Dinner
Cuisine - Seafood, American
Entree range - $6–12
Kids menu - Yes
Reservations - Accepted

Payment - All major credit cards accepted

You have to get there by boat, but that's part of the adventure. Cap's is on a small Intracoastal Waterway island, but many celebrities have found their way here since the place opened in 1928—notably Winston Churchill and Franklin Delano Roosevelt. An unusual house special is fresh hearts of palm, harvested from palm tree centers, a tasty and rare treat. Fresh fish any way is your best bet; they recommend broiled.

East Coast Burrito Factory

261 E. Commercial Boulevard, Ft. Lauderdale • (954) 772-8007

Meals served - Lunch and dinner

Cuisine - Florida, Mexican

Entree range - $6–12

Kids menu - No

Reservations - Not necessary

Payment - No credit cards

Great burritos, especially the veggie version, and they also serve huge salads. Kids go for the tacos. You can dine outdoors on the back patio.

Mama Mia Italian Ristorante

1818 S. Young Circle, Hollywood • (954) 923-0555

Meals served - Lunch and dinner

Cuisine - Italian

Entree range - Lunch, $6–12; dinner, $7–20

Kids menu - Yes

Reservations - Not accepted

Payment - Visa, MC, AmEx

Authentic Italian, especially the thin-crust pizzas. Portions are huge, so the whole family can share a large pie.

Old Florida Seafood House

1414 NE 26th Street, Wilton Manors • (954) 566-1044

Meals served - Dinner

Cuisine - Seafood

Entree range - $17–32

Kids menu - Yes

Reservations - Not accepted

Payment - Visa, MC, AmEx

The locals love this no-frills place, and it's usually packed. Fresh seafood and giant portions are the biggest reasons. Some fancy entrees, but the catch of the day any way you prefer it is always a delight.

Shirttail Charlie's

400 SW Third Avenue, Ft. Lauderdale • (954) 463-3474

Meals served - Lunch and dinner

Cuisine - Seafood

Entree range - Dinner on the docks, $7–14; main dining room, $18–30

Kids menu - Yes

Reservations - Recommended

Payment - All major credit cards accepted

Great place for kids. Interactive fishing machine for kids, billiards, complimentary boat ride after dinner. Try the conch fritters or conch chowder, any of the pastas, or fresh fish.

Miami and Miami Beach

World-renowned as an exotic vacation destination and a city that wears its reputation as a crime capital on its sleeve, Miami isn't usually thought of as a great place to bring the kids.

We disagree. Although places like South Beach are definitely adult (some would suggest R-rated) in their appeal, and the hustle and bustle of downtown will appeal only to adults and older children, Miami and its environs offer plenty of things to do that youngsters—and their folks—can enjoy. Attractions include a world-class zoo, a marine-mammal emporium, a science museum designed for young folk, and some private "jungles" that will delight the kids.

It's a city of 2 million where more people speak Spanish than English, a multicultural collage and ethnic grab bag. For Americans, Miami is an international destination that doesn't require a passport.

As in almost no other city, the cultural diversity of Miami opens the door to a world of new experiences for families. South of downtown Miami, Little Havana is the hub of a vibrant Cuban community. To the north is Little Haiti's Caribbean marketplace, an award-winning building inspired by the Iron Marketplace of Port-au-Prince, with shops offering Caribbean arts and crafts, clothing, and exotic ice creams and juices. With a strong Jewish community, Miami is home to one of the world's largest Holocaust survivor populations. And the Miccosukee Indians are still at home in the Everglades, 30 miles west of Miami, where you can visit.

How to Get to the Beach

Miami Beach offers 10 miles of sandy white beaches along the ocean from South Pointe Park in South Beach north to Sunny Isles at 192nd Street.

If you're not staying at a hotel close to the beaches, public beaches with metered parking, bathrooms, and outside showers are available along Route A1A (Collins Avenue) in Miami Beach at: 1st Street and

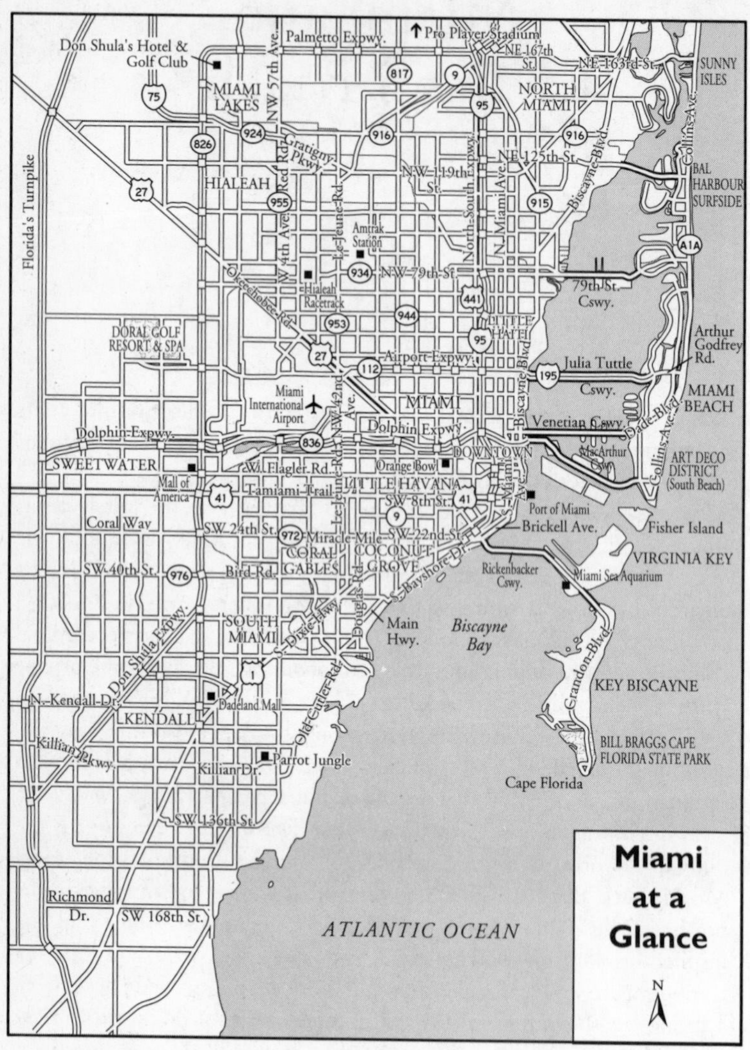

Washington Avenue (South Pointe Park); 3rd Street; 6th to 14th Streets (Lummus Park); 21st Street; 35th Street; 46th Street (next to the Eden Roc Hotel); 53rd Street; 64th Street; 73d Street (across from the North Shore Community Center); 79th to 87th Streets (North Shore State Recreation Area); 93rd Street (Surfside; a very small lot across Collins Avenue from the beach); 96th Street (another small lot); and a small lot next to the Holiday Inn on 167th Street (Sunny Isles) that charges $4 to park your car.

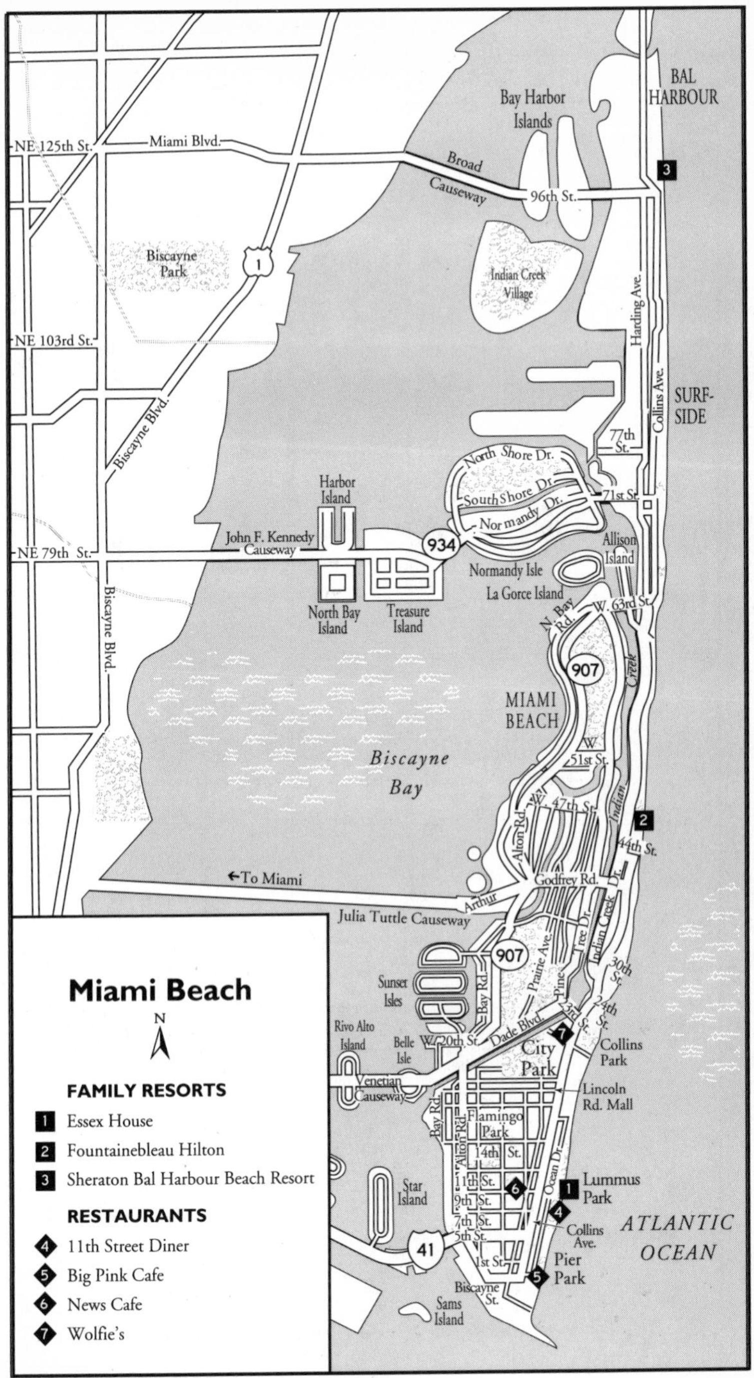

Miami Beach
N
FAMILY RESORTS
1 Essex House
2 Fountainebleau Hilton
3 Sheraton Bal Harbour Beach Resort
RESTAURANTS
4 11th Street Diner
5 Big Pink Cafe
6 News Cafe
7 Wolfie's
BAL HARBOUR
Bay Harbor Islands
NE 125th St.
Miami Blvd.
Broad Causeway
96th St.
Biscayne Park
Indian Creek Village
Harding Ave.
NE 103rd St.
Collins Ave.
SURF-SIDE
Biscayne Blvd.
77th St.
North Shore Dr.
South Shore Dr.
71st St.
Normandy Dr.
Harbor Island
John F. Kennedy Causeway
934
NE 79th St.
Allison Island
Normandy Isle
La Gorce Island
North Bay Island
Treasure Island
N. Bay Rd.
W. 63rd St.
907
MIAMI BEACH
Biscayne Bay
W 51st St.
W. 47th St.
Indian Creek
Alton Rd.
44th St.
←To Miami
Godfrey Rd.
Arthur
Julia Tuttle Causeway
Tree Dr.
Indian Creek Dr.
Prairie Ave.
Pine
30th St.
Sunset Isles
Bay Rd.
24th St.
23rd St.
Dade Blvd.
Rivo Alto Island
Belle Isle
W. 20th St.
City Park
Collins Park
Venetian Causeway
Lincoln Rd. Mall
Flamingo Park
14th St.
Star Island
11th St.
9th St.
7th St.
5th St.
Ocean Dr.
Lummus Park
Collins Ave.
ATLANTIC OCEAN
41
1st St.
Pier Park
Biscayne St.
Sams Island

Miami Area
N
FAMILY RESORTS
1 Doral Golf Resort and Spa
2 Sonesta Beach Resort
ATTRACTIONS
3 American Police Hall of Fame and Museum
4 Historical Museum of Southern Florida
5 Miami Museum of Science and Space Transit Planetarium
6 Seaquarium
7 Vizcaya Museum and Garden
Biscayne Canal
Opa-Locka Airfield
NORTH MIAMI BEACH
Haulover Beach Park
BAL HARBOUR
NE 6th Ave.
NW 135th St.
NE 135th St.
NE 123rd St.
Broad Causeway
Amelia Earhart Park
NE 125th St.
NE 125th St.
924
Gratigny Dr.
NE 119th St.
1
Gratigny Dr.
Biscayne Park
SURFSIDE
Red Rd.
Opa-Locka Canal
A1A
NE 103rd St.
NW 103rd St.
Biscayne Blvd.
Bal Harbour Beach
Collins Ave.
NW 95th St.
HIALEAH
W 29th St.
Amtrak Terminal
E 8th Ave.
NW 27th Ave.
NW 22nd Ave.
NW 79th St.
NE 79th St.
J.F. Kennedy Causeway
41st St.
85th St. Beach
E 25th St.
W 4th Ave.
Palm Ave.
E 4th Ave.
NW 17th Ave.
LITTLE HAITI
North Miami Ave.
Biscayne Blvd.
Pelican Island
Alton Rd.
E 9th St.
Dr. M. L. King Blvd.
NW 62nd St.
NE 2nd Ave.
Hialeah Dr.
NW 54th St.
NW 7th Ave.
Morningside Park
Okeechobee Rd.
Airport Expressway
112
3
Julia Tuttle Causeway
27
27
195
A1A
Miami International Airport
NW 36th St.
NW 20th St.
MIAMI BEACH
Venetian Causeway

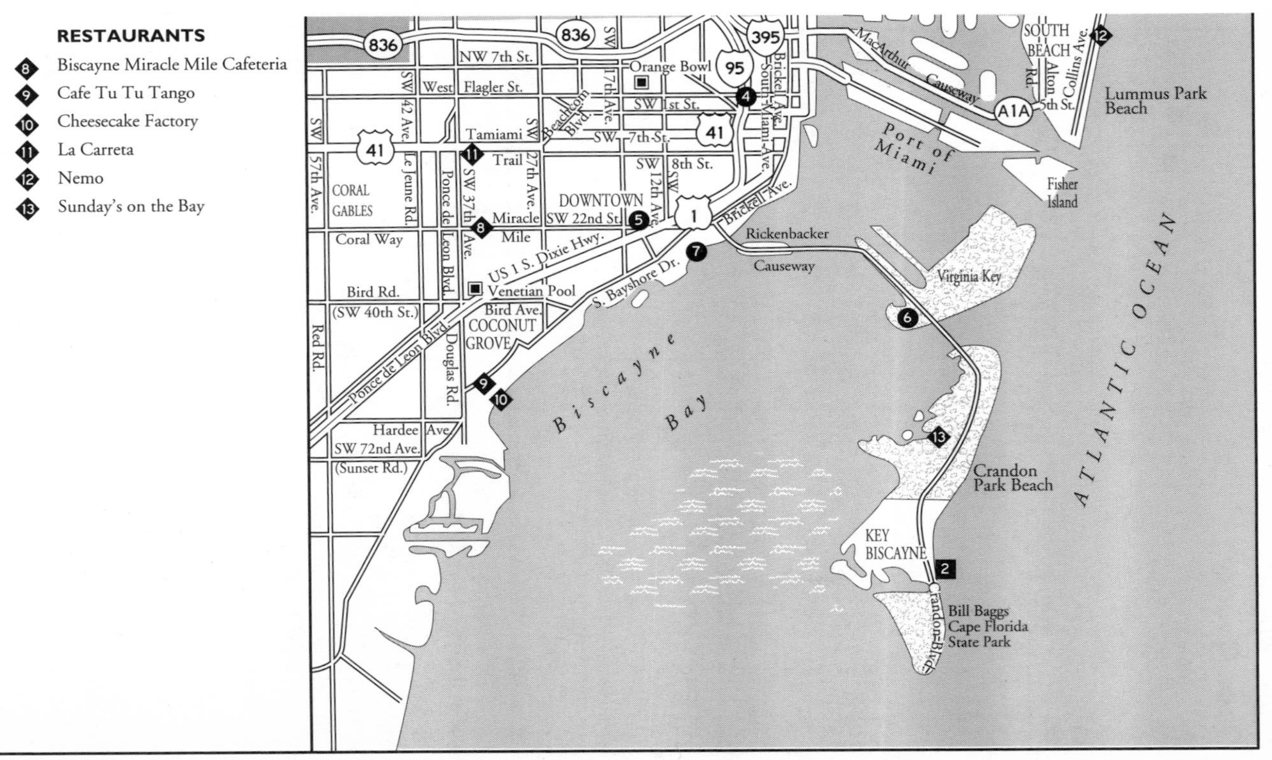
RESTAURANTS
8 Biscayne Miracle Mile Cafeteria
9 Cafe Tu Tu Tango
10 Cheesecake Factory
11 La Carreta
12 Nemo
13 Sunday's on the Bay
NW 7th St.
West Flagler St.
Orange Bowl
SW 1st St.
Tamiami Trail
SW 7th St.
SW 8th St.
Miracle Mile
DOWNTOWN
SW 22nd St.
SW 12th Ave.
SW 17th Ave.
SW 27th Ave.
SW 37th Ave.
SW 42 Ave.
SW 57th Ave.
Le Jeune Rd.
Ponce de Leon Blvd.
Beachcom Blvd.
CORAL GABLES
Coral Way
Bird Rd.
(SW 40th St.)
Red Rd.
US 1 S. Dixie Hwy.
Venetian Pool
Bird Ave.
COCONUT GROVE
Douglas Rd.
Hardee Ave.
SW 72nd Ave.
(Sunset Rd.)
S. Bayshore Dr.
Brickell Ave.
South Miami Ave.
Rickenbacker Causeway
MacArthur Causeway
Port of Miami
Fisher Island
Virginia Key
SOUTH BEACH
Alton Rd.
5th St.
Collins Ave.
Lummus Park Beach
Biscayne Bay
ATLANTIC OCEAN
Crandon Park Beach
KEY BISCAYNE
Crandon Blvd.
Bill Baggs Cape Florida State Park
836
395
95
41
1
A1A

Swimming Hazards: It's a Wild Ocean Out There

Folks on a visit to the shores of the Atlantic Ocean at Miami Beach or other South Florida beaches need to keep a few things in mind to guarantee a safe and pleasant trip. To get the low-down on beach hazards and common sense safety guidelines, we called Larry Pizzi, operations supervisor of the Miami Beach lifeguards.

On the Beach "The biggest hazard on the beach is the sun," Pizzi reports. "Even on cloudy days, the sun's ultraviolet rays filter through and you can get a really bad sunburn. Unfortunately, I hear people all the time say they can't go home without a sunburn—or no one will believe they came to Miami Beach!"

Next hazard: theft. "Be careful of your belongings on the beach," Pizzi warns. "Don't take jewelry, billfolds, or large sums of cash to the beach. Cameras are generally okay if you don't take a long walk and leave them. Just take normal precautions with your valuables."

In the Water Jellyfish, Pizzi says, top the list of hazards here. "Jellyfish can appear anytime, but are more common in the winter," he says. "Portuguese men-of-war, which are really beautiful creatures, are more common in the summer. We put out yellow warning flags to warn folks if they're in the water."

If you get stung, use a pocketknife or credit card to carefully scrape the tentacle away from the skin. "Don't rub it," Pizzi warns. "Pull it off carefully, then treat it with vinegar. Better yet, if you get stung, go to a lifeguard for help."

Sea lice—actually, the spores of Portuguese men-of-war—are invisible creatures that cause an itchy rash that's best treated with cortisone lotions. The rash can last about a week. "It's also called 'swimmers eruption,'" Pizzi adds. "It's pretty rare. But it's a good idea to avoid seaweed or anything else floating in the water, since the spores usually come into the beach on something else."

Riptides, also called undertow, usually occur when easterly winds are blowing from 15 to 20 miles an hour, creating a break in an offshore sandbar that sends water draining away from the beach.

"If you get caught in a riptide, even if you're a strong swimmer, don't fight it," Pizzi advises. "Swim parallel to the beach in the direction the water is pushing. Eventually, you'll break free. Remember that panic is the killer, and don't swim against a riptide."

When there's a riptide, a red warning flag is posted at lifeguard stations located continuously on Miami Beach from 1st to 14th Streets; at 21st, 35th, 46th, 53rd, and 64th Streets; and at North Shore State Recreation Area. A red flag is a warning not to swim, although beaches are rarely closed, and swimmers may choose to ignore the warning. Yellow flags mean caution; ask the lifeguard to tell you the specific hazard (jellyfish, riptide, etc.).

Another hazard is stingrays, which bury themselves in the sand—and occasionally get stepped on by swimmers. "They have a barb on the end of their tails which isn't poisonous, but is usually dirty, so infection is a problem," Pizzi says. "There's nothing you can do to avoid stepping on a stingray, but it's very rare."

Finally, what about everybody's favorite beach hazard—sharks?

"Shark attacks are incredibly rare, not just in Miami Beach but all over the world," Pizzi reports. "But when we get a reported sighting, we send out a boat to investigate, get the Coast Guard to send up a helicopter, and clear the beach, if necessary. We check out all the reports."

Other hazards: sport concession areas (marked with buoys), getting lost (most of the beach looks the same and lots of children and adults manage to lose the location of their cars or possessions), snorkeling and diving (mark your location with a diving flag so you're not run over by a boat), and exceeding your physical limits when swimming. "A lot of people come here when it's winter at home and they think they're in good physical shape—but they're not," Pizzi notes.

On the Water

One of the best ways to see sun-dappled Miami is from a ship, and the cruise boats that depart from downtown Miami and the marina across from the Fontainebleau Hilton on Miami Beach give visitors a chance to see the town's most spectacular sights the way they ought to be seen: from the water. Most tours are narrated in English and Spanish, and snacks and beverages are sold on board.

From Bayside, the new, two-story shopping mall by the water in downtown Miami, several large, air-conditioned tour boats leave on the hour to whisk visitors on 1-hour excursions around placid Biscayne Bay.

Tours generally leave every hour, starting at 11 a.m. until about 5:30 p.m. weekdays, and continuing until midnight on weekends. Ticket prices average $14 for adults, $7 for children ages 12 and under.

The sights include dazzling high-rise buildings downtown and the most conspicuous landmark on the water: the 65-foot Fender Stratocaster guitar rotating above the Hard Rock Cafe; its reported cost was a cool half-million dollars. Other sights on the cruise include the spiraling metal structure in Bayfront Park that's a monument to the crew of the space shuttle Challenger, and tugs, freighters, and cruise ships tied up at the Port of Miami.

Next, the tour boats swing by Fisher Island, an exclusive community of high-rise condos that can only be reached by boat or helicopter, and Miami Beach. After passing under the MacArthur Causeway connecting Miami Beach and the mainland, a number of artificial islands are next, including the aptly named Star Island and Millionaires Row. Your guide will point out the former homes of Liz Taylor, Don Johnson and Melanie Griffith, Al Capone, and other Miami notables—it seems the elusiveness of fame and the high cost of real estate dictates who stays and who leaves Star Island—and the current home of megastar Gloria Estefan.

After passing the Henry Flagler Monument and Palm Island, the tour boats swing back under the Venetian Causeway and complete their circuit of Biscayne Bay. It's a fun trip—and very scenic; (305) 577-3344.

Year-Round Sports

With top teams, world-class sport facilities, and great weather most of the year, Miami is a sports town. Joe Robbie Stadium is home to both the Miami Dolphins football team and the major league Florida Marlins baseball team.

The NBA's Miami Heat and the National Hockey League's Florida Panthers both play their games in downtown's 15,000-seat Miami Arena.

The Doral-Ryder Open welcomes the world's best golfers every March to the Doral Golf Resort and Club. And the Lipton International Players Championship at the International Tennis Center on Key Biscayne hosts the world's top tennis players each spring.

Finally, for fans of high speeds, the Marlboro Grand Prix of Miami is a world focal point for motor sports, with a race every March and year-round racing schools.

GO FLY A KITE

Skyward Kites, located at Haulover Park (10800 Collins Avenue, just north of Bal Harbour) on Miami Beach, is the place to find an astounding array of kites, wind-socks, and air bags—many floating in the breeze overhead. You can't miss it: just look up as you approach the bridge over the channel on Route A1A near Bal Harbour. A wide array of wind-borne items are for sale. The retail outlet is open from 9 a.m. to sunset daily except when it's raining; (305) 893-0906.

Family Resorts

Doral Golf Resort and Spa

4400 N.W. 87th Ave., Miami • (305) 592-2000 • www.doralresort.com

This is a win-win: championship golf for grown-ups, a fantasy pool, and other fun for kids. This 693-room, world-class spa and golf resort was undergoing a $25 million renovation at press time. You can check in and never leave the resort for the duration of your stay (though you're just 15 minutes from South Beach and other fun excursions). Along with five golf courses and the spa, there are 11 tennis courts at the Arthur Ashe Tennis Center, and the Blue Lagoon, a dreamy pool with rock facade, waterfalls, and a winding slide.

Kids ages 5–12 can learn tennis and golf from the pros at Camp Doral. Counselors also offer creative arts, fishing or just pool play. Rates start at $125 per person. Kids stay free with parents.

The Essex House

1001 Collins Avenue • (305) 534-2700, (305) 532-3927 • www.essexhotel.com

A cordial family from South America runs the Essex House, a comfortable little hotel in the Art Deco district with 60 rooms and 20 suites that have been lovingly renovated; take special note of the lobby's beautiful mural of the Everglades that was part of the restoration. The rooms and suites are spacious, and there are a swimming pool, large lobby, and courtyard to give little ones plenty of room to roam. You're a half-block from the beach and a short walk to the shops and restaurants on Lincoln Road. An ample free breakfast is offered each morning in the dining room. Rooms start at $129 in the summer, $199 in the winter, and kids stay free with parents.

Fontainebleau Hilton Resort and Towers

4441 Collins Avenue, Miami Beach • (305) 538-2000 • fax (305) 535-3299

Driving north along Miami Beach's famous Collins Avenue, look for the giant art deco mural on the exterior of the Fontainebleau. This is classic Miami Beach, a glamorous design by noted architect Morris Lapidus in the 1950s.

Today, the hotel has expanded considerably beyond its original building, covering 20 acres of oceanside gardens with 1,206 guest rooms, including 60 suites. All rooms have coffeemakers, some have refrigerators, and wet bars.

At check-in, families get a free Hilton Vacation Station Family Fun kit and free use of the resort's supply of classic toys and games. Recreation counselors also plan family barbecues, relay races, beach Olympics, and more. On the beach there are boogie boards, kayaks, paddleboats, and rafts for rent. Kids love the new 16-foot-tall octopus-shaped playland with sprays, mists, and a river raft ride.

The hotel encourages repeat visits by kids with a Jr. Travelers Program that rewards frequent visitors ages 5–12. When they visit Kids Korner, they are registered as Jr. Travelers, and with each visit they receive points redeemable for prizes.

Kids Korner is open daily, 9 a.m.–5 p.m. for $45 for a full day (includes lunch) and $25 for a half-day (no lunch). Arts and crafts, pool games, scavenger hunts, movies, and other activities are planned throughout the day. The resort also plans field trips for youngsters to attractions like Parrot Jungle and the Miami Seaquarium.

The teen program for ages 13–17 offers activities like beach volleyball, basketball contests, Ping-Pong, bingo, trivia, and water volleyball.

Some packages include free breakfast. Rates start at $220, and children ages 18 and under stay free.

Sheraton Bal Harbour Beach Resort

9701 Collins Avenue • (305) 865-7511 • fax (305) 864-2601
www.sheraton.com

Located midway between Miami and Ft. Lauderdale in the Village of Bal Harbour, this 624-room oceanfront resort (with 54 suites) caters to families—most visibly with a $12-million aquatic playground with slides, waterfalls, and a meandering design. For little ones, a wading pool and play area guarantee hours of fun.

The Harbour Kids Club for ages 5–12 has a playroom with books, puzzles, and board games. Counselors plan free activities like river pool relays, hula hoop races, and design-a-kite contests. Both full and half-day sessions are available; a full day is $45, including lunch; a half-day is $20. The resort also offers evening baby-sitting.

Each room has a coffeemaker, refrigerator, and fully stocked bar. Rates start at $225 in the summer, $279 in the winter.

Sonesta Beach Resort

350 Ocean Drive, Key Biscayne • (305) 361-2021 • fax (305) 365-2342
www.sonesta.com

The Sonesta Beach created a children's program back in 1969, long before other resorts jumped on the bandwagon. Their Just Us Kids has been operating for nearly 20 years and is still free to guests. Counselors lead morning field trips, afternoon beach and pool games, sports activities, and arts and crafts classes for children ages 5–13. Just Us Little Kids is for ages 3–4. Baby-sitters are also available. Just Us Kids starts the day at 10 a.m. and ends at 10 p.m. The only cost is for field trips—bowling, laser tag, or the Miami Seaquarium, for instance, or for lunches and dinners.

The teen program, offered Thursday, Friday, and Saturday, 5:30–10 p.m. for ages 14–17, focuses on off-property dining and entertainment. They take trips to Planet Hollywood, Hard Rock Cafe, Bayside Marketplace, and Coconut Grove.

The oceanfront resort on Key Biscayne has 292 rooms and 12 one- and two-bedroom suites. Each room has a mini-bar. Rates start at $195 in the summer, $295 in the winter.

Attractions

American Police Hall of Fame and Museum

3801 Biscayne Boulevard, Miami, at the Julia Tuttle Causeway (I-195) • (305) 573-0070 • www.aphf.com

Hours - Daily, 10 a.m.–5:30 p.m.; closed Christmas

Admission - $6 for adults, $4 for seniors ages 65 and older, $3 for children under age 12

Appeal by Age Group -

Pre-school ★	Teens ★★★	Over 30 ★★
Grade school ★★★	Young Adults ★★½	Seniors ★★½

Touring Time - Average 1½ hours; minimum 45 minutes

Rainy-Day Touring - Recommended

Author's Rating - ★½; the memorial is moving; the museum, bizarre

Restaurants - No
Alcoholic beverages - No
Handicapped access - Yes
Wheelchair rental - No
Baby stroller rental - No
Lockers - No
Pet kennels - No
Rain check - No
Private tours - Yes

Description and Comments The names, ranks, cities, and states of more than 4,000 police officers who died in the line of duty are engraved on 400 tons of white marble in the first-floor memorial. The scene is similar to the Vietnam Memorial in Washington, D.C.: flowers and mementos left by friends and relatives line the floor beneath the inscriptions. The memorial serves as a graphic reminder that a police officer is killed every 57 hours somewhere in the United States.

Upstairs, 11-year-olds will thrill to a collection of police enforcement artifacts that include a real gas chamber and electric chair ("Old Sparky"), simulated crime scenes that test powers of deduction, and displays of guns and radar units used to detect speeders.

Warning: Some of the exhibits are quite gory, such as the postelectrocution photograph of mass murderer Ted Bundy. The folks who put this museum together aren't shy about their support of capital punishment.

Coral Castle

28655 S. Federal Highway • (305) 248-6345 • www.coralcastle.com

Hours - Daily, 7 a.m.–9 p.m.

Admission - $9.75 for adults, $6.50 for seniors ages 62 and older, $5 for children ages 7–12

Appeal by Age Group -

Pre-school ★	Teens ★★	Over 30 ★★
Grade school ★★	Young Adults ★★½	Seniors ★★

Touring Time - Average 1 hour; minimum 30 minutes

Rainy-Day Touring - Not recommended

Author's Rating - ★; only visit if you've got time to spare

Restaurants - No
Alcoholic beverages - No
Handicapped access - Yes
Wheelchair rental - No
Baby stroller rental - No
Lockers - No
Pet kennels - No
Rain check - No
Private tours - Yes

Description and Comments For reasons unknown, Latvian weirdo Edward Leedskalnin (who died in 1951) carved this bizarre monument to "Sweet Sixteen," the girlfriend who jilted him back in the Old Country. He single-handedly cut and moved huge coral blocks using hand tools—a notable feat, but the results are hardly a "castle." It's essentially a courtyard filled with carvings of huge coral chairs, a table that doubles as a bird bath, a fountain, a sundial, and other stone oddities.

Some folks find the structures eerie and amazing—and, no doubt about it, the Coral Castle is genuine Florida kitsch. Our opinion: Unless you're a mechanical engineer fascinated by how this guy moved all this rock around, save yourself some money and skip it.

Fairchild Tropical Garden

10901 Old Cutler Road, Miami • (305) 667-1651

Hours - Daily, 9:30 a.m.–4:30 p.m.; closed Christmas

Admission - $8 per person, $4 ages 3–12, free for children under age 3

Appeal by Age Group -

Pre-school ★★	Teens ★★	Over 30 ★★★½
Grade school ★★½	Young Adults ★★★	Seniors ★★★★

Touring Time - Average a half-day; minimum 2 hours

Rainy-Day Touring - Not recommended

Author's Rating - ★★★★½; this manicured park filled with lush palms and exotic trees and dotted with man-made lakes is a knockout

Restaurants - Yes

Alcoholic beverages - No

Handicapped access - Yes

Wheelchair rental - No

Baby stroller rental - No

Lockers - No

Pet kennels - No

Rain check - Yes

Private tours - No

Description and Comments Fairchild Tropical Garden is the largest tropical botanical garden in the United States, with 83 beautifully landscaped acres containing plants from tropical regions around the world; its mission is education, scientific research, and display. The grounds and plant life are stunning, in spite of the beating they took from Hurricane Andrew in 1992. You don't have to be a certified tree hugger to appreciate the beauty and tranquility found here.

Fruit and Spice Park

24801 SW 187th Avenue, Homestead (located 35 miles south of Miami • from US 1, drive west on SW 248th Street • entrance is on the left after SW 187th Avenue) (305) 247-5727 • www.floridaplants.com/fruits&spice/

Hours - Daily, 10 a.m.–5 p.m.

Admission - $3.50 for adults, $1 for children under age 12

Appeal by Age Group -

Pre-school ★	Teens ★	Over 30 ★
Grade school ★	Young Adults ★	Seniors ★★

Touring Time - Average 1 hour; minimum 30 minutes beginning at 11 a.m., 1:15 and 2:30 p.m.

Rainy-Day Touring - Not recommended

Author's Rating - ★; fascinating and fun on a cool, overcast day, not so much fun in full sun

Restaurants - No

Alcoholic beverages - No

Handicapped access - Yes

Wheelchair rental - No

Baby stroller rental - No

Lockers - No

Pet kennels - No

Rain check - No

Private tours - No

Description and Comments This 35-acre park was once a delightful oasis of tropical fruit and spice trees with an abundance of shade, but Hurricane Andrew virtually flattened the park, and it will take years to regain its former loveliness. At the park entrance, you're invited to nibble samples of passion fruit, sapodilla, banana, lime, mango—whatever's ripe. Go early to avoid the sun and stroll the paths where you'll find 100 varieties of citrus and 85 kinds of bananas—markers identify each plant.

Historical Museum of Southern Florida

101 W. Flagler Street in downtown Miami, in the Metro-Dade Cultural Center • (305) 375-1492 • www.historical-museum.org

Hours - Monday–Saturday, 10 a.m.–5 p.m.; Thursday, 10 a.m.–9 p.m.; Sunday, noon–5 p.m.

Admission - $5 for adults, $2 for children ages 6–12, free for children under age 6

Appeal by Age Group -

Pre-school ★★	Teens ★★½	Over 30 ★★★
Grade school ★★★	Young Adults ★★★	Seniors ★★★

Touring Time - Average 1–2 hours; minimum 1 hour

Rainy-Day Touring - Recommended

Author's Rating - ★★★★; a spiffy museum that will entertain and educate kids and adults

Restaurants - No

Alcoholic beverages - No

Handicapped access - Yes

Wheelchair rental - No

Baby stroller rental - No
Lockers - No
Pet kennels - No
Rain check - No
Private tours - Yes

Description and Comments Displaying 10,000 years of Florida history, with lots of interactive displays (some feature earphones that let you hear jungle sounds; others are big enough to walk through), this sparkling, well-designed museum is a lot of fun. Visitors can discover the Florida that existed before the tourists came—even before people set foot in South Florida. The museum also emphasizes the rich cultural diversity of modern Florida's multiethnic population, ranging from Hispanic theater to Jewish heritage.

Kids really like the various colonial-era cannons in the historical exhibits. They'll also like climbing aboard a 1920s trolley car.

MetroZoo

12400 SW 152nd Street, Miami (take the Florida Turnpike Extension to the SW 152nd Street exit and follow the signs to the entrance) • (305) 251-0400 or 251-0401
www.miamimetrozoo.org

Hours - Daily, 9:30 a.m.–5:30 p.m. daily; open every day of the year

Admission - $8.95 for adults, $4.75 for children ages 3–12; 10% off regular admission for military, seniors, travel agents

Appeal by Age Group -

Pre-school ★★★★	Teens ★★★	Over 30 ★★★
Grade school ★★★★	Young Adults ★★★	Seniors ★★★

Touring Time - Average a half-day; minimum 2 hours

Rainy-Day Touring - Not recommended

Author's Rating - ★★★★★; it's no surprise that this is rated by experts as one of the best zoos in the world. And no cages mean that people who normally hate zoos may love this one

Restaurants - Yes
Alcoholic beverages - No
Handicapped access - Yes
Wheelchair rental - $7, 30 electric
Baby stroller rental - Yes, $6–9
Lockers - No
Pet kennels - No
Rain check - No
Private tours - Yes

Description and Comments This is a "new style" zoo that features cageless animals that roam on plots of land surrounded by moats. Start your visit with a trip on the air-conditioned Zoofari monorail, which makes a complete loop of MetroZoo in about 25 minutes. Then either get off at station 1 and begin walking toward station 2, or continue on the train to station 4 (the last stop) and walk back toward the entrance. Along the way you'll pass exhibits featuring gorillas, chimpanzees, elephants, Himalayan black bears, a white Bengal tiger, and other exotic animals. Some exhibits feature "viewing caves" that let you view animals through plate glass windows on their side of the moat. In all, there are about 260 species with more than 900 reptiles, birds, and mammals.

There's also a narrated tram tour that shows some behind-the-scenes areas such as the animal hospital. And a new play area for kids features a petting zoo.

One word of warning: in spite of the shade trees, the zoo gets extremely hot in the midday sun, so try to time your visit for early morning or late afternoon. That's also when the animals are most active. Scheduled to open in 2003 is The Wings of Asia Aviary, with about 300 birds and the ambiance of an Asian jungle.

Miami Museum of Science and Space Transit

3280 South Miami Avenue, Miami • (305) 646-4200 • www.miamisci.org

Hours - Daily, 10 a.m.–6 p.m.

Admission - Museum and planetarium: $10 for adults, $8 for students with ID and senior citizens ages 62 an older, $6 for children ages 3–12. After 4 p.m. on weekdays admission is half price; Friday nights only, $7 for adults, $4 for children and senior citizens. Laser show costs separate admission

Appeal by Age Group -

Pre-school ★★★	Teens ★★	Over 30 ★
Grade school ★★★	Young Adults ★	Seniors ★

Touring Time - Average 3 hours; minimum 2 hours

Rainy-Day Touring - Recommended

Author's Rating - ★; only fun if you have kids along

Restaurants - No

Alcoholic beverages - No

Handicapped access - Yes

Wheelchair rental - No

Baby stroller rental - No

Lockers - No

Pet kennels - No

Rain check - No

Private tours - Groups of 20 or more

Description and Comments This kid-friendly science museum and planetarium was rated the No. 1 museum in Dade County by the readers of *South Florida Parenting* magazine. While the exhibits thrill youngsters, older visitors can't help but notice the worn indoor-outdoor carpeting, the exhibits that don't work, and its overall shabby appearance. Overall, it's more like a high-tech playground for kids than a museum.

Monkey Jungle

14805 SW 216th Street • (305) 235-1611

Hours - Daily, 9:30 a.m.–5 p.m.; ticket office closes at 4 p.m.

Admission - $15.95 for adults, $9.95 for children ages 4–12

Appeal by Age Group -

Pre-school ★★★★	Teens ★★★★	Over 30 ★★★
Grade school ★★★★	Young Adults ★★★	Seniors ★★★

Touring Time - Average 2 hours; minimum 1 hour

Rainy-Day Touring - Not recommended

Author's Rating - ★★★½; a lot of fun—and it's OK to feed the primates

Restaurants - Yes

Alcoholic beverages - No

Handicapped access - Yes

Wheelchair rental - No

Baby stroller rental - No

Lockers - No

Pet kennels - No

Rain check - Yes

Private tours - No

Description and Comments Children especially love visiting this attraction, founded, by the way, in the 1930s when admission was just 10 cents. Gibbons, spider monkeys, orangutans, a gorilla, chimpanzees, and more are all close at hand as you walk through screened walkways that wind through a tropical forest. While not all the monkeys roam free—a lot of them reside in large cages located along the walkways—many primates can be seen when you pass through the larger jungle habitat.

Parrot Jungle and Gardens

11000 SW 57th Avenue (Red Road) • (305) 666-7834 • www.parrotjungle.com.
Note: *The Jungle is slated to move to Watson Island in 2003.*

Hours - Daily, 9:30 a.m.–6 p.m.

Admission - $14.95 for adults, $9.95 for children ages 3–10

Appeal by Age Group -

Pre-school ★★★★★	Teens ★★★½	Over 30 ★★★★
Grade school ★★★★★	Young Adults ★★★★	Seniors ★★★★

Touring Time - Average 3 hours; minimum 2 hours

Rainy-Day Touring - Not recommended

Author's Rating - ★★★★½; what a hoot—or, better yet, screech. Don't miss it

Restaurants - Yes

Alcoholic beverages - Yes

Handicapped access - Yes

Wheelchair rating - Yes

Baby stroller rating - Yes
Lockers - No
Pet kennels - No
Rain check - Yes
Private tours - No

Description and Comments Parrot Jungle is an old-fashioned bird sanctuary and botanical garden that also includes trained bird shows, a flock of pink flamingos, and wildlife shows. You'll find a lot more than a zillion parrots (actually, about 2,000) at Parrot Jungle. Alligators, gibbons, pink flamingos, tortoises, a children's playground, a petting zoo, and a Miccosukee Indian display are waiting to be discovered in this lush tropical garden. Fortunately, winding paths disperse the crowds that flock to this place throughout its 12 acres. Along the way you'll see more than 1,100 varieties of birds and more than 1,000 types of plants. It's a great park and a real Florida classic. By 2003, Parrot Jungle should be in its new, $46 million home on Watson Island along MacArthur Causeway connecting Miami and South Beach.

Seaquarium

4400 Rickenbacker Causeway (on Virginia Key between Key Biscayne and Miami)
(305) 361-5705

Hours - Daily, 9:30 a.m.–6 p.m.; ticket office closes at 4:30 p.m.

Admission - $221.95 for adults, $17.95 for children ages 3–9

Appeal by Age Group -

Pre-school ★★★★	Teens ★★★	Over 30 ★★½
Grade school ★★★★	Young Adults ★★★½	Seniors ★★

Touring Time - Average 4 hours; minimum 2 hours

Rainy-Day Touring - Not recommended

Author's Rating - ★★; expensive, and a bit worn around the edges

Restaurants - Yes
Alcoholic beverages - No
Handicapped access - Yes
Wheelchair rental - Yes
Baby stroller rental - Yes
Lockers - No
Pet kennels - No
Rain check - No
Private tours - No

Description and Comments Unquestionably, the hottest attraction at this tropical marine aquarium is Lolita, Seaquarium's killer whale. It's an adrenaline rush you don't want to miss when this 20-foot-long behemoth goes airborne—and lands with a splash that drenches the first 10 rows of spectators. Plan your visit around the Killer Whale Show, which takes place at 11:45 a.m. and 3:40 p.m. (Call to make sure this schedule hasn't changed.)

Other performances at Seaquarium include the "Flipper" Show, a reef aquarium presentation, the Top Deck Dolphin Show, the Golden Dome Sea Lion Show, and a shark presentation. There's also a rain forest, a sea life touch pool, a wildlife habitat, a crocodile exhibit, and a tropical aquarium to view between shows.

The Seaquarium shows are slick and well orchestrated. But like the disco music played during the performances, this marine-life park struck us as a little worn and outdated. (It's almost 40 years old.) And following the recent dose of consciousness-raising from the hit film Free Willy, a lot of folks may feel a twinge of guilt as they watch these magnificent but captive animals.

Vizcaya Museum and Garden

3521 South Miami Avenue, Miami • (305) 250-9133 • www.vizcayamuseum.com

Hours - Daily, 9:30 a.m.–5 p.m.; ticket office closes at 4:30 p.m. and the gardens close at 5:30

Admission - $10 for adults, $5 for children ages 6–12

Appeal by Age Group -

Pre-school ★	Teens ★★½	Over 30 ★★★½
Grade school ★★	Young Adults ★★★	Seniors ★★★★

Touring Time - Average 2 hours; minimum 1 hour

Rainy-Day Touring - Not recommended

Author's Rating: ★★★, the mansion; ★★★★★, the gardens

Restaurants - Yes **Alcoholic beverages -** Yes

Handicapped access - Yes **Wheelchair rental -** No

Baby stroller rental - No **Lockers -** No

Pet kennels - No **Rain check -** No

Private tours - Yes

Description and Comments Chicago industrialist James Deering built his winter home on the shores of Biscayne Bay in 1916, an era when the fabulously rich weren't shy about showing off their wealth. Vizcaya's 34 rooms are loaded with period furniture, textiles, sculptures, and paintings from the fifteenth century through the early nineteenth century. The effect is that of a great country estate that's been continuously occupied for 400 years.

Most visitors go on a guided tour of the first floor that lasts 45 minutes. (If no tour guides are available, you're given a guidebook and turned loose.) Highlights of the magnificent rooms include a rug that Christopher Columbus stood on, an ornate telephone booth (check out the early example of a dial telephone), and dramatic carved ceilings and patterned marble floors. The house also has some eccentricities: Mr. Deering didn't like doors slamming from the continuous breeze off the bay, so many doors were hung at off-angles so they would close slowly. The breeze is not as much of a problem today: the proliferation of high-rise condos on Biscayne Bay blocks much of the wind.

Family-Friendly Restaurants

11th Street Diner

1065 Washington Avenue, Miami Beach • (305) 534-6373

Meals served - Breakfast, lunch, and dinner (open 24 hours; except Tuesday nights when they close early for cleaning)

Cuisine - American classic

Entree range - $9–23

Kids menu - No, but have grilled cheese and hamburgers

Reservations - Not accepted

Payment - All major credit cards accepted (except Discover)

Miamians say the diner makes the best burgers on the beach. Philly cheese steak, tuna melt, and other sandwiches are available. Also hefty omelets and thick shakes.

Big Pink Cafe

157 Collins Avenue, Miami Beach • (305) 532-4700

Meals served - Lunch and dinner

Cuisine - American

Entree range - $8–22

Kids menu - Yes

Reservations - Accepted only for parties of 10 or more

Payment - Visa, MC, AmEx

Most popular is their unique, signature TV Dinner, served on a huge stainless steel tray with six compartments for $13.95. Everything comes in large portions: salads, burgers, pastas, wood-burning oven pizzas. And they serve breakfast all day long.

Biscayne Miracle Mile Cafeteria

147 Miracle Mile, Coral Gables • (305) 444-9005

Meals served - Lunch and dinner

Cuisine - Southern American

Entree range - $5–10

Kids menu - No

Reservations - Not necessary

Payment - Visa, MC

This old-fashioned cafeteria has been serving home-cooked meals for generations, old favorites like roast beef, fried shrimp, and baked fish. Good and cheap.

Cafe Tu Tu Tango

3015 Grand Avenue (in CocoWalk), Coconut Grove • (305) 529-2222

Meals served - Lunch and dinner

Cuisine - Spanish, international

Entree range - $5–12

Kids menu - Yes

Reservations - Priority seating

Payment - Visa, MC, AmEx

Cafe Tu Tu Tango is designed to look like an artist's loft, so it's fun for the kids to wander around and check out the original paintings in the casual place. The food is fun, too: egg rolls, pastas, pizzas, and creative salads are all perfect for sharing.

Cheesecake Factory

3015 Grand Avenue, Coconut Grove (CocoWalk) • (305) 447-9898

Meals served - Lunch and dinner; brunch Saturday and Sunday until 2 p.m.

Cuisine - Eclectic American

Entree range - $8.95–22.95

Kids menu - No, but there's a large selection for kids

Reservations - Not accepted

Payment - All major credit cards accepted

There's always a wait for a seat in this bustling restaurant, but the food—not just the cheesecake—is worth it. Pastas, salads, sandwiches all come in huge portions, so share with your child. And you have to choose from among 35 flavors, but do save room for a slice of the divine cheesecake.

La Carreta

3632 SW 8th Street, Little Havana • (305) 444-7501

Meals served - Breakfast, lunch, and dinner (open 24 hours)

Cuisine - Cuban

Entree range - $8–23

Kids menu - Yes

Reservations - Not necessary

Payment - Visa, MC, Discover

Traditional, inexpensive, and filling Cuban food is served in these cavernous restaurants.

Nemo

100 Collins Ave., South Beach • (305) 532-4550

Meals served - Lunch and dinner

Cuisine - Pan-Asian

Entree range - $9.95–23.95

Kids menu - No

Reservations - Yes

Payment - All major credit cards accepted

Dine under the shade trees at this South Beach hangout. At lunchtime, go for an all-American burger or pulled barbecue. After dark, the menu gets more exotic, with specialties like wok-charred salmon or Indian-spiced grilled pork.

News Cafe

800 Ocean Drive, South Miami Beach • (305) 538-6397

Meals served - Breakfast, lunch, and dinner

Cuisine - American

Entree range - $5–17

Kids menu - No, but smaller portions can be made to accommodate kids

Reservations - Not necessary

Payment - Visa, MC, AmEx, DC

It's on trendy South Beach, and families often come by for breakfast. If you're early enough you might get a coveted outdoor table. Food is quite good and healthful—plenty of salads, pizzas, and Key lime pie.

Sunday's on the Bay

5420 Crandon Boulevard, Key Biscayne • (305) 361-6777

Meals served - Lunch and dinner

Cuisine - Seafood

Entree range - $13.95–29.95

Kids menu - Yes, $4 and up

Reservations - Accepted

Payment - All major credit cards accepted

Most of the tables are on the porch overlooking pretty Biscayne Bay. Sunday's serves traditional fare—surf and turf, grouper, lobster, and chicken, but it's well prepared and you can't beat the view on a sunny afternoon.

Wolfie's

2038 Collins Avenue, Miami Beach • (305) 538-6626

Meals served - Breakfast, lunch, and dinner (open 24 hours)

Cuisine - Gourmet American deli

Entree range - $4.95–19.95; $7.95 early bird special

Kids menu - Yes

Reservations - Not accepted

Payment - All major credit cards accepted

Wolfie's is showing its age, but the potato pancakes, chicken soup with matzo balls, thick sandwiches, freshly baked cheesecake, and free pickles keep the regulars coming back. Wolfie's is very family-friendly; children can color their menus and "win" dessert on the house.

The Florida Keys

The Keys are a tourist, diving, and sportfishing mecca drawing a million visitors each year. US 1 stretches more than 100 miles beyond the tip of mainland South Florida, linking a string of islands that form a natural barrier between the Atlantic Ocean and the Gulf of Mexico, which ends up closer to Cuba than to the U.S. mainland. The mingling of these waters results in a fantastic array of marine life—and world-class sportfishing. Some families come to dive and snorkel in crystal-clear waters and view the only coral reef in the United States. Others explore the Keys' unusual and beautiful backcountry, which is full of birds and marine life (see pages 382–384).

One reason not to come to the Keys is to savor miles and miles of gleaming white beaches: There's no naturally occurring sand. It takes waves to make sand, and the offshore reef eliminates the surf action.

Key West is, geographically speaking, in a unique position between the Atlantic Ocean and the Gulf of Mexico. For outdoor enthusiasts, there's a wealth of things to do and see, including world-class snorkeling and scuba diving, deep-sea fishing, sight-seeing, and exploring the Dry Tortugas and Fort Jefferson, a nineteenth-century coastal fortification 70 miles west of Key West that's only accessible by boat or sea plane.

"We're on the seam of two huge bodies of water and tremendous tidal forces and flows of water wash across the Keys twice daily," explains Captain Jeff Cardenas, a retired fishing guide and owner of the Saltwater Angler, a custom fishing rod, tackle, and outdoors shop in Key West. "The result is wonderful feeding and breeding grounds for aquatic wildlife—and a tremendous water clarity. Key West is where the land runs out and the ocean takes over."

Getting There

By Plane While both Key West and Marathon (located in the Middle Keys) have small commercial airports, most folks headed to the Keys by

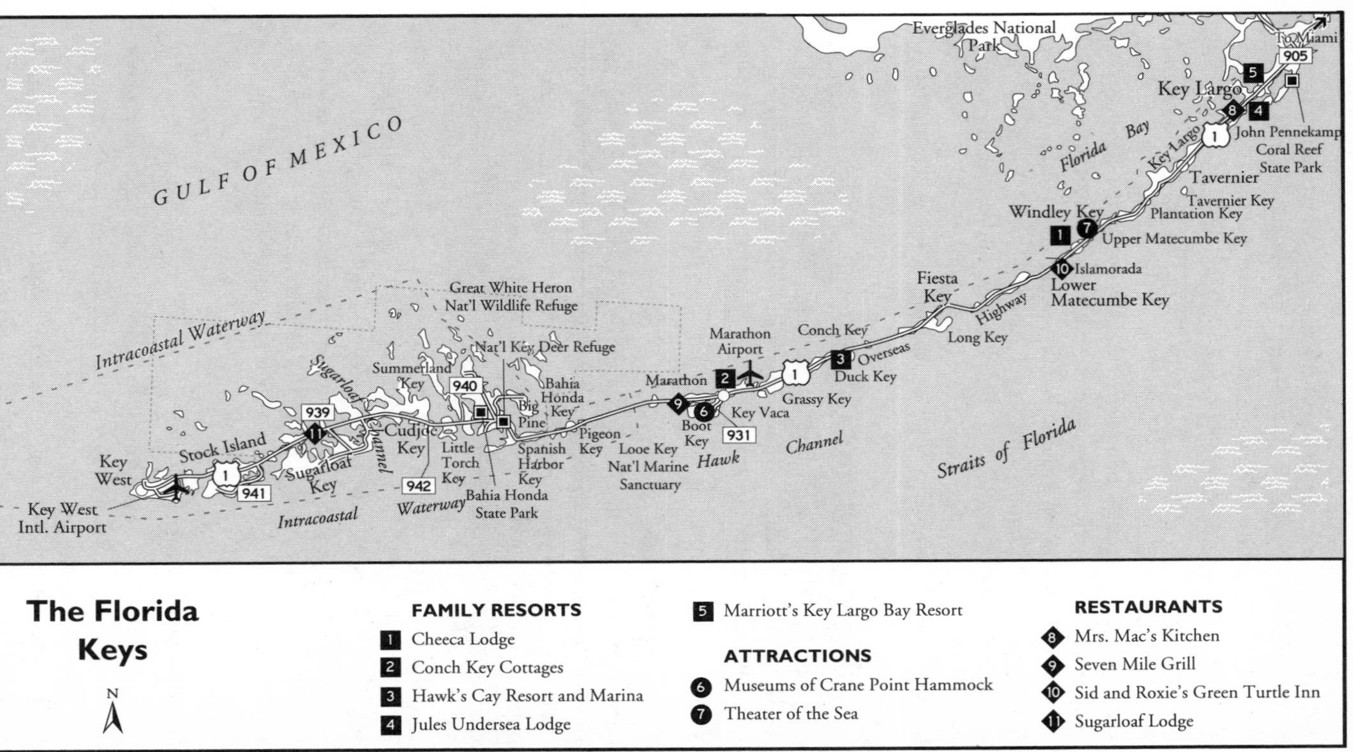
The Florida Keys
N
GULF OF MEXICO
Everglades National Park
To Miami
905
Key Largo
John Pennekamp Coral Reef State Park
Florida Bay
Key Largo
Tavernier
Tavernier Key
Plantation Key
Windley Key
Upper Matecumbe Key
Islamorada
Lower Matecumbe Key
Fiesta Key
Highway
Long Key
Conch Key
Overseas
Duck Key
Grassy Key
Marathon Airport
Marathon
Key Vaca
Boot Key
931
Great White Heron Nat'l Wildlife Refuge
Nat'l Key Deer Refuge
Intracoastal Waterway
Summerland Key
940
Bahia Honda Key
Big Pine
Pigeon Key
Looe Key Nat'l Marine Sanctuary
Hawk Channel
Straits of Florida
Spanish Harbor Key
Bahia Honda State Park
Little Torch Key
942
Cudjoe Key
Sugarloaf Channel
939
Sugarloaf Key
Stock Island
941
Key West
Key West Intl. Airport
Intracoastal Waterway
FAMILY RESORTS
1 Cheeca Lodge
2 Conch Key Cottages
3 Hawk's Cay Resort and Marina
4 Jules Undersea Lodge
5 Marriott's Key Largo Bay Resort
ATTRACTIONS
6 Museums of Crane Point Hammock
7 Theater of the Sea
RESTAURANTS
8 Mrs. Mac's Kitchen
9 Seven Mile Grill
10 Sid and Roxie's Green Turtle Inn
11 Sugarloaf Lodge

air arrive at Miami International Airport, rent a car, and drive to their final destination. You can be in the Upper Keys in about 1 hour, in Key West in 3 hours (a little longer if it's a Friday afternoon).

By Car From Miami, take the Florida Turnpike until it ends at Florida City, then take US 1 south. US 1 is mostly two-lane road as it heads over land and water on its way to Key West. During the winter, avoid driving to the Keys on Friday afternoon and evening or on Sunday evenings—the traffic is usually horrendous and multihour backups are routine. After passing Florida City, you can make a more dramatic entrance to the Keys than US 1 by hanging a left onto Card Sound Road (SR 905A). You'll miss most of the tourist traffic heading south, and the toll bridge over Card Sound offers a great view of undeveloped Key Largo and Florida Bay. (Savor the view—farther south on Key Largo, the commercialism is rampant.)

Driving through the Keys

The 112-mile Overseas Highway, sometimes called the "Highway That Goes to the Sea," leapfrogs from key to key, with lovely seascapes and a brilliant blue sky. It's fun to explore the islands along the way to Key West.

The Upper Keys

After merging back with US 1 (now called the Overseas Highway), continue south on to Key Largo. This town is close enough to Homestead and the southern 'burbs of Miami to serve as a bedroom community to the city, and strip malls, restaurants, gas stations, and fast-food joints line the highway. Keep heading south unless you want to stop at John Pennekamp Coral Reef State Park (see Family Outdoor Adventures, page 382).

Tavernier is the next town as you continue south, with Harry Harris Park, located at MM 92.5, if you need to pull over and relax. There's a small beach, barbecue pits, picnic tables, and a playground.

Past Tavernier is a 20-mile stretch of islands collectively known as Islamorada (EYE-la-ma-RAHD-a), which is best known for sportfishing, but snorkeling and diving are excellent here, too. Stop in any dive shop along the highway for more details.

The Middle Keys

South of Long Keys are the Middle Keys, with views of the water on both sides—you get the feeling you're actually off the North American continent and out to sea.

The next town is Marathon, the second-largest community in the Keys; it even has an airport. Kids enjoy Marathon's Dolphin Research

Center, a nonprofit, educational facility at MM 59. Hour-long, guided tours are Wednesday–Sunday at 10 and 11 a.m. and 12:30, 2, and 3:30 p.m. Tickets are $15 for adults, $12.50 for ages 55 and older, and $10 for children ages 4–12. Reservations aren't required; (305) 289-1121.

For a quick dip, Sombrero Beach, off the Overseas Highway at MM 50, is a family beach on the ocean with a small grassy park and picnic tables.

Next is the Seven Mile Bridge, built in the 1980s, which connects Marathon to the Lower Keys. To the right is the original bridge, built by Henry Flagler for his Overseas Railroad in the early years of the twentieth century. Today it's a fishing and jogging pier par excellence.

Little Green Signs

Those signs on the side of the road are mile markers (MM), making it easy to find places along US 1 from Key Largo to Key West. The numbers begin with 1 in Key West and go to 113 in Key Largo. If there's an *O* beside an address, it means oceanside; *B* is for bayside.

The Lower Keys

Entering the Lower Keys is like stepping back in time; it's easy to imagine that the rest of the Keys, now so commercial, must have looked like this 30 years ago. These islands are heavily wooded, primarily residential, and decidedly noncommercial.

The Lower Keys are where you find Bahia Honda State Recreation Area (see page 379), located at MM 37 and one of the loveliest spots in the Keys. Big Pine Key is home to canine-size deer, an endangered species under federal protection since 1952; the miniature white-tailed deer are found only on Big Pine Key and 16 surrounding keys. The Key Deer National Wildlife Refuge is the only wildlife refuge in the Keys accessible without taking a boat ride; your best chance to see the deer is in the early morning, late afternoon, or early evening. Take Key Deer Boulevard to Watson Boulevard to pick up information at the refuge headquarters, open Monday through Friday, 8 a.m.–5 p.m.

Looe Key National Marine Sanctuary, a submerged reef 6 miles southeast of Big Pine Key, is considered the best reef in the Keys for snorkeling, diving, fishing, and boating.

Next is Key West; as US 1 enters Key West, a sign for the far right lane reads: "Right Lane Go at All Times." Stay right and North Roosevelt Boulevard leads to Duval Street and Old Town Key West. If you go left as you enter Key West, you'll pass Houseboat Row, the Atlantic Ocean, snazzy resorts, Key West International Airport, Southernmost Point, and Old Town.

On the Water

Even kids can handle a kayak in the calm waters of the Gulf of Mexico in the Florida Keys, where you may see lobsters, turtles, stingrays, and tarpon. Reflections Kayak Nature Tours, MM 28.5, Little Torch Key will take you to Everglades National Park or Great White Heron National Wildlife Refuge for $20–140; (305) 872-4668; www.floridakeyskayak tours.com.

Operating two boats daily, 9 a.m. and 1:30 p.m., with group and private charters available, *Coral Sea* takes you out to snorkel dive and view reefs and wrecks just miles off Islamorada shores. Cost is $25–40, including equipment. The boat departs from Bud 'n' Mary's Dive Center, MM 79, Islamorada; (305) 664-2211; www.keydives.com.

Families looking for some recommendations for reputable guides and fishing boat charters available at Key West marinas can stop by the Saltwater Angler at 219 Simonton Street and talk to Captain Cardenas, who spent 10 years guiding flats fishermen in the Keys before opening his custom rod shop. He's an expert on the outdoors around Key West and happy to offer advice. Call (305) 294-3248, 9 a.m.–8 p.m. daily.

The *MV Discovery,* a glass-bottom boat with an underwater viewing room that puts you at eye level with marine life, offers trips during the summer at 11:30 a.m., noon, 2:30 p.m., and sunset, and during the winter at 10:30 a.m., 1:30 p.m., and an hour or so before sunset. Tickets for the 2-hour trip are $25 for adults and $16 for children ages 3–12; kids sail free on the first trip of the day. Sunset trip tickets are $30 for adults and $16 for children 3–12. The ship is located at the Lands End Marina, 251 Margaret Street in Key West. For more information, call (305) 293-0099; www.discoveryunderseatours.com.

A seemingly limitless number of kiosks and dive shops in Key West offer half-day snorkeling and diving trips to the reef. Shop around for the best price and most convenient departure time. If you have your own gear, you can snorkel right from the beach at Fort Zachary Taylor State Historic Site, located in the Truman Annex at Whitehead and Southard streets in Old Town Key West.

Family Resorts

Cheeca Lodge

Mile marker 82, Islamorada • (800) 327-2888 or (305) 664-4651 • fax (305) 664-2893 • www.cheeca.com

Mention kids and the Keys in the same sentence, and someone will recommend Cheeca Lodge, even other nearby hoteliers. The resort has an outstanding children's program, called Camp Cheeca, fashioned after the Aquatic Wild program developed by the State of Florida. The award-winning marine education–environmental awareness day camp for ages 6–12, is open weekends year-round and full weeks (Tuesday through Sunday) during peak season. Cost is $25 per child for a half-day, $38 full day.

Camp Cheeca's most popular activities include fishing off the resort's wooden pier, where children are taught the art of hand-lining to land a fish, canoeing at Long Key, and snorkeling at Pennekamp underwater park. Even games are designed to instruct as well as entertain; for instance, the outdoor team-building game "turtle hurdles" enacts the life cycle of an endangered sea turtle. Kids Night Out, Thursday, Friday and Saturday, $25 per child.

Grown-ups can sign up for golf clinics, tennis clinics, scuba instruction, water skiing lessons, even private swimming instructions. If you need an underwater camera, they'll supply it. And fishing is excellent, with more than 600 species in the surrounding waters. Their enviro-tours take you snorkeling or to historical islands to scout for dolphins, manatees, bald eagles, and white herons.

The resort is on 27 acres of tropical gardens, with 154 villa rooms and suites and 49 guest rooms in the main lodge. Villas have full kitchens, one or two bedrooms, and screened porches. All rooms have wet bars, and suites have microwaves, refrigerators, and coffeemakers. Rates start at $300 in the summer, $255 in the winter.

Conch Key Cottages

Mile marker 62.3, 62250 Overseas Highway, Marathon • (305) 289-1377 or (800) 330-1577 • fax (305) 743-8207 • www.florida-keys.fl.us/ckc.htm

For a laid-back family getaway, friends recommend lattice-trimmed Conch Key Cottages, 11 one-, two- and three-bedroom cottages, some with screened porches, some with back doors leading to the beach. They're all air conditioned and have televisions and full kitchens. Furnishings are reed, rattan, and wicker, with wide hammocks for afternoon naps. Laundry facilities are on the premises.

Conch Key Cottages are tucked away on their own little island, bridged by a small causeway. Hibiscus, bougainvillea, and other tropical flowers bloom nearly year-round, creating a lush, lovely getaway.

Also available, The Sand Dollar is motel a efficiency, ground level with a kitchenette, A/C, cable TV, King size bed, BBQ grill and picnic table, "Complimentary 2 person Kayak with your entire stay." Rates are $110 in the summer and $74 in the winter. This unit will accommodate two people only (No exceptions). No pets are allowed in the Cottages or the Sand Dollar. Rates start at $142–288 in the summer, $120–215 in the winter.

Hawk's Cay Resort and Marina

MM 61, Duck Key • (305) 743-7000 • www.hawkscay.com

Hawk's Cay is a longtime favorite, ideal for families with babies, toddlers, and preschoolers. The main resort sits on a 60-acre private island, wrapping around the swimming pool, beach, and lagoon, with plenty of sand toys for the kids. The Little Pirates' Club for ages 3 to 5 schedules activities Tuesday through Sunday from 9 a.m. to 1 p.m. for $30, including lunch. The children must be potty-trained. The Island Adventure Club for ages 6 to 12 features nature-oriented games, crafts, and water sports Tuesday through Sunday from 9 a.m. to 4 p.m.; cost is $40 for a full day, $30 for a half-day. Kids Night Out for ages 5–12 is every Wednesday, Friday, and Saturday 6:45–10 p.m. and includes crafts, dinner and a movie for $30.

The Hawk's Cay Dolphin Connection is a 45-minute program with 25 minutes in the water with the dolphins. Cost is $100. Two other programs—Dockside Dolphins and Dolphin Detectives (each $45)—allow guests to assist the trainers as they learn about dolphins' behavior.

There are 160 spacious rooms and 16 suites with mini-refrigerators and coffeemakers; rates start at $210 in the summer, $240 in the winter.

Jules Undersea Lodge

51 Shoreland Drive, MM 102.5, Key Largo • (305) 451-2353 • fax (305) 451-4789 • www.jul.com

Everyone in the family has to be able to scuba dive, but if you're an adventurous family with teenagers, this resort is a real hit. Diving through the tropical mangrove habitat of the Emerald Lagoon and approaching the world's only underwater hotel 30 feet beneath the ocean is an unforgettable experience—and definitely not for the claustrophobic.

Once you're dry, the 42-inch round windows in this underwater cottage provide a live show that beats any television. However, all the creature comforts are there, including air conditioning; hot showers; a well-stocked kitchen with microwave, refrigerator, and coffeemaker; books; music; and videos. And when you are tucked in at night in one of the two private bedrooms, you can watch the angelfish, parrotfish, barracuda, and snappers visit the windows. And, yes, there's a telephone. A local restaurant even delivers late-night pizza.

And you don't need to be nervous, because the place is monitored 24 hours a day, connected to the control center with an "umbilical cable" that delivers fresh air, water, power, and communications. And there's a backup system.

Free dinner and breakfast. The lodge can accommodate up to 6; rates are $250–350 a night for each diver (group rates available); children must be at least 12 years old.

Marriott's Key Largo Bay Resort

103800 Overseas Highway, MM 103.8, Key Largo • (305) 453-0000 • fax (305) 451-6054 • www.marriott.com

The Marriott Key Largo is just 45 minutes from Miami, but a world apart from the jammed highways and congestion of the city. There's plenty of kid stuff, with a daily themed Kids Club—Mardi Gras Day, Super Sports Day, and Circus Day, for example. The whole family is encouraged to join in the planned activities like poolside bingo, sand dollar painting, coconut painting, and sand art (each for a nominal fee). The Kids Club is available Wednesday through Sunday, full days (10 a.m.–4 p.m.) or half days (10 a.m.–12:30 p.m. or 1–4 p.m.). Cost is $40 a day, $20 for half a day. Kids Night Out is for ages 5–13 every Friday and Saturday from 6–10 p.m. Cost is $30. Games, pizza, and movies are on the agenda.

The Marriott has 153 rooms and suites on 17 acres of bayfront. All suites have microwaves, refrigerators, and coffeemakers. There's a little sandy beach, a nice swimming pool, and you're just a mile from John Pennekamp Underwater State Park. You can rent Waverunners, boats, snorkeling equipment, and bicycles. Rates start at $169 in the summer, $209 in the winter.

Attractions

Museums of Crane Point Hammock

On US 1 at MM 50.5, Marathon • (305) 743-9100

Hours - Monday–Saturday, 9 a.m.–5 p.m.; Sunday, noon–5 p.m.

Admission - $7.50 for adults, $6 for seniors ages 65 and older, $4 for students, free for children ages 6 and under

Appeal by Age Group -

Pre-school ★★★★	Teens ★★★	Over 30 ★★½
Grade school ★★★★	Young Adults ★★½	Seniors ★★½

Touring Time - Average 1–2 hours; minimum 1 hour

Rainy-Day Touring - Recommended

Author's Rating - ★★★; fascinating history lesson

Restaurants - No

Alcoholic beverages - No

Handicapped access - Yes

Wheelchair rental - No

Baby stroller rental - No
Lockers - No
Pet kennels - No
Rain check - Yes
Private tours - Yes

Description and Comments Includes the Museum of Natural History of the Florida Keys and the Children's Museum of the Florida Keys. A tasteful museum with exhibits on ancient Indians, pirates, wreckers, and the rail line to Key West. Kids will like the re-creation of an underwater cave, as well as the 15,000-gallon saltwater lagoon and tanks featuring spiny lobsters, an iguana, and a parrot. A separate children's museum features ten interactive exhibits, including touch tanks that let kids handle spiny sea urchins and other creatures and a corner with books and a chair for reading.

After learning about the Keys' ecology, visitors may explore the preserve's rare tropical forests on an interpretive nature trail that takes about 35 minutes to explore. Another trail leads to the Adderly Village Black Historic Site for a glimpse of what life was like in the tropics at the turn of the century. Tours are free.

Theater of the Sea

On US 1 at MM 84.5 in Islamorada • (305) 664-2431 • www.theaterofthesea.com

Hours - Daily, 9:30 a.m.–4 p.m. Holiday hours vary.

Admission - $17.75 for adults, $11.25 for children ages 3–12, free for children under 3. Group rates are available. Price of admission does not include the Dolphin Swim, boat rides, or snorkeling trips.

Appeal by Age Group -

Pre-school ★★★	Teens ★★★	Over 30 ★★★
Grade school ★★★½	Young Adults ★★★	Seniors ★★★½

Touring Time - Average a half-day; minimum 1½ hour

Rainy-Day Touring - Not recommended

Author's Rating - ★★★; plenty of interaction with all sorts of sea creatures

Restaurants - Yes
Alcoholic beverages - No
Handicapped access - Yes
Wheelchair rental - No
Baby stroller rental - No
Lockers - No
Pet kennels - No
Rain check - Yes
Private tours - Yes

Description and Comments Established in 1946, Theater of the Sea is the world's second-oldest marine park. Here, you can explore the surroundings of the deep in a natural lagoon setting. Activities at the park such as bottomless-boat rides, aquatic shows, and lagoon tours will entertain guests of all ages, as well as educate them about marine life. Children are especially drawn to the touch tank, where they can pet a shark or kiss a sea lion. Also, children of all ages are invited to take part in the shows.

Theater of the Sea will let you swim with their dolphins for $135 and with the sea lions for $90. Participants must be at least 5 years old to swim with a parent and at least 13 years old to swim without a parent. They also offer a snorkel cruise.

Family-Friendly Restaurants

Mrs. Mac's Kitchen

99336 Overseas Highway, MM 99.4, Key Largo • (305) 451-3722

Meals served - Breakfast, lunch, and dinner

Cuisine - American

Entree range - Breakfast, $3–5; lunch, $5–8; dinner, $8–22

Kids menu - Yes

Reservations - Not accepted

Payment - No credit cards

This is a tacky little roadside joint, but we think the home cookin' beats the fast-food outlets that line the highway. Sun and saltwater make you hungry, so try their stuffed pitas, burgers, or giant subs.

Seven Mile Grill

1240 Overseas Highway, MM 47, Marathon • (305) 743-4481

Meals served - Lunch and dinner

Cuisine - American

Entree range - Lunch, $4–8; dinner, $8–14

Kids menu - No, but there are hot dogs, hamburgers, and chicken fingers.

Reservations - Not accepted

Payment - Visa, MC

Opened in 1954, the grill is one of the most popular home-style eateries along the Overseas Highway. Located right at the foot of the Seven Mile Bridge, this place is as basic as it gets—20 seats at the bar and it's open to the outside no matter what the weather. Try the conch chowder or any of the fried fish. And the Key lime pie is the real thing.

Sid and Roxie's Green Turtle Inn

Overseas Highway, MM 81.5, Islamorada • (305) 664-9031

Meals served - Lunch and dinner

Cuisine - Seafood, American

Entree range - Lunch, $6–15; dinner, $15–20

Kids menu - Yes

Reservations - Recommended for dinner only

Payment - All major credit cards accepted

You can't miss the giant turtle that marks the spot for Sid and Roxie's eatery. Though Sid and Roxie are long gone, the place hasn't been updated much since the 1950s (it opened in 1947), and the food is plain and a bit old-fashioned—fresh fish or a steak with soup, potatoes, and salad. Lots of diners ask for the turtle soup, which comes from the cannery right behind the inn. Breads and pies are made from scratch.

Sugarloaf Lodge

Overseas Highway, MM 17, Sugarloaf Key • (305) 745-3741

Meals served - Breakfast, lunch, and dinner

Cuisine - American

Entree range - Breakfast, $4–5; lunch, $6–12; dinner, $7–22

Kids menu - No, but smaller portions are available for children

Reservations - Not accepted

Payment - All major credit cards accepted

Kids are welcome here, though most of the clientele are hungry fishermen. If you catch a fish, the restaurant will gladly cook it for you. Hearty breakfasts, burgers, sandwiches, and salads.

ROBBIE'S PET TARPON

If you don't want to go deep-sea fishing, here's a chance to see, and even feed, a tarpon or two. Robbie's 200-pound pets hang around the docks just waiting for a snack. Robbie's Marina, MM 77.5, Islamorada; (305) 664-9814. Open daily, 8 a.m.–5 p.m. Admission - $1 per person, $2 for a bucket of fish food; www.robbies.com.

Key West

Key West is in its own world, separate even from the rest of the Florida Keys. Its reputation as a hip and laid-back refuge has simmered for decades, with writers, poets, pirates, and dropouts taking up residence in this little piece of the tropics.

Today, there's still an aura of craziness, but mainstream tourism has taken a front seat, and the city boasts some of the finest hotels and restaurants you can imagine. Most conchs ("conks"), as the islanders call themselves, welcome visitors with open arms.

If this is your family's first trip, you might want to get oriented before you drive right into town. Park at the welcome center near the intersection of US 1 and North Roosevelt Boulevard and sign up for the next Conch Tour Train: an open-air, narrated "trolley"—really an open-air bus—that transports visitors around Key West and gives them an overview of the town.

Is it corny? You bet. The train's "engine" is a diesel-powered truck disguised as a locomotive, and it even has a whistle. But the 90-minute tour is fun and informative. It leaves daily every 30 minutes from 9 a.m. to 3:30 p.m. You can board at the Roosevelt Boulevard location or in Old Town's Mallory Square. Tickets are $20 for adults, $10 for ages 4–12. Passengers can disembark in Old Town, wander around or get lunch, and catch the next "train." Call (305) 294-5161 for more information.

Another option for a guided tour is Old Town Trolley, open-air buses that shuttle visitors on a 90-minute, narrated tour of Key West. Unlike the Conch Tour Train, you can depart at any of the 14 marked stops on the tour route and reboard another trolley later; many hotels are on the route. The tours depart daily every 30 minutes from 9 a.m. to 5:30 p.m. The tour is $20 for adults, $10 for ages 5–12. For more information, call (305) 296-6688.

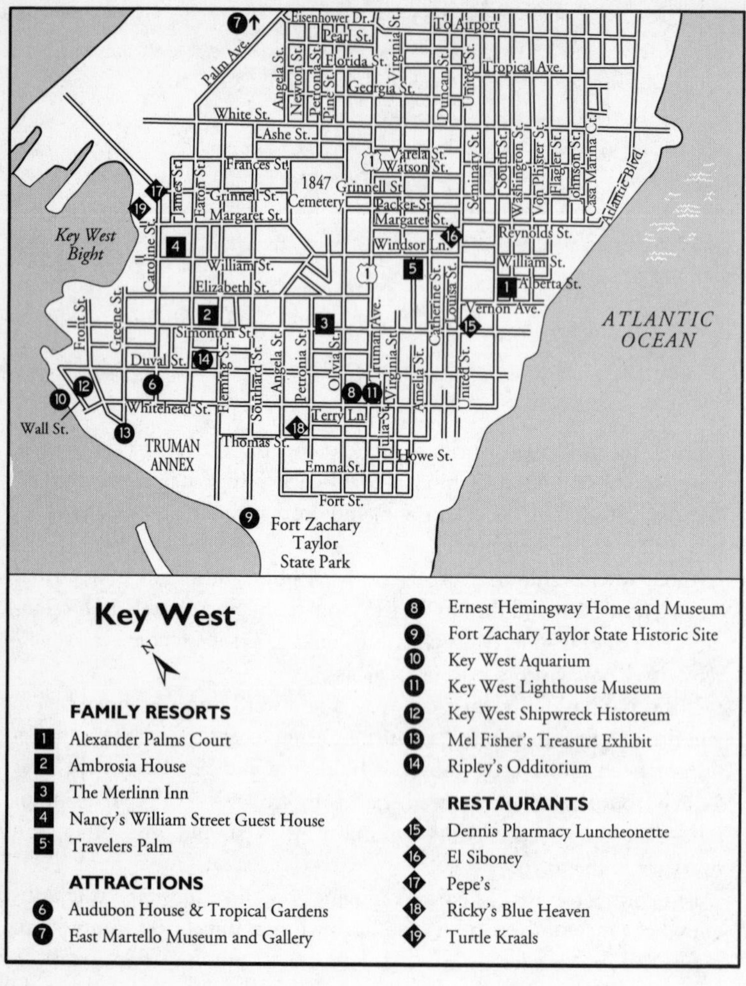

Old Town Key West

Compact Old Town, a square mile of restored houses that makes up the heart of Key West, is best viewed on foot or by bicycle. While main avenues such as Duval Street are frequently jammed with tourists, the side streets still ooze with the peculiar Key West charm that's made the town famous. As the many bike rental shops attest, Key West is a very bicycle-friendly town. Don't forget, children ages 16 and younger are required by Florida law to wear helmets.

Key West Hype

On the Gulf end of Duval Street is Mallory Square, famous for its daily sunset celebration. The "square" is in fact a cramped, old concrete wharf that hosts a mini–street festival late each afternoon. Entertainment includes a troupe of trained cats (most impressive), a bowling ball juggler, an escape artist, and musicians, but when it's high tourist season the place is packed. You'll have to carry youngsters on your shoulders or hold tight to their hands—either way they really won't get to see much because of the throngs.

Our feeling is that this famous "ritual" is touristy and overrated, at least when the crowds are overpowering.

Another overrated spot is the Southernmost Point on the Atlantic side of Duval Street—actually, a block over on parallel Whitehead Street. A huge buoy perched on land and a placard mark the point but, as any child will point out, the land continues a few yards to the water's edge—the real southernmost point. Still, you can't deny the draw of this otherwise undistinguished place: it's usually packed with tourists getting their picture taken in front of the buoy.

To really enjoy Key West, get off Duval Street, wander its back roads, visit its unique and interesting museums, and get a handle on its rich and unusual history. Slow the pace, give it a chance, and you'll soon discover Key West's charms.

Family Resorts

Alexander Palms Court

715 South Street, Key West • (800) 858-1943 or (305) 296-6413 • fax (305) 292-3975 • www.alexanderpalms.com

This renovated 1950s motel welcomes children. Just two blocks off Duval Street and three blocks from the beach, the Alexander has two suites and seven efficiencies, all with kitchens and courtyards, some with screened porches overlooking the pool. Key West's "dog beach" is two blocks away, where the animals are allowed to frolic in the sun and water. Rates start at $95 in the summer, $125 in the winter. Sorry, no pets allowed.

Ambrosia House

618 Fleming Street, Key West • (305) 294-5181 • fax (305) 296-2425 www.ambrosiahouse.com

A block off Duval Street, the Fleming Street Inn welcomes families with no extra charge for children staying with parents. There are just seven rooms and three suites in this charming inn that's nestled around a brick patio and swimming pool. All rooms have refrigerators and coffeemakers, and suites have full kitchens.

The suites are on two levels, ideal for families with older children. Rates start at $125 in the summer, $205 in the winter.

The Merlinn Inn

811 Simonton Street, Key West • (305) 296-3335 or (800) 642-4753 • fax (305) 296-3524 • www.merlinnkeywest.com

Porches, wood decks, tin roofs, and ceiling fans lend a charming, comfortable ambience to the Merlinn, located in the center of the historic district just a block off Duval Street. Kiwi, the parrot, greets you on the back porch; Buddy, the parakeet, loves to chat with guests.

There are 19 accommodations, including suites and cottages, all air conditioned and with color TVs. Some rooms have microwave, refrigerator, coffeemaker, and wet bar. A complimentary continental breakfast is served each morning out by the swimming pool. Children are allowed in cottages only. Suite rates start at $78 in the summer, $125 in the winter; cottage rates start at $139 in the summer, $179 in the winter.

Nancy's William Street Guest House

329 William Street, Key West • (305) 292-3334 • fax (305) 296-1740

Nancy Chodzin has been running this lovely little guest house for seven years, and she welcomes families with "well-behaved children." She offers four one-bedroom apartments with full kitchens and sleeper sofas in the living rooms, and if you want two bedrooms, you can have the third floor of the house to yourselves.

There's a swimming pool and gas grill with lush tropical gardens. And Nancy's is just three blocks from Duval Street. Rooms start at $79 in the summer, $89 in the winter. Apartments start at $119 in the summer, $139 in the winter.

Travelers Palm

815 Catherine Street, Key West • (800) 294-9560 • fax (305) 293-9130 www.travelerspalm.com

Travelers Palm is another cozy resort recommended by traveling families. It has five cottages and apartments covering nearly a city block in old town. All are air conditioned and comfortably furnished with full kitchens and a garden or patio. The two-bedroom apartment has a private pool, the others share a swimming pool, gas grill, and children's playground. Hammocks are strung under a thick canopy of trees for impromptu naps. Summer rates start at $118, winter rates start at $168.

Attractions

Audubon House

205 Whitehead Street, Key West • (305) 294-2116

Hours - Daily, 9:30 a.m.–5 p.m. (last tour at 4:30 p.m.)

Admission - $8.50 for adults, $7.50 for seniors, $5 for students, $3.50 for children 6–12

Appeal by Age Group -

Pre-school ★	Teens ★★	Over 30 ★★★
Grade school ★½	Young Adults ★★½	Seniors ★★★½

Touring Time - Average 45 minutes; minimum 30 minutes

Rainy-Day Touring - Recommended

Author's Rating - ★★★; a beautifully restored house and gardens

Restaurants - No

Alcoholic beverages - No

Handicapped access - Main floor

Wheelchair rental - No

Baby stroller rental - No

Lockers - No

Pet kennels - No

Rain check - No

Private tours - No

Description and Comments Audubon House is the restored home of an early nineteenth-century Key West harbor pilot and wrecker, Captain Geiger. He and his heirs lived in the house for more than 120 years, but in 1958 the deteriorating structure was slated for demolition. Through the efforts of local conservationists, the house was saved and restored, decorated with exquisite period pieces collected in Europe, and dedicated as a museum commemorating the visits of painter and ornithologist John James Audubon. The restoration inaugurated a movement that saved many historically significant Key West buildings.

Though you must walk up, don't miss the children's room on the third floor; two pairs of nineteenth-century roller skates look like forerunners of in-line skates popular today. Outside, orchid-filled trees evoke the wealthy, cosmopolitan lifestyle of early Key West residents. Check out the duplex outhouse in the corner of the garden.

East Martello Museum

3500 S. Roosevelt Boulevard, Key West • (305) 296-3913

Hours - Daily, 9:30 a.m.–5 p.m. (last admission at 4 p.m.)

Admission - $6 for adults, $4 seniors, $3 for students, $2 for children ages 7–12, free for military and for children under age 6.

Appeal by Age Group -

Pre-school ★★★★	Teens ★★★½	Over 30 ★★★
Grade school ★★★★	Young Adults ★★★	Seniors ★★★

Touring Time - Average 2 hours; minimum 1 hour
Rainy-Day Touring - Recommended
Author's Rating - ★★★; a bizarre museum with a little bit of everything
Restaurants - No
Alcoholic beverages - No
Handicapped access - Yes
Wheelchair rental - No
Baby stroller rental - No
Lockers - No
Pet kennels - No
Rain check - Yes
Private tours - Yes

Description and Comments It might be easier to catalog what you won't find here, but we'll give it a try. The low brick ceilings and arches of this old fort house a horse-drawn hearse and wicker casket (circa 1873), ship models, exhibits on Native Americans, Civil War and Spanish American War military artifacts, a hotel safe, "junkyard" art, a deep-sea diver's air suit and a wooden air pump, and a crude raft used by Cubans to escape the Castro regime. Kids can play in the "junior museum"—a tiny house that adults must stoop over to enter—located on the well-manicured grounds. There's also an art museum that features temporary exhibits.

Ernest Hemingway Home and Museum

907 Whitehead Street, Key West • (305) 294-1575

Hours - Daily, 9 a.m.–5 p.m.
Admission - $9 for adults, $5 for children ages 6–12
Appeal by Age Group -

Pre-school ★	Teens ★★½	Over 30 ★★★½
Grade school ★★	Young Adults ★★★	Seniors ★★★★

Touring Time - Average 1 hour; minimum 30 minutes
Rainy-Day Touring - Recommended
Author's Rating - ★★★★; an interesting slice of American literary history
Restaurants - No
Alcoholic beverages - No
Handicapped access - Yes
Wheelchair rental - No
Baby stroller rental - No
Lockers - No
Pet kennels - No
Rain check - No
Private tours - Yes

Description and Comments Ernest Hemingway owned this Spanish-Colonial house, built in 1870, from 1931 until his death in 1961. In his study in the loft of his pool house he wrote some of his most famous novels and short stories, including *A Farewell to Arms, The Snows of Kilimanjaro,* and *For Whom the Bell Tolls.* The spacious mansion gives visitors a glimpse into genteel life in the 1930s. Much (but not all) of the furniture and memorabilia on display belonged to Hemingway.

Fort Zachary Taylor State Historic Site

Southard Street (in the Truman Annex), Key West • (305) 292-6713

Hours - Daily, 8 a.m.–sundown

Admission - $2.50 for a car with one person, $1.50 for each additional person; $1.50 for pedestrians and bicyclists

Appeal by Age Group -

Pre-school ★★★★	Teens ★★★★	Over 30 ★★★★
Grade school ★★★★	Young Adults ★★★★	Seniors ★★★★

Touring Time - Average a half-day; minimum 2–3 hours

Rainy-Day Touring - Not recommended

Author's Rating - ★★★★; a triple hit: a neat fort, interesting history, and a beach you can snorkel from

Restaurants - Yes

Alcoholic beverages - No

Handicapped access - Yes

Wheelchair rental - No

Baby stroller rental - No

Lockers - No

Pet kennels - No

Rain check - No

Private tours - Yes

Description and Comments For 145 years Fort Zachary Taylor defended the harbor of Key West. During the Civil War it was one of four Union forts in Confederate territory that never fell into Southern hands. As a result, hundreds of cannon trained on the nearby shipping lanes kept ships bottled up in Key West throughout the Civil War. The workmanship of the exquisite brickwork throughout the fort couldn't be duplicated today.

Over the years the old fort structure has become landlocked, creating a pleasant man-made beach for swimming and snorkeling.

Key West Aquarium

1 Whitehead Street, Key West • (305) 296-2051

Hours - Daily, 10 a.m– 6 p.m.; guided tours and feedings at 11 a.m. and 1, 3, and 4:30 p.m.

Admission - $9 for adults, $4.50 for children ages 4–12. Tickets are good for 2 days

Appeal by Age Group -

Pre-school ★★★★★	Teens ★★★½	Over 30 ★★½
Grade school ★★★★	Young Adults ★★★	Seniors ★★

Touring Time - Average 1½ hours; minimum 1 hour

Rainy-Day Touring - Recommended

Author's Rating - ★★½; great for the kids, but otherwise a bit ho-hum

Restaurants - No

Alcoholic beverages - No

Handicapped access - Yes

Wheelchair rental - No

Baby stroller rental - No

Lockers - No

Pet kennels - No

Rain check - No

Private tours - Yes

Description and Comments This aquarium is small but comfortable and will especially please younger children. At the touch tank, kids can handle conch, starfish, and crabs. You'll probably never get closer to a shark unless you hook one. This aquarium has been around since 1932, the first tourist attraction built in the Florida Keys.

Key West Lighthouse Museum

938 Whitehead Street, Key West • (305) 294-0012

Hours - Daily, 9:30 a.m.–4:30 p.m.; closed Christmas

Admission - $8 for adults, $4 for students

Appeal by Age Group -

Pre-school ★★	Teens ★★★★	Over 30 ★★★★
Grade school ★★★★	Young Adults ★★★★	Seniors ★★★

Touring Time - Average 1½ hours; minimum 1 hour

Rainy-Day Touring - Not recommended

Author's Rating - ★★★★; a great view and interesting history

Restaurants - No

Alcoholic beverages - No

Handicapped access - No

Wheelchair rental - No

Baby stroller rental - No

Lockers - No

Pet kennels - No

Rain check - No

Private tours - Yes

Description and Comments Next to doing "12-ounce curls" (drinking beer) at Sloppy Joe's, a climb to the top of the lighthouse is the most rewarding workout in Key West. The 88 steps to the top lead to an impressive view of the Atlantic Ocean, the Gulf of Mexico, and cruise ships docked in the harbor.

Key West Shipwreck Historeum

1 Whitehead Street at Mallory Square, Key West • (305) 292-8990

Hours - Daily, 9:45 a.m.–4:45 p.m.; shows begin 15 minutes before and after the hour

Admission - $8 for adults, $4 for children ages 4–12, free for children under age 4

Appeal by Age Group -

Pre-school ★½	Teens ★★★	Over 30 ★★★★
Grade school ★★½	Young Adults ★★★★	Seniors ★★★★

Touring Time - Average 1 hour; minimum 45 minutes

Rainy-Day Touring - Recommended

Author's Rating - ★★★★; talented actors, interesting history

Restaurants - No

Alcoholic beverages - No

Handicapped access - No

Wheelchair rental - No

Baby stroller rental - No

Lockers - No

Pet kennels - No

Rain check - No

Private tours - Yes

Description and Comments Drift back in time as Asa Tift, a famous nineteenth-century Key West wrecker, greets you in his warehouse as a potential crew member. Listen to the story of how Key West became the "richest city in the U.S.A." when the vessel *Isaac Allerton* sank in 1856. A 20-minute video depicts the life of the wreckers and their fight to save lives and precious cargo from ships doomed by the dangerous reefs. Much of the story is told through comments and stories from some of Key West's prominent figures of the time.

Mel Fisher's Treasure Exhibit

200 Greene Street, Key West • (305) 294-2633

Hours - Daily, 9 a.m.–5 p.m.; the last video presentation is at 4:30

Admission - $7.50 for adults, $3.75 for children ages 6–12

Appeal by Age Group -

Pre-school ★★★	Teens ★★★★	Over 30 ★★★
Grade school ★★★★	Young Adults ★★★½	Seniors ★★★½

Touring Time - Average 1 hour; minimum 45 minutes

Rainy-Day Touring - Recommended

Author's Rating - ★★½; impressive booty, a small exhibit, and plenty of self-promotional schlock

Restaurants - No
Alcoholic beverages - No
Handicapped access - Yes
Wheelchair rental - No
Baby stroller rental - No
Lockers - No
Pet kennels - No
Rain check - No
Private tours - No

Description and Comments Ever dreamed of finding a trove of treasure worth millions? Well, Mel Fisher, the best-known salvager in the Keys, did—a bar of solid silver, a solid gold dinner plate, pieces of 8 in a cedar chest, and cannon and sailors' artifacts from the seventeenth century are among the items on display in this small museum. Exhibits also explain how modern treasure hunters find the ancient wrecks and bring the loot up from the bottom of the sea. Yet the relentless self-promotion and commercialism of this private museum—not to mention its small size—are a letdown.

Ripley's Odditorium

527 Duval Street, Key West • (305) 293-9686

Hours - 9 a.m.–11 p.m. every day, 365 days of the year
Admission - $12.95 for adults, $8.95 for children ages 4–12
Appeal by Age Group -

Pre-school ★★	Teens ★★★★★	Over 30 ★★
Grade school ★★★★	Young Adults ★★★	Seniors ★½

Touring Time - Average 2–3 hours; minimum 1 hour
Rainy-Day Touring - Recommended
Author's Rating - ★★ tacky, tasteless, and often hilarious; expensive, too
Restaurants - No
Alcoholic beverages - No
Handicapped access - Yes
Wheelchair rental - No
Baby stroller rental - No
Lockers - No
Pet kennels - No
Rain check - No
Private tours - No

Description and Comments Is it really Ripley, returned from the dead, who materializes at his desk and invites visitors to explore his museum? Or is it a hologram of an actor who looks vaguely like Christopher Walken wearing a smoking jacket? Who cares?

Join in the fun on an exploration of this ridiculous—and funny—"museum." You'll find oddities of questionable authenticity ("shrunken" heads), endlessly repeating film clips of human bizarreness (a guy blowing up a balloon through his eye), grainy film clips with corny narration of New Guinea natives chowing down on grubs and a roast crocodile (gross!), lots of juvenile sex teasers (walk by in one direction, you get a glimpse of a naked lady's backside, but walk by in the other direction and she's gone). It's all corny, seedy, and often quite funny.

Family-Friendly Restaurants

Dennis Pharmacy Luncheonette

1229 Simonton Street, Key West • (305) 294-1890

Meals served - Breakfast and lunch

Cuisine - Spanish, American

Entree range - $4–8.95

Kids menu - No, but small portions are available

Reservations - Not necessary

Payment - All major credit cards accepted

A Key West landmark for 35 years, this classic drugstore lunch counter is famous for daily specials and the "Cheeseburger in Paradise." They also make an excellent picadillo, with spicy ground beef spiked with olives, and traditional Cuban sandwiches. Kids love the rotating barstools and visiting the drugstore's toy department while the food is prepared.

El Siboney

900 Catherine Street, Key West • (305) 296-4184

Meals served - Lunch and dinner

Cuisine - Cuban

Entree range - $6.95–15.95

Kids menu - No, but small portions are available

Reservations - Not accepted

Payment - No credit cards

The Siboneys were Cuban Indians, and this tidy little eatery is a tribute to them. The roast pork and grilled garlic chicken keep the locals coming back, as do traditional Cuban side dishes like crusty fried plantains and garlicky yucca. Waitresses are happy to guide you through the menu.

Pepe's

806 Caroline Street, Key West • (305) 294-7192

Meals served - Breakfast, lunch, and dinner

Cuisine - American

Entree range - $3–22

Kids menu - No, but smaller portions are available for kids

Reservations - Not accepted

Payment - Visa, MC, D

Pepe's has been around since 1909. Parents might want to order the "Pepe's Steak Dinner for 2," their most-requested dish. And don't pass up the warm coconut bread if they've been baking that day. The Sunday night barbecue is a weekly tradition, as well as a full Thanksgiving dinner every Thursday. And there's a toy box to keep kids happy.

Ricky's Blue Heaven

729 Thomas Street, Key West • (305) 296-8666

Meals served - Breakfast, lunch, and dinner

Cuisine - Fine American

Entree range - Breakfast, $6–8.50; lunch, $6–12 lunch; dinner, $8.50–25.50

Kids menu - No, but smaller portions and other items on menu appeal to kids

Reservations - Not accepted, and the wait can be long

Payment - Visa, MC, D

Their backyard is very intriguing to children—heroic roosters from the days when the restaurant offered a cockfighting pit are buried in a graveyard behind the dining area. Today, hens and roosters still scratch about the dirt-floored patio among the tables. It's the kind of place that inspires songs—Ricky's is the inspiration for Jimmy Buffett's song "Blue Heaven Rendezvous."

The breakfast is ethereal; they're famous for their homemade pancakes with pure maple syrup and their homemade granola (served with cow's milk or soy milk). For lunch or dinner, try the delectable Caribbean shrimp dinner, the jerk chicken, or anything from the large selection of vegetarian items. Just save room for the flamed Banana Heaven dessert.

Turtle Kraals

231 Margaret Street, Key West • (305) 294-2640

Meals served - Lunch and dinner

Cuisine - Caribbean, Southwestern seafood

Entree range - $5.25–25.95

Kids menu - Yes

Reservations - Accepted only for groups of 15 or more

Payment - Visa, MC, D
Known for its fresh seafood and full raw bar.

Side Trips

Fort Jefferson and the Dry Tortugas For a little adventure, take a day trip to Fort Jefferson and the Dry Tortugas, a nineteenth-century coastal fortification 70 miles west of Key West that's only accessible by boat or seaplane.

Fort Jefferson is on Garden Key, a national monument administered by the National Park Service. You can explore the stone fort that was begun in 1846 and never completed, though in the late 1800s it was used as a prison.

Most families take the trip to snorkel or dive in the warm waters, abundant with fish and corals, and inhabited by four species of endangered sea turtles. (*Tortugas* is Spanish for "turtle.") If you're not a snorkeler, try the bird-watching, which is fabulous, with more than 100 species spotted, partly because Garden Key is in the path of migration for birds between North and South America.

Seaplanes of Key West offers full- and half-day flights to Fort Jefferson and the Dry Tortugas that include coolers, ice, sodas, and snorkeling gear—all you need to bring is a towel and a camera. Half-day trips depart daily in the mornings and afternoons; prices are $179 for adults, $129 for children ages 7–12, and $99 for children ages 2–6. The 70-mile flight is 40 minutes each way; the plane flies at low altitude so passengers can view the clear waters, shipwrecks, and marine life. You spend 2½ hours on the island. Full-day trips are $305 for adults, $225 for children ages 7–12, and $170 for children ages 2–6. For reservations, call (305) 294-0709.

Another option for visiting Fort Jefferson and the Dry Tortugas is the Fort Jefferson Ferry, which sails out of Lands End Marina (251 Margaret Street in Key West) for full-day excursions. The 100-foot *Yankee Freedom* boasts a large, air-conditioned salon with a chef's galley, a large sundeck, and freshwater showers for swimmers, snorkelers, and divers. The ferry departs on Monday, Wednesday, and Saturday (weather permitting) at 8 a.m. and returns at 5:30 p.m.; it's 3 hours each way, and visitors can enjoy about four hours on the island (including a complete tour of the fort). The price for the all-day trip is $109 for adults, $99 for seniors ages 62 and older, and $69 for children ages 16 and under. For schedule and booking information, call (800) 634-0939 or (305) 294-7009.

Index

Note: Resorts and restaurants are listed in separate indexes.

Hotel Index

Restaurant Index

Travel Like An Expert With The Unofficial Guides

For Travelers Who Want More Than the Official Line!

The Unofficial Guides®

Beyond Disney: Universal, SeaWorld & the Best of Central Florida
Branson, Missouri
California with Kids
Chicago
Central Italy: Florence, Rome, Tuscany & Umbria
Cruises
Disneyland®
Florida and the Keys
Florida with Kids
Golf Vacations in the Eastern U.S.
The Great Smoky & Blue Ridge Region
Inside Disney
Hawaii
Las Vegas
London
Mid-Atlantic with Kids
Mini Las Vegas
Mini-Mickey
New England & New York with Kids
New Orleans
New York City
Paris
San Francisco
Skiing in the West
Southeast with Kids
Walt Disney World®
Walt Disney World® for Grown-Ups
Walt Disney World® with Kids
Washington, D.C.
World's Best Diving Vacations

Bed & Breakfasts and Country Inns in:

California
Great Lakes States
Mid-Atlantic
New England
Northwest
Rockies
Southeast
Southwest

The Best RV & Tent Campgrounds in:

California & the West
Florida & the Southeast
Great Lakes States
Mid-Atlantic States
Northeast
Northwest & Central Plains
Southwest & South Central Plains
U.S.A.

Available at bookstores everywhere.

Unofficial Guide to Florida with Kids Reader Survey

If you would like to express your opinion about Florida or this guidebook, complete the following survey and mail it to:

Unofficial Guide Reader Survey
PO Box 43673
Birmingham, AL 35243 USA

Inclusive dates of your visit: ______________________

Members of your party:	Person 1	Person 2	Person 3	Person 4	Person 5
Gender:	M F	M F	M F	M F	M F
Age:					

Have you ever been to Florida before? ______________________
Which cities did you visit? ______________________

____

Where did you stay? ______________________
on a scale of 100 as best and 0 as worst, how would you rate:

The quality of your room?
The quietness of your room?
Staff's relations with foreigners?
The value of your room?
The reservation process?
Overall hotel satisfaction?

Did you drive? Your car or a rental? ______________________

Concerning public transportation, on a scale of 100 as best and 0 as worst, how would you rate:

Ease of use?
Cleanliness?
Airport shuttle efficiency?
Value vs. rental cars?
Hours and areas serviced?

Concerning your dining experiences:

Estimate the number of meals eaten in restaurants per day. ________
Approximately how much did your party spend on meals per day? ____
Favorite restaurants: ______________________

____

Did you buy this guide before leaving? while on your trip?

How did you hear about this guide? (check all that apply)

Loaned or recommended by a friend
Newspaper or magazine
Just picked it out on my own
Internet
Radio or TV
Bookstore salesperson
Library

Unofficial Guide to Florida with Kids Reader Survey (continued)

What other guidebooks did you use on this trip? ______________

On a scale of 100 as best and 0 as worst, how would you rate them?

Using the same scale, how would you rate *The Unofficial Guide(s)?*

____

Are *Unofficial Guides* readily available at bookstores in your area? ______

Have you used other *Unofficial Guides?* ______________

Which one(s)? ______________

Comments about your trip or *The Unofficial Guide(s):*